The Finance Center
CD–ROM and Web Site
FREE with every new textbook

The Prentice Hall Finance Center CD-ROM and Web site allow students to obtain a wealth of material that is directly linked to the book, including:

FinCoach: The Math Practice Center

Don't let math stand in the way of a good grade!

Created by Dr. Puneet Handa of the University of Iowa, FinCoach has been proven to improve students' grades by allowing them to learn and practice the math of finance on their own time and at their own speed.

myPHLIP

Your link to on-line resources.

Featuring one-click access and a personalized view of many resources, including an on-line study guide, business headlines, current events, and downloadable supplements, all created by our award-winning team of educators.

The Career Center

Explore the real world of finance.

The Career Center includes interviewing skills, interviews from professionals in the field of finance, survey of the job market, and much more!

BAII PLUS Rebate Terms and Conditions

This offer is valid only for BAII PLUS purchases between January 1, 2001 and May 1, 2003. All claims must be postmarked by July 31, 2003. Allow 8 to 10 weeks for processing. All purchases must be made in the U.S. or Canada. Rebates will be sent only to addresses in the U.S. and Canada and paid in U.S. dollars. Not redeemable at any store. Send this completed form along with the retail or on-line receipt (original or copy) and the UPC bar code to the address indicated. This original mail-in certificate must accompany your request and may not be duplicated or reproduced. Offer valid only as stated on this form. Offer void where prohibited, taxed, licensed, or restricted. Limit one rebate per household or address. Texas Instruments reserves the right to discontinue this program at any time and without notice.

Yes! I Want $5 Back On My Purchase of the BAII PLUS.

YOUR JOURNEY OF LEARNING STARTS HERE...

The next few pages reveal many of the key features that *Foundations of Finance*, Third Edition has included to help you be successful in the classroom and beyond.

The cornerstone features included in every chapter are:

10 AXIOMS These core principles of finance tie together concepts within the text. The 10 Axioms allow students to see a more complete picture.

Axiom 10:	Ethical Behavior Is Doing the Right Thing, and Ethical Dilemmas Are Everywhere in Finance

Ethics, or rather a lack of ethics in finance, is a recurring theme in the news. During the late 1980s and early 1990s the fall of Ivan Boesky and Drexel, Burnham, Lambert, and the near collapse of Salomon Brothers seemed to make continuous headlines. Meanwhile, the movie *Wall Street* was a hit at the box office and the book *Liar's Poker*, by Michael Lewis, chronicling unethical behavior in the bond markets, became a best-seller. As the lessons of Salomon Brothers and Drexel, Burnham, Lambert illustrate, ethical errors are not forgiven in the business world. Not only is acting in an ethical manner morally correct, it is congruent with our goal of maximization of shareholder wealth.

PAUSE AND REFLECT In-text inserts appear throughout the text and focus the student's attention on "the big picture." These inserts help students identify the interrelationships and motivating factors behind the core concepts.

PAUSE AND REFLECT

Keep in mind that future cash flows are assumed to occur at the end of the time period during which they accrue. For example, if a cash flow of $100 occurs in time period 5, it is assumed to occur at the end of time period 5, which is also the beginning of time period 6. In addition, cash flows that occur in time $t = 0$ occur right now; that is, they are already in present dollars.

FINANCIAL MANAGEMENT IN PRACTICE These boxes demonstrate the relevance of the topics discussed and the implementation of the theory.

FINANCIAL MANAGEMENT IN PRACTICE
Reading a Stock Quote in the *Wall Street Journal*

Below is shown a section of the *Wall Street Journal* that gives the quotes on July 8, 1999, for some of the stocks traded on the New York Stock Exchange on that date.

The stocks listed below include some familiar companies, such as General Electric (GE), General Mills, and General Motors, that are listed in the *Wall Street Journal* on a daily basis. To help us understand how to read the quotes, consider General Electric:

- The 52 week *high* column shows that General Electric stock reached a high of 117$^7/_{16}$ ($117.44) during the past year
- The 52 week *low* column shows that General Electric sold for a low of 69 ($69.00) during the past year
- The stock (GenElec) and sym (GE) columns give an abbreviated version of the corporation's name and the ticker symbol, respectively

- *Div*, the dividend column, gives the amount of dividend that General Electric paid its common stockholders in the last year; $1.40 per share
- *Yld %* (1.2) is the stock's dividend yield—the amount of the dividend divided by the day's closing price ($1.40 ÷ $117.94)
- *PE* (41) gives the current market price (117$^{15}/_{16}$ divided by the firm's earnings per share
- The amount of General Electric stock traded on July 8, 1999, is represented in the Vol 100s column, or 7,948,100 shares
- General Electric stock traded at a high price (Hi-118$^3/_4$) and a low price (Lo-114$^1/_8$) during the day
- The previous day's closing price is subtracted from the closing price (*Close*) of 117$^{15}/_{16}$ for July 8, 1999, for a net change (*Net Chg*) of + 3

| 52 Weeks | | | | | Yld | | | | | | Net |
Hi	Lo	Stock	Sym	Div	%	PE	Vol 100s	Hi	Lo	Close	Chg
118$^1/_4$	69	GenElec	GE	1.40	1.2	41	79481	118$^3/_4$	114$^1/_4$	117$^{15}/_{16}$	+ 3
39$^1/_2$	31$^1/_8$	GenGrthProp	GGP	1.96	5.6	20	779	35$^3/_4$	34$^7/_8$	35$^1/_{16}$	– $^1/_{16}$
20	7$^5/_8$	GenHouse	GHW	0.32	1.6	38	83	19$^3/_4$	19$^7/_{16}$	19$^3/_4$	+ $^1/_{16}$
47$^3/_8$	16$^{11}/_{16}$	GenInstr	GIC	...	...	...	17910	46	42$^3/_8$	43$^9/_{16}$	– 2$^{13}/_{16}$
84$^5/_{16}$	59$^1/_2$	GenMills	GIS	2.20	2.7	24	5390	82$^1/_2$	80$^{13}/_{16}$	82$^1/_4$	+ 1$^1/_4$
63$^7/_8$	30$^3/_4$	GenMotor H	GNH	...	...	...	6160	60$^3/_8$	58$^3/_4$	59$^7/_8$	– 1$^1/_4$
78$^1/_2$	38$^{13}/_{16}$	GenMotor	GM	2.00	2.9	14	26275	71$^1/_2$	69$^3/_4$	70	– 1$^{11}/_{16}$

BACK TO THE FOUNDATIONS These in-text inserts appear throughout the text to allow the student to take time out and reflect upon the meaning of the material just presented. The use of these inserts, coupled with the use of the 10 axioms, keeps the student focused on the interrelationships and motivating factors behind the concepts.

> **BACK TO THE FOUNDATIONS**
>
> Some have thought junk bonds were fundamentally different from other securities, but they are not. They are bonds with a great amount of risk, and therefore promise high expected returns. Thus, **Axiom 1: The Risk-Return Trade-off—We Won't Take on Additional Risk Unless We Expect to Be Compensated with Additional Return.**

NEW TO THIS EDITION!
FOUNDATIONS OF FINANCE, THIRD EDITION, HAS INCLUDED SEVERAL OTHER LEARNING TOOLS

> **CONCEPT CHECK**
>
> 1. What features of common stock indicate ownership in the corporation versus preferred stock or bonds?
> 2. What are the two ways that a shareholder benefits from ownership?
> 3. How does internal growth versus the infusion of new capital affect the original shareholders?
> 4. If a corporation decides to retain its earnings, when would the value of the market price actually decrease?
> 5. What is the three-step process for common stock valuation? Explain the difference in the equations for a single-holding period and multiple-holding periods.

CONCEPT CHECKS At the end of most major sections, concept checks highlight the key ideas just presented and allow students to test their understanding of the material.

> **FINANCE AND THE MULTINATIONAL FIRM: FINANCIAL STATEMENTS AND INTERNATIONAL FINANCE**
>
> As of 1999, many countries had different guidelines for firms to use in preparing financial statements. In other words, a dollar of earnings in the United States is not the same as DM 1.84 (deutsche [German] Marks) (the equivalent of a U.S. dollar based on the exchange rate). The two countries simply have different generally accepted accounting principles. In fact, the differences in accounting practices are significant enough that a firm reporting according to German standards could have $100 million in profits, but if U.S. standards are used that same company might report a loss. Just imagine what this does for an investor trying to interpret financial statements across different country boundaries.

FINANCE AND THE MULTINATIONAL FIRM Each chapter closes with a section that discusses the international aspects of the material presented in that chapter.

> **Takin' It to the Net**
>
> The rates of return in Figure 9–2 come from a company called Ibbotson Associates. Go to their home page, http://www. ibbotson.com, to see what information they provide on the Internet.

TAKIN' IT TO THE NET This new feature is found in each chapter and directs students to related Web sites.

THE SUPPORT PACKAGE

Student Study Guide   Written by the authors, the Study Guide contains several innovative features to help the student of *Foundations of Finance*. Each chapter begins with an overview of the key points, which can serve both as a preview and quick survey of the chapter content, and as a review. There are problems (with detailed solutions) and self-tests that can be used to aid in the preparation of outside assignments and to study for examinations. The problems are keyed to the end-of-chapter problems in the text in order to provide direct and meaningful student aid. Multiple-choice and true/false questions are also included to provide a self-test over the descriptive chapter material.

Instructor's Manual with Solutions   The Instructor's Manual, prepared by the authors, contains these four key elements for each chapter:

1. A chapter orientation, which offers the instructor a simple statement of the authors' intent for the chapter, and a useful point of departure for in-class lecture;
2. A chapter outline for easy reference to key issues;
3. Answers to all end-of-chapter questions in the test;
4. A second set of alternative problems with answers.

Test Bank   The Test Bank, revised for this edition by Philip T. Thames of California State University, Long Beach, provides more than 1,500 multiple-choice, true/false, and short-answer questions with complete and detailed answers. There are approximately 340 questions that are new to this edition of the Test Bank.

Prentice Hall Test Manager, Version 4.1   The Test Bank is designed for use with the Prentice Hall Test Manager, a computerized package that allows instructors to custom design, save, and generate classroom tests. The test program (in Windows format) permits instructors to edit, add, or delete questions from the test bank; edit existing graphics and create new graphics; analyze test results; and organize a database of tests and student results.

PowerPoint Presentation   Over 50 slides per chapter of new lecture notes has been prepared by Professor Anthony Byrd of the University of Central Florida. These electronic slides allow the instructor to create full-color presentations coordinated with *Foundations of Finance*, Third Edition. The PowerPoint slides are available from the Prentice Hall Web site **www.prenhall.com/keown.**

Spreadsheet Templates and Solutions   In addition to the solutions being provided in the Instructor's Manual, we have also developed **Spreadsheet Solutions** for virtually all of the end-of-chapter problems. These solutions have been prepared in Excel. The user can change the assumptions in the problem and thereby generate new solutions. (Available to download at **www.prenhall.com/keown**).

Color Transparencies   Approximately 150 four-color acetates of the major figures in the text are available.

NEW! Instructor's Resource CD-ROM   The Instructor's Resource CD-ROM includes the computerized test bank, Instructor's Manual, PowerPoint Presentations, and Transparency Masters of all the figures and tables from the text. It is dual platform for both PC and Macintosh.

TECHNOLOGY

The Prentice Hall Finance Center Web Site and CD-ROM Located in the inside back cover of this text and at **www.prenhall.com/financecenter** is the *Prentice Hall Finance Center*. This robust learning tool contains the following features all designed to increase student awareness of what finance professionals do, to ensure comprehension and mastery of the financial mathematics contained in the text, and to supply a direct link to myPHLIP—the Prentice Hall Learning on the Internet Partnership.

FINCOACH—The Financial Math Practice Center FinCoach contains an infinite number of problems and self-tests in virtually all key math topics covered in financial management. With FinCoach, students can save problems, review them, and even print them. This step-by-step guide to solving corporate finance mathematics problems allows the student to rapidly gain mastery in all mathematical challenges.

Welcome to myPHLIP

Your personal guide to the free on-line resources for your book

Featuring one click access to all of the new resources created by our award-winning team of educators, myPHLIP provides a **personalized view** of the great new resources available:

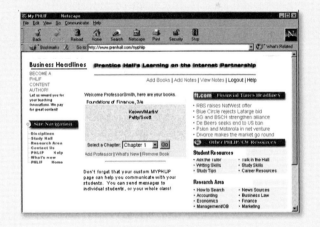

New **myPHLIP pages**—Your personal access page unites all your myPHLIP texts.

New **Notes**—Add personal notes to our resources for personal reminders and references.

New **Messages**—Instructors can send messages to individual students, or all students linked to your course.

New **Student Resources**—Add premium PHLIP resources for your students to view and download (such as our PowerPoint slides, videos, and spreadsheets).

New **Syllabus Tool**—Improved new on-line syllabus tools help you add your own personal syllabus to our site in minutes.

New **Business Headlines**—Provide links to articles in today's business news.

New **Search**—Search all PHLIP resources for relevant articles and exercises.

New **Instructor Manual**—myPHLIP Instructor Manual provides tips and suggestions from our PHLIP faculty for integrating PHLIP resources into your course.

Combined with the resources you have trusted throughout the years to provide you with the best business resources available:

✔ **In the News**—New current events articles are added throughout the year. Each article is summarized by our teams of expert professors and fully supported by exercises, activities, and instructor materials.
✔ **On-Line Study Guide**—Results from the automatically graded questions for every chapter provide immediate feedback for students that can be e-mailed to the instructor.
✔ **Research Area**—Your own personal resource library includes tutorials, descriptive links to virtual libraries, and a wealth of search engines and resources.

FOR THE PROFESSOR

✔ **Teaching Resources** include resources contributed by professors throughout the world, including teaching tips, techniques, academic papers, sample syllabi, and **Talk to the Team**, a moderated faculty chat room.
✔ **On-line faculty support** including downloadable supplements, additional cases, articles, links, and suggested answers to Current Events Activities.
✔ **What's New** gives you one click access to all newly posted PHLIP resources.
✔ **Internet Resources** provide discipline-specific sites, including preview information that allows you to review site information before you view the site, ensuring you visit the best available business resources found by our learning community.

FOR THE STUDENT

✔ **Talk to the Tutor** Virtual office hours allow students to post questions from any supported discipline and receive responses from the dedicated PHLIP/CW faculty team.
✔ **Writing Resource Center** On-line writing center provides links to on-line directories, thesauruses, writing tutors, style and grammar guides, and additional tools.
✔ **Career Center** Helps access career information, view sample resumes, even apply for jobs on-line.
✔ **Study Tips** An area for students to learn to develop better study skills.

TECHNOLOGY...
TOTAL SOLUTIONS

WebCT

Now you have the freedom to personalize your own on-line course materials! Prentice Hall Business Publishing provides the content and support you need to create and manage your own on-line course materials in WebCT. With quality materials and the best support package available, we make it easy for you to use WebCT's course management tools. WebCT is a Course Management System with robust course management tools, including page tracking, progress tracking, class and student management, grade book, communication, calendar, reporting tools, and more.

The *Foundations of Finance*, Third Edition On-line Course provides:

Customizable Content:

Use Prentice Hall materials created by professors for professors and their students.

Our development team:

- Checks course material and tests for accuracy;
- Clears permissions for content and images;
- Edits material for consistency with the supported title.

Some examples of content created for each course include:

- *Lecture Notes* containing additional exercises, discussion questions, lecture notes, and graphics created to reinforce concepts in the book.

- *Tests and Quizzes* created for each chapter give instructors hundreds of questions to select and customize for every chapter.

Instructional Design:

- *Readiness Assessment Quizzes* allow students to pre-test their understanding of chapter material.
- *Discussion Questions* are built into the lectures to encourage interpersonal relationships by asking students to discuss questions in the conference or chat rooms.
- *In-Line Exercises*, built into the lecture materials, serve as pedagogical speedbumps, requiring students to stop and make sure they understand the material.

Support: Prentice Hall Business Publishing provides the best support package available for a WebCT course.

- Business Publishing print instructor manual
- Course-specific on-line instructor manual
- Course-specific on-line student manual
- Gold Level Technical Support hotline
- Technology Enhanced Teaching course created by our WebCT team of professors and instructional designers, this course provides a background of instructional design and teaching tips for teaching an on-line course

BLACKBOARD

Easy to use, Blackboard's simple templates and tools make it easy to create, manage, and use on-line course materials.

Course Management Tools Include progress tracking, class and student management, grade book, communication, assignments, and reporting tools.

Communication Tools Blackboard offers Communication Tools such as the Virtual Classroom (chat rooms, whiteboard, slides), document sharing, and bulletin boards.

Testing Testing programs include the ability for the Instructor to create on-line quizzes and tests, and automatically grade and track results.
- Design Tools
- Blackboard's design tools and pre-set designs help you customize your course.

Content Prentice Hall content is available for each course, including additional course material, exercises, and tests.

Service
- On-line Instructor and Student Manuals
- Downloadable Instructor and Student Manuals
- On-line Tutorials
- CD Tutorials
- On-site Training

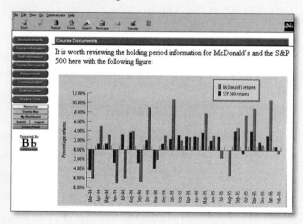

The Building Block for Your Education

KEOWN • MARTIN • PETTY • SCOTT

FOUNDATIONS OF FINANCE

Third Edition

FOUNDATIONS OF FINANCE

The Logic and Practice of Financial Management

Third Edition

PRENTICE HALL FINANCE SERIES

PERSONAL FINANCE

Keown, *Personal Finance: Turning Money into Wealth*
Trivoli, *Personal Portfolio Management: Fundamentals & Strategies*
Winger/Frasca, *Personal Finance: An Integrated Planning Approach*

INVESTMENTS

Alexander/Sharpe/Bailey, *Fundamentals of Investments*
Fabozzi, *Investment Management*
Fischer/Jordan, *Security Analysis and Portfolio Management*
Haugen, *Modern Investment Theory*
Haugen, *The New Finance*
Haugen, *The Beast on Wall Street*
Haugen, *The Inefficient Stock Market*
Sharpe/Alexander/Bailey, *Investments*
Taggart, *Quantitative Analysis for Investment Management*
Winger/Frasca, *Investments*

PORTFOLIO ANALYSIS

Alexander/Sharpe/Bailey, *Fundamentals of Investments*
Fischer/Jordan, *Security Analysis and Portfolio Management*
Haugen, *Modern Investment Theory*
Alexander/Sharpe/Bailey, *Investments*

OPTIONS/FUTURES/DERIVATIVES

Hull, *Introduction to Futures and Options Markets*
Hull, *Options, Futures, and Other Derivatives*

RISK MANAGEMENT/FINANCIAL ENGINEERING

Hull, *Financial Engineering and Risk Management*
Mason/Merton/Perold/Tufano, *Cases in Financial Engineering*

FIXED INCOME SECURITIES

Van Horne, *Financial Market, Rates and Flows*
Handa, *FinCoach: Fixed Income* (software)

BOND MARKETS

Fabozzi, *Bond Markets, Analysis and Strategies*
Van Horne, *Financial Market, Rates and Flows*

CAPITAL MARKETS

Fabozzi/Modigliani, *Capital Markets: Institutions and Instruments*
Van Horne, *Financial Market, Rates and Flows*

CORPORATE FINANCE, SURVEY OF FINANCE, & FINANCIAL ECONOMICS

Bodie/Merton, *Finance*
Emery/Finnerty/Stowe, *Principles of Financial Management*
Emery/Finnerty, *Corporate Financial Management*
Gallagher/Andrew, *Financial Management: Principles and Practices*
Haugen, *The New Finance: The Case Against Efficient Markets*
Keown/Martin/Petty/Scott, *Basic Financial Management*
Keown/Martin/Petty/Scott, *Foundations of Finance: The Logic and Practice of Financial Management*
Shapiro/Balbirer, *Modern Corporate Finance: A Multidisciplinary Approach to Value Creation*
Van Horne, *Financial Management and Policy*
Van Horne/Wachowicz, *Fundamentals of Financial Management*

INTERNATIONAL FINANCE

Baker, *International Finance: Management, Markets, and Institutions*
Grabbe, *International Financial Markets*
Rivera-Batiz/Rivera-Batiz, *International Finance and Open Economy Macroeconomics*

CAPITAL BUDGETING

Aggarwal, *Capital Budgeting Under Uncertainty*
Bierman/Smidt, *The Capital Budgeting Decision*

MERGERS/ACQUISITIONS/ TAKEOVERS

Weston/Chung/Siu, *Takeovers, Restructuring and Corporate Governance*

SHORT-TERM FINANCE

Hill/Sartoris, *Short Term Financial Management*

TAXES

Scholes/Wolfson, *Taxes and Business Strategy: A Global Planning Approach*

INSURANCE

Black/Skipper, *Life and Health Insurance*
Dorfman, *Introduction to Risk Management and Insurance*
Rejda, *Social Insurance and Economic Security*

FINANCIAL MARKETS AND INSTITUTIONS

Arshadi/Karels, *Modern Financial Intermediaries and Markets*
Dietrich, *Financial Services and Financial Institutions*
Fabozzi/Modigliani/Ferri/Jones, *Foundations of Financial Markets and Institutions*
Kaufman, *The U.S. Financial Systems*
Van Horne, *Financial Market Rates and Flows*

COMMERCIAL BANKING

Arshadi/Karels, *Modern Financial Intermediaries and Markets*
Dietrich, *Financial Services and Financial Institutions*
Sinkey, *Commercial Bank Financial Management*

ENTREPRENEURIAL FINANCE

Adelman/Marks, *Entrepreneurial Finance*
Vaughn, *Financial Planning for the Entrepreneur*

CASES IN FINANCE

May/May/Andrew, *Effective Writing: A Handbook for Finance People*

FINANCIAL STATEMENT ANALYSIS

Fraser/Ormiston, *Understanding Financial Statements*

FINANCE CENTER

For downloadable supplements and much more . . . visit us at
www.prenhall.com/financecenter

FOUNDATIONS OF FINANCE

The Logic and Practice of Financial Management

Third Edition

ARTHUR J. KEOWN   *Virginia Polytechnic and State University*
R. B. Pamplin Professor of Finance

JOHN D. MARTIN   *Baylor University*
Carr P. Collins Chair in Finance

J. WILLIAM PETTY   *Baylor University*
Carouth Professor of Entrepreneurship

DAVID F. SCOTT, JR.   *University of Central Florida*
Holder, Phillips-Schenck Chair in American
Private Enterprise and Professor of Finance

Prentice Hall

One Lake Street, Upper Saddle River, New Jersey 07458

Foundations of finance : the logic and practice of financial management / Arthur J. Keown . . . [et al.]—3rd ed.
   p. cm.
   Includes bibliographical references and index.
   ISBN 0-13-017981-7 (student)—ISBN 0-13-018368-7 (review)
   1. Corporations—Finance. I. Keown, Arthur J.
HG4026 .F67 2000
658.15—dc21

                                                      00-026814

Senior Editor: Maureen Riopelle
Managing Editor (Editorial): Gladys Soto
Editor-in-Chief: PJ Boardman
Editorial Assistant: Cheryl Clayton
Assistant Editor: Holly Jo Brown
Media Project Manager: Bill Minick
Senior Marketing Manager: Lori Braumberger
Production Editor: Carol Samet
Managing Editor (Production): Cindy Regan
Senior Manufacturing Supervisor: Paul Smolenski
Senior Prepress/Manufacturing Manager: Vincent Scelta
Design Manager: Patricia Smythe
Interior Design: Ox and Company, Inc.
Cover Illustration: Salem Krieger
Cover Design: Kevin Kall
Senior Print/Media Production Manager: Karen Goldsmith
Composition: Graphic World Publishing Services

10 9 8 7 6 5 4 3
ISBN 0-13-0179817

To my parents, from whom I learned the most.

ARTHUR J. KEOWN

In loving memory of my mother, who was ever encouraging, and to my father, whose life I seek to emulate.

JOHN D. MARTIN

To Donna, a great wife, a dedicated mother, and a fun grandmother called Nonna.

J. WILLIAM PETTY

To my wife, Peggy.

DAVID F. SCOTT, JR.

ABOUT THE AUTHORS

Arthur J. Keown is the R. B. Pamplin Professor of Finance at Virginia Polytechnic Institute and State University. He received his bachelor's degree from Ohio Wesleyan University, his M.B.A. from the University of Michigan, and his doctorate from Indiana University. An award-winning teacher, he is a member of the Academy of Teaching Excellence, has received five Certificates of Teaching Excellence at Virginia Tech, the W. E. Wine Award for Teaching Excellence, the Alumni Teaching Excellence Award, and in 1999 received the Outstanding Faculty Award from the State of Virginia. Professor Keown is widely published in academic journals. His work has appeared in *The Journal of Finance*, the *Journal of Financial Economics*, the *Journal of Financial and Quantitative Analysis*, *The Journal of Financial Research*, the *Journal of Banking and Finance*, *Financial Management*, the *Journal of Portfolio Management*, and many others. In addition to *Foundations of Finance*, two other of his books are widely used in college finance classes all over the country—*Basic Financial Management* and *Personal Finance: Turning Money Into Wealth*. Professor Keown is a Fellow of the Decision Sciences Institute, a member of the Board of Directors of the Financial Management Association, and former head of the finance department. In addition, he recently served as the co-editor of *The Journal of Financial Research* for six and a half years and is presently the co-editor of the Financial Management Association's *Survey and Synthesis* series. He lives with his wife and two children in Blacksburg, Virginia, where he collects original art from *Mad Magazine*.

John D. Martin is the Carr P. Collins Chairholder in Finance at Baylor University. He came to Baylor University in 1998 after spending eighteen years at The University of Texas at Austin where he was the Margaret and Eugene McDermott Professor of Finance. He teaches corporate finance and financial modeling, and his research interests are in corporate governance, the evaluation of firm performance, and the design of incentive compensation programs. Dr. Martin has published widely in both academic and professional journals. Included among his academic publications are papers that have appeared in the *Journal of Financial Economics*, *Journal of Finance*, *Journal of Monetary Economics*, *Journal of Financial and Quantitative Analysis*, *Financial Management*, and *Management Science*. Professional publications include papers published in *Directors and Boards*, *Financial Analysts' Journal*, *Journal of Portfolio Management*, and the *Journal of Applied Corporate Finance*. Dr. Martin is also co-author of nine books including *Basic Financial Management* (8th ed.), *Foundations of Finance* (2nd ed.), *The Theory of Finance*, *Financial Analysis* (2nd ed.), and *Value Based Management* (forthcoming Harvard Business School Press). Currently he is writing a book on value-based management for the Harvard Business School Press. He serves on the editorial boards of eight journals and has been consultant to a number of firms including Hewlett Packard, Shell Chemical, Shell E&P, Texas Instruments, and The Associates.

J. William Petty is Professor of Finance and the W. W. Caruth Chairholder of Entrepreneurship at Baylor University. He holds the Ph.D. and M.B.A. from the University of Texas at Austin, and the B.S. from Abilene Christian University. He has taught at Virginia Tech University, Texas Tech University, and served as the dean of the business school at Abilene Christian University. His research interests include corporate restructuring, acquisitions of privately held companies, shareholder value-based management, the financing of small and entrepreneurial firms, and lender-borrower relationships. He has served as the co-editor for the *Journal of Financial Research* and the editor of the *Journal of Entrepreneurial and Small Business Finance*. He has published in a number of finance journals and is the co-author of two leading corporate finance textbooks, *Basic Financial Management* and *Foundations of Finance*, and co-author of a widely used text, *Small Business Management*. Dr. Petty has worked as a consultant for oil and gas firms and consumer product companies. He has also served as a subject matter expert on a best-practices study by the American Productivity and Quality Center on the topic of shareholder value-based management. He recently served on a research team for the Australian Department of Industry to study the feasibility of establishing a public equity market for small and medium-sized enterprises in Australia.

David F. Scott Jr. received his Ph.D. from the University of Florida. He holds the M.B.A. from the University of Detroit and the B.S.B.A. from the University of Akron. He holds the Phillips-Schenck Chair in American Private Enterprise, is Executive Director of the Dr. Phillips Institute for the Study of American Business Activity, and is Professor of Finance at the University of Central Florida. He has been at UCF since 1982. From 1977 to 1982 he was Area Coordinator, then Head, Department of Finance, Insurance, and Business Law at Virginia Polytechnic Institute and State University. During 1985–1986 he was President of the Financial Management Association, an international group with 9,000 members. He was a member of the Board of Trustees of FMA from 1986 to 1993.

Dr. Scott is a member of the Board of Directors of CompDent Corporation, headquartered in Atlanta, Georgia. He has served on the Investment Policy Committee of the University of Central Florida Foundation since 1992. Dr. Scott is also past founding co-editor of the *Journal of Financial Research*, past associate editor for the *Akron Business and Economic Review*, and past associate editor for *Financial Management*. He is past president of the Southern Finance Association. In addition to *Foundations of Finance*, Dr. Scott is co-author of *Basic Financial Management*, *Cases in Finance*, and *Guide to Financial Analysis*. He is widely published in academic journals including *Financial Management*, *Engineering Economist*, *Journal of Financial and Quantitative Analysis*, *Business Economics*, and many others.

BRIEF CONTENTS

Appendixes

CONTENTS

In finance, our goal is to create wealth. This is done by providing customers with the best product and service possible, and it is the market response that determines whether we reach our goal. We are very proud of the market reaction to *Foundations of Finance*; the market's response has been overwhelming. With its success comes an even greater responsibility to deliver the finest possible textbook and supplementary package possible. We have done this with a two-pronged approach of refinement, based upon users' comments, and of remaining the innovative leaders in the field, focusing on value-added innovations.

Foundations of Finance has gained the reputation for being "intuitive"—allowing the reader "to see the forest from the trees"—and "lively and easy to read." In the third edition of *Foundations of Finance*, we have tried to build on these strengths, introducing the latest concepts and developments in finance in a practical and intuitive manner.

Pedagogy That Works

This book provides a student with a conceptual understanding of the financial decision making process, rather than just an introduction to the tools and techniques of finance. For the student, it is all too easy to lose sight of the logic that drives finance and focus instead on memorizing formulas and procedures. As a result, students have a difficult time understanding the interrelationships between the topics covered. Moreover, later in life when the problems encountered do not match the textbook presentation, students may find themselves unprepared to abstract from what they learned. To overcome this problem, the opening chapter presents ten underlying principles or axioms of finance, which serve as a springboard for the chapters and topics that follow. In essence, the student is presented with a cohesive, interrelated perspective from which future problems can be approached.

With a focus on the big picture, we provide an introduction to financial decision making rooted in current financial theory and in the current state of world economic conditions. This focus is perhaps most apparent in the attention given to the capital markets and their influence on corporate financial decisions. What results is an introductory treatment of a discipline rather than the treatment of a series of isolated problems that face the financial manager. The goal of this text is not merely to teach the tools of a discipline or trade but also to enable students to abstract what is learned to new and yet unforeseen problems—in short, to educate the student in finance.

Innovations and Distinctive Features of the Third Edition

New Chapter—Understanding Financial Statements and Cash Flows For students who need a brief refresher of accounting principles, the Understanding Financial Statements and Cash Flows chapter provides a conceptual and analytical understanding of accounting principles.

Introduction of an Integrated Learning System The text is organized around the learning objectives that appear at the beginning of each chapter to provide the instructor and student with an easy-to-use integrated learning system. Numbered icons identifying each objective appear next to the related material throughout the text and in the summary, allowing easy location of material related to each objective.

Real World Opening Vignettes Each chapter begins with a current, real-world story about a financial decision faced by a company related to the chapter material that follows. These vignettes have been carefully prepared to stimulate student interest in the topic to come and can be used as a lecture tool to stimulate class discussion.

Key Terms Identified in the Margins Key terms are highlighted in the margin with definitional material italicized in the text and can also be found in the glossary in the back of the book, making it easier for the student to check their understanding of key terms. At the end of each chapter, key terms are listed along with page numbers as a study checklist for students.

Comprehensive End-of-Chapter Problems A comprehensive problem has been added at the end of almost every chapter covering all the major topics included in that chapter. This comprehensive problem can be used as a lecture or review tool by the professor. For the student, the comprehensive end-of-chapter problems provide an opportunity to apply all the concepts presented within the chapter in a realistic setting, thereby strengthening their understanding of the material.

Financial Calculators The use of financial calculators has been integrated throughout this text, especially with respect to the presentation of the time value of money, where appropriate calculator solutions appear in the margin.

Content Updating In response to both the continued development of financial thought and reviewer comments, changes have been made in the text. Some of these changes include:

Chapter 1 In response to comments from reviewers and adopters, we have introduced a new section on "The Role of the Financial Manager in a Corporation." This section identifies both the role and the duties of the financial manager. We have also simplified the presentation of the ten axioms in such a way that they are immediately accessible to the student, regardless of his or her background.

Chapter 2 This chapter has been substantially revised, streamlined, and updated. For example, a new section on the importance of the NASDAQ system is in place, along with a section on analyzing interest rates through the use of risk premiums. Here, students work through an estimation of nominal interest rates using various risk premia. Further, the multinational firm and efficient financial markets are discussed at the chapter's end.

Chapters 3 and 4 Chapter 3 of the second edition has been expanded to two chapters to give greater attention to the basic accounting principles that students need to perform well in a finance class. Also, the perspective of cash flows has been changed from that of an accountant to that of a finance person, which means we want students to measure "free cash flows."

Chapter 5 This chapter has been updated and revised with an eye towards simplification—attempting to make the chapter more accessible to the non-accounting student.

Chapter 6 In the Time Value of Money chapter, we have introduced a number of examples aimed not only at making the material more accessible but also demonstrating the power of compounding in a fun and interesting way.

Chapters 7 through 9 In the Valuation and Risk chapters, we have added the use of Excel solutions to encourage the students to use a computer spreadsheet in their work. We have also encouraged increased use of the Internet in these chapters.

Chapters 10 and 11 The Capital Budgeting chapters, have been revised and clarified to make the material more intuitive to the student. For example, a new section on Net Present Value Profiles has been included in Chapter 10.

Chapter 12 The Cost of Capital chapter has been revised with the inclusion of an expanded section on EVA and the concept of managing for shareholder wealth.

Chapter 13 Determining the Financial Mix has been revised with a new introduction drawing on the capital structure policies of both the Coca-Cola Company and the Georgia-Pacific Corporation. This introduction is linked to a lengthier discussion of Georgia-Pacific's financial structure later in the chapter. Another real-world example is taken from the Walt Disney Company and deals with capital costs and capital structure.

Chapter 14 The Dividend Policy chapter now opens with a new introduction that focuses on the dividend choice and its relationship to two of the ten axioms that tie the entire text together. A real-world example from the Coca-Cola Company is included. In addition, a new section on dividend policy and corporate strategy has been added.

Chapter 15 The introductory Working-Capital chapter contains expanded coverage of the Cash Conversion Cycle concept using Dell Computer Corporation as an illustrative example. Dell's Cash Conversion Cycle is actually negative, indicating that it generates cash when its sales grow. We show how this is the result of tight control over receivables and inventories and the judicious use of trade credit—that is, collect early and pay late.

Chapter 16 The Liquid Assets chapter has been substantially revised, streamlined and updated to reflect recent changes in inventory and accounts receivable management.

Chapter 17 The International Business chapter has been simplified and updated with a new section on "The Euro: The New Currency of Europe."

Acknowledgments

We gratefully acknowledge the assistance, support, and encouragement of those individuals who have contributed to *Foundations of Finance*. Specifically, we wish to recognize the very helpful insights provided by many of our colleagues. For their careful comments and helpful reviews of the text, we are indebted to:

Ibrahim J. Affeneh
Indiana University of Pennsylvania

Sung C. Bae
Bowling Green State University

Laurey Berk
University of Wisconsin, Green Bay

Ronald W. Best
University of South Alabama

Stephen Black
University of Central Oklahoma

Laurence E. Blose
University of North Carolina Charlotte

Robert Boldin
Indiana University of Pennsylvania

Michael Bond
Cleveland State University

Waldo L. Born
Eastern Illinois University

Paul Bursik
St. Norbert College

Anthony K. Byrd
University of Central Florida

P. R. Chandy
University of North Texas

Santosh Choudhury
Norfolk State University

K. C. Chen
California State University, Fresno

Jeffrey S. Christensen
Youngstown State University

M.C. Chung
California State University Sacramento

Steven M. Dawson
University of Hawaii

Yashwant S. Dhatt
University of Southern Colorado

John W. Ellis
Colorado State University

Suzanne Erickson
Seattle University

Slim Feriani
George Washington University

Greg Filbeck
Miami University

Bruce Fredrikson
Syracuse University

Karen Hallows
George Mason University

Ken Halsey
Wayne State College

James D. Harriss
University of North Carolina Wilmington

Linda C. Hittle
San Diego State University

Joel Jankowski
University of Tampa

Gerry Jensen
Northern Illinois University

Steve Johnson
University of Texas at El Paso

Ravi Kamath
Cleveland State University

James D. Keys
Florida International University

Reinhold P. Lamb
University of North Carolina Charlotte

Larry Lang
University of Wisconsin

George B. F. Lanigan
University of North Carolina Greensboro

William R. Lasher
Nichols College

David E. Letourneau
Winthrop University

Ilene Levin
University of Minnesota—Duluth

Lee McClain
Western Washington University

Michael McMillan
Northern Virginia Community College

James E. McNulty
Florida Atlantic University

Grant McQueen
Brigham Young University

Judy E. Maese
New Mexico State University

Abbas Mamoozadeh
Slippery Rock University

Emil Meurer
University of New Orleans

Stuart Michelson
Eastern Illinois University

Eric J. Moon
San Francisco State University

Scott Moore
John Carroll University

Diane Morrison
University of Wisconsin at LaCrosse

Rick H. Mull
Fort Lewis College

M. P. Narayanan
University of Michigan

William E. O'Connell Jr.
College of William & Mary

Jeffrey H. Peterson
  St. Bonaventure University
Mario Picconi
  University of San Diego
Stuart Rosenstein
  Clemson University
Ivan C. Roten
  Arizona State University
Marjorie A. Rubash
  Bradley University
Joseph Stanford
  Bridgewater State College
David Suk
  Rider University
Charlene Sullivan
  Purdue University
Elizabeth Sun
  San Jose State University
R. Bruce Swensen
  Adelphi University
Philip R. Swensen
  Utah State University
Lee Tenpao
  Niagara University

Paul A. Vanderheiden
  University of Wisconsin, Eau Claire
Nikhil P. Varaiya
  San Diego State University
K. G. Viswanathan
  Hofstra University
Al Webster
  Bradley University
Patricia Webster
  Bradley University
Herbert Weinraub
  Michigan State University
Herbert Weinraub
  University of Toledo
Sandra Williams
  Moorhead State University
Tony R. Wingler
  University of North Carolina Greensboro
Wold Zemedkun
  Norfolk State University
Marc Zenner
  Indiana University

We also wish to thank a wonderful group of people at Prentice Hall. To Maureen Riopelle, our Executive Editor, we owe an immeasurable debt of gratitude. She has continued to push us to make sure that we deliver the finest possible textbook and supplementary package possible. Her efforts go well beyond what one might expect from the best of editors. We also offer our personal expression of appreciation to Gladys Soto for her editorial deftness. Not only is she bright, insightful, and attentive to detail—in short, a gifted Managing Editor—but she also made the revision a fun experience. She is a true friend. If it were not for Cheryl Clayton, something no doubt would have fallen through the cracks. Always on top of the revision process, she demonstrated coordinating skills that were simply the best. To Carol Samet, the Production Editor, we express a very special thank you for overseeing the book through a very complex production process and keeping it all on schedule while maintaining extremely high quality. Carol earns a "beyond-the-call-of duty" applause from all of us! Our appreciation to the people at Prentice Hall would be extremely incomplete without the mention of the highly professional Prentice Hall field sales people and their managers. In our opinion they are the best in the business, and we are delighted with their dedicated performance. We thank Lenda Hill and the recently retired Glenn Furney at Texas Instruments for their help in bringing to life the use of calculators in the teaching of financial management.

As a final word, we express our sincere thanks to those using *Foundations of Finance* in the classroom. We thank you for making us a part of your team. Always feel free to give any of us a call when you have questions or needs.

A. J. K.

J. D. M

J. W. P.

D. F. S.

Chapter One

Goal of the Firm • Legal Forms of Business
Organization • Federal Income Taxation •
Ten Axioms That Form the Foundations of
Financial Management • Finance and the
Multinational Firm: The New Role • Overview
of the Text

AN INTRODUCTION TO THE FOUNDATIONS OF FINANCIAL MANAGEMENT— THE TIES THAT BIND

LEARNING OBJECTIVES

AFTER READING THIS CHAPTER, YOU SHOULD BE ABLE TO:

1. Identify the goal of the firm.
2. Compare the various legal forms of business organization and explain why the corporate form of business is the most logical choice for a firm that is large or growing.
3. Describe the corporate tax features that affect business decisions.
4. Explain the 10 axioms that form the foundations of financial management.
5. Explain what has led to the era of the multinational corporation.
6. State the general topics to be covered in the remainder of this text.

In mid-1993 Volkswagen (VW) was going nowhere with its product line. The real success of the company rested on one product, the original VW Beetle. At one time they were everywhere. VW produced more than 21 million of them over a 50-year period. They were the hand-me-down cars that had that "it's-so-ugly-it's-cute" look. Plastered with Grateful Dead bumper stickers, they became the car of choice for the counterculture of the late 1960s and early 1970s. However, with time the Beetle simply lost its popularity, and eventually the Beetle line was dropped only to be replaced by the VW Rabbit, Golf, Passat, and Polo—with the Passat only lately taking on popularity.

Thus in mid-1993 in VW's design studio in Simi Valley, California, VW executives decided the time was right to bring back the old, and the New Beetle was born. A new plant was built in Puebla, Mexico, while design teams worked to refine the concept. With the Dodge/Plymouth Neon, a similarly sized car selling for about $3,000 less, how would the New Beetle be accepted by the public? Clearly, if Volkswagen had miscalculated, the company would be in trouble. Fortunately for them, they hadn't, and in March 1998 the New Beetle was introduced, and it was an eye-popping, traffic-stopping success.

How did a company like Volkswagen reinvent itself? The answer is through sound financial management. Financial management deals with the maintenance and creation of economic value or wealth by focusing on decision making with an eye toward creating wealth. As such, this text deals with financial decisions such as when to introduce a new product, when to invest in new assets, when to replace existing assets, when to borrow from banks, when to sell stocks or bonds, when to extend credit to a customer, and how much cash and inventory to maintain. All of these aspects of financial management were factors in Volkswagen's decision to introduce the New Beetle, and the end result was that this decision created wealth for Volkswagen.

WHAT'S AHEAD

In this chapter, we lay a foundation for the entire book, by discussing what finance is and then explaining the key goal that guides financial decision making: maximization of shareholder wealth. We discuss the legal and tax environment of financial decisions and describe the golden thread that ties everything together: the 10 basic axioms of finance. Finally, we briefly look at what has led to the rise in multinational corporations.

Objective 1

GOAL OF THE FIRM

In this text we designate the goal of the firm as *maximization of shareholder wealth*, by which we mean maximization of the price of the existing common stock. Not only does this goal directly benefit the shareholders of the company, but also it provides benefits to society as scarce resources are directed to their most productive use by businesses competing to create wealth. With this goal in place, our job as financial managers is to create wealth for the shareholders. To better understand this goal, we first discuss profit maximization as a possible goal for the firm. Then we compare it to maximization of shareholder wealth to see why, in financial management, the latter is the more appropriate goal for the firm.

Profit Maximization

Takin' It to the Net
As you'll soon find out, finance has a language all its own. If you ever come across terms you aren't familiar with, try looking them up in the TIAA-CREF financial dictionary http://www.tiaa-cref.org/dict.html.

In microeconomics courses, profit maximization is frequently given as the goal of the firm. Profit maximization stresses the efficient use of capital resources, but it is not specific with respect to the time frame over which profits are to be measured. Do we maximize profits over the current year, or do we maximize profits over some longer period? A financial manager could easily increase current profits by eliminating research and development expenditures and cutting down on routine maintenance. In the short run, this might result in increased profits, but this clearly is not in the best long-run interests of the firm. If we are to base financial decisions on a goal, that goal must be precise, not allow for misinterpretation, and deal with all the complexities of the real world.

In microeconomics, profit maximization functions largely as a theoretical goal, with economists using it to prove how firms behave rationally to increase profit. Unfortunately, it ignores many real-world complexities that financial managers must address in their decisions. In the more applied discipline of financial management, firms must deal every day with two major factors not considered by the goal of profit maximization: uncertainty and timing.

Microeconomics courses ignore uncertainty and risk to present theory more easily. Projects and investment alternatives are compared by examining their expected values or weighted average profits. Whether one project is riskier than another does not enter into these calculations; economists do discuss risk, but only tangentially.[1] In reality, projects differ a great deal with respect to risk characteristics, and to disregard these differences in the practice of financial management can result in incorrect decisions. As we discover later in this chapter, there is a very definite relationship between risk and expected return—that is, investors demand a higher expected return for taking on added risk—and to ignore this relationship leads to improper decision making.

Another problem with the goal of profit maximization is that it ignores the timing of the project's returns. If this goal is only concerned with this year's profits, we know it inappropriately ignores profit in future years. If we interpret it to maximize the average of future profits, it is also incorrect. Inasmuch as investment opportunities are available for money in hand, we are not indifferent to the timing of the returns. Given equivalent cash flows from profits, we want those cash flows sooner rather than later. Thus, the real-world factors of uncertainty and timing force us to look beyond a simple goal of profit maximization as a decision criterion. We now turn to an examination of a more robust goal for the firm: maximization of shareholder wealth.

Maximization of Shareholder Wealth

In formulating the goal of maximization of shareholder wealth we are doing nothing more than modifying the goal of profit maximization to deal with the complexities of the operating environment. We have chosen maximization of shareholder wealth—that is, maximization of the market value of the existing shareholders' common stock—because the effects of all financial decisions are thereby included. Investors react to poor investment or dividend decisions by causing the total value of the firm's stock to fall, and they react to good decisions by pushing up the price of the stock. In effect, under this goal, good decisions are those that create wealth for the shareholder.

Obviously, there are some serious practical problems in direct use of this goal and in using changes in the firm's stock to evaluate financial decisions. Many things affect stock prices; to attempt to identify a reaction to a particular financial decision would simply be impossible and unnecessary. To employ this goal, we need not consider every stock price change to be a market interpretation of the worth of our decisions. Other factors, such as changes in the economy, also affect stock prices. What we do focus on is the effect that our decision *should* have on the stock price if everything else were held constant. The market price of the firm's stock reflects the value of the firm as seen by its owners and takes into account the complexities and complications of the real-world risk. As we follow this goal throughout our discussions, we must keep in mind one more question: Who exactly are the shareholders? The answer: Shareholders are the legal owners of the firm.

CONCEPT CHECK

1. What are the problems with the goal of profit maximization?
2. What is the goal of the firm?

Takin' It to the Net
Given the goal of maximization of shareholder wealth, we know that if a corporation is to maximize shareholder wealth, the interests of the managers and the shareholders must be aligned. The simplest way to align these interests is to structure executive compensation packages appropriately to encourage managers to act in the best interests of shareholders. However, has executive compensation gotten out of control? Take a look at the Executive Pay Watch http://www.aflcio.org/paywatch/index.htm to see where top salaries have gone.

---

[1]See, for example, Robert S. Pindyck and Daniel Rubenfield, *Microeconomics*, 2d ed. (New York: Macmillan, 1992), pp. 244–246.

In the chapters ahead we focus on financial decisions for corporations because, although the corporation is not the only legal form of business available, it is the most logical choice for a firm that is large or growing. It is also the dominant business form in terms of sales in this country. In this section we explain why this is so. Focusing on corporations allows us to simplify the remainder of the text by following the corporate tax code, rather than examining different tax codes for different legal forms of businesses. Keep in mind that our primary purpose is to develop an understanding of the logic of financial decision making. Taxes become important only when they affect our decisions, and our discussion of the choice of the legal form of the business is directed at understanding why we limit our discussion of taxes to the corporate form.

Although numerous and diverse, the legal forms of business organization fall into three categories: the sole proprietorship, the partnership, and the corporation. To understand the basic differences between each form, we need to define each one and understand its advantages and disadvantages. As the firm grows, the advantages of the corporation begin to dominate. As a result, most large firms take on the corporate form.

Takin' It to the Net
If you're interested in starting your own business, take a look at the Small Business Administration's Web site http://www.sba.gov/. They have an on-line library with publications, free software, and all kinds of great information.

Sole Proprietorship

sole proprietorship

The **sole proprietorship** is *a business owned by an individual*. The owner maintains title to the assets and is responsible, generally without limitation, for the liabilities incurred. The proprietor is entitled to the profits from the business but must also absorb any losses. This form of business is initiated by the mere act of beginning the business operations. Typically, no legal requirement must be met in starting the operation, particularly if the proprietor is conducting the business in his or her own name. If a special name is used, an assumed-name certificate should be filed, requiring a small registration fee. Termination occurs on the owner's death or by the owner's choice. Briefly stated, the sole proprietorship is for all practical purposes the absence of any formal *legal* business structure.

Partnership

partnership

The primary difference between a partnership and a sole proprietorship is that the partnership has more than one owner. A **partnership** is *an association of two or more persons coming together as co-owners for the purpose of operating a business for profit.* Partnerships fall into two types: (1) general partnerships and (2) limited partnerships.

General Partnership

general partnership

In a **general partnership** *each partner is fully responsible for the liabilities incurred by the partnership.* Thus, any partner's faulty conduct even having the appearance of relating to the firm's business renders the remaining partners liable as well. The relationship among partners is dictated entirely by the partnership agreement, which may be an oral commitment or a formal document.

Limited Partnership

limited partnership

In addition to the general partnership, in which all partners are jointly liable without limitation, many states provide for a **limited partnership.** The state statutes permit *one or more of the partners to have limited liability, restricted to the amount of capital invested in the partnership.* Several conditions must be met to qualify as a limited partner. First, at least one general partner must remain in the association for whom the privilege of limited liability does not apply. Second, the names of the limited partners may not appear in the name of the firm. Third, the limited partners may not participate in the management of the business. If one of these restrictions is violated, all partners forfeit their right to limited liability. In essence, the intent of the statutes creating the limited partnership is to provide limited liability for a person whose interest in the partnership is purely as an investor. That individual may not assume a management function within the organization.

Corporation

The **corporation** has been a significant factor in the economic development of the United States. As early as 1819 Chief Justice John Marshall set forth the legal definition of a corporation as "an artificial being, invisible, intangible, and existing only in the contemplation of law."[2] This entity *legally functions separate and apart from its owners.* As such, the corporation can individually sue and be sued, and purchase, sell, or own property; and its personnel are subject to criminal punishment for crimes. However, despite this legal separation, the corporation is composed of owners who dictate its direction and policies. The owners elect a board of directors, whose members in turn select individuals to serve as corporate officers, including president, vice president, secretary, and treasurer. Ownership is reflected in common stock certificates, designating the number of shares owned by its holder. The number of shares owned relative to the total number of shares outstanding determines the stockholder's proportionate ownership in the business. Because the shares are transferable, ownership in a corporation may be changed by a shareholder simply remitting the shares to a new shareholder. The investor's liability is confined to the amount of the investment in the company, thereby preventing creditors from confiscating stockholders' personal assets in settlement of unresolved claims. This is an extremely important advantage of a corporation. After all, would you be willing to invest in USAir if you would be held liable if one of their planes crashed? Finally, the life of a corporation is not dependent on the status of the investors. The death or withdrawal of an investor does not affect the continuity of the corporation. The management continues to run the corporation when stock is sold or when it is passed on through inheritance.

corporation

Takin' It to the Net
Interested in doing well in this class? One place to find some extra help is the Companion Web site that accompanies this text http://cw.prenhall.com/ bookbind/pubbooks/keown/. Make sure you check it out. It has a study guide, current events, and Internet exercises.

Comparison of Organizational Forms

Owners of new businesses have some important decisions to make in choosing an organizational form. Whereas each business form seems to have some advantages over the others, the advantages of the corporation begin to dominate as the firm grows and needs access to the capital markets to raise funds.

Why Large and Growing Firms Choose the Corporate Form: Ease in Raising Capital

Because of the limited liability, the ease of transferring ownership through the sale of common shares, and the flexibility in dividing the shares, the corporation is the ideal business entity in terms of attracting new capital. In contrast, the unlimited liabilities of the sole proprietorship and the general partnership are deterrents to raising equity capital. Between the extremes, the limited partnership

---

[2] *The Trustees of Dartmouth College* v. *Woodard*, 4 Wheaton 636 (1819).

does provide limited liability for limited partners, which has a tendency to attract wealthy investors. However, the impracticality of having a large number of partners and the restricted marketability of an interest in a partnership prevent this form of organization from competing effectively with the corporation. Therefore, when developing our decision models we assume we are dealing with the corporate form. The taxes incorporated in these models deal only with the corporate tax codes. Because our goal is to develop an understanding of the management, measurement, and creation of wealth, and not to become tax experts, we only focus on those characteristics of the corporate tax code that affect our financial decisions.

The Role of the Financial Manager in a Corporation

Although a firm can assume many different organizational structures, Figure 1–1 presents a typical representation of how the finance area fits into a corporation. The Vice President for Finance, also called the Chief Financial Officer (CFO), serves under the corporation's Chief Executive Officer (CEO) and is responsible for overseeing financial planning, corporate strategic planning, and controlling the firm's cash flow. Typically, a Treasurer and Controller serve under the CFO. In a smaller firm, the same person may fill both roles, with just one office handling all the duties. The Treasurer generally handles the firm's financial activities, including cash and credit management, making capital expenditure decisions, raising funds, financial planning, and managing any foreign currency received by the firm. The Controller is responsible for managing the firm's accounting duties, including producing financial statements, cost accounting, paying taxes, and gathering and monitoring the data

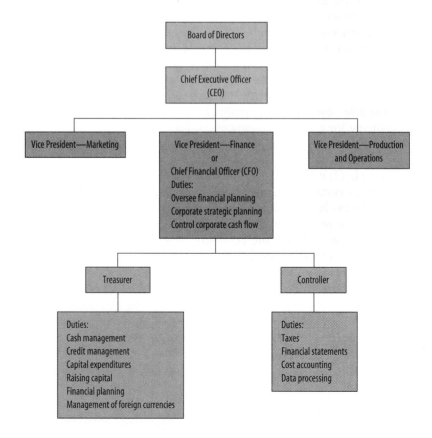

FIGURE 1–1

How the Finance Area Fits into a Corporation

necessary to oversee the firm's financial well-being. In this class, we focus on the duties generally associated with the Treasurer and on how investment decisions are made.

CONCEPT CHECK

1. What are the primary differences between a sole proprietorship, partnership, and a corporation?
2. Explain why large and growing firms tend to choose the corporate form.
3. What are the duties of the corporate treasurer? Of the corporate controller?

FEDERAL INCOME TAXATION

Objective 3

Before presenting the 10 axioms of finance that provide the conceptual underpinnings for what follow, we examine those tax features that affect our decisions. We describe the environment and set up the ground rules under which financial decisions are made. As the nation's politics change, so does the tax system. The purpose of looking at the current tax structure is not to become tax experts, but rather to gain an understanding of taxes and how they affect business decisions. There is a good chance that corporate tax rates will change significantly before you enter the workforce. However, although rates may change, taxes will continue to remain a cash outflow and therefore something to avoid. Thus, we pay close attention to which expenses are and are not deductible for tax purposes, and in doing so, focus on how taxes affect business decisions.

Objectives of Income Taxation

Originally, the sole objective of the federal government in taxing income was to generate financing for government expenditures. Although this purpose continues to be important, social and economic objectives have been added. For instance, a company may receive possible reductions in taxes if (1) it undertakes certain technological research, (2) it pays wages to certain economically disadvantaged groups, or (3) it locates in certain economically depressed areas. Other socially oriented stipulations in the tax laws include exemptions for dependents, old age, and blindness and a reduction in taxes on retirement income. In addition, the government uses tax legislation to stabilize the economy. In recessionary periods corporate taxes may be lowered to generate job growth. In short, three objectives may be given for the taxation of revenues: (1) the provision of revenues for government expenditures, (2) the achievement of socially desirable goals, and (3) economic stabilization.

Types of Taxpayers

To understand the tax system, we must first ask, "Who is the taxpayer?" For the most part, there are three basic types of taxable entities: individuals, corporations, and fiduciaries. Individuals include company employees, self-employed persons owning their own businesses, and members of a partnership. Income is reported by these

Takin' It to the Net
If you'd like some information on personal finance, take a look at the Personal Finance Navigator http://www.prenhall.com/keown, which accompanies the college textbook *Personal Finance: Turning Money Into Wealth*. When you go to this Web site, click on contents and it will take you to a table of contents that lists the chapters in the book. Each chapter has numerous links and articles of interest. In fact, there are approximately 900 links to help you plan your college finance requirements, make lease-versus-purchase decisions on a new car, get job hunting and investment information, understand tax changes, find out where to get the best loan deal, and much more.

Takin' It to the Net
Looking for tax information? The IRS has a great Web site http://www.irs.ustreas.gov/prod/cover.htm that is actually kind of fun (although nothing dealing with taxes is too much fun). It has tax information for the individual and business, along with tax statistics and downloadable forms and publications.

---

individuals in their personal tax returns.[3] The corporation, as a separate legal entity, reports its income and pays any taxes related to these profits. The owners (stockholders) of the corporation need not report these earnings in their personal tax returns, except when all or a part of the profits are distributed in the form of dividends. Finally, fiduciaries, such as estates and trusts, file a tax return and pay taxes on the income generated by the estate or trust that isn't distributed to (and included in the taxable income of) a beneficiary.

Although taxation of individual and fiduciary income is an important source of income to the government, neither is especially relevant to the financial manger. Because most firms of any size are corporations, we restrict our discussion to the corporation. A caveat is necessary, however. Tax legislation can be quite complex, with numerous exceptions to most general rules. The laws can also change quickly, and certain details discussed here may no longer apply in the near future. However, the general approach should remain the same, regardless of changes.

Computing Taxable Income

taxable income
gross income

The **taxable income** for a corporation is based on *the gross income from all sources, except for allowable exclusions, less any tax-deductible expenses.* **Gross income** equals *the firm's dollar sales from its products or services less the cost of producing or acquiring them.* Tax-deductible expenses include any operating expenses, such as marketing expenses, depreciation, and administrative expenses. Also, *interest expense* paid on the firm's outstanding debt is a tax-deductible expense. However, dividends paid to the firm's stockholders are *not* deductible expenses, but rather distributions of income. Other taxable income includes interest income and dividend income that the corporation receives.

To demonstrate how to compute a corporation's taxable income, consider the J and S Corporation, a manufacturer of home accessories. The firm, originally established by Kelly Stites, had sales of $50 million for the year. The cost of producing the accessories totaled $23 million. Operating expenses were $10 million. The corporation has $12.5 million in debt outstanding, with an 8 percent interest rate, which resulted in $1 million interest expense ($12,500,000 × .08 = $1,000,000). Management paid $1 million in dividends to the firm's common stockholders. No other income, such as interest or dividend income, was received. The taxable income for the J and S Corporation would be $16 million, as shown in Table 1–1.

Once we know the J and S Corporation's taxable income, we can next determine the amount of taxes the firm owes.

Computing the Taxes Owed

The taxes to be paid by the corporation on its taxable income are based on the corporate tax rate structure. The specific rates effective for the corporation, as of 1999, are given in Table 1–2. Under the Revenue Reconciliation Act of 1993 a new top marginal corporate tax rate of 35 percent was added for taxable income in excess of $10 million. Also, a surtax of 3 percent was imposed on taxable income between $15 million and $18,333,333. This, in combination with the previously existing 5 percent surtax on taxable income between $100,000 and $335,000, recaptures the benefits of the lower marginal rates and, as a result, both the average and marginal tax rates on taxable income above $18,333,333 become 35 percent.

---

[3]Partnerships report only the income from the partnership. The income is then reported again by each partner, who pays any taxes owed.

TABLE 1-1   J AND S CORPORATION TAXABLE INCOME

Sales		$50,000,000
Cost of goods sold		23,000,000
Gross profit		$27,000,000
Operating expenses		
Administrative expenses	$4,000,000	
Depreciation expenses	1,500,000	
Marketing expenses	4,500,000	
Total operating expenses		10,000,000
Operating income		
(earnings before interest and taxes)		$17,000,000
Other income		0
Interest expense		1,000,000
Taxable income		$16,000,000

Dividends paid to common stockholders ($1,000,000) are not tax-deductible expenses.

For example, the tax liability for the J and S Corporation, which had $16 million in taxable earnings, would be $5,530,000, calculated as follows:

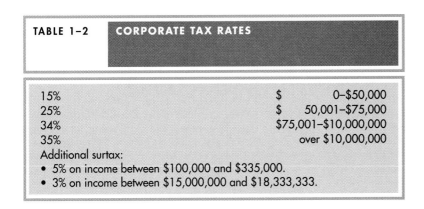

EARNINGS	×	MARGINAL TAX RATE	=	TAXES
$ 50,000	×	15%	=	$ 7,500
25,000	×	25%	=	6,250
9,925,000	×	34%	=	3,374,500
6,000,000	×	35%	=	2,100,000
				$5,488,250

Additional surtaxes:
- Add 5% surtax on income between $100,000 and $335,000 (5% × [$335,000 − $100,000])   11,750
- Add 3% surtax on income between $15,000,000 and $18,333,333 (3% × [$16,000,000 − $15,000,000])   30,000

Total tax liability $5,530,000

TABLE 1-2   CORPORATE TAX RATES

15%	$ 0–$50,000
25%	$ 50,001–$75,000
34%	$75,001–$10,000,000
35%	over $10,000,000

Additional surtax:
- 5% on income between $100,000 and $335,000.
- 3% on income between $15,000,000 and $18,333,333.

The tax rates shown in Table 1–2 are defined as the **marginal tax rates,** or *rates applicable to the next dollar of income.* For instance, if a firm has earnings of $60,000 and is contemplating an investment that would yield $10,000 in additional profits, the tax rate to be used in calculating the taxes on this added income is 25 percent; that is, the marginal tax rate is 25 percent. However, if the corporation already expects $20 million without the new investment, the extra $10,000 in earnings would be taxed at 35 percent, the marginal tax rate at the $20 million level of income. In the example, where the J and S Corporation has taxable income of $16 million, its marginal tax rate is 38 percent (this is because $16 million falls into the 35% tax bracket *with* a 3% surtax); that is, any additional income from new investments will be taxed at a rate of 38 percent. However, after taxable income exceeds $18,333,333, the marginal tax rate declines to 35 percent, when the 3 percent surtax no longer applies.

For financial decision making, it's the *marginal tax rate* rather than the average tax rate that we are concerned with. As becomes increasingly clear throughout the text, we always want to consider the tax consequences of any financial decision. The appropriate rate to be used in the analysis is the marginal tax rate, because it is this rate that will be applicable for any changes in earnings as a result of the decision being made. Thus, when making financial decisions involving taxes, always use the marginal tax rate in your calculations.[4]

The tax rate structure used in computing the J and S Corporation's taxes assumes that the income occurs in the United States. Given the globalization of the economy, it may well be that some of the income originates in a foreign country. If so, the tax rates, and the method of taxing the firm, frequently vary. As financial manager, you would minimize the firm's taxes by reporting as much income as possible in the low-tax-rate countries and as little as possible in the high-tax-rate countries. Of course, other factors, such as political risk, may discourage your efforts to minimize taxes across national borders.

Other Tax Considerations

In addition to the fundamental computation of taxes, several other aspects of the existing tax legislation have relevance for the financial manager. These are (1) the dividend income exclusion on dividends received by corporations, (2) the effects of depreciation on the firm's taxes, and (3) the recognition of capital gains and losses. Let's look at each of these tax provisions in turn.

Dividend Exclusion

A corporation may normally exclude 70 percent of any dividends received from another corporation. For instance, if corporation A owns common stock in corporation B and receives dividends of $1,000 in a given year, only $300 is subject to tax, and the remaining $700 (70 percent of $1,000) is tax exempt. If the corporation receiving the dividend income is in a 34 percent tax bracket, only $102 in taxes (34 percent of $300) will result.[5]

---

[4]On taxable income between $335,000 and $10 million, both the marginal and average tax rates equal 34 percent because of the imposition of the 5 percent surtax that applies to taxable income between $100,000 and $335,000. After the company's taxable income exceeds $18,333,333, both the marginal and average tax rates equal 35 percent because the 3 percent surtax on income between $15 million and $18,333,333 eliminates the benefits of having the first $10 million of income taxed at 34 rather than 35 percent.

[5]If corporation A owns at least 20 percent of corporation B, but less than 80 percent, 80 percent of any dividends received may be excluded from taxable income. If 80 percent or more is owned, all the dividends received may be excluded.

Depreciation

Depreciation is *the means by which an asset's value is expensed over its useful life for federal tax purposes.* Essentially, there are three methods for computing depreciation expenses: (1) straight-line depreciation, (2) the double-declining balance method, and (3) the modified accelerated cost recovery system. Any one of the three methods results in the same depreciation expense over the life of the asset; however, the last two approaches allow the firm to take the depreciation earlier as opposed to later, which in turn defers taxes until later. Assuming a time value of money, there is an advantage to using the accelerated techniques. (Chapter 6 fully explains the time value of money.) Also, management may use straight-line depreciation for reporting income to the shareholders while still using an accelerated method for calculating taxable income.

depreciation

Capital Gains and Losses

An important tax consideration before 1987 was the preferential tax treatment for **capital gains (or losses);** that is, *gains (or losses) from the sale of assets not bought or sold in the ordinary course of business.* The Tax Reform Act of 1986 repealed any special treatment of capital gains and while the Revenue Reconciliation Act of 1993 reinstituted preferential treatment in certain unique circumstances, in general, capital gains are taxed at the same rates as ordinary income. However, if a corporation has capital losses that exceed capital gains in any year, these net capital losses may not be deducted from ordinary income. The net losses may, however, be carried back and applied against net capital gains in each of the 3 years before the current year. If the loss is not completely used in the 3 prior years, any remaining loss may be carried forward and applied against any net gains in each of the next 5 years. For example, if a corporation has an $80,000 net capital loss in 1999, it may apply this loss against any net gains in 1996, 1997, and 1998. If any loss remains, it may be carried forward and applied against any gains through 2004.

capital gain (or loss)

Other Tax Concerns

As mentioned earlier, taxes are used not only to raise money, but also to promote socially desirable goals and to maintain economic stability. One way in which both of these goals are met is through the creation and retention of jobs. As a result, to keep struggling firms afloat, there is a tax provision that allows a corporation with an operating loss (which is simply a loss from operating a business) to apply this loss against income in other years. This is commonly referred to as a **net operating loss carryback and carryforward.** *This tax feature allows firms that lose money to recapture taxes they had previously paid, carrying losses back up to 2 years or forward up to 20 years to offset profits,* which hopefully allows them to deal with the problems that resulted in the loss. The bottom line is that the government wants to keep as many people employed as possible and to keep the markets as competitive as possible, and to do this they have set up a tax code that helps those in trouble stay afloat.

net operating loss carryback and carryforward

Putting It Together: An Example

To illustrate certain portions of the tax laws for a corporation, assume that the Griggs Corporation had sales during the past year of $5 million; its cost of goods sold was $3 million; and it incurred operating expenses of $1 million. In addition, it received $185,000 in interest income and $100,000 in dividend income from another

TABLE 1–3   GRIGGS CORPORATION TAX COMPUTATIONS

Sales			$ 5,000,000
Cost of goods sold			(3,000,000)
Gross profit			$ 2,000,000
Operating expenses			(1,000,000)
Operating income			$ 1,000,000
Other taxable income and expenses:			
Interest income		$185,000	
Dividend income	$ 100,000		
Less 70% exclusion	70,000	30,000	
Interest expense		(40,000)	175,000
Gain on land sale:			
Selling price		$100,000	
Cost		(50,000)	$ 50,000
Total taxable income			$ 1,225,000

Tax computation:

15% × $	50,000 =	$	7,500
25% ×	25,000 =		6,250
34% ×	1,150,000 =		391,000
	$ 1,225,000		

Add 5% surtax for income between $100,000 and $335,000	$ 11,750
Tax liability	$ 416,500

corporation. In turn, it paid $40,000 in interest and $75,000 in dividends. Finally, the company sold a piece of land for $100,000 that had cost $50,000 six years ago. Given this information, the firm's taxable income is $1,225,000 as computed in the top part of Table 1–3.

Based on the tax rates from Table 1–2, Grigg's tax liability is $416,500, as shown at the bottom of Table 1–3. Note that the $75,000 Griggs paid in dividends is not tax deductible. Also, because the firm's taxable income exceeds $335,000, and the 5 percent surtax no longer applies, the marginal tax rate and the average tax rate both equal 34 percent; that is, we could have computed Grigg's tax liability as 34 percent of $1,225,000, or $416,500.

CONCEPT CHECK

1. What is the difference between the average and marginal tax rate?
2. Are the U.S. corporate tax rates progressive? Do the largest corporations get a tax break on the first dollars they earn?
3. Because all depreciation methods result in the same depreciation expense over the life of the asset, why would a firm want to use an accelerated depreciation method rather than a straight-line method?

TEN AXIOMS THAT FORM THE FOUNDATIONS OF FINANCIAL MANAGEMENT

To the first-time student of finance, the subject matter may seem like a collection of unrelated decision rules. This could not be further from the truth. In fact, our decision rules, and the logic that underlies them, spring from 10 simple axioms that do not require knowledge of finance to understand. *However, although it is not necessary to understand finance in order to understand these axioms, it is necessary to understand these axioms in order to understand finance.* Keep in mind that although these axioms may at first appear simple or even trivial, they provide the driving force behind all that follows. These axioms weave together concepts and techniques presented in this text, thereby allowing us to focus on the logic underlying the practice of financial management.

Axiom 1: The Risk-Return Trade-off—We Won't Take on Additional Risk Unless We Expect to be Compensated with Additional Return

At some point we have all saved some money. Why have we done this? The answer is simple: to expand our future consumption opportunities. We are able to invest those savings and earn a return on our dollars because some people would rather forgo future consumption opportunities to consume more now—maybe they're borrowing money to open a new business or a company is borrowing money to build a new plant. Assuming there are a lot of different people that would like to use our savings, how do we decide where to put our money?

First, investors demand a minimum return for delaying consumption that must be greater than the anticipated rate of inflation. If they didn't receive enough to compensate for anticipated inflation, investors would purchase whatever goods they desired ahead of time or invest in assets that were subject to inflation and earn the rate of inflation on those assets. There isn't much incentive to postpone consumption if your savings are going to decline in terms of purchasing power.

Investment alternatives have different amounts of risk and expected returns. Investors sometimes choose to put their money in risky investments because these investments offer higher expected returns. The more risk an investment has, the higher will be its expected return. This relationship between risk and expected return is shown in Figure 1–2.

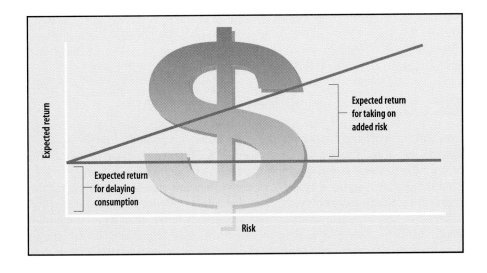

FIGURE 1-2

The Risk-Return Relationship

Notice that we keep referring to *expected* return rather than *actual* return. We may have expectations of what the returns from investing will be, but we can't peer into the future and see what those returns are actually going to be. If investors could see into the future, no one would have invested money in the medical device manufacturer Sabratek Corp., whose stock price dropped 52 percent on October 6, 1999, when it announced that it had delayed the filing of its financial reports for the second quarter with the Securities and Exchange Commission. This delayed filing led to Sabratek's delisting from NASDAQ. Until after the fact, you are never sure what the return on an investment will be. That is why General Motors bonds pay more interest than U.S. Treasury bonds of the same maturity. The additional interest convinces some investors to take on the added risk of purchasing a General Motors bond.

This risk-return relationship is a key concept as we value stocks, bonds, and proposed new projects throughout this text. We also spend some time determining how to measure risk. Interestingly, much of the work for which the 1990 Nobel Prize for Economics was awarded centered on the graph in Figure 1–2 and how to measure risk. Both the graph and the risk-return relationship it depicts reappear often in this text.

Axiom 2: The Time Value of Money—A Dollar Received Today Is Worth More Than a Dollar Received in the Future

A fundamental concept in finance is that money has a time value associated with it: A dollar received today is worth more than a dollar received a year from now. Because we can earn interest on money received today, it is better to receive money earlier rather than later. In your economics courses, this concept of the time value of money is referred to as the opportunity cost of passing up the earning potential of a dollar today.

In this text, we focus on the creation and measurement of wealth. To measure wealth or value, we use the concept of the time value of money to bring the future benefits and costs of a project back to the present. Then, if the benefits outweigh the costs, the project creates wealth and should be accepted; if the costs outweigh the benefits, the project does not create wealth and should be rejected. Without recognizing the existence of the time value of money, it is impossible to evaluate projects with future benefits and costs in a meaningful way.

To bring future benefits and costs of a project back to the present, we must assume a specific opportunity cost of money, or interest rate. Exactly what interest rate to use is determined by **Axiom 1: The Risk-Return Trade-off,** which states investors demand higher returns for taking on more risky projects. Thus, when we determine the present value of future benefits and costs, we take into account that investors demand a higher return for taking on added risk.

Axiom 3: Cash—Not Profits—Is King

In measuring wealth or value we use cash flows, not accounting profits, as our measurement tool. That is, we are concerned with when we have money in hand, when we can invest it and start earning interest on it, and when we can give it back to the shareholders in the form of dividends. Remember, it is cash flows, not profits, that are actually received by the firm and can be reinvested. Accounting profits, on the other hand, are shown when they are earned rather than when the money is actually in hand. As a result, a firm's cash flows and accounting profits may not occur together. For example, capital expenses, such as the purchase of new equipment or a building, are depreciated over several years, with the annual depreciation subtracted from profits. However, the cash flow associated with this expense generally occurs immediately. Therefore, cash outflows involving paying money out and cash inflows that can be reinvested correctly reflect the timing of the benefits and costs.

Axiom 4: Incremental Cash Flows—It's Only What Changes That Counts

In making business decisions, we are concerned with the results of those decisions: What happens if we say yes versus what happens if we say no? **Axiom 3** states that we should use cash flows to measure the benefits that accrue from taking on a new project. We are now fine-tuning our evaluation process so that we only consider incremental cash flows. The **incremental cash flow** is *the difference between the cash flows if the project is taken on versus what they will be if the project is not taken on.*

incremental cash flow

In 1997, General Mills, the maker of Cheerios, Frosted Cheerios, Apple Cinnamon Cheerios, and Multi-Grain Cheerios, introduced Team Cheerios—"3 delicious O's teamed up for one sweet crunch." Team Cheerios competed directly with General Mills' other cereals and, in particular, its Cheerios products. In fact, Team Cheerios, with its brown sugar and frosting, tastes very much like Frosted Cheerios. Certainly some of the sales dollars that ended up with Team Cheerios would have been spent on other Cheerios and General Mills products if Team Cheerios had not been available. Although General Mills was targeting younger consumers with this sweetened cereal, there is no question that Team Cheerios sales bit into—actually cannibalized—sales from Cheerios and other General Mills' lines. Realistically, there's only so much cereal anyone can eat. The *difference* between revenues General Mills generated after introducing Team Cheerios versus simply maintaining its existing line of cereals is the incremental cash flow. This difference reflects the true impact of the decision.

What is important is that we *think* incrementally. Our guiding rule in deciding whether a cash flow is incremental is to look at the company with and without the new product. In fact, let's take this incremental concept beyond cash flows and look at all consequences from all decisions on an incremental basis.

Axiom 5: The Curse of Competitive Markets—Why It's Hard to Find Exceptionally Profitable Projects

Our job as financial managers is to create wealth. Therefore, we look closely at the mechanics of valuation and decision making. We focus on estimating cash flows, determining what the investment earns, and valuing assets and new projects. However, it is easy to get caught up in the mechanics of valuation and lose sight of the process of creating wealth. Why is it so hard to find projects and investments that are exceptionally profitable? Where do profitable projects come from? The answers to these questions tell us a lot about how competitive markets operate and where to look for profitable projects.

In reality, it is much easier evaluating profitable projects than finding them. If an industry is generating large profits, new entrants are usually attracted. The additional competition and added capacity can result in profits being driven down to the required rate of return. Conversely, if an industry is returning profits below the required rate of return, then some participants in the market drop out, reducing capacity and competition. In turn, prices are driven back up. This is precisely what happened in the VCR video rental market in the mid-1980s. This market developed suddenly with the opportunity for extremely large profits. Because there were no barriers to entry, the market quickly was flooded with new entries. By 1987 the competition and price cutting produced losses for many firms in the industry, forcing them to flee the market. As the competition lessened with firms moving out of the video rental industry, profits again rose to the point where the required rate of return could be earned on invested capital.

In competitive markets, extremely large profits simply cannot exist for very long. Given that somewhat bleak scenario, how can we find good projects—that is, projects that return more than their expected rate of return given their risk level (remember Axiom 1)? Although competition makes them difficult to find, we have to invest in markets that are not perfectly competitive. The two most common ways of making markets less competitive are to differentiate the product in some key way or to achieve a cost advantage over competitors.

Product differentiation insulates a product from competition, thereby allowing a company to charge a premium price. If products are differentiated, consumer choice is no longer made by price alone. For example, many people are willing to pay a premium for Starbucks coffee. They simply want Starbucks and price is not important. In the pharmaceutical industry, patents create competitive barriers. Schering-Plough's Claritin, an allergy relief medicine, and Hoffman-La Roche's Valium, a tranquilizer, are protected from direct competition by patents.

Service and quality are also used to differentiate products. For example, Levi's has long prided itself on the quality of its jeans. As a result, it has been able to maintain its market share. Similarly, much of Toyota and Honda's brand loyalty is based on quality. Service can also create product differentiation, as shown by McDonald's fast service, cleanliness, and consistency of product that bring customers back.

Whether product differentiation occurs because of advertising, patents, service, or quality, the more the product is differentiated from competing products, the less competition it will face and the greater the possibility of large profits.

Economies of scale and the ability to produce at a cost below competition can effectively deter new entrants to the market and thereby reduce competition. Wal-Mart is one such case. For Wal-Mart, the fixed costs are largely independent of the store's size. For example, inventory costs, advertising expenses, and managerial salaries are essentially the same regardless of annual sales. Therefore, the more sales that can be built up, the lower the per-sale dollar cost of inventory, advertising, and management. Restocking from warehouses also becomes more efficient as delivery trucks can be used to full potential.

Regardless of how the cost advantage is created—by economies of scale, proprietary technology, or monopolistic control of raw materials—the cost advantage deters new market entrants while allowing production at below industry cost. This cost advantage has the potential of creating large profits.

The key to locating profitable investment projects is to first understand how and where they exist in competitive markets. Then the corporate philosophy must be aimed at creating or taking advantage of some imperfection in these markets, either through product differentiation or creation of a cost advantage, rather than looking to new markets or industries that appear to provide large profits. Any perfectly competitive industry that looks too good to be true won't be for long. It is necessary to understand this to know where to look for good projects and to accurately measure the project's cash flows. We can do this better if we recognize how wealth is created and how difficult it is to create.

Axiom 6: Efficient Capital Markets—The Markets Are Quick and the Prices Are Right

Our goal as financial managers is the maximization of shareholder wealth. How do we measure shareholder wealth? It is the value of all the shares that the shareholders own. To understand what causes stocks to change in price, as well as how securities such as bonds and stocks are valued or priced in the financial markets, it is necessary to have an understanding of the concept of **efficient markets.** *These are markets in which the values of all assets and securities at any instant in time fully reflect all available information.*

efficient markets

Whether a market is efficient has to do with the speed with which information is impounded into security prices. An efficient market is characterized by a large number of profit-driven individuals who act independently. In addition, new information regarding securities arrives in the market in a random manner. Given this setting, investors adjust to new information immediately and buy and sell the security until they feel the market price correctly reflects the new information. Under the efficient market hypothesis, information is reflected in security prices with such speed that there are no opportunities for investors to profit from publicly available information. Investors competing for profits ensure that security prices appropriately reflect the expected earnings and risks involved and thus the true value of the firm.

What are the implications of efficient markets for us? First, the price is right. Stock prices reflect all publicly available information regarding the value of the company. This means we can implement our goal of maximization of shareholder wealth by focusing on the effect each decision *should* have on the stock price if everything else is held constant. That is, over time good decisions result in higher stock prices and bad ones lower stock prices. Second, earnings manipulations through accounting changes do not result in price changes. Stock splits and other changes in accounting methods that do not affect cash flows are not reflected in prices. Market prices reflect expected cash flows available to shareholders. Thus, our preoccupation with cash flows to measure the timing of the benefits is justified.

As we will see, it is indeed reassuring that prices reflect value. It allows us to look at prices and see value reflected in them. Although it may make investing a bit less exciting, it makes corporate finance much less uncertain.

Axiom 7: The Agency Problem—Managers Won't Work for the Owners Unless It's in Their Best Interest

Although the goal of the firm is the maximization of shareholder wealth, in reality the agency problem may interfere with the implementation of this goal. The **agency problem** *results from the separation of management and the ownership of the firm.* For example, a large firm may be run by professional managers who have little or no ownership in the firm. Because of this separation of the decision makers and owners, managers may make decisions that are not in line with the goal of maximization of shareholder wealth. They may approach work less energetically and attempt to benefit themselves in terms of salary and perquisites at the expense of shareholders.

agency problem

To begin with, an agent is someone who is given the authority to act on behalf of another, referred to as the principal. In the corporate setting, the shareholders are the principals, because they are the actual owners of the firm. The Board of Directors, the CEO, the corporate executives, and all others with decision-making power are agents of the shareholders. Unfortunately, the Board of Directors, the CEO, and the other corporate executives don't always do what's in the best interest of the shareholders. Instead, they often act in their own best interest. Not only might they benefit themselves in terms of salary and perquisites, but they might also avoid any projects that have risk associated with them—even if they're great projects with huge potential returns and a small chance of failure. Why is this so? Because if the project doesn't turn out, these agents of the shareholders may lose their jobs.

The costs associated with the agency problem are difficult to measure, but occasionally we see the problem's effect in the marketplace. For example, if the market feels management of a firm is damaging shareholder wealth, we might see a positive reaction in stock price to the removal of that management. In 1989, on the day following the death of John Dorrance, Jr., chairman of Campbell's Soup, Campbell's stock price rose about 15 percent. Some investors felt that Campbell's relatively small growth in earnings might be improved with the departure of Dorrance. There was also speculation that Dorrance was the major obstacle to a possible positive reorganization.

Takin' It to the Net
For information on corporate governance, try the Corporate Governance Web site http://www.corpgov.net/, which has news links and a forum page that provides commentaries and conversations.

If the management of the firm works for the owners, who are the shareholders, why doesn't the management get fired if they don't act in the shareholders' best interest? *In theory*, the shareholders pick the corporate board of directors and the board of directors in turn picks the management. Unfortunately, *in reality* the system frequently works the other way around. Management selects the board of director nominees and then distributes the ballots. In effect, shareholders are offered a slate of nominees selected by the management. The end result is management effectively selects the directors, who then may have more allegiance to managers than to shareholders. This in turn sets up the potential for agency problems with the board of directors not monitoring managers on behalf of the shareholders as they should.

We spend considerable time discussing monitoring managers and trying to align their interests with shareholders. Managers can be monitored by auditing financial statements and managers' compensation packages. The interests of managers and shareholders can be aligned by establishing management stock options, bonuses, and perquisites that are directly tied to how closely their decisions coincide with the interest of shareholders. The agency problem will persist unless an incentive structure is set up that aligns the interests of managers and shareholders. In other words, what is good for shareholders must also be good for managers. If that is not the case, managers will make decisions in their best interest rather than maximizing shareholder wealth.

Axiom 8: Taxes Bias Business Decisions

Hardly any decision is made by the financial manager without considering the impact of taxes. When we introduced **Axiom 4,** we said that only incremental cash flows should be considered in the evaluation process. More specifically, the cash flows we consider are the *after-tax incremental cash flows to the firm as a whole.*

When we evaluate new projects, we will see income taxes play a significant role. When the company is analyzing the possible acquisition of a plant or equipment, the returns from the investment should be measured on an after-tax basis. Otherwise, the company is not evaluating the true incremental cash flows generated by the project.

The government also realizes taxes can bias business decisions and uses taxes to encourage spending in certain ways. If the government wants to encourage spending on research and development projects, it might offer an *investment tax credit* for such investments. This would have the effect of reducing taxes on research and development projects, which would in turn increase the after-tax cash flows from those projects. The increased cash flow would turn some otherwise unprofitable research and development projects into profitable projects. In effect, the government can use taxes as a tool to direct business investment to research and development projects, to the inner cities, and to projects that create jobs.

Axiom 9: **All Risk Is Not Equal—Some Risk Can Be Diversified Away, and Some Cannot**

Much of finance centers around **Axiom 1, The Risk-Return Trade-off.** But before we can fully use **Axiom 1** we must decide how to measure risk. As we will see, risk is difficult to measure. **Axiom 9** introduces you to the process of diversification and demonstrates how it can reduce risk. We also provide you with an understanding of how diversification makes it difficult to measure a project's or an asset's risk.

You are probably already familiar with the concept of diversification. There is an old saying, "don't put all your eggs in one basket." Diversification allows good and bad events or observations to cancel each other out, thereby reducing total variability without affecting expected return.

To see how diversification complicates the measurement of risk, let's look at the difficulty Louisiana Gas has in determining the level of risk associated with a new natural gas well-drilling project. Each year Louisiana Gas might drill several hundred wells, with each well having only a 1 in 10 chance of success. If the well produces, the profits are quite large, but if it comes up dry, the investment is lost. Thus, with a 90 percent chance of losing everything, we would view the project as being extremely risky. However, if each year Louisiana Gas drills 2,000 wells, all with a 10 percent, independent chance of success, then they would typically have 200 successful wells. Moreover, a bad year may result in only 190 successful wells, while a good year may result in 210 successful wells. If we look at all the wells together, the extreme good and the bad results tend to cancel each other out and the well-drilling projects taken together do not appear to have much risk or variability of possible outcome.

The amount of risk in a gas well project depends upon our perspective. Looking at the well standing alone, it looks like a lot; however, if we consider the risk that each well contributes to the overall firm risk, it is quite small. This occurs because much of the risk associated with each individual well is diversified away within the firm. The point is we can't look at a project in isolation. Later, we will see that some of this risk can be further diversified away within the shareholder's portfolio.

Perhaps the easiest way to understand the concept of diversification is to look at it graphically. Consider what happens when we combine two projects, as depicted in Figure 1–3. In this case, the cash flows from these projects move in opposite directions, and when they are combined, the variability of their combination is totally eliminated. Notice that the return has not changed—both the individual projects' and their combination's return averages 10 percent. In this case the extreme good and bad observations cancel each other out. The degree to which the total risk is reduced is a function of how the two sets of cash flows or returns move together.

As we will see for most projects and assets, some risk can be eliminated through diversification, while some risk cannot. This becomes an important distinction later in our studies. *For now, we should realize that the process of diversification can reduce risk, and as a result, measuring a project's or an asset's risk is very difficult.* A project's risk changes depending on whether you measure it standing alone or together with other projects the company may take on.

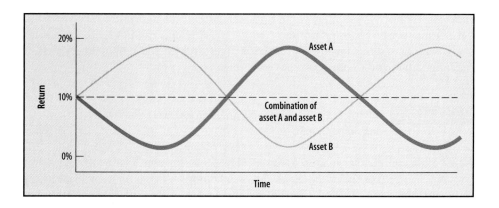

FIGURE 1–3
Reducing Risk Through Diversification

Axiom 10: Ethical Behavior Is Doing the Right Thing, and Ethical Dilemmas Are Everywhere in Finance

Ethics, or rather a lack of ethics in finance, is a recurring theme in the news. During the late 1980s and early 1990s the fall of Ivan Boesky and Drexel, Burnham, Lambert, and the near collapse of Salomon Brothers seemed to make continuous headlines. Meanwhile, the movie *Wall Street* was a hit at the box office and the book *Liar's Poker*, by Michael Lewis, chronicling unethical behavior in the bond markets, became a best-seller. As the lessons of Salomon Brothers and Drexel, Burnham, Lambert illustrate, ethical errors are not forgiven in the business world. Not only is acting in an ethical manner morally correct, it is congruent with our goal of maximization of shareholder wealth.

Ethical behavior means "doing the right thing." The difficulty arises, however, in attempting to define "doing the right thing." The problem is that each of us has his or her own set of values, which forms the basis for our personal judgments about what is the right thing to do. However, every society adopts a set of rules or laws that prescribe what it believes to be "doing the right thing." In a sense, we can think of laws as a set of rules that reflect the values of the society as a whole, as they have evolved. For purposes of this text, we recognize that individuals have a right to disagree about what constitutes "doing the right thing," and we seldom venture beyond the basic notion that ethical conduct involves abiding by society's rules. However, we point out some of the ethical dilemmas that have arisen in recent years with regard to the practice of financial management. So as we embark on our study of finance and encounter ethical dilemmas, we encourage you to consider the issues and form your own opinions. At this point you might want to look at the Ethics in Financial Management box on page 21. It illustrates that many times ethical questions are not easily answered, but they must be dealt with on a day-to-day basis.

Many students ask, "Is ethics really relevant?" This is a good question and deserves an answer. First, although business errors can be forgiven, ethical errors tend to end careers and terminate future opportunities. Why? Because *unethical behavior eliminates trust, and without trust businesses cannot interact.* Second, *the most damaging event a business can experience is a loss of the public's confidence in its ethical standards.* In finance we have seen several recent examples of such events. It was the ethical scandals involving insider trading at Drexel, Burnham, Lambert that brought down that firm. In 1991 the ethical scandals involving attempts by Salomon Brothers to corner the Treasury bill market led to the removal of its top executives and nearly put the company out of business.

Takin' It to the Net
Ethical problems seem to crop up all the time in finance. If you'd like more information on some of the worst, take a look at the Financial Scandals Web site http://www.ex.ac.uk/~RDavies/arian/scandals/. It's got information on BCCI, Barings, Daiwa, Sumitomo, Credit Lyonnais, Bre-X, Lloyds, and NASDAQ.

Is It Wrong to Tell a Lie?

In a February 1996 article in the *Journal of Business Ethics*, 400 people were asked to play the role of a fictional executive named Todd Fogler, who is faced with an ethical decision. The authors found that 47 percent of the top executives, 41 percent of the controllers, and 76 percent of the graduate-level business students they studied were willing to commit fraud by understating write-offs that cut into their companies' profits. When you hear about a study like this, the initial reaction of many students is that such ethical dilemmas are only the concerns of the top executives. They aren't—they are everywhere, and they are faced by everyone.

A teacher might not be able to change ethical standards in a college classroom, but he or she can teach students how to analyze questions so that they can bring to bear whatever ethical standards they have when they make decisions.

If you haven't already done so, there is no better time than now to develop a rule or set of rules against which you can measure the "rightness" or "wrongness" of your decisions and actions. It may be nothing more provocative than "Do unto others as you would have them do unto you." Or it may be a question or set of questions that you consistently ask: How would I feel about explaining to my parents or children what I did? How would I feel if the action I took were described, in detail, on the front page of my local newspaper? Have I avoided even the appearance of a conflict of interest in my decision? Would my action infringe on the liberty or constitutional rights of others?

Let's begin our look at ethical dilemmas in finance by asking this question: Is it wrong to tell a lie?

One of the roles of the financial manager is to transmit financial information to people outside the company. Occasionally, the facts that the financial manager must transmit and explain aren't particularly flattering to the firm. This presents the dilemma of whether it is unethical to tell a lie.

For example, at the annual stockholders' meeting a senior financial manager is reviewing her company's financial performance for the previous year. The news is not good. Sales dropped 30 percent, and profits were down 50 percent. A stockholder asks the manager, "What caused this drastic decline and has it been corrected?" The manager knows that the primary cause of the decline was a series of poor top-management decisions made over the past several years, but she also knows that's not what her colleagues want her to say. Furthermore, she personally believes the decline is far from over, but she recognizes that's not what the stockholders want to hear.

Should this financial manager lie? Is lying always wrong, or is it acceptable under certain circumstances? What, if any, would those circumstances be? What do you think?

Adapted by permission from Stephan P. Robbins, *Management*, 3rd ed., p. 11. Copyright 1991 by Prentice Hall, Inc.

Beyond the question of ethics is the question of social responsibility. In general, corporate social responsibility means that a corporation has responsibilities to society beyond the maximization of shareholder wealth. It asserts that a corporation answers to a broader constituency than shareholders alone. As with most debates that center on ethical and moral questions, there is no definitive answer. One opinion is that because financial managers are employees of the corporation, and the corporation is owned by the shareholders, the financial managers should run the corporation in such a way that shareholder wealth is maximized and then allow the shareholders to decide if they would like to fulfill a sense of social responsibility by passing on any of the profits to deserving causes. This is the view presented by Milton Friedman in the Ethics in Financial Management box. Very few corporations consistently act in this way. For example, Bristol-Myers Squibb Co. has an ambitious program to give away heart medication to those who cannot pay for it. This program came in the wake of an American Heart Association report showing that many of the nation's working poor face severe health risks because they cannot afford such medications. Clearly, Bristol-Myers

Squibb felt it had a social responsibility to provide this medicine to the poor at no cost.

How do you feel about this decision?

A Final Note on the Axioms

Hopefully, these axioms are as much statements of common sense as they are theoretical statements. These axioms provide the logic behind what is to follow. We build on them and attempt to draw out their implications for decision making. As we continue, try to keep in mind that while the topics being treated may change from chapter to chapter, the logic driving our treatment of them is constant and rooted in these 10 axioms.

CONCEPT CHECK

1. According to Axiom 1, how do investors decide where to invest their money?
2. Why is it so hard to find extremely profitable projects?
3. Why is ethics relevant?

Objective 5

FINANCE AND THE MULTINATIONAL FIRM: THE NEW ROLE

In the search for profits, U.S. corporations have been forced to look beyond our country's borders. This movement has been spurred on by the collapse of communism and the acceptance of the free market system in Third World countries. All this has taken place at a time when information technology has experienced a revolution brought on by the personal computer (PC). Concurrently, the United States went through an unprecedented period of deregulation of industries. These changes resulted in the opening of new international markets and U.S. firms experienced a period of price competition here at home that made it imperative that businesses look across borders for investment opportunities. The end result is that many U.S. companies, including General Electric, IBM, Walt Disney, American Express, and General Motors, have restructured their operations in order to expand internationally. However, not only do U.S. firms have a freer access to international markets, but also foreign firms have an easier job of entering the U.S. markets and competing with U.S. firms on their own turf.

The bottom line is what you think of as a U.S. firm may be much more of a multinational firm than you would expect. For example, Coca-Cola earns over 80% of its profits from overseas sales. Moreover, Coca-Cola earns more money from its sales in Japan than it does from all its domestic sales, and this is not uncommon. In fact, Dow Chemical, Colgate-Palmolive, 3M, Compaq, Hewlett-Packard, and Gillette make over half their sales overseas and earn over half of their profits from international sales. In addition to U.S. firms venturing abroad, foreign firms have also made their mark in the United States. You need only look to the auto industry to see what changes the entrance of Toyota, Honda, Nissan, BMW, and other foreign car manufacturers have had on the auto industry. In addition, foreigners have bought and now own such companies as Brooks Brothers, RCA, Pillsbury, A&P, 20th Century Fox, Columbia Pictures, and Firestone Tire & Rubber. Consequently, even if we wanted to, we couldn't keep all our attention focused on the United States, and even more important, we wouldn't want to ignore the opportunities that are available across international borders.

CONCEPT CHECK

1. What has brought on the era of the multinational corporation?
2. Has looking beyond U.S. borders been a profitable experience for U.S. corporations?

OVERVIEW OF THE TEXT

Objective 6

In this text we focus on the maintenance and creation of wealth. Although this involves attention to decision-making techniques, we emphasize the logic behind those techniques to ensure that you do not lose sight of the concepts driving finance and the creation of wealth. The text begins by discussing the goal of the firm, a goal that is to be used in financial decision making. It also presents the legal and tax environment in which these decisions are to be made. Because this environment sets the ground rules, it is necessary to understand it before decision rules can be formulated. The 10 guiding axioms that provide the underpinnings for what is to follow are then presented. In Chapter 2, the financial markets and interest rates are examined, looking at both the determinants of interest rates and their effect on business decisions. Chapters 3, 4, and 5 introduce the basic financial tools the financial manager uses to maintain control over the firm and its operations. These tools enable the financial manger to locate potential problem areas and plan for the future.

In Chapter 6 our focus turns to how the firm and its assets are valued. It begins with an examination of the mathematics of finance and the concept of the time value of money. An understanding of this topic allows us to compare benefits and costs that occur in different time periods. Valuation of fixed-income securities is then examined in Chapter 7. Valuation models that attempt to explain how different financial decisions affect the firm's stock price are examined in Chapter 8. We move on in Chapter 9 to develop an understanding of the meaning and measurement of risk and return.

Using the valuation principles just developed, our discussion in Chapter 10 turns to the capital-budgeting decision, which involves the financial evaluation of investment proposals in fixed assets. We then examine, in Chapter 11, the measurement of cash flows and introduce methods to incorporate risk in the analysis. In Chapter 12, we examine the financing of a firm's chosen projects, looking at what costs are associated with alternative ways of raising new funds.

Chapter 13 examines the firm's capital structure along with the impact of leverage on returns to the enterprise. It is followed in Chapter 14 with a discussion of the determination of the dividend-retained earnings decision. Chapter 15 deals with working-capital management and the management of current assets. We discuss methods for determining the appropriate investment in cash, marketable securities, inventory, and accounts receivable, as well as the risks associated with these investments and the control of these risks. Chapter 17 provides an introduction to international financial management, focusing on how financial decisions are affected by the international environment.

Milton Friedman
on the Social Responsibility of Corporations

There is a difference between acting in a socially responsible way and acting ethically. Milton Friedman does a good job of stating the argument that corporations do not have "social responsibility." This view is far from universally held. The purpose of the following is to make you think about this issue.

In a free-enterprise, private-property system, a corporate executive is an employee of the owners of the business. He has direct responsibility to his employers. That responsibility is to conduct the business in accordance with their desires, which generally will be to make as much money as possible while conforming to the basic rules of the society, both those embodied in law and those embodied in ethical custom.

Of course, the corporate executive is also a person in his own right. As a person, he may have many other responsibilities that he recognizes or assumes voluntarily—to his family, his conscience, his feelings of charity, his church, his clubs, his city, his country. He may feel impelled by these responsibilities to devote part of his income to causes he regards as worthy, to refuse to work for particular corporations, even to leave his job, for example, to join his country's armed forces. If we wish, we may refer to some of these responsibilities as "social responsibilities." But in these respects he is acting as a principal, not an agent; he is spending his own money or time or energy, not the money of his employers or the time or energy he has contracted to devote to their purposes. If these are "social responsibilities," they are the social responsibilities of individuals, not of business.

What does it mean to say that the corporate executive has a "social responsibility" in his capacity as a businessman? If this statement is not pure rhetoric, it must mean that he is to act in some way that is not in the interest of his employers. For example, that he is to refrain from increasing the price of the product in order to contribute to the social objective of preventing inflation, even though a price increase would be in the best interests of the corporation. Or that he is to make expenditures on reducing pollution beyond the amount that is in the best interests of the corporation or that is required by law in order to contribute to the social objective of improving the environment. Or that, at the expense of corporate profits, he is to hire "hard-core" unemployed instead of better-qualified available workmen to contribute to the social objective of reducing poverty.

In each of these cases, the corporate executive would be spending someone else's money for a general social interest. Insofar as his actions with his "social responsibility" reduce returns to stockholders, he is spending their money. Insofar as his actions raise the price to customers, he is spending the customers' money. Insofar as his actions lower the wages of some employees, he is spending their money.

The stockholders or the customers or the employees could separately spend their own money on the particular actions if they wished to do so. The executive is exercising a distinct "social responsibility," rather than serving as an agent of the stockholders or the customers or the employees, only if he spends the money in a different way than they would have spent it.

But if he does this, he is in effect imposing taxes, on the one hand, and deciding how the tax proceeds shall be spent, on the other.

SUMMARY

Objective 1 This chapter outlines the framework for the maintenance and creation of wealth. In introducing decision-making techniques aimed at creating wealth, we emphasize the logic behind those techniques. This chapter begins with an examination of the goal of the firm.

The commonly accepted goal of profit maximization is contrasted with the more complete goal of maximization of shareholder wealth. Because it deals well with uncertainty and time in a real-world environment, the goal of maximization of shareholder wealth is found to be the proper goal for the firm.

The legal forms of business are examined. The sole proprietorship is a business operation owned and managed by an individual. Initiating this form of business is simple and generally does not involve any substantial organizational costs. The proprietor has complete control of the firm but must be willing to assume full responsibility for its outcomes. Objective 2

The general partnership, which is simply a coming together of two or more individuals, is similar to the sole proprietorship. The limited partnership is another form of partnership sanctioned by states to permit all but one of the partners to have limited liability if this is agreeable to all partners.

The corporation increases the flow of capital from public investors to the business community. Although larger organizational costs and regulations are imposed on this legal entity, the corporation is more conducive to raising large amounts of capital. Limited liability, continuity of life, and ease of transfer in ownership, which increase the marketability of the investment, have contributed greatly in attracting large numbers of investors to the corporate environment. The formal control of the corporation is vested in the parties who own the greatest number of shares. However, day-to-day operations are managed by the corporate officers, who theoretically serve on behalf of the common stockholders.

The tax environment is presented. In introducing taxes we focus on taxes that affect our business decisions. Three taxable entities exist: the individual, including partnerships; the corporation; and the fiduciary. Only information on the corporate tax environment is given here. Objective 3

For the most part, taxable income for the corporation is equal to the firm's operating income plus capital gains less any interest expense. The corporation is allowed an income exclusion of 70 percent of the dividends received from another corporation.

Tax consequences have a direct bearing on the decisions of the financial manager. The relationships are grounded in the taxability of investment income and the difference in tax treatment for interest expense and dividend payments. Also, shareholders' tax status may influence their preference between gains from stock sale and dividends, which in turn may influence corporate dividend policy.

An examination of the 10 axioms on which finance is built is presented. The techniques and tools introduced in this text are all motivated by these 10 principles or axioms. They are: Objective 4

Axiom 1: The Risk-Return Trade-off—We Won't Take on Additional Risk Unless We Expect to Be Compensated with Additional Return
Axiom 2: The Time Value of Money—A Dollar Received Today Is Worth More Than a Dollar Received in the Future
Axiom 3: Cash—Not Profits—Is King
Axiom 4: Incremental Cash Flows—It's Only What Changes That Counts
Axiom 5: The Curse of Competitive Markets—Why It's Hard to Find Exceptionally Profitable Projects
Axiom 6: Efficient Capital Markets—The Markets Are Quick and the Prices Are Right
Axiom 7: The Agency Problem—Managers Won't Work for the Owners Unless It's in Their Best Interest
Axiom 8: Taxes Bias Business Decisions
Axiom 9: All Risk Is Not Equal—Some Risk Can Be Diversified Away, and Some Cannot
Axiom 10: Ethical Behavior Is Doing the Right Thing, and Ethical Dilemmas Are Everywhere in Finance

With the collapse of communism and the acceptance of the free market system in Third World countries, U.S. firms have been spurred on to look beyond our own boundaries for new business. The end result has been that it is not uncommon for major U.S. companies to earn over half their income from sales abroad. Objective 5

This section provides an overview of the text. Objective 6

agency problem, 17

capital gain (or loss), 11

corporation, 5

depreciation, 11

efficient markets, 17

general partnership, 4

gross income, 8

incremental cash flow, 15

limited partnership, 4

marginal tax rate, 10

net operating loss carryback and carryforward, 11

partnership, 4

sole proprietorship, 4

taxable income, 8

STUDY QUESTIONS

1-1 What are some of the problems involved in the use of profit maximization as the goal of the firm? How does the goal of maximization of shareholder wealth deal with those problems?

1-2 Compare and contrast the goals of profit maximization and maximization of shareholder wealth.

1-3 Firms often involve themselves in projects that do not result directly in profits; for example, IBM and ExxonMobil frequently support public television broadcasts. Do these projects contradict the goal of maximization of shareholder wealth? Why or why not?

1-4 What is the relationship between financial decision making and risk and return? Would all financial managers view risk-return trade-offs similarly?

1-5 Define (a) sole proprietorship, (b) partnership, and (c) corporation.

1-6 Identify the primary characteristics of each form of legal organization.

1-7 Using the following criteria, specify the legal form of business that is favored: (a) organizational requirements and costs, (b) liability of the owners, (c) continuity of business, (d) transferability of ownership, (e) management control and regulations, (f) ability to raise capital, and (g) income taxes.

1-8 Does a partnership pay taxes on its income? Explain.

1-9 When a corporation receives a dividend from another corporation, how is it taxed?

1-10 What is the purpose of the net operating loss carryback and carryforward?

SELF-TEST PROBLEM

ST-1 *(Corporate Income Tax)* The Dana Flatt Corporation had sales of $2 million this past year. Its cost of goods sold was $1.2 million, and its operating expenses were $400,000. Interest expenses on outstanding debts were $100,000, and the company paid $40,000 in preferred stock dividends. The corporation received $10,000 in preferred stock dividends and interest income of $12,000. The firm sold stock that had been owned for 2 years for $40,000; the original cost of the stock was $30,000. Determine the corporation's taxable income and its tax liability.

STUDY PROBLEMS

1-1 *(Corporate Income Tax)* The William B. Waugh Corporation is a regional Toyota dealer. The firm sells new and used trucks and is actively involved in the parts business. During the most recent year the company generated sales of $3 million. The combined cost of goods sold and the operating expenses were $2.1 million. Also, $400,000 in interest expense was paid during the year. The firm received $6,000 during the year in dividend income from 1,000 shares of common stock that had been purchased 3 years previously. However, the stock was sold toward the end of the year for $100 per share; its initial cost was $80 per share. The company also sold land that had been recently purchased and had been held for only 4 months. The selling price was $50,000; the cost was $45,000. Calculate the corporation's tax liability.

1-2 *(Corporate Income Tax)* Sales for L. B. Menielle, Inc., during the past year amounted to $5 million. The firm provides parts and supplies for oil field service companies. Gross profits for the year were $3 million. Operating expenses totaled $1 million. The interest and dividend income from securities owned were $20,000 and $25,000, respectively. The firm's interest expense was $100,000. The firm sold securities on two occasions during the year, receiving a gain of $40,000 on the first sale but losing $50,000 on the second. The stock sold first had been owned for 4 years; the stock sold second had been purchased 3 months before the sale. Compute the corporation's tax liability.

1-3 *(Corporate Income Tax)* Sandersen, Inc., sells minicomputers. During the past year the company's sales were $3 million. The cost of its merchandise sold came to $2 million, and cash operating expenses were $400,000; depreciation expense was $100,000, and the firm paid $150,000 in interest on bank loans. Also, the corporation received $50,000 in dividend income but paid $25,000 in the form of dividends to its own common stockholders. Calculate the corporation's tax liability.

1-4 *(Corporate Income Tax)* A. Don Drennan, Inc., had sales of $6 million during the past year. The company's cost of goods sold was 70 percent of sales; operating expenses, including depreciation, amounted to $800,000. The firm sold a capital asset (stock) for $75,000, which had been purchased 5 months earlier at a cost of $80,000. Determine the company's tax liability.

1-5 *(Corporate Income Tax)* The Robbins Corporation is an oil wholesaler. The company's sales last year were $1 million, with the cost of goods sold equal to $600,000. The firm paid interest of $200,000, and its cash operating expenses were $100,000. Also, the firm received $40,000 in dividend income while paying only $10,000 in dividends to its preferred stockholders. Depreciation expense was $150,000. Compute the firm's tax liability. Based on your answer, does management need to take any additional action?

1-6 *(Corporate Income Tax)* The Fair Corporation had sales of $5 million this past year. The cost of goods sold was $4.3 million, and operating expenses were $100,000. Dividend income totaled $5,000. The firm sold land for $150,000 that had cost $100,000 5 months ago. The firm received $150 per share from the sale of 1,000 shares of stock. The stock was purchased for $100 per share 3 years ago. Determine the firm's tax liability.

1-7 *(Corporate Income Tax)* Sales for J. P. Hulett, Inc., during the past year amounted to $4 million. The firm supplies statistical information to engineering companies. Gross profits totaled $1 million, and operating and depreciation expenses were $500,000 and $350,000, respectively. Dividend income for the year was $12,000. Compute the corporation's tax liability.

1-8 *(Corporate Income Tax)* Anderson & Dennis, Inc., sells computer software. The company's past year's sales were $5 million. The cost of its merchandise sold came to $3 million. Operating expenses were $175,000, plus depreciation expenses totaling $125,000. The firm paid $200,000 interest on loans. The firm sold stock during the year, receiving a $40,000 gain on a stock owned 6 years but losing $60,000 on stock held 4 months. Calculate the company's tax liability.

1-9 *(Corporate Income Tax)* G. R. Edwin, Inc., had sales of $6 million during the past year. The cost of goods sold amounted to $3 million. Operating expenses totaled $2.6 million, and interest expense was $30,000. Determine the firm's tax liability.

1-10 *(Corporate Income Tax)* The Analtoly Corporation is an electronics dealer and distributor. Sales for the last year were $4.5 million, and cost of goods sold and operating expenses totaled $3.2 million. Analtoly also paid $150,000 in interest expense, and depreciation expense totaled $50,000. In addition, the company sold securities for $120,000 that it had purchased 4 years earlier at a price of $40,000. Compute the tax liability for Analtoly.

1-11 *(Corporate Income Tax)* Utsumi Inc. supplies wholesale industrial chemicals. Last year the company had sales of $6.5 million. Cost of goods sold and operating expenses amounted to 70 percent of sales, and depreciation and interest expenses were $75,000 and $160,000, respectively. Furthermore, the corporation sold 40,000 shares of Sumitono Industries for $10 a share. These shares were purchased a year ago for $8 each. In addition, Utsumi received $60,000 in dividend income. Compute the corporation's tax liability.

---------- **COMPREHENSIVE PROBLEM** ----------

The final stage in the interview process for an Assistant Financial Analyst at Caledonia products involves a test of your understanding of basic financial concepts and of the corporate tax code. You are given the following memorandum and asked to respond to the questions. Whether or not you are offered a position at Caledonia will depend on the accuracy of your response.

To: Applicants for the position of Financial Analyst
From: Mr. V. Morrison, CEO, Caledonia Products
Re: A test of your understanding of basic financial concepts and of the Corporate Tax Code

Please respond to the following questions:

a. What are the differences between the goals of profit maximization and maximization of shareholder wealth? Which goal do you think is more appropriate?

b. What does the risk-return trade-off mean?

c. Why are we interested in cash flows rather than accounting profits in determining the value of an asset?

d. What is an efficient market and what are the implications of efficient markets for us?

e. What is the cause of the agency problem and how do we try to solve it?

f. What do ethics and ethical behavior have to do with finance?

g. Define (1) sole proprietorship, (2) partnership, and (3) corporation.

h. The Carrickfergus Corporation had sales of $4 million this past year. Its cost of goods sold was $2.4 million, and its operating expenses were $600,000. Interest expenses on outstanding debts were $300,000, and the company paid $60,000 in preferred stock dividends. The corporation received $30,000 in preferred stock dividends and interest income of $22,000. The firm sold stock that had been owned for 2 years for $100,000; the original cost of the stock was $60,000. Determine the corporation's taxable income and its tax liability.

SS-1

Sales		$2,000,000
Cost of goods sold		1,200,000
Gross profit		800,000
Tax-deductible expenses:		
Operating expenses	$400,000	
Interest expenses	100,000	500,000
		$ 300,000
Other income:		
Interest income		12,000
Preferred dividend income	$ 10,000	
Less 70% exclusion	$ 7,000	3,000
Taxable ordinary income		$ 315,000
Gain on sale:		
Selling price	$ 40,000	
Cost	30,000	10,000
Taxable income		$ 325,000
Tax liability		

$$.15 \times \$50,000 = \$ \ 7,500$$
$$.25 \times \ \ 25,000 = \ \ 6,250$$
$$.34 \times 250,000 = \ 85,000$$
$$5\% \text{ surtax} \qquad 11,250$$
$$\$110,000$$

THE FINANCIAL MARKETS AND INTEREST RATES

LEARNING OBJECTIVES

AFTER READING THIS CHAPTER, YOU SHOULD BE ABLE TO:

1. Understand the historical relationship between internally generated and externally generated sources of funds.
2. Understand the financing mix that tends to be used by firms raising long-term capital.
3. Explain why financial markets exist in a developed economy.
4. Explain the financing process by which savings are supplied and raised by major sectors in the economy.
5. Describe key components of the U.S. financial market system.
6. Understand the role of the investment-banking business in the context of raising corporate capital.
7. Distinguish between privately placed securities and publicly offered securities.
8. Be acquainted with securities flotation costs and securities markets regulations.
9. Understand the rate-of-return relationships among various classes of financing vehicles that persist in the financial markets.
10. Be acquainted with recent interest rate levels and the fundamentals of interest rate determination.
11. Explain the popular theories of the term structure of interest rates.
12. Understand the relationships among the multinational firm, efficient financial markets, and intercountry risk.

F rom February 4, 1994, through November 17, 1998, the Federal Reserve System (the Fed), the nation's central bank, voted to change the "target" federal funds rate on 14 different occasions. Eight of these interest rate changes were in the upward direction. The federal funds rate is a short-term market rate of interest, influenced by the Fed, that serves as a sensitive indicator of the direction of future changes in interest rates. In early 1994, fearing that inflationary pressures were building in the U.S. economy, the central bank raised nominal short-term interest rates to stem those pressures by slowing down aggregate economic growth. The Fed remained committed to a course of higher interest rates throughout 1994 and the first half of 1995; then on July 6, 1995, these monetary policymakers reversed course and began a series of three interest rate decreases.

For over a year, from January 31, 1996, to March 25, 1997, the Fed stayed on the sidelines and let the nation's financial markets direct the course of interest rates. However, during the first quarter of 1997, the Fed again became concerned that increased inflationary pressures were building within the U.S. economic system. For example, the national economy was growing at a faster inflation-adjusted rate in the first quarter of 1997 than had been experienced since the first quarter of 1987—the year of the major equity market crash that later occurred during October of that year. As a result, the Fed chose to raise the target federal funds rate on March 25, 1997. The March 1997 interest rate increase directed by the

31

Fed was followed by almost a year and a half of the central bank returning to the sidelines and observing the important relationship between the rate of inflation and real economic growth. But, during the fall months of 1998 unfavorable international pressures from Brazil and Russia, among others, caused the commercial lending system to pull in the reigns. This put financing strains on corporate America. Fearing a widening international economic slowdown, the Fed engineered a quick sequence of three more interest rate decreases aimed at stabilizing both the credit and equity markets. This maneuvering by the central bank did, in fact, work. These 14 policy actions and the resultant interest rate changes are shown in the accompanying table.

CHANGES IN THE TARGET FEDERAL FUNDS RATE AND COMMERCIAL BANK PRIME LENDING RATE FEBRUARY 1994–NOVEMBER 1998			
DATE	OLD TARGET RATE (%)	NEW TARGET RATE (%)	PRIME LENDING RATE (%)
		1994	
			6.00
February 4	3.00	3.25	no change
March 22	3.25	3.50	6.25
April 18	3.50	3.75	6.75
May 17	3.75	4.25	7.25
August 16	4.25	4.75	7.75
November 19	4.75	5.50	8.50
		1995	
February 1	5.50	6.00	9.00
July 6	6.00	5.75	8.75
December 19	5.75	5.50	8.50
		1996	
January 31	5.50	5.25	8.25
		1997	
March 25	5.25	5.50	8.50
		1998	
September 29	5.50	5.25	8.25
October 15	5.25	5.00	8.00
November 17	5.00	4.75	7.75

From a financial management viewpoint, the eight overt actions by the Fed to raise rates caused the *opportunity cost of funds* to rise. This means the firm's cost of capital funds rose, which in turn made it more difficult for real capital projects to be financed and included in the firm's capital budget. The six decisions to lower the target federal funds rate had the exact opposite effect, that is, the firm's cost of capital funds decreased. In this latter case, the firm can take on more capital projects.

Also note in the far right column of the table that the commercial bank prime lending rate typically changes in the same direction and at about the same time that a shift in the federal funds rate occurs. The prime lending rate is the interest rate that banks charge their *most* creditworthy customers. Thus, the transmission of the central bank's policy-move to the explicit cost of funds that the firm faces in the financial markets happens quickly. The commercial banking industry helps it along.

As you read this chapter you will learn about (1) the importance of financial markets to a developed economy, (2) how funds are raised in the financial markets, and (3) the fundamentals of interest rate determination. This will help you, as an emerging financial executive, understand the likely effects of federal monetary policy-actions on your firm's ability to do business.

WHAT'S AHEAD

At times internally generated funds will not be sufficient to finance all of the firm's proposed expenditures. In these situations, the corporation may find it necessary to attract large amounts of financial capital externally.[1] This chapter focuses on the market environment in which long-term capital is raised. It also introduces and covers the logic behind the determination of interest rates and required rates of return in the capital markets. We will explore interest rate levels and risk differentials over recent time periods and will study several theories that attempt to explain the shape of the *term structure of interest rates*. Ensuing chapters will discuss the distinguishing features of the instruments by which long-term funds are raised. Long-term funds are raised in the capital market. By the term *capital market,* we mean all institutions and procedures that facilitate transactions in long-term financial instruments (like common stocks and bonds).

Business firms in the nonfinancial corporate sector of the U.S. economy rely heavily on the nation's financial market system to raise cash. Table 2–1 displays the relative internal and external sources of funds for such corporations over the 1981–1998 period. Notice that the percentage of external funds raised in any given year can vary substantially from that of other years. In 1982, for example, the nonfinancial business sector raised only 25.4 percent of its funds by external means (in the financial markets). This was substantially less than the 39.4 percent raised externally only 1 year earlier, during 1981. In more recent years the same type of significant adjustment made by financial managers is evident. For example, during 1988 nonfinancial firms raised 36.3 percent of new funds in the external markets. By the end of 1991 this proportion dropped drastically to 9.7 percent.

Such adjustments illustrate an important point: The financial executive is perpetually on his or her toes regarding market conditions. Changes in market conditions influence the precise way corporate funds are raised.

The financial market system must be both organized and resilient. Periods of economic recession, for instance, test the financial markets and those firms that continually use the markets. Economic contractions are especially challenging to financial decision makers because all recessions are *unique*. This forces financing policies to become unique.

During the 1981–1982 recession, which lasted 16 months, interest rates remained high during the worst phases of the downturn. This occurred because policy makers at the Federal Reserve System decided to wring a high rate of inflation out of the economy by means of a tight monetary policy. Simultaneously, stock prices were depressed. These business conditions induced firms to forgo raising funds via external means. During 1982 we notice that 74.6 percent of corporate funds were generated internally (see Table 2–1).

The same general pattern followed after the 1990–1991 recession ended in the first quarter of 1991. During 1991 businesses paid down their short-term borrowings and relied on internally generated sources for 90.3 percent of their net financing needs.

Corporate profitability also plays a crucial role in the determination of the internal-external financing choice. In 1998, the U.S. economy began the eighth year of a vibrant economic expansion. The good economy translated into good corporate profits. Other things held equal, greater profits reduce the need for external financing. Thus, in 1998 the reliance by firms on external finance dropped to 16.2 percent of their total funds sources. Notice at the bottom of Table 2–1 that the simple (unweighted) average for external finance over the entire 1981–1998 period was a higher 27 percent.

The collective behavior of companies that results in firms retaining internally generated cash rather than paying it to stockholders as dividends or to creditors (bondholders)

---

[1] By *externally generated*, we mean that the funds are obtained by means *other* than through retentions or depreciation. Funds from these latter two sources are commonly called *internally generated* funds.

as interest is referred to by financial economists and analysts as the *internal capital market*.[2] This is because the firm allocates the cash flows to new projects. On the other hand, if the cash payments were made directly to stockholders and creditors, the funds would ultimately be allocated to new projects through the external capital markets.

As Figure 2–1 shows, the internal capital market accounted for 77.1 percent of nonfinancial corporations' sources of funds over the more-recent 1994–1998 period compared to 73 percent over the longer 1981–1998 period. Changing economic conditions cause this relationship to continually shift because executives continually adjust to the new information that encompasses the business cycle, interest rates, and stock prices.

As economic policy shapes the environment of the financial markets, managers must understand the meaning of the economic ups and downs and remain *flexible* in their decision-making processes.

The sums involved in tapping the capital markets can be vast. To be able to distribute and absorb security offerings of enormous size, an economy must have a well-developed financial market system. To use that system effectively, the financial officer must have a basic understanding of its structure. Accordingly, this chapter explores the rudiments of raising funds in the capital market.

TABLE 2–1	NONFINANCIAL CORPORATE BUSINESS SOURCES OF FUNDS		
YEAR	TOTAL SOURCES ($ BILLIONS)	PERCENT INTERNAL FUNDS	PERCENT EXTERNAL FUNDS
1998	830.3	83.8	16.2
1997	876.2	76.1	23.9
1996	792.4	79.6	20.4
1995	858.1	70.4	29.6
1994	729.8	75.4	24.6
1993	593.1	81.6	18.4
1992	560.5	78.2	21.8
1991	471.7	90.3	9.7
1990	535.5	76.9	23.1
1989	567.9	70.4	29.6
1988	634.2	63.7	36.3
1987	564.7	66.6	33.4
1986	538.8	62.5	37.5
1985	493.8	71.3	28.7
1984	511.4	65.8	34.2
1983	444.6	65.7	34.3
1982	331.7	74.6	25.4
1981	394.4	60.6	39.4
Mean	—	73.0	27.0

Source: *Economic Report of the President*, February 1995, p. 384; *Federal Reserve Bulletin*, April 1999, Table 1.57; and *Flow of Funds Accounts of the U.S.*, Fourth Quarter 1998, Table F. 102.

---

[2]A lengthier discussion on the relationship of the internal capital market to the external capital market is found in M. Berlin, "Jack of All Trades? Product Diversification in Nonfinancial Firms," *Business Review*, Federal Reserve Bank of Philadelphia (May–June 1999), pp. 19, 23.

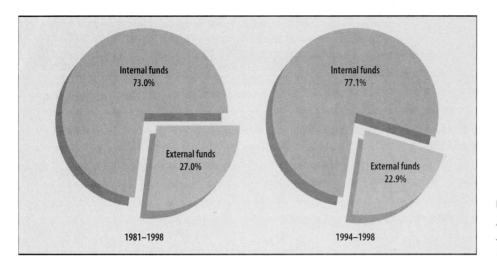

FIGURE 2-1
Nonfinancial Corporate Business Sources of Funds 1981–1998 vs. 1994–1998

CONCEPT CHECK

1. What distinguishes the internal capital market from the external capital market?
2. What important factor(s) might affect the firm's internal-external financing choice?

THE MIX OF CORPORATE SECURITIES SOLD IN THE CAPITAL MARKET

Objectives 1 and 2

When corporations decide to raise cash in the capital market, what type of financing vehicle is most favored? Many individual investors think that common stock is the answer to this question. This is understandable, given the coverage of the level of common stock prices by the popular news media. All the major television networks, for instance, quote the closing price of the Dow Jones Industrial Average on their nightly news broadcasts. Common stock, though, is not the financing method corporations most rely on; rather, they use *corporate bonds. The corporate debt markets clearly dominate the corporate equity markets when new funds are being raised.* This is a long-term relationship—it occurs year after year. Table 2–2 bears this out.

In Table 2–2 we see the total volume (in millions of dollars) of domestic corporate securities sold for cash over the 1981–1996 period. The percentage breakdown among common stock, preferred stock, and bonds is also displayed. We learn from our discussions of the cost of capital and planning the firm's financing mix that the U.S. tax system inherently favors debt as a means of raising capital. Quite simply, interest expense is deductible from other income when computing the firm's federal tax liability, whereas the dividends paid on both preferred and common stock are not.

TABLE 2-2

CORPORATE SECURITIES OFFERED FOR CASH (DOMESTIC OFFERINGS), 1981–1996

YEAR	TOTAL VOLUME ($ MILLIONS)	PERCENT COMMON STOCK	PERCENT PREFERRED STOCK	PERCENT BONDS AND NOTES
1996	502,540	16.5	6.6	76.9
1995	477,579	12.1	2.3	85.6
1994	425,620	11.2	2.9	85.9
1993	588,583	14.0	3.3	82.7
1992	456,515	12.5	4.7	82.8
1991	352,245	13.7	4.9	81.4
1990	212,712	9.1	1.9	89.0
1989	213,617	12.2	2.9	84.9
1988	244,670	14.7	2.7	82.6
1987	262,725	16.4	3.9	79.7
1986	248,722	23.7	4.9	71.4
1985	133,460	27.5	5.3	67.2
1984	95,287	23.3	4.5	72.2
1983	103,355	43.9	7.7	48.4
1982	73,397	32.3	6.7	61.0
1981	64,500	39.5	2.6	57.9
Mean	—	20.2	4.2	75.6

Source: *Economic Report of the President,* January 1989, p. 415; *Federal Reserve Bulletin,* Table 1.46, various issues.

Financial executives responsible for raising corporate cash know this. When they have a choice between marketing new bonds and marketing new preferred stock, the outcome is usually in favor of bonds. The after-tax cost of capital on the debt is less than that incurred on the preferred stock. Likewise, if the firm has unused debt capacity and the general level of equity prices is depressed, financial executives favor the issuance of debt securities over the issuance of new common stock. It is always good to keep some benchmark figures in your head. The average (unweighted) mix of corporate securities sold for cash over the 1981–1996 period follows. This *excludes* private debt placements or the bonds and notes categories would be a bit higher. Figure 2–2 illustrates this same financing pattern.

Common stock	20.2%
Preferred stock	4.2
Bonds and notes	75.6
Total	100.0%

The confirmed preference for debt financing on the part of corporate decision makers continued at a more determined pace into 1999. In fact over the 6-month

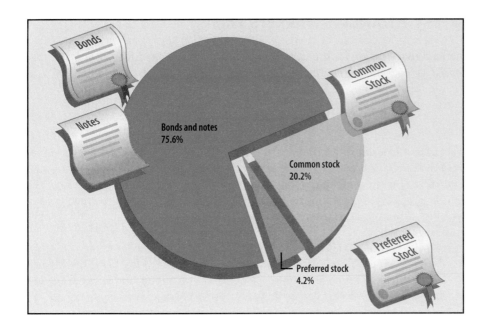

FIGURE 2–2

Corporate External Financing Patterns, 1981–1996

period ended January 1999, corporate executives raised 90.5 percent of domestic offerings through the issuance of bonds and notes and a notably lesser 9.5 percent by means of corporate equity securities.[3]

CONCEPT CHECK

1. Why might firms prefer to issue new debt securities rather than new common stock?
2. How does the U.S. tax system affect the firm's financing choices?

BACK TO THE FOUNDATIONS

Our previous discussion on the financing preferences of corporate executives provides tangible evidence of **Axiom 8: Taxes Bias Business Decisions.** The U.S. tax code allows corporations to deduct the interest expense associated with debt contracts from the income levels that are taxed. On the other hand, common and preferred stock cash dividend payments to investors are not tax deductible. Thus, the logical choice made by executives on behalf of their firms and shareholders is to finance the next dollar of externally raised capital by means of some debt contract such as bonds and notes. This decision saves the firm cash flows because the tax bill is lower. And, we remember from Chapter 1: **Axiom 3: Cash—Not Profits—Is King.** You see how it all ties together. The firm would rather have more cash, rather than less cash, and so would its stockholders.

---

[3]Calculations from the *Federal Reserve Bulletin*, Board of Governors of the Federal Reserve System (May 1999), p. A 31.

financial markets **Financial markets** are *institutions and procedures that facilitate transactions in all types of financial claims.* The purchase of your home, the common stock you may own, and your life insurance policy all took place in some type of financial market. Why do financial markets exist? What would the economy lose if our complex system of financial markets were not developed? We will address these questions here.

Some *economic units,* such as households, firms, or governments, spend more during a given period than they earn. Other economic units spend *less* on current consumption than they earn. For example, business firms in the aggregate usually spend more during a specific period than they earn. Households in the aggregate spend less on current consumption than they earn. As a result, some mechanism is needed to facilitate the transfer of savings from those economic units with a surplus to those with a deficit. That is precisely the function of financial markets. Financial markets exist in order to allocate the supply or savings in the economy to the demanders of those savings. The central characteristic of a financial market is that it acts as the vehicle through which the forces of demand and supply for a specific type of financial claim (such as a corporate bond) are brought together.

Now, why would the economy suffer without a developed financial market system? The answer is that the wealth of the economy would be less without the financial markets. The rate of capital formation would not be as high if financial markets did not exist. This means that the net additions during a specific period to the stocks of (1) dwellings, (2) productive plant and equipment, (3) inventory, and (4) consumer durables would occur at lower rates. Figure 2–3 helps clarify the rationale behind this assertion. The abbreviated balance sheets in the figure refer to firms or any other type of economic units that operate in the private as opposed to governmental sectors of the economy. This means that such units cannot issue money to finance their own activities.

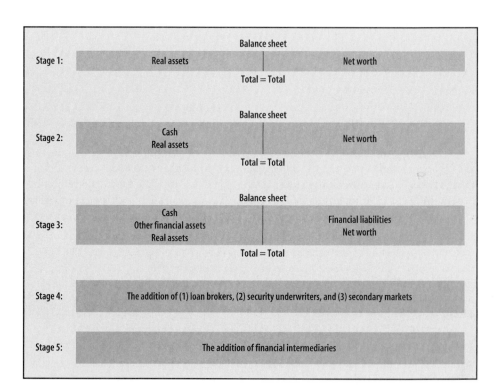

FIGURE 2–3

Development of a Financial Market System

At stage 1 in Figure 2–3 only real assets exist in the hypothetical economy. **Real assets** are *tangible assets like houses, equipment, and inventories.* They are distinguished from **financial assets,** which represent *claims for future payment on other economic units.* Common and preferred stocks, bonds, bills, and notes all are types of financial assets. If only real assets exist, then savings for a given economic unit, such as a firm, must be accumulated in the form of real assets. If the firm has a great idea for a new product, that new product can be developed, produced, and distributed only out of company savings (retained earnings). Furthermore, all investment in the new product must occur simultaneously as the savings are generated. If you have the idea, and we have the savings, there is no mechanism to transfer our savings to you. This is not a good situation.

At stage 2, paper money (cash) comes into existence in the economy. Here, at least, you can *store* your own savings in the form of money. Thus, you can finance your great idea by drawing down your cash balances. This is an improvement over stage 1, but there is still no effective mechanism to transfer our savings to you. You see, we won't just hand you our dollar bills—we'll want a receipt.

The concept of a receipt that represents the transfer of savings from one economic unit to another is a monumental advancement. The economic unit with excess savings can lend the savings to an economic unit that needs them. To the lending unit these receipts are identified as "other financial assets" in stage 3 of Figure 2–3. To the borrowing unit, the issuance of financial claims (receipts) shows up as "financial liabilities" on the stage 3 balance sheet. The economic unit with surplus savings earns a rate of return on those funds. The borrowing unit must pay that rate of return, but it has been able to finance its great idea.

In stage 4 the financial market system moves further toward full development. Loan brokers come into existence. These brokers help locate pockets of excess savings and channel such savings to economic units needing the funds. Some economic units actually purchase the financial claims of borrowing units and sell them at a higher price to other investors; this process is called *underwriting.* Underwriting is discussed in more detail later in this chapter. In addition, **secondary markets** develop. Secondary markets simply represent *trading in already existing financial claims.* If you buy your brother's General Motors common stock, you have made a secondary market transaction. Secondary markets reduce the risk of investing in financial claims. Should you need cash, you can liquidate your claims in the secondary market. This induces savers to invest in securities.

The progression toward a developed and complex system of financial markets ends with stage 5. Here, financial intermediaries come into existence. You can think of financial intermediaries as the major financial institutions you're used to dealing with. These include commercial banks, savings and loan associations, credit unions, life insurance companies, and mutual funds. Financial intermediaries share a common characteristic: They offer *their own financial claims,* called **indirect securities,** to economic units with excess savings. The proceeds from selling their indirect securities are then used to purchase the *financial claims of other economic units.* These latter claims can be called **direct securities.** Thus, a mutual fund might sell mutual fund shares (their indirect security) and purchase the common stocks (direct securities) of some major corporations. A life insurance company sells life insurance policies and purchases huge quantities of corporate bonds. Financial intermediaries thereby involve many small savers in the process of capital formation. This means there are more "good things" for everybody to buy.

A developed financial market system provides for a greater level of wealth in the economy. In the absence of financial markets, savings are not transferred to the economic units most in need of those funds. It is difficult, after all, for a household to build its own automobile. The financial market system makes it *easier* for the economy to build automobiles and all the other goods that economic units like to accumulate.

CONCEPT CHECK

1. What are financial markets?
2. Why will an economy suffer without a developed financial market system?
3. What distinguishes a real asset from a financial asset?
4. Distinguish between direct securities and indirect securities.

FINANCING OF BUSINESS: THE MOVEMENT OF FUNDS THROUGH THE ECONOMY

The movement of financial capital (funds) throughout the economy just means the movement of savings to the ultimate user of those savings. Some sectors of the economy save more than other sectors. As a result, these savings are moved to a productive use—say to manufacture that Corvette you want to buy.

The price of using someone else's savings is expressed in terms of interest rates. The financial market system helps to move funds to the most-productive end use. Those economic units with the most promising projects should be willing to bid the highest (in terms of rates) to obtain the savings. The concepts of financing and moving savings from one economic unit to another are explored in this section.

The Financing Process

We now understand the crucial role that financial markets play in a capitalist economy. At this point we take a brief look at how funds flow across some selected sectors of the U.S. economy. In addition, we focus a little more closely on the process of financial intermediation that was introduced in the preceding section. Some actual data are used to sharpen our knowledge of the financing process. We will see that financial institutions play a major role in bridging the gap between savers and borrowers in the economy. Nonfinancial corporations, we already know, are significant borrowers of financial capital.

Table 2–3 shows how funds were supplied and raised by the major sectors of the U.S. economy in 1998. Households net increase in financial liabilities exceeded their net increase in financial assets to the extent of $57.3 billion as is shown in the last column of Table 2–3. In the jargon of economics, the household sector was a *savings-deficit* sector in 1998. This financing behavior was unusual because over long periods of time the household sector is typically a major *savings-surplus* sector. This means the household sector normally is a key net supplier of funds to the financial markets. Actually, over the 5-year period of 1994–1998 the household sector supplied $338.0 billion to the markets. For all of those 5 years except 1998 the household sector was a savings-surplus sector. So why was 1998 any different? Because of prevailing low interest rates in the U.S. credit markets, households took on a huge $369.0 billion in mortgages to finance home purchases. The result made the household sector a net user of financial capital in that year.

TABLE 2-3

SECTOR VIEW OF FLOW OF FUNDS IN U.S. FINANCIAL MARKETS FOR 1998 (BILLIONS OF DOLLARS)

SECTOR	[1] FUNDS RAISED	[2] FUNDS SUPPLIED	[2] − [1] NET FUNDS SUPPLIED
Households[a]	$511.4	$454.1	$−57.3
Nonfinancial corporate business	368.0	336.6	−31.4
U.S. government	−16.0	3.1	19.1
State and local governments	81.1	86.9	5.8
Foreign	274.3	511.4	237.1

[a]Includes personal trusts and nonprofit organizations.

Source: *Flow of Funds Accounts, Fourth Quarter 1998*, Flow of Funds Section (Washington, DC; Board of Governors of the Federal Reserve System, March 12, 1999).

Notice that during 1998 the nonfinancial business sector was likewise a savings-deficit sector to the net extent of $31.4 billion. This means nonfinancial firms, such as General Motors, raised $31.4 billion more in the financial markets than they supplied to the markets. Although the nonfinancial business sector often is a savings-deficit sector, it can at times be a savings-surplus sector, depending on aggregate economic conditions. The most important of those conditions is the level of corporate profitability.

Oddly, in 1998 the U.S. government sector was a savings-surplus sector to the extent of $19.1 billion. This is an oddity because 1998 was the first year that the federal government posted a budget surplus since 1969; the last time before that was 1960. So you see the federal government has been a "quasi-permanent" savings-deficit sector since 1960. That's a long time and it's also a politically sensitive relationship that garners much ink in Washington, D.C.

Table 2–3 further highlights how important foreign financial investment is to the activity of the U.S. economy. In 1998, the foreign sector supplied a net $237.1 billion to the domestic capital markets. Back in 1982, the foreign sector raised—rather than supplied—$29.9 billion in the U.S. financial markets! This illustrates the dynamic nature of financial management.

Thus we have seen that the financial market system must exist to facilitate the orderly and efficient flow of savings from the surplus sectors to the deficit sectors of the economy. Over long periods, the nonfinancial business sector is typically dependent on the household sector to finance its investment needs. Foreign financing also plays an important role in the U.S. economy.

Movement of Savings

Figure 2–4 provides a useful way to summarize our discussion of (1) why financial markets exist and (2) the movement of funds through the economy. It also serves as an introduction to the role of the investment banker—a subject discussed in detail later in this chapter.

We see that savings are ultimately transferred to the business firm in need of cash in three ways.

1. The direct transfer of funds. Here the firm seeking cash sells its securities directly to savers (investors) who are willing to purchase them in hopes of earning a

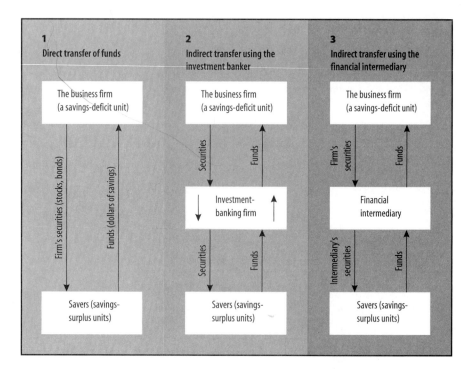

FIGURE 2–4

Three Ways to Transfer Financial Capital in the Economy

reasonable rate of return. New business formation is a good example of this process at work. The new business may go directly to a saver or group of savers called venture capitalists. The venture capitalists lend funds to the firm or take an equity position in the firm if they feel the product or service the new firm hopes to market will be successful.

2. Indirect transfer using the investment banker. In a common arrangement under this system, the managing investment-banking house forms a syndicate of several investment bankers. The syndicate buys the entire issue of securities from the firm that is in need of financial capital. The syndicate then sells the securities at a higher price than it paid for them to the investing public (the savers). Salomon Smith Barney and Goldman Sachs are examples of investment-banking firms. They tend to be called "houses" by those who work in the financial community. Notice that under this second method of transferring savings, the securities being issued just pass through the investment-banking firm. They are not transformed into a different type of security.

3. Indirect transfer using the financial intermediary. This is the type of system life insurance companies and pension funds operate within. The financial intermediary collects the savings of individuals and issues its own (indirect) securities in exchange for these savings. The intermediary then uses the funds collected from the individual savers to acquire the business firm's (direct) securities, such as stocks and bonds.

CONCEPT CHECK

1. What is the difference between a savings-surplus sector and a savings-deficit sector? Give an example of each.
2. Why can't all sectors be savings-deficit sectors?

We all benefit from the three transfer mechanisms displayed in Figure 2–4. Capital formation and economic wealth are greater than they would be in the absence of this financial market system.

COMPONENTS OF THE U.S. FINANCIAL MARKET SYSTEM

Numerous approaches exist for classifying the securities markets. At times, the array can be confusing. An examination of four sets of dichotomous terms can help provide a basic understanding of the structure of the U.S. financial markets.

Public Offerings and Private Placements

When a corporation decides to raise external capital, those founds can be obtained by making a public offering or a private placement. In a **public offering** *both individual and institutional investors have the opportunity to purchase the securities.* The securities are usually made available to the public at large by a managing investment-banking firm and its underwriting (risk-taking) syndicate. The firm does not meet the ultimate purchasers of the securities in the public offering. The public market is an impersonal market.

public offering

In a **private placement,** also called a **direct placement,** the securities are offered and sold to a *limited number of investors.* The firm will usually hammer out, on a face-to-face basis with the prospective buyers, the details of the offering. In this setting the investment-banking firm may act as a finder by bringing together potential lenders and borrowers. The private placement market is a more personal market than its public counterpart.

private placement
direct placement

Primary Markets and Secondary Markets

Primary markets are *those in which securities are offered for the first time to potential investors.* A new issue of common stock by AT&T is a primary market transaction. This type of transaction increases the total stock of financial assets outstanding in the economy.

primary markets

As mentioned in our discussion of the development of the financial market system, *secondary markets* represent transactions in currently outstanding securities. If the first buyer of the AT&T stock subsequently sells it, he or she does so in the secondary market. All transactions after the initial purchase take place in the secondary market. The sales do *not* affect the total stock of financial assets that exist in the economy. Both the money market and the capital market, described next, have primary and secondary sides.

Money Market and Capital Market

Money Market

The key distinguishing feature between the money and capital markets is the maturity period of the securities traded in them. The **money market** refers to *all institutions and procedures that provide for transactions in short-term debt instruments* generally issued by borrowers with very high credit ratings. By financial convention, *short-term* means maturity periods of 1 year or less. Notice that equity instruments, either common or preferred, are not traded in the money market. The major instruments issued and traded are U.S. Treasury bills, various federal agency securities, bankers' acceptances, negotiable certificates of deposit, and commercial paper. Keep in mind that the money market is an intangible market.

money market

You do not walk into a building on Wall Street that has the words "Money Market" etched in stone over its arches. Rather, the money market is primarily a telephone market.

capital market

Capital Market

The **capital market** refers to *all institutions and procedures that provide for transactions in long-term financial instruments. Long-term* here means having maturity periods that extend beyond one year. In the broad sense this encompasses term loans and financial leases, corporate equities, and bonds. The funds that comprise the firm's capital structure are raised in the capital market. Important elements of the capital market are the organized security exchanges and the over-the-counter markets.

Organized Security Exchanges and Over-the-Counter Markets

organized security exchanges

over-the-counter markets

Organized security exchanges are *tangible entities;* they physically occupy space (such as a building or part of a building), and *financial instruments are traded on their premises.* The **over-the-counter markets** include *all security markets except the organized exchanges.* The money market, then, is an over-the-counter market. Because both markets are important to financial officers concerned with raising *long-term capital,* some additional discussion is warranted.

Organized Security Exchanges

For practical purposes there are seven major security exchanges in the United States: (1) New York Stock Exchange, (2) American Stock Exchange, (3) Chicago Stock Exchange, (4) Pacific Stock Exchange, (5) Philadelphia Stock Exchange, (6) Boston Stock Exchange, and (7) Cincinnati Stock Exchange. The New York Stock Exchange (NYSE) and the American Stock Exchange (AMEX) are called *national* exchanges, whereas the others are loosely described as *regionals.* All seven of these active exchanges are registered with the Securities and Exchange Commission (SEC). Firms whose securities are traded on the registered exchanges must comply with reporting requirements of both the specific exchange and the SEC.

An indication of the importance of the NYSE to our financial market system is reflected in something known as "consolidated tape volume." The Consolidated Tape prints all of the transactions on stocks that are listed on the NYSE and are traded on other organized markets. These markets include the exchanges mentioned earlier plus over-the-counter markets. In 1997, the NYSE accounted for 83.7 percent of consolidated volume.[4]

Another example of the stature of the NYSE is provided by the sheer number of companies that have various security issues listed on this exchange. In 1997, the NYSE handled the listings of 3,047 firms—up from 2,907 in 1996. By contrast, the other organized exchange with a national following—the AMEX—handled the security issues of 771 companies. The AMEX tends to deal in the securities of firms that have a national interest, but are smaller in operating size than the NYSE-listed firms.

The business of an exchange, including securities transactions, is conducted by its *members.* Members are said to occupy "seats." There are 1,366 seats on the NYSE, a number that has remained constant since 1953. Major brokerage firms own seats on the exchanges. An officer of the firm is designated to be the member of the

---

[4]New York Stock Exchange, *Fact Book* (New York, 1998), p. 27.

exchange, and this membership permits the brokerage house to use the facilities of the exchange to effect trades. During 1997 the prices of seats that were exchanged for cash ranged from a low of $1,175,000 to a high of $1,750,000.[5]

Stock Exchange Benefits Both corporations and investors enjoy several benefits provided by the existence of organized security exchanges. These include

1. Providing a continuous market. This may be the most important function of an organized security exchange. A continuous market provides a series of continuous security prices. Price changes from trade to trade tend to be smaller than they would be in the absence of organized markets because there is a relatively large sales volume in each security, trading orders are executed quickly, and the range between the price asked for a security and the offered price tends to be narrow. The result is that price volatility is reduced.

2. Establishing and publicizing fair security prices. An organized exchange permits security prices to be set by competitive forces. They are not set by negotiations off the floor of the exchange, where one party might have a bargaining advantage. The bidding process flows from the supply and demand underlying each security. This means the specific price of a security is determined in the manner of an auction. In addition, the security prices determined at each exchange are widely publicized.

3. Helping business raise new capital. Because a continuous secondary market exists where prices are competitively determined, it is easier for firms to float new security offerings successfully. This continuous pricing mechanism also facilitates the determination of the offering price of a new issue. This means that comparative values are easily observed.

Listing Requirements To receive the benefits provided by an organized exchange, the firm must seek to have its securities listed on the exchange. An application for listing must be filed and a fee paid. The requirements for listing vary from exchange to exchange; those of the NYSE are the most stringent. The general criteria for listing fall into these categories: (1) profitability, (2) size, (3) market value, and (4) public ownership. To give you the flavor of an actual set of listing requirements, those set forth by the NYSE are displayed in Table 2–4.

Over-the-Counter Markets

Many publicly held firms do not meet the listing requirements of major stock exchanges. Others may want to avoid the reporting requirements and fees required to maintain listing. As an alternative their securities may trade in the over-the-counter markets. On the basis of sheer numbers (not dollar volume), more stocks are traded over-the-counter than on organized exchanges. As far as secondary trading in corporate bonds is concerned, the over-the-counter markets are where the action is. In a typical year, more than 90 percent of corporate bond business takes place over-the-counter.

Most over-the-counter transactions are done through a loose network of security traders who are known as broker-dealers and brokers. Brokers do not purchase securities for their own account, whereas dealers do. Broker-dealers stand ready to buy and sell specific securities at selected prices. They are said to "make a market" in those securities. Their profit is the spread or difference between the price they pay for a security (bid price) and the price at which they sell the security (asked price).

---

[5]New York Stock Exchange, *Fact Book* (New York, 1998), p. 77.

TABLE 2-4	NYSE LISTING REQUIREMENTS

Profitability
Earnings before taxes (EBT) for the most recent year must be at least $2.5 million. For the 2 years preceding that, EBT must be at least $2.0 million.

Size
Net tangible assets must be at least $40.0 million.

Market Value[a]
The market value of publicly held stock must be at least $40.0 million.

Public Ownership
There must be at least 1.1 million publicly held common shares.
There must be at least 2,000 holders of 100 shares or more.

[a]The market value is tied to the level of common stock prices prevailing in the marketplace at the time of the listing application. From time to time, the $40.0 million requirement noted above may be lessened. Under current regulations of the NYSE, the requirement can never be less than $9.0 million.

Source: New York Stock Exchange, *1997 Fact Book* (New York, 1998), p. 37.

Price Quotes and the NASDAQ

Takin' It to the Net
A fine source of up-to-the-minute price quotes for securities listed or traded on the NASDAQ, AMEX, or NYSE is provided at the Nasdaq Stock Market's Web site. Go to http://www.nasdaq.com. Price and volume data for certain indices like that of the NASDAQ and the Dow Jones Industrial Average are continuously displayed. In June 1998, the Nasdaq Stock Market, Inc. and the AMEX announced the creation of a strategic alliance to provide market participants with timely information and enhanced order execution capabilities. The latter extended to international trading.

The availability of prices is not as continuous in the over-the-counter market as it is on an organized exchange. Since February 8, 1971, however, when a computerized network called NASDAQ came into existence, the availability of prices in this market has improved substantially. NASDAQ stands for National Association of Security Dealers Automated Quotation system. It is a telecommunications system that provides a national information link among the brokers and dealers operating in the over-the-counter markets. Subscribing traders have a terminal that allows them to obtain representative bids and ask prices for thousands of securities traded over-the-counter. NASDAQ is a quotation system, not a transactions system. The final trade is still consummated by direct negotiation between traders.

The NASDAQ system has become an increasingly important element of the U.S. financial market system in recent years. It provides a nationwide communications element that was lacking in the over-the-counter side of the securities markets. In 1997, the NASDAQ accounted for almost 40 percent of equity market trading in the United States as measured in dollar volume. The 1997 comparison across exchanges and systems as a percentage of total equity market dollar volume is shown in the following table.

EXCHANGE OR SYSTEM	PERCENT OF EQUITY DOLLAR VOLUME
NASDAQ	39.7
NASDAQ Market Maker Trading in Exchange Listed Securities	4.9
AMEX	1.2
Regional Exchanges	3.1
NYSE	51.1

The Nasdaq Stock Market Inc. describes itself as a "screen-based, floorless market." It now is actually home to the securities of more companies than the NYSE; in 1997 some 5,487 public companies had securities traded by means of the NASDAQ system. It has become highly popular as the trading mechanism of choice of several fast growth sectors in the United States, including the high technology sector. The common stock of computer chip maker Intel Corporation, for example, is traded via the NASDAQ.[6]

NASDAQ price quotes for many stocks are published daily in the *Wall Street Journal*. This same financial newspaper also publishes prices on hundreds of other stocks traded over-the-counter. Local papers supply prices on stocks of regional interest.

CONCEPT CHECK

1. Explain the difference between (a) public offerings and private placements, (b) primary markets and secondary markets, (c) the money market and the capital market, and (d) tangible-organized security exchanges and over-the-counter markets.
2. Name the benefits derived from the existence of stock exchanges.
3. Briefly describe what is meant by the "NASDAQ system."

THE INVESTMENT BANKER

Objective 6

We touched briefly on the investment-banking industry and the investment banker earlier in this chapter when we described various methods for transferring financial capital (see Figure 2–4). The investment banker is to be distinguished from the commercial banker in that the former's organization is not a permanent depository for funds. For the moment, it is important for you to learn about the role of the investment banker in the funding of commercial activity because of the importance of this institution within the financial market system.

Most corporations do not raise long-term capital frequently. The activities of working-capital management go on daily, but attracting long-term capital is, by comparison, episodic. The sums involved can be huge, so these situations are considered of great importance to financial managers. Because most managers are unfamiliar with the subtleties of raising long-term funds, they enlist the help of an expert. That expert is an investment banker.

Definition

The **investment banker** is *a financial specialist involved as an intermediary in the merchandising of securities.* He or she acts as a "middle person" by facilitating the flow of savings from those economic units that want to invest to those units that want to raise funds. We use the term investment banker to refer both to a given individual and to the organization for which such a person works, variously known as an investment-banking

investment banker

---

[6]The Nasdaq Stock Market, *1998 Fact Book & Company Directory* (Washington, DC), pp. 1, 9.

firm or an investment-banking house. Although these firms are called investment bankers, they perform no depository or lending functions. The activities of commercial banking and investment banking as we know them today were separated by the Banking Act of 1933 (also known as the Glass-Steagall Act of 1933). Then, after considerable political debate, the Financial Modernization Act was passed by the U.S. Congress on November 12, 1999. This recent legislation is also referred to as the Gramm-Leach-Bliley Act of 1999, in honor of its congressional sponsors. The Act actually repealed the depression-era Glass-Steagall Act and is aimed at increasing competitiveness among modern financial services companies. Through the creation of operating subsidiaries, the Act provides for business combinations among banks, underwriters of financial securities (investment bankers), insurance firms, and securities brokers. Here we focus on investment banking and its important middleman role. That is most easily understood in terms of the basic functions of investment banking.

Functions

The investment banker performs three basic functions: (1) underwriting, (2) distributing, and (3) advising.

Underwriting

underwriting

The term **underwriting** is borrowed from the field of insurance. It means *assuming a risk*. The investment banker assumes the risk of selling a security issue at a satisfactory price. A satisfactory price is one that generates a profit for the investment banking house.

syndicate

The procedure goes like this. The managing investment banker and its syndicate will buy the security issue from the corporation in need of funds. The **syndicate** is *a group of other investment bankers who are invited to help buy and resell the issue*. The managing house is the investment-banking firm that originated the business because its corporate client decided to raise external funds. On a specific day, the firm that is raising capital is presented with a check in exchange for the securities being issued. At this point the investment-banking syndicate owns the securities. The corporation has its cash and can proceed to use it. The firm is now immune from the possibility that the security markets might turn sour. If the price of the newly issued security falls below that paid to the firm by the syndicate, the syndicate will suffer a loss. The syndicate, of course, hopes that the opposite situation will result. Its objective is to sell the new issue to the investing public at a price per security greater than its cost.

Distributing

Once the syndicate owns the new securities, it must get them into the hands of the ultimate investors. This is the distribution or selling function of investment banking. The investment banker may have branch offices across the Untied States, or it may have an informal arrangement with several security dealers who regularly buy a portion of each new offering for final sale. It is not unusual to have 300 to 400 dealers involved in the selling effort. The syndicate can properly be viewed as the security wholesaler, and the dealer organization can be viewed as the security retailer.

Advising

The investment banker is an expert in the issuance and marketing of securities. A sound investment-banking house will be aware of prevailing market conditions and can relate those conditions to the particular type of security that should be sold at a given time. Business conditions may be pointing to a future increase in interest rates. The investment banker might advise the firm to issue its bonds in a timely fashion to avoid the higher yields that are forthcoming. The banker can analyze the firm's capital structure and make recommendations as to what general source of capital should be issued. In many instances the firm will invite its investment banker to sit on the board of directors. This permits the banker to observe corporate activity and make recommendations on a regular basis.

Distribution Methods

Several methods are available to the corporation for placing new security offerings in the hands of final investors. The investment banker's role is different in each of these. Sometimes, in fact, it is possible to bypass the investment banker. These methods are described in this section. Private placements, because of their importance, are treated separately later in the chapter.

Negotiated Purchase

In a negotiated underwriting, the firm that needs funds makes contact with an investment banker, and deliberations concerning the new issue begin. If all goes well, a *method* is negotiated for determining the price the investment banker and the syndicate will pay for the securities. For example, the agreement might state that the syndicate will pay $2 less than the closing price of the firm's common stock on the day before the offering date of a new stock issue. The negotiated purchase is the most prevalent method of securities distribution in the private sector. It is generally thought to be the most profitable technique as far as investment bankers are concerned.

Competitive Bid Purchase

The method by which the underwriting group is determined distinguishes the competitive bid purchase from the negotiated purchase. In a competitive underwriting, several underwriting groups bid for the right to purchase the new issue from the corporation that is raising funds. The firm does not directly select the investment banker. The investment banker that underwrites and distributes the issue is chosen by an auction process. The syndicate willing to pay the greatest dollar amount per new security will win the competitive bid.

Most competitive bid purchases are confined to three situations, compelled by legal regulations: (1) railroad issues, (2) public utility issues, and (3) state and municipal bond issues. The argument in favor of competitive bids is that any undue influence of the investment banker over the firm is mitigated and the price received by the firm for each security should be higher. Thus, we would intuitively suspect that the cost of capital in a competitive bid situation would be less than in a negotiated purchase situation. Evidence on this question, however, is mixed. One problem with the competitive bid purchase as far as the fund-raising firm is concerned is that the benefits gained from the advisory function of the investment banker are lost. It may be necessary to use an investment banker for advisory purposes and then by law exclude the banker from the competitive bid process.

Commission or Best-Efforts Basis

Here, the investment banker acts as an agent rather than as a principal in the distribution process. The securities are *not* underwritten. The investment banker attempts to sell the issue in return for a fixed commission on each security actually sold. Unsold securities are returned to the corporation. This arrangement is typically used for more speculative issues. The issuing firm may be smaller or less established than the investment banker would like. Because the underwriting risk is not passed on to the investment banker, this distribution method is less costly to the issuer than a negotiated or competitive bid purchase. On the other hand, the investment banker only has to give it his or her "best effort." A successful sale is not guaranteed.

Privileged Subscription

Occasionally, the firm may feel that a distinct market already exists for its new securities. When a *new issue is marketed to a definite and select group of investors*, it is called a **privileged subscription.** Three target markets are typically involved: (1) current stockholders, (2) employees, or (3) customers. Of these, distributions directed at current stockholders are the most prevalent. Such offerings are called *rights offerings.* In a privileged subscription the investment banker may act only as a selling agent. It is also possible that the issuing firm and the investment banker might sign a *standby agreement*, which would obligate the investment banker to underwrite the securities that are not accepted by the privileged investors.

Direct Sale

In a **direct sale** *the issuing firm sells the securities directly to the investing public without involving an investment banker.* Even among established corporate giants this procedure is relatively rare. A variation of the direct sale, though, was used more frequently in the 1970s than in previous decades. This involves the private placement of a new issue by the fund-raising corporation *without* the use of an investment banker as an intermediary. Texaco, Mobil Oil, and International Harvester (now Navistar) are examples of large firms that have followed this procedure.

Industry Leaders

All industries have their leaders, and investment banking is no exception. We have discussed investment bankers in general at some length in this chapter. Table 2–5 gives us some idea who the major players are within the investment-banking industry. It lists the top 10 houses in 1998 based on the dollar volume of security issues that were managed.

Notice in Table 2–5 that the U.S. investment banking industry is a highly concentrated one. The top four bankers with regard to underwriting volume during 1998 accounted for a full 50.8 percent of the total market. Such concentration was up from 47.4 percent just 2 years earlier in 1996. This degree of concentration is pervasive over time. The upshot is it is most difficult to successfully launch a new investment banking firm. The barriers to market entry are steep.

TABLE 2–5	LEADING U.S. INVESTMENT BANKERS, 1998

FIRM	UNDERWRITING VOLUME ($ BILLIONS)	PERCENT OF MARKET
1. Merrill Lynch	304.1	16.7
2. Salomon Smith Barney	225.1	12.4
3. Morgan Stanley Dean Witter	203.3	11.2
4. Goldman Sachs	191.7	10.5
5. Lehman Brothers	147.2	8.1
6. Credit Suisse First Boston	126.9	7.0
7. J.P. Morgan	89.0	4.9
8. Bear Stearns	83.2	4.6
9. Chase Manhattan	70.9	3.9
10. Donaldson, Lufkin & Jenrette	60.6	3.3

Source: Securities Data Co. as reported in the *Wall Street Journal* (January 4, 1999), p. R39.

PRIVATE PLACEMENTS

Objective 7

Private placements are an alternative to the sale of securities to the public or to a restricted group of investors through a privileged subscription. Any type of security can be privately placed (directly placed). This market, however, is clearly dominated by debt issues. Thus, we restrict this discussion to debt securities. From year to year the volume of private placements varies greatly. However, the private placement market is always a significant portion of the U.S. capital market. In fact, according to the Federal Reserve, the private placement side of the corporate debt market represented 26.6 percent of total domestically placed debt issues for the 10-year period ending in 1994.

The major investors in private placements are large financial institutions. Based on the volume of securities purchased, the three most important investor groups are (1) life insurance companies, (2) state and local retirement funds, and (3) private pension funds.

In arranging a private placement the firm may (1) avoid the use of an investment banker and work directly with the investing institutions or (2) engage the services of an investment banker. If the firm does not use an investment banker, of course, it does not have to pay a fee. Conversely, investment bankers can provide valuable advice in the private placement process. They are usually in contact with several major institutional investors; thus, they will know if a firm is in a position to invest in its proposed offering, and they can help the firm evaluate the terms of the new issue.

Private placements have advantages and disadvantages compared with public offerings. The financial manager must carefully evaluate both sides of the question. The advantages associated with private placements are these:

1. **Speed.** The firm usually obtains funds more quickly through a private placement than a public offering. The major reason is that registration of the issue with the SEC is not required.

2. **Reduced flotation costs.** These savings result because the lengthy registration statement for the SEC does not have to be prepared, and the investment-banking underwriting and distribution costs do not have to be absorbed.

3. **Financing flexibility.** In a private placement the firm deals on a face-to-face basis with a small number of investors. This means that the terms of the issue can be tailored to meet the specific needs of the company. For example, all of the funds need not be taken by the firm at once. In exchange for a commitment fee the firm can "draw down" against the established amount of credit with the investors. This provides some insurance against capital market uncertainties, and the firm

does not have to borrow the funds if the need does not arise. There is also the possibility of renegotiation. The terms of the debt issue can be altered. The term to maturity, the interest rate, or any restrictive covenants can be discussed among the affected parties.

The following disadvantages of private placements must be evaluated:

1. Interest costs. It is generally conceded that interest costs on private placements exceed those of public issues. Whether this disadvantage is enough to offset the reduced flotation costs associated with a private placement is a determination the financial manager must make. There is some evidence that on smaller issues, say $500,000 as opposed to $30 million, the private placement alternative would be preferable.

2. Restrictive covenants. Dividend policy, working-capital levels, and the raising of additional debt capital may all be affected by provisions in the private-placement debt contract. This is not to say that such restrictions are always absent in public debt contracts. Rather, the financial officer must be alert to the tendency for these covenants to be especially burdensome in private contracts.

3. The possibility of future SEC registration. If the lender (investor) should decide to sell the issue to a public buyer before maturity, the issue must be registered with the SEC. Some lenders, then, require that the issuing firm agree to a future registration at their option.

CONCEPT CHECK

1. Within the financial markets, what do we mean by "private placements"?

2. What are the possible advantages and disadvantages of private placements?

Objective 8 **FLOTATION COSTS**

flotation costs   The firm raising long-term capital incurs two types of **flotation costs:** (1) *the underwriter's spread* and (2) *issuing costs.* Of these two costs, the underwriter's spread is the larger. The *underwriter's spread* is simply the difference between the gross and net proceeds from a given security issue expressed as a percent of the gross proceeds. The *issue costs* include (1) printing and engraving, (2) legal fees, (3) accounting fees, (4) trustee fees, and (5) several other miscellaneous components. The two most significant issue costs are printing and engraving and legal fees.

Data published by the SEC have consistently revealed two relationships about flotation costs. First, the costs associated with issuing common stock are notably greater than the costs associated with preferred stock offerings. In turn, preferred stock costs exceed those of bonds. Second, flotation costs (expressed as a percent of gross proceeds) decrease as the size of the security issue increases.

In the first instance, the stated relationship reflects the fact that issue costs are sensitive to the risks involved in successfully distributing a security issue. Common stock is riskier to own than corporate bonds. Underwriting risk is, therefore, greater with common stock than with bonds. Thus, flotation costs just mirror these risk relationships. In the second case, a portion of the issue costs is fixed. Legal fees and accounting costs are good examples. So, as the size of the security issue rises, the fixed component is spread over a larger gross proceeds base. As a consequence, average flotation costs vary inversely with the size of the issue.

CONCEPT CHECK

1. What are the two major categories of flotation costs?
2. Are flotation costs greater for a new bond issue or a new common stock issue?

REGULATION

Since late 1986, public interest has been renewed in the regulation of the country's financial markets. The key event was a massive insider trading scandal that made the name Ivan F. Boesky one of almost universal recognition—but, unfortunately, in a negative sense. This was followed by the October 19, 1987, crash of the equity markets. More recently, in early 1990, the investing community (both institutional and individual) became increasingly concerned over a weakening in the so-called junk bond market. The upshot of all of this enhanced awareness is a new appreciation of the crucial role that regulation plays in the financial system.

Following the severe economic downturn of 1929–1932, Congressional action was taken to provide for federal regulation of the securities markets. State statutes (blue sky laws) also govern the securities markets where applicable, but the federal regulations are clearly more pressing and important. The major federal regulations are reviewed here.

Primary Market Regulations

The new issues market is governed by the Securities Act of 1933. The intent of the act is important. It aims to provide potential investors with accurate, truthful disclosure about the firm and the new securities being offered to the public. This does *not* prevent firms from issuing highly speculative securities. The SEC says nothing whatsoever about the possible investment worth of a given offering. It is up to the investor to separate the junk from the jewels. The SEC does have the legal power and responsibility to enforce the 1933 act.

Full public disclosure is achieved by the requirement that the issuing firm file a registration statement with the SEC containing requisite information. The statement details particulars about the firm and the new security being issued. During a minimum 20-day waiting period, the SEC examines the submitted document. In numerous instances the 20-day wait has been extended by several weeks. The SEC can ask for additional information that was omitted in order to clarify the original document. The SEC can also order the offering to be stopped.

During the registration process a preliminary prospectus (the red herring) may be distributed to potential investors. When the registration is approved, the final prospectus must be made available to the prospective investors. The prospectus is actually a condensed version of the full registration statement. If, at a later date, the information in the registration statement and the prospectus is found to be lacking, purchasers of the new issue who incurred a loss can sue for damages. Officers of the issuing firm and others who took part in the registration and marketing of the issue may suffer both civil and criminal penalties.

Generally, the SEC defines public issues as those that are sold to more than 25 investors. Some public issues need not be registered. These include the following:

1. Relatively small issues for which the firm sells less than $1.5 million of new securities per year. Such issues of less than $1.5 million are not entirely regulation free. They are monitored through what is usually called the *small-issues exemption*. These small issues, then, fall under the auspices of Regulation A, which is just a very short offering statement compared to the full-blown registration statement. The later is onerous, often ending up in the 50- to 100-page range.
2. Issues that are sold entirely intrastate.
3. Issues that are basically short-term instruments. This translates into maturity periods of 270 days or less.
4. Issues that are already regulated or controlled by some other federal agency. Examples include the Federal Power Commission (public utilities) and the Interstate Commerce Commission (railroads).

Secondary Market Regulations

Secondary market trading is regulated by the Securities Exchange Act of 1934. This act created the SEC to enforce federal securities laws. The Federal Trade Commission enforced the 1933 act for 1 year. The major aspects of the 1934 act can be best presented in outline form:

1. Major security exchanges must register with the SEC. This regulates the exchanges and places reporting requirements on the firms whose securities are listed on them.
2. Insider trading is regulated. Insiders can be officers, directors, employees, relatives, major investors, or anyone having information about the operation of the firm that is not public knowledge. If an investor purchases the security of the firm in which the investor is an insider, he or she must hold it for at least 6 months before disposing of it. Otherwise, profits made from trading the stock within a period of less than 6 months must be returned to the firm. Furthermore, insiders must file with the SEC a monthly statement of holdings and transactions in the stock of their corporation.[6]
3. Manipulative trading of securities by investors to affect stock prices is prohibited.
4. The SEC is given control over proxy procedures.
5. The Board of Governors of the Federal Reserve System is given responsibility for setting margin requirements. This affects the flow of credit into the securities markets. Buying securities on margin simply means using credit to acquire a portion of the subject financial instruments.

---

[6]On November 14, 1986, the SEC announced that Ivan F. Boesky had admitted to illegal inside trading after an intensive investigation. Boesky at the time was a very well-known Wall Street investor, speculator, and arbitrageur. Boesky was an owner or part owner in several companies, including an arbitrage fund named Ivan F. Boesky & Co. L. P. Boesky agreed to pay the U.S. government $50 million, which represented a return of illegal profits, another $50 million in civil penalties; to withdraw permanently from the securities industry; and to plead guilty to criminal charges. The far-reaching investigation continued into 1987 and implicated several other prominent investment figures.

More Recent Regulatory Developments: The Securities Acts Amendments of 1975

The Securities Acts Amendments of 1975 touched on three important issues. First, Congress mandated the creation of a national market system (NMS). Only broad goals for this national exchange were identified by Congress. Implementation details were left to the SEC and, to a much lesser extent, the securities industry in general. Congress was really expressing its desire for (1) widespread application of auction market trading principles, (2) a high degree of competition across markets, and (3) the use of modern electronic communication systems to link the fragmented markets in the country into a true NMS. The NMS is still a goal toward which the SEC and the securities industry are moving. Agreement as to its final form and an implementation date have not occurred.

A second major alteration in the habits of the securities industry also took place in 1975. This was the elimination of fixed commissions (fixed brokerage rates) on public transactions in securities. This was closely tied to the desire for an NMS in that fixed brokerage fees provided no incentive for competition among brokers. A third consideration of the 1975 amendments focused on such financial institutions as commercial banks and insurance firms. These financial institutions were prohibited from acquiring membership on stock exchanges in order to reduce or save commissions on their own trades.

Shelf Registration

On March 16, 1982, the SEC began a new procedure for registering new issues of securities. Formally it is called SEC Rule 415; informally the process is known as a **shelf registration,** or a **shelf offering.** The essence of the process is rather simple. Rather than go through the lengthy, full registration process each time the firm plans an offering of securities, it can get a blanket order approved by the SEC. *A master registration statement that covers the financing plans of the firm over the coming 2 years is filed with the SEC.* On approval, the firm can market some or all of the securities over this 2-year period. The securities are sold in a piecemeal fashion, or "off the shelf." Before each specific offering, a short statement about the issue is filed with the SEC.

shelf registration
shelf offering

Corporations raising funds approve of this new procedure. The tedious, full registration process is avoided with each offering pulled off the shelf. This should result in a saving of fees paid to investment bankers. Moreover, an issue can more quickly be brought to the market. Also, if market conditions change, an issue can easily be redesigned to fit the specific conditions of the moment.

As is always the case, there is another side to the story. Recall that the reason for the registration process in the first place is to give investors useful information about the firm and the securities being offered. Under the shelf registration procedure some of the information about the issuing firm becomes old as the 2-year horizon unfolds. Some investment bankers feel they do not have the proper amount of time to study the firm when a shelf offering takes place. This is one of those areas of finance where more observations are needed before any final conclusions can be made. Those observations will only come with the passage of time.

CONCEPT CHECK

1. What are the main elements of the Securities Act of 1933 and the Securities Exchange Act of 1934?
2. What is meant by "insider trading"?
3. What is a "shelf registration"?

Objective 9 **RATES OF RETURN IN THE FINANCIAL MARKETS**

Earlier in this chapter in discussing "the financing process" we noted that net users of funds (savings-deficit economic units) must compete with one another for the funds supplied by net savers (savings-surplus economic units). Consequently, to obtain financing for projects that will benefit the firm's stockholders, that firm must offer the supplier (savings-surplus unit) a rate of return *competitive* with the next best investment alternative available to that saver (investor). This *rate of return on the next best investment alternative to the saver* is known as the supplier's **opportunity cost of funds.** The opportunity cost concept is crucial in financial management and is referred to often.

opportunity cost of funds

Next we review the levels and variability in rates of return that have occurred over the lengthy period of 1926–1998. This review focuses on returns from a wide array of financial instruments. In both Chapters 9 and 12 we discuss at length the concept of an *overall* cost of capital. Part of that overall cost of capital is attributed to interest rate levels at given points in time. So we follow this initial broad look at interest rate levels with a discussion of the more recent period of 1981–1998.

Rates of Return over Long Periods

History can tell us a great deal about the returns that investors earn in the financial markets. A primary source for a historical perspective comes from Ibbotson and Sinquefield's *Stocks, Bonds, Bills, and Inflation*, which examines the realized rates of return for a wide variety of securities spanning the period from 1926 through 1998.[7] As part of their study, Ibbotson and Sinquefield calculated the average annual rates of return investors earned over the preceding 73 years, along with the average inflation rate for the same period. They also calculated the standard deviations of the returns for each type of security. The concept of standard deviation comes from our statistical colleagues, who use this measurement to indicate quantitatively how much

---

[7]Roger G. Ibbotson and Rex A. Sinquefield, *Stocks, Bonds, Bills, and Inflation: Historical Returns* (Chicago: Ibbotson Associates, 1999).

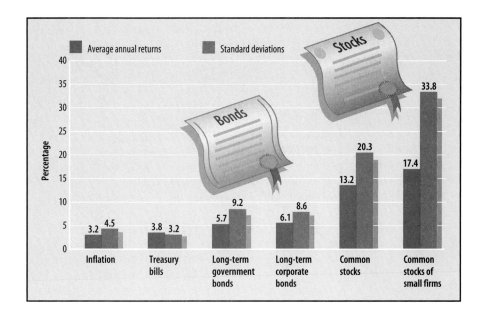

FIGURE 2–5

Average Annual Returns and Standard Deviations of Returns, 1926–1998

Source: *Stocks, Bonds, Bills, and Inflation: 1999 Yearbook.* Based on copyrighted works by Ibbotson and Sinquefield. All rights reserved. Used with permission.

dispersion or variability there is around the mean, or average, value of the item being measured—in this case, the rates of return in the financial markets.

Ibbotson and Sinquefield's results are summarized in Figure 2–5. These returns represent the average inflation rate and the average observed rates of return for different types of securities. The average inflation rate was 3.2 percent for the period covered by the study. We refer to this rate as the "inflation-risk premium." The investor who earns only the rate of inflation has earned no "real return." That is, the *real return* is the return earned above the rate of increase in the general price level for goods and services in the economy, which is the inflation rate. In addition to the danger of not earning above the inflation rate, investors are concerned about the risk of the borrower defaulting or failing to repay the loan when due. Thus, we would expect a default-risk premium for long-term corporate bonds over long-term government bonds. The premium for 1926–1998, as shown in Figure 2–5, was 0.4 percent, or what is called 40 basis points (6.1 percent on long-term corporate bonds minus 5.7 percent on long-term government bonds). We would also expect an even greater risk premium for common stocks vis-à-vis long-term corporate bonds, since the variability in average returns is greater for common stocks. The Ibbotson and Sinquefield study verifies such a risk premium, with common stocks (all firms) earning 7.1 percent more than the rate earned on long-term corporate bonds (13.2 percent for common stocks minus 6.1 percent for long-term corporate bonds).

Remember that these returns are "averages" across many securities and over an extended period of time. However, these averages reflect the conventional wisdom regarding risk premiums: The greater the risk, the greater will be the expected returns. Such a relationship is shown in Figure 2–6, where the average returns are plotted against their standard deviations; note that higher average returns have historically been associated with higher dispersion in these returns.

Interest Rate Levels over Recent Periods

Objective 10

The *nominal* interest rates on some key fixed-income securities are displayed within both Table 2–6 and Figure 2–7 for the most recent 1981–1998 time frame. The rate

FIGURE 2–6

*Rates of Return and
Standard Deviations,
1926–1998*

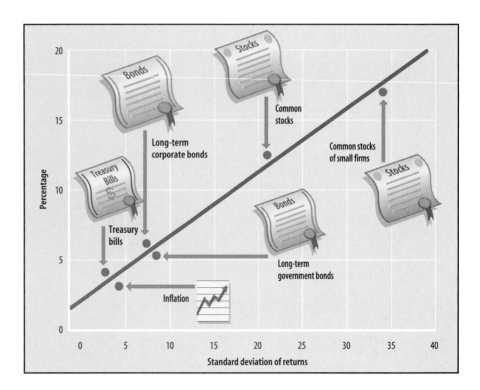

of inflation at the consumer level is also presented in those two exhibits. This allows us to observe quite easily several concepts that were mentioned in the section above. Specifically, we can observe (1) the inflation-risk premium, (2) the default-risk premium across the several instruments, and (3) the approximate real return for each instrument. Looking at the mean (average) values for each security and the inflation rate at the bottom of Table 2–6 will facilitate the discussion.

Notice that the average inflation rate over this more recent period is higher than reported in the longer period covered by the Ibbotson and Sinquefield analysis. Over the period 1981–1998 the consumer price index (December to December change) increased by an average of 3.64 percent each year. According to the logic of the financial markets, investors *require* a nominal rate of interest that exceeds the inflation rate or else their realized *real* return will be negative. Earning a negative return over long periods of time (e.g., 18 years) is not very smart.

Table 2–6 indicates that investor rationality prevailed. For example, the average return premium demanded on U.S. Treasury bills with a 3-month maturity was 3.09 percent (or 309 basis points) in excess of the inferred inflation-risk premium of 3.64 percent. That is, an average 6.73 percent yield on Treasury bills over the period *minus* the average inflation rate of 3.64 percent over the same period produces a premium of 3.09 percent. This 3.09 percent can be thought of as the real risk-free short-term interest rate that prevailed over the 1981–1998 period.

The default-risk premium is also evident in Table 2–6 and Figure 2–7. If we arrange the securities in these two exhibits from low risk to high risk, the following tabulation results:

Security	Average Yield
3-month Treasury bills	6.73
30-year Treasury bonds	8.81
Aaa corporate bonds	9.53

TABLE 2–6

	3-MONTH TREASURY BILLS	30-YEAR TREASURY BONDS	AAA RATED CORPORATE BONDS	INFLATION RATE
INTEREST RATE LEVELS AND INFLATION RATES 1981–1998				
YEAR	(%)	(%)	(%)	(%)
1981	14.08	13.44	14.17	8.9
1982	10.69	12.76	13.79	3.9
1983	8.63	11.18	12.04	3.8
1984	9.52	12.39	12.71	4.0
1985	7.49	10.79	11.37	3.8
1986	5.98	7.80	9.02	1.1
1987	5.82	8.58	9.38	4.4
1988	6.68	8.96	9.71	4.4
1989	8.12	8.45	9.26	4.6
1990	7.51	8.61	9.32	6.1
1991	5.42	8.14	8.77	3.1
1992	3.45	7.67	8.14	2.9
1993	3.02	6.59	7.22	2.7
1994	4.29	7.37	7.97	2.7
1995	5.51	6.88	7.59	2.5
1996	5.02	6.71	7.37	3.3
1997	5.07	6.61	7.26	1.7
1998	4.81	5.58	6.53	1.6
Mean	6.73	8.81	9.53	3.64

Source: *Federal Reserve Bulletin,* various issues, and *Federal Reserve Statistical Releases* H.15 (519), G.13 (415), various issues.

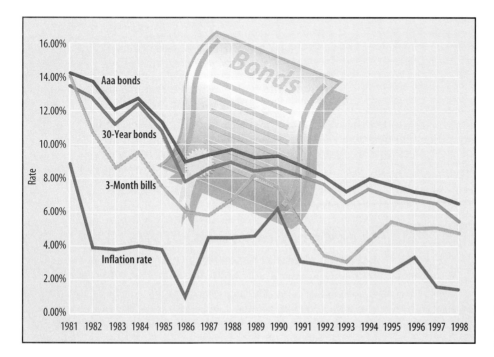

FIGURE 2–7

Interest Rate Levels and Inflation Rates, 1981–1998

Again, the basic rationale of the financial markets prevailed. The default-risk premium on high-rated (Aaa) corporate bonds relative to long-term Treasury bonds of 30-year maturity was 0.72 percent.

The array above can also be used to identify another factor that affects interest rate levels. It is referred to as the "maturity premium." This maturity premium arises even if securities possess equal (or approximately equal) odds of default. This is the case with Treasury bills and Treasury bonds, for instance, because the full faith and credit of the U.S. government stands behind these financial contracts. They are considered risk free (i.e., possessing no chance of default).

Notice that Treasury bonds with a 30-year maturity commanded a 2.08 percent yield differential over the shorter, 3-month-to-maturity Treasury bonds. This provides an estimate of the maturity premium demanded by investors over this specific **maturity premium** 1981–1998 period. More precisely, the **maturity premium** can be defined as:

The additional return required by investors in longer-term securities (bonds in this case) to compensate them for the greater risk of price fluctuations on those securities caused by interest rate changes.

When you study the basic mathematics of financial decisions in Chapter 6 and the characteristics of fixed-income securities in Chapter 7, you learn how to quantify this maturity premium that is imbedded in nominal interest rates.

One other type of risk premium that helps determine interest rate levels needs to be identified and defined. It is known as the "liquidity premium." The **liquidity premium** **liquidity premium** is defined as:

The additional return required by investors in securities that cannot be quickly converted into cash at a reasonably predictable price.

The secondary markets for small-bank stocks, especially community banks, provide a good example of the liquidity premium. A bank holding company that trades on the New York Stock Exchange, such as SunTrust Bank, will be more liquid to investors than, say, the common stock of Citizens National Bank of Leesburg, Florida. Such a liquidity premium is reflected across the spectrum of financial assets, from bonds to stocks.

CONCEPT CHECK

1. What is the "opportunity cost of funds"?
2. Over long periods of time is the "real rate of return" higher on common stocks or long-term government bonds?
3. Distinguish between the concepts of the "inflation-risk premium" and "default-risk premium."
4. Distinguish between the concepts of the "maturity premium" and "liquidity premium."

BACK TO THE FOUNDATIONS

Our first axiom, **Axiom 1: The Risk-Return Trade-off—We Won't Take on Additional Risk Unless We Expect to Be Compensated with Additional Return**, established the fundamental risk-return trade-offs that govern the financial markets. We are now trying to provide you with an understanding of the kinds of risks that are rewarded in the risk-return trade-off presented in **Axiom 1**.

Our review of rates of return and interest rate levels in the financial markets permits us to synthesize our introduction to the different types of risks that impact interest rates. We can, thereby, generate a simple equation with the **nominal** (i.e., observed) **rate of interest** being the output variable from the equation. The nominal interest rate, also called the "quoted" rate, *is the interest rate paid on debt securities without an adjustment for any loss in purchasing power.* It is the rate that you would read about in the *Wall Street Journal* for a specific fixed-income security. That equation follows:

nominal rate of interest

$$k = k^* + IRP + DRP + MP + LP \qquad (2\text{--}1)$$

where: k = the nominal or observed rate of interest on a specific fixed-income security.

k^* = the real risk-free rate of interest; it is the required rate of interest on a fixed-income security that has no risk and in an economic environment of zero inflation. This can be reasonably thought of as the rate of interest demanded by investors in U.S. Treasury securities during periods of no inflation.

IRP = the inflation-risk premium.

DRP = the default-risk premium.

MP = the maturity premium.

LP = the liquidity premium.

Sometimes in analyzing interest rate relationships over time it is of use to focus on what is called the "nominal risk-free rate of interest." Again, by nominal we mean "observed." So let us designate the nominal risk-free interest rate as k_{rf}. Drawing, then, on our previous discussions and notation we can write this expression for k_{rf}:

$$k_{rf} = k^* + IRP \qquad (2\text{--}2)$$

This equation says that the nominal risk-free rate of interest is equal to the real risk-free interest rate plus the inflation-risk premium. It also provides a quick and *approximate* way of estimating the risk-free rate of interest, k^*, by solving directly for this rate. The basic relationship in equation (2–2) contains important information for the financial decision maker. It has also for years been the subject of fascinating and lengthy discussions among financial economists.

Estimating Specific Interest Rates Using Risk Premiums: An Example

By using our knowledge of various risk premia as contained in equation (2–1) the financial manager can generate useful information for the firm's financial planning process. For instance, if the firm is about to offer a new issue of corporate bonds to the investing marketplace, it is possible for the financial manager or analyst to estimate what interest rate (yield) would satisfy the market and help ensure that the bonds are actually bought by investors. It would be unwise for the firm to offer too high of a yield because it will incur unnecessary interest expense that will negatively impact earnings. On the other hand, offering too low of a yield will hinder the bonds from being attractive to investors (savers) in a competitive marketplace. The following example should help clarify and illustrate this situation.

Problem Situation

You have been asked to provide a reasonable estimate of the nominal interest rate for a new issue of Aaa-rated bonds to be offered by Big Truck Producers, Inc. The

Takin' It to the Net
Timely data that enables you to estimate your own inflation-risk premium (IRP) is available at http://stats.bls.gov/newsrelease/cpi.nws.htm. This site from the U.S. Bureau of Labor Statistics gives you the current consumer price index report. Note that you do not enter "www" with this site.

final format that the chief financial officer (CFO) of Big Truck has requested is that of equation (2–1). Your assignment also requires that you consult the data in Table 2–6.

Some agreed-upon procedures related to generating estimates for key variables in equation (2–1) follow:

1. The financial market environment over the 1996–1998 period is considered representative of the prospective tone of the market near the time of offering the new bonds to the investing public. This means that 3-year averages are used as benchmarks for some of the variable estimates. All estimates are rounded off to hundredths of a percent; thus, 6.288 becomes 6.29%.
2. The real risk-free rate of interest is the difference between the calculated average yield on 3-month Treasury bills and the inflation rate.
3. The default-risk premium is estimated by the difference between the average yield on Aaa-rated bonds and 30-year Treasury bonds.
4. The maturity premium is estimated by the difference between the average yield on 30-year Treasury bonds and 3-month Treasury bills.
5. Big Truck's bonds will be traded on the New York Exchange for Bonds so the liquidity premium will be slight. It will be greater than zero, however, because the secondary market for the firm's bonds is more uncertain than that of some other truck producers. It is estimated at 3 basis points. A basis point is one-hundredth of one percent.

Now place your output into the format of equation (2–1) so that the nominal interest rate can be estimated and the size of each variable can also be inspected for reasonableness and discussion with the CFO.

Solution
Let's look at the building blocks that comprise our forecast of the nominal interest rate on Big Truck's new issue of bonds. The nominal rate (k) that is forecast to satisfy the market is 7.08%. The following tables illustrate how we obtained this estimate. The top portion generates the 3-year averages thought to be representative of the basic financial market environment. The bottom portion is a worksheet that "builds up" the nominal interest rate. It's just equation (2–1) in worksheet form.

YEAR	(1) 3-MONTH TREASURY BILLS (%)	(2) 30-YEAR TREASURY BONDS (%)	(3) AAA-RATED CORPORATE BONDS (%)	(4) INFLATION RATE (%)
1996	5.02	6.71	7.37	3.30
1997	5.07	6.61	7.26	1.70
1998	4.81	5.58	6.53	1.60
Mean	4.97	6.30	7.05	2.20

Thus, the real risk-free rate of interest is estimated to be 2.77 percent; it is the difference between the 3-year average yield on 3-month Treasury bills and the inflation rate (column 1 minus column 4). In similar fashion, the inflation-risk premium of 2.20 percent *(IRP)* is the 3-year average of the change in the inflation rate (column 4). The default-risk premium *(DRP)* is the difference in the 3-year average

TABLE COLUMNS (FROM PREVIOUS TABLE)	EQUATION (2–1)	
(1) − (4)	k^*	2.77
	+	+
(4)	IRP	2.20
	+	+
(3) − (2)	DRP	0.75
	+	+
(2) − (1)	MP	1.33
	+	+
Given	LP	0.03
	=	=
	k	7.08

rates that were available to investors in Aaa-rated bonds and Treasury bonds with a 30-year maturity (column 3 minus column 2). The maturity premium *(MP)* of 1.33 percent is the difference in the 3-year average rates that were earned by investors in 30-year Treasury bonds and 3-month Treasury bills (column 2 minus column 1). And, the liquidity premium *(LP)* of 3 basis points was estimated for us by a sharp financial analyst like yourself.

When we put this altogether as an estimate of the nominal interest rate needed to satisfy the financial markets on Big Truck's new bond issue, we have:

$k = k^* + IRP + DRP + MP + LP$ = nominal rate on Big Truck's bonds,
$k = 2.77 + 2.20 + 0.75 + 1.33 + 0.03 = 7.08\%$

Understanding this analysis will help you deal with the comprehensive problem at the end of this chapter. We now move to an examination of the relationship between real and nominal interest rates.

The Effects of Inflation on Rates of Return and the Fisher Effect

When a rate of interest is quoted, it is generally the nominal, or observed rate. The **real rate of interest,** on the other hand, represents *the rate of increase in actual purchasing power, after adjusting for inflation.* For example, if you have $100 today and lend it to someone for a year at a nominal rate of interest of 11.3 percent, you will get back $111.30 in 1 year. But if during the year prices of goods and services rise by 5 percent, it will take $105 at year end to purchase the same goods and services that $100 purchased at the beginning of the year. What was your increase in purchasing power over the year? The quick and dirty answer is found by subtracting the inflation rate from the nominal rate, $11.3\% - 5\% = 6.3\%$, but this is not exactly correct. To be more precise, let the nominal rate of interest be represented by k_{rf}, the anticipated rate of inflation by *IRP*, and the real rate of interest by k^*. Using these notations, we can express the relationship among the nominal interest rate, the rate of inflation, and the real rate of interest as follows:

real rate of interest

$$1 + k_{rf} = (1 + k^*)(1 + IRP) \qquad (2\text{--}3)$$

or

$$k_{rf} = k^* + IRP + (k^* \cdot IRP)$$

Consequently, the nominal rate of interest (k_{rf}) is equal to the sum of the real rate of interest (k^*), the inflation rate (IRP), and the product of the real rate and the inflation rate. This relationship among nominal rates, real rates, and the rate of inflation has come to be called the *Fisher effect*.[8] It means that the observed nominal rate of interest includes both the real rate and an *inflation premium* as noted in the previous section.

Substituting into equation (2–3) using a nominal rate of 11.3 percent and an inflation rate of 5 percent, we can calculate the real rate of interest, k^*, as follows:

$$k_{rf} = k^* + IRP + (k^* \cdot IRP)$$
$$.113 = k^* + .05 + .05k^*$$
$$k^* = .06 = 6\%$$

Thus, at the new higher prices, your purchasing power will have increased by only 6 percent, although you have $11.30 more than you had at the start of the year. To see why, let's assume that at the outset of the year one unit of the market basket of goods and services costs $1, so you could purchase 100 units with your $100. At the end of the year you have $11.30 more, but each unit now costs 1.05 (remember the 5 percent rate of inflation). How many units can you buy at the end of the year? The answer is $111.30 ÷ $1.05 = 106, which represents a 6 percent increase in real purchasing power.[9]

Inflation and Real Rates of Return: The Financial Analyst's Approach

Although the algebraic methodology presented in the previous section is strictly correct, few practicing analysts or executives use it. Rather, they employ some version of the following relationship, an approximation method, to estimate the real rate of interest over a selected past time frame.

(nominal interest rate) − (inflation rate) = real interest rate

The concept is straightforward, but implementation requires that several judgments be made. For example, which interest rate series and maturity period should be used? Suppose we settle for using some U.S. Treasury security as a surrogate for a nominal risk-free interest rate. Then, should we use the yield on 3-month U.S. Treasury bills or, perhaps, that on 30-year Treasury bonds? There is no absolute answer to the question.

So, we can have a real risk-free short-term interest rate, as well as a real risk-free long-term interest rate, and several variations in between. In essence, it just depends on what the analyst wants to accomplish. We could also calculate the real rate of interest on some rating class of corporate bonds (like Aaa-rated bonds) and have a risky real rate of interest as opposed to a real risk-free interest rate.

Further, the choice of a proper inflation index is equally challenging. Again, we have several choices. We could use the consumer price index, the producer price index for finished goods, or some price index out of the national income accounts,

---

[8]This relationship was analyzed many years ago by Irving Fisher. For those who want to explore "Fisher's theory of interest" in more detail, a fine overview is contained in Peter N. Ireland, "Long-Term Interest Rates and Inflation: A Fisherian Approach," *Federal Reserve Bank of Richmond, Economic Quarterly* 82 (Winter 1996), pp. 22–26.

[9]In Chapter 6 we study more about the time value of money.

such as the gross domestic product chain price index. Again, there is no precise scientific answer as to which specific price index to use. Logic and consistency do narrow the boundaries of the ultimate choice.

Let's tackle a very basic (simple) example. Suppose that an analyst wants to estimate the approximate real interest rate on (1) 3-month Treasury bills, (2) 30-year Treasury bonds, and (3) Aaa-rated corporate bonds over the 1981–1998 time frame. Further, the annual rate of change in the consumer price index (measured from December to December) is considered a logical measure of past inflation experience. Most of our work is already done for us in Table 2–6. Some of the data from Table 2–6 are displayed below.

SECURITY	MEAN NOMINAL YIELD (%)	MEAN INFLATION RATE (%)	INFERRED REAL RATE (%)
Treasury bills	6.73	3.64	3.09
Treasury bonds	8.81	3.64	5.17
Corporate bonds	9.53	3.64	5.89

Notice that the mean yield over the 18 years from 1981 to 1998 on all three classes of securities has been used as a reasonable proxy for the ex-post return. Likewise, the mean inflation rate over the same time period has been used as an estimate of the inflation-risk premium (IRP from our earlier notation). The last column provides the approximation for the real interest rate on each class of securities.

Thus, over the 18-year examination period the real rate of interest on 3-month Treasury bills was 3.09 percent versus 5.17 percent on 30-year Treasury bonds, versus 5.89 percent on Aaa-rated corporate bonds. These three estimates (approximations) of the real interest rate provide a rough guide to the increase in real purchasing power associated with an investment position in each security. Remember that the real rate on the corporate bonds is expected to be greater than that on long-term government bonds because of the default-risk premium (DRP) placed on the corporate securities. We move in the next section to a discussion of the maturity premium (MP).

CONCEPT CHECK

1. What is the "nominal rate of interest"? Explain how it differs from the "real rate of interest."
2. Write an equation that includes the building blocks of the nominal rate of interest.

THE TERM STRUCTURE OF INTEREST RATES

Objective 12

The relationship between a debt security's rate of return and the length of time until the debt matures is known as the **term structure of interest rates** or the **yield to maturity.** For the relationship to be meaningful to us, all the factors other than maturity, meaning factors such as the chance of the bond defaulting, must be held constant.

term structure of interest rates
yield to maturity

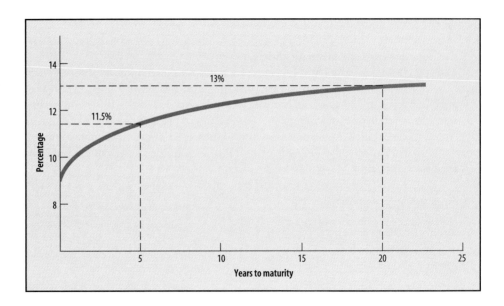

FIGURE 2–8

*The Term Structure of
Interest Rates*

Thus, *the term structure reflects observed rates or yields on similar securities, except for the length of time until maturity, at a particular moment in time.*

Figure 2–8 shows an example of the term structure of interest rates. The curve is upward sloping, indicating that longer terms to maturity command higher returns, or yields. In this hypothetical term structure, the rate of interest on a 5-year note or bond is 11.5 percent, whereas the comparable rate on a 20-year bond is 13 percent.

Observing Historical Term Structures of Interest Rates

As we might expect, the term structure of interest rates changes over time, depending on the environment. The particular term structure observed today may be quite different from the term structure a month ago and different still from the term structure 1 month from now. A perfect example of the changing term structure, or yield curve, was witnessed during the early days of the Persian Gulf crisis in August 1990. Figure 2–9 shows the yield curves 1 day before the Iraqi invasion of Kuwait and then

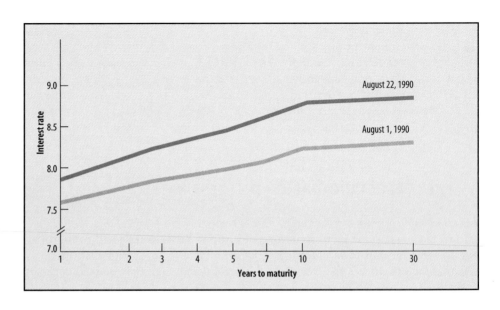

FIGURE 2–9

*Changes in the Term
Structure of Interest Rates
for Government Securities
at the Outbreak of the
Persian Gulf Crisis*

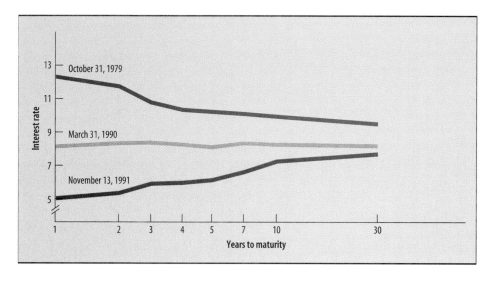

FIGURE 2-10

Historical Term Structures of Interest Rates for Government Securities

again just 3 weeks later. The change is noticeable, particularly for long-term interest rates. Investors quickly developed new fears about the prospect of increased inflation to be caused by the crisis and consequently increased their required rates of return. Although the upward-sloping term-structure curves in Figures 2–8 and 2–9 are the ones most commonly observed, yield curves can assume several shapes. Sometimes the term structure is downward sloping; at other times it rises and then falls (hump-backed); and at still other times it may be relatively flat. Figure 2–10 shows some yield curves at different points in time.

Trying to Explain the Shape of the Term Structure

A number of theories may explain the shape of the term structure of interest rates at any point. Three possible explanations are prominent: (1) the unbiased expectations theory, (2) the liquidity preference theory, and (3) the market segmentation theory.[10] Let's look at each in turn.

The Unbiased Expectations Theory

The **unbiased expectations theory** says that *the term structure is determined by an investor's expectations about future interest rates.*[11] To see how this works, consider the following investment problem faced by Mary Maxell. Mary has $10,000 that she wants to invest for 2 years, at which time she plans to use her savings to make a down payment on a new home. Wanting not to take any risk of losing her savings, she decides to invest in U.S. government securities. She has two choices. First, she can purchase a government security that matures in 2 years, which offers her an interest rate of 9 percent per year. If she does this, she will have $11,881 in 2 years, calculated as follows:[12]

unbiased expectations theory

---

[10]See Richard Roll, *The Behavior of Interest Rates: An Application of the Efficient Market Model to U.S. Treasury Bills* (New York: Basic Books, 1970).

[11]Irving Fisher thought of this idea in 1896. The theory was later refined by J. R. Hicks in *Value and Capital* (London: Oxford University Press, 1946) and F. A. Lutz and V. C. Lutz in *The Theory of Investment in the Firm* (Princeton, NJ: Princeton University Press, 1951).

[12]We could also calculate the principal plus interest for Mary's investment using the following compound interest equation: $\$10,000(1 + .09)^2 = \$11,881$. We study the mathematics of compound interest in Chapter 6.

Principal amount	$10,000
Plus: Year 1 interest (.09 × $10,000)	900
Principal plus interest at the end of year 1	$10,900
Plus: Year 2 interest (.09 × $10,900)	981
Principal plus interest at the end of year 2	$11,881

Alternatively, Mary could buy a government security maturing in 1 year that pays an 8 percent rate of interest. She would then need to purchase another 1-year security at the end of the first year. Which alternative Mary chooses obviously depends in part on the rate of interest she expects to receive on the government security she will purchase a year from now. We cannot tell Mary what the interest rate will be in a year; however, we can at least calculate the rate that will give her the same two-year total savings she would get from her first choice, or $11,881. The interest rate can be calculated as follows:

Savings needed in 2 years	$11,881
Savings at the end of year 1	
$10,000(1 + .08)	$10,800
Interest needed in year 2	$1,081

For Mary to receive $1,081 in the second year, she would have to earn about 10 percent on her second-year investment, computed as follows:

$$\frac{\text{interest received in year 2}}{\text{investment made at beginning of year 2}} = \frac{\$1,081}{\$10,800} = 10\%$$

So the term structure of interest rates for our example consists of the 1-year interest rate of 8 percent and the 2-year rate of 9 percent. This exercise also gives us information about the *expected* 1-year rate for investments made 1 year hence. In a sense, the term structure contains implications about investor expectations of future interest rates; thus, this explains the unbiased expectations theory of the term structure of interest rates.

Although we can see a relationship between current interest rates with different maturities and the investor's expectations about future interest rates, is this the whole story? Are there influences other than the investor's expectations about future interest rates? Probably, so let's continue to think about Mary's dilemma.

Liquidity Preference Theory

In presenting Mary's choices, we have suggested that she would be indifferent to a choice between the 2-year government security offering a 9 percent return and two consecutive 1-year investments offering 8 and 10 percent, respectively. However, that would be so only if she is unconcerned about the risk associated with not knowing the rate of interest on the second security as of today. If Mary is risk averse (that is, she dislikes risk), she might not be satisfied with expectations of a 10 percent return on the second 1-year government security. She might require some additional expected return to be truly indifferent. Mary might in fact decide that she will expose herself to the uncertainty of future interest rates only if she can reasonably *expect* to earn an additional .5 percent in interest, or 10.5 percent, on the second 1-year investment. This *risk premium* (additional required interest rate) to compensate for the risk of changing future interest rates is nothing more than the maturity premium (MP) introduced earlier, and this concept underlies the liquidity preference theory of the term structure.[13] In the **liquidity preference theory,** *investors require maturity premiums to compensate them for buying securities that expose them to the risks of fluctuating interest rates.*

liquidity preference theory

Market Segmentation Theory

The **market segmentation theory** of the term structure of interest rates is built on the notion that legal restrictions and personal preferences limit choices for investors to certain ranges of maturities. For example, commercial banks prefer short- to medium-term maturities as a result of the short-term nature of their deposit liabilities. They prefer not to invest in long-term securities. Life insurance companies, on the other hand, have long-term liabilities, so they prefer longer maturities in investments. At the extreme, the market segmentation theory implies that *the rate of interest for a particular maturity is determined solely by demand and supply for a given maturity and that it is independent of the demand and supply for securities having different maturities.* A more moderate version of the theory allows investors strong maturity preferences, but it also allows them to modify their feelings and preferences if significant yield inducements occur.

market segmentation theory

CONCEPT CHECK

1. Identify three prominent theories that attempt to explain the term structure of interest rates.
2. Which shape of the yield curve is considered to be the most typical?

FINANCE AND THE MULTINATIONAL FIRM: EFFICIENT FINANCIAL MARKETS AND INTERCOUNTRY RISK

Objective 13

In this chapter we have discussed and demonstrated that the United States has a highly developed, complex, and competitive system of financial markets that allows for the quick transfer of savings from those economic units with a surplus of savings to those economic units with a savings deficit. Such a system of robust and credible financial markets allows great ideas (e.g., the personal computer) to be financed and increases the overall wealth of the given economy. Real capital formation, such as a Ford Motor Company manufacturing plant in Livonia, Michigan, is enhanced by the financial market mechanism.

One major reason underdeveloped countries are indeed underdeveloped is that they lack a financial market system that has the confidence of those who must use it—such as the multinational firm. The multinational firm with cash to invest in foreign markets will weigh heavily the integrity of both the financial system and the political system of the prospective foreign country.

---

[13]This theory was first presented by John R. Hicks in *Value and Capital* (London: Oxford University Press, 1946), pp. 141–145, with the risk premium referred to as the liquidity premium. For our purposes we use the term *maturity premium (MP)* to describe this risk premium, thereby keeping our terminology consistent within this chapter.

A lack of integrity on either the financial side or the political stability side retards direct investment in the lesser developed nation. Consider the Walt Disney Company headquartered in Burbank, California. Disney common stock trades on the NYSE (ticker symbol DIS), although the firm has significant overseas real investments in projects known as the Disneyland Paris Resort and Tokyo Disneyland. Disney has confidence in the French financial markets, those of western Europe, and Japan. For example, Disney executives launched three new projects in Japan during 1998—a new theme park and two new hotels.[14] However, Disney did not launch any new projects in Thailand, where the basic currency—called the "baht"—lost a full 98 percent of its value against the U.S. dollar over the short period from June 1997 to February 1998. Profits generated in Thailand and measured by the baht would have bought significantly fewer U.S. dollars after the devaluation. This type of situation is typically referred to as exchange rate risk. Currencies, too, trade within financial markets and those risks are closely studied by wise multinational firms.

CONCEPT CHECK

1. Identify one major reason why underdeveloped countries remain underdeveloped.
2. Give an example of "foreign exchange risk".

SUMMARY

This chapter centers on the market environment in which corporations raise long-term funds, including the structure of the U.S. financial markets, the institution of investment banking, and the various methods for distributing securities. It also discusses the role of interest rates in allocating savings to ultimate investment.

Objectives 1 and 2

Mix of corporate securities sold

When corporations go to the capital market for cash, the most favored financing method is debt. The corporate debt markets clearly dominate the equity markets when new funds are raised. The U.S. tax system inherently favors debt capital as a fund-raising method. In an average year over the 1981–1996 period, bonds and notes made up 75.6 percent of external cash that was raised.

Primarily because of the transactions costs involved, corporations prefer to finance new investments out of internally generated funds before external sources of funds are tapped. Table 2–1 showed that from 70.4 to 90.3 percent of business sources of funds over the 1990–1998 period were generated via internal sources.

Objective 3

Why financial markets exist

The function of financial markets is to allocate savings efficiently in the economy to the ultimate demander (user) of the savings. In a financial market the forces of supply and demand for a specific financial instrument are brought together. The wealth of an economy would not be as great as it is without a fully developed financial market system.

Objective 4

Financing of business

Every year households are a net supplier of funds to the financial markets. The nonfinancial business sector is usually a net borrower of funds. Both life insurance companies and

---

[14]The Walt Disney Company, *Annual Report*, 1998, pp. 24–25, 57.

private pension funds are important buyers of corporate securities. Savings are ultimately transferred to the business firm seeking cash by means of (1) the direct transfer, (2) the indirect transfer using the investment banker, or (3) the indirect transfer using the financial intermediary.

Components of the U.S. financial market system

Objective 5

Corporations can raise funds through public offerings or private placements. The public market is impersonal in that the security issuer does not meet the ultimate investors in the financial instruments. In a private placement, the securities are sold directly to a limited number of institutional investors.

The primary market is the market for new issues. The secondary market represents transactions in currently outstanding securities. Both the money and capital markets have primary and secondary sides. The money market refers to transactions in short-term debt instruments. The capital market, on the other hand, refers to transactions in long-term financial instruments. Trading in the money and capital markets can occur in either the organized security exchanges or the over-the-counter market. The money market is exclusively an over-the-counter market.

Investment banker

Objective 6

The investment banker is a financial specialist involved as an intermediary in the merchandising of securities. He or she performs the functions of (1) underwriting, (2) distributing, and (3) advising. Major methods for the public distribution of securities include (1) the negotiated purchase, (2) the competitive bid purchase, (3) the commission or best-efforts basis, (4) privileged subscriptions, and (5) direct sales. The direct sale bypasses the use of an investment banker. The negotiated purchase is the most profitable distribution method to the investment banker. It also provides the greatest amount of investment-banking services to the corporate client.

Private placements

Objective 7

Privately placed debt provides an important market outlet for corporate bonds. Major investors in this market are (1) life insurance firms, (2) state and local retirement funds, and (3) private pension funds. Several advantages and disadvantages are associated with private placements. The financial officer must weigh these attributes and decide if a private placement is preferable to a public offering.

Flotation costs

Objective 8

Flotation costs consist of the underwriter's spread and issuing costs. The flotation costs of common stock exceed those of preferred stock, which, in turn, exceed those of debt. Moreover, flotation costs as a percent of gross proceeds are inversely related to the size of the security issue.

Regulation

Objective 9

The new issues market is regulated at the federal level by the Securities Act of 1933. It provides for the registration of new issues with the SEC. Secondary market trading is regulated by the Securities Exchange Act of 1934. The Securities Acts Amendments of 1975 placed on the SEC the responsibility for devising a national market system. This concept is still being studied. The shelf registration procedure (SEC Rule 415) was initiated in March 1982. Under this regulation and with the proper filing of documents, firms that are selling new issues do not have to go through the old, lengthy registration process each time the firm plans an offering of securities.

The logic of rates of return and interest rate determination

Objectives 10–12

The financial markets give managers an informed indication of investors' opportunity costs. The more efficient the market, the more informed the indication. This information is a useful input about the rates of return that investors require on financial claims. In turn, this becomes useful to financial managers as they estimate the overall cost of capital used as a screening rate in the capital budgeting process.

Rates of return on various securities are based on the underlying supply of loanable funds (savings) and demand for those loanable funds. In addition to a risk-free return, investors will want to be compensated for the potential loss of purchasing power resulting from inflation. Moreover, investors require a greater return the greater the default-risk, maturity premium, and liquidity premium are on the securities being analyzed.

Objective 13

The Multinational Firm: Efficient Financial Markets and Intercountry Risk

A system of robust and credible financial markets allows great ideas to be financed and increases the overall wealth of the given economy. The multinational firm with cash to invest in foreign markets will weigh heavily the integrity of both the financial system and the political system of the prospective foreign country where the proposed investment project will be domiciled. A lack of integrity on either the financial side or the political stability side retards direct investment in a lesser-developed nation.

KEY TERMS

capital market, 44

direct placement, 43

direct sale, 50

direct securities, 39

financial assets, 39

financial markets, 38

flotation costs, 52

indirect securities, 39

investment banker, 47

liquidity preference theory, 69

liquidity premium, 60

market segmentation theory, 69

maturity premium, 60

money market, 43

nominal rate of interest, 61

opportunity cost of funds, 56

organized security exchanges, 44

over-the-counter markets, 44

primary markets, 43

private placement, 43

privileged subscription, 50

public offering, 43

real assets, 39

real rate of interest, 63

secondary markets, 39

shelf offering, 55

shelf registration, 55

syndicate, 48

term structure of interest rates, 65

unbiased expectations theory, 67

underwriting, 48

yield to maturity, 65

STUDY QUESTIONS

2-1 What are financial markets? What function do they perform? How would an economy be worse off without them?

2-2 Define in a technical sense what we mean by *financial intermediary*. Give an example of your definition.

2-3 Distinguish between the money and capital markets.

2-4 What major benefits do corporations and investors enjoy because of the existence of organized security exchanges?

2-5 What are the general categories examined by an organized exchange in determining whether an applicant firm's securities can be listed on it? (Specific numbers are not needed here, but rather areas of investigation.)

2-6 Why do you think most secondary-market trading in bonds takes place over-the-counter?

2-7 What is an investment banker, and what major functions does he or she perform?

2-8 What is the major difference between a negotiated purchase and a competitive bid purchase?

2-9 Why is an investment-banking syndicate formed?

2-10 Why might a large corporation want to raise long-term capital through a private placement rather than a public offering?

2-11 As a recent business school graduate, you work directly for the corporate treasurer. Your corporation is going to issue a new security and is concerned with the probable flotation costs. What tendencies about flotation costs can you relate to the treasurer?

2-12 When corporations raise funds, what type of financing vehicle (instrument or instruments) is most favored?

2-13 What is the major (most significant) savings-surplus sector in the U.S. economy?

2-14 Identify three distinct ways that savings are ultimately transferred to business firms in need of cash.

2-15 Explain the term *opportunity cost* with respect to cost of funds to the firm.

2-16 Compare and explain the historical rates of return for different types of securities.

2-17 Explain the impact of inflation on rates of return.

2-18 Define the term *structure of interest rates.*

2-19 Explain the popular theories for the rationale of the term structure of interest rates.

STUDY PROBLEMS

2-1 *(Real Interest Rates: Financial Analyst's Method)* The CFO of your firm has asked you for an approximate answer to this question: What was the increase in real purchasing power associated with both 3-month Treasury bills and 30-year Treasury bonds over the 1991–1995 period? Hints: (1) Consult Table 2–6 in the text, and (2) simple averages on the key variables will provide a defensible response to your boss. Also, the chief financial officer wants a short explanation should the 3-month real rate turn out to be *less* than the 30-year real rate.

2-2 *(Inflation and Interest Rates)* What would you expect the nominal rate of interest to be if the real rate is 4 percent and the expected inflation rate is 7 percent?

2-3 *(Inflation and Interest Rates)* Assume the expected inflation rate to be 4 percent. If the current real rate of interest is 6 percent, what ought the nominal rate of interest be?

2-4 *(Inflation and Interest Rates)* Assume the expected inflation rate to be 5 percent. If the current real rate of interest is 7 percent, what would you expect the nominal rate of interest to be?

2-5 *(Term Structure of Interest Rates)* You want to invest your savings of $20,000 in government securities for the next 2 years. Currently, you can invest either in a security that pays interest of 8 percent per year for the next 2 years or in a security that matures in 1 year but pays only 6 percent interest. If you make the latter choice, you would then reinvest your savings at the end of the first year for another year.

  a. Why might you choose to make the investment in the 1-year security that pays an interest rate of only 6 percent, as opposed to investing in the 2-year security paying 8 percent? Provide numerical support for your answer. Which theory of term structure have you supported in your answer?

  b. Assume your required rate of return on the second-year investment is 11 percent; otherwise, you will choose to go with the 2-year security. What rationale could you offer for your preference?

COMPREHENSIVE PROBLEM

You have been asked to provide a reasonable estimate of the nominal interest rate for a new issue of Aaa-rated bonds to be offered by Big Truck Producers, Inc. The final format that the chief financial officer of Big Truck has requested is that of equation (2–1) in the text. Your assignment also requires that you consult the data in Table 2–6.

Some agreed-upon procedures related to generating estimates for key variables in equation (2–1) follow.

a. The financial market environment over the 1993–1995 period is considered representative of the prospective tone of the market near the time of offering the new bonds to the investing public. This means that 3-year averages will be used as benchmarks for some of the variable estimates. All estimates are rounded off to hundredths of a percent; thus, 6.288 becomes 6.29 percent.

b. The real risk-free rate of interest is the difference between the calculated average yield on 3-month Treasury bills and the inflation rate.

c. The default-risk premium is estimated by the difference between the average yield on Aaa-rated bonds and 30-year Treasury bonds.

d. The maturity premium is estimated by the difference between the average yield on 30-year Treasury bonds and 3-month Treasury bills.

e. Big Truck's bonds will be traded on the New York Exchange for Bonds so the liquidity premium will be slight. It will be greater than zero, however, because the secondary market for the firm's bonds is more uncertain than that of some other truck producers. It is estimated at 3 basis points. A basis point is one hundredth of 1 percent.

Now place your output into the format of equation (2–1) so that the nominal interest rate can be estimated and the size of each variable can also be inspected for reasonableness and discussion with the CFO.

Chapter Three

Income Statement • Balance Sheet •

Measuring Cash Flows • Finance and the

Multinational Firm: Financial Statements and

International Finance

UNDERSTANDING FINANCIAL STATEMENTS AND CASH FLOWS

LEARNING OBJECTIVES

AFTER READING THIS CHAPTER, YOU SHOULD BE ABLE TO:

1. Compute a company's profits as reflected by an income statement.
2. Determine a firm's accounting book value, as presented in a balance sheet.
3. Measure a company's free cash flows, both from an operating perspective and a financing perspective.
4. Explain the difficulty in comparing financial statements of U.S. firms and foreign companies.

Evaluating the performance of a firm using its financial statements can be a tricky business. The difficulty is generally not due to deliberate attempts by corporate managers and their accountants to mislead you. The problem relates to the substantial flexibility inherent in the set of rules and principles that accountants follow in preparing a firm's financial statements (generally accepted accounting principles, or GAAP). For example, consider the words of wisdom offered by Warren Buffet, one of the most successful investors ever.

The term "earnings" has a precise ring to it. And when an earnings figure is accompanied by an unqualified auditor's certificate, a naive reader might think it comparable in certitude to pi, calculated to dozens of decimal places. In reality, however, earnings can be as pliable as putty when a charlatan heads the company reporting them. . . .

So where does this leave the analyst who attempts to evaluate the financial performance of a firm using its financial statements? The answer is that one must indeed "look through" the numbers in the statements and seek to understand the subtle differences in accounting practice and the effect that they can have on reported earnings. Analyzing financial performance using accounting statements is not simply a mechanical process. It requires the analyst not only to "crunch the numbers" but to understand where the numbers came from.

With this caveat in mind, we begin our study of how to interpret and use a firm's financial statements.

Takin' It to the Net
Click on http://www.reportgallery.com/ for a listing of 2,200 different annual reports. Find a company that is of interest to you and read the letter to shareholders. Is there anything mentioned in the letter that reveals the management's view of their role of creating value for the stockholders?

Let's begin our study by looking at the format and content of the following basic financial statements: the income statement, the balance sheet, and the firm's cash flows.

Objective 1

INCOME STATEMENT

income statement (profit and loss statement)

An **income statement,** or **profit and loss statement,** *indicates the amount of profits generated by a firm over a given time period, often a year.* In its most basic form, the income statement may be represented as follows:

$$\text{Sales} - \text{Expenses} = \text{Profits}$$

Thus, the income statement answers the question, How profitable is the business? In providing this answer, the income statement reports financial information related to five broad areas of business activity:

1. **Revenue (sales)**—*money derived from selling the company's product or service*
2. **Cost of goods sold**—*the cost of producing or acquiring the goods or services to be sold*
3. **Operating expenses**—*expenses related to (1) marketing and distributing the product or service to the customer and (2) administering the business*
4. **Financing costs** of doing business—*the interest paid to the firm's creditors and the dividends paid to preferred stcockholders (but not dividends paid to common stockholders)*
5. **Tax expenses**—*amount of taxes owed based on a firm's taxable imcome*

revenue (sales)
cost of goods sold
operating expenses

financing costs

tax expenses

Thus, we would expect that:

1. The higher (lower) a firm's revenues or sales, the higher (lower) its profits will be.
2. The lower (higher) the costs of producing a product, the higher (lower) its profits will be.
3. The lower (higher) a company's operating expenses (which consist of marketing expenses, administration expenses, and depreciation expenses), the higher (lower) its profits will be.
4. The less (more) interest and preferred stock dividends a company pays, the higher (lower) its profits will be.
5. The less (more) taxes a company pays, the higher (lower) its profits will be.

In short, combining higher (lower) sales with lower (higher) costs and expenses yields a firm higher (lower) profits.

All of these "income statement activities" are presented graphically in Figure 3–1. We observe that the top portion of Figure 3–1, beginning with sales and continuing down through the **operating income or earnings before interest and taxes,** is affected solely by the first three activities listed—sales, cost of acquiring the firm's product or service, and operating expenses. To this point, no financing costs are included. In other words, the operating profits are unaffected by how the company is being financed. The firm may be financed entirely by its owners (shareholders) without incurring any debt, or it may be financed in part by the owners (shareholders) and in part by borrowing money (incurring debt). In either case, operating profits are the same. In other words, operating profits (earnings before interest and taxes) represent the firm's profits that are available to all the firm's investors, both debt holders and shareholders.

operating income (earnings before interest and taxes)

Below the line reporting operating income in Figure 3–1, we see the results of the firm's financing decisions, along with the taxes that are due on the company's income. Here the company's *financing costs* are shown, first in the form of *interest expenses* and then *preferred dividends.* The tax rates imposed on the company's **earnings before taxes** determine the amount of the *tax liability,* or the *tax expenses.*[1] The final number, **net income available to common stockholders** (commonly called **net income),** is the *income that may be distributed to the company's owners or reinvested in the company,* provided of course there is cash available to do so. As we shall see later, however, the fact that a firm has a positive net income does not necessarily mean it has any cash—possibly a surprising result to us, but one we shall come to understand.

earnings before taxes

net income available to common stockholders (net income)

Income Statement: The McDonald's Corporation

An example of an income statement is provided in Table 3–1 for the McDonald's Corporation. As shown in the table, McDonald's had sales of $11,508 million for the

---

[1]Notice that interest is a tax-deductible expense, while preferred dividends are paid after taxes have been calculated.

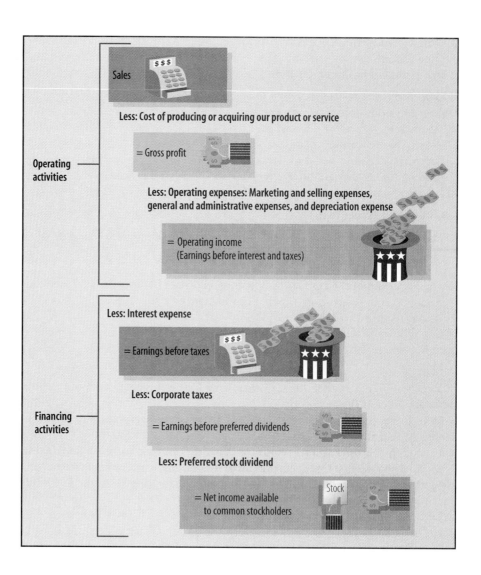

FIGURE 3–1

The Income Statement:
An Overview

12-month period ending December 31, 1997, and the cost of goods sold was $6,537 million. (The numbers for McDonald's are expressed in millions, so McDonald's sales were actually about $11.5 billion, with cost of goods sold over $6.5 billion.) The result is a gross profit of $4,971 million ($4.97 billion). The firm then had $2,177 million in operating expenses, which included marketing expenses, general and administrative expenses, and depreciation expenses. After deducting operating expenses, the firm's operating profits (earnings before interest and taxes) amounted to $2,794 million ($2.8 billion). This amount represents the before-tax profits generated as if the McDonald's Corporation were an all-equity company. To this point, we have calculated the profits resulting only from operating activities, as opposed to financing decisions such as how much debt or equity is used to finance the company's operations.[2]

_____

[2]The McDonald's Corporation financial statements presented in this chapter have been simplified considerably with some loss of accuracy in details, but so doing avoids unnecessary complexity.

TABLE 3-1 THE MCDONALD'S CORPORATION INCOME STATEMENT FOR YEAR ENDED 1997 ($ MILLIONS)

Sales		$11,508
Cost of goods sold		6,537
Gross profits		$ 4,971
Marketing expenses and general and administrative expenses	$ 1,832	
Depreciation expense	345	
Total operating expenses		$ 2,177
Operating profits		$ 2,794
Interest expenses		387
Earnings before taxes		$ 2,407
Income taxes		765
Earnings before preferred stock dividends		$ 1,642
Preferred stock dividends		25
Net income available to common stockholders		$ 1,617

Net income available to common stockholders	$ 1,617
Common stock dividends	688
Change in retained earnings	$ 929

We next deduct McDonald's interest expense (the amount paid for using debt financing) of $387 million to arrive at the company's earnings before tax of $2,407 million ($2.4 billion). We then deduct the income taxes of $765 million to give us $1,642 million in earnings before preferred stock dividends. Finally we subtract a meager (meager for McDonald's) $25 million in preferred stock dividends to arrive at the company's net income available to common stockholders of $1,617 million ($1.6 billion).

Although not technically part of the income statement, we have added a box at the bottom of the table that shows what happened to the firm's $1,617 million net income. The firm paid $688 million in dividends to its common stockholders, leaving $929 million to be retained within the company. As we will see shortly, the firm's retained earnings reported in the balance sheet increased by this same amount of $929 million.[3]

What conclusion can we draw from McDonald's income statement? Well, for one thing, we learn that for every $1 in sales, McDonald's earned about 43¢ in gross profits ($4,971 gross profits ÷ $11,508 sales), 24¢ in operating profits ($2,794 operating profits ÷ $11,508 sales), and 14¢ in net income ($1,617 net income ÷ $11,508 sales). Only by estimating if these profit-to-sales levels are high enough that shareholder value is being created can we know if these results are good. We might also gain some insights if we could see how McDonald's performance compares with its competition (more about this in Chapter 4). For the time being, simply remember that profit-to-sales relationships are important in assessing a firm's performance.

Takin' It to the Net
Go to http://www.lucent.com/press/0499/990422.coa.html for the April 1999 Lucent Technologies press release regarding their income statement. Look for key words from this chapter (e.g., revenue, gross profits, and net income).

Takin' It to the Net
See Intel's 1998 Annual Report at http://www.intel.com/intel/annual98/letter.htm for their letter to the stockholders, the firm's vision, and financial information.

[3]We are "fudging" here. In McDonald's actual balance sheet, retained earnings did not increase precisely by the $930 million. There were a number of other complicating adjustments made to retained earnings, but nothing that we need to be concerned about.

Objective 2

BALANCE SHEET

balance sheet

Whereas the income statement reports the results from operating the business for a period of time, such as a year, the **balance sheet** provides a *snapshot of the firm's financial position at a specific point in time*, presenting its asset holdings, liabilities, and owner-supplied capital. In its simplest form, a balance sheet follows this formula:

Total assets = Outstanding debt + shareholders' equity

Assets represent the resources owned by the firm, whereas the liabilities and shareholders' equity indicate how those resources are financed.

The difference between the timing of an income statement and a balance sheet may be represented graphically as follows.

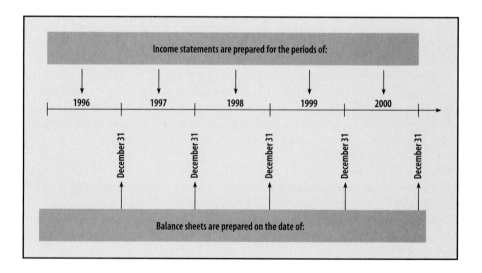

Here we see five periods of operations from 1996 through 2000. There would be an income statement for the period of January 1 through December 31 for each of the 5 years' operations and a balance sheet reporting the company's financial position as of December 31 of each year. Thus, the balance sheet on December 31, 2000, is a statement of the company's financial position at that particular date, which is the result of all financial transactions since the company began its operations.

Figure 3–2 gives us the basic components of a balance sheet. On the left side of Figure 3–2, the firm's assets are listed according to their type; on the right side, we

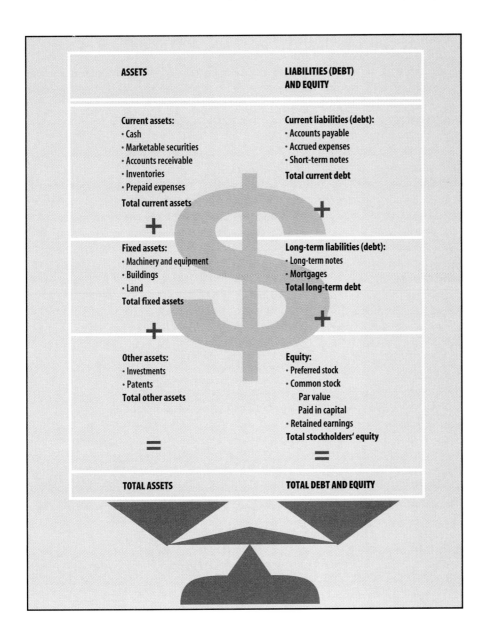

ASSETS	LIABILITIES (DEBT) AND EQUITY
Current assets: • Cash • Marketable securities • Accounts receivable • Inventories • Prepaid expenses **Total current assets**	**Current liabilities (debt):** • Accounts payable • Accrued expenses • Short-term notes **Total current debt**
+	**+**
Fixed assets: • Machinery and equipment • Buildings • Land **Total fixed assets**	**Long-term liabilities (debt):** • Long-term notes • Mortgages **Total long-term debt**
+	**+**

Other assets:
• Investments
• Patents
Total other assets
	Equity:
	• Preferred stock
	• Common stock
	   Par value
	   Paid in capital
	• Retained earnings
	Total stockholders' equity

=	**=**
TOTAL ASSETS	**TOTAL DEBT AND EQUITY**

FIGURE 3–2
The Balance Sheet: An Overview

see a listing of the different sources of financing a company could use to finance its assets.

Types of Assets

As shown in Figure 3–2, a company's assets fall into three categories: (1) current assets, (2) fixed assets, and (3) other assets.

Current Assets

Current assets, or **gross working capital,** as it is sometimes called, *comprise those assets that are relatively liquid, that is, those that are expected to be converted into cash within a year.* Current assets primarily include cash, accounts receivable, inventories, and prepaid expenses.

current assets
(gross working capital)

- **Cash.** Every firm must have cash for current business operations. A reservoir of cash is needed because of the unequal flow of funds into (cash receipts) and out of (cash expenditures) the business. The amount of the cash balance is determined not only by the volume of sales, but also by the predictability of cash receipts and cash payments.

accounts receivable

- **Accounts receivable.** The firm's **accounts receivable** *consists of payments due from its customers who buy on credit.*

inventory

- **Inventories. Inventory** *consists of the raw materials, work in process, and the final products held by a firm for eventual sale.*

prepaid expenses

- **Prepaid expenses.** A company often needs to prepay some of its expenses. For example, insurance premiums may be due before coverage begins, or rent may have to be paid in advance. Thus, **prepaid expenses** *are those cash payments recorded on the balance sheet as current assets and then shown as an expense in the income statement as they are used.*

Fixed Assets

fixed assets

Fixed assets *include machinery and equipment, buildings, and land.* Some businesses are more capital-intensive than others; for example, a manufacturer would typically be more capital-intensive than a wholesale operation and, therefore, have more fixed assets.

Other Assets

other assets

Other assets *are all assets that are not current assets or fixed assets,* including for example, intangible assets such as patents, copyrights, and goodwill.

In reporting the dollar amounts of the various types of assets described above, the conventional practice is to report the value of the assets and liabilities on a historical cost basis. Thus, the balance sheet is not intended to represent the current market value of the company, but rather *reports the historical transactions recorded at*

accounting book value

their cost, or what we call a firm's **accounting book value.** Determining a fair value of the business is a different matter.

Types of Financing

We now turn to the right side of the balance sheet in Figure 3–2, labeled "Liabilities (Debt) and Equity," which indicates how the firm finances its assets. Financing

debt

comes from two main sources: debt (liabilities) and equity. **Debt** *is money that has been*

equity

borrowed and must be repaid at some predetermined date. **Equity,** on the other hand, *represents the shareholders' investment in the company.*

Debt Capital

debt capital
current debt

Debt capital *is financing provided by a creditor.* As shown in Figure 3–2, it is divided into (1) current, or short-term, debt and (2) long-term debt. **Current debt,** or short-term liabilities, *includes borrowed money that must be repaid within the next 12 months.* Sources of current debt include the following:

accounts payable

- **Accounts payable** *represents credit extended by suppliers to a firm when it purchases inventories.* The purchasing firm may have 30 or 60 days before paying for inventory that has been purchased. This form of credit extension is also called trade credit.

other payables

- **Other payables** include *interest payable and income taxes payable that are owed and will come due within the year.*

accrued expenses

- **Accrued expenses** *are short-term liabilities that have been incurred in the firm's operations, but not yet paid.* For example, employees perform work that may not be paid for until the following week or month, which are recorded as accrued wages.

- **Short-term notes** *represent amounts borrowed from a bank or other lending source that are due and payable within 12 months.*

Long-Term Debt

Long-term debt *includes loans from banks or other sources that lend money for longer than 12 months.* For example, a firm might borrow money for 5 years to buy equipment, or for as long as 25 to 30 years to purchase real estate, such as a warehouse or office building.

Equity

Equity includes the shareholders' investment—both preferred stockholders and common stockholders—in the firm.

- **Preferred stockholders** *receive a dividend that is fixed in amount.* In the event of liquidation of the firm, these stockholders are paid after the firm's creditors, but before the common stockholders.
- **Common stockholders** *are the residual owners of a business.* They receive whatever is left over—good or bad—after the creditors and preferred stockholders are paid. The amount of a firm's common equity as reported in the balance sheet is equal to (1) the amount the company received from selling stock to investors plus (2) the firm's retained earnings. *The amount the firm receives from selling stock is recorded in the common equity section in the accounts of* **par value and paid-in capital.**[4] These amounts may be offset by *any stock that has been repurchased by the company,* which is typically shown as **treasury stock. Retained earnings** is *the cumulative total of all the net income over the firm's life less the common stock dividends that have been paid over the years.* Thus, the common equity capital consists of the following:

```
common shareholder' equity = common stock issued − common
stock repurchased + cumulative net income over the firm's life −
total dividends paid over the firm's life
```

which is shown in the balance sheet as:

```
Common shareholders' equity = (par value + paid-in capital) −
treasury stock + retained earnings
```

Balance Sheet: The McDonald's Corporation

Balance sheets for the McDonald's Corporation are presented in Table 3–2 for both December 31, 1996, and December 31, 1997, along with the changes in each amount between years. By referring to the two balance sheets, we can see the financial position of the firm both at the beginning and end of 1997. Furthermore, by examining the two balance sheets, along with the income statement for 1997, we have a more complete picture of the firm's operations. We are then able to see what McDonald's looked like at the beginning of 1997 (balance sheet on December 31, 1996), what happened during the year (income statement for 1997), and the final outcome at the

---

[4]At times, the financial statement does not separate out the par value and paid in capital and just shows the combined amounts as "common stock."

short-term notes

long-term debt

preferred stockholders

common stockholders

par value and paid-in capital

treasury stock
retained earnings

Assets	1996	1997	Change
Cash	$ 332	$ 341	$ 9
Accounts receivable	495	484	(11)
Inventories	70	71	1
Prepaid expenses	208	247	39
Total current assets	$ 1,105	$ 1,143	$ 38
Gross fixed assets	$19,134	$20,088	$ 954
Accumulated depreciation	(4,782)	(5,127)	(345)
Net fixed assets	$14,352	$14,961	$ 609
Investments	779	702	(77)
Other assets	1,152	1,436	284
Total assets	$17,388	$18,242	$ 854

Liabilities and Equity	1996	1997	Change
Liabilities			
Short-term notes payable	$ 693	$ 1,629	$ 936
Accounts payable	638	651	13
Taxes payable	23	53	30
Accrued expenses	782	652	(130)
Total current liabilities	$ 2,136	$ 2,985	$ 849
Long-term debt	6,533	6,325	(208)
Total liabilities	$ 8,669	$ 9,310	$ 641
Equity			
Preferred stock	$ 165	$ 80	$ (85)
Common stock:			
Par value and paid-in capital	$ 583	$ 708	$ 125
Retained earnings	10,998	11,927	929
Treasury stock	(3,027)	(3,783)	(756)
Total common equity	$ 8,554	$ 8,852	$ 298
Total equity	8,719	8,932	213
Total liabilities and equity	17,388	$18,242	$ 854

end of the year (balance sheet on December 31, 1997). Our perspective of 1997 is shown graphically in Figure 3–3.

    The balance sheet data for the McDonald's Corporation show that the firm ended the prior year (1996) with about $17.4 billion ($17,358 million) in assets, compared to $18.2 billion ($18,242 million) a year later at the end of 1997. Practically all of this growth was in long-term assets, namely, an increase of $954 million in gross fixed assets, also called plant and equipment, and a $284 million increase in other assets. In the bottom half of the balance sheet, we should notice the growth in debt and equity primarily occurred in the short-term notes payable (an increase of $936 million), along with an increase in retained earnings of $929 million. These increases in debt (liabilities) and equity were offset in part by a decrease of $208 million in long-term debt.

    To help us gain an even better grasp of McDonald's financial position on December 31, 1997, we have graphed the major types of assets and debt and equity in Figure 3–4. In looking at this graph, we have to be struck by the large proportion of the firm's assets that are invested in fixed assets—almost $15 billion in fixed assets

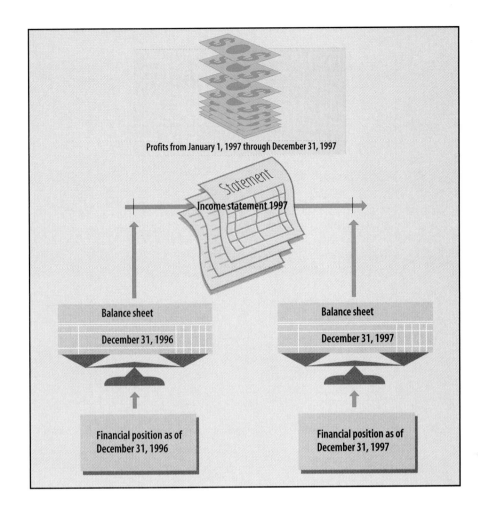

Profits from January 1, 1997 through December 31, 1997

Statement

Income statement 1997

| Balance sheet | Balance sheet |
| December 31, 1996 | December 31, 1997 |

| Financial position as of December 31, 1996 | Financial position as of December 31, 1997 |

FIGURE 3–3

Visual Perspective of the Relationship between the McDonald's Corporation Balance Sheets and Income Statement

of the $18.2 billion in total assets. Also, there are two other relationships that can be observed in Figure 3–4: (1) the level of McDonald's net working capital and (2) the firm's mix of debt to equity used in financing the company. Let's consider each.

Net Working Capital

Earlier we said that the term *current assets* is also called *gross working capital*. We can now define **net working capital** *as current assets less current liabilities (current assets − current liabilities)*. Thus, net working capital compares the amount of current assets (assets that should convert into cash within the next 12 months) to the current liabilities (debt that will be due within 12 months). For McDonald's, its net working capital is a negative $1,842 million ($1,143 million current assets − $2,985 million current debt). This is quite unusual; most firms have a positive net working capital by a substantial margin. McDonald's clearly does not choose to maintain a large amount of liquid assets (assets that can easily be converted into cash).

To better understand the small investment in accounts receivable and inventories and the large amounts in fixed assets, we have to think about the nature of McDonald's business. For a restaurant business, inventories are small—you don't want to keep a lot of lettuce on hand. Also, many of the restaurants are owned by franchisees and not the McDonald's Corporation itself; thus, McDonald's has no inventory whatsoever related to these units. Regarding accounts receivable, the business is largely a cash operation, with the receivables being primarily money owed the

net working capital

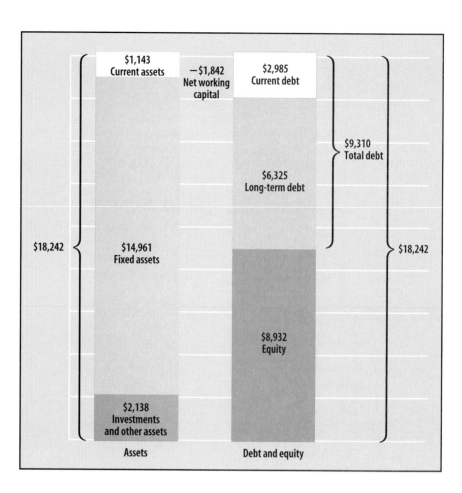

FIGURE 3–4

*McDonald's Corporation
1997 Balance Sheet*

firm by the franchises. On the other hand, the McDonald's Corporation owns the real estate for all the stores, whether company-owned or a franchise, which explains the large amount of fixed assets. So by looking at the financial statements for the McDonald's Corporation, we have gained a better understanding of the business.

Debt/Equity Mix

debt/equity mix

A firm's **debt-to-equity mix** *is the amount of debt a firm borrows per dollar of equity.* We can also see that by the end of 1997, McDonald's was financing its assets about half (actually 51%) from debt and half from equity. The debt-equity relationship is an important one to lenders and investors, as we will see on numerous occasions in our studies.

CONCEPT CHECK

1. Regarding the time frame reported, how is the balance sheet different from the income statement?
2. State the basic balance sheet formula and its meaning.
3. What is the definition of a firm's "accounting book value"?
4. What are the two principal sources of financing? What do these sources consist of?

Although an income statement measures a company's profits, profits are not the same as cash flows; profits are calculated on an *accrual* basis rather than a *cash* basis. **Accrual-basis accounting** *records income when it is earned, whether or not the income has been received in cash, and records expenses when they are incurred, even if money has not actually been paid out.* For example, sales reported in the income statement include both cash sales and credit sales. Therefore, sales for a given year do not correspond exactly to the actual cash collected from sales. Similarly, a firm must purchase inventory, but some of the purchases are financed by credit rather than by immediate cash payment. Also, under the accrual system, the purchase of equipment that will last for more than a year is not shown as an expense in the income statement. Instead, the amount is recorded as an asset and then depreciated over its useful life. An annual depreciation expense (this is not a cash flow) is recorded as a way to match the use of the asset with sales generated from its use. **Cash-basis accounting,** on the other hand, *reports income when cash is received and records expenses when they are paid.*

accrual-basis accounting

cash-basis accounting

In measuring cash flows, we could use the conventional accountant's presentation called a *statement of cash flows*; however, we are more interested in considering cash flows from the perspective of the firm's shareholders and its investors, rather than from an accounting viewpoint. We will instead measure *the cash flow that is free and available to be distributed to the firm's investors, both debt and equity investors,* or what we will call **free cash flows.** Thus, what follows is similar to a conventional cash flow statement presented as part of a company's financial statements, but "not exactly."

free cash flows

We should begin by recognizing an important financial principle. *The cash flows that are generated through a firm's operations and investments in assets always equal its cash flows paid to—or received by—the company's investors (both creditors and stockholders).* They have to be equal. That is, a firm's operating free cash flows must equal its financing free cash flows, as represented by the following equation:

$$\text{operating free cash flows} = \text{financing free cash flows}$$

As a result, we either can calculate a firm's free cash flows from an operating perspective or a financing perspective. Either way, we will get the same answer. However, the two calculations give us different perspectives about the firm's cash flows, not to mention serving as a check that we have correctly computed the cash flows. So, let's look at each approach for measuring a company's cash.

Calculating Free Cash Flows: An Operating Perspective

A firm's **free cash flows,** from an **operating perspective,** *is the after tax cash flows generated from operations less the firm's investments in assets.* It is this same amount that is available for distributing to the firm's investors. That is, a firm's free cash flows for a given period is equal to:

free cash flows (operating perspective)

after-tax cash flow from operations
less
the investment (increase) in net operating working capital
less
investments in fixed assets (plant and equipment) and other assets

Thus, the procedure for computing a firm's free cash flows on an operating basis involves three steps:

1. Convert the income statement from an accrual basis to a cash basis (compute after-tax cash flows from operations).
2. Calculate the investment in *net* working capital.
3. Compute investments made in fixed assets and other assets (investment activities).

For the first step, we compute after-tax cash flows from operations as follows:

---

operating income (earnings before interest and taxes)

+ depreciation

= earnings before interest, taxes, depreciation, and amortization (EBITDA)

− cash tax payments

= after-tax cash flows from operations

In the foregoing calculation, we determine **earnings before interest, taxes, depreciation, and amortization (EBITDA)** by adding back depreciation to operating income because depreciation is not a cash expense. Also, we should note that the actual *cash* tax payments are not necessarily equal to the tax expense reported in the income statement. The provision for taxes in the income statement is the amount attributable to income reported, but the company may be permitted to defer the payment (or sometimes a firm may have to prepay taxes).

Thus, the **cash tax payment** *is equal to the provision for taxes reported in the income statement less (plus) any increase (decrease) in accrued or deferred taxes in the balance sheet.*

For the second step, the increase in net operating working capital is equal to the:

(change in current assets) − (change in non-interest-bearing current liabilities)

Earlier, we said that *net working capital* is equal to current assets minus current or short-term debt. However, in computing free cash flows, we only consider the **non-interest-bearing current liabilities** incurred in the normal day-to-day operating activities of buying and selling the firm's goods, such as accounts payable and accrued wages. Any interest-bearing debt (that is, where you pay interest for the use of the money) is included in computing free cash flows from a financing perspective because borrowing money is a financing activity.

Finally, the third step involves computing the change in *gross* fixed assets (and not *net* fixed assets) and any other assets that are on the balance sheet not already considered.

The McDonald's Corporation's Free Cash Flows (Operating Perspective)

The cash flow for McDonald's Corporation in 1997 is presented in Table 3–3, along with an indication as to the source of the data—whether the number came from the income statement or represents a change in the balance sheet. Simply put, it shows how the profits for the year combine with all the changes in the balance sheets to affect the company's cash flow. (The calculations in Table 3–3 are divided into the three steps previously listed for determining a firm's cash flows.)

As shown in Table 3–3, McDonald's cash flows are determined as follows:

1. Start with McDonald's operating income of $2,794 million ($2.79 billion).
2. Because the $345 million in depreciation was not a cash outflow, add it to the $2,794 million operating income figure.
3. Subtract the cash taxes—the actual amount of taxes paid ($735 million), as opposed to the amount shown in the income statement ($765 million).
4. Subtract the increase in the firm's net operating working capital ($155 million), which is equal to the increase in current assets ($38 million), plus the decreases in non-interest-bearing current liabilities, such as accounts payable and accruals ($117 million). (Note that we excluded changes in taxes payable because it was already recognized when computing cash taxes.)

TABLE 3–3	MCDONALD'S CORPORATION OPERATING FREE CASH FLOWS FOR THE YEAR ENDING DECEMBER 31, 1997 (IN $ MILLIONS)		

| | | Information from: | |
		INCOME STATEMENT	BALANCE SHEETS
Step 1: Compute after-tax cash flows from operations			
Operating income (EBIT)		$2,794 ‡	
Depreciation		345 ‡	
Earnings before interest, tax, depreciation, and amortization (EBITDA)		$3,139	
Tax expense	$ 765	‡	
Less the change in income tax payable	30		‡
Cash taxes		735	
After-tax cash flows from operations		$2,404	
Step 2: Compute the change in net operating working capital			
Change in current assets:			
Change in cash	$ 9		‡
Change in accounts receivable	(11)		‡
Change in inventories	1		‡
Change in prepaid expenses	39		‡
Change in current assets	$ 38		
Change in non-interest-bearing operating current debt:			
Change in accounts payable	$ 13		‡
Change in accrued expenses	(130)		‡
Change in non-interest-bearing current debt	$ (117)		
Change in net operating working capital (current assets − non-interest-bearing current debt)		$ 155	
Step 3: Compute the change in fixed assets and other assets			
Change in long-term assets:			
Purchase of fixed assets	$ 954		‡
Change in investments	(77)		‡
Change in other assets	284		‡
Net cash used for investments		$1,161	
Operating cash flows		$1,088	
(After-tax operating cash flows − change in net working capital − change in long-term assets)			

Takin' It to the Net

Go to http://www.toolkit.cch.com/text/p06_4100.asp for the Business Owner's Toolkit for "Understanding How Cash Flow Works."

5. Subtract the $1,161 million increase in long-term assets, which results from a $954 million increase in gross fixed assets, a $77 million decrease in investments, and a $284 million increase in other assets.

Given the above computations, we see that the firm's free cash flows are positive in the amount of $1,088 million. Although $2,404 million was generated from operations, part of this amount was consumed by the increases in net operating working capital ($155 million) and the investments in long-term assets ($1,161 million).

So where did McDonald's $1,088 in free cash flows go? It went to the investors. Let's compute the free cash flows from a financing perspective to confirm that they received the money.

Calculating Free Cash Flows: A Financing Perspective

free cash flows (financing perspective)

We now compute **free cash flows** from a **financing perspective.** This free cash flow measurement *is equal to the cash that is distributed to or received from the firm's investors.* Specifically, free cash flows from a financing perspective are equal to:

FINANCIAL MANAGEMENT IN PRACTICE

Earnings or Cash: Which Is Better?

A number of stock analysts at investment houses such as J.P. Morgan and Goldman Sachs are converting from using earnings to cash flows when valuing stocks.

Cash-flow valuations were favored by many of the "raiders" in the 1980s who wanted to see how much debt companies could suffer and still survive. But today's stock analysts are coming around to cash flow because they say it ignores accounting tricks and thus shows the true economic health of companies.

"The reported profits number is now considered an accounting fiction," says Michael Mayo, a bank analyst at First Boston. Cash-flow valuations are now in vogue in the cable, high-tech, Internet, pharmaceutical, and financial-services sectors.

Some analysts argue that cash flow may better estimate companies' true growth rates. For example, in 1999 analysts projected that Citigroup Inc. and Wells Fargo & Co. would report above-average future earnings growth, partly because of events stemming from mergers. Mr. Mayo contended that these events could "potentially inflate the banks' future reported earnings, relative to cash flow." He warned that

investors might overlook that the banks aren't creating as much value as reported profits suggest.

Analysts say that when cash flow is lower than reported earnings, it is a sign that profits are coming from items other than cash—including possible accounting tricks. For example, before it restated its 1997 numbers because of alleged accounting irregularities, Sunbeam Corp. reported $109 million in net profits for 1997. But at the same time, Sunbeam reported $8 million in net outflows of cash for the year, which suggests that reported earnings may have come instead from possible accounting manipulations.

There is an even more impressive indication than anecdotal evidence that cash flow is coming to have greater importance in the views of analysts. According to a study by Rick Escherich, a managing director in J.P. Morgan M&A group, 72 percent of 178 investment bankers surveyed publish a cash-flow earnings multiple. Escherich commented, "Fifteen years ago, there was very little emphasis on cash flow."

Source: Elizabeth MacDonald, "Analysts Increasingly Look to Cash Flow Over Earnings," *Wall Street Journal,* April 1, 1999, p. C2. The *Wall Street Journal.* © 1993 by Dow Jones & Co., Inc. All rights reserved.

```
┌─────────────────────────────────────────────────────────────────┐
│ Interest payments to creditors                                     │
│                                                                    │
│   ┌─────────────────────────────────────────────────────────┐    │
│   │   + decrease in debt principal                           │    │
│   │  or                                                      │    │
│   │   − increase in debt principal                           │    │
│   └─────────────────────────────────────────────────────────┘    │
│                                                                    │
│ plus dividends paid to stockholders                                │
│                                                                    │
│   ┌─────────────────────────────────────────────────────────┐    │
│   │   + decrease in stock                                    │    │
│   │  or                                                      │    │
│   │   − increase in stock                                    │    │
│   └─────────────────────────────────────────────────────────┘    │
└─────────────────────────────────────────────────────────────────┘
```

Thus, to compute free cash flows from a financing perspective, we do the following:

1. *Compute the actual interest paid to creditors.* To calculate the interest payment to creditors, we begin with the interest expense shown in the income statement. However, because some of this interest may have only been accrued for income purposes and not yet paid, we subtract any increase in interest payable to arrive at the actual interest paid.
2. *Determine if the company repaid any debt principal to the creditors (creditors receive cash) or increased debt principal (creditors provide cash to the firm).* This amount is found by computing the change in debt principal.
3. *Ascertain if any dividends were paid to (received by) the stockholders.*
4. *Determine if any new stock was issued (investors provide cash to the firm) or if the firm repurchased stock from investors (investors receive cash from the firm).* Here we take the change in the par value and paid-in capital for any stock issued and the change in treasury stock (stock that has been repurchased).

To conclude, free cash flows from a financing perspective are simply the net cash flows received by the firm's investors or, if negative, the cash flows that the investors are paying into the firm. In the latter situation, the investors are putting money into the firm because the firm's free cash flows are negative, thereby requiring an infusion of capital by the investors.

The McDonald's Corporation's Free Cash Flows (Financing Perspective)

For McDonald's, the financing cash flows paid to the firm's investors are shown in Table 3–4, which are again based on data from McDonald's 1997 income statement and the two balance sheets (December 31, 1996 and 1997). We compute the interest received by the investors by taking the interest expense in the income statement ($387 million) and subtracting the increase in interest payable. However, because there was no interest payable, interest expense is the same as interest paid. Next, we calculate the changes in debt principal and then add the dividends received by the investors. Finally, we calculate the change in stock, which was a negative $631 million. The reduction in stock is equal to the change in par value and paid-in capital ($125 million) less the increase in treasury stock ($756 million), or $125 million − $756 million = −$631 million. The net decrease in stock indicates that the shareholders received $631 million in cash.

TABLE 3–4	MCDONALD'S FINANCING FREE CASH FLOWS FOR THE YEAR ENDING DECEMBER 31, 1997

			Information from:	
			INCOME STATEMENT	BALANCE SHEETS
Interest paid to—received by—investors	$ 387		‡	
Less change in interest payable	0			‡
Interest received by investors		$ 387		
Plus decrease in long-term debt		208		‡
Less increase in short-term debt		(936)		‡
Plus preferred stock dividends		25	‡	
Plus common stock dividends		688	‡	
Plus decrease in preferred stock		85		‡
Plus decrease in common stock		631		‡
Net cash flows to investors (financing cash flows)		$1,088		

As we expected, in 1997 the investors received more money from the company than they invested. In fact, they received $1,088 million—the exact amount of the firm's free cash flows from an operating perspective. As we noted earlier, the cash flows generated by a company must equal the cash flowing to or from the investors.

The McDonald's Corporation: What Have We Learned?

Based on our review of the McDonald's Corporation's financial statements, we can now draw some conclusions. To this point, we have learned that:

- For every dollar of sales, McDonald's earns 24¢ in operating income and 14¢ in net income.
- McDonald's has little in the way of current assets, especially accounts receivable and inventory. Most of the firm's investments are in fixed assets.
- The firm finances its assets from an almost equal split of debt and equity.
- McDonald's has positive free cash flows, which means that in net the firm is returning cash to its investors.
- The company used a portion of its after-tax cash flows from operations to expand the asset base, particularly fixed assets.

Takin' It to the Net

Go to www.mcdonalds.com/corporate/investor/financialinfo/annualreport/index.html for the 1998 financial statements for McDonald's. How do they compare to the 1997 financial statements presented in this chapter?

CONCEPT CHECK

1. Why can an income statement not provide a measurement of the firm's cash flows?
2. What is the relationship between a firm's operating and financing free cash flows?
3. When computing a firm's operating free cash flows, why is it necessary to adjust operating income for increases (decreases) in net working capital and fixed assets?
4. What impact does positive or negative operating cash flows have on financing cash flows?

- The primary cash flows going to the investors were interest, dividends, the repayment of long-term debt, and the company repurchasing stock. However, short-term lenders provided the firm additional financing.

FINANCE AND THE MULTINATIONAL FIRM: FINANCIAL STATEMENTS AND INTERNATIONAL FINANCE

Objective 4

As of 1999, many countries had different guidelines for firms to use in preparing financial statements. In other words, a dollar of earnings in the United States is not the same as DM 1.84 (deutsche [German] Marks) (the equivalent of a U.S. dollar based on the exchange rate). The two countries simply have different generally accepted accounting principles. In fact, the differences in accounting practices are significant enough that a firm reporting according to German standards could have $100 million in profits, but if U.S. standards are used that same company might report a loss. Just imagine what this does for an investor trying to interpret financial statements across different country boundaries.

As a result of this situation, the International Accounting Standards Committee (IASC), a private body supported by the worldwide accounting profession, is trying to develop international financial reporting standards that will minimize the problem. The need for international standards became increasingly urgent as a result of the Asian crisis, which called attention to the perils of lax accounting in many of the Asian countries.

In spite of the work to standardize accounting practices around the world, the U.S. accounting profession has rejected efforts toward international standards. On the other hand, both the U.S. Congress and the New York Stock Exchange want to see more foreign companies list their stocks on their exchange; thus, they have encouraged the Securities and Exchange Commission (SEC) to accept the new international standards. Even so, the SEC has instead insisted that foreign companies seeking to list their shares in the United States must follow U.S. accounting standards, as developed by the Financial Accounting Standards Board (FASB). Despite the push for acceptable uniform standards, this is not an issue that will resolve itself quickly. Only time will tell what will happen.

--- SUMMARY ---

Compute a company's profits, as reflected by an income statement.

Objective 1

A firm's profits may be viewed as follows:

Gross profit = sales − cost of goods sold

Earnings before interest and tax (operating profits) = sales − cost of goods sold − operating expenses

Net profits (net income) = sales − cost of goods sold − operating expenses − interest expense − taxes − preferred stock dividends

The following five activities drive a company's profits:

1. Revenue derived from selling the company's product or service
2. Cost of producing or acquiring the goods or services to be sold
3. Operating expenses related to (1) marketing and distributing the product or service to the customer and (2) administering the business
4. Financing costs of doing business—namely, the interest paid to the firm's creditors
5. Payment of taxes

Objective 2   **Determine a firm's accounting book value, as presented in a balance sheet.**
The balance sheet presents a companies assets and liabilities as of a specific date. Total assets must equal debt plus equity. The assets include current assets, fixed assets, and other assets. Debt includes short-term and long-term debt. Equity includes common stock and retained earnings. All the numbers in a balance sheet are based on historical costs. As such, they are considered to equal the firm's accounting book value, as opposed to its market value.

Objective 3   **Measure a company's free cash flows, both from an operating perspective and a financing perspective.**
Free cash flow is the cash that is distributed to or received from the firm's investors. Free cash flow can be computed from an operating or a financing perspective. In either case, they are equal. That is,

Free cash flow from an:

Operating perspective	Financing perspective
Earnings before interest, taxes, depreciation, and amortization (EBITDA) − taxes − additional investments in assets	Interest and dividend payments + decreases in debt and stock or − increases in debt and stock

The two are equal (=).

Objective 4   **Explain the difficulty in comparing financial statements of U.S. firms and foreign companies.**
Accounting practices in foreign countries are significantly different from the United States. Thus, it is difficult to compare financial results of two companies from different countries.

KEY TERMS

revenue (sales), 77

short-term notes, 83

tax expenses, 77

treasury stock, 83

STUDY QUESTIONS

3-1. A company's financial statements consist of the balance sheet, income statement, and statement of cash flows.
  a. Describe the nature of the balance sheet and the income statement.
  b. Why have we not used the conventional statement of cash flows in our presentation, computing instead what we call free cash flows?
3-2. What are the differences between gross profits, operating profits, and net income?
3-3. What is the difference between dividends and interest expense?
3-4. Why is it that the preferred stockholders' equity section of the balance sheet would change only when new shares are sold or repurchased, whereas the common equity section would change from year to year regardless of whether new shares are bought or sold?
3-5. What is net working capital? How is it different from gross working capital? What is the difference between interest-bearing debt and non-interest-bearing debt?
3-6. Discuss the reasons why one firm could have positive cash flows and be headed for financial trouble, while another firm with negative cash flows could actually be in a good financial position.
3-7. Why is the examination of only the balance sheet and income statement not adequate in evaluating a firm?
3-8. Why do a firm's free cash flows from an operating perspective have to equal its free cash flows from a financing perspective?

SELF-TEST PROBLEMS

ST-1. *(Measuring cash flows)* Given the information below for the M & G Corporation, compute the firm's free cash flows for the year 2000, first from an operating perspective and then from a financing perspective. What do you learn about the firm from these computations?

M & G CORPORATION BALANCE SHEET
FOR DECEMBER 31, 1999 AND 2000

	1999	2000
Cash	$ 9,000	$ 500
Accounts receivable	12,500	16,000
Inventories	29,000	45,500
Total current assets	$ 50,500	$ 62,000
Land	20,000	26,000
Buildings and equipment	70,000	100,000
Less: allowance for depreciation	(28,000)	(38,000)
Total fixed assets	$ 62,000	$ 88,000
Total assets	$112,500	$150,000
Accounts payable	$ 10,500	$ 22,000
Short-term bank notes	17,000	47,000
Total current liabilities	$ 27,500	$ 69,000
Long-term debt	28,750	22,950
Common stock	31,500	31,500
Retained earnings	24,750	26,550
Total debt and equity	$112,500	$150,000

M & G CORPORATION INCOME STATEMENT FOR THE YEARS ENDING DECEMBER 31, 1999 AND 2000		
	1999	2000
Sales (all credit)	$125,000	$160,000
Cost of goods sold	75,000	96,000
Gross profit	$ 50,000	$ 64,000
Operating expenses		
Fixed cash operating expenses	$ 21,000	$ 21,000
Variable operating expenses	12,500	16,000
Depreciation	4,500	10,000
Total operating expenses	$ 38,000	$ 47,000
Earnings before interest and taxes	$ 12,000	$ 17,000
Interest expense	3,000	6,100
Earnings before taxes	$ 9,000	$ 10,900
Taxes	4,500	5,450
Net income	$ 4,500	$ 5,450

STUDY PROBLEMS

3-1. *(Review of financial statements)* Prepare a balance sheet and income statement as of December 31, 2000, for Belmond, Inc., from the following information.

Inventory	$ 6,500
Common stock	45,000
Cash	16,550
Operating expenses	1,350
Notes payable	600
Interest expense	900
Depreciation expense	500
Net sales	12,800
Accounts receivable	9,600
Accounts payable	4,800
Long-term debt	55,000
Cost of goods sold	5,750
Buildings and equipment	122,000
Accumulated depreciation	34,000
Taxes	1,440
General and Administrative Expense	850
Retained earnings	?

3-2. *(Review of financial statements)* Prepare a balance sheet and income statement as of December 31, 2000, for the Warner Company from the following scrambled list of items.

Depreciation	$ 66,000
Cash	225,000
Long-term debt	334,000
Sales	573,000
Accounts payable	102,000
General and Administrative Expense	79,000
Buildings and equipment	895,000
Notes payable	75,000

Accounts receivable	153,000
Interest expense	4,750
Accrued expenses	7,900
Common stock	289,000
Cost of goods sold	297,000
Inventory	99,300
Taxes	50,500
Accumulated depreciation	263,000
Prepaid expenses	14,500
Taxes payable	53,000
Retained earnings	262,900

3-3. *(Free cash flow analysis)* Interpret the information below regarding the Westlake Corporation's free cash flows.

WESTLAKE CORPORATION FREE CASH FLOWS

Free Cash Flows—Operating Perspective		
Operating income (EBIT)		$1,020
Depreciation		125
Earnings before interest, tax, depreciation, and amortization (EBITDA)		$1,145
Tax expense	$ 325	
Less the change in income tax payable	35	
Cash taxes		290
After-tax cash flows from operations		$ 855
Change in net working capital		
Change in current assets:		
Change in cash	$ 226	
Change in accounts receivable	112	
Change in inventories	302	
Change in current assets		$ 640
Change in non-interest-bearing current debt		
Change in accounts payable	$ 116	
Change in accruals	85	
Change in non-interest-bearing operating current debt		201
Change in net operating working capital		$ 439
(current assets − non-interest-bearing current debt)		
Change in long-term assets:		
Purchase of fixed assets		1,064
Free cash flows		$ (648)
Free Cash Flows—Financing Perspective		
Interest paid to—received by—investors	$ 231	
Less change in interest payable	(45)	
Interest received by investors		$ 276
Issue long-term debt		(550)
Increase in short-term debt		(126)
Issue common stock		(312)
Common stock dividends		64
Free cash flow—financing perspective		$ (648)

3-4. *(Free cash flow analysis)* Interpret the information below regarding the Maness Corporation's free cash flows.

MANESS CORPORATION FREE CASH FLOWS		
Free Cash Flows—Operating Perspective		
Operating income (EBIT)		$ 954
Depreciation		60
Earnings before interest, tax, depreciation, and amortization (EBITDA)		$1,014
Tax expense	$ 360	
Less the change in income tax payable	40	
Cash taxes		320
After-tax cash flows from operations		$ 694
Change in net working capital		
Change in current assets:		
Change in cash	$ (250)	
Change in accounts receivable	(89)	
Change in inventories	(560)	
Change in current assets		$ (899)
Change in non-interest-bearing current debt		
Change in accounts payable	$ (100)	
Change in accruals	(75)	
Change in non-interest-bearing operating current debt		$ (175)
Change in net operating working capital		$ (724)
(current assets − non-interest-bearing current debt)		
Change in long-term assets:		
Sale of fixed assets		(2,161)
Free Cash Flows—Operating Perspective		$3,579
Free Cash Flows—Financing Perspective		
Interest paid to—received by—investors	$ 319	
Less change in interest payable	(45)	
Interest received by investors		$ 364
Repayment of long-term debt		877
Increase in short-term debt		(27)
Repurchase in common stock		1,024
Common stock dividends		1,341
Free cash flows—financing perspective		$3,579

3-5. *(Measuring cash flows)* Calculate the free cash flows for Pamplin, Inc. for the year ended December 31, 2000, both from an operating and a financing perspective. Interpret your results.

PAMPLIN INC. BALANCE SHEET AT 12/31/1999 AND 12/31/2000

Assets

	1999	2000
Cash	$ 200	$ 150
Accounts receivable	450	425
Inventory	550	625
Current assets	$1,200	$1,200
Plant and equipment	$2,200	$2,600
Less: accumulated depreciation	(1,000)	(1,200)
Net plant and equipment	$1,200	$1,400
Total assets	$2,400	$2,600

Liabilities and Owners Equity

	1999	2000
Accounts payable	$ 200	$ 150
Notes payable—current (9%)	0	150
Current liabilities	$ 200	$ 300
Bonds (8 1/3% interest)	$ 600	$ 600
Owners' equity		
Common stock	$ 300	$ 300
Paid-in capital	600	600
Retained earnings	700	800
Total owners' equity	$1,600	$1,700
Total liabilities and owners' equity	$2,400	$2,600

PAMPLIN INC. INCOME STATEMENT FOR YEARS ENDING 12/31/1999 AND 12/31/2000

		1999		2000
Sales (all credit)		$1,200		$1,450
Cost of goods sold		700		850
Gross profit		$ 500		$ 600
Operating expenses	30		40	
Depreciation	220	250	200	240
Operating income		$ 250		$ 360
Interest expense		50		64
Net income before taxes		$ 200		$ 296
Taxes (40%)		80		118
Net income		$ 120		$ 178

3-6. *(Measuring cash flows)* Calculate the free cash flows for the Waterhouse Co. for the year ended December 31, 2000, both from an operating and a financing perspective. Interpret your results.

WATERHOUSE CO. BALANCE SHEET FOR 12/31/1999 AND 12/31/2000		
	1999	2000
Cash	$ 75,000	$ 82,500
Receivables	102,000	90,000
Inventory	168,000	165,000
Prepaid expenses	12,000	13,500
Total current assets	$357,000	$351,000
Gross fixed assets	325,500	468,000
Accumulated depreciation	(94,500)	(129,000)
Patents	61,500	52,500
Total assets	$649,500	$742,500
Accounts payable	$124,500	$112,500
Taxes payable	97,500	105,000
Total current liabilities	$222,000	$217,500
Mortgage payable	150,000	0
Preferred stock	0	225,000
Additional paid-in capital—preferred	0	6,000
Common stock	225,000	225,000
Retained earnings	52,500	69,000
Total liabilities and equity	$649,500	$742,500

Additional Information

1. The only entry in the accumulated depreciation account is the depreciation expense for the period.
2. The only entries in the retained earning account are for dividends paid in the amount of $18,000 and for the net income for the year.
3. Expenses include a $9,000 amortization of patents.
4. The income statement for 2000 is as follows:

WATERHOUSE CO. INCOME STATEMENT FOR YEAR ENDED 12/31/2000	
Sales (all credit)	$187,500
Cost of goods sold	111,000
Gross profit	76,500
Operating expenses	32,000
Provision for taxes	10,000
Net income	$ 34,500
(Cost of goods sold included depreciation expense of $34,500)	

3-7. *(Measuring cash flows)* Calculate the free cash flows for T.P. Jarmon Company for the year ended December 31, 2000, both from an operating and a financing perspective. Interpret your results.

T. P. JARMON COMPANY BALANCE SHEET
FOR 12/31/1999 AND 12/31/2000

Assets	1999	2000
Cash	$ 15,000	$ 14,000
Marketable securities	6,000	6,200
Accounts receivable	42,000	33,000
Inventory	51,000	84,000
Prepaid rent	1,200	1,100
Total current assets	$115,200	$138,300
Net plant and equipment	286,000	270,000
Total assets	$401,200	$408,300

Liabilities and Equity	1999	2000
Accounts payable	$ 48,000	$ 57,000
Notes payable	15,000	13,000
Accruals	6,000	5,000
Total current liabilities	$ 69,000	$ 75,000
Long-term debt	$160,000	$150,000
Common stockholders' equity	$172,200	$183,300
Total liabilities and equity	$401,200	$408,300

T. P. JARMON COMPANY INCOME STATEMENT
FOR THE YEAR ENDED 12/31/2000

Sales (all credit)		$600,000
Less: cost of goods sold		460,000
Gross profits		$140,000
Less: operating and interest expenses		
General and administrative	$ 30,000	
Interest	10,000	
Depreciation	30,000	
Total		70,000
Earnings before taxes		$ 70,000
Less: taxes		27,100
Net income available to common stockholders		$ 42,900
Less: cash dividends		31,800
Change in retained earnings		$ 11,100

3-8. *(Measuring cash flows)* Calculate the free cash flows for Abrams Manufacturing Company for the year ended December 31, 2000, both from an operating and a financing perspective. Interpret your results.

ABRAMS MANUFACTURING COMPANY BALANCE SHEET FOR 12/31/1999 AND 12/31/2000		
	1999	2000
Cash	$ 89,000	$100,000
Accounts receivable	64,000	70,000
Inventory	112,000	100,000
Prepaid expenses	10,000	10,000
Total current assets	275,000	280,000
Plant and equipment	238,000	311,000
Accumulated depreciation	(40,000)	(66,000)
Total assets	$473,000	$525,000
Accounts payable	$ 85,000	$ 90,000
Accrued liabilities	68,000	63,000
Total current debt	153,000	153,000
Mortgage payable	70,000	0
Preferred stock	0	120,000
Common stock	205,000	205,000
Retained earnings	45,000	47,000
Total debt and equity	$473,000	$525,000

ABRAMS MANUFACTURING COMPANY INCOME STATEMENT FOR THE YEAR ENDED 12/31/2000	
	2000
Sales (all credit)	$184,000
Cost of goods sold	60,000
Gross profit	$124,000
Selling, general, and administrative expenses	44,000
Depreciation expense	26,000
Operating income	$ 54,000
Interest expense	4,000
Earnings before taxes	$ 50,000
Taxes	16,000
Preferred stock dividends	10,000
Net income	$ 24,000

Additional Information

1. The only entry in the accumulated depreciation account is for year 2000 depreciation.
2. The firm paid $22,000 in common stock dividends during 2000.

The financial statements both for PepsiCo and Coca-Cola are provided below.
   a. How much profit is each company making per dollar of sales?
   b. Calculate the free cash flows (operating and financing) for the two firms. Compare your findings.

PEPSICO, INC. INCOME STATEMENT
FOR YEAR ENDING 1997

Net sales		$20,917
Cost and expenses, net		
Costs of sales	$7,618	
Selling, general, and administrative expenses	9,241	
Impairment of long-lived assets	290	
Depreciation expense	1,106	$18,255
Operating profit		$ 2,662
Interest expense		(478)
Interest income		$ 125
Extraordinary items		$ 651
Income before income taxes		$ 2,960
Provision for income taxes		818
Net income		$ 2,142

Note: Impairment of long-lived assets (plant and equipment or fixed assets) is a noncash expense, similar to depreciation.

PEPSICO, INC. BALANCE SHEET
DECEMBER 31, 1996 AND 1997

	1997	1996
Assets		
Current assets		
Cash and cash equivalents	$ 2,883	$ 786
Accounts and notes receivable, less allowance $150 in 1997 and $151 in 1996	2,150	2,516
Inventories	732	1,038
Prepaid expenses	486	799
Total current assets	$ 6,251	$ 5,139
Investments in unconsolidated affiliates	1,201	1,375
Property, plant, and equipment, net	6,261	10,191
Intangible assets, net	5,855	7,136
Other assets	533	671
Total assets	$20,101	$24,512
Liabilities and Shareholders' Equity		
Current liabilities		
Accounts payable	$ 1,047	$ 1,565
Accrued expenses	1,125	1,420
Short-term borrowings	0	26
Income taxes payable	640	487
Other current liabilities	1,445	1,641
Total current liabilities	$ 4,257	$ 5,139
Long-term debt	4,946	8,439
Other liabilities	2,265	2,533
Deferred income taxes	1,697	1,778
Shareholders' equity		
Capital stock, par value $1^2/_3$ cents per share: authorized 1,800 shares, issued 863 shares	$ 29	$ 29
Capital in excess of par value	1,314	1,201
Retained earnings	11,239	8,851
Currency translation adjustment and other	(660)	(435)
	$11,922	$9,646
Less: treasury stock, at cost: 75 shares and 73 shares in 1995 and 1994, respectively	(4,986)	(3,023)
Total shareholders' equity	$ 6,936	$ 6,623
Total liabilities and shareholders' equity	$20,101	$24,512

Note: The change in retained earnings equals $2,142 net income plus $992 gain from sale of the restaurant business less $746 dividend payments.

COCA-COLA CO.
INCOME STATEMENT FOR YEAR ENDING 1997 ($ MILLIONS)

Sales		$18,868
Cost of goods sold	$5,631	
Selling and administrative expenses	7,792	
Depreciation and amortization	384	13,807
Operating profits		$ 5,061
Interest expense		258
Extraordinary items		1,252
Earnings before tax		$ 6,055
Provision for taxes		1,926
Net income		4,129

COCA-COLA CO. BALANCE SHEET
DECEMBER 31, 1996 AND 1997 ($ MILLIONS)

	1997	1996
Cash and cash equivalents	$ 1,843	$ 1,658
Accounts receivable (net)	1,639	1,641
Inventories	959	952
Other current assets	1,528	1,659
Total current assets	$ 5,969	$ 5,910
Gross plant and equipment	$ 5,771	$ 5,581
Accumulated depreciation	2,028	2,031
Net plant and equipment	$ 3,743	$ 3,550
Investments	4,437	3,432
Intangibles	727	753
Other assets	2,064	2,516
Total assets	$16,940	$16,161
Debt and equity		
Long-term debt due in one year	$ 397	$ 9
Notes payable	2,677	3,388
Accounts payable	2,279	2,055
Taxes payable	1,056	1,037
Other current liabilities	970	917
Total current liabilities	$ 7,379	$ 7,406
Long-term debt	801	1,116
Deferred taxes	448	301
Other liabilities	1,001	1,182
Shareholders' equity		
Common stock	$ 861	$ 858
Capital surplus	1,477	997
Retained earnings	16,555	14,621
Less treasury stock	(11,582)	(10,320)
Total shareholders' equity	$ 7,311	$ 6,156
Total liabilities and equity	$16,940	$16,161

Note: The change in retained earnings is equal to the $4,129 net income less $814 currency translation losses and less $1,381 in dividend payments.

SS-1

M & G INDUSTRIES FREE CASH FLOWS FOR THE YEAR ENDED DECEMBER 31, 2000		
Free cash flows: Operating Perspective		
Operating income		$ 17,000
Plus depreciation expense		10,000
Less tax expense		(5,450)
Less change in income tax payable		0
After-tax cash flows from operations		$ 21,550
Change in net operating working capital		
Change in cash	$ (8,500)	
Change in accounts receivable	3,500	
Change in inventories	16,500	
Change in accounts payable	(11,500)	
Change in net operating working capital		$ 0
Change in fixed assets and land		
Purchase of plant and equipment	$ 30,000	
Purchase of land	6,000	
Change in fixed assets and land		$ 36,000
Free cash flows (operating perspective)		$ (14,450)
Free cash flows: Financing Perspective		
Increase in short-term notes		$ (30,000)
Decrease in long-term notes		5,800
Dividends		3,650
Interest income		6,100
Financing cash flows		$ (14,450)

Chapter Four

Financial Ratio Analysis • The DuPont Analysis:
An Integrative Approach to Ratio Analysis •
Limitations of Ratio Analysis • Firm Performance
and Shareholder Value

EVALUATING A FIRM'S FINANCIAL PERFORMANCE

LEARNING OBJECTIVES

AFTER READING THIS CHAPTER, YOU SHOULD BE ABLE TO:

1. Calculate a comprehensive set of financial ratios and use them to evaluate the financial health of a company.

2. Apply the DuPont analysis in evaluating the firm's performance.

3. Explain the limitations of ratio analysis.

4. Link firm performance to creating shareholder value.

One of the oldest methods for evaluating a firm's financial performance is the DuPont system of financial analysis. The DuPont analysis "is a good tool for getting people started in understanding how they can have an impact on results," says Doug McCallen, budgets and forecasts manager at construction and mining equipment maker Caterpillar Inc.

Using return on assets as a primary performance measure and setting targets for each part of the organization, Caterpillar can determine when a problem is related to operating efficiency versus utilization. The results have been phenomenal, McCallen says. The firm's return on assets has reached double digits, accompanied by record profits in 13 of the past 15 quarters.

Nucor Corp., a $4 billion-a-year producer of steel and steel products, has been using return on assets employed to measure performance in its facilities for years, with good results. "Number one, it's simple," says Sam Siegel, vice chairman and chief financial officer. "All of our people understand it." Each facility aims for a 25 percent or greater return on assets employed, which is calculated before the effects of federal income tax, interest expense, and corporate overhead.

Other managers are choosing *economic value added (EVA®)* as the way to measure a firm's financial performance, arguing that the DuPont model leaves room for managers to make shortsighted decisions that boost return on investment without real improvement in the business. "Ratio measures can be very misleading and create conflicts between management and shareholders," warns Dennis Uyemura, senior vice president in charge of financial institutions at Stern Stewart & Co., the consulting firm that developed the EVA® framework.

Nucor's decision to stick with DuPont reflects a pragmatic view of metrics. "I don't say it's the best way," Siegel concedes. "All I say is that it has worked for us."

How to measure a company's financial performance has created quite a debate, and one that you will better understand after reading this chapter.

Source: Robin Goldwyn Blumenthal, "Tis the Gift to Be Simple: Why the 80-year-old DuPont Model Still Has Fans," *CFO Magazine*, January 1998.

FINANCIAL RATIO ANALYSIS

In Chapter 3, we examined financial statements in absolute dollar terms for the purpose of coming to understand a firm's financial position. We used the financial statements for the McDonald's Corporation to illustrate the format and content of the statements and to demonstrate an important financial measurement—free cash flows. We next want to restate the *accounting data in relative terms*, or what we call **financial ratios.** Financial ratios help us identify some of the financial strengths and weaknesses of a company. The ratios give us two ways of making meaningful comparisons of a firm's financial data: (1) we can examine the ratios across time (say for the last 5 years) to identify any trends; and (2) we can compare the firm's ratios with those of other firms.

financial ratios

Mathematically, a financial ratio is nothing more than a ratio whose numerator and denominator are comprised of financial data. Sound simple? Well, in concept it is. The objective in using a ratio when analyzing financial information is simply to standardize the information being analyzed so that comparisons can be made between ratios of different firms or possibly the same firm at different points in time. So try to keep this in mind as you read through the discussion of financial ratios. All we are doing is trying to standardize financial data so that we can make comparisons with industry norms or other standards.

In comparing our firm with other companies, we could select a peer group of companies, or we could use industry norms published by firms such as Dun & Bradstreet, Robert Morris Associates, Standard & Poor's, and Prentice Hall. Dun & Bradstreet, for instance, annually publishes a set of 14 key ratios for each of 125 lines of business. Robert Morris Associates, the association of bank loan and credit officers, publishes a set of 16 key ratios for more than 350 lines of business. In both cases, the ratios are classified by industry and by firm size to provide the basis for more meaningful comparisons.

In learning about ratios, we could simply study the different types or categories of ratios, or we could use ratios to answer some important questions about a firm's operations. We prefer the latter approach and have chosen the following four questions as a map in using financial ratios:

1. How liquid is the firm?
2. Is management generating adequate operating profits on the firm's assets?
3. How is the firm financing its assets?
4. Are the owners (stockholders) receiving an adequate return on their investment?

Takin' It to the Net
Go to American Express Exchange at http://www. americanexpress.com/smallbusiness/resources/managing/ratios. shtml for a listing of source directories for common ratios within specific industries.

Let's look at each of these questions in turn. In doing so, we will use the McDonald's Corporation to illustrate the use of ratios in answering these questions. For ease of reference, we have again shown McDonald's financial statements in Tables 4–1 and 4–2.

Question 1: How Liquid Is the Firm?

The **liquidity** of a business is defined as its *ability to meet maturing debt obligations.* That is, does or will the firm have the resources to pay the creditors when the debt comes due?

liquidity

There are two ways to approach the liquidity question. First, we can look at the firm's assets that are relatively liquid in nature and compare them to the amount of

TABLE 4–1   MCDONALD'S CORPORATION 1997 INCOME STATEMENT
($ MILLIONS)

Sales		$11,508
Cost of goods sold		6,537
Gross profits		$ 4,971
Marketing expenses and general and administrative expenses	$ 1,832	
Depreciation expense	345	
Total operating expenses		$ 2,177
Operating profits		$ 2,794
Interest expenses		387
Earnings before taxes		$ 2,407
Income taxes		765
Net income before preferred stock dividends		$ 1,642
Preferred stock dividends		25
Net income available to common stockholders		$ 1,617

Assets	
Cash	$ 341
Accounts receivables	484
Inventories	71
Prepaid expenses	247
Total current assets	$ 1,143
Gross fixed assets	$20,088
Accumulated depreciation	5,127
Net fixed assets	$14,961
Investments	702
Other assets	1,436
Total assets	$18,242
Liabilities and Equity	
Liabilities (debt):	
Short-term notes payable	$ 1,629
Accounts payable	651
Taxes payable	53
Accrued expenses	652
Total current liabilities	$ 2,985
Long-term debt	6,325
Total liabilities	$ 9,310
Equity:	
Preferred stock	$ 80
Common stock:	
Par value and paid in capital	$ 708
Retained earnings	11,927
Treasury stock	(3,783)
Total common equity	$ 8,852
Total equity	$ 8,932
Total liabilities (debt) and equity	$18,242

the debt coming due in the near term.[1] Second, we can look at how quickly the firm's liquid assets are being converted into cash.

Measuring Liquidity: Approach 1

The first approach compares (a) cash and the assets that should be converted into cash within the year with (b) the debt (liabilities) that is coming due and payable within the year. The assets here are the *current assets*, and the debt is the *current liabilities* in the balance sheet. Thus, we could use the following measure, called the **current ratio,** to estimate a company's relative liquidity:

current ratio

$$\text{current ratio} = \frac{\text{current assets}}{\text{current liabilities}} \qquad (4\text{--}1)$$

Furthermore, remembering that the three primary current assets include (1) cash, (2) accounts receivable, and (3) inventories, we could make our measure of liquidity more restrictive by *excluding inventories*, the least liquid of the current assets, in the numerator. This revised ratio is called the **acid-test** (or **quick**) **ratio,** and is calculated as follows:

acid-test (quick) ratio

$$\text{acid-test ratio} = \frac{\text{current assets} - \text{inventories}}{\text{current liabilities}} \qquad (4\text{--}2)$$

To demonstrate how to compute the current ratio and acid-test ratio, we will use the 1997 balance sheet for the McDonald's Corporation (refer to Table 4–2). To have a standard for comparison, we use the industry norms published by Robert Morris Associates.

McDonald's Corporation	Industry Average
$\text{current ratio} = \dfrac{\text{current assets}}{\text{current liabilities}}$	
$= \dfrac{\$1,143\text{M}}{\$2,985\text{M}} = 0.38$	0.70
$\text{acid-test ratio} = \dfrac{\text{current assets} - \text{inventories}}{\text{current liabilities}}$	
$= \dfrac{\$1,143\text{M} - \$71\text{M}}{\$2,985\text{M}} = 0.36$	0.40

So, in terms of the current ratio and acid-test ratio, McDonald's is significantly less liquid than the average firm. McDonald's only has $0.38 in current assets for every $1 in current liabilities (debt), compared to $0.70 for comparable firms, and only $0.36 in current assets less inventories per $1 of current debt, compared to $0.40 for the peer group. Given the conventional wisdom that firms should maintain about $2 in current assets for every $1 in current debt—an idea that fails to recognize the unique needs of various companies—McDonald's, and even the industry itself, is less liquid than most other companies.

---

[1]This approach has long been used in the finance community; however, it really measures solvency, not liquidity. A firm is solvent when its assets exceed its liabilities, which is in essence what we will be measuring by this approach. For an in-depth discussion of this issue, see Chapter 2 of Terry S. Maness and John T. Zietlow, *Short-Term Financial Management* (New York: Dryden Press, 1997).

Measuring Liquidity: Approach 2

The second view of liquidity examines the firm's ability to convert accounts receivable and inventory into cash on a timely basis. The conversion of accounts receivable into cash may be measured by computing *how long it takes to collect the firm's receivables;* that is, how many days of sales are outstanding in the form of accounts receivable? We can answer this question by computing the **average collection period:**

average collection period

$$\text{average collection period} = \frac{\text{accounts receivable}}{\text{daily credit sales}} \qquad (4\text{--}3)$$

If we assume all the McDonald's Corporation's 1997 sales ($11,508 million in Table 4–1) to be credit sales, as opposed to some cash sales, then the firm's average collection period is 15.3 days, compared to an industry norm of 6.5 days:

McDonald's Corporation   **Industry Average**

$$\begin{matrix} \text{average} \\ \text{collection} \\ \text{period} \end{matrix} = \frac{\text{accounts receivable}}{\text{daily credit sales}}$$

$$= \frac{\$484M}{\$11,508M \div 365} = 15.3 \text{ days} \qquad 6.5 \text{ days}$$

Thus, McDonald's does not collect its receivables as quickly as the average firm in the comparison group—15.3 days compared to only 6.5 days for the industry. The short collection period for the industry is undoubtedly the result of being in the restaurant industry, which has more cash sales than most industries. By our using total sales, as opposed to credit sales, in our calculation, we have understated the actual collection period, both for McDonald's and for the industry. Nevertheless, the fact remains that McDonald's does extend longer credit terms than do its competitors.

accounts receivable turnover

We could have reached the same conclusion by measuring *how many times accounts receivable are "rolled over" during a year,* or the **accounts receivable turnover.** For instance, the McDonald's Corporation turns its receivables over 23.8 times a year.[2]

McDonald's Corporation   **Industry Average**

$$\begin{matrix} \text{accounts} \\ \text{receivable} \\ \text{turnover} \end{matrix} = \frac{\text{credit sales}}{\text{accounts receivable}} \qquad (4\text{--}4)$$

$$= \frac{\$11,508M}{\$484M} = 23.8 \text{ times/year} \qquad 56.2 \text{ times/year}$$

Whether we use the average collection period or the accounts receivable turnover ratio, the conclusion is the same. The McDonald's Corporation is slower at collecting its receivables than competing firms.[3]

---

[2]We could also measure the accounts receivable turnover by dividing 365 days by the average collection period: 365/15.3 = 23.8

[3]Although it will not be discussed here, one tool for further assessing the liquidity of a firm's receivables is an aging of accounts receivable schedule. Such a schedule identifies the number and dollar value of accounts outstanding for various periods. For example, accounts that are less than 10 days old, 11 to 20 days, and so forth might be examined. Still another way to construct the schedule would involve analyzing the length of time to eventual collection of accounts over a past period. For example, how many accounts were outstanding less than 10 days when collected, between 11 and 20 days, and so forth.

We now want to know the same thing for inventories that we just determined for accounts receivable: *How many times are we turning over inventories during the year?* In this manner, we gain some insight into the liquidity of inventories. The **inventory turnover ratio** is calculated as follows:

inventory turnover ratio

$$\text{inventory turnover} = \frac{\text{cost of goods sold}}{\text{inventory}} \qquad (4\text{--}5)$$

Note that sales in this ratio is replaced by cost of goods sold. Because the inventory (the denominator) is measured at cost, we want to use a cost-based measure of sales in the numerator. Otherwise, our answer would vary from one firm to the next solely because of differences in how each firm marks up its sales over costs.[4]

Given that the McDonald's Corporation's cost of goods sold was $6,537 million (Table 4–1) and its inventory was $71 million (Table 4–2) the firm's 1997 inventory turnover, along with the industry average, is as follows:

McDonald's Corporation	**Industry Average**

$$\frac{\text{inventory}}{\text{turnover}} = \frac{\text{cost of goods sold}}{\text{inventory}}$$

$$= \frac{\$6,537M}{\$71M} = 92 \text{ times/year} \qquad 35 \text{ times/year}$$

Given these results, we can conclude that McDonald's is clearly excellent in its management of inventory, turning its inventory over 92 times per year compared to 35 times for the industry. In other words, McDonald's sells its inventory in 4 days on average (365 days ÷ 92 times), while the average firm takes 10 days (365 days ÷ 35 times).

Thus, when it comes to McDonald's liquidity, we see that the firm has low current and acid-test ratios, but that the firm collects its receivables in about 15 days and turns its inventory over 92 times per year, indicating that these assets are relatively liquid.

Question 2: Is Management Generating Adequate Operating Profits on the Firm's Assets?

We now begin a different line of thinking that will carry us through all the remaining questions. At this point, we want to know if the profits are sufficient relative to the assets being invested. The question is similar to a question one might ask about the interest being earned on a savings account at the bank. When you invest $1,000 in a savings account and receive $40 in interest during the year, you are earning a 4 percent return on your investment ($40 ÷ $1,000 = .04 = 4%). With respect to the McDonald's Corporation, we want to know something similar: the rate of return management is earning on the firm's assets.

In answering this question, we have several choices as to how we measure profits: gross profits, operating profits, or net income. Gross profits would not be an acceptable choice because it does not include some important information, such as the cost of marketing and distributing the firm's product. Thus, we should choose between operating profits and net income. For our purposes, we prefer to use operating profits, because this measure of firm profits is calculated before the costs of the company's financing policies have been deducted. Because financing is explicitly considered in our next question, we want to isolate only the operating aspects of the

Takin' It to the Net
Go to SOHO Guidebook's presentation of business ratios at http://www.toolkit.cch.com/text/P06_7100.asp. Select the link on "liquidity ratios" for 09explanations and examples of these ratios.

---

[4]Whereas our logic may be correct to use cost of goods sold in the numerator, practicality may dictate that we use sales instead. Some suppliers of industry group norm data use sales in the numerator. Thus, for consistency in our comparisons, we too may need to use sales.

company's profits at this point. In this way, we are able to compare the profitability of firms with different debt-to-equity mixes. Therefore, to examine the *level of operating profits relative to the assets*, we would use the **operating income return on investment (OIROI)**:

$$\text{operating income return on investment} = \frac{\text{operating income}}{\text{total assets}} \quad (4\text{–}6)$$

The operating income return on investment for the McDonald's Corporation for 1997 (based on the financial data in Tables 4–1 and 4–2), and the corresponding industry norm, are shown below:

McDonald's Corporation   **Industry Average**

$$\begin{aligned}
\text{operating income} \atop \text{return on investment} &= \frac{\text{operating income}}{\text{total assets}} \\
&= \frac{\$2,794\text{M}}{\$18,242\text{M}} = .153 = 15.3\% \qquad 11.6\%
\end{aligned}$$

Hence, we see that the McDonald's Corporation is earning an above-average return on investment relative to the average firm in the industry. Management is generating more income on $1 of assets than similar firms.[5]

If we were the managers of the McDonald's Corporation, we should not be satisfied with merely knowing that we are earning more than a competitive return on the firm's assets. We should also want to know *why we are above average*. To understand this issue, we may separate the operating income return on investment, OIROI, into two important pieces: the operating profit margin and the total asset turnover. The firm's OIROI is a multiple of these two ratios and may be shown algebraically as follows:

$$\text{OIROI} = (\text{operating profit margin}) \times (\text{total asset turnover}) \quad (4\text{–}7\text{a})$$

or more completely,

$$\text{OIROI} = \frac{\text{operating income}}{\text{sales}} \times \frac{\text{sales}}{\text{total assets}} \quad (4\text{–}7\text{b})$$

The first component of the OIROI, the **operating profit margin,** is an extremely important variable in understanding a *company's operating profitability*. It is important that we know exactly what drives this ratio. In coming to understand the ratio, think about the makeup of the ratio, which may be expressed as follows:

$$\text{operating profit margin} = \frac{\text{operating income}}{\text{sales}}$$

$$= \frac{\text{total} \atop \text{sales} - \text{cost of} \atop \text{goods sold} - \text{general and} \atop \text{administrative} \atop \text{expenses} - \text{marketing} \atop \text{expenses}}{\text{sales}} \quad (4\text{–}8)$$

---

[5]The **return on assets (ROA)** is often used as an indicator of a firm's profitability and is measured as follows: *return on assets = net income ÷ total assets.*

We choose not to use this ratio because *net income* is influenced by operating decisions and how the firm is financed. We want to restrict our attention only to operating activities; financing is considered later in questions 3 and 4. Nevertheless, sometimes the industry norm for operating income return on investment is not available. Instead, return on assets is provided. If so, we have no option but to use the return on assets for measuring the firm's profitability.

Because total sales equals the number of units sold times the sales price per unit, and the cost of goods sold equals the number of units sold times the cost of goods sold per unit, we may conclude that the driving forces of the operating profit margin are the following:

1. The number of units of product sold[6]
2. The average selling price for each product unit
3. The cost of manufacturing or acquiring the firm's product
4. The ability to control general and administrative expenses
5. The ability to control expenses in marketing and distributing the firm's product

These influences are also apparent simply by looking at the income statement and thinking about what is involved in determining the firm's operating profits or income.[7]

As shown in Equation 4–9, the **total asset turnover** is the second component of the operating income return on investment. *The total asset turnover measures the dollar sales per one dollar of assets.* The ratio is calculated as follows:

total asset turnover

$$\text{total asset turnover} = \frac{\text{sales}}{\text{total assets}} \qquad (4\text{–}9)$$

This ratio indicates how efficiently a firm is using its assets in generating sales. For instance, if Company A can generate $3 in sales with $1 in assets, compared to $2 in sales per asset dollar for Company B, we may say that Company A is using its assets more efficiently in generating sales, which is a major determinant in the firm's operating income return on investment.

Let's again return to the McDonald's Corporation to apply the above concepts. Continuing to rely on the firm's financial statements in Tables 4–1 and 4–2, we can compute the operating profit margin and total asset turnover for McDonald's as follows:

Takin' It to the Net
Go to SOHO Guidebook's presentation of business ratios at http://www.toolkit.cch.com/text/P06_7100.asp. Select the link on "efficiency ratios" for explanations and examples of these ratios.

McDonald's Corporation	**Industry Average**

$$\frac{\text{operating}}{\text{profit margin}} = \frac{\text{operating income}}{\text{sales}}$$

$$= \frac{\$2,794\text{M}}{\$11,508\text{M}} = .243 = 24.3\% \qquad 6.1\%$$

McDonald's Corporation	**Industry Average**

$$\frac{\text{total asset}}{\text{turnover}} = \frac{\text{sales}}{\text{total assets}}$$

$$= \frac{\$11,508\text{M}}{\$18,242\text{M}} = 0.63 \qquad 1.90$$

---

[6]The number of units affects the operating profit margin only if some of the firm's costs and expenses are fixed. If a company's expenses are all variable in nature, then the ratio would not change as the number of units sold increases or decreases, because the numerator and the denominator would change at the same rate.

[7]We could have used the **net profit margin,** rather than the operating profit margin, which is measured as follows: net profit margin = net income ÷ sales. The net profit margin *measures the amount of net income per $1 of sales.* However, because net income includes both operating expenses and interest expense, this ratio is influenced both by operating activities and financing activities. We prefer to defer the effect of financing decisions until questions 3 and 4, which follow shortly.

net profit margin

Recalling that:

$$\text{OIROI} = \left(\begin{array}{c} \text{operating} \\ \text{profit margin} \end{array} \right) \times \left(\begin{array}{c} \text{total asset} \\ \text{turnover} \end{array} \right)$$

we see that for the McDonald's Corporation,

$$\text{OIROI}_{\text{McD}} = 24.3\% \times .63 = 15.3\%$$

and for the industry, this same ratio is

$$\text{OIROI}_{\text{ind}} = 6.1\% \times 1.90 = 11.6\%$$

Clearly, the McDonald's Corporation is more than competitive when it comes to keeping costs and expenses in line relative to sales, as is reflected by the operating profit margin. In other words, management is extremely effective in managing the five driving forces of the operating profit margin listed above. In terms of its high operating profit margin, McDonald's has no equal. However, when we look at the total asset turnover, we can see that the firm is not using its assets efficiently. The McDonald's Corporation generates only about $.63 in sales per dollar of assets, whereas the competition produces $1.90 in sales from every dollar in assets.

We should not stop here with our analysis of McDonald's asset utilization; we should dig deeper. We have concluded that the assets are not being used efficiently, but now we should try to determine which assets are the problem. Are we overinvested in all assets or more so in accounts receivable or inventory or fixed assets? To answer this question, we merely examine the turnover ratios for the primary assets held by the firm—accounts receivable, inventories, and fixed assets. We have already calculated these ratios for accounts receivable and inventories, which are repeated as follows:

McDonald's Corporation		**Industry Average**
Accounts receivable turnover:		
$\dfrac{\text{credit sales}}{\text{accounts receivable}} = \dfrac{\$11,508M}{\$484M} = 23.8$		56.2
Inventory turnover:		
$\dfrac{\text{cost of goods sold}}{\text{inventory}} = \dfrac{\$6,537M}{\$71M} = 92$		35

fixed assets turnover   We next calculate a firm's **fixed assets turnover** as follows:

$$\begin{array}{c} \text{fixed assets} \\ \text{turnover} \end{array} = \frac{\text{sales}}{\text{fixed assets}} \tag{4-10}$$

For the McDonald's Corporation:

		Industry Average
$\begin{array}{c}\text{fixed}\\\text{assets}\\\text{turnover}\end{array} = \dfrac{\text{sales}}{\text{net fixed assets}} = \dfrac{\$11,508M}{\$14,961M} = 0.77$		3.2

McDonald's Corporation's situation is now clearer. The company has excessive accounts receivables, which we had known from our earlier discussions, and also there is too large an investment in fixed assets for the sales being produced. It would appear that these two asset categories are not being managed well, and the consequence is a lower overall or total asset turnover ratio. Moreover, given the far greater amount invested in fixed assets ($15 billion) than accounts receivable ($484 million)—see the balance sheet in Table 4–2—the heart of the problem is with the firm's large amount of fixed assets relative to the firm's sales.

Question 3: How Is the Firm Financing its Assets?

We now turn for the moment to the matter of how the firm is financed. (We shall return to the firm's profitability shortly.) The basic issue is the use of debt versus equity: Do we finance the assets more by debt or equity? (We use the terms *debt* and *liabilities* interchangeably.) In answering this question, we use two ratios. (Many more could be used.) First, we simply ask *what percentage of the firm's assets are financed by debt*, including *both* short-term and long-term debt, realizing the remaining percentage must be financed by equity. We would compute the **debt ratio** as follows:[8]

debt ratio

$$\text{debt ratio} = \frac{\text{total debt}}{\text{total assets}} \qquad (4\text{--}11)$$

For the McDonald's Corporation, debt as a percentage of total assets is 51 percent (taken from McDonald's balance sheet in Table 4–2) compared to an industry norm of 69 percent. The computation is as follows:

McDonald's Corporation **Industry Average**

$$\text{debt ratio} = \frac{\text{total debt}}{\text{total assets}}$$

$$= \frac{\$9,310\text{M}}{\$18,242\text{M}} = 0.51 = 51\% \qquad 69\%$$

Thus, the McDonald's Corporation uses significantly less debt than the average firm in the industry.

Our second perspective regarding the firm's financing decisions comes by looking at the income statement. When we borrow money, there is a minimum requirement that the firm pay the interest on the debt. Thus, it is informative to compare the amount of operating income that is available to service the interest with the amount of interest that is to be paid. Stated as a ratio, we compute *the number of times we are earning our interest*. Thus, a **times interest earned** ratio is commonly used when examining the firm's debt position and is computed in the following manner:

times interest earned

$$\text{times interest earned} = \frac{\text{operating income}}{\text{interest}} \qquad (4\text{--}12)$$

Based on the income statement for the McDonald's Corporation (Table 4–1), the firm's times interest earned is 7.22, computed as follows:

McDonald's Corporation **Industry Average**

$$\frac{\text{times interest}}{\text{earned}} = \frac{\text{operating income}}{\text{interest}}$$

$$= \frac{\$2,794\text{M}}{\$387\text{M}} = 7.22 \qquad 3.3$$

---

[8]We will often see the relationship stated in terms of debt to equity, or the debt-equity ratio, rather than debt to total assets. We come to the same conclusion with either ratio.

Thus, the McDonald's Corporation is able to service its interest expense without any great difficulty. In fact, the firm's operating income could fall to as little as one-seventh (1/7.22) its current level and still have the income to pay the required interest. We should remember, however, that interest is not paid with income but with cash and that the firm may be required to repay some of the debt principal, as well as the interest. Thus, the times interest earned is only a crude measure of the firm's capacity to service its debt. Nevertheless, it does give us a general indication of a company's debt capacity.

Question 4: Are the Owners (Stockholders) Receiving an Adequate Return on Their Investment?

return on common equity

Our one remaining question looks at the *accounting return on the common stockholders' investment* or **return on common equity**; that is, we want to know if the earnings available to the firm's owners or common equity investors is attractive when compared to the returns of owners of companies in the industry.

We measure the return to the owners as follows:

$$\text{return on common equity} = \frac{\text{net income}}{\text{common equity (including par, paid in capital, and retained earnings} - \text{treasury stock)}} \quad (4\text{--}13)$$

The returns on common equity for the McDonald's Corporation and the industry are 18.1 percent and 12.8 percent, respectively:

McDonald's Corporation   **Industry Average**

$$\text{return on common equity} = \frac{\text{net income}}{\text{common equity}}$$

$$= \frac{\$1,617M}{\$8,852M} = .183 = 18.3\% \qquad 12.78$$

The owners of the McDonald's Corporation are more than receiving a return on their investment equivalent to what owners involved with competing businesses receive. However, we should also ask, "*How* is the firm creating such good returns for its shareholders?" To answer, we need to draw on what we have already learned, namely that:

1. The McDonald's Corporation is more profitable in its operations than its competitors. (Remember, the operating income return on investment, OIROI, was 15.3 percent for McDonald's compared to 11.6 percent for the competition.) Thus, this fact would suggest that McDonald's should have a higher return on common equity.
2. On the other hand, McDonald's uses considerably less debt (more equity) financing than does the average firm in the industry, which lowers the return on common equity. As we will see shortly, the more debt a firm uses, the higher its return on equity will be, provided that the firm is earning a return on investment greater than its cost of debt. Thus, the competition, on average, provides a higher return for its shareholders by using more debt, not by being better at generating profits on the firm's assets. That's the good news. The bad news for the competitors' shareholders is the more debt a firm uses, the greater the company's financial risk, which translates to more risk for the shareholders as well.

To help us understand the foregoing conclusion about the reason for McDonald's higher return on common equity and its implications, consider the following example.

The Effect of Using Debt on Net Income

Firms A and B are identical in size, both having $1,000 in total assets and both having an operating income return on investment of 14 percent. However, they are different in one respect: Firm A uses no debt, but Firm B finances 60 percent of its investments with debt at an interest cost of 10 percent. For the sake of simplicity, we will assume there are no income taxes. The financial statements for the two companies would be as follows:

	FIRM A	FIRM B
Total assets	$1,000	$1,000
Debt (10% interest rate)	$ 0	$ 600
Equity	1,000	400
Total debt and equity	$1,000	$1,000
Operating income (OIROI – 14%)	$ 140	$ 140
Interest expense (10%)	0	60
Net income	$ 140	$ 80

Computing the return on common equity for both companies, we see that Firm B has a much more attractive return to its owners, 20 percent compared to Firm A's 14 percent.

$$\text{return on equity} = \frac{\text{net income}}{\text{common equity}}$$

$$\text{Firm A: } = \frac{\$140}{\$1,000} = .14 = 14\% \quad \text{Firm B: } \frac{\$80}{\$400} = .20 = 20\%$$

Why the difference? The answer is straightforward. Firm B is earning 14 percent on its investments, but is only having to pay 10 percent for its borrowed money. The difference between the return on the firm's investments and the interest rate, 14 percent less the 10 percent, goes to the owners, thus boosting Firm B's return on equity above that of Firm A. We are seeing the results of favorable financial leverage at work, where we borrow at 10 percent and invest at 14 percent. The result is an increase in the return on equity.

If debt enhances the owners' returns, why would we not use lots of it all the time? We may continue our example to find the answer. Assume now that the economy falls into a deep recession, business declines sharply, and Firms A and B only earn a 6 percent operating income return on investment. Let's recompute the return on common equity now.

	FIRM A	FIRM B
Operating income (OIROI = 6%)	$60	$60
Interest expense	0	60
Net income	$60	$ 0
Return on common equity:		

$$\text{Firm A: } \frac{\$60}{\$1,000} = .06 = 6\% \qquad \text{Firm B: } \frac{\$0}{\$400} = .00 = 0\%$$

Now the use of leverage has a negative influence on the return on equity, with Firm B earning less than Firm A for its owners. This results from the fact that now

Firm B earns less than the interest rate of 10 percent; consequently, the equity investors have to make up the difference. Thus, financial leverage is a two-edged sword; when times are good, financial leverage can make them very, very good, but when times are bad, financial leverage makes them very, very bad. Thus, financial leverage can potentially enhance the returns of the equity investors, but it also increases the uncertainty or risk for the owners.

Let's review what we have learned about the use of financial ratios in evaluating a company's financial position. We have presented all the ratios for the McDonald's Corporation in Table 4–3. The ratios are grouped by the issue being addressed: liquidity, operating profitability, financing, and profits for the owners. As before, we use some ratios for more than one purpose, namely the turnover ratios for accounts receivable and inventories. These ratios have implications both for the firm's liquidity and its profitability; thus, they are listed in both areas. Also, we have included both average collection period and accounts receivable turnover; typically, we would only use one in our analysis, because they are just different ways of expressing the same thing.

Takin' It to the Net
Go to SOHO Guidebook's presentation of business ratios at http://www.toolkit.cch.com/text/P06_7100.asp. Select the link on "profitability ratios" for explanations and examples of these ratios.

CONCEPT CHECK

1. How can financial ratios be used to make valuable comparisons?
2. The financial ratios outlined in this chapter have been developed to answer what four important questions?
3. Which number in the income statement should be used in measuring profitability relative to total assets and why?
4. What are the two driving forces behind the operating income return on investment?
5. What is the relationship between the use of debt and the return on common equity for shareholders?

Objective 2

THE DUPONT ANALYSIS: AN INTEGRATIVE APPROACH TO RATIO ANALYSIS

In the previous section, we used ratio analysis to answer four questions thought to be important in understanding a company's financial position. The last three of the four questions dealt with a company's earnings capabilities and the common stockholders' return on the equity capital. In our analysis, we measured the return on equity as follows:

$$\text{return on common equity} = \frac{\text{net income}}{\text{common equity}} \qquad (4\text{–}14)$$

DuPont analysis

Another approach can be used to evaluate a firm's return on equity. The **DuPont analysis,** is *a method used to analyze a firm's profitability and return on equity.* Figure 4-1 shows graphically the DuPont technique, modified somewhat from the original format developed by the management at the DuPont Corporation. Beginning at the top of the figure, we see that the return on common equity is calculated as follows:

$$\text{return on common equity} = (\text{return on assets}) \div \left(\frac{\text{common equity}}{\text{total assets}} \right) \qquad (4\text{–}15)$$

TABLE 4-3 MCDONALD'S CORPORATION 1997 FINANCIAL RATIO ANALYSIS

FINANCIAL RATIOS	MCDONALD'S CORPORATION	INDUSTRY AVERAGE
1. Firm Liquidity		
current ratio $= \dfrac{\text{current assets}}{\text{current liabilities}}$	$\dfrac{\$1,143M}{\$2,985M} = 0.38$	0.70
acid-test ratio $= \dfrac{\text{current assets} - \text{inventories}}{\text{current liabilities}}$	$\dfrac{\$1,143M - \$71M}{\$2,985M} = 0.36$	0.40
average collection period $= \dfrac{\text{accounts receivable}}{\text{daily credit sales}}$	$\dfrac{\$484M}{\$11,508M \div 365} = 15.3$	6.5 days
accounts receivable turnover $= \dfrac{\text{credit sales}}{\text{accounts receivable}}$	$\dfrac{\$11,508M}{\$484M} = 23.8$	56.2 times/yr
inventory turnover $= \dfrac{\text{cost of goods sold}}{\text{inventory}}$	$\dfrac{\$6,537M}{\$71M} = 92$	35 times/yr
2. Operating Profitability		
operating income return on investment $= \dfrac{\text{operating income}}{\text{total assets}}$	$\dfrac{\$2,794M}{\$18,242M} = 15.3\%$	11.6%
operating profit margin $= \dfrac{\text{operating income}}{\text{sales}}$	$\dfrac{\$2,794M}{\$11,508M} = 24.3\%$	6.1%
total asset turnover $= \dfrac{\text{sales}}{\text{total assets}}$	$\dfrac{\$11,508M}{\$18,242M} = 0.63$	1.9
accounts receivable turnover $= \dfrac{\text{credit sales}}{\text{accounts receivable}}$	$\dfrac{\$11,508M}{\$484M} = 23.8$	56.2 times/yr
inventory turnover $= \dfrac{\text{cost of goods sold}}{\text{inventory}}$	$\dfrac{\$6,537M}{\$71M} = 92$	35 times/yr
fixed assets turnover $= \dfrac{\text{sales}}{\text{net fixed assets}}$	$\dfrac{\$11,508M}{\$14,961M} = 0.77$	3.2
3. Financing Decisions		
debt ratio $= \dfrac{\text{total debt}}{\text{total assets}}$	$\dfrac{\$9,310M}{\$18,242M} = 51\%$	69%
times interest earned $= \dfrac{\text{operating income}}{\text{interest}}$	$\dfrac{\$2,794M}{\$387M} = 7.22$	3.3
4. Return on common equity		
return on common equity $= \dfrac{\text{net income}}{\text{common equity}}$	$\dfrac{\$1,617M}{\$8,852M} = 18.3\%$	12.78%

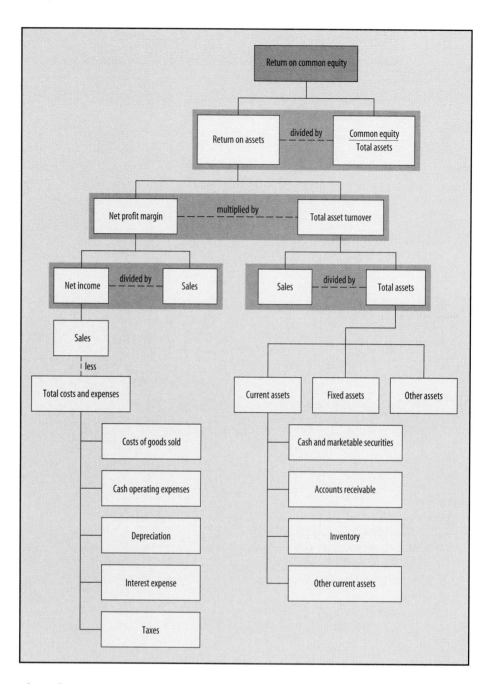

FIGURE 4-1
DuPont Analysis

where the return on assets, or ROA, equals:

$$\text{return on assets} = \frac{\text{net income}}{\text{total assets}} \qquad (4\text{--}16)$$

Thus, we see that the return on equity is a function of (1) the firm's overall profitability (net income relative to the amount invested in assets), and (2) the amount of common equity used to finance the assets. We also know that the return on assets may be represented as follows:

$$\text{return on assets} = (\text{net profit margin}) \times (\text{total asset turnover})$$
$$= \left(\frac{\text{net income}}{\text{sales}}\right) \times \left(\frac{\text{sales}}{\text{total assets}}\right) \qquad (4\text{--}17)$$

Combining equations (4–15) and (4–17) gives us the basic DuPont equation that shows the firm's return on equity as follows:

$$\begin{array}{l} \text{return on} \\ \text{common equity} \end{array} = \left(\begin{array}{c} \text{net profit} \\ \text{margin} \end{array}\right) \times \left(\begin{array}{c} \text{total asset} \\ \text{turnover} \end{array}\right) \div \left(\dfrac{\text{common equity}}{\text{total assets}}\right)$$

$$= \left(\dfrac{\text{net income}}{\text{sales}}\right) \times \left(\dfrac{\text{sales}}{\text{total assets}}\right) \div \left(\dfrac{\text{common equity}}{\text{total assets}}\right) \quad \text{(4–18)}$$

Using the DuPont equation and the diagram in Figure 4–1 allows management to see more clearly what drives the return on equity and the interrelationships among the net profit margin, the asset turnover, and the common equity ratio. Management is provided with a road map to follow in determining their effectiveness in managing the firm's resources to maximize the return earned on the owners' investment. In addition, the manager or owner can determine why that particular return was earned.

Let's return to the McDonald's Corporation to demonstrate the use of the DuPont analysis. Taking the information from the McDonald's Corporation's 1997 income statement (Table 4–1) and balance sheet as of December 31, 1997 (Table 4–2), we can calculate the company's return on equity as follows:

$$\begin{array}{l} \text{return} \\ \text{on equity} \end{array} = \left(\dfrac{\text{net income}}{\text{sales}}\right) \times \left(\dfrac{\text{sales}}{\text{total assets}}\right) \div \left(\dfrac{\text{common equity}}{\text{total assets}}\right)$$

$$= \left(\dfrac{\$1,617}{\$11,508}\right) \times \left(\dfrac{\$11,508}{\$18,242}\right) \div \left(\dfrac{\$8,852}{\$18,242}\right)$$

$$= 0.141 \times 0.631 \div 0.485$$

$$= 0.183 = 18.3\%$$

We can also visualize the relationships graphically for the McDonald's Corporation, as shown in Figure 4–2.

If the McDonald's Corporation's management wants to improve the company's return on equity, they should carefully examine Figure 4–2 for possible avenues. As we study the figure, we quickly see that improvement in the return on equity can come in one or more of four ways:

1. Increase sales without a disproportionate increase in costs and expenses.
2. Reduce the firm's cost of goods sold or operating expenses shown in the lefthand side of Figure 4–2.
3. Increase the sales relative to the asset base, either by increasing sales or by reducing the amounts invested in company assets. From our earlier examination of the McDonald's Corporation, we learned that the firm had excessive accounts receivables and fixed assets. Thus, management needs to reduce these assets to the lowest point possible, which would in turn result in an increase in the return on assets and then the return on equity.
4. Increase the use of debt relative to equity, but only to the extent that it does not unduly jeopardize the firm's financial position.

The choice between using the four-question approach as described earlier or the DuPont analysis is largely a matter of personal preference. Both approaches are intended to let us see the variables that determine a firm's profitability. There are, however, limitations to either technique because of the inherent limitations in using financial ratios—a topic addressed in the next section.

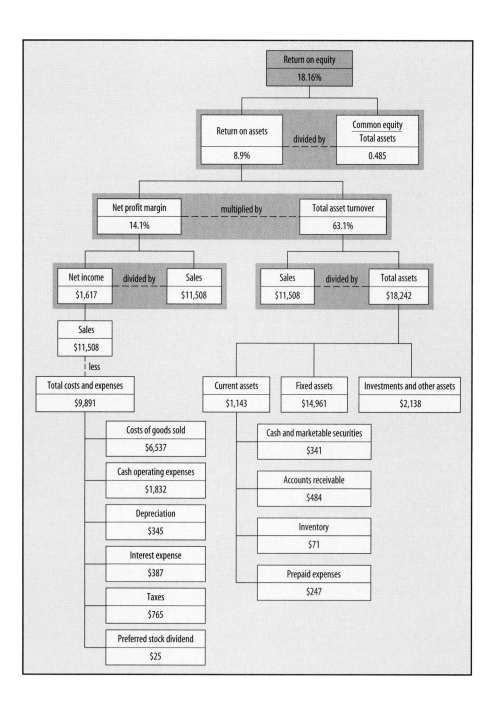

FIGURE 4–2

DuPont Analysis: McDonald's Corporation

CONCEPT CHECK

1. In the DuPont analysis, the return on equity is the function of what two factors?

2. What four ways can be utilized by a firm to improve return on equity?

LIMITATIONS OF RATIO ANALYSIS

We have shown how financial ratios may be used to understand a company's financial position, but anyone who works with these ratios ought to be aware of the limitations involved in their use. The following list includes some of the more important pitfalls that may be encountered in computing and interpreting financial ratios:

1. It is sometimes difficult to identify the industry category to which a firm belongs when the firm engages in multiple lines of business. Thus, we frequently must select our own set of peer firms and construct tailor-made norms.

2. Published industry averages are only approximations and provide the user with general guidelines rather than scientifically determined averages of the ratios of all or even a representative sample of the firms within an industry.

3. Accounting practices differ widely among firms and can lead to differences in computed ratios. For example, the use of last-in, first-out (LIFO) in inventory valuation can, in a period of rising prices, lower the firm's inventory account and increase its inventory turnover ratio as compared with that of a firm that uses first-in, first-out (FIFO). In addition, firms may choose different methods of depreciating their fixed assets.

4. Financial ratios can be too high or too low. For example, a current ratio that exceeds the industry norm may signal the presence of excess liquidity, which results in a lowering of overall profits in relation to the firm's investment in assets. On the other hand, a current ratio that falls below the norm indicates the possibility that the firm has inadequate liquidity and may at some future date be unable to pay its bills on time.

5. An industry average may not provide a desirable target ratio or norm. At best, an industry average provides a guide to the financial position of the average firm in the industry. It does not mean it is the ideal or best value for the ratio. Thus, we may choose to compare our firm's ratios with a self-determined peer group or even a single competitor.[9]

6. Many firms experience seasonality in their operations. Thus, balance sheet entries and their corresponding ratios will vary with the time of year when the statements are prepared. To avoid this problem, an average account balance should be used (for several months or quarters during the year) rather than the year-end total. For example, an average of month-end inventory balances might be used to compute a firm's inventory turnover ratio when the firm is subject to a significant seasonality in its sales (and correspondingly in its investment in inventories).

In spite of their limitations, financial ratios provide us with a very useful tool for assessing a firm's financial conditions. We should, however, be aware of these potential weaknesses when performing a ratio analysis. In many cases the real value derived from analyzing financial ratios is that they tell us what questions to ask.

---

[9]See Donald F. Cunningham and John T. Rose, "Industry Norms in Financial Statement Analysis: A Comparison of RMA and D&B Benchmark Data," *The Credit and Financial Management Review*, 1995, pp. 42-48, for a comparison of the industry financial ratios provided by Robert Morris Associates with those of Dun & Bradstreet. They find significant differences within the same industry classifications. This finding points out the need to carefully consider the choice of an industry norm. In fact, your analysis may require that you construct your own norm from, say, a list of the four or five firms in a particular industry that might provide the most appropriate standard of comparison for the firm being analyzed.

CONCEPT CHECK

1. Why is it difficult to create industry categories, especially among larger companies?
2. What differences in accounting practices create problems in using financial ratios?
3. Why should a firm be careful when making comparisons with industry norms?

| Objective 4 | FIRM PERFORMANCE AND SHAREHOLDER VALUE |

Up to this point, we have considered firm performance only from an accounting perspective. Questions 2 and 4 of our four-question approach have specifically measured the rate of return on the firm's total assets (operating income return on investment) and the return earned on the shareholders' investment (return on equity). We suggested that these returns should be compared with returns earned by other firms in comparable businesses or against norms to see how management is doing with the firm's assets. However, in none of our discussions have we connected these return measurements to the financial goal of the firm, that of creating shareholder value. For instance, we observed that McDonald's is earning a 15-percent operating income return on investment, compared to about 12 percent by a peer group of companies. We concluded that management is performing better than its competition, but we never said whether McDonald's is creating or destroying shareholder value from its investments.

How is shareholder value created or destroyed? Quite simply, shareholder value is created when a firm earns a rate of return on the capital invested in excess of the investors' required rate of return. If we invest in a firm and have a 12-percent required rate of return and the firm earns 15 percent on our capital, then management is creating value for the investor. If instead, the firm only earns 10 percent, then investor value is being destroyed. This concept, although followed faithfully by many firms when making accept/reject decisions on large capital investments in plant and equipment, has traditionally not been part of management's thought process in evaluating firm—and management—performance. Instead, most managers are more focused on the accounting results—earnings growth, profit margins, and the return on equity.

More recently, attention has been given to determining whether a firm's management is in fact creating shareholder value on all the capital invested and linking their compensation, mostly through bonuses, to the amount of shareholder value created. Although several techniques have been developed for assessing whether management is creating shareholder value, the one seeming to capture the most attention presently is economic value added (EVA®). This approach, developed by the consulting firm Stern Stewart & Co., is an attempt to measure a firm's *economic* profit rather than *accounting* profit in a given year. Economic profits assign a cost to the equity capital (the opportunity cost of the funds provided by the shareholders) in addition to the interest cost on the firm's debt; many accountants only recognize the interest expense as a financing cost. For example, assume a firm has total assets of $1,000 and is financed 40 percent with debt ($400) and 60 percent with equity ($600). If the interest rate on the debt is 10 percent, the interest cost is $40 ($400 × 10%) and would be reported in the income statement. However, there would be no cost shown for the equity financing. On the other hand, to compute economic profits, we recognize not only the interest cost, but also the opportunity cost of the $600 equity. That is, if the shareholders could earn 15 percent on another investment of similar risk (their opportunity cost is therefore 15 percent), then we should count this cost just as surely as we do the interest payment.[10] Thus in computing economic profits, we would subtract not only the $40 in interest, but also $90 ($600 equity × 15%) as the cost of equity. Thus economic profits exist only if our operating profits exceed $130 ($40 + $90).[11] Stated as a percentage, the firm must earn at least a 13-percent operating income return on its investment ($130 ÷ $1,000) in order to meet the investors' required rates of return.

In this context, EVA® (the value created for the shareholders) is computed as follows:

$$EVA^{®} = (r - k) \times C \qquad \text{(4–19)}$$

where r = the firm's operating income return on invested capital
  k = the total cost of all capital, both debt and equity
  C = amount of capital (total assets) invested in the firm

That is, the value created by management is determined by the amount the firm earns on its invested capital relative to the cost of these funds—both debt and equity—and the amount of capital invested in the firm. Continuing with our previous example, assume that our company is earning a 16-percent operating return on its assets (capital). Then we could say that the firm's economic value added is $30, determined as follows:

$$EVA^{®} = (16\% - 13\%) \times \$1,000$$

$$= \$30$$

The foregoing explains the EVA® concept in its simplest form. However, computing EVA requires our converting a firm's financial statement from an accountant's perspective (GAAP) to an economic book value. This process is much more involved than is being presented here, but we have at least an understanding of the basic premises involved in its computation. For now, we simply want to remember that management should be working to create shareholder value, and ideally, the evaluation of management's performance should be tied to that objective. Taken alone, financial ratios fail to capture this important dimension of financial management and should therefore be used with a measure of caution. Much more will be said about the goal of creating shareholder value as we continue our study of finance.

----------------------------------- SUMMARY -----------------------------------

Calculate a comprehensive set of financial ratios and use them to evaluate the financial health of a company

Objective 1

Financial ratios are the principal tool of financial analysis. Sometimes referred to simply as benchmarks, ratios standardize financial information so that comparisons can be made between firms of varying sizes.

Two groups find financial ratios useful. The first is comprised of managers who use them to measure and track company performance over time. The focus of their analysis is frequently related to various measures of profitability used to evaluate the performance of the firm from the perspective of the owners. The second group of users of financial ratios includes

---

[10]In Chapter 13, we explain much more about the investor's opportunity cost of funds and how that is used to compute a cost of capital for the firm.

[11]We are ignoring the affect of taxes in these computations for simplicity's sake. The basic idea is the same.

analysts external to the firm who, for one reason or another, have an interest in the firm's economic well-being. An example of this group would be a loan officer of a commercial bank who wishes to determine the credit worthiness of a loan applicant. Here the focus of the analysis is on the firm's previous use of financial leverage and its ability to pay the interest and principal associated with the loan request.

Financial ratios may be used to answer at least four questions: (1) How liquid is the company? (2) Is management effective at generating operating profits on the firm's assets? (3) How is the firm financed? (4) Are the returns earned by the common stockholders adequate?

Two methods may be used in analyzing financial ratios. The first involves trend analysis for the firm over time; the second involves making ratio comparisons with industry norms or a selected peer group of similar firms. In our example, industry norms were chosen for analyzing the financial position of the McDonald's Corporation.

Objective 2

Apply the DuPont analysis in evaluating the firm's performance

Another approach frequently used to evaluate a firm's profitability and the return on equity is the DuPont analysis. The basic format of the DuPont analysis dissects the return on equity into three drivers, represented as follows:

$$\text{return on equity} = \left(\frac{\text{net income}}{\text{sales}} \right) \times \left(\frac{\text{sales}}{\text{total assets}} \right) \div \left(1 - \frac{\text{total debt}}{\text{total assets}} \right)$$

Objective 3

Explain the limitations of ratio analysis

The following limitations may be encountered in computing and interpreting financial ratios:

1. It is sometimes difficult to identify an appropriate industry category.
2. Published industry averages are only approximations rather than scientifically determined averages.
3. Accounting practices differ widely among firms and can lead to differences in computed ratios.
4. Some financial ratios can be too high or too low, which makes the results more difficult to interpret.
5. An industry average may not provide a desirable target ratio or norm.
6. Many firms experience seasonality in their operations. Thus, ratios will vary with the time of year when the statements are prepared.

In spite of their limitations, financial ratios provide us with a very useful tool for assessing a firm's financial condition.

Objective 4

Link firm performance and shareholder value

Financial ratios provide a popular way to evaluate a firm's financial performance. However, when evaluating a company's use of assets (capital) to create firm value, financial ratio analysis may not be enough. Economic value added (EVA)® is one approach (there are others) being used by managements to evaluate their firm's performance in terms of shareholder value creation. EVA is equal to the return on invested capital less the investors' opportunity cost of the funds times the total amount of capital invested.

--- **KEY TERMS** ---

accounts receivable turnover ratio, 112	fixed assets turnover, 116
acid-test (quick) ratio, 111	inventory turnover ratio, 113
average collection period, 112	liquidity, 109
current ratio, 111	net profit margin, 115
debt ratio, 117	operating income return on investment (OIROI), 114
DuPont analysis, 120	
financial ratios, 109	operating profit margin, 114

return on assets, 114

return on common equity, 118

times interest earned, 117

total asset turnover, 115

STUDY QUESTIONS

4-1 Describe the "four-question approach" to using financial ratios.

4-2 Discuss briefly the two perspectives that can be taken in performing ratio analysis.

4-3 Where can we obtain industry norms? What are the limitations of industry average ratios? Discuss briefly.

4-4 What is liquidity, and what is the rationale for its measurement?

4-5 Distinguish between the operating income return on investment and the operating profit margin.

4-6 Why is operating income return on investment a function of operating profit margin and total asset turnover?

4-7 What is the difference between gross profit margin, operating profit margin, and net profit margin?

4-8 Explain what drives a company's return on common equity.

4-9 What is economic value added? Why is it used?

SELF-TEST PROBLEMS

ST-1 *(Ratio Analysis and Short-term Liquidity)* Ray's Tool and Supply Company of Austin, Texas, has been expanding its level of operation for the past 2 years. The firm's sales have grown rapidly as a result of the expansion in the Austin economy. However, Ray's is a privately held company, and the only source of available funds it has is a line of credit with the firm's bank. The company needs to expand its inventories to meet the needs of its growing customer base but also wishes to maintain a current ratio of at least 3. If Ray's current assets are $6 million, and its current ratio is now 4, how much can it expand its inventories (financing the expansion with its line of credit) before the target current ratio is violated?

ST-2 *(Ratio Analysis)* The statements for M & G Industries are presented below:

M & G INDUSTRIES BALANCE SHEET
FOR DECEMBER 31, 1999 AND 2000

	1999	2000
Cash	$ 9,000	$ 500
Accounts receivable	12,500	16,000
Inventories	29,000	45,500
Total current assets	$ 50,500	$ 62,000
Land	20,000	26,000
Buildings and equipment	70,000	100,000
Less: allowance for depreciation	(28,000)	(38,000)
Total fixed assets	$62,000	$ 88,000
Total assets	$112,500	$150,000
Accounts payable	$ 10,500	$ 22,000
Short-term bank notes	17,000	47,000
Total current liabilities	$ 27,500	$ 69,000
Long-term debt	28,750	22,950
Common stock	31,500	31,500
Retained earnings	24,750	26,550
Total debt and equity	$112,500	$150,000

M & G INDUSTRIES INCOME STATEMENT
FOR THE YEARS ENDED DECEMBER 31, 1999 AND 2000

	1999	2000
Sales (all credit)	$125,000	$160,000
Cost of goods sold	75,000	96,000
Gross profit	$ 50,000	$ 64,000
Operating expenses		
Fixed cash operating expenses	$ 21,000	$ 21,000
Variable operating expenses	12,500	16,000
Depreciation	4,500	10,000
Total operating expenses	$ 38,000	$ 47,000
Earnings before interest and taxes	$ 12,000	$ 17,000
Interest expense	3,000	6,100
Earnings before taxes	$ 9,000	$ 10,900
Taxes	4,500	5,450
Net income	$ 4,500	$ 5,450

a. Based on the preceding statements, complete the following table:

M & G INDUSTRIES RATIO ANALYSIS

	INDUSTRY AVERAGES	ACTUAL 1999	ACTUAL 2000
Current ratio	1.80		
Acid-test ratio	0.70		
Average collection period	37.00		
Inventory turnover	2.50		
Debt ratio	58%		
Times interest earned	3.80		
Gross profit margin	38%		
Operating profit margin	10%		
Total asset turnover	1.14		
Fixed asset turnover	1.40		
Operating income return on investment	11.4%		
Return on total assets	4.0%		
Return on common equity	9.5%		

b. Evaluate the firm's financial position using the "four-question approach" described in the chapter.

4-1 *(Ratio Analysis)* The Mitchem Marble Company has a target current ratio of 2.0 but has experienced some difficulties financing its expanding sales in the past few months. At present the firm has a current ratio of 2.5 with current assets of $2.5 million. If Mitchem expands its receivables and inventories using its short-term line of credit, how much additional short-term funding can it borrow before its current ratio standard is reached?

4-2 *(Ratio Analysis)* The balance sheet and income statement for the J. P. Robard Mfg. Company are as follows:

BALANCE SHEET ($000)	
Cash	$ 500
Accounts receivable	2,000
Inventories	1,000
Current assets	3,500
Net fixed assets	4,500
Total assets	$8,000
Accounts payable	$1,100
Accrued expenses	600
Short-term notes payable	300
Current liabilities	$2,000
Long-term debt	2,000
Owners' equity	4,000
Total liabilities and owners' equity	$8,000

INCOME STATEMENT ($000)	
Net sales (all credit)	$8,000
Cost of goods sold	(3,300)
Gross profit	4,700
Operating expenses (includes $500 depreciation)	(3,000)
Operating income	1,700
Interest expense	(367)
Earnings before taxes	$1,333
Income taxes (40%)	(533)
Net income	$ 800

Calculate the following ratios:

Current ratio	Operating income return on investment
Times interest earned	Debt ratio
Inventory turnover	Average collection period
Total asset turnover	Fixed asset turnover
Operating profit margin	Gross profit margin
	Return on equity

4-3 *(Analyzing Operating Income Return on Investment)* The R. M. Smithers Corporation earned an operating profit margin of 10 percent based on sales of $10 million and total assets of $5 million last year.

    a. What was Smithers' total asset turnover ratio?

    b. During the coming year the company president has set a goal of attaining a total asset turnover of 3.5. How much must firm sales rise, other things being the same, for the goal to be achieved? (State your answer in both dollars and percentage increase in sales.)

    c. What was Smithers' operating income return on investment last year? Assuming the firm's operating profit margin remains the same, what will the operating income return on investment be next year if the total asset turnover goal is achieved?

4-4 *(Using Financial Ratios)* The Brenmar Sales Company had a gross profit margin (gross profits ÷ sales) of 30 percent and sales of $9 million last year. Seventy-five percent of the firm's sales are on credit and the remainder are cash sales. Brenmar's current assets equal $1.5 million, its current liabilities equal $300,000, and it has $100,000 in cash plus marketable securities.

    a. If Brenmar's accounts receivable are $562,500, what is its average collection period?

    b. If Brenmar reduces its average collection period to 20 days, what will be its new level of accounts receivable?

    c. Brenmar's inventory turnover ratio is 9 times. What is the level of Brenmar's inventories?

4-5 *(Ratio Analysis)* Using Pamplin Inc.'s financial statements shown on the following pages:

    a. Compute the following ratios for both 1999 and 2000.

INDUSTRY NORM 2000	
Current ratio	5.00
Acid-test (quick) ratio	3.00
Inventory turnover	2.20
Average collection period	90.00
Debt ratio	0.33
Times interest earned	7.00
Total asset turnover	0.75
Fixed asset turnover	1.00
Operating profit margin	20%
Return on common equity	9%

    b. How liquid is the firm?

    c. Is management generating adequate operating profit on the firm's assets?

    d. How is the firm financing its assets?

    e. Are the common stockholders receiving a good return on their investment?

PAMPLIN INC. BALANCE SHEET
AT 12/31/1999 AND 12/31/2000

Assets

	1999	2000
Cash	$ 200	$ 150
Accounts receivable	450	425
Inventory	550	625
Current assets	$1,200	$1,200
Plant and equipment	$2,200	$2,600
Less: accumulated depreciation	(1,000)	(1,200)
Net plant and equipment	$1,200	$1,400
Total assets	$2,400	$2,600

Liabilities and Owners' Equity

	1999	2000
Accounts payable	$ 200	$ 150
Notes payable—current (9%)	0	150
Current liabilities	$ 200	$ 300
Bonds (8$^1/_3$% interest)	$ 600	$ 600
Owners' equity		
Common stock	$ 300	$ 300
Paid in capital	600	600
Retained earnings	700	800
Total owners' equity	$1,600	$1,700
Total liabilities and owners' equity	$2,400	$2,600

PAMPLIN INC. INCOME STATEMENT
FOR YEARS ENDING 12/31/1999 AND 12/31/2000

	1999		2000	
Sales (all credit)		$1,200		$1,450
Cost of goods sold		700		850
Gross profit		$ 500		$ 600
Operating expenses	30		40	
Depreciation	220	250	200	240
Operating income		$ 250		$ 360
Interest expense		50		64
Net income before taxes		$ 200		$ 296
Taxes (40%)		80		118
Net income		$ 120		$ 178

4-6 *(Financial Ratios—Investment Analysis)* The annual sales for Salco, Inc., were $4.5 million last year. The firm's end-of-year balance sheet appeared as follows:

Current assets	$ 500,000	Liabilities	$1,000,000
Net fixed assets	1,500,000	Owners' equity	1,000,000
	$2,000,000		$2,000,000

The firm's income statement for the year was as follows:

Sales	$ 4,500,000
Less: cost of goods sold	(3,500,000)
Gross profit	$ 1,000,000
Less: operating expenses	(500,000)
Operating income	$ 500,000
Less: interest expense	(100,000)
Earnings before taxes	$ 400,000
Less: taxes (50%)	(200,000)
Net income	$ 200,000

a. Calculate Salco's total asset turnover, operating profit margin, and operating income return on investment.

b. Salco plans to renovate one of its plants, which will require an added investment in plant and equipment of $1 million. The firm will maintain its present debt ratio of .5 when financing the new investment and expects sales to remain constant, while the operating profit margin will rise to 13 percent. What will be the new operating income return on investment for Salco after the plant renovation?

c. Given that the plant renovation in part b occurs and Salco's interest expense rises by $50,000 per year, what will be the return earned on the common stockholders' investment? Compare this rate of return with that earned before the renovation.

4-7 *(Financial Analysis)* The T. P. Jarmon Company manufactures and sells a line of exclusive sportswear. The firm's sales were $600,000 for the year just ended, and its total assets exceeded $400,000. The company was started by Mr. Jarmon just 10 years ago and has been profitable every year since its inception. The chief financial officer for the firm, Brent Vehlim, has decided to seek a line of credit from the firm's banks totaling $80,000. In the past, the company has relied on its suppliers to finance a large part of its needs for inventory. However, in recent months tight money conditions have led the firm's suppliers to offer sizable cash discounts to speed up payments for purchases. Mr. Vehlim wants to use the line of credit to supplant a large portion of the firm's payables during the summer months, which are the firm's peak seasonal sales period.

The firm's two most recent balance sheets were presented to the bank in support of its loan request. In addition, the firm's income statement for the year just ended was provided to support the loan request. These statements are found in the following tables:

T. P. JARMON COMPANY, BALANCE SHEET FOR 12/31/1999 AND 12/31/2000

Assets

	1999	2000
Cash	$ 15,000	$ 14,000
Marketable securities	6,000	6,200
Accounts receivable	42,000	33,000
Inventory	51,000	84,000
Prepaid rent	1,200	1,100
Total current assets	$115,200	$138,300
Net plant and equipment	286,000	270,000
Total assets	$401,200	$408,300

Liabilities and Equity

	1999	2000
Accounts payable	$ 48,000	$ 57,000
Notes payable	15,000	13,000
Accruals	6,000	5,000
Total current liabilities	$ 69,000	$ 75,000
Long-term debt	$160,000	$150,000
Common stockholders' equity	$172,200	$183,300
Total liabilities and equity	$401,200	$408,300

T. P. JARMON COMPANY, INCOME STATEMENT FOR THE YEAR ENDED 12/31/2000

Sales (all credit)		$600,000
Less: cost of goods sold		460,000
Gross profits		$140,000
Less: operating and interest expenses		
General and administrative	$ 30,000	
Interest	10,000	
Depreciation	30,000	
Total		70,000
Earnings before taxes		$ 70,000
Less: taxes		27,100
Net income available to common stockholders		$ 42,900
Less: cash dividends		31,800
Change in retained earnings		$ 11,100

Jan Fama, associate credit analyst for the Merchants National Bank of Midland, Michigan, was assigned the task of analyzing Jarmon's loan request.

a. Calculate the financial ratios for 2000 corresponding to the industry norms provided as follows:

	RATIO NORM
Current ratio	1.8
Acid-test ratio	0.9
Debt ratio	0.5
Times interest earned	10.0
Average collection period	20.0
Inventory turnover	
(based on cost of goods sold)	7.0
Return on common equity	12.0%
Gross profit margin	25.0%
Operating income return on investment	16.8%
Operating profit margin	14.0%
Total asset turnover	1.20
Fixed asset turnover	1.80

b. Which of the ratios reported above in the industry norms do you feel should be most crucial in determining whether the bank should extend the line of credit?

c. Compute Jarmon's free cash flows for the year ended December 31, 2000. Interpret your findings.

d. Use the information provided by the financial ratios and the cash flow statement to decide if you would support making the loan.

e. Use the DuPont analysis to evaluate the firm's financial position.

4-8 *(Economic Value Added)* Stegemoller Inc.'s management wants to evaluate its firm's prior-year performance in terms of its contribution to shareholder value. This past year, the firm earned an operating income return on investment of 12 percent, compared to an industry norm of 11 percent. It has been estimated that the firm's investors have an opportunity cost on their funds of 14 percent. The firm's total assets for the year were $100 million. Compute the amount of economic value created or destroyed by the firm. How does your finding support or fail to support what you would conclude using ratio analysis to evaluate the firm's performance?

─────── **COMPREHENSIVE PROBLEM** ───────

Return to the Chapter 3 comprehensive problem (pp. 103–105) in which we presented the financial statements for PepsiCo and Coca-Cola. These two firms are considered to be in the beverages industry (Standard Industrial Code 2080).

a. Go to your library and find industry norms for the beverages industry.

b. Are there any ratios that are not provided for the industry that prevent you from using the "four-question approach" as described in this chapter? How would you adapt your approach to compensate for any missing industry norms?

c. Compute the financial ratios for both firms for 2000, and using your industry norms, evaluate the firm in the following areas:

(1) liquidity

(2) operating profitability

(3) financing policies

(4) return on the shareholders' investment

SS-1 Note that Ray's current ratio before the inventory expansion is as follows:

$$\text{current ratio} = \$6,000,000/\text{current liabilities} = 4$$

Thus, the firm's level of current liabilities is $1.5 million. If the expansion in inventories is financed entirely with borrowed funds, then the change in inventories is equal to the change in current liabilities, and the firm's current ratio after the expansion can be defined as follows:

$$\text{current ratio} = \frac{\$6,000,000 + \text{change in inventory}}{\$1,500,000 + \text{change in inventory}} = 3$$

Note that we set the new current ratio equal to the firm's target of 3. Solving for the change in inventory in the above equation, we determine that the firm can expand its inventories by $750,000 and finance the expansion with current liabilities and still maintain its target current ratio.

SS-2

a.

M & G INDUSTRIES RATIO ANALYSIS			
	INDUSTRY AVERAGES	ACTUAL 1999	ACTUAL 2000
Current ratio	1.80	1.84	0.90
Acid-test ratio	0.70	0.78	0.24
Average collection period (based on a 365-day year and end-of-year figures)	37.00	36.50	36.50
Inventory turnover	2.50	2.59	2.11
Debt ratio	58%	50%	61.3%
Times interest earned	3.80	4.00	2.79
Gross profit margin	38%	40%	40%
Operating profit margin	10%	9.6%	10.6
Total asset turnover	1.14	1.11	1.07
Fixed asset turnover	1.40	2.02	1.82
Operating income return on investment	11.4%	10.67%	11.3%
Return on common equity	9.5%	8.0%	9.4%

b. M & G's liquidity is poor, as suggested by the low current ratio and acid-test ratio; also, inventories are turning slowly. In 2000, management is doing a satisfactory job at generating profits on the firm's operating assets, as indicated by the operating income return on investment. Note that the operating income return on investment in 2000 is average, owing to a slightly above average operating profit margin combined with a slightly below average asset turnover. The problem with the asset turnover ratio comes from a slow inventory turnover.

M & G has increased its use of debt to the point of using slightly more debt than the average company in the industry. As a result, the firm's coverage of interest has decreased to a point well below the industry norm.

Financial Forecasting • Sustainable Rate of Growth • Limitations of the Percent of Sales Forecast Method • Cash Budgeting

FINANCIAL FORECASTING, PLANNING, AND BUDGETING

LEARNING OBJECTIVES

AFTER READING THIS CHAPTER, YOU SHOULD BE ABLE TO:

1. Use the percent of sales method to forecast the financing requirements of a firm.
2. Calculate a firm's sustainable rate of growth.
3. Describe the limitations of the percent of sales forecast method.
4. Prepare a cash budget and use it to evaluate the amount and timing of a firm's financing needs.

Forecasting is an integral part of the planning process, yet there are countless examples where our ability to predict the future is simply awful. Declining birthrates during the seventies was widely attributed to the women's liberation movement. Believing that the lower birthrates were permanent, school administrators began closing elementary schools. Then in the eighties birthrates and consequently school enrollments increased again as a result of the fact that childless couples had simply deferred having children until later in life. Still another example of poor forecasting relates to projections of oil prices that were prevalent during the mid-1980s. Oil prices were roughly $30 a barrel and many firms were developing new reserves that would cost well over this amount to produce. Why? Oil prices were projected to continue to rise and many thought the price might eventually reach $50 a barrel by the end of the decade. Then in January 1986 the collapse of the oil producers' cartel in combination with the benefits of energy conservation efforts produced a dramatic drop in oil prices to below $10 a barrel. Although these cases are dramatic they are by no means unique.

If forecasting the future is so difficult, and plans are built on forecasts, why do firms engage in planning efforts? Obviously, they do, but why? The answer, oddly enough, does not lie in the accuracy of the firm's projections, for planning offers its greatest value when the future is the most uncertain. The reason is that planning is the process of thinking about what the future might bring and devising strategies for dealing with the likely outcomes. Planning is thinking in advance, and thinking in advance provides an opportunity to devise contingency plans that can be quickly and easily initiated should the need arise. This increased speed of response to uncertain events means that the firm can reduce the costs of responding to adverse circumstances and quickly respond to take advantage of unexpected opportunities.

Objective 1

FINANCIAL FORECASTING

Forecasting in financial management is used to estimate a firm's future financial needs. The basic steps involved in predicting those financing needs are the following: *Step 1:* Project the firm's sales revenues and expenses over the planning period. *Step 2:* Estimate the levels of investment in current and fixed assets that are necessary to support the projected sales. *Step 3:* Determine the firm's financing needs throughout the planning period.

Sales Forecast

The key ingredient in the firm's planning process is the sales forecast. This projection is generally derived using information from a number of sources. At a minimum, the sales forecast for the coming year would reflect (1) any past trend in sales that is expected to carry through into the new year, and (2) the influence of any events that might materially affect that trend.[1] An example of the latter is the initiation of a major advertising campaign or a change in the firm's pricing policy.

Forecasting Financial Variables

Traditional financial forecasting takes the sales forecast as a given and makes projections of its impact on the firm's various expenses, assets, and liabilities. The most commonly used method for making these projections is the percent of sales method.

Percent of Sales Method of Financial Forecasting

The **percent of sales method** involves *estimating the level of an expense, asset, or liability for a future period as a percent of the sales forecast.* The percentage used can come from the most recent financial statement item as a percent of current sales, from an average computed over several years, from the judgment of the analyst, or from some combination of these sources.

Table 5–1 presents a complete example that uses the percent of sales method of financial forecasting. In this example each item in the firm's balance sheet that varies with sales is converted to a percentage of 2000 sales of $10 million. The forecast of the new balance for each item is then calculated by multiplying this percentage times the $12 million in projected sales for the 2001 planning period. The method of forecasting future financing is not as precise or detailed as the method using a cash budget, which is presented later; however, it offers a relatively low-cost and easy-to-use first approximation of the firm's financing needs for a future period.

Note that in the example in Table 5–1, both current and fixed assets are assumed to vary with the level of firm sales. This means that the firm does not have sufficient productive capacity to absorb a projected increase in sales. Thus, if sales were to rise by $1, fixed assets would rise by $.40, or 40 percent of the projected increase in sales. If the fixed assets the firm currently owns were sufficient to support the projected level of new sales, then fixed assets would not be converted to a percent of sales and would be projected to remain unchanged for the period being forecast.

Also, we note that accounts payable and accrued expenses are the only liabilities allowed to vary with sales. Both these liability accounts might reasonably be expected to rise and fall with the level of firm sales; hence the use of the percent of sales forecast. Because these two categories of current liabilities normally vary directly with the level of sales, they are often referred to as sources of **spontaneous financing**, which include *the trade credit and other accounts payable that arise "spontaneously in the firm's day-to-day operations."* Chapter 15, which discusses working-capital management, has more to say about these forms of financing. Notes payable, long-term debt, common stock, and paid-in capital are not assumed to vary directly with the level of firm sales. These sources of financing are termed **discretionary financing,** *which require an explicit decision on the part of the firm's management every time funds are raised. An example is a bank note that requires negotiations be undertaken and an agreement signed setting forth the terms and conditions for the financing.* Finally, we note that the level of retained earnings does vary with estimated sales. The predicted change in the level of retained earnings equals the estimated after-tax profits (projected net income) equal to 5 percent of sales or $600,000 less the common stock dividends of $300,000.

Takin' It to the Net
To get economy wide data on business, interest rates, and a wide range of economic time series see http://www.stls.frb.org/fred/. Often industry historical sales data for specific industries are available. For example, historical industry sales for semiconductors can be found at http://www. eb-mag.com/registrd/research/semicon/index.htm.

percent of sales method

spontaneous financing

discretionary financing

---

[1]A complete discussion of forecast methodologies is outside the scope of this book. The interested reader will find the following reference helpful: Paul Newbold and Theodore Bos, *Introductory Business Forecasting 2nd* (Cincinnati: Southwestern, 1994).

ASSETS	PRESENT (2000)	PERCENT OF SALES (2000 SALES = $10M)	PROJECTED (BASED ON 2001 SALES = $12M)
Current assets	$2.0M	$\frac{\$2M}{\$10M} = 20\%$	$.2 \times \$12M = \$2.4M$
Net fixed assets	$4.0M	$\frac{\$4M}{\$10M} = 40\%$	$.4 \times \$12M = \underline{\$4.8M}$
Total	$6.0M		$7.2M
Liabilities and Owners' Equity			
Accounts payable	$1.0M	$\frac{\$1M}{\$10M} = 10\%$	$.10 \times \$12M = \$1.2M$
Accrued expenses	1.0M	$\frac{\$1M}{\$10M} = 10\%$	$.10 \times \$12M = \$1.2M$
Notes payable	.5M	NA[a]	No change .5M
Long-term debt	$2.0M	NA[a]	No change 2.0M
Total liabilities	$4.5M		$4.9M
Common stock	$ .1M	NA[a]	No change $ .1M
Paid-in capital	.2M	NA[a]	No change .2M
Retained earnings	1.2M		1.2M [.05 × $12M × (1 − .5)] = 1.5M[b]
Common equity	$1.5M		$1.8M
Total	$6.0M		Total financing provided $6.7M
			Discretionary financing needed .5M[c]
			Total $7.2M

[a]Not applicable. These accounts balances are assumed not to vary with sales.

[b]Projected retained earnings equals the beginning level ($1.2M) plus projected net income less than any dividends paid. In this case net income is projected to equal 5 percent of sales, and dividends are projected to equal half of net income: .05 × $12M × (1 − .5) = $300,000.

[c]Discretionary financing needed equals projected total assets ($7.2M) less projected total liabilities ($4.9M) less projected common equity ($1.8), or $7.2M − 4.9M − 1.8M = $500,000.

Thus, using the example from Table 5–1, we estimate that firm sales will increase from $10 million to $12 million, which will cause the firm's need for total assets to rise to $7.2 million. These assets will then be financed by $4.9 million in existing liabilities plus spontaneous liabilities; $1.8 million in owner funds, including $300,000 in retained earnings from next year's sales; and finally, $500,000 in discretionary financing, which can be raised by issuing notes payable, selling bonds, offering an issue of stock, or some combination of these sources.

In summary, we can estimate the firm's discretionary financing needs (DFN), using the percent of sales method of financial forecasting, by following a four-step procedure:

Step 1: Convert each asset and liability account that varies directly with firm sales to a percent of the current year's sales.

Example   **Current Assets as a Percent of Sales**

$$\frac{\text{current assets}}{\text{sales}} = \frac{\$2M}{\$10M} = .2 \text{ or } 20\%$$

Now You See It . . .

Cash flow is at least as important a measure of corporate health as reported earnings. But put a dozen investors in a room and you'll get almost as many different definitions.

After grappling with the problem for more than six years, the Financial Accounting Standards Board has come up with the beginnings of a more precise definition. It would require all companies to use the same format to explain how cash and cash equivalents change from one reporting period to the next. The proposal still leaves companies with room for flexibility but will make investors' lives much easier. Why? Companies will have to show sources and uses of cash in three areas: operations, investing, and financing.

Let's take a specific case: Lowe's Cos., the North Carolina-based retailer of building materials. The company said in its annual report that cash flow amounted to $2.31 per share in 1985 as compared with $2.20 the year before. An investor looking at these numbers might have assumed Lowe's had plenty of cash left over for dividends and other purposes.

Not necessarily so. Although Lowe's used a generally accepted definition of cash flow, it was not a strict definition. It failed to subtract the cash absorbed by higher inventories and receivables. Lowe's ended the year with hardly more cash than it started the year, and its long-term debt almost doubled from 1984 to 1985—despite the positive cash flow.

Does it really matter how you measure cash flow? Very much. While Lowe's is healthy—the increased inventory and receivables simply reflect growth in revenues—there are situations where a company can go broke while reporting positive cash flow. How can this be? Simple.

Suppose inventories and receivables rise faster than sales, reflecting slow pay by customers on unsold goods. Under the simpler method of reporting cash flow (which would not include working-capital components), such a company could report a positive cash flow even while it was fast running out of cash.

When the smoke clears, investors will still need to do lots of homework. It's never enough to know just what the numbers are. You still have to figure out what the numbers mean. Again, Lowe's is an example. Even if it were forced to report a negative cash flow, it would still be a very healthy business; it would cease being one only if inventories and receivables increased faster than sales and the company's credit were deteriorating.

When it comes to some things, the more you try simplifying them, the more complicated they become.

Source: Excerpted by permission of Forbes (February 9, 1987): 70. © Forbes Inc. 1987

Step 2: Project the level of each asset and liability account in the balance sheet using its percent of sales multiplied by projected sales or by leaving the account balance unchanged where the account does not vary with the level of sales.

Example **Predicting Current Assets**

$$\text{projected current assets} =$$
$$\text{projected sales} \times \frac{\text{current assets}}{\text{sales}} = \$12M \times .2 = \$2.4M$$

Step 3: Project the addition to retained earnings available to help finance the firm's operations. This equals projected net income for the period less planned common stock dividends.

Example **Predicting Additional Retained Earnings**

$$\text{projected addition to retained earnings} =$$
$$\text{projected sales} \times \frac{\text{net income}}{\text{sales}} \times \left(1 - \frac{\text{cash dividends}}{\text{net income}}\right)$$
$$= \$12M \times .05 \times (1 - .5) = \$300,000$$

Financial Forecasting, Planning, and Budgeting   **143**

Step 4: Project the firm's DFN as the projected level of total assets less projected liabilities and owners' equity.

> **Example** **Predicting Discretionary Financing Needs**
>
> discretionary financing needed =
> projected total assets − projected total liabilities − projected owner's equity
> = $7.2M − $4.9M − $1.8M = $500,000

Analyzing the Effects of Profitability and Dividend Policy on DFN

Projecting discretionary financing needed we can quickly and easily evaluate the sensitivity of our projected financing requirements to changes in key variables. For example, using the information from the preceding example, we evaluate the effect of net profit margins (NPMs) equal to 1 percent, 5 percent, and 10 percent in combination with dividend payout ratios of 30 percent, 50 percent, and 70 percent as follows:

DISCRETIONARY FINANCING NEEDED FOR VARIOUS NET PROFIT MARGINS AND DIVIDEND PAYOUT RATIOS			

Net Profit Margin	Dividend Payout Ratios (Dividends ÷ Net Income)		
	30%	50%	70%
1%	$716,000	$740,000	$764,000
5%	380,000	500,000	620,000
10%	(40,000)	200,000	440,000

If these values for the NPM represent reasonable estimates of the possible ranges of values the firm might experience, and if the firm is considering dividend payouts ranging from 30 percent to 70 percent, then we estimate that the firm's financing requirements will range from ($40,000), which represents a surplus of $40,000, to a situation where it would need to acquire $764,000. Lower NPMs mean higher funds requirements. Also, higher dividend payout percentages, other things remaining constant, lead to a need for more discretionary financing. This is a direct result of the fact that a high-dividend-paying firm retains less of its earnings.

Analyzing the Effects of Sales Growth on a Firm's DFN

In Figure 5–1 we analyzed the DFN for a firm whose sales were expected to grow from $10 million to $12 million during the coming year. Recall that the 20 percent expected increase in sales led to an increase in the firm's needs for financing in the amount of $500,000. We referred to this added financing requirement as the firm's DFN because all these funds must be raised from sources, such as bank borrowing or a new equity issue, which require that management exercise its discretion in selecting the source. In this section we want to investigate how a firm's DFN varies with different rates of anticipated growth in sales.

Table 5–2 contains an expansion of the financial forecast found in Table 5–1. Specifically, we use the same assumptions and prediction methods that underlie Table 5–1 but apply them to sales growth rates of −5 percent to 20 percent DFN for

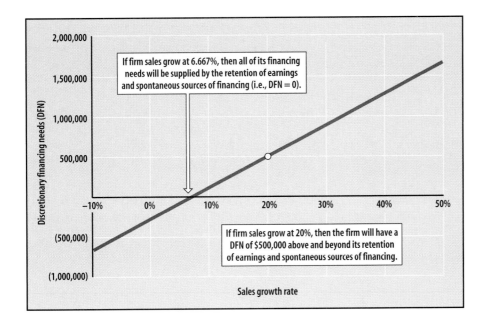

Box in chart: If firm sales grow at 6.667%, then all of its financing needs will be supplied by the retention of earnings and spontaneous sources of financing (i.e., DFN = 0).

Box in chart: If firm sales grow at 20%, then the firm will have a DFN of $500,000 above and beyond its retention of earnings and spontaneous sources of financing.

Y-axis: Discretionary financing needs (DFN)

X-axis: Sales growth rate

FIGURE 5–1

Sales Growth and the Discretionary Financing Needs of the Firm

these sales growth rates ranges from ($625,000) to $500,000. When DFN is negative, this means that the firm has more money than it needs to finance the assets used to generate the projected sales. Alternatively, when DFN is positive, this means that the firm must raise additional funds in this amount either by borrowing or issuing stock. We can calculate DFN using the following relationship:

$$\text{DFN} = \begin{bmatrix} \text{predicted} \\ \text{change in} \\ \text{total assets} \end{bmatrix} - \begin{bmatrix} \text{predicted} \\ \text{change in} \\ \text{spontaneous liabilities} \end{bmatrix} - \begin{bmatrix} \text{predicted} \\ \text{change in} \\ \text{retained earnings} \end{bmatrix} \quad (5\text{–}1)$$

Notice that in defining DFN we only consider changes in spontaneous liabilities, which you will recall are those liabilities that arise more or less automatically in the course of doing business (examples include accrued expenses and accounts payable). In Table 5–1 the only liabilities that are allowed to change with sales are spontaneous liabilities so that we can calculate the change in spontaneous liabilities simply by comparing total liabilities at the current sales level with total liabilities for the predicted sales level.

Equation (5–1) can be used to estimate the DFN numbers found in Table 5–2. For example, where sales are expected to grow at a rate of 10 percent (i.e., *g* equals 10 percent), DFN can be calculated as follows:

$$\text{DFN}(g = 10\%) = (\$6{,}600{,}000 - 6{,}000{,}000) - (\$4{,}700{,}000 - 4{,}500{,}000) - (\$1{,}475{,}000 - 1{,}200{,}000) = \$125{,}000$$

Sometimes analysts prefer to calculate a firm's **external financing needs (EFN),** which include *all the firm's needs for financing beyond the funds provided internally through the retention of earnings.* Thus,

$$\text{EFN} = \begin{bmatrix} \text{predicted} \\ \text{change in} \\ \text{total assets} \end{bmatrix} - \begin{bmatrix} \text{predicted} \\ \text{change in} \\ \text{retained earnings} \end{bmatrix} \quad (5\text{–}2)$$

For an anticipated growth in sales of 10 percent, EFN equals $325,000. The difference between EFN and DFN equals the $200,000 in added spontaneous financing

Takin' It to the Net

An increasing variety of software products are becoming available to support a firm's efforts to build financial forecasts and model its financial requirements. For example, visit http://www.dataper. demon.co.uk/prophecy.html.

external financing needs

TABLE 5–2   **DFN AND THE RATE OF GROWTH IN FIRM SALES**

			Growth Rate in Firm Sales			
			−10%	0%	10%	20%
				Pro Forma Income Statements		
Current Sales (2000)	$10,000,000	Sales	9,000,000	10,000,000	11,000,000	12,000,000
Net Income ÷ Sales	5%	Net Income	450,000	500,000	550,000	600,000
Dividends ÷ Earnings	50%	Dividends	225,000	250,000	275,000	300,000
ASSETS		FORECAST MODEL		PRO FORMA BALANCE SHEETS		
Current assets	2,000,000	20% of sales	1,800,000	2,000,000	2,200,000	2,400,000
Net fixed assets	4,000,000	40% of sales	3,600,000	4,000,000	4,400,000	4,800,000
Total assets	6,000,000		5,400,000	6,000,000	6,600,000	7,200,000
LIABILITIES AND OWNERS' EQUITY						
Accounts payable	1,000,000	10% of sales	900,000	1,000,000	1,100,000	1,200,000
Accrued expenses	1,000,000	10% of sales	900,000	1,000,000	1,100,000	1,200,000
Notes payable	500,000	Constant	500,000	500,000	500,000	500,000
Current liabilities	2,500,000		2,300,000	2,500,000	2,700,000	2,900,000
Long-term debt	2,000,000	Constant	2,000,000	2,000,000	2,000,000	2,000,000
Total liabilities	4,500,000		4,300,000	4,500,000	4,700,000	4,900,000
Common stock	100,000	Constant	100,000	100,000	100,000	100,000
Paid-in capital	200,000	Constant	200,000	200,000	200,000	200,000
Retained earnings	1,200,000	Plus new retained earnings	1,425,000	1,450,000	1,475,000	1,500,000
Common equity	1,500,000		1,725,000	1,750,000	1,775,000	1,800,000
Total financing requirements = total assets			5,400,000	6,000,000	6,600,000	7,200,000
Total financing available			6,025,000	6,250,000	6,475,000	6,700,000
Discretionary financing needed (DFN) = Total Assets − Total Financing Available			(625,000)	(250,000)	125,000	500,000

that the firm anticipates receiving when its sales rise from $10 million to $11 million. We prefer to use the DFN concept because it focuses the analyst's attention on the amount of funds that the firm must actively seek to meet the firm's financing requirements.

Figure 5–1 contains a graphic representation of the relationship between growth rates for sales and DFN. The straight line in the graph depicts the level of DFN for each of the different rates of growth in firm sales. For example, if sales grow by 20 percent, then the firm projects a DFN of $500,000, which must be raised externally by borrowing or a new equity offering. Note that where firm sales grow at 6.667 percent, the firm's DFN will be exactly zero. For firms that have limited sources of external financing or choose to grow through internal finance plus spontaneous financing, it is important that they be able to estimate the sales growth rate that they can "afford," which in this case is 6.667 percent.

The Sustainable Rate of Growth

sustainable rate of growth

The **sustainable rate of growth** (g^*) represents *the rate at which a firm's sales can grow if it wants to maintain its present financial ratios and* does not *want to resort to the sale of new equity shares.*[2] A simple formula can be derived for g^* where we assume that a firm's assets and liabilities all grow at the same rate as its sales, that is,

$$\text{sustainable rate of growth } (g^*) = \text{ROE } (1 - b) \qquad (5\text{--}3)$$

ROE is the firm's return on equity, which was defined in Chapter 3 as follows:

$$\text{ROE} = \frac{\text{net income}}{\text{common equity}}$$

and b is the firm's dividend payout ratio, that is, $\frac{\text{dividends}}{\text{net income}}$. The term $(1 - b)$ is sometimes referred to as the **plowback ratio** since it indicates *the fraction of earnings that are reinvested or plowed back into the firm.* Equation (5–3) is deceptively simple. Recall that ROE can also be written as follows:

plowback ratio

$$\text{ROE} = \left(\frac{\text{net income}}{\text{sales}} \right) \times \left(\frac{\text{sales}}{\text{assets}} \right) \times \left(\frac{\text{total assets}}{\text{common equity}} \right)$$

Consequently, a firm's sustainable rate of growth is determined by its ROE (i.e., its anticipated NPM, asset turnover, and capital structure), as well as its dividend policy.

Example **Calculating the Sustainable Rate of Growth**

Consider the three firms found below:

FIRM	NET PROFIT MARGIN	ASSET TURNOVER	LEVERAGE	PLOWBACK RATIO	g^*
A	15%	2	0.3	50%	4.5%
B	15%	2	0.3	100%	9.0%
C	15%	2	0.5	100%	15.0%

---

[2]For an extensive discussion of this concept see Robert C. Higgins, "Sustainable Growth with Inflation," *Financial Management* (Autumn 1981): 36–40.

Comparing Firms A and B we see that the only difference is that Firm A pays out half its earnings in common dividends (i.e., plows back half its earnings) whereas Firm B retains or plows back all of its earnings. The net result is that Firm B with its added source of internal equity financing can grow at twice the rate of Firm A (9 percent compared to only 4.5 percent). Similarly, comparing Firms B and C we note that they differ only in that Firm B finances only 30 percent of its assets with equity whereas Firm C finances 50 percent of its assets with equity. The result is that Firm C's sustainable rate of growth is 15 percent compared to only 9 percent for Firm B.

Before leaving our discussion of the sustainable rate of growth concept, it is important that we stress the underlying assumptions behind equation (5-2). For this equation to accurately depict a firm's sustainable rate of growth, the following assumptions must hold: First, the firm's assets must vary as a constant percent of sales (i.e., even fixed assets expand and contract directly with the level of firm sales). Second, the firm's liabilities must all vary directly with firm sales. This means that the firm's management will expand its borrowing (both spontaneous and discretionary) in direct proportion with sales to maintain its present ratio of debt to assets. Finally, the firm pays out a constant proportion of its earnings in common stock dividends regardless of the level of firm sales. Because all three of these assumptions are only rough approximations to the way that firms actually behave, equation (5–3) provides a crude approximation of the firm's actual sustainable rate of growth. However, an estimate of g^* using equation (5–3) can be a very useful first step in the firm's financial planning process.

CONCEPT CHECK

1. What is a firm's sustainable rate of growth?
2. How is a firm's sustainable rate of growth related to the firm's profitability and dividend policy?

Limitations of the Percent of Sales Forecast Method

The percent of sales method of financial forecasting provides reasonable estimates of a firm's financing requirements only where asset requirements and financing sources can be accurately forecast as a constant percent of sales. For example, predicting inventories using the percent of sales method involves the following predictive equation, where the subscript t refers to the period that is being forecast.

$$\text{inventories}_t = \left[\frac{\text{inventories}}{\text{sales}} \right] \cdot \text{sales}_t$$

Figure 5–2a depicts this predictive relationship. Note that the percent of sales predictive model is simply a straight line that passes through the origin (i.e., has a zero intercept). There are some fairly common instances in which this type of relationship fails to describe the relationship between an asset category and sales. Two such examples involve assets for which there are scale economies and assets that must be purchased in discrete quantities ("lumpy assets").

Economies of scale are sometimes realized from investing in certain types of assets. For example, a new computer system may support a firm's operations over a wide range of firm sales. This means that these assets do not increase in direct proportion to sales. Figure 5–2b reflects one instance in which the firm realizes

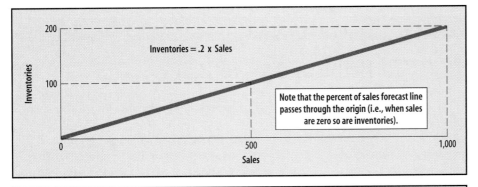

FIGURE 5-2a
Percent of Sales Forecast

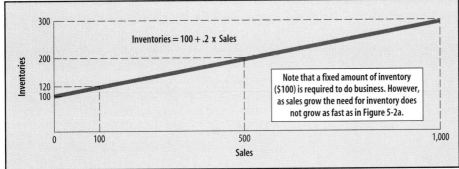

FIGURE 5-2b
Economies of Scale

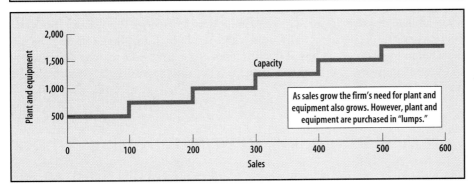

FIGURE 5-2c
Economies of Scale and Lumpy Investments

economies of scale from its investment in inventory. Note that inventories as a percent of sales decline from 120 percent of sales or $120 when sales are $100, to 30 percent of sales or $300 when sales equal $1,000. This reflects the fact that there is a fixed component of inventories (in this case $100) that the firm must have on hand regardless of the level of sales, plus a variable component (20 percent of sales). In this instance the predictive equation for inventories is as follows:

$$\text{inventories}_t = a + b\ \text{sales}_t$$

In this example, a is equal to 100 and b equals .20.[3]

Figure 5–2c is an example of *lumpy assets*, that is, assets that must be purchased in large, nondivisible components. For example, if the firm spends $500 on plant and equipment, it can produce up to $100 in sales per year. If it spends another $500 (for

---

[3]Economies of scale are evidenced by the nonzero intercept value. However, scale economies can also result in nonlinear relationships between sales and a particular asset category. Later, when we discuss cash management, we will find that one popular cash management model predicts a nonlinear relationship between the optimal cash balance and the level of cash transactions.

a total of $1,000), then it can support sales of $200 per year, and so forth. Note that when a block of assets is purchased, it creates excess capacity until sales grow to the point where the capacity is fully used. The result is a step function like the one depicted in Figure 5–2c. Thus, if the firm does not expect sales to exceed the current capacity of its plant and equipment, there would be no projected need for added plant and equipment capacity.

FINANCIAL PLANNING AND BUDGETING

As we noted earlier, the principal virtue of the percent of sales method of financial forecasting is its simplicity. To obtain a more precise estimate of the amount and timing of the firm's future financing needs, we require a cash budget. The percent of sales method of financial forecasting provides a very useful, low-cost forerunner to the development of the more detailed cash budget, which the firm will ultimately use to estimate its financing needs.

BACK TO THE FOUNDATIONS

Budgets have many important uses; however, their use as a tool of managerial control is critically important and often overlooked in the study of financial management. **Axiom 7: The Agency Problems—Managers Won't Work for Owners Unless It's in Their Best Interest** speaks to the root source of the problem, and budgets provide one tool for attempting to deal with it. Specifically, budgets provide management with a tool for evaluating performance and consequently maintaining a degree of control over employee actions.

Budget Functions

A **budget** is simply *a forecast of future events.* For example, students preparing for final exams make use of time budgets to help them allocate their limited preparation time among their courses. Students also must budget their financial resources among competing uses, such as books, tuition, food, rent, clothes, and extracurricular activities.

budget

Budgets perform three basic functions for a firm. First, they indicate the amount and timing of the firm's needs for future financing. Second, they provide the basis for taking corrective action in the event budgeted figures do not match actual or realized figures. Third, budgets provide the basis for performance evaluation and control. Plans are carried out by people, and budgets provide benchmarks that management can use to evaluate the performance of those responsible for carrying out those plans and, in turn, to control their actions. Thus, budgets are valuable aids in both the planning and controlling aspects of the firm's financial management.

CONCEPT CHECK

1. What, in words, is the fundamental relationship (equation) used in making percent of sales forecasts?
2. Under what circumstances does a firm violate the basic relationship underlying the percent of sales forecast method?

The Cash Budget

Objective 4

The **cash budget** represents a *detailed plan of future cash flows* and is composed of four elements: cash receipts, cash disbursements, net change in cash for the period, and new financing needed.

cash budget

Example Constructing a Cash Budget

To demonstrate the construction and use of the cash budget, consider Salco Furniture Company, Inc., a regional distributor of household furniture. Management is in the process of preparing a monthly cash budget for the upcoming 6 months (January through June 2001). Salco's sales are highly seasonal, peaking in the months of March through May. Roughly 30 percent of Salco's sales are collected 1 month after the sale, 50 percent 2 months after the sale, and the remainder during the third month following the sale.

Salco attempts to pace its purchases with its forecast of future sales. Purchases generally equal 75 percent of sales and are made 2 months in advance of anticipated sales. Payments are made in the month following purchases. For example, June sales are estimated at $100,000, thus April purchases are .75 × $100,000 = $75,000. Correspondingly, payments for purchases in May equal $75,000. Wages, salaries, rent, and other cash expenses are recorded in Table 5–3, which gives Salco's cash budget for the 6-month period ended in June 2001. Additional expenditures are recorded in the cash budget related to the purchase of equipment in the amount of $14,000 during February and the repayment of a $12,000 loan in May. In June Salco will pay $7,500 interest on its $150,000 in long-term debt for the period of January–June 2001. Interest on the $12,000 short-term note repaid in May for the period January through May equals $600 and is paid in May.

Salco currently has a cash balance of $20,000 and wants to maintain a minimum balance of $10,000. Additional borrowing necessary to maintain that minimum balance is estimated in the final section of Table 5-3. Borrowing takes place at the beginning of the month in which the funds are needed. Interest on borrowed funds equals 12 percent per annum or 1 percent per month, and is paid in the month following the one in which funds are borrowed. Thus, interest on funds borrowed in January will be paid in February equal to 1 percent of the loan amount outstanding during January.

The financing-needed line in Salco's cash budget determines that the firm's cumulative short-term borrowing will be $36,350 in February, $65,874 in March, $86,633 in April, and $97,599 in May. In June the firm will be able to reduce its borrowing to $79,875. Note that the cash budget indicates not only the amount of financing needed during the period but also when the funds will be needed.

Fixed versus Flexible Budgets

The cash budget given in Table 5–3 on pages 154–155 for Salco, Inc., is an example of a fixed budget. Cash flow estimates are made for a single set of monthly sales estimates. Thus, the estimates of expenses and new financing needed are meaningful only for the level of sales for which they were computed. To avoid this limitation, several budgets corresponding to different sets of sales estimates can be prepared. Such flexible budgeting fulfills two basic needs: First, it gives information regarding the firm's possible financing needs, and second, it provides management with a control mechanism. That is, management can compare actual performance against budgeted figures. In this way management can evaluate the performance of subordinates who are responsible for the various cost and revenue items contained in the budget.

This second function deserves some additional comment. Some costs vary with the actual level of sales experienced by the firm. Thus, if the budget is to be used as a standard for performance evaluation or control, it must be constructed to match realized sales and production figures. This can involve much more than simply adjusting cost figures up or down in proportion to the deviation of actual from planned sales; that is, costs may not vary in strict proportion to sales, just as inventory levels may not vary as a constant percent of sales. Thus, preparation of a flexible budget involves reestimating all the cash expenses that would be incurred at each of several possible sales levels. This process might utilize a variation of the percent of sales method discussed earlier.

Budget Period

There are no strict rules for determining the length of the budget period. However, as a general rule, it should be long enough to show the effect of management policies yet short enough that estimates can be made with reasonable accuracy. Applying this rule of thumb to the Salco example in Table 5–3, it appears that the 6-month budget period is too short because we cannot tell whether the planned operations of the firm will be successful over the coming fiscal year. That is, for most of the first 6-month period, the firm is operating with a cash flow deficit. If this does not reverse in the latter 6 months of the year, then a reevaluation of the firm's plans and policies is clearly in order.

Longer-range budgets are also prepared in the form of the capital-expenditure budget. These budgets detail the firm's plans for acquiring plant and equipment over

Being Honest About the Uncertainty of the Future

Put yourself in the shoes of Ben Tolbert, who is the CFO of Bonajet Enterprises. Ben's CEO is scheduled to meet with a group of outside analysts tomorrow to discuss the firm's financial forecast for the last quarter of the year. Ben's analysis suggests that there is a very real prospect that the coming quarter's results could be very disappointing. How would you handle Ben's dilemma?

As Ben looks over a draft of the report he must submit to the company CEO, he becomes increasingly concerned. Although the forecast is below initial expectations, this is not what worries Ben. The problem is that some of the basic assumptions underlying his prediction might not come true. If this is the case, then the company's performance for the last quarter of the year will be dramatically below its annual forecast. The result would be a potentially severe reaction in the investment community causing a downward adjustment of unknown proportions in the firm's stock price.

Bonajet's CEO is a no-nonsense guy who really doesn't like to see his CFO hedge his predictions, so Ben is under pressure to decide whether to ignore the downside prospects or make them known to his CEO. Complicating matters is the fact that the worst-case scenario would probably give rise to a reorganization of Bonajet that would lead to substantial layoffs of its workforce. Here is Ben's dilemma: What should he tell the CEO in their meeting tomorrow morning?

CONCEPT CHECK

1. What is a cash budget and how is it used in financial planning?
2. What is a fixed cash budget and how does it differ from a flexible cash budget?
3. How long should a firm's budget period be?

---

a 5-year, 10-year, or even longer period. Furthermore, firms often develop comprehensive long-range plans extending up to 10 years into the future. These plans are generally not as detailed as the annual cash budget, but they do consider such major components as sales, capital expenditures, new-product development, capital funds acquisition, and employment needs.

COMPUTERIZED FINANCIAL PLANNING

Personal computers and spreadsheet software have reduced the tedium of the planning and budgeting process immensely. The number and variety of financial spreadsheet programs has expanded dramatically since the introduction of the original VisiCalc program. These include Lotus 1-2-3 and Excel, among others. In addition, there is a growing set of products referred to as "expert systems," which attempt to mimic the decisions of experts. To date, these efforts have produced a limited number of financial applications software related to such things as the capital-budgeting decision, but they offer an opportunity to expand the capabilities of the financial manager of the future.

TABLE 5–3	SALCO FURNITURE CO., INC., CASH BUDGET FOR THE 6 MONTHS ENDED JUNE 30, 2001

WORKSHEET	OCT.	NOV.	DEC.	JAN.
Sales	$55,000	$62,000	$50,000	$60,000
Collections:				
First month (30%)				15,000
Second month (50%)				31,000
Third month (20%)				11,000
Total				$57,000
Purchases (75% of sales in two months)			$56,250	66,000
Payments (one-month lag)				$56,250
Cash budget				
Cash receipts				
Collections (see worksheet)				$57,000
Cash disbursements:				
Payments (see worksheet)				$56,250
Wages and salaries				3,000
Rent				4,000
Other expenses				1,000
Interest expense on existing debt ($12,000 note and $150,000 in long-term debt)				
Taxes				
Purchase of equipment				
Loan repayment ($12,000 note due in May)				
Total disbursements:				$64,250
Net monthly change				$ (7,250)
Plus: Beginning cash balance				20,000
Less: Interest on short-term borrowing				—
Equals: Ending cash balance before short-term no borrowing				$12,750
Financing needed[a]				—
Ending cash balance				$12,750
Cumulative borrowing				—

[a]The amount of financing that is required to raise the firm's ending cash balance up to its $10,000 desired cash balance.

[b]Negative financing needed simply means the firm has excess cash that can be used to retire a part of its short-term borrowing from prior months.

SUMMARY

Objective 1   This chapter develops the role of forecasting within the context of the firm's financial-planning activities. Forecasts of the firm's sales revenues and related expenses provide the basis for projecting future financing needs. The most popular method for forecasting financial variables is the percent of sales method.

FEB.	MAR.	APR.	MAY	JUNE	JULY	AUG.
$75,000	$88,000	$100,000	$110,000	$100,000	$80,000	$75,000
18,000	22,500	26,400	30,000	33,000		
25,000	30,000	37,500	44,000	50,000		
12,400	10,000	12,000	15,000	17,600		
55,400	62,500	75,900	89,000	100,600		
75,000	82,500	75,000	60,000	56,250		
66,000	75,000	82,500	75,000	60,000		
55,400	62,500	75,900	89,000	100,600		
66,000	75,000	82,500	75,000	60,000		
10,000	7,000	8,000	6,000	4,000		
4,000	4,000	4,000	4,000	4,000		
500	1,200	1,500	1,500	1,200		
			600			
				7,500		
	4,460			5,200		
14,000						
			12,000			
94,500	91,660	96,000	99,100	81,900		
(39,100)	(29,160)	(20,100)	(10,100)	18,700		
12,750	10,000	10,000	10,000	10,000		
—	(364)	(659)	(866)	(976)		
(26,350)	(19,524)	(10,759)	(966)	27,724		
36,350	29,524	20,759	10,966	(17,724)[b]		
10,000	10,000	10,000	10,000	10,000		
36,350	65,874	86,633	97,599	79,875		

A firm's sustainable rate of growth is the maximum rate at which its sales can grow if it is to maintain its present financial ratios and not have to resort to issuing new equity. We calculate the sustainable rate of growth as follows:

Objective 2

$$\text{sustainable rate of growth } (g^*) = \text{ROE } (1 - b)$$

where ROE is the return earned on common equity and b is the dividend payout ratio (i.e., the ratio of dividends to earnings). Consequently, a firm's sustainable rate of growth increases with ROE and decreases with the fraction of its earnings paid out in dividends.

Objective 3
The percent of sales method presumes that the asset or liability being forecast is a constant percent of sales for all future levels of sales. There are instances when this assumption is not reasonable and consequently the percent of sales method does not provide reasonable predictions. One such instance arises when there are economies of scale in the use of the asset being forecast. For example, the firm may need at least $10 million in inventories to open its doors and operate even for sales as low as $100 million per year. If sales double to $200 million, inventories may only increase to $15 million. Thus, inventories do not increase with sales in a constant proportion. A second situation in which the percent of sales method fails to work properly is when asset purchases are lumpy. That is, if plant capacity must be purchased in $50 million increments, then plant and equipment will not remain a constant percent of sales.

How serious are these possible problems and should we use the percent of sales method? Even in the face of these problems, the percent of sales method predicts reasonably well when predicted sales levels do not differ drastically from the level used to calculate the percent of sales. For example, if the current sales level used in calculating percent of sales for inventories is $40 million, then we can feel more comfortable forecasting the level of inventories corresponding to a new sales level of $42 million than when sales are predicted to rise to $60 million.

Objective 4
The cash budget is the primary tool of financial forecasting and planning. It contains a detailed plan of future cash flow estimates and is comprised of four elements or segments: cash receipts, cash disbursements, net change in cash for the period, and new financing needed. Once prepared, the cash budget also serves as a tool for monitoring and controlling the firm's operations. By comparing actual cash receipts and disbursements to those in the cash budget, the financial manager can gain an appreciation for how well the firm is performing. In addition, deviations from the plan serve as an early warning system to signal the onset of financial difficulties ahead.

--- **KEY TERMS** ---

budget, 151	percent of sales method, 141
cash budget, 151	plowback ratio, 147
discretionary financing, 141	spontaneous financing, 141
external financing needs, 145	sustainable rate of growth, 147

--- **STUDY QUESTIONS** ---

5-1 Discuss the shortcomings of the percent of sales method of financial forecasting.
5-2 Explain how a fixed cash budget differs from a variable or flexible cash budget.
5-3 What two basic needs does a flexible (variable) cash budget serve?
5-4 What would be the probable effect on a firm's cash position of the following events?
    a. Rapidly rising sales
    b. A delay in the payment of payables
    c. A more liberal credit policy on sales (to the firm's customers)
    d. Holding larger inventories
5-5 How long should the budget period be? Why would a firm not set a rule that all budgets be for a 12-month period?
5-6 A cash budget is usually thought of as a means of planning for future financing needs. Why would a cash budget also be important for a firm that has excess cash on hand?

5-7 Explain why a cash budget would be of particular importance to a firm that experiences seasonal fluctuations in its sales.

─────────────────── SELF-TEST PROBLEMS ───────────────────

ST-1 *(Financial Forecasting)* Use the percent of sales method to prepare a pro forma income statement for Calico Sales Co., Inc. Projected sales for next year equal $4 million. Cost of goods sold equals 70 percent of sales, administrative expense equals $500,000, and depreciation expense is $300,000. Interest expense equals $50,000 and income is taxed at a rate of 40 percent. The firm plans to spend $200,000 during the period to renovate its office facility and will retire $150,000 in notes payable. Finally, selling expense equals 5 percent of sales.

ST-2 *(Cash Budget)* Stauffer, Inc., has estimated sales and purchase requirements for the last half of the coming year. Past experience indicates that it will collect 20 percent of its sales in the month of the sale, 50 percent of the remainder 1 month after the sale, and the balance in the second month following the sale. Stauffer prefers to pay for half its purchases in the month of the purchase and the other half the following month. Labor expense for each month is expected to equal 5 percent of that month's sales, with cash payment being made in the month in which the expense is incurred. Depreciation expense is $5,000 per month; miscellaneous cash expenses are $4,000 per month and are paid in the month incurred. General and administrative expenses of $50,000 are recognized and paid monthly. A $60,000 truck is to be purchased in August and is to be depreciated on a straight-line basis over 10 years with no expected salvage value. The company also plans to pay a $9,000 cash dividend to stockholders in July. The company feels that a minimum cash balance of $30,000 should be maintained. Any borrowing will cost 12 percent annually, with interest paid in the month following the month in which the funds are borrowed. Borrowing takes place at the beginning of the month in which the need for funds arises. For example, if during the month of July the firm should need to borrow $24,000 to maintain its $30,000 desired minimum balance, then $24,000 will be taken out on July 1 with interest owed for the entire month of July. Interest for the month of July would then be paid on August 1. Sales and purchase estimates are shown below. Prepare a cash budget for the months of July and August (cash on hand June 30 was $30,000, while sales for May and June were $100,000 and purchases were $60,000 for each of these months).

MONTH	SALES	PURCHASES
JULY	$120,000	$50,000
AUGUST	150,000	40,000
SEPTEMBER	110,000	30,000

─────────────────── STUDY PROBLEMS ───────────────────

5-1 *(Financial Forecasting)* Zapatera Enterprises is evaluating its financing requirements for the coming year. The firm has only been in business for 1 year, but its CFO predicts that the firm's operating expenses, current assets, net fixed assets, and current liabilities will remain at their current proportion of sales.

Last year Zapatera had $12 million in sales with net income of $1.2 million. The firm anticipates that next year's sales will reach $15 million with net income rising to $2 million. Given its present high rate of growth, the firm retains all its earnings to help defray the cost of new investments.

The firm's balance sheet for the year just ended is found below:

ZAPATERA INTERPRISES, INC.		
Balance Sheet		
	12/31/2000	% OF SALES
Current assets	$3,000,000	25%
Net fixed assets	6,000,000	50%
Total	$9,000,000	
Liabilities and Owners' Equity		
Accounts payable	$3,000,000	25%
Long-term debt	2,000,000	NAª
Total liabilities	$5,000,000	
Common stock	1,000,000	NA
Paid-in capital	1,800,000	NA
Retained earnings	1,200,000	
Common equity	4,000,000	
Total	$9,000,000	

ªNot applicable. This figure does not vary directly with sales and is assumed to remain constant for purposes of making next year's forecast of financing requirements.

Estimate Zapatera's total financing requirements (i.e., total assets) for 2001 and its net funding requirements (DFN).

MONTH	SALES	MONTH	SALES
January	$15,000	March	$30,000
February	20,000	April (projected)	40,000

5-2 *(Pro Forma Accounts Receivable Balance Calculation)* On March 31, 2000, the Sylvia Gift Shop had outstanding accounts receivable of $20,000. Sylvia's sales are roughly evenly split between credit and cash sales, with the credit sales collected half in the month after the sale and the remainder 2 months after the sale. Historical and projected sales for the gift shop are given below:
  a. Under these circumstances, what should the balance in accounts receivable be at the end of April?
  b. How much cash did Sylvia realize during April from sales and collections?

5-3 *(Financial Forecasting)* Sambonoza Enterprises projects its sales next year to be $4 million and expects to earn 5 percent of that amount after taxes. The firm is currently in the process of projecting its financing needs and has made the following assumptions (projections):
  1. Current assets will equal 20 percent of sales, while fixed assets will remain at their current level of $1 million.
  2. Common equity is currently $0.8 million, and the firm pays out half its after-tax earnings in dividends.
  3. The firm has short-term payables and trade credit that normally equal 10 percent of sales, and has no long-term debt outstanding.

What are Sambonoza's financing needs for the coming year?

5-4 *(Financial Forecasting—Percent of Sales)* Tulley Appliances, Inc., projects next year's sales to be $20 million. Current sales are at $15 million based on current assets of $5 million and fixed assets of $5 million. The firm's net profit margin is 5 percent after taxes. Tulley forecasts that current assets will rise in direct proportion to the increase in sales, but fixed assets will increase by only $100,000. Currently, Tulley has $1.5 million in accounts payable (which vary directly with sales), $2 million in long-term debt (due in 10 years), and common equity (including $4 million in retained earnings) totaling $6.5 million. Tulley plans to pay $500,000 in common stock dividends next year.

a. What are Tulley's total financing needs (i.e., total assets) for the coming year?

b. Given the firm's projections and dividend payment plans, what are its discretionary financing needs?

c. Based on your projections, and assuming that the $100,000 expansion in fixed assets will occur, what is the largest increase in sales the firm can support without having to resort to the use of discretionary sources of financing?

5-5 *(Pro Forma Balance Sheet Construction)* Use the following industry-average ratios to construct a pro forma balance sheet for Carlos Menza, Inc.

Total asset turnover	2 times
Average collection period (assume 365-day year)	9 days
Fixed asset turnover	5 times
Inventory turnover (based on cost of goods sold)	3 times
Current ratio	2 times
Sales (all on credit)	$4.0 million
Cost of goods sold	75% of sales
Debt ratio	50%

	Current liabilities	
Cash	Long-term debt	
Accounts receivable	Common stock plus	_____
Net fixed assets $_____	Retained earnings $_____	

5-6 *(Cash Budget)* The Sharpe Corporation's projected sales for the first 8 months of 2001 are as follows:

January	$ 90,000	May	$300,000
February	120,000	June	270,000
March	135,000	July	225,000
April	240,000	August	150,000

Of Sharpe's sales, 10 percent is for cash, another 60 percent is collected in the month following sales, and 30 percent is collected in the second month following sales. November and December sales for 2000 were $220,000 and $175,000, respectively.

Sharpe purchases its raw materials 2 months in advance of its sales equal to 60 percent of their final sales price. The supplier is paid 1 month after it makes delivery. For example, purchases for April sales are made in Febuary and payment is made in March.

In addition, Sharpe pays $10,000 per month for rent and $20,000 each month for other expenditures. Tax repayments of $22,500 are made each quarter, beginning in March.

The company's cash balance at December 31, 2000, was $22,000; a minimum balance to maintain the cash balance would be paid off in the month following the month of financing if sufficient funds are available. Interest on short-term loans (12 percent) is paid monthly. Borrowing to meet estimated monthly cash needs takes place at the beginning of the month. Thus, if in the month of April the firm expects to have a need for an additional $60,500, these funds would be borrowed at the beginning of April with interest of $605 ($.12 \times 1/12 \times $60,500$) owed for April and paid at the beginning of May.

    a. Prepare a cash budget for Sharpe covering the first 7 months of 2001.

    b. Sharpe has $200,000 in notes payable due in July that must be repaid or renegotiated for an extension. Will the firm have ample cash to repay the notes?

5-7 *(Percent of Sales Forecasting)* Which of the following accounts would most likely vary directly with the level of firm sales? Discuss each briefly.

	YES	NO		YES	NO
Cash	____	____	Notes payable	____	____
Marketable securities	____	____	Plant and equipment	____	____
Accounts payable	____	____	Inventories	____	____

5-8 *(Financing Forecasting—Percent of Sales)* The balance of the Thompson Trucking Company (TTC) follows:

THOMPSON TRUCKING COMPANY BALANCE SHEET, DECEMBER 31, 2000 ($ MILLIONS)			
Current assets	$10	Accounts payable	$ 5
Net fixed assets	15	Notes payable	0
Total	$25	Bonds payable	10
		Common equity	10
		Total	$25

TTC had sales for the year ended 12/31/2000 of $50 million. The firm follows a policy of paying all net earnings out to its common stockholders in cash dividends. Thus, TTC generates no funds from its earnings that can be used to expand its operations. (Assume that depreciation expense is just equal to the cost of replacing worn-out assets.)

    a. If TTC anticipates sales of $80 million during the coming year, develop a pro forma balance sheet for the firm for 12/31/01. Assume that current assets vary as a percent of sales, net fixed assets remain unchanged, accounts payable vary as a percent of sales, and use notes payable as a balancing entry.

    b. How much "new" financing will TTC need next year?

    c. What limitations does the percent of sales forecast method suffer from? Discuss briefly.

5-9 *(Financial Forecasting—Discretionary Financing Needs)* The most recent balance sheet for the Armadillo Dog Co. is shown in the following table. The company is about to embark on an advertising campaign, which is expected to raise sales from the current level of $5 million to $7 million by the end of next year. The firm is currently operating at full capacity and will have to increase its investment in both current and fixed assets to support the projected level of new sales. In fact, the firm estimates that both categories of assets will rise in direct proportion to the projected increase in sales.

ARMADILLO DOG BISCUIT CO., INC. ($ MILLIONS)			
	PRESENT LEVEL	PERCENT OF SALES	PROJECTED LEVEL
Current assets	$2.0		
Net fixed assets	3.0		
Total	$5.0		
Accounts payable	$0.5		
Accrued expense	0.5		
Noes payable	—		
Current liabilities	$1.0		
Long-term debt	$2.0		
Common stock	0.5		
Retained earnings	1.5		
Common equity	$2.0		
Total	$5.0		

The firm's net profits were 6 percent of the current year's sales but are expected to rise to 7 percent of next year's sales. To help support its anticipated growth in asset needs next year, the firm has suspended plans to pay cash dividends to its stockholders. In past years a $1.50 per share dividend has been paid annually.

Armadillo's payables and accrued expenses are expected to vary directly with sales. In addition, notes payable will be used to supply the funds needed to finance next year's operations and not forthcoming from other sources.

a. Fill in the table and project the firm's needs for discretionary financing. Use notes payable as the balancing entry for future discretionary financing needs.

b. Compare Armadillo's current ratio and debt ratio (total liabilities/total assets) before the growth in sales and after. What was the effect of the expanded sales on these two dimensions of Armadillo's financial condition?

c. What difference, if any, would have resulted if Armadillo's sales had risen to $6 million in 1 year and $7 million only after 2 years? Discuss only; no calculations required.

5-10 *(Forecasting Discretionary Financing Needs)* Fishing Charter, Inc., estimates that it invests 30¢ in assets for each dollar of new sales. However, 5¢ in profits are produced by each dollar of additional sales, of which 1¢ can be reinvested in the firm. If sales rise from their current level of $5 million by $500,000 next year, and the ratio of spontaneous liabilities to sales is 15¢, what will be the firm's need for discretionary financing? *(Hint:* In this situation you do not know what the firm's existing level of assets is, nor do you know how those assets have been financed. Thus you must estimate the change in financing needs and match this change with the expected changes in spontaneous liabilities, retained earnings, and other sources of discretionary financing.)

5-11 *(Preparation of a Cash Budget)* Harrison Printing has projected its sales for the first 8 months of 2001 as follows:

January	$100,000	April	$300,000	July	$200,000
February	120,000	May	275,000	August	180,000
March	150,000	June	200,000		

Harrison collects 20 percent of its sales in the month of the sale, 50 percent in the month following the sale, and the remaining 30 percent 2 months following the sale. During November and December of 2000 Harrison's sales were $220,000 and $175,000, respectively.

Harrison purchases raw materials 2 months in advance of its sales equal to 65 percent of its final sales. The supplier is paid 1 month after delivery. Thus, purchases for April sales are made in February and payment is made in March.

In addition, Harrison pays $10,000 per month for rent and $20,000 each month for other expenditures. Tax prepayments of $22,500 are made each quarter beginning in March. The company's cash balance as of December 31, 2000 was $22,000; a minimum balance of $20,000 must be maintained at all times to satisfy the firm's bank line of credit agreement. Harrison has arranged with its bank for short-term credit at an interest rate of 12 percent per annum (1 percent per month) to be paid monthly. Borrowing to meet estimated monthly cash needs takes place at the end of the month, and interest is not paid until the end of the following month. Consequently, if the firm were to need to borrow $50,000 during the month of April, then it would pay $500 (= .01 × $50,000) in interest during May. Finally, Harrison follows a policy of repaying its outstanding short-term debt in any month in which its cash balance exceeds the minimum desired balance of $20,000.

a. Harrison needs to know what its cash requirements will be for the next 6 months so that it can renegotiate the terms of its short-term credit agreement with its bank, if necessary. To evaluate this problem, the firm plans to evaluate the impact of a ± 20 percent variation in its monthly sales efforts. Prepare a 6-month cash budget for Harrison and use it to evaluate the firm's cash needs.

b. Harrison has a $20,000 note due in June. Will the firm have sufficient cash to repay the loan?

5-12 *(Sustainable Rate of Growth)* ADP, Inc., is a manufacturer of specialty circuit boards in the personal computer industry. The firm has experienced phenomenal sales growth over its short 5-year life. Selected financial statement data are found in the following table:

	2000	1999	1998	1997	1996
Sales	$3,000	$2,200	$1,800	$1,400	$1,200
Net income	150	110	90	70	60
Assets	2,700	1,980	1,620	1,260	1,080
Dividends	60	44	36	28	24
Common equity	812	722	656	602	560
Liabilities	1,888	1,258	964	658	520
Liabilities and equity	2,700	1,980	1,620	1,260	1,080

a. Calculate ADP's sustainable rate of growth for each of the 5 years of its existence.

b. Compare the actual rates of growth in sales to the firm's sustainable rates calculated in part a. How has ADP been financing its growing asset needs?

5-13 *(Sustainable Rate of Growth)* The Carrera Game Company has experienced a 100 percent increase in sales over the last 5 years. The company president, Jack Carrera, has become increasingly alarmed by the firm's rising debt level even in the face of continued profitability.

	2000	1999	1998	1997	1996
Sales	$60,000	$56,000	$48,000	$36,000	$30,000
Net income	3,000	2,800	2,400	1,800	1,500
Assets	54,000	50,400	43,200	32,400	27,000
Dividends	1,200	1,120	960	720	600
Common equity	21,000	19,200	17,520	16,080	15,000
Liabilities	33,000	31,200	25,680	16,320	12,000
Liabilities and equity	54,000	50,400	43,200	32,400	27,000

a. Calculate the debt-to-assets ratio, return on common equity, actual rate of growth in firm sales, and retention ratio for each of the 5 years of data provided above.

b. Calculate the sustainable rates of growth for Carrera for each of the last 5 years. Why has the firm's borrowing increased so dramatically?

5-14 *(Forecasting Inventories)* Findlay Instruments produces a complete line of medical instruments used by plastic surgeons and has experienced rapid growth over the last 5 years. In an effort to make more accurate predictions of its financing requirements, Findlay is currently attempting to construct a financial-planning model based on the percent of sales forecasting method. However, the firm's chief financial analyst (Sarah Macias) is concerned that the projections for inventories will be seriously in error. She recognizes that the firm has begun to accrue substantial economies of scale in its inventory investment and has documented this fact in the following data and calculations:

YEAR	SALES (000)	INVENTORY (000)	% OF SALES
1996	$15,000	1,150	7.67%
1997	18,000	1,180	6.56%
1998	17,500	1,175	6.71%
1999	20,000	1,200	6.00%
2000	25,000	1,250	5.00%
		Average	6.39%

a. Plot Findlay's sales and inventories for the last 5 years. What is the relationship between these two variables?

b. Estimate firm inventories for 2001 when firm sales are projected to reach $30 million. Use the average percent of sales for the last 5 years, the most recent percent of sales, and your evaluation of the true relationship between the sales and inventories from part a to make three predictions.

COMPREHENSIVE PROBLEM

Phillips Petroleum is an integrated oil and gas company with headquarters in Bartlesville, Oklahoma, where it was founded in 1917. The company engages in petroleum exploration and production worldwide. In addition, it engages in natural gas gathering and processing, as well as petroleum refining and marketing primarily in the United States. The company has three operating groups—Exploration and Production, Gas and Gas Liquids, and Downstream Operations, which encompasses Petroleum Products and Chemicals.

In the mid 1980s Phillips engaged in a major restructuring following two failed takeover attempts, one led by T. Boone Pickins and the other by Carl Ichan.* The restructuring resulted in a $4.5 billion plan to exchange a package of cash and debt securities for roughly half the company's shares and to sell $2 billion worth of assets. Phillip's long-term debt increased from $3.4 billion in late 1984 to a peak of $8.6 billion in April 1985.

During 1992 Phillips was able to strengthen its financial structure dramatically. Its subsidiary Phillips Gas Company completed an offering of $345 million of Series A 9.32% Cumulative Preferred Stock. As a result of these actions and prior year's debt reductions, the company lowered its long-term debt-to-capital ratio over the last 5 years from 75 percent to 55 percent. In addition, the firm refinanced over a billion dollars of its debt at reduced rates. A company spokesman said that "Our debt-to-capital ratio is still on the high side, and we'll keep working to bring it down. But the cost of debt is manageable, and we're beyond the point where debt overshadows everything else we do."[†]

---

*This discussion is based on a story in the *New York Times*, January 7, 1986.

[†]From *SEC Online*, 1992.

	1986	1987	1988	1989	1990	1991	1992
Sales	$10,018.00	$10,917.00	$11,490.00	$12,492.00	$13,975.00	$13,259.00	$12,140.00
Net income	228.00	35.00	650.00	219.00	541.00	98.00	270.00
EPS	0.89	0.06	2.72	0.90	2.18	0.38	1.04
Current assets	2,802.00	2,855.00	3,062.00	2,876.00	3,322.00	2,459.00	2,349.00
Total assets	12,403.00	12,111.00	11,968.00	11,256.00	12,130.00	11,473.00	11,468.00
Current liabilities	2,234.00	2,402.00	2,468.00	2,706.00	2,910.00	2,503.00	2,517.00
Long-term debt	8,175.00	7,887.00	7,387.00	6,418.00	6,505.00	6,113.00	5,894.00
Total liabilities	10,409.00	10,289.00	9,855.00	9,124.00	9,411.00	8,716.00	8,411.00
Preferred stock	270.00	205.00	0.00	0.00	0.00	0.00	359.00
Common equity	1,724.00	1,617.00	2,113.00	2,132.00	2,719.00	2,757.00	2,698.00
Dividends per share	2.02	1.73	1.34	0.00	1.03	1.12	1.12

Source: Phillips Annual Reports for the years 1986–1992.

Highlights of Phillips' financial condition spanning the years 1986–1992 are found in the accompanying table. These data reflect the modern history of the company as a result of its financial restructuring following the downsizing and reorganization of Phillips' operations begun in the mid-1980s.

Phillips' management is currently developing its financial plans for the next 5 years and wants to develop a forecast of its financing requirements. As a first approximation they have asked you to develop a model that can be used to make "ballpark" estimates of the firm's financing needs under the proviso that existing relationships found in the firm's financial statements remain the same over the period. Of particular interest is whether Phillips will be able to further reduce its reliance on debt financing. You may assume that Phillips' projected sales (in millions) for 1993 through 1997 are as follows: $13,000; $13,500; $14,000; $14,500; and $15,500.

a. Project net income for 1993–1997 using the percent of sales method based on an average of this ratio for 1986–1992.

b. Project total assets and current liabilities for the period 1993–1997 using the percent of sales method and your sales projections from part a.

c. Assuming that common equity increases only as a result of the retention of earnings and holding long-term debt and preferred stock equal to their 1992 balances, project Phillips' discretionary financing needs for 1993–1997. (*Hint:* Assume that total asset and current liabilities vary as a percent of sales as per your answers to part b above. In addition, assume that Phillips plans to continue to pay its dividends of $1.12 per share in each of the next 5 years.)

SS-1

CALICO SALES CO., INC., PRO FORMA INCOME STATEMENT		
Sales		$4,000,000
Cost of goods sold (70%)		(2,800,000)
Gross profit		1,200,000
Operating expense		
Selling expense (5%)	$200,000	
Administrative expense	500,000	
Depreciation expense	300,000	(1,000,000)
Net operating income		200,000
Interest		(50,000)
Earnings before taxes		150,000
Taxes (40%)		(60,000)
Net income		$90,000

Although the office renovation expenditure and debt retirement are surely cash outflows, they do not enter the income statement directly. These expenditures affect expenses for the period's income statement only through their effect on depreciation and interest expense. A cash budget would indicate the full cash impact of the renovation and debt retirement expenditures.

	MAY	JUNE	JULY	AUGUST
Sales	$100,000	$100,000	$120,000	$ 150,000
Purchases	60,000	60,000	50,000	40,000
Cash receipts:				
Collections from month of sale (20%)	20,000	20,000	24,000	30,000
1 month later (50% of uncollected amount)		40,000	40,000	48,000
2 months later (balance)			40,000	40,000
Total receipts			$ 104,000	$ 118,000
Cash disbursements:				
Payments for purchases—				
From 1 month earlier			$ 30,000	$ 25,000
From current month			$ 25,000	20,000
Total			$ 55,000	$ 45,000
Miscellaneous cash expenses			4,000	4,000
Labor expense (5% of sales)			6,000	7,500
General and administrative expense				
($50,000 per month)			50,000	50,000
Truck purchase			0	60,000
Cash dividends			9,000	—
Total disbursements			$(124,000)	$(166,500)
Net change in cash			(20,000)	(48,500)
Plus: beginning cash balance			30,000	30,000
Less: interest on short-term borrowing				
(1% prior month's borrowing)				(200)
Equals: ending cash balance—without borrowing			10,000	(18,700)
Financing needed to reach target cash balance			20,000	48,700
Cumulative borrowing			$ 20,000	$ 68,700

Compound Interest and Future Value • Present Value • Annuities • Annuities Due • Amortized Loans • Compound Interest with Nonannual Periods • Present Value of an Uneven Stream • Perpetuities • Finance and the Multinational Firm: The Time Value of Money

THE TIME VALUE OF MONEY

LEARNING OBJECTIVES

AFTER READING THIS CHAPTER, YOU SHOULD BE ABLE TO:

1. Explain the mechanics of compounding, that is, how money grows over time when it is invested.
2. Discuss the relationship between compounding and bringing money back to the present.
3. Define an ordinary annuity and calculate its compound or future value.
4. Differentiate between an ordinary annuity and an annuity due, and determine the future and present value of an annuity due.
5. Determine the future or present value of a sum when there are nonannual compounding periods.
6. Determine the present value of an uneven stream of payments.
7. Determine the present value of a perpetuity.
8. Explain how the international setting complicates the time value of money.

In business, there is probably no other single concept with more power or applications than that of the time value of money. In his landmark book, *A History of Interest Rates,* Sidney Homer noted that if $1,000 were invested for 400 years at 8 percent interest, it would grow to $23 quadrillion—that would work out to approximately $5 million per person on earth. He was not giving a plan to make the world rich, but effectively pointing out the power of the time value of money.

The time value of money is certainly not a new concept. Benjamin Franklin had a good understanding of how it worked when he left £1,000 each to Boston and Philadelphia. With the gift, he left instructions that the cities were to lend the money, charging the going interest rate, to worthy apprentices. Then, after the money had been invested in this way for 100 years, they were to use a portion of the investment to build something of benefit to the city and hold some back for the future. Two hundred years later, Franklin's Boston gift resulted in the construction of the Franklin Union, has helped countless medical students with loans, and still has over $3 million left in the account. Philadelphia, likewise, has reaped a significant reward from his gift. Bear in mind that all this has come from a gift of £2,000 with some serious help from the time value of money.

The power of the time value of money can also be illustrated through a story Andrew Tobias tells in his book *Money Angles.* There he tells of a peasant who wins a chess tournament put on by the king. The king then asks the peasant what he would like as the prize. The peasant answers that he would like for his village one piece of grain to be placed on the first square of his chessboard, two pieces of grain on the second square, four pieces on the third, eight on the fourth, and so forth. The king, thinking he was getting off easy, pledged on his word of honor that it would be done. Unfortunately for the king, by the time all 64 squares on the chessboard were filled, there were 18.5 million trillion grains of wheat on the board—the kernels were compounding at a rate of 100 percent over the 64 squares of the chessboard. Needless to say, no one in the village ever went hungry, in fact, that is so much wheat that if the kernels were one-quarter inch long (quite frankly, I have no idea how long a kernel of wheat is, but Andrew Tobias' guess is one-quarter inch), if laid end to end, they could stretch to the sun and back 391,320 times.

Understanding the techniques of compounding and moving money through time are critical to almost every business decision. It will help you to understand such varied things as how stocks and bonds are valued, how to determine the value of a new project, how much you should save for children's education, and how much your mortgage payments will be.

WHAT'S AHEAD

In the next five chapters, we focus on determining the value of the firm and the desirability of investment proposals. A key concept that underlies this material is the *time value of money;* that is, a dollar today is worth more than a dollar received a year from now. Intuitively this idea is easy to understand. We are all familiar with the concept of interest. This concept illustrates what economists call an *opportunity cost* of passing up the earning potential of a dollar today. This opportunity cost is the time value of money.

In evaluating and comparing investment proposals, we need to examine how dollar values might accrue from accepting these proposals. To do this, all dollar values must first be comparable; because a dollar received today is worth more than a dollar received in the future, we must move all dollar flows back to the present or out to a common future date. An understanding of the time value of money is essential, therefore, to an understanding of financial management, whether basic or advanced.

BACK TO THE FOUNDATIONS

In this chapter we develop the tools to incorporate **Axiom 2: The Time Value of Money— A Dollar Received Today Is Worth More Than a Dollar Received in the Future** into our calculations. In coming chapters we use this concept to measure value by bringing the benefits and costs from a project back to the present.

Objective 1

COMPOUND INTEREST AND FUTURE VALUE

Most of us encounter the concept of compound interest at an early age. Anyone who has ever had a savings account or purchased a government savings bond has received compound interest. **Compound interest** occurs when *interest paid on the investment*

compound interest

during the first period is added to the principal; then, during the second period, interest is earned on this new sum.

For example, suppose we place $100 in a savings account that pays 6 percent interest, compounded annually. How will our savings grow? At the end of the first year we have earned 6 percent, or $6 on our initial deposit of $100, giving us a total of $106 in our savings account. The mathematical formula illustrating this phenomenon is

$$FV_1 = PV(1 + i) \qquad\qquad (6\text{--}1)$$

where FV_1 = the future value of the investment at the end of one year
i = the annual interest (or discount) rate
PV = the present value, or original amount invested at the beginning of the first year

In our example

$$
\begin{aligned}
FV_1 &= PV(1 + i) \\
&= \$100(1 + .06) \\
&= \$100(1.06) \\
&= \$106
\end{aligned}
$$

Carrying these calculations one period further, we find that we now earn the 6 percent interest on a principal of $106, which means we earn $6.36 in interest during the second year. Why do we earn more interest during the second year than we did during the first? Simply because we now earn interest on the sum of the original principal, or present value, and the interest we earned in the first year. In effect we are now earning interest on interest; this is the concept of compound interest. Examining the mathematical formula illustrating the earning of interest in the second year, we find

$$FV_2 = FV_1(1 + i) \qquad\qquad (6\text{--}2)$$

which, for our example, gives

$$
\begin{aligned}
FV_2 &= \$106(1.06) \\
&= \$112.36
\end{aligned}
$$

Looking back at equation (6–1), we can see that FV_1, or $106, is actually equal to $PV(1 + i)$, or $100(1 + .06)$. If we substitute these values into equation (6–2), we get

$$
\begin{aligned}
FV_2 &= PV(1 + i)(1 + i) \\
&= PV(1 + i)^2 \qquad\qquad (6\text{--}3)
\end{aligned}
$$

Carrying this forward into the third year, we find that we enter the year with $112.36 and we earn 6 percent, or $6.74 in interest, giving us a total of $119.10 in our savings account. Expressing this mathematically:

$$
\begin{aligned}
FV_3 &= FV_2(1 + i) \\
&= \$112.36(1.06) \\
&= \$119.10 \qquad\qquad (6\text{--}4)
\end{aligned}
$$

If we substitute the value in equation (6–3) for FV_2 into equation (6–4), we find

$$
\begin{aligned}
FV_3 &= PV(1 + i)(1 + i)(1 + i) \\
&= PV(1 + i)^3 \qquad\qquad (6\text{--}5)
\end{aligned}
$$

By now a pattern is becoming apparent. We can generalize this formula to illustrate the value of our investment if it is compounded annually at a rate of i for n years to be

$$FV_n = PV(1 + i)^n \qquad (6\text{--}6)$$

where FV_n = the future value of the investment at the end of n years
n = the number of years during which the compounding occurs
i = the annual interest (or discount) rate
PV = the present value or original amount invested at the beginning of the first year

Table 6–1 illustrates how this investment of $100 would continue to grow for the first 10 years at a compound interest rate of 6 percent. Notice how the amount of interest earned annually increases each year. Again, the reason is that each year interest is received on the sum of the original investment plus any interest earned in the past.

When we examine the relationship between the number of years an initial investment is compounded for and its future value as shown graphically in figure 6–1, we see that we can increase the future value of an investment by either increasing the number of years for which we let it compound or by compounding it at a higher interest rate. We can also see this from equation (6–6) because an increase in either i or n while PV is held constant results in an increase in FV_n.

PAUSE AND REFLECT

Keep in mind that future cash flows are assumed to occur at the end of the time period during which they accrue. For example, if a cash flow of $100 occurs in time period 5, it is assumed to occur at the end of time period 5, which is also the beginning of time period 6. In addition, cash flows that occur in time $t = 0$ occur right now; that is, they are already in present dollars.

TABLE 6-1 **ILLUSTRATION OF COMPOUND INTEREST CALCULATIONS**

YEAR	BEGINNING VALUE	INTEREST EARNED	ENDING VALUE
1	$100.00	$6.00	$106.00
2	106.00	6.36	112.36
3	112.36	6.74	119.10
4	119.10	7.15	126.25
5	126.25	7.57	133.82
6	133.82	8.03	141.85
7	141.85	8.51	150.36
8	150.36	9.02	159.38
9	159.38	9.57	168.95
10	168.95	10.13	179.08

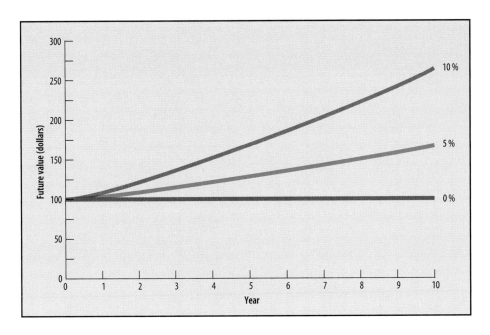

Example

If we place $1,000 in a savings account paying 5 percent interest compounded annually, how much will our account accrue to in 10 years? Substituting $PV = \$1,000$, $i = 5$ percent, and $n = 10$ years into equation (6–6), we get

$$
\begin{aligned}
FV_n &= PV(1 + i)^n \\
&= \$1,000(1 + .05)^{10} \\
&= \$1,000(1.62889) \\
&= \$1,628.89
\end{aligned}
\tag{6-6}
$$

Thus, at the end of 10 years we will have $1,628.89 in our savings account.

Because determining future value can be quite time-consuming when an investment is held for a number of years, the **future-value interest factor** for i and n **($FVIF_{i,n}$)** defined as $(1 + i)^n$, has been compiled in the back of the book for various values of i and n. An abbreviated compound interest or future-value interest factor table appears in Table 6–2, with a more comprehensive version of this table appearing in Appendix B at the back of this book. Alternatively, the $FVIF_{i,n}$ values could easily be determined using a calculator. Note that the compounding factors given in these tables represent the value of $1 compounded at rate i at the *end* of the nth year. Thus, to calculate the future value of an initial investment we need only to determine the $FVIF_{i,n}$ using a calculator or the tables at the end of the text and multiply this times the initial investment. In effect, we can rewrite equation (6–6) as follows:

future-value interest factor

$$
FV_n = PV(FVIF_{i,n})
\tag{6-6a}
$$

Example

If we invest $500 in a bank where it will earn 8 percent compounded annually, how much will it be worth at the end of 7 years? Looking at Table 6–2 in the row $n = 7$ and column $i = 8$ percent, we find that $FVIF_{8\%, 7 \text{ yr}}$ has a value of 1.714. Substituting this into equation (6–6a), we find

TABLE 6–2

$FVIF_{i,n}$, or the Compound Sum of $1

N	1%	2%	3%	4%	5%	6%	7%	8%	9%	10%
1	1.010	1.020	1.030	1.040	1.050	1.060	1.070	1.080	1.090	1.100
2	1.020	1.040	1.061	1.082	1.102	1.124	1.145	1.166	1.188	1.210
3	1.030	1.061	1.093	1.125	1.158	1.191	1.225	1.260	1.295	1.331
4	1.041	1.082	1.126	1.170	1.216	1.262	1.311	1.360	1.412	1.464
5	1.051	1.104	1.159	1.217	1.276	1.338	1.403	1.469	1.539	1.611
6	1.062	1.126	1.194	1.265	1.340	1.419	1.501	1.587	1.677	1.772
7	1.072	1.149	1.230	1.316	1.407	1.504	1.606	1.714	1.828	1.949
8	1.083	1.172	1.267	1.369	1.477	1.594	1.718	1.851	1.993	2.144
9	1.094	1.195	1.305	1.423	1.551	1.689	1.838	1.999	2.172	2.358
10	1.105	1.219	1.344	1.480	1.629	1.791	1.967	2.159	2.367	2.594
11	1.116	1.243	1.384	1.539	1.710	1.898	2.105	2.332	2.580	2.853
12	1.127	1.268	1.426	1.601	1.796	2.012	2.252	2.518	2.813	3.138
13	1.138	1.294	1.469	1.665	1.886	2.133	2.410	2.720	3.066	3.452
14	1.149	1.319	1.513	1.732	1.980	2.261	2.579	2.937	3.342	3.797
15	1.161	1.346	1.558	1.801	2.079	2.397	2.759	3.172	3.642	4.177

$$FV_n = PV(FVIF_{8\%, \, 7 \, \text{yr}})$$
$$= \$500(1.714)$$
$$= \$857$$

Thus, we will have $857 at the end of 7 years.

In the future we will find several uses for equation (6–6); not only can we find the future value of an investment, but we can also solve for PV, i, or n. In any case, you will be given three of the four variables and will have to solve for the fourth. ■

PAUSE AND REFLECT

As you read through the chapter it is a good idea to solve the problems as they are presented. If you just read the problems, the principles behind them often do not sink in. The material presented in this chapter forms the basis for the rest of the course; therefore, a good command of the concepts underlying the time value of money is extremely important.

Example

Let's assume that the DaimlerChrysler Corporation has guaranteed that the price of a new Jeep will always be $20,000, and you'd like to buy one but currently have only $7,752. How many years will it take for your initial investment of $7,752 to grow to $20,000 if it is invested at 9 percent compounded annually? We can use equation (6–6a) to solve for this problem as well. Substituting the known values in equation (6–6a), you find

$$FV_n = PV(FVIF_{i,n})$$

$$\$20,000 = \$7,752(FVIF_{9\%, \, n \, \text{yr}})$$

$$\frac{\$20,000}{\$7,752} = \frac{\$7,752(FVIF_{9\%, \, n \, \text{yr}})}{\$7,752}$$

$$2.58 = FVIF_{9\%, \, n \, \text{yr}}$$

Thus you are looking for a value of 2.58 in the $FVIF_{i,n}$ tables, and you know it must be in the 9% column. To finish solving the problem, look down the 9% column for the value closest to 2.58. You find that it occurs in the $n = 11$ row. Thus it will take 11 years for an initial investment of $7,752 to grow to $20,000 if it is invested at 9 percent compounded annually.

Example

Now let's solve for the compound annual growth rate, and let's go back to that Jeep that always costs $20,000. In 10 years, you'd really like to have $20,000 to buy a new Jeep, but you only have $11,167. At what rate must your $11,167 be compounded annually for it to grow to $20,000 in 10 years? Substituting the known variables into equation (6–6a), you get

$$FV_n = PV(FVIF_{i,n})$$
$$\$20,000 = \$11,167(FVIF_{i,\ 10\ yr})$$
$$\frac{\$20,000}{\$11,167} = \frac{\$11,167\ (FVIF_{i,\ 10\ yr})}{\$11,167}$$
$$1.791 = FVIF_{i,\ 10\ yr}$$

You know to look in the $n = 10$ row of the $FVIF_{i,n}$ tables for a value of 1.791, and you find this in the $i = 6\%$ column. Thus if you want your initial investment of $11,167 to grow to $20,000 in 10 years, you must invest it at 6 percent.

Example

At what rate must $100 be compounded annually for it to grow to $179.10 in 10 years? In this case we know the initial investment, $PV = \$100$; the future value of this investment at the end of n years, $FV_n = \$179.10$; and the number of years that the initial investment will compound for, $n = 10$ years. Substituting into equation (6–6), we get

$$FV_n = PV(1 + i)^n$$
$$\$179.10 = \$100(1 + i)^{10}$$
$$1.791 = (1 + i)^{10} \tag{6–6}$$

We know to look in the $n = 10$ row of the $FVIF_{i,n}$ table for a value of 1.791, and we find this in the $i = 6$ percent column. Thus, if we want our initial investment of $100 to accrue to $179.10 in 10 years, we must invest it at 6 percent.

Just how powerful is the time value of money? Manhattan Island was purchased by Peter Minuit from the Indians in 1624 for $24 in "knickknacks" and jewelry. If at the end of 1624 the Indians had invested their $24 at 8 percent compounded annually, it would be worth over $88.6 trillion today (by the end of 2000, 376 years later). That's certainly enough to buy back all of Manhattan—in fact, with $88 trillion in the bank, the $70 to $80 billion you'd have to pay to buy back all of Manhattan would seem like pocket change. This story illustrates the incredible power of time in compounding. There simply is no substitute for it.

Moving Money Through Time with the Aid of a Financial Calculator

Time value of money calculations can be made simple with the aid of a *financial calculator*. In solving time value of money problems with a financial calculator, you will be given three of four variables and will have to solve for the fourth. Before presenting any solutions using a financial calculator, we introduce the calculator's five most common keys. (In most time value of money problems, only four of these keys are relevant.) These keys are:

Takin' It to the Net
There are a number of calculators on the Internet aimed at not only moving money through time, but also solving other problems that involve the time value of money. One great site for financial calculators is Kiplinger Online Calculators http://www.kiplinger.com/calc/calchome.html.

MENU KEY	DESCRIPTION
N	Stores (or calculates) the total number of payments or compounding periods.
I/Y	Stores (or calculates) the interest or discount rate.
PV	Stores (or calculates) the present value of a cash flow or series of cash flows.
FV	Stores (or calculates) the future value, that is, the dollar amount of a final cash flow or the compound value of a single flow or series of cash flows.
PMT	Stores (or calculates) the dollar amount of each annuity payment deposited or received at the end of each year.

When you use a financial calculator, remember that outflows generally have to be entered as negative numbers. In general, each problem will have two cash flows: one an outflow with a negative value, and one an inflow with a positive value. The idea is that you deposit money in the bank at some point in time (an outflow), and at some other point in time you take money out of the bank (an inflow). Also, every calculator operates a bit differently with respect to entering variables. Needless to say, it is a good idea to familiarize yourself with exactly how your calculator functions.

Takin' It to the Net
Another excellent site that provides financial calculators is Money Advisors http://www.moneyadvisor.com/calc/. This site has, among other things, a loan calculator, retirement spending calculator, present value calculator, and calculators for future value of an annuity calculation.

As previously stated, in any problem you will be given three of four variables. These four variables will always include N and I/Y; in addition, two out of the final three variables—PV, FV, and PMT—will also be included. To solve a time value of money problem using a financial calculator, all you need to do is enter the appropriate numbers for three of the four variables and then press the key of the final variable to calculate its value. It is also a good idea to enter zero for any of the five variables not included in the problem in order to clear that variable.

Now let's solve the previous example using a financial calculator. We were trying to find at what rate $100 must be compounded annually for it to grow to $179.10 in 10 years. The solution using a financial calculator would be as follows:

Step 1: Input Values of Known Variables		
DATA INPUT	FUNCTION KEY	DESCRIPTION
10	N	Stores N = 10 years
−100	PV	Stores PV = −$100
179.10	FV	Stores FV = $179.10
0	PMT	Clears PMT to = 0
Step 2: Calculate the Value of the Unknown Variable		
FUNCTION KEY	ANSWER	DESCRIPTION
CPT		
I/Y	6.00%	Calculates I/Y = 6.00%

Any of the problems in this chapter can easily be solved using a financial calculator; and the solutions to many examples using a Texas Instruments BAII Plus financial calculator are provided in the margins. If you are using the TI BAII Plus, make sure that you have selected both the "END MODE" and "one payment per year" (P/Y = 1). This sets the payment conditions to a maximum of one payment per period occurring at the end of the period. One final point, you will notice that solutions using the present-value tables versus solutions using a calculator may vary slightly—a result of rounding errors in the tables.

For further explanation of the TI BAII Plus, see Appendix A at the end of the book.

Obviously, the choice of the interest rate plays a critical role in how much an investment grows, but do small changes in the interest rate have much of an impact on future values? To answer this question, let's look back to Peter Minuit's purchase of Manhattan. If the Indians had invested their $24 at 10 percent rather than 8 percent compounded annually at the end of 1624, they would have over $88 quadrillion by the end of 2000 (376 years later). That is 88 followed by 15 zeros or $88,000,000,000,000,000. Actually, that is enough to buy back not only Manhattan Island, but the entire world and still have plenty left over! Now let's assume a lower interest rate—say 6 percent. In that case the $24 would have only grown to a mere $78.6 billion—less than one–one hundedth of what it grew to at 8 percent, and less than one-millionth of what it would have grown to at 10 percent. With today's real estate prices, you'd have a tough time buying Manhattan, and if you did, you probably couldn't pay your taxes! To say the least, the interest rate is extremely important in investing.

CONCEPT CHECK

1. Axiom 2 states that "a dollar received today is worth more than a dollar received in the future," explain this statement.
2. How does compound interest differ from simple interest?
3. Explain the formula $FV_n = PV(1 + i)^n$

PRESENT VALUE

Up to this point we have been moving money forward in time; that is, we know how much we have to begin with and are trying to determine how much that sum will grow in a certain number of years when compounded at a specific rate. We are now going to look at the reverse question: What is the value in today's dollars of a sum of money to be received in the future? The answer to this question will help us determine the desirability of investment projects in Chapters 10 and 11. In this case we are moving future money back to the present. We will determine the **present value** of a lump sum, which in simple terms is the *current value of a future payment*. In fact, we will be doing nothing other than inverse compounding. The differences in these techniques come about merely from the investor's point of view. In compounding we talked about the compound interest rate and the initial investment; in determining the present value we will talk about the discount rate and present value of future cash flows. Determination of the discount rate is the subject of Chapter 12 and can be defined as the rate of return available on an investment of equal risk to what is being discounted. Other than that, the technique and the terminology remain the same, and the mathematics are simply reversed. In equation (6–6) we were attempting to

present value

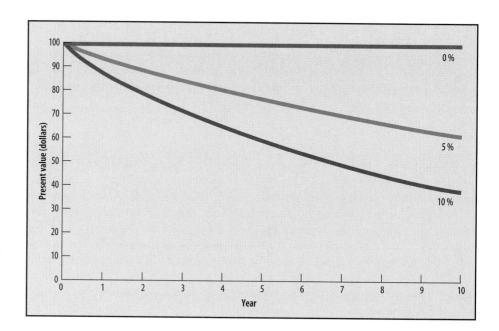

FIGURE 6-2

Present Value of $100 to Be Received at a Future Date and Discounted Back to the Present at 0, 5, and 10 Percent

determine the future value of an initial investment. We now want to determine the initial investment or present value. By dividing both sides of equation (6–6) by $(1 + i)^n$, we get

$$PV = FV_n \left[\frac{1}{(1 + i)^n} \right]$$

(6–7)

where FV_n = the future value of the investment at the end of n years
n = the number of years until the payment will be received
i = the annual discount (or interest) rate
PV = the present value of the future sum of money

Because the mathematical procedure for determining the present value is exactly the inverse of determining the future value, we also find that the relationships among n, i, and PV are just the opposite of those we observed in future value. The present value of a future sum of money is inversely related to both the number of years until the payment will be received and the discount rate. This relationship is shown in Figure 6–2.

PAUSE AND REFLECT

Although the present value equation [equation (6–7)] is used extensively in evaluating new investment proposals, it should be stressed that the present value equation is actually the same as the future value or compounding equation [equation (6–6)], where it is solved for *PV*.

Example

What is the present value of $500 to be received 10 years from today if our discount rate is 6 percent? Substituting $FV_{10} = \$500$, $n = 10$, and $i = 6$ percent into equation (6–7), we find

TABLE 6-3

N	1%	2%	3%	4%	5%	6%	7%	8%	9%	10%
1	.990	.980	.971	.962	.952	.943	.935	.926	.917	.909
2	.980	.961	.943	.925	.907	.890	.873	.857	.842	.826
3	.971	.942	.915	.889	.864	.840	.816	.794	.772	.751
4	.961	.924	.888	.855	.823	.792	.763	.735	.708	.683
5	.951	.906	.863	.822	.784	.747	.713	.681	.650	.621
6	.942	.888	.837	.790	.746	.705	.666	.630	.596	.564
7	.933	.871	.813	.760	.711	.655	.623	.583	.547	.513
8	.923	.853	.789	.731	.677	.627	.582	.540	.502	.467
9	.914	.837	.766	.703	.645	.592	.544	.500	.460	.424
10	.905	.820	.744	.676	.614	.558	.508	.463	.422	.386
11	.896	.804	.722	.650	.585	.527	.475	.429	.388	.350
12	.887	.789	.701	.625	.557	.497	.444	.397	.356	.319
13	.879	.773	.681	.601	.530	.469	.415	.368	.326	.290
14	.870	.758	.661	.577	.505	.442	.388	.340	.299	.263
15	.861	.743	.642	.555	.481	.417	.362	.315	.275	.239

TABLE 6-3 $PVIF_{i,n}$, or the Present Value of $1

$$PV = \$500 \left[\frac{1}{(1 + .06)^{10}} \right]$$

$$= \$500 \left(\frac{1}{1.791} \right)$$

$$= \$500(.558)$$

$$= \$279$$

Thus, the present value of the $500 to be received in 10 years is $279.

To aid in the computation of present values, the **present-value interest factor** for i and n (**$PVIF_{i,n}$**), defined as $[1/(1 + i)^n]$, has been compiled for various combinations of i and n and appears in Appendix C at the back of this book. An abbreviated version of Appendix C appears in Table 6–3. A close examination shows that the values in Table 6–3 are merely the inverse of those found in Table 6–2 and Appendix B. This, of course, is as it should be because the values in Appendix B are $(1 + i)^n$ and those in Appendix C are $[1/(1 + i)^n]$. Now, to determine the present value of a sum of money to be received at some future date, we need only determine the value of the appropriate $PVIF_{i,n}$, either by using a calculator or consulting the tables, and multiply it by the future value. In effect we can use our new notation and rewrite equation (6–7) as follows:

$$PV = FV_n(PVIF_{i,n}) \tag{6–7a}$$

present-value interest factor

CALCULATOR SOLUTION

Data Input	Function Key
10	N
6	1/Y
100	FV
0	PMT

Function Key	Answer
CPT	
PV	−55.84

Example

You're on vacation in a rather remote part of Florida and see an advertisement stating that if you take a sales tour of some condominiums "you will be given $100 just for taking the tour." However, the $100 that you get is in the form of a savings bond that will not pay you the $100 for 10 years. What is the present value of $100 to be received 10 years from today if your discount rate is 6 percent? By looking at the $n = 10$ row and $i = 6\%$ column of Table 6–3, you find the

$PVIF_{6\%, \ 10 \ yr}$ is .558. Substituting $FV_{10} = \$100$ and $PVIF_{6\%, \ 10 \ yr} = .558$ into equation (6–7a), you find

$$PV = \$100 \ (PVIF_{6\%, \ 10 \ yr})$$
$$= \$100(.558)$$
$$= \$55.80$$

Thus, the value in today's dollars of that $100 savings bond is only $55.80.

Dealing with Multiple, Uneven Cash Flows

Again, we only have one present-value–future-value equation; that is, equations (6–6) and (6–7) are identical. We have introduced them as separate equations to simplify our calculations; in one case we are determining the value in future dollars and in the other case the value in today's dollars. In either case the reason is the same: to compare values on alternative investments and to recognize that the value of a dollar received today is not the same as that of a dollar received at some future date. We must measure the dollar values in dollars of the same time period. For example, if we looked at these projects, one that promised $1,000 in 1 year, one that promised $1,500 in 5 years, and one that promised $2,500 in 10 years, the concept of present value allows us to bring their flows back to the present and make those projects comparable. Moreover, because all present values are comparable (they are all measured in dollars of the same time period), we can add and subtract the present value of inflows and outflows to determine the present value of an investment. Let's now look at an example of an investment that has two cash flows in different time periods and determine the present value of this investment.

Example

What is the present value of an investment that yields $500 to be received in 5 years and $1,000 to be received in 10 years if the discount rate is 4 percent? Substituting the values of $n = 5$, $i = 4$ percent, and $FV_5 = \$500$; and $n = 10$, $i = 4$ percent, and $FV_{10} = \$1,000$ into equation (6–7) and adding these values together, we find

$$PV = \$500 \left[\frac{1}{(1 \ + \ .04)^5} \right] + \$1,000 \left[\frac{1}{(1 \ + \ .04)^{10}} \right]$$
$$= \$500(PVIF_{4\%, \ 5 \ yr}) + \$1,000(PVIF_{4\%, \ 10 \ yr})$$
$$= \$500(.822) + \$1,000(.676)$$
$$= \$411 + \$676$$
$$= \$1,087$$

CONCEPT CHECK

1. What is the relationship between the present value equation (6–7) and the future value or compounding equation (6–6)?
2. Why is the present value of a future sum always less than that sum's future value?

Again, present values are comparable because they are measured in the same time period's dollars.

ANNUITIES

Objective 3

An **annuity** is a *series of equal dollar payments for a specified number of years.* When we talk about annuities we are referring to **ordinary annuities** unless otherwise noted. With an ordinary annuity *the payments occur at the end of each period.* Because annuities occur frequently in finance—for example, as bond interest payments—we treat them specially. Although compounding and determining the present value of an annuity can be dealt with using the methods we have just described, these processes can be time-consuming, especially for larger annuities. Thus, we have modified the formulas to deal directly with annuities.

annuity
ordinary annuities

Compound Annuities

A **compound annuity** involves *depositing or investing an equal sum of money at the end of each year for a certain number of years and allowing it to grow.* Perhaps we are saving money for education, a new car, or a vacation home. In any case we want to know how much our savings will have grown by some point in the future.

compound annuity

Actually, we can find the answer by using equation (6–6), our compounding equation, and compounding each of the individual deposits to its future value. For example, if to provide for a college education we are going to deposit $500 at the end of each year for the next 5 years in a bank where it will earn 6 percent interest, how much will we have at the end of 5 years? Compounding each of these values using equation (6–6), we find that we will have $2,818.50 at the end of 5 years.

Takin' It to the Net
USA Today also has a selection of on-line calculators http://www.usatoday.com/money /calculat/mcfront.htm aimed at helping you with all kinds of personal finance questions involving the time value of money.

$$FV_5 = \$500(1 + .06)^4 + \$500(1 + .06)^3 + \$500(1 + .06)^2$$
$$+ \$500(1 + .06) + \$500$$

$$= \$500(1.262) + \$500(1.191) + \$500(1.124)$$
$$+ \$500(1.060) + \$500$$

$$= \$631.00 + \$595.50 + \$562.00 + \$530.00 + \$500.00$$
$$= \$2,818.50$$

From examining the mathematics involved and the graph of the movement of money through time in Table 6–4, we can see that this procedure can be generalized to

$$FV_n = PMT \left[\sum_{t=0}^{n-1} (1 + i)^t \right] \qquad (6\text{–}8)$$

where FV_n = the future value of the annuity at the end of the nth year
PMT = the annuity payment deposited or received at the end of each year
i = the annual interest (or discount) rate
n = the number of years for which the annuity will last

To aid in compounding annuities, the **future-value interest factor for an annuity** for i and n (**$FVIFA_{i,n}$**), defined as $\left[\sum_{t=0}^{n-1} (1 + i)^t \right]$, is provided in Appendix D for various combinations of n and i; an abbreviated version is shown in Table 6–5.[1]

future-value interest factor for an annuity

---

[1]Another useful analytical relationship for FV_n is $FV_n = PMT[(1 + i)^n - 1]/i$.

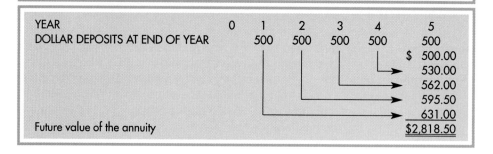

TABLE 6-4	ILLUSTRATION OF A 5-YEAR $500 ANNUITY COMPOUNDED AT 6 PERCENT

YEAR	0	1	2	3	4	5
DOLLAR DEPOSITS AT END OF YEAR		500	500	500	500	500
						$ 500.00
						530.00
						562.00
						595.50
						631.00
Future value of the annuity						$2,818.50

CALCULATOR SOLUTION

Data Input	Function Key
5	N
6	I/Y
0	PV
500	PMT
Function Key	Answer
CPT	
FV	−2,818.55

Using this new notation, we can rewrite equation (6–8) as follows:

$$FV_n = PMT\,(FVIFA_{i,n}) \qquad \text{(6–8a)}$$

Reexamining the previous example, in which we determined the value after 5 years of $500 deposited in the bank at 6 percent at the end of each of the next 5 years, we would look in the $i = 6$ percent column and $n = 5$ row and find the value of the $FVIFA_{6\%,\,5\,yr}$ to be 5.637. Substituting this value into equation (6–8a), we get

$$FV_5 = \$500(5.637)$$
$$= \$2,818.50$$

This is the same answer we obtained earlier using equation (6–6).

Rather than ask how much we will accumulate if we deposit an equal sum in a savings account each year, a more common question is how much we must

TABLE 6-5	$FVIFA_{i,n}$, OR THE SUM OF AN ANNUITY OF $1 FOR n YEARS

N	1%	2%	3%	4%	5%	6%	7%	8%	9%	10%
1	1.000	1.000	1.000	1.000	1.000	1.000	1.000	1.000	1.000	1.000
2	2.010	2.020	2.030	2.040	2.050	2.060	2.070	2.080	2.090	2.100
3	3.030	3.060	3.091	3.122	3.152	3.184	3.215	3.246	3.278	3.310
4	4.060	4.122	4.184	4.246	4.310	4.375	4.440	4.506	4.573	4.641
5	5.101	5.204	5.309	5.416	5.526	5.637	5.751	5.867	5.985	6.105
6	6.152	6.308	6.468	6.633	6.802	6.975	7.153	7.336	7.523	7.716
7	7.214	7.434	7.662	7.898	8.142	8.394	8.654	8.923	9.200	9.487
8	8.286	8.583	8.892	9.214	9.549	9.897	10.260	10.637	11.028	11.436
9	9.368	9.755	10.159	10.583	11.027	11.491	11.978	12.488	13.021	13.579
10	10.462	10.950	11.464	12.006	12.578	13.181	13.816	14.487	15.193	15.937
11	11.567	12.169	12.808	13.486	14.207	14.972	15.784	16.645	17.560	18.531
12	12.682	13.412	14.192	15.026	15.917	16.870	17.888	18.977	20.141	21.384
13	13.809	14.680	15.618	16.627	17.713	18.882	20.141	21.495	22.953	24.523
14	14.947	15.974	17.086	18.292	19.598	21.015	22.550	24.215	26.019	27.975
15	16.097	17.293	18.599	20.023	21.578	23.276	25.129	27.152	29.361	31.772

deposit each year to accumulate a certain amount of savings. This problem frequently occurs with respect to saving for large expenditures and pension funding obligations.

For example, we may know that we need $10,000 for education in 8 years; how much must we deposit in the bank at the end of each year at 6 percent interest to have the college money ready? In this case we know the values of n, i, and FV_n in equation (6–8); what we do not know is the value of PMT. Substituting these example values in equation (6–8), we find

$$\$10{,}000 = \left[PMT \sum_{t=0}^{8-1} (1 + .06)^t \right]$$

$$\$10{,}000 = PMT(FVIFA_{6\%,\ 8\ yr})$$

$$\$10{,}000 = PMT(9.897)$$

$$\frac{\$10{,}000}{\$9.897} = PMT$$

$$\$1{,}010.41 = PMT$$

Thus, we must deposit $1,010.41 in the bank at the end of each year for 8 years at 6 percent interest to accumulate $10,000 at the end of 8 years.

Example

How much must we deposit in an 8 percent savings account at the end of each year to accumulate $5,000 at the end of 10 years? Substituting the values $FV_{10} = \$5{,}000$, $n = 10$, and $i = 8$ percent into equation (6–8), we find

$$\$5{,}000 = PMT \left[\sum_{t=0}^{10-1} (1 + .08)^t \right] = PMT(FVIFA_{8\%,\ 10\ yr})$$

$$\$5{,}000 = PMT(14.487)$$

$$\frac{\$5{,}000}{14.487} = PMT$$

$$\$345.14 = PMT$$

Thus, we must deposit $345.14 per year for 10 years at 8 percent to accumulate $5,000.

CALCULATOR SOLUTION

Data Input	Function Key
8	N
6	I/Y
10,000	FV
0	PV

Function Key	Answer
CPT	
PMT	−1,010.36

CALCULATOR SOLUTION

Data Input	Function Key
10	N
8	I/Y
5,000	FV
0	PV

Function Key	Answer
CPT	
PMT	−345.15

PAUSE AND REFLECT

A timeline often makes it easier to understand time value of money problems. By visually plotting the flow of money you can better determine which formula to use. Arrows placed above the line are inflows, whereas arrows below the line represent outflows. One thing is certain: Timelines reduce errors.

Present Value of an Annuity

Pension funds, insurance obligations, and interest received from bonds all involve annuities. To compare them, we need to know the present value of each. Although we can

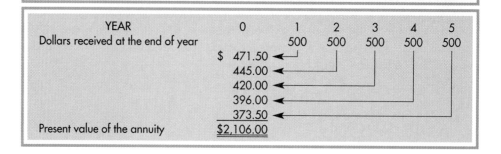

TABLE 6-6 ILLUSTRATION OF A 5-YEAR $500 ANNUITY DISCOUNTED TO THE PRESENT AT 6 PERCENT

YEAR	0	1	2	3	4	5
Dollars received at the end of year		500	500	500	500	500
	$ 471.50					
	445.00					
	420.00					
	396.00					
	373.50					
Present value of the annuity	$2,106.00					

find this by using the present-value table in Appendix C, this can be time-consuming, particularly when the annuity lasts for several years. For example, if we wish to know what $500 received at the end of the next 5 years is worth to us given the appropriate discount rate of 6 percent, we can simply substitute the appropriate values into equation (6–7), such that

$$PV = \$500 \left[\frac{1}{(1 + .06)} \right] + \$500 \left[\frac{1}{(1 + .06)^2} \right] + \$500 \left[\frac{1}{(1 + .06)^3} \right]$$

$$+ \$500 \left[\frac{1}{(1 + .06)^4} \right] + \$500 \left[\frac{1}{(1 + .06)^5} \right]$$

$$= \$500(.943) + \$500(.890) + \$500(.840) + \$500(.792) + \$500(.747)$$

$$= \$2,106$$

Thus, the present value of this annuity is $2,106.00. From examining the mathematics involved and the graph of the movement of these funds through time in Table 6–6, we see that we are simply summing up the present value of each cash flow. Thus, this procedure can be generalized to

$$PV = PMT \left[\sum_{t = 1}^{n} \frac{1}{(1 + i)^t} \right] \qquad (6–9)$$

where PMT = the annuity payment deposited or received at the end of each year
i = the annual discount (or interest) rate
PV = the present value of the future annuity
n = the number of years for which the annuity will last

To simplify the process of determining the present value of an annuity, the **present-value interest factor for an annuity** for i and n ($PVIFA_{i,n}$), defined as $\left[\sum_{t = 1}^{n} \frac{1}{(1 + i)^t} \right]$ has been compiled for various combinations of i and n in Appendix E with an abbreviated version provided in Table 6–7.[2]

present-value-interest factor for an annuity

---

[2]Another useful analytical relationship for PV is $PV = PMT[1 - 1/(1 + i)^n]/i$.

N	1%	2%	3%	4%	5%	6%	7%	8%	9%	10%
1	0.990	0.980	0.971	0.962	0.952	0.943	0.935	0.926	0.917	0.909
2	1.970	1.942	1.913	1.886	1.859	1.833	1.808	1.783	1.759	1.736
3	2.941	2.884	2.829	2.775	2.723	2.673	2.624	2.577	2.531	2.487
4	3.902	3.808	3.717	3.630	3.546	3.465	3.387	3.312	3.240	3.170
5	4.853	4.713	4.580	4.452	4.329	4.212	4.100	3.993	3.890	3.791
6	5.795	5.601	5.417	5.242	5.076	4.917	4.767	4.623	4.486	4.355
7	6.728	6.472	6.230	6.002	5.786	5.582	5.389	5.206	5.033	4.868
8	7.652	7.326	7.020	6.733	6.463	6.210	5.971	5.747	5.535	5.335
9	8.566	8.162	7.786	7.435	7.108	6.802	6.515	6.247	5.995	5.759
10	9.471	8.983	8.530	8.111	7.722	7.360	7.024	6.710	6.418	6.145
11	10.368	9.787	9.253	8.760	8.306	7.887	7.499	7.139	6.805	6.495
12	11.255	10.575	9.954	9.385	8.863	8.384	7.943	7.536	7.161	6.814
13	12.134	11.348	10.635	9.986	9.394	8.853	8.358	7.904	7.487	7.103
14	13.004	12.106	11.296	10.563	9.899	9.295	8.746	8.244	7.786	7.367
15	13.865	12.849	11.938	11.118	10.380	9.712	9.108	8.560	8.061	7.606

TABLE 6–7 $PVIFA_{i,n}$, or the Present Value of an Annuity of $1

Using this new notation we can rewrite equation (6–9) as follows:

$$PV = PMT(PVIFA_{i,n}) \qquad (6\text{–}9a)$$

Solving the previous example to find the present value of $500 received at the end of each of the next 5 years discounted back to the present at 6 percent, we look in the $i = 6$ percent column and $n = 5$ row and find the $PVIFA_{6\%,\,5\,yr}$ to be 4.212. Substituting the appropriate values into equation (6–9a), we find

$$PV = \$500(4.212)$$
$$= \$2,106$$

This, of course, is the same answer we calculated when we individually discounted each cash flow to the present. The reason is that we really only have *one* table; the Table 6–7 value for an *n*-year annuity for any discount rate i is merely the sum of the first *n* values in Table 6–3. We can see this by comparing the value in the present-value-of-an-annuity table (Table 6–8) for $i = 8$ percent and $n = 6$ years, which is 4.623, with the sum of the values in the $i = 8$ percent column and $n = 1, \ldots, 6$ rows of the present-value table (Table 6–3), which is equal to 4.623, as shown in Table 6–8.

Example

What is the present value of a 10-year $1,000 annuity discounted back to the present at 5 percent? Substituting $n = 10$ years, $i = 5$ percent, and $PMT = \$1,000$ into equation (6–9), we find

$$PV = \$1,000\left[\sum_{t=1}^{10} \frac{1}{(1 + .05)^t}\right] = \$1,000(PVIFA_{5\%,\,10\,yr})$$

Determining the value for the $PVIFA_{5\%,\,10\,yr}$ from Table 6–7, row $n = 10$, column $i = 5$ percent, and substituting it in, we get

$$PV = \$1,000(7.722)$$
$$= \$7,722$$

CALCULATOR SOLUTION

Data Input	Function Key
10	N
5	I/Y
1,000	PMT
0	FV

Function Key	Answer
CPT	
PV	−7,721.73

TABLE 6–8	PRESENT VALUE OF A 6-YEAR ANNUITY DISCOUNTED AT 8 PERCENT

One dollar received at the end of year 　　1　2　3　4　5　6
Preset value
.926
.857
.794
.735
.681
.630
4.623 Present value of the annuity

Thus, the present value of this annuity is $7,722.

As with our other compounding and present-value tables, given any three of the four unknowns in equation (6–9), we can solve for the fourth. In the case of the present-value-of-an-annuity table we may be interested in solving for *PMT*, if we know *i*, *n*, and *PV*. The financial interpretation of this action would be: How much can be withdrawn, perhaps as a pension or to make loan payments, from an account that earns *i* percent compounded annually for each of the next *n* years if we wish to have nothing left at the end of *n* years? For example, if we have $5,000 in an account earning 8 percent interest, how large an annuity can we draw out each year if we want nothing left at the end of 5 years? In this case the present value, *PV*, of the annuity is $5,000, *n* = 5 years, *i* = 8 percent, and *PMT* is unknown. Substituting this into equation (6–9), we find

$$\$5,000 = PMT(3.993)$$
$$\$1,252.19 = PMT$$

Thus, this account will fall to zero at the end of 5 years if we withdraw $1,252.19 at the end of each year.

CONCEPT CHECK

1. Could you determine the future value of a 3-year annuity using the formula for the future value of a single cash flow? How?
2. What is the $PVIFA_{10\%,\,3\,yr}$? Now add up the values for the $PVIF_{10\%,\,n\,yr}$. For $n = 1, 2$, and 3. What is this value? Why do these values have the relationship they do?

Objective 4　　**ANNUITIES DUE**

annuity due　　Because **annuities due** are really just *ordinary annuities where all the annuity payments have been shifted forward by 1 year*, compounding them and determining their present value is actually quite simple. Remember, with an annuity due, each annuity payment occurs at the beginning of each period rather than at the end of the period. Let's first look at how this affects our compounding calculations.

Because an annuity due merely shifts the payments from the end of the year to the beginning of the year, we now compound the cash flows for one additional year. Therefore, the compound sum of an annuity due is simply

$$FV_n(\text{annuity due}) = PMT(FVIFA_{i,n})(1 + i) \qquad \text{(6–10)}$$

For example, earlier we calculated the value of a 5-year ordinary annuity of $500, invested in the bank at 6 percent to be $2,818.50. If we now assume this to be a 5-year annuity due, its future value increases from $2,818.50 to $2,987.61.

$$\begin{aligned} FV_5 &= \$500(FVIFA_{6\%,\ 5\ yr})\ (1 + .06) \\ &= \$500(5.637)(1.06) \\ &= \$2,987.61 \end{aligned}$$

Likewise, with the present value of an annuity due, we simply receive each cash flow 1 year earlier—that is, we receive it at the beginning of each year rather than at the end of each year. Thus, because each cash flow is received 1 year earlier, it is discounted back for one less period. To determine the present value of an annuity due, we merely need to find the present value of an ordinary annuity and multiply that by $(1 + i)$, which in effect cancels out 1 year's discounting.

$$PV(\text{annuity due}) = PMT(PVIFA_{i,n})(1 + i) \qquad \text{(6–11)}$$

Reexamining the earlier example in which we calculated the present value of a 5-year ordinary annuity of $500 given an appropriate discount rate of 6 percent, we now find that if it is an annuity due rather than an ordinary annuity, the present value increases from $2,106 to $2,232.36,

$$\begin{aligned} PV &= \$500(PVIFA_{6\%,\ 5\ yr})(1 + .06) \\ &= \$500(4.212)(1.06) \\ &= \$2,232.36 \end{aligned}$$

The result of all this is that both the future and present values of an annuity due are larger than those of an ordinary annuity because in each case all payments are received earlier. Thus, when *compounding* an annuity due, it compounds for one additional year, whereas when *discounting* an annuity due, the cash flows are discounted for one less year. Although annuities due are used with some frequency in accounting, their usage is quite limited in finance. Therefore, in the remainder of this text, whenever the term *annuity* is used, you should assume that we are referring to an ordinary annuity.

Takin' It to the Net
The FinanCenter Web site http://www.financenter.com/ has a great selection of Internet calculators. In fact, many of the calculators used on the Internet actually have been developed by the FinanCenter.

Example

The Virginia State Lottery runs like most other state lotteries: You must select 6 out of 44 numbers correctly in order to win the jackpot. If you come close, there are some significantly lesser prizes, which we ignore for now. For each million dollars in the lottery jackpot you receive $50,000 per year for 20 years, and your chance of winning is 1 in 7.1 million. A recent advertisement for the Virginia State Lottery went as follows: "Okay, you got two kinds of people. You've got the kind who play Lotto all the time, and the kind who play Lotto some of the time. You know, like only on a Saturday when they stop in at the store on the corner for some peanut butter cups and diet soda and the jackpot happens to be really big. I mean, my friend Ned? He's like, "Hey, it's only $2 million this week." Well, hellloooo, anybody home? I mean, I don't know about you, but I wouldn't mind having a measly 2 mill coming *my* way. . . ."

What is the present value of these payments? The answer to this question depends on what assumption you make as to the time value of money. In this case, let's assume that your required rate of return on an investment with this level of risk is 10 percent. Keeping in mind that the Lotto is an annuity due—that is on a $2 million lottery you would get $100,000 immediately and $100,000 at the end of each of the next 19 years. Thus, the present value of this 20-year annuity due discounted back to present at 10 percent becomes:

$$
\begin{aligned}
PV_{\text{annuity due}} &= PMT(PVIFA_{i\%, \, n \text{ yr}})(1 + i) \\
&= \$100,000(PVIFA_{10\%, \, 20 \text{ yr}})(1 + .10) \\
&= \$100,000(8.514)(1.10) \\
&= \$851,400(1.10) \\
&= \$936,540.
\end{aligned}
$$

Thus, the present value of the $2 million Lotto jackpot is less than $1 million if 10 percent is the appropriate discount rate. Moreover, because the chance of winning is only 1 in 7.1 million, the expected value of each dollar "invested" in the lottery is only (1/7.1 million) × ($936,540) = 13.19¢. That is, for every dollar you spend on the lottery you should expect to get, *on average*, about 13 cents back—not a particularly good deal. While this ignores the minor payments for coming close, it also ignores taxes. In this case, it looks like "my friend Ned" is doing the right thing by staying clear of the lottery. Obviously, the main value of the lottery is entertainment. Unfortunately, without an understanding of the time value of money, it can sound like a good investment.

CONCEPT CHECK

1. How does an annuity due differ from an ordinary annuity?
2. Why are both the future and present values greater for an annuity?

AMORTIZED LOANS

amortized loan

This procedure of solving for *PMT*, the annuity payment value when *i*, *n*, and *PV* are known, is also used to determine what payments are associated with paying off a loan in equal installments over time. *Loans that are paid off this way, in equal periodic payments*, are called **amortized loans.** For example, suppose a firm wants to purchase a piece of machinery. To do this, it borrows $6,000 to be repaid in four equal payments at the end of each of the next 4 years, and the interest rate that is paid to the lender is 15 percent on the outstanding portion of the loan. To determine what the annual payments associated with the repayment of this debt will be, we simply use equation (6–9) and solve for the value of *PMT*, the annual annuity. Again we know three of the four values in that equation, *PV*, *i*, and *n*. *PV*, the present value of the future annuity, is $6,000; *i*, the annual interest rate, is 15 percent; and *n*, the number of years for which the annuity will last, is 4 years. *PMT*, the annuity payment received (by the

$$FV_5 = \$100 \left(1 + \frac{.12}{4}\right)^{4 \cdot 5}$$

$$= \$100 \, (1 + .03)^{20}$$

$$= \$100 \, (1.806)$$

$$= \$180.60$$

Thus, we will have \$180.60 at the end of 5 years. Notice that the calculator solution is slightly different because of rounding errors in the tables, and that it also takes on a negative value.

CONCEPT CHECK

1. Why does the future value of a given amount increase when interest is compounded nonannually as opposed to annually?
2. How do you adjust the present and future value formulas when interest is compounded monthly?

PRESENT VALUE OF AN UNEVEN STREAM

Objective 6

Although some projects will involve a single cash flow and some annuities, many projects will involve uneven cash flows over several years. Chapter 10, which examines investments in fixed assets, presents this situation repeatedly. There we will be comparing not only the present value of cash flows between projects but also the cash inflows and outflows within a particular project, trying to determine that project's present value. However, this will not be difficult because the present value of any cash flow is measured in today's dollars and thus can be compared, through addition for inflows and subtraction for outflows, to the present value of any other cash flow also measured in today's dollars. For example, if we wished to find the present value of the following cash flows:

YEAR	CASH FLOW	YEAR	CASH FLOW
1	$500	6	500
2	200	7	500
3	−400	8	500
4	500	9	500
5	500	10	500

given a 6-percent discount rate, we would merely discount the flows back to the present and total them by adding in the positive flows and subtracting the negative ones. However, this problem is complicated by the annuity of \$500 that runs from years 4 through 10. To accommodate this, we can first discount the annuity back to the beginning of period 4 (or end of period 3) by multiplying it by the value of

TABLE 6-11

$PVIFA_{6\%,\ 7\ yr}$ and get its present value at that point in time. We then multiply this value times the $PVIF_{6\%,\ 3\ yr}$ in order to bring this single cash flow (which is the present value of the 7-year annuity) back to the present. In effect we discount twice, first back to the end of period 3, then back to the present. This is shown graphically in Table 6–11 and numerically in Table 6–12. Thus, the present value of this uneven stream of cash flows is $2,657.94.

Example

What is the present value of an investment involving $200 received at the end of years 1 through 5, a $300 cash outflow at the end of year 6, and $500 received at the end of years 7 through 10, given a 5-percent discount rate? Here we have two annuities, one that can be discounted directly back to the present by multiplying it by the value of the $PVIFA_{5\%,\ 5\ yr}$ and one that must be discounted twice to bring it back to the present. This second annuity, which is a 4-year annuity, must first be discounted back to the beginning of period 7 (or end of period 6) by multiplying it by the value of the $PVIFA_{5\%,\ 4\ yr}$. Then the present value of this annuity at the end of period 6 (which can be viewed as a single cash flow) must be discounted back to the present by multiplying it by the value of the $PVIF_{5\%,\ 6\ yr}$.

To arrive at the total present value of this investment, we subtract the present value of the $300 cash outflow at the end of year 6 from the sum of the present value of the two annuities. Table 6–13 shows this graphically; Table 6–14 gives the calculations. Thus, the present value of this series of cash flows is $1,964.66.

TABLE 6-12

1. Present value of $500 received at the end of 1 year = $500(.943) = $ 471.50
2. Present value of $200 received at the end of 2 years = $200(.890) =   178.00
3. Present value of a $400 outflow at the end of 3 years = −400(.840) =   −336.00
4. (a) Value at the end of year 3 and a $500 annuity, years 4 through 10 = $500(5.582) = $2,791.00
    (b) Present value of $2,791.00 received at the end of year 3 = $2,791(.840) =   2,344.44
5. Total present value = $2,657.94

YEAR	0	1	2	3	4	5	6	7	8	9	10
Dollars received at end of year		200	200	200	200	200	−300	500	500	500	500

$ 865.80
−223.80
$1,773
1,322.66
Total present value $1,964.66

Remember, once the cash flows from an investment have been brought back to the present they can be combined by adding and subtracting to determine the project's total present value.

CONCEPT CHECK

1. If you wanted to calculate the present value of an investment that produced cash flows of $100 received at the end of year 1 and $700 at the end of year 2, how would you do it?

PERPETUITIES

Objective 7

A **perpetuity** is *an annuity that continues forever*; that is, every year from its establishment this investment pays the same dollar amount. An example of a perpetuity is preferred stock that pays a constant dollar dividend infinitely. Determining the present value of a perpetuity is delightfully simple; we merely need to divide the constant flow by the discount rate. For example, the present value of a $100 perpetuity

perpetuity

TABLE 6-14	DETERMINATION OF THE PRESENT VALUE OF AN EXAMPLE WITH UNEVEN STREAM INVOLVING TWO ANNUITIES DISCOUNTED TO THE PRESENT AT 5 PERCENT

1. Present value of first annuity, years 1 through 5 = $200(4.329) $ 865.80
2. Present value of $300 cash outflow = −$300(.746) =   −223.80
3. (a) Value at end of year 6 of second annuity, years 7 through 10 = $500(3.546) = $1,773.00
   (b) Present value of $1,773.00 received at the end of year 6 = $1,773.00(.746) =   1,322.66
4. Total present value = $1,964.66

discounted back to the present at 5 percent is $100/.05 = $2,000. Thus, the equation representing the present value of a perpetuity is

$$PV = \frac{PP}{i}$$

(6–13)

where PV = the present value of the perpetuity
PP = the constant dollar amount provided by the perpetuity
i = the annual interest (or discount) rate

Example

What is the present value of a $500 perpetuity discounted back to the present at 8 percent? Substituting PP = $500 and i = .08 into equation (6–11), we find

$$PV = \frac{\$500}{.08} = \$6,250$$

Thus, the present value of this perpetuity is $6,250.

CONCEPT CHECK

1. What is a perpetuity?
2. When the i, the annual interest (or discount) rate, increases, what happens to the present value of a perpetuity? Why?

Objective 8   **THE MULTINATIONAL FIRM: THE TIME VALUE OF MONEY**

From **Axiom 1: The Risk-Return Tradeoff—We Won't Take on Additional Risk Unless We Expect to be Compensated with Additional Return,** we found that investors demand a return for delaying consumption, as well as an additional return for taking on added risk. The discount rate that we use to move money through time should reflect this return for delaying consumption; and as the Fisher effect showed in Chapter 2, this discount rate should reflect anticipated inflation. In the United States, anticipated inflation is quite low, although it does tend to fluctuate over time. Elsewhere in the world, however, the inflation rate is difficult to predict because it can be dramatically high and undergo huge fluctuations.

Let's look at Argentina, keeping in mind that similar examples abound in Central and South America and Eastern Europe. At the beginning of 1992, Argentina introduced the fifth currency in 22 years, the new peso. The austral, the currency that was replaced, was introduced in June 1985 and was initially equal in value to $1.25 U.S. currency. Five and a half years later it took 100,000 australs to equal $1. Inflation had reached the point where the stack of money needed to buy a candy bar was bigger and weighed more than the candy bar itself, and many workers received their weeks' wages in grocery bags. Needless to say, if we were to move australs through time, we would have to use an extremely high interest or discount rate. Unfortunately, in countries suffering from hyperinflation, inflation rates tend to fluctuate dramatically, and this makes estimating the expected inflation rate even more difficult. For example, in 1989 the inflation rate in Argentina was 4,924 percent; in 1990 it dropped to 1,344 percent; in 1991 it was only 84 percent; in 1992, only 18 percent; and in 1997 it had fallen to 0.3 percent. However, as inflation in

Argentina dropped, inflation in Brazil heated up, going from 426 percent in 1991, to 1,094 percent in 1995. In fact, in the first 3 months of 1999, prices in Brazil rose by 35 percent. Finally, at the extreme, in 1993 in Serbia the inflation rate reached 360,000,000,000,000,000 percent.

The bottom line on all this is that because of the dramatic fluctuations in inflation that can take place in the international setting, choosing the appropriate discount rate of moving money through time is an extremely difficult process.

CONCEPT CHECK

1. How does the international setting complicate the choice of the appropriate interest rate to use when discounting cash flows back to the present?

TABLE 6-15 SUMMARY OF TIME VALUE OF MONEY EQUATIONS[a]

CALCULATION	EQUATION	
Future value of a single payment	$FV_n = PV(1 + i)^n = PV(FVIF_{i,n})$	Objective 1
Present value of a single payment	$PV = FV_n \left[\dfrac{1}{(1 + i)^n} \right] = FV_n(PVIF_{i,n})$	Objective 2
Future value of an annuity	$FV_n = PMT \left[\displaystyle\sum_{t=0}^{n-1} (1 + i)^t \right] = PMT(FVIFA_{i,n})$	Objective 3
Present value of an annuity	$PV = PMT \left[\displaystyle\sum_{t=1}^{n} \dfrac{1}{(1 + i)^t} \right] = PMT(PVIFA_{i,n})$	
Future value of an annuity due	$FV_n(\text{annuity due}) = PMT(FVIFA_{i,n})(1 + i)$	Objective 4
Present value of an annuity due	$PV(\text{annuity due}) = PMT(PVIFA_{i,n})(1 + i)$	
Future value of a single payment with nonannual compounding	$FV_n = PV\left(1 + \dfrac{i}{m}\right)^{mn}$	Objective 5
Present value of a perpetuity	$PV = \dfrac{PP}{i}$	Objective 7

Notations: FV_n = the future value of the investment at the end of n years
  n = the number of years until payment will be received or during which compounding occurs
  i = the annual interest or discount rate
  PV = the present value of the future sum of money
  m = the number of times compounding occurs during the year
  PMT = the annuity payment deposited or received at the end of each year
  PP = the constant dollar amount provided by the perpetuity

[a]Related tables appear in Appendixes B through E at the end of the book.

SUMMARY

To make decisions, financial managers must compare the costs and benefits of alternatives that do not occur during the same time period. Whether to make profitable investments or to take advantage of favorable interest rates, financial decision making requires an understanding of the time value of money. Managers who use the time value of money in all of their financial calculations assure themselves of more logical decisions. The time value process first makes all dollar values comparable; because money has a time value, it moves all dollar flows either back to the present or out to a common future date. All time value formulas presented in this chapter actually stem from the single compounding formula $FV_n = PV(1 + i)^n$. The formulas are used to deal simply with common financial situations, for example, discounting single flows, compounding annuities, and discounting annuities. Table 6–15 on the previous page provides a summary of these calculations.

Objective 6

Objective 8

Because of the dramatic fluctuations in inflation that can take place in the international setting, choosing the appropriate discount rate of moving money through time is an extremely difficult process.

KEY TERMS

amortized loan, 186

annuity, 179

annuity due, 184

compound annuity, 179

compound interest, 168

future-value interest factor ($FVIF_{i,n}$), 171

future-value interest factor for an annuity ($FVIFA_{i,n}$), 179

ordinary annuity, 179

perpetuity, 191

present value, 175

present-value interest factor ($PVIF_{i,n}$), 177

present-value interest factor for an annuity ($PVIFA_{i,n}$), 182

STUDY QUESTIONS

6-1 What is the time value of money? Why is it so important?

6-2 The processes of discounting and compounding are related. Explain this relationship.

6-3 How would an increase in the interest rate (i) or a decrease in the holding period (n) affect the future value (FV_n) of a sum of money? Explain why.

6-4 Suppose you were considering depositing your savings in one of three banks, all of which pay 5 percent interest; bank A compounds annually, bank B compounds semi-annually, and bank C compounds daily. Which bank would you choose? Why?

6-5 What is the relationship between the $PVIF_{i,n}$ (Table 6–3) and the $PVIFA_{i,n}$ (Table 6–7)? What is the $PVIFA_{10\%, \, 10 \, yr}$? Add up the values of the $PVIF_{10\%, \, n}$, for $n = 1, \ldots, 10$. What is this value? Why do these values have the relationship they do?

6-6 What is an annuity? Give some examples of annuities. Distinguish between an annuity and a perpetuity.

SELF-TEST PROBLEMS

ST-1 You place $25,000 in a savings account paying an annual compound interest of 8 percent for 3 years and then move it into a savings account that pays 10 percent interest compounded annually. How much will your money have grown at the end of 6 years?

ST-2 You purchase a boat for $35,000 and pay $5,000 down and agree to pay the rest over the next 10 years in 10 equal annual end-of-the-year payments that include principal payments plus 13 percent compound interest on the unpaid balance. What will be the amount of each payment?

STUDY PROBLEMS

6-1 *(Compound Interest)* To what amount will the following investments accumulate?
   a. $5,000 invested for 10 years at 10 percent compounded annually
   b. $8,000 invested for 7 years at 8 percent compounded annually
   c. $775 invested for 12 years at 12 percent compounded annually
   d. $21,000 invested for 5 years at 5 percent compounded annually

6-2 *(Compound Value Solving for n)* How many years will the following take?
   a. $500 to grow to $1,039.50 if invested at 5 percent compounded annually
   b. $35 to grow to $53.87 if invested at 9 percent compounded annually
   c. $100 to grow to $298.60 if invested at 20 percent compounded annually
   d. $53 to grow to $78.76 if invested at 2 percent compounded annually

6-3 *(Compound Value Solving for i)* At what annual rate would the following have to be invested?
   a. $500 to grow to $1,948.00 in 12 years
   b. $300 to grow to $422.10 in 7 years
   c. $50 to grow to $280.20 in 20 years
   d. $200 to grow to $497.60 in 5 years

6-4 *(Present Value)* What is the present value of the following future amounts?
   a. $800 to be received 10 years from now discounted back to the present at 10 percent
   b. $300 to be received 5 years from now discounted back to the present at 5 percent
   c. $1,000 to be received 8 years from now discounted back to the present at 3 percent
   d. $1,000 to be received 8 years from now discounted back to the present at 20 percent

6-5 *(Compound Annuity)* What is the accumulated sum of each of the following streams of payments?
   a. $500 a year for 10 years compounded annually at 5 percent
   b. $100 a year for 5 years compounded annually at 10 percent
   c. $35 a year for 7 years compounded annually at 7 percent
   d. $25 a year for 3 years compounded annually at 2 percent

6-6 *(Present Value of an Annuity)* What is the present value of the following annuities?
   a. $2,500 a year for 10 years discounted back to the present at 7 percent
   b. $70 a year for 3 years discounted back to the present at 3 percent
   c. $280 a year for 7 years discounted back to the present at 6 percent
   d. $500 a year for 10 years discounted back to the present at 10 percent

6-7 *(Compound Value)* Stanford Simmons, who recently sold his Porsche, placed $10,000 in a savings account paying annual compound interest of 6 percent.
   a. Calculate the amount of money that will have accrued if he leaves the money in the bank for 1, 5, and 15 years.
   b. If he moves his money into an account that pays 8 percent or one that pays 10 percent, rework part (a) using these new interest rates.
   c. What conclusions can you draw about the relationship between interest rates, time, and future sums from the calculations you have completed in this problem.

6-8 *(Compound Interest with Nonannual Periods)* Calculate the amount of money that will be in each of the following accounts at the end of the given deposit period.

ACCOUNT	AMOUNT DEPOSITED	ANNUAL INTEREST RATE	COMPOUNDING PERIOD (COMPOUNDED EVERY __ MONTHS)	DEPOSIT PERIOD (YEARS)
Theodore Logan III	$ 1,000	10%	12	10
Vernell Coles	95,000	12	1	1
Thomas Elliott	8,000	12	2	2
Wayne Robinson	120,000	8	3	2
Eugene Chung	30,000	10	6	4
Kelly Cravens	15,000	12	4	3

6-9 *(Compound Interest with Nonannual Periods)*
   a. Calculate the future sum of $5,000 given that it will be held in the bank 5 years at an annual interest rate of 6 percent.
   b. Recalculate part (a) using a compounding period that is (1) semiannual and (2) bimonthly.
   c. Recalculate parts (a) and (b) for a 12-percent annual interest rate.
   d. Recalculate part (a) using a time horizon of 12 years (annual interest rate is still 6 percent).
   e. With respect to the effect of changes in the stated interest rate and holding periods on future sums in parts (c) and (d), what conclusions do you draw when you compare these figures with the answers found in parts (a) and (b)?

6-10 *(Solving for i with Annuities)* Nicki Johnson, a sophomore mechanical engineering student, receives a call from an insurance agent, who believes that Nicki is an older woman ready to retire from teaching. He talks to her about several annuities that she could buy that would guarantee her an annual fixed income. The annuities are as follows:

ANNUITY	INITIAL PAYMENT INTO ANNUITY (AT $t = 0$)	AMOUNT OF MONEY RECEIVED PER YEAR	DURATION OF ANNUITY (YEARS)
A	$50,000	$8,500	12
B	$60,000	$7,000	25
C	$70,000	$8,000	20

If Nicki could earn 11 percent on her money by placing it in a savings account, should she place it instead in any of the annuities? Which ones, if any? Why?

6-11 *(Future Value)* Sales of a new finance book were 15,000 copies this year and were expected to increase by 20 percent per year. What are expected sales during each of the next 3 years? Graph this sales trend and explain.

6-12 *(Future Value)* Reggie Jackson, formerly of the New York Yankees, hit 41 home runs in 1980. If his home-run output grew at a rate of 10 percent per year, what would it have been over the following 5 years?

6-13 *(Loan Amortization)* Mr. Bill S. Preston, Esq., purchased a new house for $80,000. He paid $20,000 down and agreed to pay the rest over the next 25 years in 25 equal annual end-of-year payments that include principal payments plus 9 percent compound interest on the unpaid balance. What will these equal payments be?

6-14 (*Solving for PMT of an Annuity*) To pay for your child's education you wish to have accumulated $15,000 at the end of 15 years. To do this you plan on depositing an equal amount into the bank at the end of each year. If the bank is willing to pay 6 percent compounded annually, how much must you deposit each year to obtain your goal?

6-15 (*Solving for i in Compound Interest*) If you were offered $1,079.50 10 years from now in return for an investment of $500 currently, what annual rate of interest would you earn if you took the offer?

6-16 (*Future Value of an Annuity*) In 10 years you are planning on retiring and buying a house in Oviedo, Florida. The house you are looking at currently costs $100,000 and is expected to increase in value each year at a rate of 5 percent. Assuming you can earn 10 percent annually on your investments, how much must you invest at the end of each of the next 10 years to be able to buy your dream home when you retire?

6-17 (*Compound Value*) The Aggarwal Corporation needs to save $10 million to retire a $10 million mortgage that matures in 10 years. To retire this mortgage, the company plans to put a fixed amount into an account at the end of each year for 10 years, with the first payment occurring at the end of 1 year. The Aggarwal Corporation expects to earn 9 percent annually on the money in this account. What equal annual contribution must it make to this account to accumulate the $10 million in 10 years.

6-18 (*Compound Interest with Nonannual Periods*) After examining the various personal loan rates available to you, you find that you can borrow funds from a finance company at 12 percent compounded monthly or from a bank at 13 percent compounded annually. Which alternative is more attractive?

6-19 (*Present Value of an Uneven Stream of Payments*) You are given three investment alternatives to analyze. The cash flows from these three investments are as follows:

	INVESTMENT		
END OF YEAR	A	B	C
1	$10,000		$10,000
2	10,000		
3	10,000		
4	10,000		
5	10,000	$10,000	
6		10,000	50,000
7		10,000	
8		10,000	
9		10,000	
10		10,000	10,000

Assuming a 20 percent discount rate, find the present value of each investment.

6-20 (*Present Value*) The Kumar Corporation is planning on issuing bonds that pay no interest but can be converted into $1,000 at maturity, 7 years from their purchase. To price these bonds competitively with other bonds of equal risk, it is determined that they should yield 10 percent, compounded annually. At what price should the Kumar Corporation sell these bonds?

6-21 (*Perpetuities*) What is the present value of the following?
  a. A $300 perpetuity discounted back to the present at 8 percent
  b. A $1,000 perpetuity discounted back to the present at 12 percent
  c. A $100 perpetuity discounted back to the present at 9 percent
  d. A $95 perpetuity discounted back to the present at 5 percent

6-22 (*Solving for n with Nonannual Periods*) About how many years would it take for your investment to grow fourfold if it were invested at 16 percent compounded semi-annually?

6-23 *(Complex Present Value)* How much do you have to deposit today so that beginning 11 years from now you can withdraw $10,000 a year for the next 5 years (periods 11 through 15) plus an *additional* amount of $20,000 in that last year (period 15)? Assume an interest rate of 6 percent.

6-24 *(Loan Amortization)* On December 31, Beth Klemkosky bought a yacht for $50,000, paying $10,000 down and agreeing to pay the balance in 10 equal annual end-of-year installments that include both the principal and 10 percent interest on the declining balance. How big would the annual payments be?

6-25 *(Solving for i of an Annuity)* You lend a friend $30,000, which your friend will repay in 5 equal annual end-of-year payments of $10,000, with the first payment to be received 1 year from now. What rate of return does your loan receive?

6-26 *(Solving for i in Compound Interest)* You lend a friend $10,000, for which your friend will repay you $27,027 at the end of 5 years. What interest rate are you charging your "friend"?

6-27 *(Loan Amortization)* A firm borrows $25,000 from the bank at 12 percent compounded annually to purchase some new machinery. This loan is to be repaid in equal annual installments at the end of each year over the next 5 years. How much will each annual payment be?

6-28 *(Present Value Comparison)* You are offered $1,000 today, $10,000 in 12 years, or $25,000 in 25 years. Assuming that you can earn 11 percent on your money, which should you choose?

6-29 *(Compound Annuity)* You plan on buying some property in Florida 5 years from today. To do this you estimate that you will need $20,000 at that time for the purchase. You would like to accumulate these funds by making equal annual deposits in your savings account, which pays 12 percent annually. If you make your first deposit at the end of this year and you would like your account to reach $20,000 when the final deposit is made, what will be the amount of your deposits?

6-30 *(Complex Present Value)* You would like to have $50,000 in 15 years. To accumulate this amount you plan to deposit each year an equal sum in the bank, which will earn 7 percent interest compounded annually. Your first payment will be made at the end of the year.

  a. How much must you deposit annually to accumulate this amount?

  b. If you decide to make a large lump-sum deposit today instead of the annual deposits, how large should this lump-sum deposit be? (Assume you can earn 7 percent on this deposit.)

  c. At the end of 5 years you will receive $10,000 and deposit this in the bank toward your goal of $50,000 at the end of 15 years. In addition to this deposit, how much must you deposit in equal annual deposits to reach your goal? (Again assume you can earn 7 percent on this deposit.)

6-31 *(Comprehensive Present Value)* You are trying to plan for retirement in 10 years, and currently you have $100,000 in a savings account and $300,000 in stocks. In addition you plan on adding to your savings by depositing $10,000 per year in your savings account at the end of each of the next 5 years and then $20,000 per year at the end of each year for the final 5 years until retirement.

  a. Assuming your savings account returns 7 percent compounded annually while your investment in stocks will return 12 percent compounded annually, how much will you have at the end of 10 years? (Ignore taxes.)

  b. If you expect to live for 20 years after you retire, and at retirement you deposit all of your savings in a bank account paying 10 percent, how much can you withdraw each year after retirement (20 equal withdrawals beginning one year after you retire) to end up with a zero balance at death?

6-32 *(Loan Amortization)* On December 31, Son-Nan Chen borrowed $100,000, agreeing to repay this sum in 20 equal annual end-of-year installments that include both the principal and 15 percent interest on the declining balance. How large will the annual payments be?

6-33 *(Loan Amortization)* To buy a new house you must borrow $150,000. To do this you take out a $150,000, 30-year, 10 percent mortgage. Your mortgage payments, which are made at the end of each year (one payment each year), include both principal and 10 percent interest on the declining balance. How large will your annual payments be?

6-34 *(Present Value)* The state lottery's million-dollar payout provides for $1 million to be paid over 19 years in $50,000 amounts. The first $50,000 payment is made immediately, and the 19 remaining $50,000 payments occur at the end of each of the next 19 years. If 10 percent is the appropriate discount rate, what is the present value of this stream of cash flows? If 20 percent is the appropriate discount rate, what is the present value of the cash flows?

6-35 *(Solving for* i *in Compound Interest—Financial Calculator Needed)* In September 1963 the first issue of the comic book *X-MEN* was issued. The original price for that issue was 12¢. By September 1999, 36 years later, the value of this comic book had risen to $6,500. What annual rate of interest would you have earned if you had bought the comic in 1963 and sold it in 1999?

6-36 *(Comprehensive Present Value)* You have just inherited a large sum of money and you are trying to determine how much you should save for retirement and how much you can spend now. For retirement you will deposit today (January 1, 2000) a lump sum in a bank account paying 10 percent compounded annually. You don't plan on touching this deposit until you retire in 5 years (January 1, 2005), and you plan on living for 20 additional years and then dropping dead on December 31, 2024. During your retirement you would like to receive income of $50,000 per year to be received the first day of each year, with the first payment on January 1, 2005, and the last payment on January 1, 2024. Complicating this objective is your desire to have one final 3-year fling during which time you'd like to track down all the living original members of "Leave It to Beaver" and "The Brady Bunch" and get their autographs. To finance this you want to receive $250,000 on January 1, 2020, and *nothing* on January 1, 2021, and January 1, 2022, as you will be on the road. In addition, after you pass on (January 1, 2025), you would like to have a total of $100,000 to leave to your children.

a. How much must you deposit in the bank at 10 percent on January 1, 2000, to achieve your goal? (Use a timeline to answer this question.)

b. What kinds of problems are associated with this analysis and its assumptions?

COMPREHENSIVE PROBLEM

For your job as the business reporter for a local newspaper, you are given the task of putting together a series of articles that explains the power of the time value of money to your readers. Your editor would like you to address several specific questions in addition to demonstrating for the readership the use of the time value of money techniques by applying them to several problems. What would be your response to the following memorandum from your editor:

TO: Business Reporter

FROM: Perry White, Editor, *Daily Planet*

RE: Upcoming Series on the Importance and Power of the Time Value of Money

In your upcoming series on the time value of money, I would like to make sure you cover several specific points. In addition, before you begin this assignment, I want to make sure we are all reading from the same script, as accuracy has always been the cornerstone of the *Daily Planet*. In this regard, I'd like a response to the following questions before we proceed:

a. What is the relationship between discounting and compounding?

b. What is the relationship between the $PVIF_{i,n}$ and $PVIFA_{i,n}$?

c. (1) What will $5,000 invested for 10 years at 8 percent compounded annually grow to?

(2) How many years will it take $400 to grow to $1,671, if it is invested at 10 percent compounded annually?

(3) At what rate would $1,000 have to be invested to grow to $4,046 in 10 years?

d. Calculate the future sum of $1,000, given that it will be held in the bank for 5 years and earn 10 percent compounded semiannually?

e. What is an annuity due? How does this differ from an ordinary annuity?

f. What is the present value of an ordinary annuity of $1,000 per year for 7 years discounted back to the present at 10 percent? What would be the present value if it were an annuity due?

g. What is the future value of an ordinary annuity of $1,000 per year for 7 years compounded at 10 percent? What would be the future value if it were an annuity due?

h. You have just borrowed $100,000, and you agree to pay it back over the next 25 years in 25 equal end-of-year annual payments that include the principal payments plus 10 percent compound interest on the unpaid balance. What will be the size of these payments?

i. What is the present value of a $1,000 perpetuity discounted back to the present at 8 percent?

j. What is the present value of a $1,000 annuity for 10 years with the first payment occurring at the end of year 10 (that is, ten $1,000 payments occurring at the end of year 10 through year 19), given an appropriate discount rate of 10 percent?

k. Given a 10 percent discount rate, what is the present value of a perpetuity of $1,000 per year if the first payment does not begin until the end of year 10?

------------ **SELF-TEST SOLUTIONS** ------------

SS-1

This is a compound interest problem in which you must first find the future value of $25,000 growing at 8 percent compounded annually for 3 years and then allow that future value to grow for an additional 3 years at 10 percent. First, the value of the $25,000 after 3 years growing at 8 percent is

$$FV_3 = PV(1 + i)^n$$
$$FV_3 = \$25,000(1 + .08)^3$$
$$FV_3 = \$25,000(1.260)$$
$$FV_3 = \$31,500$$

Thus, after 3 years you have $31,500. Now this amount is allowed to grow for 3 years at 10 percent. Plugging this into equation (6–6), with $PV = \$31,500$, $i = 10$ percent, and $n = 3$ years, we solve for FV_3.

$$FV_3 = \$31,500(1 + .10)^3$$
$$FV_3 = \$31,500(1.331)$$
$$FV_3 = \$41,926.50$$

Thus, after 6 years the $25,000 will have grown to $41,926.50.

SS-2

This loan amortization problem is actually just a present-value-of-an-annuity problem in which we know the values of i, n, and PV and are solving for PMT. In this case the value of i is 13 percent, n is 10 years, and PV is $30,000. Substituting these values into equation (6–9) we find

$$\$30,000 = PMT \left[\sum_{t=1}^{10} \frac{1}{(1 + .13)^t} \right]$$
$$\$30,000 = PMT(5.426)$$
$$\$5,528.93 = PMT$$

VALUATION AND CHARACTERISTICS OF BONDS

LEARNING OBJECTIVES

AFTER READING THIS CHAPTER, YOU SHOULD BE ABLE TO:

1. Distinguish between different kinds of bonds.
2. Explain the more popular features of bonds.
3. Define the term *value* as used for several different purposes.
4. Explain the factors that determine value.
5. Describe the basic process for valuing assets.
6. Estimate the value of a bond.
7. Compute a bond-holder's expected rate of return.
8. Explain three important relationships that exist in bond valuation.

Practically all companies use debt to finance their firms, and many of those companies issue bonds, just one form of debt. Bonds provide investors a fixed income each year in the form of interest. Just as you can open a savings account at a bank and earn interest on your savings, so you can buy a bond that pays interest and then repays your principal on a designated date when the bond matures. Many of these bonds are traded in the public capital markets. Three examples of companies that have issued bonds to investors include the computer firm, IBM; the telephone company, Pacific Bell; and the athletic wear business, Converse. Each of these bonds pay $70 in interest each year on a bond that will repay the investor $1,000 when it matures. However, while these bonds are similar in terms of their interest payment, investors do not value them the same. In mid-1999, they were selling for the following amounts:

Pacific Bell	$1,040
IBM	$1,000
Converse	$ 481

Why would there be differences in the values of these bonds? Why would Pacific Bell's bonds be worth more than IBM's bonds? And why would the Converse bonds be so "cheap"? They all pay the same amount of interest. Why would an investor pay $1,000 for a bond that promises $70 in interest, when they could buy Converse bonds for only $481? Or a more general question, "What determines a bond's value?" Read on and you will find the answer to this puzzle.

We now begin our study by considering the different kinds of bonds.

| Objective 1 | **TYPES OF BONDS** |

bond

A **bond** is a *type of debt or long-term promissory note, issued by the borrower, promising to pay its holder a predetermined and fixed amount of interest per year.* However, there are a wide variety of such creatures. Just to mention a few, we have

- Debentures
- Subordinated debentures
- Mortgage bonds
- Eurobonds
- Zero and very low coupon bonds
- Junk bonds

The following sections briefly explain each of these types of bonds.

Debentures

debenture

The term **debenture** applies to *any unsecured long-term debt.* Because these bonds are unsecured, the earning ability of the issuing corporation is of great concern to the bondholder. They are also viewed as being more risky than secured bonds and as a result must provide investors with a higher yield than secured bonds provide. Often the issuing firm attempts to provide some protection to the holder of the bond by prohibiting the firm from issuing more secured long-term debt that would further tie up the firm's assets and leave the bondholders less protected. To the issuing firm, the major advantage of debentures is that no property has to be secured by them. This allows the firm to issue debt and still preserve some future borrowing power.

Subordinated Debentures

Many firms have more than one issue of debentures outstanding. In this case a hierarchy may be specified, in which some debentures are given *subordinated standing in case of insolvency.* The claims of the **subordinated debentures** are honored only after the claims of secured debt and unsubordinated debentures have been satisfied.

subordinated debentures

Mortgage Bonds

A **mortgage bond** is a *bond secured by a lien on real property.* Typically, the value of the real property is greater than that of the mortgage bonds issued. This provides the mortgage bondholders with a margin of safety in the event the market value of the secured property declines. In the case of foreclosure, the trustees have the power to sell the secured property and use the proceeds to pay the bondholders. In the event that the proceeds from this sale do not cover the bonds, the bondholders become general creditors, similar to debenture bondholders, for the unpaid portion of the debt.

mortgage bond

Eurobonds

Eurobonds are not so much a different type of security. They are simply securities, in this case *bonds, issued in a country different from the one in whose currency the bond is denominated.* For example, a bond that is issued in Europe or in Asia by an American company and that pays interest and principal to the lender in U.S. dollars would be considered a Eurobond. Thus, even if the bond is not issued in Europe, it merely needs to be sold in a country different from the one in whose currency it is denominated to be considered a Eurobond. The Eurobond market actually had its roots in the 1950s and 1960s as the U.S. dollar became increasingly popular because of its role as the primary international reserve. In recent years as the U.S. dollar has gained a reputation for being one of the most stable currencies, demand for Eurobonds has increased. The primary attractions of Eurobonds to borrowers, aside from favorable rates, are the relative lack of regulation (Eurobonds are not registered with the Securities and Exchange Commission [SEC]), less rigorous disclosure requirements than those of the SEC, and the speed with which they can be issued. Interestingly, not only are Eurobonds not registered with the SEC, but U.S. citizens and residents may not be offered them during their initial distribution.

Eurobonds

Zero and Very Low Coupon Bonds

Zero and very low coupon bonds allow the issuing firm to issue *bonds at a substantial discount from their $1,000 face value with a zero or very low coupon rate.* The investor receives a large part (or all with zero coupon bonds) of the return from the appreciation of the bond. For example, in 1998, 21st Century Telecom Group, Inc., a telecommunications firm, issued $43 million of debt maturing in 2008 with a zero coupon rate. These bonds were sold at a 57 percent discount from their par value; that is, investors only paid $433 for a bond with a $1,000 par value. Investors who purchased these bonds for $433 and hold them until they mature in 2008 will receive an 8.8-percent yield to maturity, with all of this yield coming from appreciation of the bond. On the other hand, 21st Century Telecom Group, Inc., will have no cash outflows until these bonds mature; however, at that time it will have to pay back $100 million even though they only received $43 million when the bonds were first issued.

zero and very low coupon bonds

As with any form of financing, there are both advantages and disadvantages of issuing zero or very low coupon bonds. As already mentioned, the disadvantage is, when the bonds mature, 21st Century Group will face an extremely large cash outflow, much greater than the cash inflow it experienced when the bonds were first issued. The advantages of zero and low coupon bonds are, first, that annual cash outflows associated with interest payments do not occur with zero coupon bonds and are at a relatively low level with low coupon bonds. Second, because there is relatively strong investor demand for this type of debt, prices tend to be bid up and yields tend to be bid down. That is to say, 21st Century Telecom Group was able to issue zero coupon bonds at about half a percent less than it would have been if they had been traditional coupon bonds. Finally, 21st Century Telecom Group is able to deduct the annual amortization of the discount from taxable income, which will provide a positive annual cash flow to 21st Century Telecom Group.

Junk Bonds (High-Yield Bonds)

Junk bonds (high-yield bonds)

Junk bonds are high-risk debt with *ratings of BB or below* by Moody's and Standard & Poor's. The lower the rating, the higher the chance of default; the lowest class is CC for Standard & Poor's and Ca for Moody's. Originally, the term was used to describe bonds issued by "fallen angels"; that is, firms with sound financial histories that were facing severe financial problems and suffering from poor credit ratings.

Junk bonds are also called **high-yield bonds** for the high interest rates they pay the investor, typically having an interest rate of between 3 and 5 percent more than AAA grade long-term debt.

Before the mid-1970s, smaller firms simply did not have access to the capital markets because of the reluctance of investors to accept speculative grade bonds. However, by the late 1980s, junk bonds became the way to finance hostile takeovers—buying a firm without the management's approval. For example, the purchase of RJR Nabisco for some $20 billion by the investment group KKR was largely accomplished by junk bond financing. However, the eventual bankruptcy of Drexel Burnham Lambert, the investment banker most responsible for developing a large junk bond market, the jailing of the "king of junk bonds" Michael Milken, and increasing interest rates brought an end to the extensive use of junk bonds for financing corporate takeovers. (Michael Milken, a partner at Drexel Burnham Lambert, used to have an annual conference in Beverly Hills, California, nicknamed "The Predator's Ball" for attracting takeover investors and corporate raiders who needed junk bond financing to accomplish their takeovers.)

When corporate takeovers subsided from their highs, most people thought the junk bond was forever dead. By 1990, the junk bond market was virtually nonexistent. Then, in 1992, with investors looking for higher interest rates and a rebounding economy, the junk bond market was revitalized. The following year, new junk bond issues reached a record $62 billion. Also, by 1995, less than 20 percent of the proceeds from junk bonds were being used to finance mergers and acquisitions, compared to 60 percent in the 1980s. In addition, in 1995, more than 800 companies had issued junk bonds, up from several hundred in the 1980s. Then in early 1998, the junk bond market suffered a sudden, jarring setback that led to the market for these bonds essentially dying. By year-end 1998, the capital market had returned to relatively moderate levels, in part because the Federal Reserve lowered interest rates. The borrowers in the 1990s came from a variety of industries, including manufacturing, media, retailing, consumer products, financial services, and housing. Also, credit quality improved. Only 17 percent of new issues in 1995 fell into the lower ratings of creditworthiness, compared with 66 percent in 1988.

Issuing Junk Bonds: A Case Example

On the matter of junk bonds, Lea Carty, an economist at the bondrating agency Moody's Investors Service in New York, says, "The junk bond market is here to stay. It's become a very important form of financing for younger, riskier firms." One such young, risky company is CommNet.

CommNet, which went public in 1986 and had yet to make a profit by 1995, is an example of a hot, young company that issued junk bonds. A 10-year-old firm with $90 million in sales was one of the first companies in the cellular telephone industry to use junk bond financing in 1993. The company's first issue raised $100 million to expand CommNet's eight-state rural telephone systems. The company sold more junk bonds in 1995, raising $80 million by selling 10-year notes with an 11.25 percent coupon.

Proceeds from CommNet's second junk sale were used to pay investors of convertible stock. A conventional bank loan wasn't a viable alternative because banks don't allow companies to buy back stock with bank proceeds, he said.

The firm's chief financial officer, Dan Dwyer, remembers the experience this way: "I think it was a combination of the quality of our company and market timing. The company's philosophy chose to sell bonds instead of stock in hopes of increasing value to shareholders."

Dwyer doesn't rule out a third junk bond issue in the future. "If we see an acquisition opportunity out there, we may well be back in the high-yield market," he said.

Source: John Accola, "Junk is Looking Good: Denver Companies Find Raising Cash with Risky Securities Easy as ATM," *Rocky Mountain News,* January 14, 1996, p. 80A. Denver: Denver Publishing Company. Reprinted with permission of the Denver *Rocky Mountain News.*

BACK TO THE FOUNDATIONS

Some have thought junk bonds were fundamentally different from other securities, but they are not. They are bonds with a great amount of risk, and therefore promise high expected returns. Thus, **Axiom 1: The Risk-Return Trade-off—We Won't Take on Additional Risk Unless We Expect to Be Compensated with Additional Return.**

As we begin the new millennium, junk bonds will continue to play an important role in the financing of many middle-sized firms. Mutual funds and pension funds, who owned 40 percent of all junk bonds in 1995, should continue to provide an active market for such securities. So, contrary to the conventional wisdom of the early 1990s, the junk bond market is alive and well.

CONCEPT CHECK

1. What is the difference in the nature and associated risk between debentures, subordinated debentures, and mortgage bonds? How would investors respond to the varying types of risk?
2. How does an investor receive a return from a zero or very low coupon bond? Why would a company be able to deduct amortized interest over the life of the bond even though there are no cash outflows associated with interest?
3. Why do junk bonds typically have a higher interest rate than other types of bonds? Why has this market been revitalized?

Now that you have an understanding of the kinds of bonds firms might issue, let's look at some of the characteristics and terminology of bonds.

TERMINOLOGY AND CHARACTERISTICS OF BONDS

Before valuing bonds, we first need to understand the terminology related to bonds. We should also know the different types of bonds that exist. Then we will be better prepared to determine the value of a bond.

When a firm or nonprofit institution needs financing, one source is *bonds*. As already noted, this type of financing instrument is simply a long-term promissory note, issued by the borrower, promising to pay its holder a predetermined and fixed amount of interest each year. Some of the more important terms and characteristics that you might hear about bonds are as follows:

Takin' It to the Net
Click on http://invest-faq. com/vse/bonds-a-basics.html to view the Virtual Stock Exchange's discussion on bond basics, then click on "bonds" for 10 other related articles.

- Claims on assets and income
- Par value
- Coupon interest rate
- Maturity
- Indenture
- Current yield
- Bond ratings

Let's consider each in turn.

Claims on Assets and Income

In the case of insolvency, claims of debt in general, including bonds, are honored before those of both common stock and preferred stock. However, different types of debt may also have a hierarchy among themselves as to the order of their claim on assets.

Bonds also have a claim on income that comes ahead of common and preferred stock. In general if interest on bonds is not paid, the bond trustees can classify the firm as insolvent and force it into bankruptcy. Thus, the bondholder's claim on income is more likely to be honored than that of common and preferred stockholders, whose dividends are paid at the discretion of the firm's management.

Par Value

par value of a bond

The **par value of a bond** is its *face value that is returned to the bondholder at maturity.* In general, corporate bonds are issued in denominations of $1,000, although there are some exceptions to this rule. Also, when bond prices are quoted, either by financial managers or in the financial press, prices are generally expressed as a percentage of the bond's par value. For example, a Revlon bond was recently quoted in the *Wall Street Journal* as selling for $96^1/_4$. That does not mean you can buy the bond for $96.25. It means that this bond is selling for $96^1/_4$ percent of its par value of $1,000. Hence, the market price of this bond is actually $962.50. At maturity in 2008 the bondholder will receive the $1,000.

Coupon Interest Rate

coupon interest rate

The **coupon interest rate** on a bond indicates the *percentage of the par value of the bond that will be paid out annually in the form of interest.* Thus, regardless of what happens to the price of a bond with an 8 percent coupon interest rate and a $1,000 par value, it will pay out $80 annually in interest until maturity (.08 × $1,000 = $80).

Bondholders Beware

We have learned that the bond rating attached to a bond when it is issued does not necessarily continue with it until maturity. In fact, with all the debt that corporations piled on in the late 1980s, it seemed that the only direction debt ratings went was down. The ethical question here: Does management have a duty to bondholders to watch out for their interests? Is just living by the letter of the bond covenants—while working hard to evade them—all right?

Let's look at a couple of examples that have infuriated bondholders. In early 1988, Shearson Lehman Hutton helped sell $1 billion of RJR Nabisco bonds. About 6 months later Shearsen helped Kohlberg Kravis Roberts (KKR), an investment banker, buy RJR. The way the purchase was arranged, RJR issued large amounts of new debt, driving the market value of the previously issued bonds down by $100 million. Needless to say, a lot of bondholders were angry.

Texaco is another company that has worked around bond covenants. Several years ago, Pennzoil sued Texaco for $10 billion and won the case. To minimize damage to shareholders as a result of their court battle with Pennzoil, Texaco filed for Chapter 11 bankruptcy protection. The company entered bankruptcy, bond interest payments were passed, and later it emerged from bankruptcy with its credit standing unchanged.

Was what Shearson did—to issue then destroy—unethical? Should Texaco have used bankruptcy to protect its shareholders at the expense of its bondholders? What do you think?

Maturity

The **maturity** of a bond indicates *the length of time until the bond issuer returns the par value to the bondholder and terminates or redeems the bond.*

maturity

Indenture

An **indenture** is the *legal agreement between the firm issuing the bonds and the bond trustee who represents the bondholders.* The indenture provides the specific terms of the loan agreement, including a description of the bonds, the rights of the bondholders, the rights of the issuing firm, and the responsibilities of the trustee. This legal document may run 100 pages or more in length, with the majority of it devoted to defining protective provisions for the bondholder. The bond trustee, usually a banking institution or trust company, is then assigned the task of overseeing the relationship between the bondholder and the issuing firm, protecting the bondholder, and seeing that the terms of the indenture are carried out.

indenture

Typically, the restrictive provisions included in the indenture attempt to protect the bondholders' financial position relative to that of other outstanding securities. Common provisions involve (1) prohibiting the sale of accounts receivable, (2) limiting common stock dividends, (3) restricting the purchase or sale of fixed assets, and (4) setting limits on additional borrowing. Not allowing the sale of accounts receivable is specified because such sales would benefit the firm's short-run liquidity position at the expense of its future liquidity position. Common stock dividends may not be allowed if the firm's liquidity falls below a specified level, or the maximum dividend payout may be limited to some fraction, say 50 percent or 60 percent of earnings under any circumstance. Fixed-asset restrictions generally require lender permission before the liquidation of any fixed asset or prohibit the use of any existing fixed asset as collateral on new loans. Constraints on additional borrowing usually involve limiting the amount and type of additional long-term debt that can be issued. All these restrictions have one thing in common: They attempt to prohibit actions that would improve the status of other securities at the expense of bonds and to protect the status of bonds from being weakened by any managerial action.

Current Yield

current yield

The **current yield** on a bond refers to the *ratio of the annual interest payment to the bond's current market price*. If, for example, we have a bond with an 8-percent coupon interest rate, a par value of $1,000, and a market price of $700, it would have a current yield of

$$\text{current yield} = \frac{\text{annual interest payment}}{\text{market price of the bond}} \qquad (7\text{--}1)$$

$$= \frac{0.08 \times \$1000}{\$700} = \frac{\$80}{\$700} = 0.114 = 11.4\%$$

Bond Ratings

John Moody first began to rate bonds in 1909; since that time three rating agencies—Moody's, Standard and Poor's, and Fitch Investor Services—have provided ratings on corporate bonds. These ratings involve a judgment about the future risk potential of the bond. Although they deal with expectations, several historical factors seem to play a significant role in their determination. Bond ratings are favorably affected by (1) a greater reliance on equity as opposed to debt in financing the firm, (2) profitable operations, (3) a low variability in past earnings, (4) large firm size, and (5) little use of subordinated debt. In turn, the rating a bond receives affects the rate of return demanded on the bond by the investors. The poorer the bond rating, the higher the rate of return demanded in the capital markets. Table 7–1 provides an example and description of these ratings. Thus, bond ratings are extremely important for the financial manager. They provide an indicator of default risk that in turn affects the rate of return that must be paid on borrowed funds.

BACK TO THE FOUNDATIONS

When we say that a lower bond rating means a higher interest rate charged by the investors (bondholders), we are observing an application of **Axiom 1: The Risk-Return Trade-off—We Won't Take on Additional Risk Unless We Expect to Be Compensated with Additional Return.**

We are now ready to think about bond valuation. But, to begin, we must first clarify precisely what we mean by value. Next, we need to understand the basic concepts of valuation and the process for valuing an asset. Then we may apply these concepts to valuing a bond—and in Chapter 8 to valuing stocks.

TABLE 7–1   STANDARD & POOR'S CORPORATE BOND RATINGS

AAA This is the highest rating assigned by Standard and Poor's for debt obligation and indicates an extremely strong capacity to pay principal and interest.

AA Bonds rated AA also qualify as high-quality debt obligations. Their capacity to pay principal and interest is very strong, and in the majority of instances, they differ from AAA issues only in small degree.

A Bonds rated A have a strong capacity to pay principal and interest, although they are somewhat more susceptible to the adverse effects of changes in circumstances and economic conditions.

BBB Bonds rated BBB are regarded as having an adequate capacity to pay principal and interest. Whereas they normally exhibit adequate protection parameters, adverse economic conditions or changing circumstances are more likely to lead to a weakened capacity to pay principal and interest for bonds in this category than for bonds in the A category.

BB Bonds rated BB, B, CCC, and CC are regarded, on balance, as predominantly
B speculative with respect to the issuer's capacity to pay interest and repay principal
CCC in accordance with the terms of the obligation.
CC BB indicates the lowest degree of speculation and CC the highest. While such bonds will likely have some quality and protective characteristics, these are outweighed by large uncertainties or major risk exposures to adverse conditions.

C The rating C is reserved for income bonds on which no interest is being paid.

D Bonds rated D are in default, and payment of principal and/or interest is in arrears.

Plus (+) or Minus (−): To provide more detailed indications of credit quality, the ratings from AA to BB may be modified by the addition of a plus or minus sign to show relative standing within the major rating categories.

Source: Standard & Poor's Fixed Income Investor, Vol. 8 (1980). Reprinted by permission.

CONCEPT CHECK

1. What are some of the important features of a bond? Which features determine the cash flows associated with a bond?
2. What restrictions are typically included in an indenture in order to protect the bondholder?
3. How does the bond rating affect an investor's required rate of return? What actions could a firm take to receive a more favorable rating?

DEFINITIONS OF VALUE

Objective 3

The term *value* is often used in different contexts, depending on its application. Examples of different uses of this term include the following:

Book value is the *value of an asset as shown on a firm's balance sheet*. It represents the historical cost of the asset rather than its current worth. For instance, the book value of a company's preferred stock is the amount the investors originally

book value

paid for the stock and therefore the amount the firm received when the stock was issued.

liquidation value

Liquidation value is the *dollar sum that could be realized if an asset were sold individually and not as part of a going concern*. For example, if a firm's operations were discontinued and its assets were divided up and sold, the sales price would represent the asset's liquidation value.

market value

The **market value** of an asset is the *observed value for the asset in the marketplace*. This value is determined by supply and demand forces working together in the marketplace, where buyers and sellers negotiate a mutually acceptable price for the asset. For instance, the market price for Ford common stock on June 20, 1999, was $34. This price was reached by a large number of buyers and sellers working through the New York Stock Exchange. In theory, a market price exists for all assets. However, many assets have no readily observable market price because trading seldom occurs. For instance, the market price for the common stock of Blanks Engraving, a Dallas-based, family-owned firm, would be more difficult to establish than the market value of J. C. Penney's common stock.

intrinsic or economic value
fair value

The **intrinsic or economic value** of an asset—also called the **fair value**—is the *present value of the asset's expected future cash flows*. This value is the amount an investor should be willing to pay, given the amount, timing, and riskiness of future cash flows. Once the investor has estimated the intrinsic value of a security, this value could be compared with its market value when available. If the intrinsic value is greater than the market value, then the security is undervalued in the eyes of the investor. Should the market value exceed the investor's intrinsic value, then the security is overvalued.

We hasten to add that if the securities market is working efficiently, the market value and the intrinsic value of a security will be equal. Whenever a security's intrinsic value differs from its current market price, the competition among investors seeking opportunities to make a profit will quickly drive the market price back to its intrinsic value. Thus, we may define an **efficient market** as *one in which the values of all securities at any instant fully reflect all available public information, which results in the market value and the intrinsic value being the same*. If the markets are efficient, it is extremely difficult for an investor to make extra profits from an ability to predict prices.

efficient market

BACK TO THE FOUNDATIONS

The fact that investors have difficulty identifying stocks that are undervalued relates to **Axiom 6: Efficient Capital Markets—The Markets Are Quick and the Prices Are Right.** In an efficient market, the price reflects all available public information about the security, and therefore, it is priced fairly.

The idea of market efficiency has been the backdrop for an intense battle between professional investors and university professors. The academic community has contended that someone throwing darts at the list of securities in the *Wall Street Journal* could do as well as a professional money manager. Market professionals retort that academicians are grossly mistaken in this view. The war has been intense but also one that the student of finance should find intriguing, and it can be followed each month in the *Wall Street Journal*, where the investment performance of dart throwers and different professional investors are compared. Through June 1998, there had been 109 contests between these rivals. The score: 68 for the professional managers and 41 for the dart throwers. Also, as aptly expressed by one teacher, the

Central Puerto SA Credit Rating Lowered

The following news announcement was released regarding Standard & Poor's lowering its corporate credit rating on Central Puerto SA, an Argentinian company, to BB− from BB and the company's $150 million unsecured Euro medium-term notes to A+ from AA−. The announcement read as follows:

The downgrade reflects "weaker than expected financial ratios mainly due to the higher tax burden imposed by the tax reform legislation passed in December 1998 and weaker than expected electricity market prices (without considering exceptional weather conditions) stemming from slower projected demand growth over the near term," S & P said.

In addition, the rating agency said, the company is evaluating the expansion of generating capacity at its Loma de la Lata's plant, incorporating combined-cycle technology, which would represent a further increase in the company's leverage level.

"The new rating incorporates the potential for cash flow volatility associated with generation operations in a competitive power market," S & P said.

The rating agency expects Central Puerto's competitive position to improve with the start-up of the new combined cycle facility and an improved financial profile beginning 2002.

Source : "Central Puerto SA Corporate Credit Rating Cut to BB− by S & P," Dow Jones Newswires, June 18, 1999.

---

real point about efficient markets is that an investor should throw a large wet towel at the *Wall Street Journal*, not a dart. That is, we want to be broadly diversified with a large group of stocks, not just one. For example, when the professional investors are compared with the performance of the 30 companies represented on the Dow Jones Industrial Index they have won only 57 of the contests. The importance of diversification is explained in Chapter 9.

Takin' It to the Net

For the Bond Market's Association Guide to "Seven Steps to Educate Yourself About Investing in Bonds," go to their Web site http://www.investinginbonds.com/. Also available are articles on the bond market, buying and selling, and taxation.

CONCEPT CHECK

1. Explain the difference between the four different values of a bond. Why should the market value equal the intrinsic value?
2. How does risk play a role in the three basic factors of asset valuation?

DETERMINANTS OF VALUE

Objective 4

For our purposes, *the value of an asset is its intrinsic value or the present value of its expected future cash flows*, where these cash flows are discounted back to the present using the investor's required rate of return. This statement is true for valuing all assets and serves as the basis of almost all that we do in finance. Thus, value is affected by three elements:

1. The amount and timing of the asset's expected cash flows
2. The riskiness of these cash flows
3. The investor's required rate of return for undertaking the investment

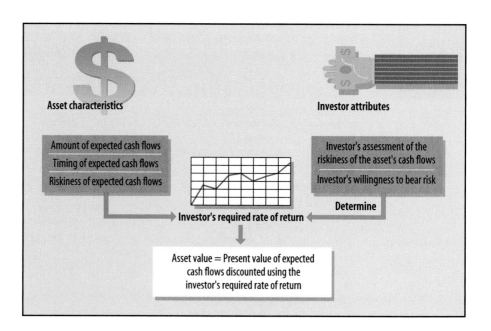

FIGURE 7–1

*Basic Factors Determining
an Asset's Value*

The first two factors are characteristics of the asset; the third one, the required rate of return, is the minimum rate of return necessary to attract an investor to purchase or hold a security, which is determined by *the rates of return available on similar investments*, or what is called the **opportunity cost of funds.** This rate must be high enough to compensate the investor for the risk perceived in the asset's future cash flows. (The required rate of return is explained more fully in Chapter 9.)

opportunity cost of funds

BACK TO THE FOUNDATIONS

Our discussions should remind us of three of our axioms that help us understand finance:

Axiom 1: The Risk-Return Trade-off—We Won't Take on Additional Risk Unless We Expect to Be Compensated with Additional Return.

Axiom 2: The Time Value of Money—A Dollar Received Today Is Worth More Than a Dollar Received in the Future.

Axiom 3: Cash—Not Profits—Is King.

Determining the economic worth or value of an asset always relies on these three axioms. Without them, we would have no basis for explaining value. With them, we can know that the amount and timing of cash, not earnings, drive value. Also, we must be rewarded for taking risk; otherwise, we will not invest.

Figure 7-1 depicts the basic factors involved in valuation. As the figure shows, finding the value of an asset involves the following steps:

1. Assessing the asset's characteristics, which include the amount and timing of the expected cash flows and the riskiness of these cash flows
2. Determining the investor's required rate of return, which embodies the investor's attitude about assuming risk and perception of the riskiness of the asset

3. Discounting the expected cash flows back to the present, using the investor's required rate of return as the discount rate

Thus, intrinsic value is a function of the cash flows yet to be received, the riskiness of these cash flows, and the investor's required rate of return.

CONCEPT CHECK

1. What are the three important elements of asset valuation?

VALUATION: THE BASIC PROCESS

The valuation process can be described as follows: It is assigning value to an asset by calculating the present value of its expected future cash flows using the investor's required rate of return as the discount rate. The investor's required rate of return, k, is determined by the level of the risk-free rate of interest and the risk premium that the investor feels is necessary to compensate for the risks assumed in owning the asset. Therefore, a basic security valuation model can be defined mathematically as follows:

$$V = \frac{C_1}{(1 + k)^1} + \frac{C_2}{(1 + k)^2} + \cdots + \frac{C_n}{(1 + k)^n} \qquad (7\text{-}2)$$

or

$$V = \sum_{t=1}^{n} \frac{C_t}{(1 + k)^t}$$

where C_t = cash flow to be received at time t
  V = the intrinsic value or present value of an asset producing expected future cash flows, C_t, in years 1 through n
  k = the investor's required rate of return

Using equation (7-2), there are three basic steps in the valuation process:

Step 1: Estimate the C_t in equation (7-2), which is the amount and timing of the future cash flows the security is expected to provide.
Step 2: Determine k, the investor's required rate of return.
Step 3: Calculate the intrinsic value, V, as the present value of expected future cash flows discounted at the investor's required rate of return.

Equation (7-2), which measures the present value of future cash flows, is the basis of the valuation process. It is the most important equation in this chapter, because all the remaining equations in this chapter and in Chapters 8 and 9 are merely reformulations of this one equation. If we understand equation (7-2), all the valuation work we do, and a host of other topics as well, will be much clearer in our minds.

CONCEPT CHECK

1. What two factors determine an investor's required rate of return?
2. How does the required rate of return affect a bond's value?

FIGURE 7–2
*Data Requirements for
Bond Valuation*

With the foregoing principles of valuation as our foundation, let's now look at how bonds are valued.

Objective 6 **BOND VALUATION**

The value of a bond is the present value both of future interest to be received and the par or maturity value of the bond. It's that simple.

The process for valuing a bond, as depicted in Figure 7–2, requires knowing three essential elements: (1) the amount and timing of the cash flows to be received by the investor, (2) the time to maturity of the loan, and (3) the investor's required rate of return. The amount of cash flows is dictated by the periodic interest to be received and by the par value to be paid at maturity. Given these elements, we can compute the value of the bond, or the present value.

Example

Consider a bond issued by American Airlines with a maturity date of 2020 and a stated coupon rate of 10.2 percent.[1] In 1999, with 21 years left to maturity, investors owning the bonds are requiring an 8-percent rate of return. We can calculate the value of the bonds to these investors using the following three-step valuation procedure:

Step 1: Estimate the amount and timing of the expected future cash flows. Two types of cash flows are received by the bondholder:

    a. Annual interest payments equal to the coupon rate of interest times the face value of the bond. In this example, the bond's coupon interest rate is 10.2 percent; thus the annual interest payment is $102 = .102 \times \$1,000$. Assuming that 1999 interest payments have already been made, these cash flows will be received by the bondholder in each of the 21 years before the bond matures (2000 through 2020 = 21 years).

    b. The face value of the bond of $1,000 to be received in 2020. To summarize, the cash flows received by the bondholder are as follows:

Takin' It to the Net
Go to http://www.
fitchibca.com for the latest Fitch
IBCA.'s press releases on their
bond ratings.

YEARS	1	2	3	4	...	20	21
	$102	$102	$102	$102	...	$102	$ 102
							+$1,000
							$1,102

---

[1]American Airlines pays interest to its bondholders on a semiannual basis on January 15 and July 15. However, for the moment, assume the interest is to be received annually. The effect of semiannual payments is examined later.

Reading a Bond Quote in the *Wall Street Journal*

Below is shown a section of the *Wall Street Journal* that gives the quotes on June 17, 1999, for some of the corporate bonds traded on the New York Stock Exchange on that date.

Bond	Cur Yld	Vol	Close	Net Chg
ChespkE $9\frac{5}{8}$ 05	10.4	21	$92\frac{1}{2}$	$+ \ 1\frac{1}{2}$
ChespkE $8\frac{1}{2}$ 12	10.8	65	$78\frac{7}{8}$	$- \ 3\frac{1}{8}$
ChckFul 7s 12	CV	16	$123\frac{3}{4}$	$+ \ \frac{1}{8}$
Clardge $11\frac{3}{4}$ 02f	...	10	60	$- \ 2$
ClrkOil $9\frac{1}{2}$ 04	9.4	238	$100\frac{7}{8}$	$- \ \frac{1}{8}$
CoeurDA $7\frac{1}{4}$ 05	CV	100	60	$- \ \frac{1}{2}$
Couer $6\frac{3}{8}$ 04	CV	40	$59\frac{3}{4}$	$+ \ \frac{1}{4}$
CompUSA $9\frac{1}{2}$ 00	9.5	64	$100\frac{1}{4}$	$+ \ \frac{1}{4}$
CouPort $10\frac{1}{2}$ 04	33.3	12	$31\frac{1}{2}$	$+ \ \frac{1}{2}$
Convrse 7s 04	CV	27	$48\frac{1}{4}$	$+ \ \frac{7}{8}$
DRHrtn 10s 06	9.7	20	103	$+ \ \frac{7}{8}$
DataGen 6s 04	CV	53	$86\frac{3}{4}$	$- \ 1\frac{1}{8}$

The bonds shown in the list above as "ChespkE $9\frac{5}{8}$ 05" were issued by Chesapeake Electric, they pay a $9\frac{5}{8}$-percent coupon interest rate (indicated by the "$9\frac{5}{8}$"), or $96.25 interest paid annually (actually $48.13 paid semiannually) on a par value of $1,000, and they mature in 2005 (05 is the last two digits of the year the bonds mature). The closing price of the bonds on June 17, 1999, was $92\frac{1}{2}$, which is stated as a percentage of the bond's $1,000 par value; thus, the bond's closing price on June 17 was $925 = .925 × $1,000. The current yield on the bonds is 10.4 percent, calculated as the annual interest divided by the closing price, or $96.25/$925 = 10.4%. During the trading day, 21 bonds were traded on the exchange, as reflected by the "Vol" heading.* Finally, the net change ("Net Chg") in the price of the bond from the previous day's close was an increase of $1\frac{1}{2}$ percent.

---

*There may have been a lot more than 21 bonds changing hands on June 17, 1999. Many bond trades are negotiated directly between institutional investors or through bankers and are not listed in the *Wall Street Journal.*

Step 2: Determine the investor's required rate of return by evaluating the riskiness of the bond's future cash flows. An 8-percent required rate of return for the bondholders is given. In Chapter 9, we learn how this rate is determined. For now, simply realize that the investor's required rate of return is equal to a rate earned on a risk-free security plus a risk premium for assuming risk.

Step 3: Calculate the intrinsic value of the bond as the present value of the expected future interest and principal payments discounted at the investor's required rate of return.

The present value of American Airlines bonds is found as follows:

$$\text{bond value} = V_b = \frac{\$ \text{ interest in year 1}}{(1 + \text{required rate of return})^1}$$

$$+ \frac{\$ \text{ interest in year 2}}{(1 + \text{required rate of return})^2} \qquad (7-3a)$$

$$+ \cdots + \frac{\$ \text{ interest in year 21}}{(1 + \text{required rate of return})^{21}}$$

$$+ \frac{\$ \text{ par value of bond}}{(1 + \text{required rate of return})^{21}}$$

or, summing over the interest payments,

$$V_b = \underbrace{\sum_{t=1}^{21} \frac{\$ \text{ interest in year } t}{(1 + \text{required rate of return})^t}}_{\text{present value of interest}} + \underbrace{\frac{\$ \text{ par value of bond}}{(1 + \text{required rate of return})^{21}}}_{\text{present value of par value}}$$

The foregoing equation is a restatement in a slightly different form of equation (7–2). Recall that equation (7–2) states that the value of an asset is the present value of future cash flows to be received by the investor.

Using I_t to represent the interest payment in year t, M to represent the bond's maturity (or par) value, and k_b to equal the bondholder's required rate of return, we may express the value of a bond maturing in year n as follows:

$$V_b = \sum_{t=1}^{n} \frac{\$ I_t}{(1 + k_b)^t} + \frac{\$ M}{(1 + k_b)^n} \qquad (7-3b)$$

Finding the value of the American Airlines bonds may be represented graphically as follows:

YEAR	0	1	2	3	4	5	6	⋯	21
Dollars received at end of year		$102	$102	$102	$102	$102	$102	⋯	$ 102 $1,000 $1,102
Present value	$1,220 ◄								

CALCULATOR SOLUTION

Data Input	Function key
21	N
8	I/Y
102	PMT
1000	FV

Function key	Answer
CPT PV	− 1,220

Using the TI BAII Plus, we find the value of the bond to be $1,220, as calculated in the margin.[2] Thus, if investors consider 8 percent to be an appropriate required rate of return in view of the risk level associated with American Airlines bonds, paying a price of $1,220 would satisfy their return requirement.

_____

[2]As noted in Chapter 6, we are using the TI BAII Plus. You may want to return to the Chapter 6 section "Moving Money through Time with the Aid of a Financial Calculator" or Appendix A, to see a more complete explanation of using the TI BAII Plus. For an explanation of other calculators, see the study guide that accompanies this text.

We can also solve for the value of American Airlines' bonds using a spreadsheet. The solution using Excel appears as follows:

	A	B	C	D
1	Required rate of return	Rate	0.08	
2	Years left to maturity	Nper	21	
3	Annual interest payment	Pmt	102	
4	Future value	FV	1,000	
5	Present value	PV	($1,220)	
6			↑	
7				
8				
9	Equation: = PV (Rate, Nper, Pmt, FV) = PV (C1, C2, C3, C4)			

Semiannual Interest Payments

In the preceding American Airlines illustration, the interest payments were assumed to be paid annually. However, companies typically pay interest to bondholders semiannually. For example, consider Alaskan Airlines' bonds maturing in 14 years that pay $68.75 per year, but disburses the interest semiannually ($34.375 each January 15 and July 15).

Several steps are involved in adapting equation (7–3b) for semiannual interest payments.[3] First, thinking in terms of *periods* instead of years, a bond with a life of n years paying interest semiannually has a life of $2n$ periods. In other words, a 5-year bond ($n = 5$) that remits its interest on a semiannual basis actually makes

---

[3]The logic for calculating the value of a bond that pays interest semiannually is similar to the material presented in Chapter 6 where compound interest with nonannual periods was discussed.

10 payments. Yet although the number of periods has doubled, the *dollar* amount of interest being sent to the investors for each period and the bondholders' required rate of return are half of the equivalent annual figures. I_t becomes $I_t/2$ and k_b is changed to $k_b/2$; thus, for semiannual compounding, equation (7–3b) becomes

$$V_b = \sum_{t=1}^{2n} \frac{\$I_t/2}{\left(1 + \dfrac{k_b}{2}\right)^t} + \frac{\$M}{\left(1 + \dfrac{k_b}{2}\right)^{2n}} \tag{7-4}$$

Alternatively, using the notations introduced in Chapter 6 for discounting cash flows, the above equation may be restated as follows:

$$V_b = (\$I_t \div 2)(PVIFA_{k_b/2,\ 2n}) + \$M(PVIF_{k_b/2,\ 2n}) \tag{7-5}$$

Assuming the Alaskan Airlines bondholders' annual required rate of return is 7.2 percent, we can use the TI BAII Plus calculator in the margin to find the bond value, but now assuming semiannual interest payments. Thus, the value of a bond paying $34.375 in semiannual interest for 14 years, where the investor has a 7.2 percent required rate of return, would be $972.

This solution can be found using a spreadsheet that would look as follows:

	A	B	C	D
1	Required rate of return	Rate	0.036	
2	Years left to maturity	Nper	28	
3	Annual interest payment	Pmt	34.375	
4	Future value	FV	1,000	
5	Present value	PV	($972)	
6			↑	
7				
8				
9	Equation: = PV (Rate, Nper, Pmt, FV) = PV (C1, C2, C3, C4)			

CONCEPT CHECK

1. What does it mean if your required rate of return for investing in a bond is different from the expected rate of return implied by its current market price? As an investor, what would you do if this were true?
2. How do semiannual payments affect the asset valuation equation?

THE BONDHOLDER'S EXPECTED RATE OF RETURN (YIELD TO MATURITY)

Theoretically, each investor could have a different required rate of return for a particular security. However, the financial manager is only interested in the required rate of return that is implied by the market prices of the firm's securities. In other words, the consensus of a firm's investors about the expected rate of return is reflected in the current market price of the stock.

expected rate of return

To measure the bondholder's **expected rate of return**, $\bar{k}_b$, we would find the *discount rate that equates the present value of the future cash flows (interest and maturity* *value) with the current market price of the bond.*[4] The expected rate of return for a bond is also the *rate of return the investor will earn if the bond is held to maturity*, or the **yield to maturity.** Thus, when referring to bonds, the terms *expected rate of return* and *yield to maturity* are often used interchangeably.

yield to maturity

To illustrate this concept, consider the Brister Corporation's bonds, which are selling for $1,100. The bonds carry a coupon interest rate of 9 percent and mature in 10 years. (Remember, the coupon rate determines the interest payment—coupon rate × par value.)

In determining the expected rate of return $(\overline{k}_b)$, implicit in the current market price, we need to find the rate that discounts the anticipated cash flows back to a present value of $1,100, the current market price (P_0) for the bond.

Finding the expected rate of return for a bond using the present value tables is done by trial and error. We have to keep trying new rates until we find the discount rate that results in the present value of the future interest and maturity value of the bond just equaling the current market value of the bond. If the expected rate is somewhere between rates in the present value tables, we then must interpolate between the rates.

For our example, if we try 7 percent, the bond's present value is $1,140.16. Because the present value of $1,140.16 is greater than the market price of $1,100, we should next try a higher rate. Increasing the discount rate, say, to 8 percent gives a present value of $1,066.90. (These computations are shown below.) Now the present value is less than the market price; thus, we know that the investor's expected rate of return is between 7 percent and 8 percent.

		7%		8%	
YEARS	CASH FLOW	PRESENT VALUE FACTORS	PRESENT VALUE	PRESENT VALUE FACTORS	PRESENT VALUE
1–10	$90 per year	7.024	$ 632.16	6.710	$ 603.90
10	$1,000 in year 10	0.508	508.00	0.463	$ 463.00
		Present value at 7%	$1,140.16	Present value at 8%	$1,066.90

CALCULATOR SOLUTION

Data Input	Function key
10	N
1100	PV
90	+/− PMT
1000	+/− FV
Function key	Answer
CPT I/Y	7.54

The actual expected return for the Brister Corporation bondholders is 7.54 percent, which may be found by using the TI BAII Plus calculator as presented in the margin, or by using a computer spreadsheet shown as follows:

	A	B	C	D
1	Years left to maturity	Nper	10	
2	Annual interest payment	Pmt	90	
3	Present value	PV	−1100	
4	Future value	FV	1,000	
5	Required rate of return	Rate	7.54%	
6			↑	
7				
8				
9				
10	Equation: = RATE (Nper, Pmt, −PV, FV) = RATE (C1, C2, C3, C4)			

---

[4]When we speak of computing an expected rate of return, we are not describing the situation very accurately. Expected rates of return are ex ante (before the fact) and are based on "expected and unobservable future cash flows" and, therefore, can only be "estimated."

BOND VALUATION: THREE IMPORTANT RELATIONSHIPS

We have now learned to find the value of a bond (V_b), given (1) the amount of interest payments (I_t), (2) the maturity value (M), (3) the length of time to maturity (n periods), and (4) the investor's required rate of return, k_b. We also know how to compute the expected rate of return ($\bar{k}_b$), which also happens to be the current interest rate on the bond, given (1) the current market value (P_0), (2) the amount of interest payments (I_t), (3) the maturity value (M), and (4) the length of time to maturity (n periods). We now have the basics. But let's go further in our understanding of bond valuation by studying several important relationships.

First Relationship

The value of a bond is inversely related to changes in the investor's present required rate of return (the current interest rate). In other words, as interest rates increase (decrease), the value of the bond decreases (increases).

To illustrate, assume that an investor's required rate of return for a given bond is 12 percent. The bond has a par value of $1,000 and annual interest payments of $120, indicating a 12-percent coupon interest rate ($120 ÷ $1,000 = 12\%$). Assuming a 5-year maturity date, the bond would be worth $1,000, computed as follows:

$$V_b = \frac{\$I_1}{(1 + k_b)^1} + \cdots + \frac{\$I_n}{(1 + k_b)^n} + \frac{\$M}{(1 + k_b)^n} \qquad (7\text{–}3b)$$

$$= \sum_{t=1}^{n} \frac{\$I_t}{(1 + k_b)^t} + \frac{\$M}{(1 + k_b)^n}$$

$$= \sum_{t=1}^{5} \frac{\$120}{(1 + 0.12)^t} + \frac{\$1,000}{(1 + 0.12)^5}$$

Using present value tables we have:

$$V_b = \$120(PVIFA_{12\%,\ 5\ yr}) + \$1,000(PVIF_{12\%,\ 5\ yr})$$
$$V_b = \$120(3.605) + \$1,000(0.567)$$
$$= \$432.60 + \$567.00$$
$$= \$999.60 \cong \$1,000.00$$

If, however, the investor's required rate of return increases from 12 percent to 15 percent, the value of the bond would decrease to $899.24, computed as follows:

$$V_b = \$120(PVIFA_{15\%,\ 5\ yr}) + \$1,000(PVIF_{15\%,\ 5\ yr})$$
$$V_b = \$120(3.352) + \$1,000(0.497)$$
$$= \$402.24 + \$497.00$$
$$= \$899.24$$

On the other hand, if the investor's required rate of return decreases to 9 percent, the bond would increase in value to $1,116.80:

$$V_b = \$120(PVIFA_{9\%,\ 5\ yr}) + \$1,000(PVIF_{9\%,\ 5\ yr})$$
$$V_b = \$120(3.890) + \$1,000(0.650)$$
$$= \$466.80 + \$650.00$$
$$= \$1,116.80$$

This inverse relationship between the investor's required rate of return and the value of a bond is presented in Figure 7–3. Clearly, as an investor demands a higher

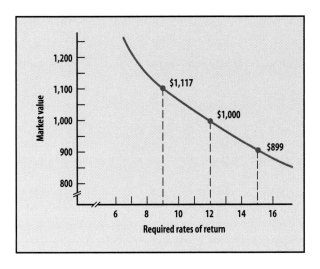

FIGURE 7-3

Value and Required Rates for a 5-Year Bond at 12 Percent Coupon Rate

rate of return, the value of the bond decreases. The higher rate of return the investor desires can be achieved only by paying less for the bond. Conversely, a lower required rate of return yields a higher market value for the bond.

Changes in bond prices represent an element of uncertainty for the bond investor. If the current interest rate (required rate of return) changes, the price of the bond also fluctuates. An increase in interest rates causes the bondholder to incur a loss in market value. Because future interest rates and the resulting bond value cannot be predicted with certainty, a bond investor is exposed to the *risk of changing values as interest rates vary*. This risk has come to be known as **interest rate risk.**

interest rate risk

Second Relationship

The market value of a bond will be less than the par value if the investor's required rate of return is above the coupon interest rate; but it will be valued above par value if the investor's required rate of return is below the coupon interest rate.

Using the previous example, we observed that:

Takin' It to the Net
Go to www.dowjones.com. Type "bonds" in the Business Search column for the latest articles related to current bond issues.

1. The bond has a *market* value of $1,000, equal to the par or maturity value, when the investor's required rate of return equals the 12-percent coupon interest rate. In other words, if

$$required \ rate = coupon \ rate, \text{ then } market \ value = par \ value$$
$$12\% \quad = \quad 12\% \quad , \text{ then} \quad \$1,000 \quad = \quad \$1,000$$

2. When the required rate is 15 percent, which exceeds the 12-percent coupon rate, the market value falls below par value to $899.24; that is, if

$$required \ rate > coupon \ rate, \text{ then } market \ value < par \ value$$
$$15\% \quad > \quad 12\% \quad , \text{ then} \quad \$899.24 \quad < \quad \$1,000$$

In this case the *bond sells at a discount below par value;* thus, it is called a **discount bond.**

discount bond

3. When the required rate is 9 percent, or less than the 12 percent coupon rate, the market value, $1,116.80, exceeds the bond's par value. In this instance, if

$$required\ rate < coupon\ rate,\ then\ market\ value > par\ value$$
$$9\% \quad < \quad 12\% \quad ,\ then\ \$1{,}116.80\ >\ \$1{,}000$$

premium bond

The *bond is now selling at a premium above par value*; thus, it is a **premium bond.**

Third Relationship

Long-term bonds have greater interest rate risk than do short-term bonds.

As already noted, a change in current interest rates (required rate of return) causes an inverse change in the market value of a bond. However, the impact on value is greater for long-term bonds than it is for short-term bonds.

In Figure 7–3 we observed the effect of interest rate changes on a 5-year bond paying a 12-percent coupon interest rate. What if the bond did not mature until 10 years from today instead of 5 years? Would the changes in market value be the same? Absolutely not. The changes in value would be more significant for the 10-year bond. For example, if we vary the current interest rates (the bondholder's required rate of return) from 9 percent to 12 percent and then to 15 percent, as we did earlier with the 5-year bond, the values for both the 5-year and the 10-year bonds are as shown below.

	Market Value for a 12% Coupon-Rate Bond Maturing In	
REQUIRED RATE	5 YEARS	10 YEARS
9%	$1,116.80	$1,192.16
12	1,000.00	1,000.00
15	899.24	849.28

Using these values and the required rates, we can graph the changes in values for the two bonds relative to different interest rates. These comparisons are provided in Figure 7–4. The figure clearly illustrates that the price of a long-term bond (say, 10 years) is more responsive or sensitive to interest rate changes than the price of a short-term bond (say, 5 years).

The reason long-term bond prices fluctuate more than short-term bond prices in response to interest rate changes is simple. Assume an investor bought a 10-year bond yielding a 12-percent interest rate. If the current interest rate for bonds of similar risk increased to 15 percent, the investor would be locked into the lower rate for 10 years. If, on the other hand, a shorter-term bond had been purchased—say, one maturing in 2 years—the investor would have to accept the lower return for only 2 years and not the full 10 years. At the end of year 2, the investor would receive the maturity value of $1,000 and could buy a bond offering the higher 15-percent rate for the remaining 8 years. Thus, interest rate risk is determined, at least in part, by the length of time an investor is required to commit to an investment. However, the holder of a long-term bond may take some comfort from the fact that long-term interest rates are usually not as volatile as short-term rates. If the short-term rate changed 1 percentage point, for example, it would not be unusual for the long-term rate to change only .3 percentage points.

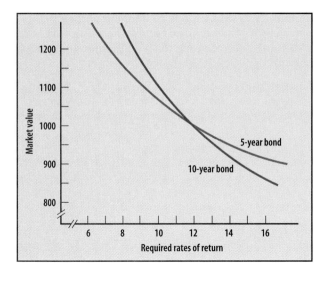

FIGURE 7–4

Market Values of a 5-Year and a 10-Year Bond at Different Required Rates of Return

CONCEPT CHECK

1. As interest rates increase, why does the price of a long-term bond decrease more than a short-term bond?
2. Why does a bond sell at a discount when the coupon rate is lower than the required rate of return and vice versa?

SUMMARY

Valuation is an important issue if we are to manage the company effectively. An understanding of the concepts and how to compute the value of a security underlie much of what we do in finance and in making correct decisions for the firm as a whole. Only if we know what matters to our investors can we maximize the firm's value.

Distinguish between different kinds of bonds   Objective 1

There are a variety of types of bonds, including:

• Debentures
• Subordinated debentures
• Mortgage bonds
• Eurobonds
• Zero and very low coupon bonds
• Junk bonds

Explain the more popular features of bonds   Objective 2

Some of the more popular terms and characteristics that you might hear about bonds include the following:

• Claims on assets and income
• Par value
• Coupon interest rate
• Maturity
• Indenture
• Current yield
• Bond ratings

Objective 3	**Define the term *value* as used for several different purposes**
	Value is defined differently depending on the context. But for us, value is the present value of future cash flows expected to be received from an investment discounted at the investor's required rate of return.
Objective 4	**Explain the determinants of value**
	Three basic factors determine an asset's value: (1) the amount and timing of future cash flows, (2) the riskiness of the cash flows, and (3) the investor's attitude about the risk.
Objective 5	**Describe the basic process for valuing assets**
	The valuation process can be described as follows: It is assigning value to an asset by calculating the present value of its expected future cash flows using the investor's required rate of return as the discount rate. The investor's required rate of return, k, equals the risk-free rate of interest plus a risk premium to compensate the investor for assuming risk.
Objective 6	**Estimate the value of a bond**
	The value of a bond is the present value both of future interest to be received and the par or maturity value of the bond.
Objective 7	**Compute a bondholder's expected rate of return**
	To measure the bondholder's expected rate of return, we find the discount rate that equates the present value of the future cash flows (interest and maturity value) with the current market price of the bond. The expected rate of return for a bond is also the rate of return the investor will earn if the bond is held to maturity, or the yield to maturity.
Objective 8	**Explain three important relationships that exist in bond valuation**
	Certain key relationships exist in bond valuation, these being:

1. A decrease in interest rates (required rates of return) will cause the value of a bond to increase; an interest rate increase will cause a decrease in value. The change in value caused by changing interest rates is called interest rate risk.
2. If the bondholder's required rate of return (current interest rate):
   a. Equals the coupon interest rate, the bond will sell at par, or maturity value.
   b. Exceeds the bond's coupon rate, the bond will sell below par value, or at a discount.
   c. Is less than the bond's coupon rate, the bond will sell above par value, or at a premium.
3. A bondholder owning a long-term bond is exposed to greater interest rate risk than one owning a short-term bond.

--- **KEY TERMS** ---

bond, 202

book value, 209

coupon interest rate, 206

current yield, 208

debenture, 202

discount bond, 221

efficient market, 210

eurobonds, 203

expected rate of return, 218

fair value, 210

high-yield bonds, 204

indenture, 207

interest rate risk, 221

intrinsic or economic value, 210

junk bonds (high-yield bonds), 204

liquidation value, 210

market value, 210

maturity, 207

mortgage bond, 203

opportunity cost of funds, 212

par value of a bond, 206

premium bond, 222

subordinated debentures, 203

yield to maturity, 219

zero and very low coupon bonds, 203

7-1 Distinguish between debentures and mortgage bonds.

7-2 Define (a) Eurobonds, (b) zero coupon bonds, and (c) junk bonds.

7-3 Describe the bondholder's claim on the firm's assets and income.

7-4 a. How does a bond's par value differ from its market value?

   b. Explain the difference between a bond's coupon interest rate, the current yield, and a bondholder's required rate of return.

7-5 What factors determine a bond's rating? Why is the rating important to the firm's manager?

7-6 What are the basic differences between book value, liquidation value, market value, and intrinsic value?

7-7 What is a general definition of the intrinsic value of a security?

7-8 Explain the three factors that determine the intrinsic or economic value of an asset.

7-9 Explain the relationship between an investor's required rate of return and the value of a security.

7-10 Define the bondholder's expected rate of return.

SELF-TEST PROBLEMS

ST-1 *(Bond Valuation)* Trico bonds have a coupon rate of 8 percent, a par value of $1,000, and will mature in 20 years. If you require a return of 7 percent, what price would you be willing to pay for the bond? What happens if you pay *more* for the bond? What happens if you pay *less* for the bond?

ST-2 *(Bond Valuation)* Sunn Co.'s bonds, maturing in 7 years, pay 8 percent interest on a $1,000 face value. However, interest is paid semiannually. If your required rate of return is 10 percent, what is the value of the bond? How would your answer change if the interest were paid annually?

ST-3 *(Bondholder's Expected Rate of Return)* Sharp Co. bonds are selling in the market for $1,045. These 15-year bonds pay 7 percent interest annually on a $1,000 par value. If they are purchased at the market price, what is the expected rate of return?

STUDY PROBLEMS

7-1 *(Bond Valuation)* Calculate the value of a bond that expects to mature in 12 years and has a $1,000 face value. The coupon interest rate is 8 percent, and the investor's required rate of return is 12 percent.

7-2 *(Bond Valuation)* Enterprise, Inc., bonds have a 9-percent coupon rate. The interest is paid semiannually, and the bonds mature in 8 years. Their par value is $1,000. If your required rate of return is 8 percent, what is the value of the bond? What is the value if the interest is paid annually?

7-3 *(Bondholder's Expected Rate of Return)* The market price is $900 for a 10-year bond ($1,000 par value) that pays 8 percent interest (4 percent semiannually). What is the bond's expected rate of return?

7-4 *(Bond Valuation)* Exxon 20-year bonds pay 9 percent interest annually on a $1,000 par value. If bonds sell at $945, what is the bond's expected rate of return?

7-5 *(Bondholder's Expected Rate of Return)* Zenith Co.'s bonds mature in 12 years and pay 7 percent interest annually. If you purchase the bonds for $1,150, what is your expected rate of return?

7-6 *(Bond Valuation)* National Steel 15-year, $1,000 par value bonds pay 8 percent interest annually. The market price of the bonds is $1,085, and your required rate of return is 10 percent.

   a. Compute the bond's expected rate of return.
   b. Determine the value of the bond to you, given your required rate of return.
   c. Should you purchase the bond?

7-7 *(Bond Valuation)* You own a bond that pays $100 in annual interest, with a $1,000 par value. It matures in 15 years. Your required rate of return is 12 percent.

   a. Calculate the value of the bond.
   b. How does the value change if your required rate of return (1) increases to 15 percent or (2) decreases to 8 percent?
   c. Explain the implications of your answers in part b as they relate to interest rate risk, premium bonds, and discount bonds.
   d. Assume that the bond matures in 5 years instead of 15 years. Recompute your answers in part b.
   e. Explain the implications of your answers in part d as they relate to interest rate risk, premium bonds, and discount bonds.

7-8 *(Bond Valuation)* Arizona Public Utilities issued a bond that pays $80 in annual interest, with a $1,000 par value. It matures in 20 years. Your required rate of return is 7 percent.

   a. Calculate the value of the bond.
   b. How does the value change if your required rate of return (1) increases to 10 percent or (2) decreases to 6 percent?
   c. Explain the implications of your answers in part b as they relate to interest rate risk, premium bonds, and discount bonds.
   d. Assume that the bond matures in 10 years instead of 20 years. Recompute your answers in part b.
   e. Explain the implications of your answers in part d as they relate to interest rate risk, premium bonds, and discount bonds.

7-9 *(Bond Valuation—Zero Coupon)* The Kumar Corporation is planning on issuing bonds that pay no interest but can be converted into $1,000 at maturity, seven years from their purchase. To price these bonds competitively with other bonds of equal risk, it is determined that they should yield 10 percent, compounded annually. At what price should the Kumar Corporation sell these bonds?

7-10 *(Bond Values)* You are examining three bonds with par value of $1,000 (you receive $1,000 at maturity) and are concerned with what would happen to their market value if interest rates (or the market discount rate) changed. The three bonds are:

Bond A—A bond with 3 years left to maturity that pays 10 percent per year compounded semiannually.

Bond B—A bond with 7 years left to maturity that pays 10 percent per year compounded semiannually.

Bond C—A bond with 20 years left to maturity that pays 10 percent per year compounded semiannually.

What would be the value of these bonds if the market discount rate were

   a. 10 percent per year compounded semiannually?
   b. 4 percent per year compounded semiannually?
   c. 16 percent per year compounded semiannually?
   d. What observations can you make about these results?

COMPREHENSIVE PROBLEM

Below are data on $1,000 par value bonds issued by Time Warner, Nations Bank (now Bank of America), and Hilton Hotels at the end of 1996. Assume you are thinking about buying these bonds as of January 2000. Answer the following questions for each of these bonds:

a. Calculate the values of the bonds if your required rates of return are as follows: Time Warner, 8 percent; Nations Bank, 6 percent; and Hilton Hotels, 9 percent; where

	TIME WARNER	NATIONS BANK	HILTON HOTELS
Coupon interest rates	7.975%	6.60%	7.56%
Years to maturity	5	10	17

b. At the end of 1996, the bonds were selling for the following amounts:

Time Warner $1,064
Nations Bank $ 978
Hilton Hotels $1,004

What were the expected rates of return for each bond?

c. How would the value of the bonds change if (1) your required rate of return (k_b) increases 2 percentage points or (2) decreases 2 percentage points?

d. Explain the implications of your answers in part b in terms of interest rate risk, premium bonds, and discount bonds.

e. Should you buy the bonds? Explain.

SELF-TEST SOLUTIONS

SS-1

$$\text{value } (V_b) = \sum_{t=1}^{20} \frac{\$80}{(1.07)^t} + \frac{\$1,000}{(1.07)^{20}}$$

Thus,

$$
\begin{aligned}
\text{present value of interest: } \$\ 80(10.594) &= \$\ \ 847.52 \\
\text{present value of par value: } \$1,000(0.258) &= \underline{\$\ \ 258.00} \\
\text{value } (V_b) &= \underline{\$1,105.52}
\end{aligned}
$$

If you pay more for the bond, your required rate of return will not be satisfied. In other words, by paying an amount for the bond that exceeds $1,105.52, the expected rate of return for the bond is less than the required rate of return. If you have the opportunity to pay less for the bond, the expected rate of return exceeds the 7-percent required rate of return.

SS-2

If interest is paid semiannually:

$$\text{value } (V_b) = \sum_{t=1}^{14} \frac{\$40}{(1 + 0.05)^t} + \frac{\$1,000}{(1 + 0.05)^{14}}$$

Thus,

$$
\begin{aligned}
\$40(9.899) &= \$395.96 \\
\$1,000(0.505) &= \underline{\ \ 505.00} \\
\text{value } (V_b) &= \underline{\$900.96}
\end{aligned}
$$

If interest is paid annually:

$$\text{value } (V_b) = \sum_{t=1}^{7} \frac{\$80}{(1.10)^t} + \frac{\$1,000}{(1.10)^7}$$

$$V_b = \$80(4.868) + \$1,000(0.513)$$
$$V_b = \$902.44$$

<table>
<tr><th colspan="2">CALCULATOR SOLUTION</th></tr>
<tr><th>Data Input</th><th>Function key</th></tr>
<tr><td>15</td><td>N</td></tr>
<tr><td>70</td><td>+/− PMT</td></tr>
<tr><td>1000</td><td>+/− FV</td></tr>
<tr><td>1045</td><td>PV</td></tr>
<tr><th>Function key</th><th>Answer</th></tr>
<tr><td>CPT I/Y</td><td>6.52</td></tr>
</table>

SS-3

$$\$1,045 = \sum_{t=1}^{15} \frac{\$70}{(1 + \overline{k}_b)^t} + \frac{\$1,000}{(1 + \overline{k}_b)^{15}}$$

At 6%: $\$70(9.712) + \$1,000(0.417) = \$1,096.84$
At 7%: Value must equal $\$1,000$.

Interpolation:

$$\text{Expected rate of return: } \overline{k}_b = 6\% + \frac{\$51.84}{\$96.84}(1\%) = 6.54\%$$

Chapter Eight

Preferred Stock • Common Stock • The

Stockholder's Expected Rate of Return

VALUATION AND CHARACTERISTICS OF STOCK

LEARNING OBJECTIVES

AFTER READING THIS CHAPTER, YOU SHOULD BE ABLE TO:

1. Identify the basic characteristics and features of preferred stock.
2. Value preferred stock.
3. Identify the basic characteristics and features of common stock.
4. Value common stock.
5. Calculate a stock's expected rate of return

During the 1990s, a record number of privately owned companies issued stock for the first time to the public—often called initial public offerings (IPOs). Some of the more well-known ones included Netscape and Planet Hollywood. However, their stories could be told by many other young firms from cosmetics makers to oil companies, all having one thing in common, a need for additional equity capital for growth. One such firm is Broadcom.

Broadcom makes chips that help bring Internet access to television screens through cable lines. The firm, which had one of 1998's most successful IPOs, announced that it would issue another 3 million shares as a follow-on to the initial offering. The firm was planning to use the funds for needed working capital and acquisition of capital equipment. The company said the original shareholders will not receive any proceeds from the sale of shares.

During 1998, the firm's shares had traded as high as $89.75 and as low as $47. In April of that year, shares of Broadcom surged more than 123 percent in their first day of trading on the NASDAQ. The investment bankers helping with the offering included Morgan Stanley Dean Witter, BT Alex Brown, Credit Suisse First Boston, Hambrecht & Quist, and Merrill.

The managers of firms wanting to issue stock, whether for the first time or not, need to have a clear understanding of the features of stock and how stock is valued.

PREFERRED STOCK

preferred stock

Preferred stock is often referred to as a *hybrid security* because it has *many characteristics of both common stock and bonds.* Preferred stock is similar to common stock in that (1) it has no fixed maturity date, (2) failure to pay dividends does not bring on bankruptcy, and (3) dividends are not deductible for tax purposes. On the other hand, preferred stock is similar to bonds in that dividends are limited in amount.

The size of the preferred stock dividend is generally fixed either as a dollar amount or as a percentage of the par value. For example, Texas Utility Electric has preferred stock outstanding that pays an annual dividend of $2.05, while Pacific Telesis has some 7.56-percent preferred stock outstanding. The Pacific Telesis preferred stock has a par value of $25; hence, each share pays 7.56% × $25, or $1.89 in dividends annually.

To begin, we first discuss several features associated with almost all preferred stock. Then we take a brief look at methods of retiring preferred stock. We close by learning how to value preferred stock.

| Objective 1 | ## Features of Preferred Stock |

Although each issue of preferred stock is unique, a number of characteristics are common to almost all issues. Some of these more frequent traits include

- Multiple classes of preferred stock
- Preferred stock's claim on assets and income
- Cumulative dividends
- Protective provisions
- Convertibility
- Retirement features

All these features are presented in the discussion that follows.

Multiple Classes

If a company desires, it can issue more than one series or class of preferred stock, and each class can have different characteristics. In fact, it is quite common for firms that issue preferred stock to issue more than one series. For example, Philadelphia Electric has 13 different issues of preferred stock outstanding. These issues can be further differentiated in that some are convertible into common stock and others are not, and they have varying protective provisions in the event of bankruptcy.

Claim on Assets and Income
Preferred stock has priority over common stock with regard to claims on assets in the case of bankruptcy. The preferred stock claim is honored after that of bonds and before that of common stock. Multiple issues of preferred stock may be given an order of priority. Preferred stock also has a claim on income before common stock. That is, the firm must pay its preferred stock dividends before it pays common stock dividends. Thus, in terms of risk, preferred stock is safer than common stock because it has a prior claim on assets and income. However, it is riskier than long-term debt because its claims on assets and income come after those of bonds.

Cumulative Dividends
Most preferred stocks carry a **cumulative feature** that *requires all past unpaid preferred stock dividends be paid before any common stock dividends are declared.* The purpose is to provide some degree of protection for the preferred shareholder. Without a cumulative feature, there would be no reason why preferred stock dividends would not be omitted or passed when common stock dividends were passed.

cumulative feature

Protective Provisions
In addition to the cumulative feature, protective provisions are common to preferred stock. These **protective provisions** generally *allow for voting rights in the event of nonpayment of dividends, or they restrict the payment of common stock dividends if sinking-fund payments are not met or if the firm is in financial difficulty.* For example, consider

protective provisions

Reading a Stock Quote in the *Wall Street Journal*

Below is shown a section of the *Wall Street Journal* that gives the quotes on July 8, 1999, for some of the stocks traded on the New York Stock Exchange on that date.

The stocks listed below include some familiar companies, such as General Electric (GE), General Mills, and General Motors, that are listed in the *Wall Street Journal* on a daily basis. To help us understand how to read the quotes, consider General Electric:

- The 52 week *high* column shows that General Electric stock reached a high of $117^7/_{16}$ ($117.44) during the past year
- The 52 week *low* column shows that General Electric sold for a low of 69 ($69.00) during the past year
- The *stock* (GenElec) and *sym* (GE) columns give an abbreviated version of the corporation's name and the ticker symbol, respectively

- *Div*, the dividend column, gives the amount of dividend that General Electric paid its common stockholders in the last year; $1.40 per share
- *Yld %* (1.2) is the stock's dividend yield—the amount of the dividend divided by the day's closing price ($1.40 ÷ $117.94)
- *PE* (41) gives the current market price ($117^{15}/_{16}$ divided by the firm's earnings per share
- The amount of General Electric stock traded on July 8, 1999, is represented in the *Vol 100s* column, or 7,948,100 shares
- General Electric stock traded at a high price (Hi-$118^3/_4$) and a low price (Lo-$114^1/_8$) during the day
- The previous day's closing price is subtracted from the closing price *(Close)* of $117^{15}/_{16}$ for July 8, 1999, for a net change *(Net Chg)* of + 3

| 52 Weeks | | | | | Yld | | | | | | Net |
Hi	Lo	Stock	Sym	Div	%	PE	Vol 100s	Hi	Lo	Close	Chg
$118^3/_4$	69	GenElec	GE	1.40	1.2	41	79481	$118^3/_4$	$114^1/_8$	$117^{15}/_{16}$	$+\ 3$
$39^1/_4$	$31^1/_8$	GenGrthProp	GGP	1.96	5.6	20	779	$35^3/_8$	$34^7/_8$	$35^1/_{16}$	$-\ ^1/_{16}$
20	$7^3/_8$	GenHouse	GHW	0.32	1.6	38	83	$19^5/_8$	$19^7/_{16}$	$19^5/_8$	$+\ ^3/_{16}$
$47^7/_8$	$16^{11}/_{16}$	GenInstr	GIC	...	...		17910	46	$42^5/_8$	$43^3/_{16}$	$-\ 2^{13}/_{16}$
$84^{11}/_{16}$	$59^3/_{16}$	GenMills	GIS	2.20	2.7	24	5390	$82^1/_2$	$80^{15}/_{16}$	$82^1/_8$	$+\ 1^1/_4$
$63^7/_8$	$30^3/_8$	GenMotor H	GNH		...	...	6160	$60^5/_{16}$	$58^3/_4$	$59^1/_8$	$-\ 1^1/_4$
$78^1/_2$	$38^{15}/_{16}$	GenMotor	GM	2.00	2.9	14	26275	$71^1/_2$	$69^3/_4$	70	$-\ 1^{11}/_{16}$

Takin' It to the Net
The Web site for the New York Stock Exchange http://www. nyse.com describe how shares are traded on the NYSE.

Tenneco Corporation and Reynolds Metals preferred stocks. The Tenneco preferred stock has a protective provision that provides preferred stockholders with voting rights whenever six quarterly dividends are in arrears. At that point the preferred shareholders are given the power to elect a majority of the board of directors. The Reynolds Metals preferred stock includes a protective provision that precludes the payment of common stock dividends during any period in which the preferred stock sinking fund is in default. Both provisions, which give protection beyond that provided by the cumulative provision and thereby reduce shareholder risk, are desirable. Because of these protective provisions, investors do not require as high a rate of return. That is, they will accept a lower dividend payment.

Convertibility

convertible preferred stock

Much of the preferred stock that is issued today is **convertible preferred stock;** that is, *at the discretion of the holder the stock can be converted into a predetermined number of shares of common stock*. In fact, today about one-third of all preferred stock issued has a convertibility feature. The convertibility feature is, of course, desirable to the investor and thus reduces the cost of the preferred stock to the issuer.

Retirement Features

Although preferred stock does not have a set maturity associated with it, issuing firms generally provide for some method for retiring the stock.

Callable Preferred   Most preferred stock has some type of **call provision** associated with it. A call provision *entitles a company to repurchase its preferred stock (or bonds) from their holders at stated prices over a given time period.* In fact, the Securities and Exchange Commission discourages firms from issuing preferred stock without some call provision.

call provision

The call feature on preferred stock usually involves an initial premium of approximately ten percent above the par value or issuing price of the preferred stock. Then, over time, the call premium generally falls. By setting the initial call price above the initial issue price and allowing it to decline slowly over time, the firm protects the investor from an early call that carries no premium. A call provision also allows the issuing firm to plan the retirement of its preferred stock at predetermined prices.

Sinking-Fund Provision   A **sinking-fund provision** *requires the firm periodically to set aside an amount of money for the retirement of its preferred stock.* This money is then used to purchase the preferred stock in the open market or to call the stock, whichever method is cheaper. Although preferred stock does not have a maturity date associated with it, the use of a call provision in addition to a sinking fund can effectively create a maturity date. For instance, the Xerox Corporation has two preferred stock issues, one that has a 7-year sinking-fund provision and another with a 17-year sinking fund. Another firm, the SCANA Corporation, a $4.5 billion energy-based holding company in South Carolina, has preferred stock outstanding that is both callable and has a sinking-fund provision. By the terms of the issue, the stock's call premium above its par value is not to exceed the amount of the annual dividend, and the firm was to retire $2.4 million per year from 1996 through the year 2000.

sinking-fund provision

Valuing Preferred Stock

Objective 2

As already explained, the owner of preferred stock generally receives a constant dividend from the investment in each period. In addition, most preferred stocks are perpetuities (nonmaturing). In this instance, finding the value (present value) of preferred stock, V_{ps}, with a level cash-flow stream continuing indefinitely, may best be explained by an example.

Example

Consider AT&T's preferred stock issue. In similar fashion to valuing bonds in Chapter 7, we use a three-step valuation procedure.

Step 1: Estimate the amount and timing of the receipt of the future cash flows the preferred stock is expected to provide. AT&T's preferred stock pays an annual dividend of $3.64. The shares do not have a maturity date; that is, they are a perpetuity.

Step 2: Evaluate the riskiness of the preferred stock's future dividends and determine the investor's required rate of return. The investor's required rate of return is assumed to equal 7.28 percent.[1]

---

[1] For now the required rate of return is given, but in the next chapter we learn more about measuring an investor's required rate of return. Trust us for now.

Step 3: Calculate the economic or intrinsic value of the share of preferred stock, which is the present value of the expected dividends discounted at the investor's required rate of return. The valuation model for a share of preferred stock, V_{ps}, is therefore defined as follows:

$$V_{ps} = \frac{\text{dividend in year 1}}{(1 + \text{required rate of return})^1}$$

$$+ \frac{\text{dividend in year 2}}{(1 + \text{required rate of return})^2}$$

$$+ \cdots + \frac{\text{dividend in infinity}}{(1 + \text{required rate of return})^\infty} \qquad (8\text{--}1)$$

$$= \frac{D_1}{(1 + k_{ps})^1} + \frac{D_2}{(1 + k_{ps})^2} + \cdots + \frac{D_\infty}{(1 + k_{ps})^\infty}$$

$$V_{px} = \sum_{t=1}^{\infty} \frac{D_t}{(1 + k_{ps})^t}$$

Notice that Equation (8–1) is a restatement in a slightly different form of equation (7–2) in Chapter 7. Recall that equation (7–2) states that the value of an asset is the present value of future cash flows to be received by the investor.

Because the dividends in each period are equal for preferred stock, equation (8–1) can be reduced to the following relationship[2]:

$$V_{ps} = \frac{\text{annual dividend}}{\text{required rate of return}} = \frac{D}{k_{ps}} \qquad (8\text{--}2)$$

Equation (8–2) represents the present value of an infinite stream of cash flows, where the cash flows are the same each year. We can determine the value of the AT&T preferred stock, using equation (8–2), as follows:

$$V_{ps} = \frac{D}{k_{ps}} = \frac{\$3.64}{0.0728} = \$50$$

■

---

[2] To verify this result, consider the following equation:

(i)
$$V_{ps} = \frac{D_1}{(1 + k_{ps})^1} + \frac{D_2}{(1 + k_{ps})^2} + \cdots + \frac{D_n}{(1 + k_{ps})^n}$$

If we multiply both sides of this equation by $(1 + k_{ps})$, we have

(ii)
$$V_{ps}(1 + k_{ps}) = D_1 + \frac{D_2}{(1 + k_{ps})} + \cdots + \frac{D_n}{(1 + k_{ps})^{n-1}}$$

Subtracting (i) from (ii) yields

$$V_{ps}(1 + k_{ps} - 1) = D_1 - \frac{D_n}{(1 + k_{ps})^n}$$

As n approaches infinity, $D_n/(1 + k_{ps})$ approaches zero. Consequently,

$$V_{ps}k_{ps} = D_1 \text{ and } V_{ps} = \frac{D_1}{k_{ps}}$$

Since $D_1 = D_2 = \cdots = D_n$ we need not designate the year. Therefore,

(iii)
$$V_{ps} = \frac{D}{k_{ps}}$$

In summary, the value of a preferred stock is the present value of all future dividends. But because most preferred stocks are nonmaturing—the dividends continue to infinity—we therefore rely on a shortcut for finding value as represented by equation (8–2).

Takin' It to the Net
Visit the NASDAQ home page, http://www.nasdaq.com/ for symbol lookups, NASDAQ earning surprises, and other site press releases.

BACK TO THE FOUNDATIONS

Valuing preferred stock relies on three of our axioms presented in Chapter 1, namely:

Axiom 1: The Risk-Return Trade-off—We Won't Take on Additional Risk Unless We Expect to Be Compensated with Additional Return.

Axiom 2: The Time Value of Money—A Dollar Received Today Is Worth More Than a Dollar Received in the Future.

Axiom 3: Cash—Not Profits—Is King.

Determining the economic worth or value of an asset always relies on these three axioms. Without them, we would have no basis for explaining value. With them, we can know that the amount and timing of cash, not earnings, drive value. Also, we must be rewarded for taking risk; otherwise, we will not invest.

CONCEPT CHECK

1. What features of preferred stock are different from bonds?
2. What provisions are available to protect a preferred stockholder?
3. What cash flows associated with preferred stock are included in valuation model (8–1)? Why is the valuation model simplified in equation (8–2)?

COMMON STOCK

Common stock is *a certificate that indicates ownership in a corporation.* In effect, bondholders and preferred stockholders can be viewed as creditors, whereas the common stockholders are the true owners of the firm. Common stock does not have a maturity date, but exists as long as the firm does. Nor does common stock have an upper limit on its dividend payments. Dividend payments must be declared each period (usually quarterly) by the firm's board of directors. In the event of bankruptcy the common stockholders, as owners of the corporation, will not receive any payment until the firm's creditors, including the bondholders and preferred shareholders, have been satisfied.

common stock

In examining common stock, we first look at several of its features or characteristics. Then we focus on valuing common stock.

Features or Characteristics of Common Stock

Objective 3

We now examine common stock's claim on income and assets, stockholder voting rights, preemptive rights, and the meaning and importance of its limited-liability feature.

Berkshire Hathaway Issues New Class B Stock

If you look in the *Wall Street Journal* at the shares traded on the New York Stock Exchange, you might be surprised to see that one firm, Berkshire Hathaway, has shares that trade at $72,300 per share (as of July 8, 1999). The firm, founded and operated by Warren Buffett, began as an insurance company in Omaha, Nebraska, and has since grown into a multibillion-dollar enterprise that now owns a portfolio of companies. But few of us could afford to buy very many—if even one—of the shares. So Buffett made a decision to issue some class B shares that would be priced at a small portion of the original shares. The following is a Dow Jones News Service release (when the stock was selling for *only* $33,400) announcing the new shares.

Berkshire Hathaway Class B Shares Priced at $1,110
OMAHA, Neb. (Dow Jones)—Berkshire Hathaway, Inc.'s (BRK) offer of 450,000 new class B shares was priced at $1,100 each.

In a press release, the company said its class A common shares closed today at $33,400. The company has said the class B shares would come to market at about one-thirtieth of the price of the class A shares.

The offering may be increased to 517,500 shares of the lower-priced stock if the underwriter, Salomon Brothers, Inc., exercises its overallotment option in full.

Berkshire Hathaway, which is about 40% owned by Warren Buffett, is an insurance holding company.

Source: "Berkshire Hathaway Class B Shares Priced at $1110," *Dow Jones Newswires,* July 1999.

Claim on Income

As the owners of a corporation, the common shareholders have the right to the residual income after bondholders and preferred stockholders have been paid. This income may be paid directly to the shareholders in the form of dividends or retained and reinvested by the firm. Although it is obvious the shareholder benefits immediately from the distribution of income in the form of dividends, the reinvestment of earnings also benefits the shareholder. Plowing back earnings into the firm results in an increase in the value of the firm, in its earning power, and in its future dividends. This action in turn results in an increase in the value of the stock. In effect, residual income is distributed directly to shareholders in the form of dividends or indirectly in the form of capital gains on their common stock.

The right to residual income has both advantages and disadvantages for the common stockholder. The advantage is that the potential return is limitless. Once the claims of the most senior securities (bonds and preferred stock) have been satisfied, the remaining income flows to the common stockholders in the form of dividends or capital gains. The disadvantage is that if the bond and preferred stock claims on income totally absorb earnings, common shareholders receive nothing. In years when earnings fall, it is the common shareholder who suffers first.

Claim on Assets

Just as common stock has a residual claim on income, it also has a residual claim on assets in the case of liquidation. Only after the claims of debt holders and preferred stockholders have been satisfied do the claims of common shareholders receive any consideration. Unfortunately, when bankruptcy does occur, the claims of the common shareholders generally go unsatisfied. This residual claim on assets adds to the risk of common stock. Thus, while common stock has historically provided a large return, averaging 13 percent annually since the late 1920s, it also has large risks associated with it.

What Does a Stock Look Like?

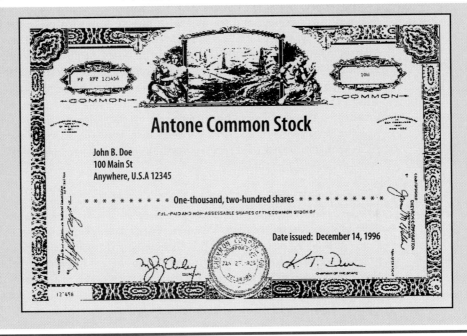

Voting Rights

The common stock shareholders are entitled to elect the board of directors, and are in general, the only security holders given a vote. However, with the merger boom of the 1980s, dual classes of common stock with different voting rights emerged as a defensive tactic used to prevent takeovers.

Common shareholders not only have the right to elect the board of directors, they also must approve any change in the corporate charter. A typical charter change might involve the authorization to issue new stock or perhaps to accept a merger proposal.

Voting for directors and charter changes occurs at the corporation's annual meeting. Although shareholders may vote in person, the majority generally vote by proxy. A **proxy** *gives a designated party the temporary power of attorney to vote for the signee at the corporation's annual meeting.* The firm's management generally solicits proxy votes and, if the shareholders are satisfied with its performance, has little problem securing them. However, in times of financial distress or when management takeovers are threatened, **proxy fights**—*battles between rival groups for proxy votes*—occur.

While each share of stock carries the same number of votes, the voting procedure is not always the same from company to company. The two procedures commonly used are majority and cumulative voting. Under **majority voting,** *each share of stock allows the shareholder one vote, and each position on the board of directors is voted on separately.* Because each member of the board of directors is elected by a simple majority, a majority of shares has the power to elect the entire board of directors.

proxy

proxy fight

majority voting

With **cumulative voting,** *each share of stock allows the shareholder a number of votes equal to the number of directors being elected.* The shareholder can then cast all of his or her votes for a single candidate or split them among the various candidates. The advantage of a cumulative voting procedure is that it gives minority shareholders the power to elect a director.

In theory, the shareholders pick the corporate board of directors, generally through proxy voting, and the board of directors in turn picks the management. Unfortunately, in reality the system frequently works the other way around. Management selects both the issues and the board of director nominees and then distributes the proxy ballots. In effect, shareholders are offered a slate of nominees selected by management from which to choose. The end result is that management effectively selects the directors, who then may have more allegiance to the managers than to the shareholders. This in turn sets up the potential for agency problems in which a divergence of interests between managers and shareholders is allowed to exist, with the board of directors not monitoring the managers on behalf of the shareholders as they should.

Preemptive Rights

The **preemptive right** *entitles the common shareholder to maintain a proportionate share of ownership in the firm.* When new shares are issued, common shareholders have the first right of refusal. If a shareholder owns 25 percent of the corporation's stock, then he or she is entitled to purchase 25 percent of the new shares. *Certificates issued to the shareholders giving them an option to purchase a stated number of new shares of stock at a specified price during a 2- to 10-week period* are called

rights. These rights can be exercised (generally at a price set by management below the common stock's current market price), allowed to expire, or sold in the open market.

Limited Liability

Although the common shareholders are the actual owners of the corporation, their *liability in the case of bankruptcy is limited to the amount of their investment.* The advantage is that investors who might not otherwise invest their funds in the firm become

willing to do so. This **limited liability** feature aids the firm in raising funds.

Objective 4 ■ Valuing Common Stock

Like bonds and preferred stock, a common stock's value is equal to the present value of all future cash flows expected to be received by the stockholder. However, in contrast to bonds, common stock does not promise its owners interest income or a maturity payment at some specified time in the future. Nor does common stock entitle the holder to a predetermined constant dividend, as does preferred stock. For common stock, the dividend is based on the profitability of the firm and on management's decision to pay dividends or to retain the profits for reinvestment purposes. As a consequence, dividend streams tend to increase with the growth in corporate earnings. Thus, the growth of future dividends is a prime distinguishing feature of common stock.

The Growth Factor in Valuing Common Stock

What is meant by the term *growth* when used in the context of valuing common stock? A company can grow in a variety of ways. It can become larger by borrowing money to invest in new projects. Likewise, it can issue new stock for expansion.

What Do You Tell Your Shareholders?

If you want a higher share price, what would you tell your investors? Suppose that someone asks you whether your company's share price is too high, too low, or just right. What should you say? If you think the answer depends on the circumstances, then you had best think again.

Most chief executives understand that they are, above all, salespersons, trying to convince the financial markets that their company is a good buy. But whereas ordinary salespeople are told that the customer is always right, most CEOs act as if the investors are always wrong. The CEO complains about the market's short-term focus and has little appreciation for analysts who follow the firm's stock.

Pleasing investors, however, is becoming more complicated. Besides the usual backward-looking financial measures, investors also want managers to be specific about their firms' future prospects, and they want more nonfinancial information to help them fill in the picture. Some advocates also want firms to provide more details about their "corporate governance" practices, such as boardroom procedures and ethical guidelines.

In a study by Shelley Taylor & Associates, "The Care and Feeding of Institutional Investors," the researchers examined the demands of the largest institutional investors in America, Britain, and continental Europe, and compared these with what firms actually disclose. The study found that investors rate one measure above all else: *free cash flow.*

Most managers, however, have refused to believe this. Instead, they continue to rely on accrual accounting measures to make decisions, frequently destroying value in the process. This has discouraged firms from being frank with shareholders. Although the disclosure of cash flow itself is easy enough (and is required by many accounting standards), Shelley Taylor's research suggests that information that helps investors gauge future cash flows is guarded closely.

There was another interesting finding. Of the 19 kinds of corporate-governance information considered, only one—executive pay—ranked among the top 20 issues investors care about. Specifically, they are concerned about the way in which pay relates to performance, not with just the amount. The rationale: an executive's incentives have a large effect on future performance.

Management could also acquire another company to merge with the existing firm, which would increase the firm's assets. In all these cases, the firm is growing through the use of new financing, by issuing debt or common stock. Although management could accurately say that the firm has grown, the original stockholders may or may not participate in this growth. Growth is realized through the infusion of new capital. The firm size has clearly increased, but unless the original investors increase their investment in the firm, they will own a smaller portion of the expanded business.

Another means of growing is **internal growth,** which requires that *management retain some or all of the firm's profits for reinvestment in the firm*, resulting in the growth of future earnings and, hopefully, the value of the common stock. This process underlies the essence of potential growth for the firm's current stockholders and is the only relevant growth for our purposes in valuing a firm's common shares.[3]

internal growth

---

[3]We are not arguing that the existing common stockholders never benefit from the use of external financing; however, such benefit is nominal if capital markets are efficient.

Takin' It to the Net
Visit the "Big Charts" Web site
http://www.bigcharts.com/ for
reports and charting on all areas
of NYSE, NASDAQ, S&P 500,
and other indexes.

Example

To illustrate the nature of internal growth, assume that the return on equity for PepsiCo is 16 percent.[4] If PepsiCo's management decides to pay all the profits out in dividends to its stockholders, the firm will experience no growth internally. It might become larger by borrowing more money or issuing new stock, but internal growth will come only through the retention of profits. If, on the other hand, PepsiCo retained all the profits, the stockholders' investment in the firm would grow by the amount of profits retained, or by 16 percent. If, however, management kept only 50 percent of the profits for reinvestment, the common shareholders' investment would increase only by half of the 16 percent return on equity, or by 8 percent. We can express this relationship by the following equation:

$$g = ROE \times r \tag{8-3}$$

where g = the growth rate of future earnings and the growth in the common
          stockholders' investment in the firm
   ROE = the return on equity (net income/common book value)
     r = *the company's percentage of profits retained*, called the **profit-retention rate**[5]

profit-retention rate

Therefore, if only 25 percent of the profits were retained by PepsiCo, we would expect the common stockholders' investment in the firm and the value of the stock price to increase or grow by 4 percent; that is,

$$g = 16\% \times 0.25 = 4\%$$

In summary, common stockholders frequently rely on an increase in the stock price as a source of return. If the company is retaining a portion of its earnings for reinvestment, future profits and dividends should grow. This growth should be reflected in an increased market price of the common stock in future periods, provided that the return on the funds reinvested exceeds the investor's required rate of return. Therefore, both types of return (dividends and price appreciation) must be recognized in valuing common stock.

To explain this process, let us consider how an investor might value a common stock that is to be held for only 1 year.

Common Stock Valuation—Single Holding Period

For an investor holding a common stock for only 1 year, the value of the stock should equal the present value of both the expected dividend to be received in 1 year, D_1, and the anticipated market price of the share at year end, P_1. If k_{cs} represents a common stockholder's required rate of return, the value of the security, V_{cs}, would be

$$V_{cs} = \text{present value of dividend in 1 year } (D_1)$$
$$+ \text{ present value of market price in 1 year } (P_1)$$
$$= \frac{D_1}{(1 + k_{cs})} = \frac{P_1}{(1 + k_{cs})} \tag{8-4}$$

---

[4]The return on equity is the accounting rate of return on the common shareholder's investment in the company and is computed as follows:

$$\text{return on equity} = \frac{\text{net income}}{\text{(par value + paid-in capital + retained earnings)}}$$

dividend-payout ratio

[5]The retention rate is also equal to (1 − the percentage of profits paid out in dividends). *The percentage of profits paid out in dividends* is often called the **dividend-payout ratio.**

Suppose an investor is contemplating the purchase of RMI common stock at the beginning of this year. The dividend at year end is expected to be $1.64, and the market price by the end of the year is projected to be $22. If the investor's required rate of return is 18 percent, the value of the security would be

$$V_{cs} = \frac{\$1.64}{1 + .18} + \frac{\$22}{1 + .18}$$
$$= \$1.39 + \$18.64$$
$$= \$20.03$$

Once again we see that valuation is a three-step process. First, we estimate the expected future cash flows from common stock ownership (a $1.64 dividend and a $22 end-of-year expected share price). Second, we determine the investor's required rate of return based on the riskiness of the expected cash flows (assumed to be 18 percent). Finally, we discount the expected dividend and end-of-year share price back to the present at the investor's required rate of return. The result is $20.03.

In summary, the intrinsic value of a common stock, like preferred stock, is the present value of all future dividends. And we have the same problem we had with preferred stock: It is hard to value cash flows that continue in perpetuity. So we must make some assumptions about the expected growth of future dividends. If, for example, we assume that dividends grow at a constant rate forever, we can then calculate the value (present value) of the stock.

Common Stock Valuation—Multiple Holding Periods

Because common stock has no maturity date and is frequently held for many years, a **multiple-holding-period valuation model** is needed. This model is *an equation used to value stock that has no maturity date, but continues in perpetuity (or as long as the firm exists)*. The general common stock valuation model can be defined as follows:

multiple-holding-period valuation model

$$V_{cs} = \frac{D_1}{(1 + k_{cs})^1} + \frac{D_2}{(1 + k_{cs})^2} + \cdots + \frac{D_n}{(1 + k_{cs})^n} + \cdots + \frac{D_\infty}{(1 + k_{cs})^\infty} \quad (8\text{–}5)$$

PAUSE AND REFLECT

Turn back to Chapter 7, and compare equation (7–2) with equation (8–5). Equation (8–5) is merely a restatement in a slightly different form of equation (7–2). Recall that equation (7–2), which is the basis for our work in valuing securities, states that the value of an asset is the present value of future cash flows to be received by the investor. Equation (8–5) is simply applying equation (7–2) to valuing common stock.

Equation (8–5) indicates that we are discounting the dividend at the end of the first year, D_1, back 1 year; the dividend in the second year, D_2, back 2 years; the dividend in the nth year back n years; and the dividend in infinity back an infinite number of years. The required rate of return is k_{cs}. In using equation (8–5), note that the value of the stock is established at the beginning of the year, say January 1, 2000. The most recent past dividend, D_0, would have been paid the previous day, December 31, 1999. Thus, if we purchased the stock on January 1, the first dividend would be received in 12 months, on December 31, 2000, which is represented by D_1.

Fortunately, equation (8–5) can be reduced to a much more manageable form if dividends grow each year at a constant rate, g. The constant-growth common-stock valuation equation may be presented as follows.[6]

$$\text{common stock value} = \frac{\text{dividend in year 1}}{\text{required rate of return} - \text{growth rate}} \tag{8-8}$$

$$V_{cs} = \frac{D_1}{k_{cs} - g}$$

Consequently, the intrinsic value (present value) of a share of common stock whose dividends grow at a constant annual rate can be calculated using equation (8–8). Although the interpretation of this equation may not be intuitively obvious, simply remember that it solves for the present value of the future dividend stream growing at a rate, g, to infinity, assuming that k_{cs} is greater than g.

Example

Consider the valuation of a share of common stock that paid a $2 dividend at the end of the last year and is expected to pay a cash dividend every year from now to infinity. Each year the dividends are expected to grow at a rate of 10 percent. Based on an assessment of the riskiness of the common stock, the investor's required rate of return is 15 percent. Using this information, we would compute the value of the common stock as follows:

1. Because the $2 dividend was paid last year (actually, yesterday), we must compute the next dividend to be received, that is, D_1, where

$$\begin{aligned} D_1 &= D_0(1 + g) \\ &= \$2(1 + .10) \\ &= \$2.20 \end{aligned}$$

---

[6]Where common stock dividends grow at a constant rate of g every year, we can express the dividend in any year in terms of the dividend paid at the end of the previous year, D_0. For example, the expected dividend 1 year hence is simply $D_0(1 + g)$. Likewise, the dividend at the end of t years is $D_0(1 + g)^t$. Using this notation, the common-stock valuation equation in (8–5) can be rewritten as follows:

$$V_{cs} = \frac{D_0(1 + g)^1}{(1 + k_{cs})^1} + \frac{D_0(1 + g)^2}{(1 + k_{cs})^2} + \cdots + \frac{D_0(1 + g)^n}{(1 + k_{cs})^n} + \cdots + \frac{D_0(1 + g)^\infty}{(1 + k_{cs})^\infty} \tag{8-6}$$

If both sides of equation (8–6) are multiplied by $(1 + k_{cs})/(1 + g)$ and then equation (8–5) is subtracted from the product, the result is

$$\frac{V_{cs}(1 + k_{cs})}{1 + g} - V_{cs} = D_0 - \frac{D_0(1 + g)^\infty}{(1 + k_{cs})^\infty} \tag{8-7}$$

If $k_{cs} > g$, which normally should hold, $[D_0(1 + g)^\infty/(1 + k_{cs})^\infty]$ approaches zero. As a result,

$$\frac{V_{cs}(1 + k_{cs})}{1 + g} - V_{cs} = D_0$$

$$V_{cs}\left(\frac{1 + k_{cs}}{1 + g}\right) - V_{cs}\left(\frac{1 + g}{1 + g}\right) = D_0$$

$$V_{cs}\left[\frac{(1 + k_{cs}) - (1 + g)}{1 + g}\right] = D_0$$

$$V_{cs}(k_{cs} - g) = D_0(1 + g)$$

$$V_{cs} = \frac{D_1}{k_{cs} - g} \tag{8-8}$$

2. Now, using equation (8–8),

$$V_{cs} = \frac{D_1}{k_{cs} - g}$$
$$= \frac{\$2.20}{.15 - .10}$$
$$= \$44$$

Takin' It to the Net
The CBS Market Watch
http://cbs.marketwatch.com has daily market data for analyst changes, IPO's, buybacks, and other market press releases. Check the Mutual Funds or Personal Finance section for resources on individual financing.

We have argued that the value of a common stock is equal to the present value of all future dividends, which is without question a fundamental premise of finance. In practice, however, managers, along with many security analysts, often talk about the relationship between stock value and earnings, rather than dividends. We would encourage you to be very cautious in using earnings to value a stock. Even though it may be a popular practice, the evidence available suggests that investors look to the cash flows generated by the firm, not the earnings, for value. A firm's value truly is the present value of the cash flow it produces.

We now turn to our last issue in stock valuation, that of the stockholder's expected returns, a matter of key importance to the financial manager.

CONCEPT CHECK

1. What features of common stock indicate ownership in the corporation versus preferred stock or bonds?
2. What are the two ways that a shareholder benefits from ownership?
3. How does internal growth versus the infusion of new capital affect the original shareholders?
4. If a corporation decides to retain its earnings, when would the value of the market price actually decrease?
5. What is the three-step process for common stock valuation? Explain the difference in the equations for a single-holding period and multiple-holding periods.

THE STOCKHOLDER'S EXPECTED RATE OF RETURN

As stated in Chapter 7, the expected rate of return on a bond is the return the bondholder expects to receive on the investment by paying the existing market price for the security. This rate of return is of interest to the financial manager because it tells the manager about the investor's expectations. The same can be said for the financial manager needing to know the expected rate of return of the firm's stockholders, which is the topic of this section.

The Preferred Stockholder's Expected Rate of Return

In computing the preferred stockholder's expected rate of return, we use the valuation equation for preferred stock. Earlier, equation (8–2) specified the value of a preferred stock, V_{ps}, as

$$V_{ps} = \frac{\text{annual dividend}}{\text{required rate of return}} = \frac{D}{k_{ps}} \tag{8-2}$$

Solving equation (8–2) for k_{ps}, we have

$$k_{ps} = \frac{\text{annual dividend}}{\text{value}} = \frac{D}{V_{ps}} \tag{8-9}$$

Thus, a preferred stockholder's *required* rate of return simply equals the stock's annual dividend divided by the intrinsic value. We may also restate equation (8–9) to solve for a preferred stock's *expected* rate of return, k_{ps}, as follows[7]:

$$\overline{k}_{ps} = \frac{\text{annual dividend}}{\text{market price}} = \frac{D}{P_{ps}} \qquad (8\text{–}10)$$

Note that we have merely substituted the current market price, P_{ps}, for the intrinsic value, V_{ps}. The expected rate of return, $\overline{k}_{ps}$, therefore equals the annual dividend relative to the price the stock is presently selling for, P_{ps}. Thus, the **expected rate of return, $\overline{k}_{ps}$,** is *the rate of return the investor can expect to earn from the investment if bought at the current market price.* For example, if the present market price of preferred stock is $50 and it pays a $3.64 annual dividend, the expected rate of return implicit in the present market price is

expected rate of return

$$\overline{k}_{ps} = \frac{D}{P_{ps}} = \frac{\$3.64}{\$50} = 7.28\%$$

Therefore, investors (who pay $50 per share for a preferred security that is paying $3.64 in annual dividends) are expecting a 7.28-percent rate of return.

The Common Stockholder's Expected Rate of Return

The valuation equation for common stock was defined earlier in equation (8–5) as

$$\text{value} = \frac{\text{dividend in year 1}}{(1 + \text{required rate of return})^1}$$

$$+ \frac{\text{dividend in year 2}}{(1 + \text{required rate of return})^2}$$

$$+ \cdots + \frac{\text{dividend in year infinity}}{(1 + \text{required rate of return})^\infty}$$

$$V_{cs} = \frac{D_1}{(1 + k_{cs})^1} + \frac{D_2}{(1 + k_{cs})^2} + \cdots + \frac{D_\infty}{(1 + k_{cs})^\infty} \qquad (8\text{–}5)$$

$$V_{cs} = \sum_{t=1}^{\infty} \frac{D_t}{(1 + k_{cs})^t}$$

Owing to the difficulty of discounting to infinity, we made the key assumption that the dividends, D_t, increase at a constant annual compound growth rate of g. If this assumption is valid, equation (8–5) was shown to be equivalent to

$$\text{common stock value} = \frac{\text{dividend in year 1}}{\text{required rate of return} - \text{growth rate}} \qquad (8\text{–}8)$$

$$V_{cs} = \frac{D_1}{k_{cs} - g}$$

Thus, V_{cs} represents the maximum value that an investor having a required rate of return of k_{cs}, would pay for a security having an anticipated dividend in year 1 of

---

[7]We will use $\overline{k}$ to represent a security's *expected* rate of return versus k for the investor's *required* rate of return.

D_1 that is expected to grow in future years at rate g. Solving equation (8–8) for k_{cs} we can compute the common stockholder's required rate of return as follows[8]:

$$k_{cs} = \frac{D_1}{V_{cs}} + g \qquad (8\text{–}11)$$

$$\uparrow \qquad\qquad \uparrow$$

dividend   annual
yield   growth
rate

From this equation, the common stockholder's required rate of return is equal to the dividend yield plus a growth factor. Although the growth rate, g, applies to the growth in the company's dividends, given our assumptions the stock's value may also be expected to increase at the same rate. For this reason, g represents the annual percentage growth in the stock value. In other words, the investor's required rate of return is satisfied by receiving dividends and capital gains, as reflected by the expected percentage growth rate in the stock price.

As was done for preferred stock earlier, we may revise equation (8–11) to measure a common stock's *expected* rate of return, $\bar{k}_{cs}$. Replacing the intrinsic value, V_{cs}, in equation (8–11) with the stock's current market price, P_{cs}, we may express the stock's expected rate of return as follows:

$$\bar{k}_{cs} = \frac{\text{dividend in year 1}}{\text{market price}} + \text{growth} = \frac{D_1}{P_{cs}} + g \qquad (8\text{–}12)$$

As an example of computing the expected rate of return for a common stock where dividends are anticipated to grow at a constant rate to infinity, assume that a firm's common stock has a current market price of $44. If the expected dividend at the conclusion of this year is $2.20 and dividends and earnings are growing at a 10-percent annual rate (last year's dividend was $2), the expected rate of return implicit in the $44 stock price is as follows:

$$\bar{k}_{cs} = \frac{\$2.20}{\$44} + 10\% = 15\%$$

BACK TO THE FOUNDATIONS

We have just learned that on average, the expected return will be equal to the investor's required rate of return. This equilibrium condition is achieved by investors paying for an asset only the amount that will exactly satisfy their required rate of return. Thus, finding the expected rate of return based on the current market price for the security relies on two of the axioms given in Chapter 1:

Axiom 1: The Risk-Return Trade-off—We Won't Take on Additional Risk Unless We Expect to Be Compensated with Additional Return.

Axiom 2: The Time Value of Money—A Dollar Received Today Is Worth More Than a Dollar Received in the Future.

---

[8]At times the expected dividend at year end (D_1) is not given. Instead, we might only know the most recent dividend (paid yesterday), that is, D_0. If so, equation (8–8) must be restated as follows:

$$V_{cs} = \frac{D_1}{(k_{cs} - g)} = \frac{D_0(1 + g)}{(k_{cs} - g)}$$

Takin' It to the Net
Visit Spreadware's Web site http://spreadware.com to look at some of the many methods of their software products used to estimate a firm's value.

As a final note, we should understand that the *expected* rate of return implied by a given market price equals the *required* rate of return for investors at the margin. For these investors, the expected rate of return is just equal to their required rate of return, and therefore they are willing to pay the current market price for the security. These investors' required rate of return is of particular significance to the financial manager, because it represents the cost of new financing to the firm.

CONCEPT CHECK

1. In computing the required rate of return, why should the growth factor be added to the dividend yield?
2. How does an efficient market affect the required and expected rates of return?

SUMMARY

Valuation is an important process in financial management. An understanding of valuation, both the concepts and procedures, supports the financial officer's objective of maximizing the value of the firm.

Identify the basic characteristics and features of preferred stock
Objective 1

Preferred stock has no fixed maturity date and the dividends are fixed in amount. Some of the more common characteristics of preferred stock include the following:

- There are multiple classes of preferred stock.
- Preferred stock has a priority of claim on assets and income over common stock.
- Any dividends, if not paid as promised, must be paid before any common stock dividends may be paid; that is, they are cumulative.
- Protective provisions are included in the contract with the shareholder to reduce the investor's risk.
- Many preferred stocks are convertible into common stock shares.

In addition there are provisions frequently used to retire an issue of preferred stock, such as the ability of the firm to call its preferred stock or to use a sinking-fund provision.

Value preferred stock
Objective 2

Value is the present value of future cash flows discounted at the investor's required rate of return. Although the valuation of any security entails the same basic principles, the procedures used in each situation vary. For example, we learned in Chapter 7 that valuing a bond involves calculating the present value of future interest to be received plus the present value of the principle returned to the investor at the maturity of the bond.

For securities with cash flows that are constant in each year but where there is no specified maturity, such as preferred stock, the present value equals the dollar amount of the annual dividend divided by the investor's required rate of return; that is,

$$\frac{\text{preferred}}{\text{stock value}} = \frac{\text{annual dividend}}{\text{required rate of return}}$$

Identify the basic characteristics and features of common stock
Objective 3

Common stock involves ownership in the corporation. In effect, bondholders and preferred stockholders can be viewed as creditors, while the common stockholders are the owners of the firm. Common stock does not have a maturity date, but exists as long as the firm does. Nor does common stock have an upper limit on its dividend payments. Dividend payments must be declared by the firm's board of directors before they are issued. In the event of bankruptcy, the common stockholders, as owners of the corporation, cannot exercise claims on assets until the firm's creditors, including the bondholders and preferred shareholders, have been satisfied. However, common stockholders' liability is limited to the amount of their investment.

The common stockholders are entitled to elect the board of directors and are in general the only security holders given a vote. Common shareholders have the right to elect the board of directors and to approve any change in the corporate charter. While each share of stock carries the same number of votes, the voting procedure is not always the same from company to company.

The preemptive right entitles the common shareholder to maintain a proportionate share of ownership in the firm.

Objective 4
Value common stock
For common stock where the future dividends are expected to increase at a constant growth rate, value may be given by the following equation:

$$\frac{\text{common}}{\text{stock value}} = \frac{\text{dividend in year 1}}{\text{required rate of return} - \text{growth rate}}$$

Growth here relates to *internal* growth only, in which management retains part of the firm's profit to be reinvested and thereby grow the firm—as opposed to growth through issuing of new stock or acquiring another firm.

Growth in and of itself does not mean that we are creating value for the stockholders. Only if we are reinvesting at a rate of return greater than the investors' required rate of return will growth result in increased value to the firm. In fact, if we are investing at rates less than the required rate of return for investors, the value of the firm will actually decline.

Objective 5
Calculate a stock's expected rate of return
The expected rate of return on a security is the required rate of return of investors who are willing to pay the present market price for the security, but no more. This rate of return is important to the financial manager because it equals the required rate of return of the firm's investors.

The expected rate of return for preferred stock is computed as follows:

$$\frac{\text{expected return,}}{\text{preferred stock}} = \frac{\text{annual dividend}}{\text{market price}}$$

The expected rate of return for common stock is calculated as follows:

$$\frac{\text{expected return,}}{\text{common stock}} = \frac{\text{dividend in year 1}}{\text{market price}} + \frac{\text{dividend}}{\text{growth rate}}$$

--- **KEY TERMS** ---

call provision, 233

common stock, 235

convertible preferred stock, 232

cumulative feature, 231

cumulative voting, 238

dividend-payout ratio, 240

expected rate of return, 245

internal growth, 239

limited liability, 238

majority voting, 237

multiple-holding-period valuation model, 241

preemptive right, 238

preferred stock, 230

profit-retention rate, 240

protective provisions, 231

proxy, 237

proxy fight, 237

rights, 238

sinking-fund provision, 233

8-1 Why is preferred stock referred to as a hybrid security? It is often said to combine the worst features of common stock and bonds. What is meant by this statement?

8-2 Inasmuch as preferred stock dividends in arrears must be paid before common stock dividends, should they be considered a liability and appear on the right-hand side of the balance sheet?

8-3 Why would a preferred stockholder want the stock to have a cumulative dividend feature and protective provisions?

8-4 Why is preferred stock frequently convertible? Why would it be callable?

8-5 Compare valuing preferred stock and common stock.

8-6 Define the investor's expected rate of return.

8-7 State how the investor's expected rate of return is computed.

8-8 The common stockholders receive two types of return from their investment. What are they?

SELF-TEST PROBLEMS

ST-1 *(Preferred Stock Valuation)*   What is the value of a preferred stock where the dividend rate is 16 percent on a $100 par value? The appropriate discount rate for a stock of this risk level is 12 percent.

ST-2 *(Preferred Stockholder Expected Return)*   You own 250 shares of Dalton Resources preferred stock, which currently sells for $38.50 per share and pays annual dividends of $3.25 per share.
  a. What is your expected return?
  b. If you require an 8-percent return, given the current price, should you sell or buy more stock?

ST-3 *(Preferred Stock Valuation)*   The preferred stock of Armlo pays a $2.75 dividend. What is the value of the stock if your required return is 9 percent?

ST-4 *(Common Stock Valuation)*   Crosby Corporation common stock paid $1.32 in dividends last year and is expected to grow indefinitely at an annual 7 percent rate. What is the value of the stock if you require an 11-percent return?

ST-5 *(Common Stockholder Expected Return)*   Blackburn & Smith common stock currently sells for $23 per share. The company's executives anticipate a constant growth rate of 10.5 percent and an end-of-year dividend of $2.50.
  a. What is your expected rate of return?
  b. If you require a 17-percent return, should you purchase the stock?

STUDY PROBLEMS

8-1 *(Preferred Stock Valuation)* What is the value of a preferred stock where the dividend rate is 14 percent on a $100 par value? The appropriate discount rate for a stock of this risk level is 12 percent.

8-2 *(Preferred Stockholder Expected Return)* Solitron preferred stock is selling for $42.16 and pays $1.95 in dividends. What is your expected rate of return if you purchase the security at the market price?

8-3 *(Preferred Stockholder Expected Return)* You own 200 shares of Somner Resources preferred stock, which currently sells for $40 per share and pays annual dividends of $3.40 per share.
  a. What is your expected return?
  b. If you require an 8-percent return, given the current price, should you sell or buy more stock?

8-4 *(Common Stock Valuation)* You intend to purchase Marigo common stock at $50 per share, hold it 1 year, and sell after a dividend of $6 is paid. How much will the stock price have to appreciate for you to satisfy your required rate of return of 15 percent?

8-5 *(Common Stockholder Expected Return)* Made-It common stock currently sells for $22.50 per share. The company's executives anticipate a constant growth rate of 10 percent and an end-of-year dividend of $2.

    a. What is your expected rate of return if you buy the stock for $22.50?

    b. If you require a 17-percent return, should you purchase the stock?

8-6 *(Common Stock Valuation)* Header Motor, Inc., paid a $3.50 dividend last year. At a constant growth rate of 5 percent, what is the value of the common stock if the investors require a 20-percent rate of return?

8-7 *(Measuring Growth)* Given that a firm's return on equity is 18 percent and management plans to retain 40 percent of earnings for investment purposes, what will be the firm's growth rate?

8-8 *(Common Stockholder Expected Return)* The common stock of Zaldi Co. is selling for $32.84. The stock recently paid dividends of $2.94 per share and has a projected constant growth rate of 9.5 percent. If you purchase the stock at the market price, what is your expected rate of return?

8-9 *(Common Stock Valuation)* Honeywag common stock is expected to pay $1.85 in dividends next year, and the market price is projected to be $42.50 by year end. If the investor's required rate of return is 11 percent, what is the current value of the stock?

8-10 *(Common Stockholder Expected Return)* The market price for Hobart common stock is $43. The price at the end of 1 year is expected to be $48, and dividends for next year should be $2.84. What is the expected rate of return?

8-11 *(Preferred Stock Valuation)* Pioneer preferred stock is selling for $33 in the market and pays a $3.60 annual dividend.

    a. What is the expected rate of return on the stock?

    b. If an investor's required rate of return is 10 percent, what is the value of the stock for that investor?

    c. Should the investor acquire the stock?

8-12 *(Common Stock Valuation)* The common stock of NCP paid $1.32 in dividends last year. Dividends are expected to grow at an 8-percent annual rate for an indefinite number of years.

    a. If NCP's current market price is $23.50, what is the stock's expected rate of return?

    b. If your required rate of return is 10.5 percent, what is the value of the stock for you?

    c. Should you make the investment?

8-13 *(Preferred Stock Valuation)* Calculate the value of a preferred stock that pays a dividend of $6 per share and your required rate of return is 12 percent.

8-14 *(Measuring Growth)* Pepperdine, Inc.'s return on equity is 16 percent and the management plans to retain 60 percent of earnings for investment purposes. What will be the firm's growth rate?

--- **COMPREHENSIVE PROBLEM** ---

You are considering three investments. The first is a bond that is selling in the market at $1,100. The bond has a $1,000 par value, pays interest at 13 percent, and is scheduled to mature in 15 years. For bonds of this risk class you believe that a 14-percent rate of return should be required. The second investment that you are analyzing is a preferred stock ($100 par value) that sells for $90 and pays an annual dividend of $13. Your required rate of return for this stock is 15 percent. The last investment is a common stock ($25 par value) that recently paid a $2 dividend. The firm's earnings per share has increased from $3 to $6 in 10 years, which also reflects the expected growth in dividends per share for the indefinite future. The stock is selling for $20, and you think a reasonable required rate of return for the stock is 20 percent.

   a. Calculate the value of each security based on your required rate of return.
   b. Which investment(s) should you accept? Why?
   c. **1.** If your required rates of return changed to 12 percent for the bond, 14 percent for the preferred stock, and 18 percent for the common stock, how would your answers change to parts a and b?
       2. Assuming again that your required rate of return for the common stock is 20 percent, but the anticipated constant growth rate changes to 12 percent, how would your answers to parts a and b change?

SELF-TEST SOLUTIONS

SS-1

$$\text{value } (V_{ps}) = \frac{0.16 \times \$100}{0.12}$$

$$= \frac{\$16}{0.12}$$

$$= \$133.33$$

SS-2

a. $\text{Expected return} = \dfrac{\text{dividend}}{\text{market price}} = \dfrac{\$3.25}{\$38.50} = 0.0844 = 8.44\%$

b. Given your 8 percent required rate of return, the stock is worth $40.62 to you:

$$\text{value} = \frac{\text{dividend}}{\text{required rate of return}} = \frac{\$3.25}{0.08} = \$40.62$$

Because the expected rate of return (8.44%) is greater than your required rate of return (8%) or because the current market price ($38.50) is less than $40.62, the stock is undervalued and you should buy.

SS-3

$$\text{value } (V_{ps}) = \frac{\text{dividend}}{\text{required rate of return}} = \frac{\$2.75}{0.09} = \$30.56$$

SS-4

$$\text{value } (V_{cs}) = \left(\frac{\text{last year dividend } (1 + \text{growth rate})}{\text{required rate of return} - \text{growth rate}} \right)$$

$$= \frac{\$1.32(1.07)}{0.11 - 0.07}$$

$$= \$35.31$$

SS-5

a.

$$\text{expected rate of return } (\bar{k}_{cs}) = \frac{\text{dividend in year 1}}{\text{market price}} + \text{growth rate}$$

$$\bar{k}_{cs} = \frac{\$2.50}{\$23.00} + 0.105 = 0.2137$$

$$\bar{k}_{cs} = 21.37\%$$

b.

$$V_{cs} = \frac{\$2.50}{0.17 - 0.105} = \$38.46$$

The expected rate of return exceeds your required rate of return, which means that the value of the security to you is greater than the current market price. Thus, you should buy the stock.

Chapter Nine

Expected Return Defined and Measured • Risk
Defined and Measured • Rates of Return: The
Investor's Experience • Risk and Diversification
• The Investor's Required Rate of Return

THE MEANING AND MEASUREMENT OF RISK AND RETURN

LEARNING OBJECTIVES

AFTER READING THIS CHAPTER, YOU SHOULD BE ABLE TO:

1. Define and measure the expected rate of return of an individual investment.

2. Define and measure the riskiness of an individual investment.

3. Compare the historical relationship between risk and rates of return in the capital markets.

4. Explain how diversifying investments affects the riskiness and expected rate of return of a portfolio or combination of assets.

5. Explain the relationship between an investor's required rate of return on an investment and the riskiness of the investment.

One of the most important concepts in all of finance deals with risk and return, and our first axiom addresses this topic. As an illustration of risk and return, consider what was happening with the stock prices of the various Internet companies during 1998 and early 1999.

From January 1, 1998, through April 16, 1999, the stock prices of Internet companies, such as Amazon.com, increased in value a whopping 572 percent, compared to 36 percent for most large company stocks. Most of us wish that we had been so "smart" as to buy a group of these Internet stocks. But then on April 19, 1999, the stock prices of Internet companies declined 17 percent on average, all within a matter of a few hours. Even some of the big high-tech stocks, such as Cisco, AOL, and Microsoft fell almost 6 percent. If you had owned these stocks, you might have been worried. However, these highly volatile price changes are part of the landscape if you buy and sell Internet stocks. Only 2 months before these share declined in April, the average Internet stock price fell 36 percent over a 2-week period.

Just to give one more example, on March 31, 1999, Priceline.com, which lets consumers bid on discounted items on the Net, issued stock to the public for the first time. The price was $16. In short order, the price increased to $91. On the fateful April 19 fall out, the stock price fell from $81 to $59.

Clearly, owning Internet stocks has not been for the faint of heart. In other words, these stocks may produce

WHAT'S AHEAD

The need to recognize risk in financial decisions has already been apparent in earlier chapters. In Chapter 2, we referred to the discount rate or the interest rate as the opportunity cost of funds, but we did not look at the causes for why that rate might be high or low. For example, we did not explain why in August 1999 you could buy bonds issued by AT&T that promised to pay a 6.5-percent rate of return, or why you could buy Polaroid Corporation bonds that would give you a 9.2-percent rate of return, provided that both firms make the payments to the investors as promised. Then in Chapters 7 and 8 when valuing bonds, preferred stock, and common stock, we suggested there is a relationship between an investor's required rate of return and the riskiness of the investment, but we gave little, if any, explanation.

In this chapter, we learn that risk is an integral force underlying rates of return. To begin our study, we define expected return and risk and offer suggestions as to how these important concepts of return and risk can be measured quantitatively. We also compare the historical relationship between risk and rates of return. We then explain how diversifying investments can affect the expected return and riskiness of those investments. We also consider how the riskiness of an investment should affect the required rate of return on an investment.

Let's begin our study by looking at what we mean by the expected rate of return and how it can be measured.

high rates of returns to their owners, but they are risky investments, as demonstrated by their high volatility. As the owner of Internet stocks, you may eat well if they continue to increase in the future, but you certainly won't sleep very well some nights. Welcome to the world of high risk.

BACK TO THE FOUNDATIONS

This chapter has one primary objective, that of helping us understand **Axiom 1: The Risk-Return Trade-off—We Won't Take on Additional Risk Unless We Expect to Be Compensated with Additional Return.**

Objective 1

EXPECTED RETURN DEFINED AND MEASURED

The expected benefits or returns an investment generates come in the form of cash flows. Cash flows, not accounting profits, is the relevant variable the financial manager uses to measure returns. This principle holds true regardless of the type of security, whether it is a debt instrument, preferred stock, common stock, or any mixture of these (such as convertible bonds).

Accurately measuring expected future cash flows is not easy in a world of uncertainty. To illustrate, assume you are considering an investment costing $10,000, for which the future cash flows from owning the security depend on the state of the economy, as estimated in Table 9–1.

TABLE 9-1

| | | | PERCENTAGE |
STATE OF THE ECONOMY	PROBABILITY OF THE STATES[a]	CASH FLOWS FROM THE INVESTMENT	RETURNS (CASH FLOW ÷ INVESTMENT COST)
Economic recession	20%	$1,000	10% ($1,000 ÷ $10,000)
Moderate economic growth	30%	1,200	12% ($1,200 ÷ $10,000)
Strong economic growth	50%	1,400	14% ($1,400 ÷ $10,000)

[a]The probabilities assigned to the three possible economic conditions have to be determined subjectively, which requires management to have a thorough understanding of both the investment cash flows and the general economy.

BACK TO THE FOUNDATIONS

Remember that future cash flows, not the reported earnings figure, determine the investor's rate of return. That is, **Axiom 3: Cash—Not Profits—Is King.**

In any given year, the investment could produce any one of three possible cash flows, depending on the particular state of the economy. With this information, how should we select the cash flow estimate that means the most for measuring the investment's expected rate of return? One approach is to calculate an *expected* cash flow. The expected cash flow is simply the weighted average of the *possible* cash flow outcomes such that the weights are the probabilities of the occurrence of the various states of the economy. Let X_i designate the ith possible cash flow, n reflect the number of possible states of the economy, and $P(X_i)$ indicate the probability that the ith cash flow or state of economy will occur. The expected cash flow, $\overline{X}$, may then be calculated as follows:

$$\overline{X} = P(X_1)X_1 + P(X_2)X_2 + \cdots + P(X_n)X_n \qquad (9\text{--}1)$$

or

$$\overline{X} = \sum_{i=1}^{n} P(X_i)X_i$$

For the present illustration:

$$\overline{X} = (.2)(\$1,000) + (.3)(\$1,200) + (.5)(\$1,400) = \$1,260$$

In addition to computing an expected dollar return from an investment, we can also calculate an **expected rate of return** earned on the $10,000 investment. Similar to the expected cash flow, the expected rate of return is *a weighted average of all the possible returns, weighted by the probability that each return will occur.* As the last column in Table 9–1 shows, the $1,400 cash inflow, assuming strong economic growth, represents a 14-percent return ($1,400 ÷ $10,000). Similarly, the $1,200 and $1,000 cash flows result in 12 percent and 10 percent returns, respectively. Using these percentage returns in place of the dollar amounts, the expected rate of return, $\overline{k}$, can be expressed as follows:

expected rate of return

$$\overline{k} = P(k_1)k_1 + P(k_2)k_2 + \cdots + P(k_n)k_n \qquad (9\text{--}2)$$

or

$$\overline{k} = \sum_{i=1}^{n} P(k_i)k_i$$

In our example:

$$\bar{k} = (.2)(10\%) + (.3)(12\%) + (.5)(14\%) = 12.6\%$$

With our concept and measurement of expected returns, let's consider the other side of the investment coin: risk.

CONCEPT CHECK

1. When we speak of "benefits" from investing in an asset, what do we mean?
2. Why is it difficult to measure future cash flows?
3. Define "expected rate of return."

Objective 2 **RISK DEFINED AND MEASURED**

Because we live in a world where events are uncertain, the way we see risk is vitally important in almost all dimensions of our life. The Greek poet and statesman Solon, writing in the sixth century B.C., put it this way:

> There is risk in everything that one does, and no one knows where he will make his landfall when his enterprise is at its beginning. One man, trying to act effectively, fails to foresee something and falls into great and grim ruination, but to another man, one who is acting ineffectively, a god gives good fortune in everything and escape from his folly.[1]

Solon would have given more of the credit to Zeus than we would for the outcomes of our ventures. However, his insight reminds us that little is new in this world, including the need to acknowledge and compensate as best we can for the risks we encounter. In fact, the significance of risk and the need for understanding what it means in our lives is noted by Peter Bernstein in the following excerpt[2]:

> What is it that distinguishes the thousands of years of history from what we think of as modern times? The answer goes way beyond the progress of science, technology, capitalism, and democracy.
>
> The distant past was studded with brilliant scientists, mathematicians, inventors, technologists, and political philosophers. Hundreds of years before the birth of Christ, the skies had been mapped, the great library of Alexandria built, and Euclid's geometry taught. Demand for technological innovation in warfare was as insatiable then as it is today. Coal, oil, iron, and copper have been at the service of human beings for millennia, and travel and communication mark the very beginnings of recorded civilization.
>
> The revolutionary idea that defines the boundary between modern times and the past is the mastery of risk: the notion that the future is more than a whim of the gods and that men and women are not passive before nature. Until human beings discovered a way across that boundary, the

---

[1]Translated by Arthur W. H. Adkins from the Greek text of Solon's poem "Prosperity, Justice, and the Hazards of Life," in M. L. West, ed., *Iambi et Elegi Gracci ante Alexandrum Canttati*, vol. 2 (Oxford: Clarendon Press, 1972).

[2]Peter Bernstein, *Against the Gods, the Remarkable Story of Risk*. John Wiley & Sons, Inc., New York, 1996, p. 1.

future was a mirror of the past or the murky domain of oracles and sooth-sayers who held a monopoly over knowledge of anticipated events.

In our study of risk, we want to consider these questions:

1. What is risk?
2. How do we know the amount of risk associated with a given investment; that is, how do we measure risk?
3. If we choose to diversify our investments by owning more than one asset, as most of us do, will such diversification reduce the riskiness of our combined portfolio of investments?

What Is Risk?

Without intending to be trite, risk means different things to different people, depending on the context and on how they feel about taking chances. For the student, risk is the possibility of failing an exam or the chance of not making his or her best grades. For the coal miner or the oil field worker, risk is the chance of an explosion in the mine or at the well site. For the retired person, risk means perhaps not being able to live comfortably on a fixed income. For the entrepreneur, risk is the chance that a new venture will fail.

While certainly acknowledging these different kinds of risk, we limit our atten- **risk** tion to the risk inherent in an investment. In this context, **risk** is the *potential vari- ability in future cash flows.* The wider the range of possible events that can occur, the greater the risk. If we think about it, this is a relatively intuitive concept.

To help us grasp the fundamental meaning of risk within this context, consider two possible investments:

1. The first investment is a U.S. Treasury bill, a government security that matures in 90 days and promises to pay an annual return of 6 percent. If we purchase and hold this security for 90 days, we are virtually assured of receiving no more and no less than 6 percent on annualized basis. For all practical purposes, the risk of loss is nonexistent.
2. The second investment involves the purchase of the stock of a local publishing company. Looking at the past returns of the firm's stock, we have made the fol- lowing estimate of the annual returns from the investment:

CHANCE OF OCCURRENCE	RATE OF RETURN ON INVESTMENT
1 chance in 10 (10%)	0%
2 chances in 10 (20%)	5%
4 chances in 10 (40%)	15%
2 chances in 10 (20%)	25%
1 chance in 10 (10%)	30%

Investing in the publishing company could conceivably provide a return as high as 30 percent if all goes well, or no return (0 percent) if everything goes against the firm. However, in future years, both good and bad, we could expect a 15-percent return on average.[3]

---

[3]We assume that the particular outcome or return earned in 1 year does *not* affect the return earned in the subsequent year. Technically speaking, the distribution of returns in any year is assumed to be independ- ent of the outcome in any prior year.

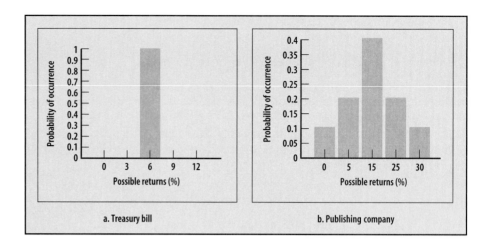

FIGURE 9–1

Probability Distribution of Returns

a. Treasury bill

b. Publishing company

$$\overline{k} = (.10)(0\%) + (.20)(5\%) + (.40)(15\%) + (.20)(25\%) + (.10)(30\%)$$
$$= 15\%$$

Comparing the Treasury bill investment with the publishing company investment, we see that the Treasury bill offers an expected 6-percent annualized rate of return, whereas the publishing company has an expected rate of return of 15 percent. However, our investment in the publishing firm is clearly more "risky"—that is, there is greater uncertainty about the final outcome. Stated somewhat differently, there is a greater variation or dispersion of possible returns, which in turn implies greater risk.[4] Figure 9–1 shows these differences graphically in the form of discrete probability distributions.

Although the return from investing in the publishing firm is clearly less certain than for Treasury bills, quantitative measures of risk are useful when the difference between two investments is not so evident. The standard deviation (σ) is such a measure. The **standard deviation** is simply the square root of the *weighted average squared deviation of each possible return from the expected return*; that is,

standard deviation

$$\sigma = \sqrt{\sum_{i=1}^{n} (k_i - \overline{k})^2 \, P(k_i)} \tag{9–3}$$

where n = the number of possible outcomes or different rates of return on the investment

k_i = the value of the *i*th possible rate of return

$\overline{k}$ = the expected value of the rates of return

$P(k_i)$ = the chance or probability that the *i*th outcome or return will occur

For the publishing company, the standard deviation would be 9.22 percent, determined as follows:

$$\sigma = \left[\begin{array}{ll} (\ 0\% - 15\%)^2(.10) & + (\ 5\% - 15\%)^2(.20) \\ + (15\% - 15\%)^2(.40) & + (25\% - 15\%)^2(.20) \\ + (30\% - 15\%)^2(.10) & \end{array} \right]^{1/2}$$

$$= \sqrt{85\%} = 9.22\%$$

---

[4]How can we possibly view variations above the expected return as risk? Should we even be concerned with the positive deviations above the expected return? Some would agree and view risk as only the negative variability in returns from a predetermined minimum acceptable rate of return. However, as long as the distribution of returns is symmetrical, the same conclusions will be reached.

Although the standard deviation of returns provides us with a quantitative measure of an asset's riskiness, how should we interpret the result? What does it mean? Is the 9.22-percent standard deviation for the publishing company investment good or bad? First, we should remember that statisticians tell us that two-thirds of the time an event will fall within one standard deviation of the expected value (assuming the distribution is normally distributed; that is, it is shaped like a bell). Thus, given a 15-percent expected return and a standard deviation of 9.22 percent for the publishing company investment, we may reasonably anticipate that the actual returns will fall between 5.78 percent and 24.22 percent (15% ± 9.22%) two-thirds of the time—not much certainty with this investment.

A second way of answering the question about the meaning of the standard deviation comes by comparing the investment in the publishing firm against other investments. The attractiveness of a security with respect to its return and risk cannot be determined in isolation. Only by examining other available alternatives can we reach a conclusion about a particular investment's risk. For example, if another investment, say an investment in a firm that owns a local radio station, has the same expected return as the publishing company, 15 percent, but with a standard deviation of 7 percent, we would consider the risk associated with the publishing firm, 9.22 percent, to be excessive. In the technical jargon of modern portfolio theory, the radio company investment is said to "dominate" the publishing firm investment. In commonsense terms, this means that the radio company investment has the same expected return as the publishing company investment but is less risky.

What if we compare the investment in the publishing company with one in a quick oil-change franchise, an investment in which the expected rate of return is an attractive 24 percent but where the standard deviation is estimated at 13 percent? Now what should we do? Clearly, the oil-change franchise has a higher expected rate of return, but it also has a larger standard deviation. In this example, we see that the real challenge in selecting the better investment comes when one investment has a higher expected rate of return but also exhibits greater risk. *Here the final choice is determined by our attitude toward risk, and there is no single right answer.* You might select the publishing company, while I might choose the oil-change investment, and neither of us would be wrong. We would simply be expressing our tastes and preferences about risk and return.

1. How is risk defined?
2. How does the standard deviation help us to measure the riskiness of an investment?
3. Does greater risk imply a bad investment?

| Objective 3 | RATES OF RETURN: THE INVESTOR'S EXPERIENCE |

In speaking of expected rates of return and risk, we have mostly used hypothetical examples; however, it is also interesting to look at returns that investors have actually received. Such information is readily available. For example, Ibbotson and Sinquefield have provided annual rates of return as far back as 1926.[5] In their results, they summarize, among other things, the annual returns for six portfolios of securities made up of

1. Common stocks of large companies
2. Common stocks of small firms
3. Long-term corporate bonds
4. Long-term U.S. government bonds
5. Intermediate-term U.S. government bonds
6. U.S. Treasury bills

Before comparing these returns, we should think about what to expect. First, we would intuitively expect a Treasury bill to be the least risky of the six portfolios. Because a Treasury bill has a short-term maturity date, the price is less volatile (less risky) than the price of an intermediate- or long-term government security. In turn, because there is a chance of default on a corporate bond, which is essentially nonexistent for government securities, a long-term government bond is less risky than a long-term corporate bond. Finally, common stock of large companies is more risky than a corporate bond, with small-company stocks being more risky than the portfolio of large-firm stocks.

With this in mind, we could reasonably expect different rates of return to the holders of these varied securities. If the market rewards an investor for assuming risk, the average annual rates of return should increase as risk increases.

A comparison of the annual rates of return for the six respective portfolios for the years 1926–1998 is provided in Figure 9–2. Four aspects of these returns are included: (1) the nominal average annual rate of return; (2) the standard deviation of the returns, which measures the volatility or riskiness of the portfolio returns; (3) the real average annual rate of return, which is the nominal return less the inflation rate; and (4) the risk premium, which represents the additional return received beyond the risk-free rate (Treasury bill rate) for assuming risk. Also, a frequency distribution of returns is provided. Looking first at the two columns of average annual returns and standard deviations, we gain a good overview of the risk-return relationships that have existed over the 73 years ending in 1998. For the most part, there has been a positive relationship between risk and return, with Treasury bills being least risky

[5]Roger G. Ibbotson and Rex A. Sinquefield, *Stocks, Bonds, Bills, and Inflation: 1998 Yearbook* (1926–1998) (Chicago: Dow Jones–Irwin, 1999).

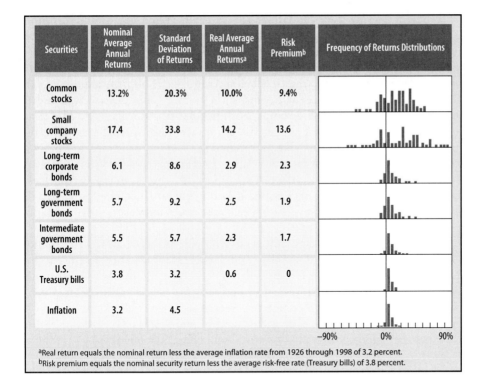

Securities	Nominal Average Annual Returns	Standard Deviation of Returns	Real Average Annual Returns[a]	Risk Premium[b]	Frequency of Returns Distributions
Common stocks	13.2%	20.3%	10.0%	9.4%	
Small company stocks	17.4	33.8	14.2	13.6	
Long-term corporate bonds	6.1	8.6	2.9	2.3	
Long-term government bonds	5.7	9.2	2.5	1.9	
Intermediate government bonds	5.5	5.7	2.3	1.7	
U.S. Treasury bills	3.8	3.2	0.6	0	
Inflation	3.2	4.5			

[a]Real return equals the nominal return less the average inflation rate from 1926 through 1998 of 3.2 percent.
[b]Risk premium equals the nominal security return less the average risk-free rate (Treasury bills) of 3.8 percent.

FIGURE 9–2
Annual Rates of Return, 1926–1998

Source: Summary Statistics of Annual Total Returns: 1926 to 1998. *1999 Yearbook.* Copyright © 1999 Ibbotson Assoc., Inc. Based on copyrighted works by Ibbotson and Sinquefield. All rights reserved. Used with permission.

and small company common stocks being most risky. However, long-term government bonds have been more risky than corporate bonds. This aberration has largely been the result of the 5 years from 1977 through 1981, a period when interest rates rose to all-time highs, which had a significantly negative impact on bond prices.

The return information in Figure 9–2 clearly demonstrates that only common stock has in the long run served as an inflation hedge and provided any substantial risk premium. However, it is equally apparent that the common stockholder is exposed to sizable risk, as demonstrated by a 20.3-percent standard deviation for large-company stocks and a 33.8-percent standard deviation for small-company stocks. In fact, in the 1926–1998 time frame, common shareholders of large firms received negative returns in 20 of the 73 years, compared with only 1 (1938) in 73 for Treasury bills.

Takin' It to the Net
The rates of return in Figure 9–2 come from a company called Ibbotson Associates. Go to their home page, http://www.ibbotson.com, to see what information they provide on the Internet.

CONCEPT CHECK

1. What is the additional compensation called for assuming greater risk?
2. In Figure 9–2, which rate of return is the risk-free rate? Why?

RISK AND DIVERSIFICATION

Objective 4

From the preceding discussions, we can define risk as the variability of anticipated returns as measured by the standard deviation. However, more can be said about risk, especially as to its nature, when we own more than one asset in our investment portfolio. Let's consider for the moment how risk is affected if we diversify our investment by holding a variety of securities.

To begin, assume that the date is July 1, 1999. When you awake this morning, you follow your daily routine, which includes reading the *Wall Street Journal*. You always begin by scanning "What's News—Business and Finance," with an eye for anything related to the stocks you own—and there they are. Two of your stocks made the front page, the first being Motorola. The firm announced that profits had declined 32 percent because of a cellular-phone price war and the declining demand for computer chips, both products Motorola sells. The result: Motorola's stock fell 15 percent on the announcement. That hurts! The only consolation is the article on Nike, another one of your investments. For Nike, profits were up 38 percent as the result of an unexpected surge in sales. In response, the company's stock increased 4.3 percent—not as much as your loss in Motorola, but it helps. You also notice that these events occurred on a day that the overall market on the New York Stock Exchange increased only one-half of 1 percent.

Clearly, what we have described about Motorola and Nike were events unique to these two companies, and as we would expect, the investors reacted accordingly; that is, the value of the stock changed in light of the new information. While we might have wished we had owned only Nike stock at the time, most of us would prefer to avoid such uncertainties; that is, we are risk averse. Instead, we would like to reduce the risk associated with our investment portfolio, without having to accept a lower expected return. Good news: It is possible by diversifying our portfolio!

Diversifying Away the Risk

If we diversify our investments across different securities rather than invest in only one stock, the variability in the returns of our portfolio should decline. The reduction in risk will occur if the stock returns within our portfolio do not move precisely together over time—that is, if they are not perfectly correlated. Figure 9–3 shows graphically what we may expect to happen to the variability of returns as we add additional stocks to the portfolio. The reduction occurs because some of the volatility in returns of a stock are unique to that security. The unique variability of a single stock tends to be countered by the uniqueness of another security. However, we should not expect to eliminate all risk from our portfolio. In practice, it would be rather difficult to cancel all the variations in returns of a portfolio, because stock prices have some tendency to move together. Thus, we can divide the total risk (total variability) of our portfolio into two types of risk: (1) **company-unique risk** or **unsystematic risk** and (2) **market risk** or **systematic risk.** Company-unique risk might also be called **diversifiable risk,** in that it *can be diversified away.* Market risk is **nondiversifiable risk;** it *cannot be eliminated through random diversification.* These two types of risk are shown graphically in Figure 9–3. Total risk declines until we have approximately 20 securities, and then the decline becomes very slight.

The remaining risk, which would typically be about 40 percent of the total risk, is the portfolio's systematic or market risk. At this point, our portfolio is highly correlated with all securities in the marketplace. Events that affect our portfolio now are not so much unique events as changes in the general economy, major political events, and sociological changes. Examples include changes in interest rates in the economy, changes in tax legislation that affect all companies, or increasing public concern about the effect of business practices on the environment.

Because we can remove the company-unique or unsystematic risk, there is no reason to believe the market will reward us with additional returns for assuming risk

company-unique risk
unsystematic risk
market risk
systematic risk
diversifiable risk
nondiversifiable risk

Negotiating a Deal—The Old-Fashioned Way

Warren Buffet is world renowned as an investor. The stock of his firm, Berkshire Hathaway, traded at a price of about $32,000 per share in 1996. His philosophy is to invest in only a small number of companies and then be actively involved with the management. The following is an excerpt from the 1993 Berkshire Hathaway annual report, and gives us a great (and unique) example of a business transaction based not on the technicalities of a long and involved contract, but on trust. Buffet writes:

Mrs. B—Rose Blumkin—had her 100th birthday on December 3, 1993. (The candles cost more than the cake.) That was a day on which the store was scheduled to be open in the evening. Mrs. B, who works seven days a week, for however many hours the store operates, found the proper decision quite obvious: She simply postponed her party until an evening when the store was closed.

Mrs. B's story is well known but worth telling again. She came to the United States 77 years ago, unable to speak English and devoid of formal schooling. In 1937, she founded the Nebraska Furniture Mart with $500. Last year the store had sales of $200 million, a larger amount by far than that recorded by any other home furnishings store in the United States. Our part in all of this began ten years ago when Mrs. B sold control of the business to Berkshire Hathaway, a deal we completed without obtaining audited financial statements, checking real estate records, or getting any warranties. In short, her word was good enough for us.

Naturally, I was delighted to attend Mrs. B's birthday party. After all, she's promised to attend *my* 100th.

Source: Berkshire Hathway, Inc., 1993 Annual Report, Omaha, Nebraska, pages 19–20.

that could be avoided by simply diversifying. Our measure of risk should therefore measure how responsive a stock or portfolio is to changes in a market portfolio, such as the New York Stock Exchange or the S&P 500 Index.[6]

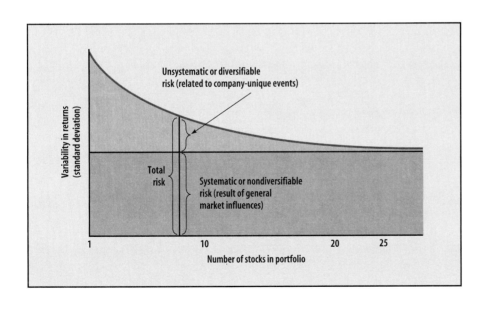

FIGURE 9–3
Variability of Returns Compared with Size of Portfolio

---

[6]The New York Stock Exchange Index is an index that reflects the performance of all stocks listed on the New York Stock Exchange. The Standard & Poor's (S&P) 500 Index is similarly an index that measures the combined stock-price performance of the companies that constitute the 500 largest companies in the United States, as designated by Standard & Poor's.

Measuring Market Risk

To help clarify the idea of systematic risk, let's examine the relationship between the common stock returns of McDonald's Corporation and the returns of the S&P 500 Index. The monthly returns for the McDonald's Corporation and the S&P 500 Index for the 24 months ending April 1999 are presented in Table 9–2 and Figure 9–4. These *monthly returns*, or **holding-period returns,** as they are often called, are calculated as follows.[7]

holding-period returns

$$k_t = \frac{P_t}{P_{t-1}} - 1 \tag{9–4}$$

where k_t = the holding-period return in month t for a particular firm like McDonald's or for a portfolio such as the S&P 500 Index

P_t = a firm's stock price like McDonald's (or the S&P 500 Index) at the end of month t

For instance, the holding-period return for McDonald's and the S&P 500 Index for the first month, May 1997, is computed as follows:

$$\text{McDonald's return} = \frac{\text{stock price end of May 1997}}{\text{stock price end of April 1997}} - 1$$

$$= \frac{25.13}{26.75} - 1 = -.0607 = -6.07\%$$

$$\text{S\&P 500 Index return} = \frac{\text{index value end of May 1997}}{\text{index value end of April 1997}} - 1$$

$$= \frac{848.28}{801.34} - 1 = .0586 = 5.86\%$$

At the bottom of Table 9–2, we have also computed the averages of the returns for the 24 months, both for McDonald's and the S&P 500 Index, and the standard deviation for these returns. Because we are using historical return data, we assume each observation has an equal probability of occurrence. Thus, the average return, $\bar{k}$, is found by summing the returns and dividing by the number of months; that is,

$$\frac{\text{average}}{\text{return}} = \bar{k} = \frac{\sum\limits_{t=1}^{n} \text{return in month } t}{\text{number of months}} = \frac{\sum\limits_{t=1}^{n} (k_t)}{n} \tag{9–6}$$

and the standard deviation σ is computed as:

$$\frac{\text{standard}}{\text{deviation}} = \sqrt{\frac{\sum\limits_{t=1}^{n} (\text{return in month } t - \text{average return})^2}{\text{number of months} - 1}} \tag{9–7}$$

$$\sigma = \sqrt{\frac{\sum\limits_{t=1}^{n} (k_t - \bar{k})^2}{n - 1}}$$

---

[7]For simplicity's sake, we are ignoring the dividend that the investor receives from the stock as part of the total return. In other words, letting D_t equal the dividend received by the investor in month t, the holding-period return would more accurately be measured as

$$k_t = \frac{P_t + D_t}{P_{t-1}} - 1 \tag{9–5}$$

MONTH AND YEAR	McDonald's		S&P 500 Index	
	PRICES	RETURNS (%)	PRICES	RETURNS (%)
1997				
April	26.75		801.34	
May	25.13	−6.06	848.28	5.86
June	24.16	−3.86	885.14	4.35
July	26.88	11.26	954.29	7.81
August	23.66	−11.98	899.47	−5.74
September	23.81	0.63	947.28	5.32
October	22.41	−5.88	914.62	−3.45
November	24.25	8.21	955.40	4.46
December	23.88	−1.53	970.43	1.57
1998				
January	23.56	−1.34	980.28	1.02
February	27.28	15.79	1,049.34	7.04
March	30.00	9.97	1,101.75	4.99
April	30.94	3.13	1,111.75	0.91
May	32.81	6.04	1,090.82	−1.88
June	34.50	5.15	1,133.84	3.94
July	33.41	−3.16	1,120.67	−1.16
August	28.19	−15.62	957.28	−14.58
September	29.84	5.85	1,017.01	6.24
October	33.53	12.37	1,098.67	8.03
November	35.03	4.47	1,163.63	5.91
December	38.41	9.65	1,229.23	5.64
1999				
January	39.41	2.60	1,279.64	4.10
February	42.50	7.84	1,238.33	−3.23
March	45.31	6.61	1,286.37	3.88
April	42.38	−6.47	1,335.18	3.79
Average monthly return		2.24		2.28
Standard deviation		7.91		5.20

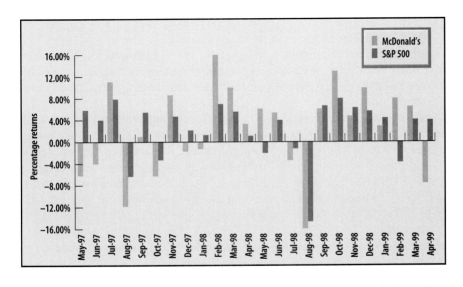

FIGURE 9-4

Monthly Holding-Period Returns: McDonald's Corporation and the S&P 500 Index, May 1997–April 1999

Source: Standard & Poor's 500 Guide, 1999 Edition. Standard & Poor's Corp, 1999.

In looking at Table 9–2 and Figure 9–4, we notice the following things about McDonald's holding-period returns over the 2 years ending in April 1999, these being:

1. McDonald's stockholders have had about the same average monthly returns as the average stock in the S&P 500 Index, 2.24 percent compared to 2.28 percent.
2. The bad news is McDonald's greater volatility of returns—in other words, greater risk—as evidenced by McDonald's higher standard deviation. As shown at the bottom of Table 9–2, the standard deviation of the returns is 7.91 percent for McDonald's versus 5.2 percent for the S&P 500 Index. McDonald's more volatile returns are also evident in Figure 9–4, where we see the McDonald's returns frequently being higher and lower than the corresponding S&P 500 returns.
3. We should also notice the tendency of McDonald's stock price to increase (decrease) when the value of the S&P 500 Index increases (decreases). In 17 of the 24 months, McDonald's returns were positive (negative) when the S&P 500 Index returns were positive (negative). That is, there is a positive, although not perfect, relationship between McDonald's stock returns and the S&P 500 Index returns.

With respect to our third observation, that there is a relationship between the stock returns with McDonald's and the S&P 500 Index, it is helpful to see this relationship by graphing McDonald's returns against the S&P 500 Index returns. We provide such a graph in Figure 9–5. In the figure, we have plotted McDonald's returns on the vertical axis and the returns for the S&P 500 Index on the horizontal axis. Each of the 24 dots in the figure represent the returns the McDonald's and the S&P 500 Index for a particular month. For instance, the returns for November 1998 for McDonald's and the S&P 500 Index were 4.47 percent and 5.91 percent, respectively, which are noted in the figure.

characteristic line

In addition to the dots in the graph, we have drawn a line of "best fit," which we call the **characteristic line.** *The slope of the characteristic line measures the average relationship between a stock's returns and those of the S&P 500 Index:* or stated differently, *the slope of the line indicates the average movement in a stock's price to a movement in the S&P 500 Index price.* For McDonald's, the slope of the line is 1.1, which simply equals the rise of the line relative to the run of the line.[8] A slope of 1.1, as for McDonald's, means that as the market return (S&P 500 Index returns) increases or decreases one percentage point, the return for McDonald's on average increases or decreases 1.1 percentage points.

beta

We can also think of the 1.1 slope of the characteristic line as indicating that McDonald's returns are 1.1 times as volatile on average as those of the overall market (S&P 500 Index). This slope has come to be called **beta** in investor jargon, and *measures the average relationship between a stock's returns and the market's returns.* It is a term you will see almost any time you read an article written by a financial analyst about the riskiness of a stock.

Looking once again at Figure 9–5, we see that the dots (returns) are scattered all about the characteristic line—most of the returns do not fit neatly on the characteristic line. That is, the average relationship may be 1.1, but the variation in McDonald's returns is only partly explained by the stock's average relationship with the S&P 500 Index. There are other driving forces unique to McDonald's that also affect the firm's stock returns. (Earlier, we called this company-unique risk.) If we

---

[8]Linear regression is the statistical technique used to determine the slope of the line of best fit.

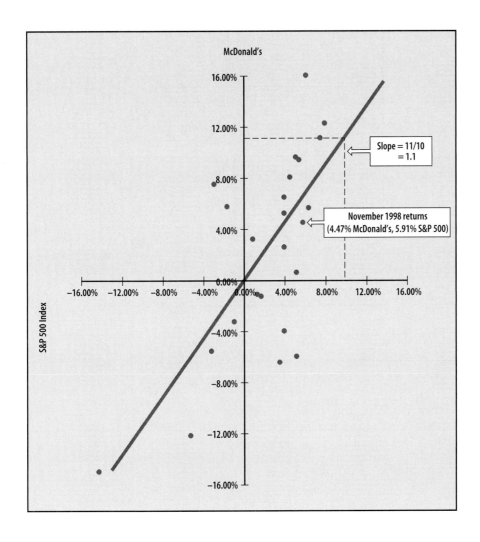

FIGURE 9–5

Monthly Holding-Period Returns of McDonald's Corporation and the S&P 500 Index, May 1997–April 1999

were, however, to diversify our holdings and own, say, 20 stocks with betas of 1.1, we could essentially eliminate the variation about the characteristic line. That is, we would remove almost all the volatility in returns, except for what is caused by the general market, which is represented by the slope of the line in Figure 9–5. If we plotted the returns of our 20-stock portfolio against the S&P 500 Index, the points in our new graph would fit nicely along a straight line with a slope of 1.1, which means that the beta of the portfolio is also 1.1. The new graph would look something like the one shown in Figure 9–6. In other words, by diversifying our portfolio, we can essentially eliminate the variations about the characteristic line, leaving only the variation in returns for a company that comes from variations in the general market returns.

So beta—the slope of the characteristic line—is a measure of a firm's market risk or systematic risk, which is the risk that remains for a company even after we have diversified our portfolio. It is this risk—and only this risk—that matters for investors who have broadly diversified portfolios.

While we have said that beta is a measure of a stock's systematic risk, how should we interpret a specific beta? For instance, when is a beta considered low and when is it considered high? In general, a stock with a beta of zero has no systematic risk; a stock with a beta of 1 has systematic or market risk equal to the

FIGURE 9–6

Holding-Period Returns: Hypothetical Portfolio and the S&P 500 Index

"typical" stock in the marketplace; and a stock with a beta exceeding 1 has more market risk than the typical stock. Most stocks, however, have betas between 0.60 and 1.60.

We should also realize that calculating beta is no exact science. The final estimate of a firm's beta is heavily dependent on one's methodology. For instance, it matters whether you use 24 months in your measurement or 60 months, as most professional investment companies do. Take our computation of McDonald's beta. We said McDonald's beta was 1.1, but Standard & Poor's and Value Line, two well-known investment services, have estimated McDonald's beta to be 1.01 and 1.05, respectively. The difference in results can be observed by comparing Standard & Poor's and Value Line's beta estimates for a number of firms as follows:

	STANDARD & POOR'S	VALUE LINE
Coca-Cola	1.00	1.10
Exxon	0.62	0.85
Ford	0.94	1.15
General Electric	1.15	1.20
IBM	1.25	1.05
Merck	0.93	1.05
Nike	0.99	0.85
PepsiCo	1.44	0.95
Wal-Mart	0.86	1.00

Thus, although close in many instances, even the professionals may not agree in their measurement of a given firm's beta.

To this point, we have talked about measuring an individual stock's beta. We will now consider how to measure the beta for a portfolio of stocks.

Measuring a Portfolio's Beta

What if we were to diversify our portfolio, as we have just suggested, but instead of acquiring stocks with the same beta as McDonald's (1.1) we buy 8 stocks with betas of 1.0 and 12 stocks with betas of 1.5. What would the beta of our portfolio become? As it works out, the **portfolio beta** is merely the average of the individual stock betas. Actually, the portfolio beta is a *weighted average of the individual security's betas, with the weights being equal to the proportion of the portfolio invested in each security.* Thus, the beta (β) of a portfolio consisting of *n* stocks is equal to:

portfolio beta

$$\beta_{portfolio} = \sum_{j=1}^{n} \left[(\text{percentage invested in stock } j) \times (\beta \text{ of stock } j) \right] \quad \text{(9-8)}$$

So, assuming we bought equal amounts of each stock in our new 20-stock portfolio, the beta would simply be 1.3, calculated as follows:

$$\text{portfolio beta} = \left(\frac{8}{20} \times 1.0 \right) + \left(\frac{12}{20} \times 1.50 \right)$$
$$= 1.3$$

Thus, whenever the general market increases or decreases 1 percent, our new portfolio's returns would change 1.3 percent on average, which says that our new portfolio has more systematic or market risk than the market has as a whole.

We can conclude that the beta of a portfolio is determined by the betas of the individual stocks. If we have a portfolio consisting of stocks with low betas, then our portfolio will have a low beta. The reverse is true as well. Figure 9–7 presents these situations graphically.

Before leaving the subject of risk and diversification, we want to share a study that demonstrates the effects of diversifying our investments, not just across different stocks, but across different types of securities.

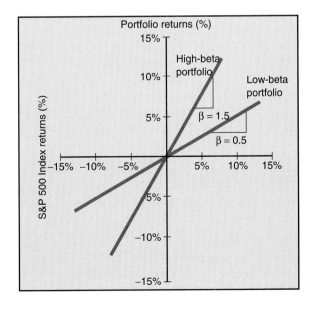

FIGURE 9–7

Holding-Period Returns: High- and Low-Beta Portfolios and the S&P 500 Index

Risk and Diversification Demonstrated[9]

Having described the effect of diversification on risk and return in a general way, let's now look at some actual numbers to demonstrate how risk and return changes as you diversify your portfolio. As it was earlier in the chapter, our source of information is Ibbotson Associates, a firm that gathers extensive return data on a large group of investments.

To show the effect of diversification on risk and rates of return, Ibbotson compared three portfolios (A, B, and C), consisting of the following investments:

TYPES OF SECURITIES	Investment Mix in Portfolio (%)		
	A	B	C
Short-term government securities (Treasury bills)	0	63	34
Long-term government bonds	100	12	14
Large-company stocks	_0_	_25_	_52_
	100	100	100

Figure 9–8 shows the average returns and standard deviations of the three portfolios. The results show that an investor can use diversification to improve the risk return characteristics of a portfolio. Specifically, we can see that

1. Portfolio A, which consists entirely of long-term government bonds, has an average annual return of 5.5 percent with a standard deviation of 11.3 percent.[10]

2. In portfolio B, we have diversified across all three security types, with the majority of the funds (63%) now invested in Treasury bills and a lesser amount (25%) in stocks. The effects are readily apparent. The average returns of the two portfolios are identical, but the risk associated with portfolio B is almost half that of portfolio A—a standard deviation of 6.1 percent for portfolio B compared to 11.3 percent for portfolio A. Notice that risk has been reduced in portfolio B even though stocks, a far more risky security, have been included in the portfolio. How could this be? Quite simply, stocks behave differently than both government bonds and Treasury bills, with the effect being a less risky (lower standard deviation) portfolio.

3. While portfolio B demonstrates how an investor can reduce risk while keeping returns constant, portfolio C, with its increased investment in stocks (52%), shows how an investor can increase average returns while keeping risk constant. This portfolio has a risk level identical to that of long-term government bonds alone (portfolio A), but achieves a higher average return of 8 percent, compared to 5.5 percent for the government bond portfolio.

The conclusion to be drawn from this example is clear. The market rewards diversification. We can indeed lower risk without sacrificing expected returns, and/or we can increase expected returns without having to assume more risk by diversifying our investments.

Takin' It to the Net
Go to http://www.ibbotson. com/research/papers/Small_ Stock_Betas/default.asp to download an article (click on "Download PDF") by Ibbotson, Kaplan, and Peterson for a discussion on computing betas of small firms.

---

[9]This presentation is taken from material developed by Ibbotson Associates, Chicago. Copyright © 1994.

[10]In this example, Ibbotson Associates use 1970–1993 data to compute the standard deviation for the long-term government bonds; all other computations use the total 1926–1993 time frame.

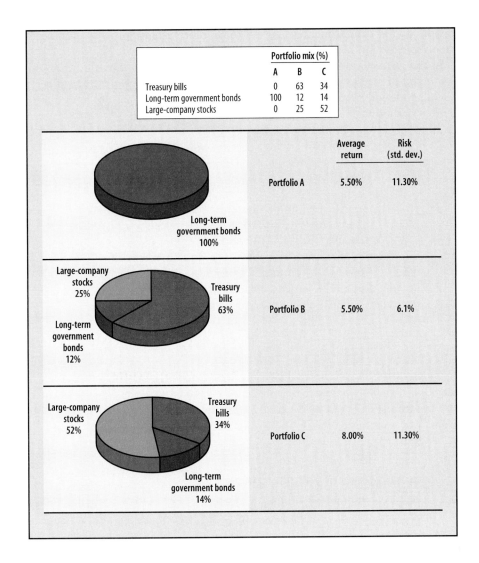

	Portfolio mix (%)		
	A	B	C
Treasury bills	0	63	34
Long-term government bonds	100	12	14
Large-company stocks	0	25	52

	Average return	Risk (std. dev.)
Portfolio A	5.50%	11.30%
Portfolio B	5.50%	6.1%
Portfolio C	8.00%	11.30%

Portfolio A — Long-term government bonds 100%

Portfolio B — Large-company stocks 25%, Treasury bills 63%, Long-term government bonds 12%

Portfolio C — Large-company stocks 52%, Treasury bills 34%, Long-term government bonds 14%

FIGURE 9–8

The Effect of Diversification on Average Return and Risk

Source: Adapted from Ibbotson Associates, Inc. Copyright © 1994, Ibbotson Assoc, Inc., Chicago.

This example gives us real-world evidence as to the merits of diversification; however, a clarification is in order. Note that the diversification in our example is across different asset types—Treasury bills versus long-term government bonds versus common stocks. *Diversifying among different kinds of assets* is called **asset allocation,** as compared to diversification within the different asset classes. The benefit we receive from diversifying is far greater through effective asset allocation than it is from astutely selecting individual stocks to include within an asset category. For instance, Brinson, Singer, and Beebower studied quarterly data from 82 large U.S. pension funds over the period 1977–1987.[11] They found that the asset allocation decision accounted for over 91 percent of the differences among the returns of pension funds. Deciding what specific securities to hold accounted for only 4.6 percent of the variation in the different pension returns.[12] The point is

asset allocation

---

[11]Gary P. Brinson, Ronald F. Singer, and Gilbert L. Beebower, "Determinants of Portfolio Performance," *Financial Analysts Journal* May–June 1991.

[12]It is also interesting to know that Brinson, Singer, and Beebower found that timing investments explained a meager 1.8 percent of the variation in pension fund returns. That is, none of the investors of these pension funds were any better than their peers at timing market movements when making investments.

investors in the capital markets should focus more attention on asset allocation than on selecting individual securities.

In the next section, we complete our study of risk and returns by connecting risk—market or systematic risk, that is—to the investor's *required* rate of return. After all, although risk is an important issue, it is primarily important in its effect on the investor's required rate of return.

CONCEPT CHECK

1. Give specific examples of systematic and unsystematic risk. How many different securities must be owned to essentially diversify away unsystematic risk?
2. What method is used to measure a firm's market risk?
3. After reviewing Figure 9–5, explain the difference between the plotted dots and the firm's characteristic line. What must be done to eliminate the variations?

Objective 5 **THE INVESTOR'S REQUIRED RATE OF RETURN**

In this section, we examine the concept of the investor's required rate of return, especially as it relates to the riskiness of an asset, and then we see how the required rate of return might be measured.

The Required Rate of Return Concept

required rate of return

opportunity cost of funds

An investor's **required rate of return** can be defined as the *minimum rate of return necessary to attract an investor to purchase or hold a security.* This definition considers the investor's **opportunity cost of funds** of making an investment; *the next-best invest-ment.* This forgone return is an opportunity cost of undertaking the investment and consequently is the investor's required rate of return. In other words, we invest with the intention of achieving a rate of return sufficient to warrant making the invest-ment. The investment will be made only if the purchase price is low enough relative to expected future cash flows to provide a rate of return greater than or equal to our required rate of return.

To help us better understand the nature of an investor's required rate of return, we can separate the return into its basic components: the risk-free rate of return plus a risk premium. Expressed as an equation:

$$k = k_{rf} + k_{rp} \qquad (9\text{--}9)$$

where k = the investor's required rate of return
k_{rf} = the risk-free rate of return
k_{rp} = the risk premium

risk-free rate of return

The risk-free rate of return rewards us for deferring consumption, and not for assuming risks; that is, the risk-free return reflects the basic fact that we invest today so that we can consume more later. By itself, the **risk-free rate of return** is the *required rate of return, or discount rate, for riskless investments.* Typically, our measure for the risk-free rate of return is the U.S. Treasury bill rate.

The Investor and Asset Allocation

As suggested in this chapter, how an investor allocates his or her assets is important in terms of the resulting returns and the variability of these returns over time. As we have also noted, stocks are more volatile in their returns than bonds or Treasury bills. The importance of this issue for investors was captured in an article appearing in the *Wall Street Journal*. Some of the author's ideas follow.

Amid the recent market turmoil, maybe you are wondering whether you really have the right mix of investments. Here are a few thoughts to keep in mind:

TAKING STOCK

If you are a bond investor who is petrified of stocks, the wild price swings of the past few weeks have probably confirmed all your worst suspicions. But the truth is, adding stocks to your bond portfolio could bolster your returns without boosting your portfolio's overall gyrations.

How can that be? While stocks and bonds often move up and down in tandem, this isn't always the case, and sometimes stocks rise when bonds are tumbling. That happened in this year's [1996] first six months, when U.S. stock-mutual funds soared 10.8% while taxable bonds slipped 0.3%, according to Lipper Analytical Services.

Indeed, Chicago researchers Ibbotson Associates figures a portfolio that's 100% in longer-term government bonds has the same risk profile as a mix that includes 83% in longer-term government bonds and 17% in the blue chip stocks that constitute Standard & Poor's 500 stock index.

But while the risk level is similar, the bond-stock mix had better returns over the past 25 years, gaining 10.2% a year, compared with 9.6% for longer-term government bonds alone. The bottom line? Everybody should own some stocks. Even cowards.

SAME GREAT TASTE, EVEN MORE FILLING

All right, you will buy a few stocks. But you are sticking strictly to the blue chips. A good move? Here's another fun fact from Ibbotson Associates.

The Chicago firm calculates that a portfolio that's 100% in the S&P 500 is about as risky as a mix that includes 73% S&P 500, 6% smaller company stocks and 21% foreign stocks. But the globally diverse portfolio was more rewarding over the past 25 years, climbing 12.9% a year, compared with 12.2% for the S&P 500. If you're going to own stocks, it clearly pays to diversify.

Source: Jonathan Clements, "The Right Mix: Fine-tuning a Portfolio to Make Money and Sleep Soundly," *Wall Street Journal*, July 23, 1996, C1.

The **risk premium,** k_{rp} is the *additional return we must expect to receive for assuming risk.* As the level of risk increases, we will demand additional expected returns. Even though we may or may not actually receive this incremental return, we must have reason to expect it; otherwise, why expose ourselves to the chance of losing all or part of our money?

risk premium

Example

Assume you are considering the purchase of a stock that you believe will provide a 14-percent return over the next year. If the expected risk-free rate of return, such as the rate of return for 90-day Treasury bills, is 5 percent, then the risk premium you are demanding to assume the additional risk is 9 percent (14% − 5%). ∎

Measuring the Required Rate of Return

We have seen that (1) systematic risk is the only relevant risk—the rest can be diversified away, and (2) the required rate of return, k, equals the risk-free rate, k_{rf} plus a risk premium, k_{rp}. We may now examine how we actually estimate investors' required rates of return. Looking back at equation (9–9), the really tough task is estimating the risk premium.

Does Beta Always Work?

At the start of 1998, Apple Computer was in deep trouble. As a result, its stock price fluctuated wildly—far more than other computer firms, such as IBM. However, based on the capital asset pricing model (CAPM) and its measure of beta, the required return of Apple's investors would have been only 8 percent at the time, compared to 12 percent for IBM's stockholders. Equally interesting, when Apple's situation improved in the spring of that year and its share price became less volatile, Apple's investors, at least according to the CAPM, would have required a rate of return of 11 percent—a 3 percentage-point increase from the earlier required rate of return. That is not what intuition would suggest should have happened.

So what should we think? Just when Apple's future was most in doubt and its shares most volatile, its beta was only 0.47, suggesting that Apple's stock was only half as volatile as the overall stock market. In reality, beta is meaningless here. The truth is that Apple was in such dire condition that its stock price simply decoupled itself from the stock market. So as IBM and its peer stock prices moved up and down with the rest of the market, Apple shares reacted solely to news about the company, without regard for the market's movements. Beta

thus created the false impression that Apple shares were more stable than the stock market.

The lesson here is that beta may at times be misleading when used with individual companies. Instead, its use is far more reliable when applied to a portfolio of companies. A firm that was interested in acquiring Apple Computer in 1998, for instance, most likely would not have been planning to buy other computer companies in the same circumstances. If an interested acquirer used beta in computing the required rate of return for the acquisition, it would without a doubt have overvalued Apple.

So does that mean that CAPM is worthless? No, not as long as company-unique risk is not the main driving force in a company's stock price movements, or if investors are able to diversify away specific company risk. Then they would bid up the price of such shares until they reflect only market risk. For example, a mutual fund that specializes in "distress stocks" might purchase a number of "Apple Computer companies," each with its own problems, but for different reasons. For such investors, beta works pretty well. Thus, the moral of the story is to exercise common sense and judgment when using beta.

capital asset pricing model
(CAPM)

The finance profession has had difficulty in developing a practical approach to measure the investor's required rate of return; however, financial managers often use a method called the **capital asset pricing model (CAPM).** The capital asset pricing model is *an equation that equates the expected rate of return on a stock to the risk-free rate plus a risk premium for the stock's systematic risk.* Although certainly not without its critics, the CAPM provides an intuitive approach for thinking about the return that an investor should require on an investment, given the asset's systematic or market risk.

Equation (9–9) provides the natural starting point for measuring the investor's required rate of return and sets us up for using the CAPM. Rearranging this equation to solve for the risk premium (k_{rp}), we have

$$k_{rp} = k - k_{rf} \qquad\text{(9–10)}$$

which simply says that the risk premium for a security, k_{rp}, equals the required return, k, less the risk-free rate existing in the market, k_{rf}. For example, if the required return is 15 percent and the risk-free rate is 5 percent, the risk premium is 10 percent. Also, if the required return for the market portfolio, k_m is 12 percent, and the risk-free rate, k_{rf} is 5 percent, the risk premium, k_{rp} for the market would be 7 percent. This 7-percent risk premium would apply to any security having systematic (nondiversifiable) risk equivalent to the general market, or a beta of 1.

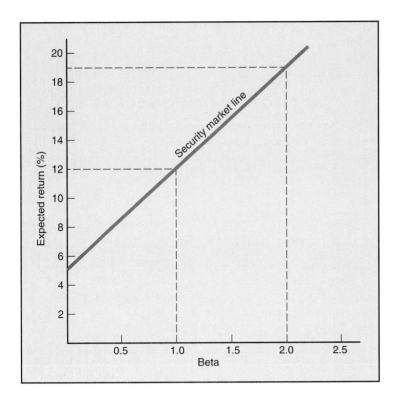

Security Market Line

In this same market, a security with a beta of 2 should provide a risk premium of 14 percent, or twice the 7-percent risk premium existing for the market as a whole. Hence, in general, the appropriate required rate of return for the jth security, k_j, should be determined by

$$k_j = k_{rf} + \beta_j(k_m - k_{rf}) \qquad (9\text{-}11)$$

Equation (9-11) is the CAPM. This equation designates the risk-return trade-off existing in the market, where risk is defined in terms of beta. Figure 9-9 graphs the CAPM as the **security market line**.[13] The security market line is *the graphic representation of the CAPM, where the line shows the appropriate required rate of return given a stock's systematic risk.* As presented in this figure, securities with betas equal to 0, 1, and 2 should have required rates of return as follows:

security market line

If $\beta_j = 0$: $k_j = 5\% + 0(12\% - 5\%) = 5\%$
If $\beta_j = 1$: $k_j = 5\% + 1(12\% - 5\%) = 12\%$
If $\beta_j = 2$: $k_j = 5\% + 2(12\% - 5\%) = 19\%$

---

[13]Two key assumptions are made in using the security market line. First, we assume that the marketplace where securities are bought and sold is highly efficient. Market efficiency indicates that the price of an asset responds quickly to new information, thereby suggesting that the price of a security reflects all available information. As a result, the current price of a security is considered to represent the best estimate of its future price. Second, the model assumes that a perfect market exists. A perfect market is one in which information is readily available to all investors at a nominal cost. Also, securities are assumed to be infinitely divisible, with any transaction costs incurred in purchasing or selling a security being negligible. Furthermore, investors are assumed to be single-period wealth maximizers who agree on the meaning and significance of the available information. Finally, within the perfect market, all investors are *price takers*, which simply means that a single investor's actions cannot affect the price of a security. These assumptions are obviously not descriptive of reality. However, from the perspective of positive economics, the mark of a good theory is the accuracy of its predictions, not the validity of the simplifying assumptions that underlie its development.

where the risk-free rate, k_{rf}, is 5 percent and the required return for the market portfolio, k_m, is 12 percent.

BACK TO THE FOUNDATIONS

The conclusion of the matter is that **Axiom 1** is alive and well. It tells us, **We Won't Take on Additional Risk Unless We Expect to Be Compensated with Additional Return.** That is, there is a risk-return trade-off in the market.

CONCEPT CHECK

1. How does opportunity cost affect an investor's required rate of return?
2. What are the two components of the investor's required rate of return?
3. How does beta fit into factoring the risk premium in the CAPM equation?
4. Assuming the market is efficient, what is the relationship between a stock's price and the security market line?

SUMMARY

Takin' It to the Net
Go to http://www.ibbotson.com/news/dow_forecast.asp to see a prediction for the stock market for the year 2025.

In Chapter 2, we referred to the discount rate as the interest rate or the opportunity cost of funds. At that point, we considered a number of important factors that influence interest rates, including the price of time, expected or anticipated inflation, and risk premium related to maturity (liquidity) and variability of future returns.

In this chapter, we have returned to our study of rates of return, and looked ever so carefully at the relationship between risk and rates of return.

Objective 1

Define and measure the expected rate of return of an individual investment
In a world of uncertainty, we cannot make forecasts with certitude. Thus, we must speak in terms of *expected* events. The expected return on an investment may therefore be stated as a weighted average of all the possible returns, weighted by the probability that each return will occur.

Objective 2

Define and measure the riskiness of an individual investment
Risk for our purposes is the variability of returns and may be measured by the standard deviation.

Objective 3

Compare the historical relationship between risk and rates of return in the capital markets
Ibbotson and Sinquefield have provided us with annual rates of return earned on different types of security investments as far back as 1926. They summarize, among other things, the annual returns for six portfolios of securities made up of

1. Common stocks of large companies
2. Common stocks of small firms
3. Long-term corporate bonds
4. Long-term U.S. government bonds
5. Intermediate-term U.S. government bonds
6. U.S. Treasury bills

A comparison of the annual rates of return for these respective portfolios for the years 1926–1998 shows a positive relationship between risk and return, with Treasury bills being least risky and common stocks of small firms being most risky. From the data, we are able to see the benefit of diversification in terms of improving the return-risk relationship. Also, the data clearly demonstrate that only common stock has in the long run served as an inflation hedge, and that risk associated with common stock can be reduced if investors are patient in receiving their returns.

Explain how diversifying our investments affects the riskiness and expected rate of return of a portfolio or combination of assets

Objective 4

We made an important distinction between nondiversifiable risk and diversifiable risk. We concluded that the only relevant risk, given the opportunity to diversify our portfolio, is a security's nondiversifiable risk, which we called by two other names: systematic risk and market-related risk.

Explain the relationship between an investor's required rate of return on an investment and the riskiness of the investment

Objective 5

The capital asset pricing model provides an intuitive framework for understanding the risk-return relationship. The CAPM suggests that investors determine an appropriate required rate of return, depending upon the amount of systematic risk inherent in a security. This minimum acceptable rate of return is equal to the risk-free rate plus a risk premium for assuming risk.

KEY TERMS

asset allocation, 271

beta, 266

capital asset pricing model (CAPM), 274

characteristic line, 266

company-unique risk (see unsystematic risk), 262

diversifiable risk (see unsystematic risk), 262

expected rate of return, 255

holding-period returns, 264

market risk (see systematic risk), 262

nondiversifiable risk (see systematic risk), 262

opportunity cost of funds, 272

portfolio beta, 269

required rate of return, 272

risk, 257

risk premium, 273

risk-free rate of return, 272

security market line, 275

standard deviation, 258

systematic risk, 262

unsystematic risk, 262

STUDY QUESTIONS

9-1 a. What is meant by the investor's required rate of return?
   b. How do we measure the riskiness of an asset?
   c. How should the proposed measurement of risk be interpreted?

9-2 What is (a) unsystematic risk (company-unique or diversifiable risk) and (b) systematic risk (market or nondiversifiable risk)?

9-3 What is the meaning of beta? How is it used to calculate k, the investor's required rate of return?

9-4 Define the security market line. What does it represent?

9-5 How do we measure the beta for a portfolio?

9-6 If we were to graph the returns of a stock against the returns of the S&P 500 Index, and the points did not follow a very ordered pattern, what could we say about that stock? If the stock's returns tracked the S&P 500 returns very closely, then what could we say?

9-7 Over the past six decades, we have had the opportunity to observe the rates of return and variability of these returns for different types of securities. Summarize these observations.

9-8 Describe the potential effect on returns by diversifying your portfolio.

SELF-TEST PROBLEMS

ST-1 *(Expected Return and Risk)* Universal Corporation is planning to invest in a security that has several possible rates of return. Given the following probability distribution of returns, what is the expected rate of return on the investment? Also compute the standard deviation of the returns. What do the resulting numbers represent?

PROBABILITY	RETURN
.10	−10%
.20	5%
.30	10%
.40	25%

ST-2 *(Capital Asset Pricing Model)* Using the CAPM, estimate the appropriate required rate of return for the three stocks listed below, given that the risk-free rate is 5 percent and the expected return for the market is 17 percent.

STOCK	BETA
A	.75
B	.90
C	1.40

ST-3 *(Average Expected Return and Risk)* Given the holding-period returns shown below, calculate the average returns and the standard deviations for the Kaifu Corporation and for the market.

MONTH	KAIFU CORP.	MARKET
1	4%	2%
2	6	3
3	0	1
4	2	−1

ST-4 *(Holding-Period Returns)* From the price data that follow, compute holding-period returns for periods 2 through 4.

PERIOD	STOCK PRICE
1	$10
2	13
3	11
4	15

ST-5 *(Security Market Line)*

 a. Determine the expected return and beta for the following portfolio:

STOCK	PERCENTAGE OF PORTFOLIO	BETA	EXPECTED RETURN
1	40%	1.00	12%
2	25	0.75	11
3	35	1.30	15

 b. Given the information above, draw the security market line and show where the securities fit on the graph. Assume that the risk-free rate is 8 percent and that the expected return on the market portfolio is 12 percent. How would you interpret these findings?

STUDY PROBLEMS

9-1 *(Expected Rate of Return and Risk)* Pritchard Press, Inc., is evaluating a security. One-year Treasury bills are currently paying 9.1 percent. Calculate the investment's expected return and its standard deviation. Should Pritchard invest in this security?

PROBABILITY	RETURN
.15	5%
.30	7%
.40	10%
.15	15%

9-2 *(Expected Rate of Return and Risk)* Syntex, Inc. is considering an investment in one of two common stocks. Given the information that follows, which investment is better, based on risk (as measured by the standard deviation) and return?

Common Stock A		Common Stock B	
PROBABILITY	RETURN	PROBABILITY	RETURN
.30	11%	.20	−5%
.40	15%	.30	6%
.30	19%	.30	14%
		.20	22%

9-3 *(Expected Rate of Return and Risk)* Friedman Manufacturing, Inc. has prepared the following information regarding two investments under consideration. Which investment should be accepted?

Common Stock A		Common Stock B	
PROBABILITY	RETURN	PROBABILITY	RETURN
.20	−2%	.10	4%
.50	18%	.30	6%
.30	27%	.40	10%
		.20	15%

9-4 *(Required Rate of Return Using CAPM)*
    a. Compute a fair rate of return for Intel common stock, which has a 1.2 beta. The risk-free rate is 6 percent and the market portfolio (New York Stock Exchange stocks) has an expected return of 16 percent.
    b. Why is the rate you computed a fair rate?

9-5 *(Estimating Beta)* From the graph below relating the holding-period returns for Aram, Inc. to the S&P 500 Index, estimate the firm's beta.

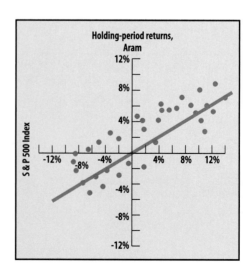

9-6 *(Capital Asset Pricing Model)* Johnson Manufacturing, Inc. is considering several investments. The rate on Treasury bills is currently 6.75 percent, and the expected return for the market is 12 percent. What should be the required rates of return for each investment (using the CAPM)?

SECURITY	BETA
A	1.50
B	.82
C	.60
D	1.15

9-7 *(Capital Asset Pricing Model)* CSB, Inc. has a beta of .765. If the expected market return is 11.5 percent and the risk-free rate is 7.5 percent, what is the appropriate required return of CSB (using the CAPM)?

9-8 *(Capital Asset Pricing Model)* The expected return for the general market is 12.8 percent, and the risk premium in the market is 4.3 percent. Tasaco, LBM, and Exxos have betas of .864, .693, and .575, respectively. What are the corresponding required rates of return for the three securities?

9-9 *(Computing Holding-Period Returns)*
  a. From the price data below, compute the holding-period returns for Asman and Salinas for periods 2 through 4.

PERIOD	ASMAN	SALINAS
1	$10	$30
2	12	28
3	11	32
4	13	35

  b. How would you interpret the meaning of a holding-period return?

9-10 *(Measuring Risk and Rates of Return)*
  a. Given the holding-period returns shown below, compute the average returns and the standard deviations for the Zemin Corporation and for the market.

MONTH	ZEMIN CORP.	MARKET
1	6%	4%
2	3	2
3	−1	1
4	−3	−2
5	5	2
6	0	2

  b. If Zemin's beta is 1.54 and the risk-free rate is 8 percent, what would be an appropriate required return for an investor owning Zemin? (*Note:* Because the above returns are based on monthly data, you will need to annualize the returns to make them compatible with the risk-free rate. For simplicity, you can convert from monthly to yearly returns by multiplying the average monthly returns by 12.)

c. How does Zemin's historical average return compare with the return you believe to be a fair return, given the firm's systematic risk?

9-11 *(Portfolio Beta and Security Market Line)* You own a portfolio consisting of the following stocks:

STOCK	PERCENTAGE OF PORTFOLIO	BETA	EXPECTED RETURN
1	20%	1.00	16%
2	30	0.85	14
3	15	1.20	20
4	25	0.60	12
5	10	1.60	24

The risk-free rate is 7 percent. Also, the expected return on the market portfolio is 15.5 percent.

a. Calculate the expected return of your portfolio. (*Hint:* The expected return of a portfolio equals the weighted average of the individual stock's expected return, where the weights are the percentage invested in each stock.)

b. Calculate the portfolio beta.

c. Given the information above, plot the security market line on paper. Plot the stocks from your portfolio on your graph.

d. From your plot in part c, which stocks appear to be your winners and which ones appear to be losers?

e. Why should you consider your conclusion in part d to be less than certain?

9-12 *(Expected Return, Standard Deviation, and Capital Asset Pricing Model)* Below you will find the end-of-month prices for both the Standard & Poor's 500 Index and Coca-Cola common stock.

a. Using the data below, calculate the holding-period returns for each of the months.

MONTH AND YEAR	Prices	
	S&P 500	COCA-COLA
1998		
April	$1,111.75	$75.88
May	1,090.82	78.38
June	1,133.84	85.50
July	1,120.67	80.50
August	957.28	65.13
September	1,017.01	57.63
October	1,098.67	67.56
November	1,163.63	70.06
December	1,229.23	67.00
1999		
January	1,279.64	65.31
February	1,238.33	63.88
March	1,286.37	61.38
April	1,335.18	68.06

b. Calculate the average monthly return and the standard deviation of these returns both for the S&P 500 and Coca-Cola.

c. Develop a graph that shows the relationship between the Coca-Cola stock returns and the S&P 500 Index (show the Coca-Cola returns on the vertical axis and the S&P 500 Index returns on the horizontal axis as done in Figure 9–5).

d. From your graph, describe the nature of the relationship between Coca-Cola stock returns and the returns for the S&P 500 Index.

COMPREHENSIVE PROBLEM

Note: Although not absolutely necessary, you are advised to use a computer spreadsheet to work the following problem.

a. Use the price data from the table on the following page for the Standard & Poor's 500 Index, Bristol Myers Squibb, and General Electric to calculate the holding-period returns for the 24 months from May 1997 through April 1999.

MONTH AND YEAR	Prices		
	S&P 500	BRISTOL	GE
1997			
April	801.34	32.75	55.50
May	848.28	36.69	60.38
June	885.14	40.50	65.00
July	954.29	39.16	70.13
August	899.47	38.00	62.56
September	947.28	41.38	68.06
October	914.62	43.94	64.63
November	955.40	46.81	73.88
December	970.43	47.31	73.38
1998			
January	980.28	49.84	77.50
February	1,049.34	50.09	77.75
March	1,101.75	52.16	86.19
April	1,111.75	52.94	85.19
May	1,090.82	53.75	83.38
June	1,133.84	57.47	90.88
July	1,120.67	56.97	89.44
August	957.28	48.94	80.00
September	1,017.01	51.94	79.56
October	1,098.67	55.34	87.50
November	1,163.63	61.00	90.38
December	1,229.23	66.91	102.00
1999			
January	1,279.64	64.13	104.88
February	1,238.33	62.97	100.31
March	1,286.37	64.13	110.63
April	1,335.18	63.56	105.38

b. Calculate the average monthly holding-period returns and the standard deviation of these returns for the S&P 500 Index, Bristol Myers Squibb, and General Electric.

c. Plot (1) the holding-period returns for Bristol Myers Squibb against the Standard & Poor's 500 Index, and (2) the General Electric holding-period returns against the Standard & Poor's 500 Index. (Use Figure 9–5 as the format for your graph.)

d. From your graphs in part c, describe the nature of the relationship between the Bristol Myers Squibb stock returns and the returns for the S&P 500 Index. Make the same comparison for General Electric.

e. Assume that you have decided to invest one-half of your money in Bristol Myers Squibb and the remaining in General Electric. Calculate the monthly holding-period returns for your two-stock portfolio. (*Hint:* The monthly return for the portfolio is the average of the two stocks' monthly returns.)

f. Plot the returns of your two-stock portfolio against the Standard & Poor's 500 Index as you did for the individual stocks in part c. How does this graph compare to the graphs for the individual stocks? Explain the difference.

g. Below you are provided the returns on an *annualized* basis that were realized from holding long-term government bonds during 1997, 1998, and 1999. Calculate the average *monthly* holding-period returns and the standard deviations of these returns. (*Hint:* You will need to convert the annual returns to monthly returns by dividing each return by 12 months.)

MONTH AND YEAR	ANNUALIZED RATE OF RETURN (%)
1997	
May	6.94
June	6.77
July	6.51
August	6.58
September	6.50
October	6.33
November	6.11
December	5.99
1998	
January	5.81
February	5.89
March	5.95
April	5.92
May	5.93
June	5.70
July	5.68
August	5.54
September	5.20
October	5.01
November	5.25
December	5.06
1999	
January	5.16
February	5.37
March	5.58
April	5.70

h. Now assuming that you have decided to invest equal amounts of money in Bristol Myers Squibb, General Electric, and long-term government securities, calculate the monthly returns for your three-asset portfolio. What are the average return and the standard deviation?

i. Make a comparison of the average returns and the standard deviations for all the individual assets and the two portfolios that we designed. What conclusions can be reached by your comparison?

j. According to Standard & Poor's, the betas for Bristol Myers Squibb and General Electric are 1.11 and 1.21, respectively. Compare the meaning of these betas relative to the standard deviations calculated above.

k. The Treasury bill rate at the end of April 1999 was approximately 5.5 percent. Given the betas for Bristol Myers Squibb and General Electric and using the above data for the S&P 500 Index as a measure for the market portfolio expected return, estimate an appropriate required rate of return given the level of systematic risk for each stock.

SELF-TEST SOLUTIONS

SS-1

(A)	(B)	EXPECTED RETURN $(\bar{k})$	WEIGHTED DEVIATION
PROBABILITY $P(k_i)$	RETURN (k_i)	$(A) \times (B)$	$(k_i - \bar{k})^2 P(k_i)$
.10	−10%	−1%	52.9%
.20	5	1	12.8
.30	10	3	2.7
.40	25	10	57.6
		$\bar{k} = 13\%$	$\sigma^2 = 126.0\%$
			$\sigma = 11.22\%$

From our studies in statistics, we know that if the distribution of returns were normal, then Universal could expect a return of 13 percent with a 67 percent possibility that this return would vary up or down by 11.22 percent between 1.78 percent (13% − 11.22%) and 24.22 percent (13% + 11.22%). However, it is apparent from the probabilities that the distribution is not normal.

SS-2

Stock A:	5% + .75 (17% − 5%) = 14.0%
Stock B:	5% + .90 (17% − 5%) = 15.8
Stock C:	5% + 1.40 (17% − 5%) = 21.8

SS-3

Kaifu

Average return: $\dfrac{4\% + 6\% + 0\% + 2\%}{4} = 3\%$

Standard deviation:

$$\sqrt{\dfrac{\begin{array}{l}(4\% - 3\%)^2 \\ +(6\% - 3\%)^2 \\ +(0\% - 3\%)^2 \\ +(2\% - 3\%)\end{array}}{4 - 1}} = 2.58\%$$

Market

Average return: $\dfrac{2\% + 3\% + 1\% - 1\%}{4} = 1.25\%$

Standard deviation:

$$\sqrt{\dfrac{\begin{array}{l}(2\% - 1.25\%)^2 \\ +(3\% - 1.25\%)^2 \\ +(1\% - 1.25\%)^2 \\ +(-1\% - 1.25\%)^2\end{array}}{4 - 1}} = 1.71\%$$

SS-4

TIME	STOCK PRICE	HOLDING-PERIOD RETURN
1	$10	
2	13	($13 ÷ $10) − 1 = 30.0%
3	11	($11 ÷ $13) − 1 = −15.4
4	15	($15 ÷ $11) − 1 = 36.4

SS-5

a. Portfolio expected return:

$$(.4 \times 12\%) + (.25 \times 11\%) + (.35 \times 15\%) = 12.8\%$$

Portfolio beta:

$$(.4 \times 1) + (.25 \times .75) + (.35 \times 1.3) = 1.04$$

b.

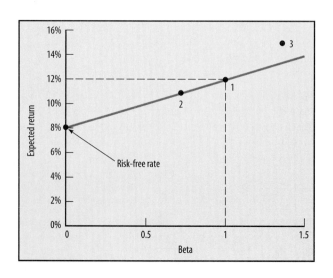

Stocks 1 and 2 seem to be right in line with the security market line, which suggests that they are earning a fair return, given their systematic risk. Stock 3, on the other hand, is earning more than a fair return (above the security market line). We might be tempted to conclude that security 3 is undervalued. However, we may be seeing an illusion; it is possible to misspecify the security market line by using bad estimates in our data.

CAPITAL-BUDGETING TECHNIQUES AND PRACTICE

LEARNING OBJECTIVES

AFTER READING THIS CHAPTER, YOU SHOULD BE ABLE TO:

1. Discuss the difficulty encountered in finding profitable projects in competitive markets and the importance of the search.

2. Determine whether or not a new project should be accepted or rejected using the payback period, the net present value, the profitability index, and the internal rate of return.

3. Explain how the capital-budgeting decision process changes when a dollar limit is placed on the dollar size of the capital budget.

4. Discuss the problems encountered in project ranking.

5. Explain the importance of ethical considerations in capital-budgeting decisions.

6. Discuss the trends in the use of different capital-budgeting criteria.

7. Explain how foreign markets provide opportunities for finding new capital-budgeting projects.

In 1999, Universal Studios, owned by The Seagram Company, unveiled its "Islands of Adventure" theme park. This 110-acre park is chock-full of rides and other attractions, a total of 23 in all, located on five theme-based islands. You can take a trek through Jurassic Park, featuring three 24-foot-long, state-of-the-art robotic triceratops that actually respond to visitors—flinching their muscles and even spitting water on guests as they make their way through the island. Marvel Super Hero Island is host to three high-speed roller coasters—the Incredible Hulk; the inverted twin Dueling Dragons; and the Amazing Adventures of Spiderman, a one-of-a-kind simulator that combines 3-D with live motion. With two theme park giants, seven major theme parks, and over 80 "fun zones" in and around the Orlando area, the battle is on for the tourists' dollars. But regardless of what the competition has come up with in the past, Disney has continued to dominate the amusement industry in Orlando.

Given the history and legend of Disney World, it was not an easy decision to challenge the champ. Moreover, the stakes involved are so large that the outcome of this decision will have a major effect on Universal's and Seagram's future. To challenge Disney's dominance in this market, Universal committed $2.6 billion to the project. Whether this was a good or a bad decision only time will tell. Early reports indicate that Universal has come up with a winner, but it's going to be tough dethroning Disney as the ruler of Orlando. How did Universal go about deciding to spend

WHAT'S AHEAD

In this chapter we look first at the difficulties associated with finding profitable projects. Four capital-budgeting criteria are subsequently provided for evaluating capital investments, followed by a discussion of the problems created when the number of projects that can be accepted or the total budget is limited. We then examine capital budgeting in practice and close with a discussion of how foreign markets can provide capital-budgeting projects.

billions and challenge Disney? They did it using the decision criteria we examine in this chapter.

This chapter is actually the first of two chapters dealing with the decision-making process regarding investment in fixed assets—that is, should a proposed project be accepted or should it be rejected? We refer to this process as capital budgeting. In this chapter we look at methods used to evaluate new projects. In deciding whether to accept a new project, we focus on cash flows. Cash flows represent the benefits generated from accepting a capital-budgeting proposal. We will assume we know what level of cash flows are generated by a project and work on determining whether that project should be accepted. In Chapter 11 we examine what a relevant cash flow is and how we measure it, and also look at how risk enters into this process.

| Objective 1 | **FINDING PROFITABLE PROJECTS** |

capital budgeting

Without question it is easier to *evaluate profitable projects or investments in fixed assets*, a process referred to as **capital budgeting,** than it is to find them. In competitive markets, generating ideas for profitable projects is extremely difficult. The competition is brisk for new profitable projects, and once they have been uncovered competitors generally rush in, pushing down prices and profits. For this reason a firm must have a systematic strategy for generating capital-budgeting projects. Without this flow of new projects and ideas, the firm cannot grow or even survive for long, being forced to live off the profits from existing projects with limited lives. So where do these ideas come from for new products, or for ways to improve existing products or make them more profitable? The answer is from inside the firm—from everywhere inside the firm.

BACK TO THE FOUNDATIONS

The fact that profitable projects are difficult to find relates directly to **Axiom 5: The Curse of Competitive Markets—Why It's Hard to Find Exceptionally Profitable Projects.** When we introduced that axiom we stated that successful investments involve the reduction of competition by creating barriers to entry either through product differentiation or cost advantages. The key to locating profitable projects is to understand how and where they exist.

Takin' It to the Net
Capital budgeting not only involves coming up with new products, but also with new ways of selling old products. A good example of this is the battle between Amazon.com (http://www.amazon.com/) and Barnes and Noble, which introduced BarnesandNoble.com (http://www.barnesandnoble.com/) in 1997 after giving Amazon.com a 2-year lead. Take a look at these two sites. Which one do you think will dominate in the future and why?

Typically, a firm has a research and development (R&D) department that searches for ways of improving on existing products or finding new products. These ideas may come from within the R&D department or be based on referral ideas from executives, sales personnel, anyone in the firm, or even from customers. For example, at Ford Motor Company before the 1990s, ideas for product improvement had typically been generated in Ford's R&D department. Unfortunately, this strategy was not enough to keep Ford from losing much of its market share to the Japanese.

In an attempt to cut costs and improve product quality, Ford moved from strict reliance on an R&D department to seeking the input of employees at all levels for new ideas. Bonuses are now provided to workers for their cost-cutting suggestions, and assembly-line personnel who can see the production process from a hands-on point of view are now brought into the hunt for new projects. The effect on Ford has been positive and significant. Although not all suggested projects prove to be profitable, many new ideas generated from within the firm turn out to be good ones.

CONCEPT CHECK

1. Why is it so difficult to find an exceptionally profitable project?
2. Why is the search for new profitable projects so important?

CAPITAL-BUDGETING DECISION CRITERIA

Objective 2

In deciding whether to accept a new project, we focus on cash flows. Cash flows represent the benefits generated from accepting a capital-budgeting proposal. In this chapter we assume a given cash flow is generated by a project and work on determining whether that project should be accepted.

We consider four commonly used criteria for determining acceptability of investment proposals. The first one is the least sophisticated, in that it does not incorporate the time value of money into its calculations; the other three do take it into account. For the time being, the problem of incorporating risk into the capital-budgeting decision is ignored. This issue is examined in Chapter 11. In addition, we assume that the appropriate discount rate, required rate of return, or cost of capital is given. The determination of the cost of capital is the topic of Chapter 12.

Payback Period

The **payback period** is the *number of years needed to recover the initial cash outlay*. Because this criterion measures how quickly the project will return its original investment, it deals with cash flows, which measure the true timing of the benefits, rather than accounting profits. Unfortunately, it also ignores the time value of money and does not discount these cash flows back to the present. The accept/reject criterion centers on whether the project's payback period is less than or equal to the firm's maximum desired payback period. For example, if a firm's maximum desired payback period is 3 years and an investment proposal requires an initial cash outlay of $10,000 and yields the following set of annual cash flows, what is its payback period? Should the project be accepted?

payback period

YEAR	AFTER-TAX CASH FLOW
1	$2,000
2	4,000
3	3,000
4	3,000
5	1,000

TABLE 10-1	**PAYBACK PERIOD EXAMPLE**	

	Projects	
	A	B
Initial cash outlay	−$10,000	−$10,000
Annual net cash inflows		
Year 1	$ 6,000	$ 5,000
2	4,000	5,000
3	3,000	0
4	2,000	0
5	1,000	0

In this case, after 3 years the firm will have recaptured $9,000 on an initial investment of $10,000, leaving $1,000 of the initial investment to be recouped. During the fourth year a total of $3,000 will be returned from this investment, and, assuming it will flow into the firm at a constant rate over the year, it will take one-third of the year ($1,000/$3,000) to recapture the remaining $1,000. Thus, the payback period on this project is three and a third years, which is more than the desired payback period. Using the payback period criterion, the firm would reject this project without even considering the $1,000 cash flow in year 5.

Although the payback period is used frequently, it does have some rather obvious drawbacks that are best demonstrated through the use of an example. Consider two investment projects, A and B, that involve an initial cash outlay of $10,000 each and produce the annual cash flows shown in Table 10–1. Both projects have a payback period of 2 years; therefore, in terms of the payback period criterion both are equally acceptable. However, if we had our choice, it is clear we would select A over B, for at least two reasons. First, regardless of what happens after the payback period, project A returns our initial investment to us earlier within the payback period. Thus, because there is a time value of money, the cash flows occurring within the payback period should not be weighted equally, as they are. In addition, all cash flows that occur after the payback period are ignored. This violates the principle that investors desire more in the way of benefits rather than less—a principle that is difficult to deny, especially when we are talking about money.

Although these deficiencies limit the value of the payback period as a tool for investment evaluation, the payback period has several positive features. First, it deals with cash flows, as opposed to accounting profits, and therefore focuses on the true timing of the project's benefits and costs, even though it does not adjust the cash flows for the time value of money. Second, it is easy to visualize, quickly understood, and easy to calculate. Finally, although the payback period has serious deficiencies, it is often used as a rough screening device to eliminate projects whose returns do not materialize until later years. This method emphasizes the earliest returns, which in all likelihood are less uncertain, and provides for the liquidity needs of the firm. Although its advantages are certainly significant, its disadvantages severely limit its value as a discriminating capital-budgeting criterion.

Net Present Value

net present value (NPV)

The **net present value (NPV)** of an investment proposal is equal to the *present value of its annual net cash flows after taxes less the investment's initial outlay*. The net present value can be expressed as follows:

BACK TO THE FOUNDATIONS

The final three capital-budgeting criteria all incorporate **Axiom 2: The Time Value of Money—A Dollar Received Today Is Worth More Than a Dollar Received in the Future** in their calculations. If we are at all to make rational business decisions we must recognize that money has a time value. In examining the following three capital-budgeting techniques, you will notice that this axiom is the driving force behind each of them.

$$NPV = \sum_{t=1}^{n} \frac{ACF_t}{(1 + k)^t} - IO \qquad (10\text{--}1)$$

where ACF_t = the annual after-tax cash flow in time period t (this can take on either positive or negative values)

k = the appropriate discount rate; that is, the required rate of return or cost of capital[1]

IO = the initial cash outlay

n = the project's expected life

The project's NPV gives a measurement of the net value of an investment proposal in terms of today's dollars. Because all cash flows are discounted back to the present, comparing the difference between the present value of the annual cash flows and the investment outlay does not violate the time value of money assumption. The

Takin' It to the Net
The same principles that guide us in capital-budgeting decisions also guide our decisions in personal finance. If you'd like to see an excellent selection of personal finance calculators check out the FinanCenter Web site (http://www.financenter.com/).

---

[1]The required rate of return or cost of capital is the rate of return necessary to justify raising funds to finance the project or, alternatively, the rate of return necessary to maintain the firm's current market price per share. These terms are defined in greater detail in Chapter 12.

difference between the present value of the annual cash flows and the initial outlay determines the net value of accepting the investment proposal in terms of today's dollars. Whenever the project's NPV is greater than or equal to zero, we will accept the project; whenever the NPV is negative, we will reject the project. If the project's NPV is zero, then it returns the required rate of return and should be accepted. This accept/reject criterion is illustrated below:

$$NPV \geq 0.0: \text{accept}$$
$$NPV < 0.0: \text{reject}$$

The following example illustrates the use of NPV as a capital-budgeting criterion.

Example

Ski-Doo is considering new machinery that would reduce manufacturing costs associated with its Mach Z snowmobile for which the after-tax cash flows are shown in Table 10–2. If the firm has a 12-percent required rate of return, the present value of the after-tax cash flow is $47,678, as calculated in Table 10–3. Subtracting the $40,000 initial outlay leaves an NPV of $7,678. Because this value is greater than zero, the NPV criterion indicates that the project should be accepted. ■

Note in the Ski-Doo example that the worth of the NPV calculation is a function of the accuracy of cash flow predictions.

The NPV criterion is the capital-budgeting decision tool we find most favorable for several reasons. First of all, it deals with cash flows rather than accounting profits. In this regard it is sensitive to the true timing of the benefits resulting from the project. Moreover, recognizing the time value of money allows comparison of the benefits and costs in a logical manner. Finally, because projects are accepted only if a positive NPV is associated with them, the acceptance of a project using this criterion will increase the value of the firm, which is consistent with the goal of maximizing the shareholders' wealth.

The disadvantage of the NPV method stems from the need for detailed, long-term forecasts of cash flows accruing from the project's acceptance. Despite this drawback, the NPV is the most theoretically correct criterion that we will examine. The following example provides an additional illustration of its application.

Example

A firm is considering the purchase of a new computer system, which will cost $30,000 initially, to aid in credit billing and inventory management. The after-tax

TABLE 10–2	NPV ILLUSTRATION OF SKI-DOO'S INVESTMENT IN NEW MACHINERY

	AFTER-TAX CASH FLOW
Initial outlay	−$40,000
Inflow year 1	15,000
Inflow year 2	14,000
Inflow year 3	13,000
Inflow year 4	12,000
Inflow year 5	11,000

TABLE 10-3

CALCULATION FOR NPV ILLUSTRATION OF INVESTMENT IN NEW MACHINERY

	AFTER-TAX CASH FLOW	PRESENT VALUE FACTOR AT 12 PERCENT	PRESENT VALUE
Inflow year 1	15,000	.893	$13,395
Inflow year 2	14,000	.797	11,158
Inflow year 3	13,000	.712	9,256
Inflow year 4	12,000	.636	7,632
Inflow year 5	11,000	.567	6,237
Present value of cash flows			$47,678
Initial outlay			− 40,000
Net present value			$ 7,678

cash flows resulting from this project are provided in Table 10–4. The required rate of return demanded by the firm is 10 percent. To determine the system's NPV, the 3-year $15,000 cash flow annuity is first discounted back to the present at 10 percent. From Appendix E in the back of this book, we find that $PVIFA_{10\%, 3 \text{ yr}}$ is 2.487. Thus, the present value of this $15,000 annuity is $37,305.

Seeing that the cash inflows have been discounted back to the present, they can now be compared with the initial outlay because both of the flows are now stated in terms of today's dollars. Subtracting the initial outlay ($30,000) from the present value of the cash inflows ($37,305), we find that the system's NPV is $7,305. Because the NPV on this project is positive, the project should be accepted.

Profitability Index (Benefit-Cost Ratio)

The **profitability index (PI),** or **benefit-cost ratio,** is the *ratio of the present value of the future net cash flows to the initial outlay.* Although the NPV investment criterion gives a measure of the absolute dollar desirability of a project, the profitability index provides a relative measure of an investment proposal's desirability—that is, the ratio of the present value of its future net benefits to its initial cost. The profitability index can be expressed as follows:

profitability index (PI or benefit-cost ratio)

$$PI = \frac{\sum_{t=1}^{n} \frac{ACF_t}{(1 + k)^t}}{IO}$$

(10–2)

TABLE 10-4 | **NPV EXAMPLE PROBLEM OF COMPUTER SYSTEM**

	AFTER-TAX CASH FLOW
Initial outlay	−$30,000
Inflow year 1	15,000
Inflow year 2	15,000
Inflow year 3	15,000

where ACF_t = the annual after-tax cash flow in time period t (this can take on either positive or negative values)

k = the appropriate discount rate; that is, the required rate of return or cost of capital

IO = the initial cash outlay

n = the project's expected life

The decision criterion is accept the project if the PI is greater than or equal to 1.00, and reject the project if the PI is less than 1.00.

$$PI \geq 1.0: \text{accept}$$
$$PI < 1.0: \text{reject}$$

Looking closely at this criterion, we see that it yields the same accept/reject decision as does the NPV criterion. Whenever the present value of the project's net cash flows is greater than its initial cash outlay, the project's NPV will be positive, signaling a decision to accept. When this is true, then the project's PI will also be greater than 1 because the present value of the net cash flows (the *PI*'s numerator) is greater than its initial outlay (the *PI*'s denominator). Thus, these two decision criteria will always yield the same decision, although they will not necessarily rank acceptable projects in the same order. This problem of conflicting ranking is dealt with at a later point.

Because the NPV and PI criteria are essentially the same, they have the same advantages over the other criteria examined. Both employ cash flows, recognize the timing of the cash flows, and are consistent with the goal of maximization of shareholders' wealth. The major disadvantage of the PI criterion, similar to the NPV criterion, is that it requires long, detailed cash flow forecasts.

Example

A firm with a 10-percent required rate of return is considering investing in a new machine with an expected life of 6 years. The after-tax cash flows resulting from this investment are given in Table 10–5. Discounting the project's future net cash flows back to the present yields a present value of $53,667; dividing this value by the initial outlay of $50,000 gives a profitability index of 1.0733, as shown in Table 10–6. This tells us that the present value of the future benefits accruing from this project is 1.0733 times the level of the initial outlay. Because the profitability index is greater than 1.0, the project should be accepted. ∎

TABLE 10–5	PI ILLUSTRATION OF INVESTMENT IN NEW MACHINERY

	AFTER-TAX CASH FLOW
Initial outlay	−$50,000
Inflow year 1	15,000
Inflow year 2	8,000
Inflow year 3	10,000
Inflow year 4	12,000
Inflow year 5	14,000
Inflow year 6	16,000

TABLE 10-6	CALCULATION FOR PI ILLUSTRATION OF INVESTMENT IN NEW MACHINERY		

	AFTER-TAX CASH FLOW	PRESENT VALUE FACTOR AT 10 PERCENT	PRESENT VALUE
Initial outlay	−$50,000	1.000	−$50,000
Inflow year 1	15,000	0.909	13,635
Inflow year 2	8,000	0.826	6,608
Inflow year 3	10,000	0.751	7,510
Inflow year 4	12,000	0.683	8,196
Inflow year 5	14,000	0.621	8,694
Inflow year 6	16,000	0.564	9,024

$$PI = \frac{\sum_{t=1}^{n} \frac{ACF_t}{(1+k)^t}}{IO}$$

$$= \frac{\$13,635 + \$6,608 + \$7,510 + \$8,196 + \$8,694 + \$9,024}{\$50,000}$$

$$= \frac{\$53,667}{\$50,000}$$

$$= 1.0733$$

Internal Rate of Return

internal rate of return (IRR)

The **internal rate of return (IRR)** attempts to answer the question, what rate of return does this project earn? For computational purposes, the internal rate of return is defined as *the discount rate that equates the present value of the project's future net cash flows with the project's initial cash outlay*. Mathematically, the internal rate of return is defined as the value *IRR* in the following equation:

$$IO = \sum_{t=1}^{n} \frac{ACF_t}{(1+IRR)^t} \qquad (10\text{–}3)$$

where ACF_t = the annual after-tax cash flow in time period t (this can take on either positive or negative values)

IO = the initial cash outlay

n = the project's expected life

IRR = the project's internal rate of return

In effect, the IRR is analogous to the concept of the yield to maturity for bonds, which was examined in Chapter 7. In other words, a project's IRR is simply the rate of return that the project earns.

The decision criterion is to accept the project if the IRR is greater than or equal to the required rate of return. We reject the project if its IRR is less than the required rate of return. This accept/reject criterion can be stated as:

$IRR \geq$ required rate of return: accept
$IRR <$ required rate of return: reject

If the IRR on a project is equal to the shareholders' required rate of return, then the project should be accepted because the firm is earning the rate that its shareholders are requiring. However, the acceptance of a project with an IRR below the investors' required rate of return will decrease the firm's stock price.

If the NPV is positive, then the IRR must be greater than the required rate of return, k. Thus, all the discounted cash flow criteria are consistent and will give similar accept/reject decisions. In addition, because the internal rate of return is another discounted cash flow criterion, it exhibits the same general advantages and disadvantages as both the NPV and PI, but has an additional disadvantage of being tedious to calculate if a financial calculator is not available.

Computing the IRR with a Financial Calculator

With today's calculators, the determination of an IRR is merely a matter of a few keystrokes. In Chapter 6, whenever we were solving time value of money problems for i, we were really solving for the IRR. For instance, in the example on page 173, when we solved for the rate that $100 must be compounded annually for it to grow to $179.10 in 10 years, we were actually solving for that problem's IRR. Thus, with financial calculators we need only input the initial outlay, the cash flows and their timing, and then input the function key "I/Y" or the "IRR" button to calculate the IRR. On some calculators it is necessary to press the compute key, CPT, before pressing the function key to be calculated.

Computing the IRR for Even Cash Flows

In this section we are going to put our calculators aside and obtain a better understanding of the IRR by examining the mathematical process of calculating internal rates of return.

The calculation of a project's IRR can either be very simple or relatively complicated. As an example of a straightforward solution, assume that a firm with a required rate of return of 10 percent is considering a project that involves an initial outlay of $45,555. If the investment is taken, the after-tax cash flows are expected to be $15,000 per annum over the project's 4-year life. In this case, the internal rate of return is equal to IRR in the following equation:

$$\$45,555 = \frac{\$15,000}{(1 + IRR)^1} + \frac{\$15,000}{(1 + IRR)^2} + \frac{\$15,000}{(1 + IRR)^3} + \frac{\$15,000}{(1 + IRR)^4}$$

From our discussion of the present value of an annuity in Chapter 6, we know that this equation can be reduced to

$$\$45,555 = \$15,000 \left[\sum_{t=1}^{4} \frac{1}{(1 + IRR)^t} \right]$$

Appendix E gives values for the $PVIFA_{i,\,n}$ for various combinations of i and n, which further reduces this equation to

$$\$45,555 = \$15,000\ (PVIFA_{i,\,4\,yr})$$

Dividing both sides by $15,000, this becomes

$$3.037 = PVIFA_{i,\,4\,yr}$$

Hence, we are looking for $PVIFA_{i,\,4\,yr}$ of 3.037 in the 4-year row of Appendix E. This value occurs when i equals 12 percent, which means that 12 percent is the IRR for the investment. Therefore, because 12 percent is greater than the 10-percent required return, the project should be accepted.

Computing the IRR for Uneven Cash Flows

Unfortunately, although solving for the IRR is quite easy when using a financial calculator or spreadsheet, it can be solved directly in the tables only when the future after-tax net cash flows are in the form of an annuity or a single payment. With a calculator the process is simple: One need only key in the initial cash outlay, the cash flows and their timing, and press the "IRR" button. When a financial calculator is not available and these flows are in the form of an uneven series of flows, a trial-and-error approach is necessary. To do this, we first determine the present value of the future after-tax net cash flows using an arbitrary discount rate. If the present value of the future cash flows at this discount rate is larger than the initial outlay, the rate is increased; if it is smaller than the initial outlay, the discount rate is lowered and the process begins again. This search routine is continued until the present value of the future after-tax cash flows is equal to the initial outlay. The interest rate that creates this situation is the IRR. This is the same basic process that a financial calculator uses to calculate an IRR.

To illustrate the procedure, consider an investment proposal that requires an initial outlay of $3,817 and returns $1,000 at the end of year 1, $2,000 at the end of year 2, and $3,000 at the end of year 3. In this case, the IRR must be determined using trial and error. This process is presented in Table 10–7, in which an arbitrarily selected discount rate of 15 percent was chosen to begin the process. Obviously, 15 percent isn't the IRR for this project because the present value of the inflows discounted back to present at 15 percent ($4,356) doesn't equal the initial outlay ($3,815). How do we make the present value of the future cash flows smaller? We raise the discount rate. Thus, we tried 20 percent next. Again, 20 percent isn't the IRR for this project because the present value of the inflows discounted back to present at 20 percent ($3,958) doesn't equal the initial outlay ($3,815), although it's closer than it was at 15 percent. Once more, we need to make the present value of the future cash flows smaller so we try a higher discount rate—22 percent. At 22 percent we have found the project's IRR because the present value of the future cash flows equals the initial outlay. The project's IRR is then compared with the firm's required rate of return, and if the IRR is the larger, the project is accepted.

Example

A firm with a required rate of return of 10 percent is considering three investment proposals. Given the information in Table 10–8, management plans to calculate the IRR for each project and determine which projects should be accepted.

Because project A is an annuity, we can easily calculate its internal rate of return by determining the $PVIFA_{i,\,4\,\mathrm{yr}}$ necessary to equate the present value of the future cash flows with the initial outlay. This computation is done as follows:

$$IO = \sum_{t=1}^{n} \frac{ACF_t}{(1 + IRR)^t}$$

$$\$10,000 = \sum_{t=1}^{4} \frac{\$3,362}{(1 + IRR)^t}$$

$$\$10,000 = \$3,362 \, (PVIFA_{i,\,4\,\mathrm{yr}})$$
$$2.974 = (PVIFA_{i,\,4\,\mathrm{yr}})$$

We are looking for a $PVIFA_{i,\,4\,\mathrm{yr}}$ of 2.974, in the four-year row of Appendix E, which occurs in the $i = 13$ percent column. Thus, 13 percent is the IRR. Because this rate is greater than the firm's required rate of return of 10 percent, the project should be accepted.

Project B involves the single future cash flow of $13,605, resulting from an initial outlay of $10,000; thus, its IRR can be determined directly from the present-value table in Appendix C as follows:

TABLE 10-7	COMPUTING IRR FOR UNEVEN CASH FLOWS WITHOUT A FINANCIAL CALCULATOR

Initial outlay	−$3,817
Inflow year 1	1,000
Inflow year 2	2,000
Inflow year 3	3,000

Solution:

Step 1: Pick an arbitrary discount rate and use it to determine the present value of the inflows.

Step 2: Compare the present value of the inflows with the initial outlay; if they are equal you have determined the IRR.

Step 3: If the present value of the inflows is larger (less than) than the initial outlay, raise (lower) the discount rate.

Step 4: Determine the present value of the inflows and repeat Step 2.

1. Try $i = 15$ percent:

	NET CASH FLOWS	PRESENT VALUE FACTOR AT 15 PERCENT	PRESENT VALUE
Inflow year 1	$1,000	.870	$ 870
Inflow year 2	2,000	.756	1,512
Inflow year 3	3,000	.658	1,974
Present value of inflows			$4,356
Initial outlay			−$3,817

2. Try $i = 20$ percent:

	NET CASH FLOWS	PRESENT VALUE FACTOR AT 20 PERCENT	PRESENT VALUE
Inflow year 1	$1,000	.833	$ 833
Inflow year 2	2,000	.694	1,388
Inflow year 3	3,000	.579	1,737
Present value of inflows			$3,958
Initial outlay			−3,817

3. Try $i = 22$ percent:

	NET CASH FLOWS	PRESENT VALUE FACTOR AT 22 PERCENT	PRESENT VALUE
Inflow year 1	$1,000	.820	$ 820
Inflow year 2	2,000	.672	1,344
Inflow year 3	3,000	.551	1,653
Present value of inflows			$3,817
Initial outlay			−$3,817

TABLE 10-8	THREE IRR INVESTMENT PROPOSAL EXAMPLES

	A	B	C
Initial outlay	−$10,000	−$10,000	−$10,000
Inflow year 1	3,362	0	1,000
Inflow year 2	3,362	0	3,000
Inflow year 3	3,362	0	6,000
Inflow year 4	3,362	13,605	7,000

$$IO = \frac{ACF_t}{(1 + IRR)^t}$$

$$\$10{,}000 = \frac{\$13{,}605}{(1 + IRR)^4}$$

$$\$10{,}000 = \$13{,}605 \; (PVIF_{i,\,4\,yr})$$
$$.735 = (PVIF_{i,\,4\,yr})$$

This tells us that we should look for a $PVIF_{i,\,4\,yr}$ of .735 in the 4-year row of Appendix C, which occurs in the $i = 8$ percent column. We may therefore conclude that 8 percent is the internal rate of return. Because this rate is less than the firm's required rate of return of 10 percent, project B should be rejected.

The uneven nature of the future cash flows associated with project C necessitates the use of the trial-and-error method. The IRR for project C is equal to the value *IRR* in the following equation:

$$\$10{,}000 = \frac{\$1{,}000}{(1 + IRR)^1} + \frac{\$3{,}000}{(1 + IRR)^2} + \frac{\$6{,}000}{(1 + IRR)^3} + \frac{\$7{,}000}{(1 + IRR)^4} \quad (10\text{--}4)$$

Arbitrarily selecting a discount rate of 15 percent and substituting it into equation (10–4) for *IRR* reduces the right-hand side of the equation to $11,090, as shown in Table 10–9. Therefore, because the present value of the future cash flows is larger than the initial outlay, we must raise the discount rate to find the project's IRR. Substituting 20 percent for the discount rate, the right-hand side of equation (10–4) now becomes $9,763. Because this is less than the initial outlay of $10,000, we must now decrease the discount rate. In other words, we know that the IRR for this project is between 15 and 20 percent. Because the present value of the future flows discounted back to present at 20 percent was only $237 too low, a discount rate of 19 percent is selected. As shown in Table 10–9, a discount rate of 19 percent reduces the present value of the future inflows down to $10,009, which is approximately the same as the initial outlay. Consequently, project C's IRR is approximately 19 percent.[2] Because the IRR is greater than the firm's required rate of return of 10 percent, this investment should be accepted. ∎

Viewing the NPV–IRR Relationship: The Net Present Value Profile

Perhaps the easiest way to understand the relationship between the IRR and the NPV value is to view it graphically through the use of a **net present value profile.** A net present value profile is simply *a graph showing how a project's NPV changes as the discount rate changes.* To graph a project's net present value profile you simply need to determine the project's NPV first using a 0-percent discount rate, then slowly increasing the discount rate until a representative curve has been plotted. How does

net present value profile

---

[2]If desired, the actual rate can be more approximated through interpolation as follows:

DISCOUNT RATE	PRESENT VALUE		
19%	$10,009	} difference $9	} difference $246
IRR	10,000		
20%	9,763		

Thus, *IRR* = 19% + ($9/246) × 1% = 19.04%

TABLE 10-9 COMPUTING IRR FOR PROJECT C

Try i = 15 percent:

	NET CASH FLOWS	PRESENT VALUE FACTOR AT 15 PERCENT	PRESENT VALUE
Inflow year 1	$1,000	.870	$ 870
Inflow year 2	3,000	.756	2,268
Inflow year 3	6,000	.658	3,948
Inflow year 4	7,000	.572	4,004
Present value of inflows			$11,090
Initial outlay			−$10,000

Try i = 20 percent:

	NET CASH FLOWS	PRESENT VALUE FACTOR AT 20 PERCENT	PRESENT VALUE
Inflow year 1	$1,000	.833	$ 833
Inflow year 2	3,000	.694	2,082
Inflow year 3	6,000	.579	3,474
Inflow year 4	7,000	.482	3,374
Present value of inflows			$ 9,763
Initial outlay			−$10,000

Try i = 19 percent:

	NET CASH FLOWS	PRESENT VALUE FACTOR AT 19 PERCENT	PRESENT VALUE
Inflow year 1	$1,000	.840	$ 840
Inflow year 2	3,000	.706	2,118
Inflow year 3	6,000	.593	3,558
Inflow year 4	7,000	.499	3,493
Present value of inflows			$10,009
Initial outlay			−$10,000

the IRR enter into the net present value profile? The IRR is the discount rate at which the NPV is zero.

Let's look at an example of a project that involves an after-tax initial outlay of $105,517 with after-tax cash flows expected to be $30,000 per year over the project's 5-year life. Calculating the NPV of this project at several different discounts rates results in the following:

Discount Rate	Project's NPV
0%	$44,483
5%	$24,367
10%	$ 8,207
13%	$ 0
15%	−$ 4,952
20%	−$15,798
25%	−$24,839

Plotting these values yields the net present value profile in Figure 10–1.

Where is the IRR in this figure? Recall that the IRR is the discount rate that equates the present value of the inflows with the present value of the outflows;

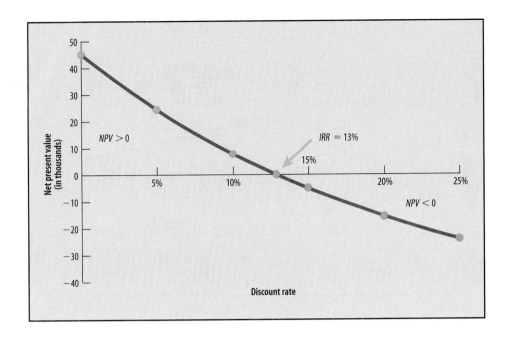

FIGURE 10-1
Net Present Value Profile

thus, the IRR is the point where the NPV is equal to zero—in this case, 13 percent.

From the net present value profile you can easily see how a project's NPV varies inversely with the discount rate—as the discount rate is raised, the NPV drops. By analyzing a project's net present value profile you can also see how sensitive the project is to your selection of the discount rate. The more sensitive the NPV is to the discount rate, the more important it is that you use the correct one in your calculations.

Complications with IRR: Multiple Rates of Return

Although any project can have only one NPV and one PI, a single project under certain circumstances can have more than one IRR. The reason for this can be traced to the calculations involved in determining the IRR. Equation (10–3) states that the IRR is the discount rate that equates the present value of the project's future net cash flows with the project's initial outlay:

$$IO = \sum_{t=1}^{n} \frac{ACF_t}{(1 + IRR)^t} \qquad (10\text{–}3)$$

However, because equation (10–3) is a polynomial of a degree n, it has n solutions. Now if the initial outlay (*IO*) is the only negative cash flow and all the annual after-tax cash flows (ACF_t) are positive, then all but one of these n solutions is either a negative or imaginary number and there is no problem. But problems occur when there are sign reversals in the cash flow stream; in fact, there can be as many solutions as there are sign reversals. A normal pattern with a negative initial outlay and positive annual after-tax cash flows after that (−, +, +, +, ⋯, +) has only one sign reversal, hence only one positive IRR. However, a pattern with more than one sign reversal can have more than one IRR[3]:

---

[3]This example is taken from James H. Lorie and Leonard J. Savage, "Three Problems in Rationing Capital," *Journal of Business* 28 (October 1955): 229–39.

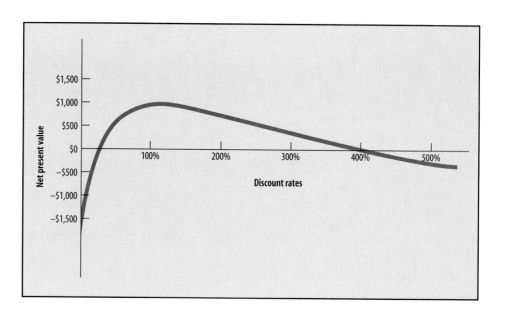

FIGURE 10-2
Multiple IRRs

	AFTER-TAX CASH FLOW
Initial outlay	−$ 1,600
Inflow year 1	+$10,000
Inflow year 2	−$10,000

In this pattern of cash flows there are two sign reversals, from −$1,600 to +$10,000 and then from +$10,000 to −$10,000, so there can be as many as two positive IRRs that will make the present value of the future cash flows equal to the initial outlay. In fact, two internal rates of return solve this problem, 25 percent and 400 percent. Graphically what we are solving for is the discount rate that makes the project's NPV equal to zero; as Figure 10–2 illustrates, this occurs twice.

Which solution is correct? The answer is that neither solution is valid. Although each fits the definition of IRR, neither provides any insight into the true project returns. In summary, when there is more than one sign reversal in the cash flow stream, the possibility of multiple IRRs exists, and the normal interpretation of the IRR loses its meaning. In this case, try the NPV criterion instead.

> **CONCEPT CHECK**
>
> 1. Name the four capital-budgeting criteria discussed in this section.
> 2. What are some of the shortcomings of the payback period? Why do you think it is used as frequently as it is?
> 3. Which of the capital-budgeting criteria lead to the same accept/reject decisions for independent projects?

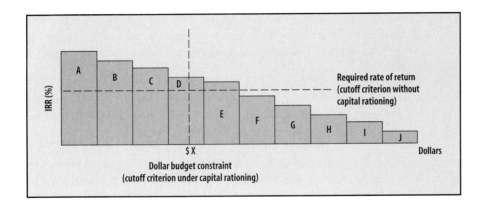

FIGURE 10–3
Projects Ranked by IRR

CAPITAL RATIONING

Objective 3

The use of our capital-budgeting decision rules developed in this chapter implies that the size of the capital budget is determined by the availability of acceptable investment proposals. However, a firm may *place a limit on the dollar size of the capital budget*. This situation is called **capital rationing**. As we will see, an examination of capital rationing not only better enables us to deal with complexities of the real world but also serves to demonstrate the superiority of the NPV method over the IRR method for capital budgeting.

capital rationing

Using the IRR as the firm's decision rule, a firm accepts all projects with an IRR greater than the firm's required rate of return. This rule is illustrated in Figure 10–3 where projects A through E would be chosen. However, when capital rationing is imposed, the dollar size of the total investment is limited by the budget constraint. In Figure 10–3 the budget constraint of $X precludes the acceptance of an attractive investment, project E. This situation obviously contradicts prior decision rules. Moreover, the solution of choosing the projects with the highest IRR is complicated by the fact that some projects may be indivisible; for example, it is meaningless to recommend that half project D be acquired.

PAUSE AND REFLECT

It is always somewhat uncomfortable to deal with problems associated with capital rationing because, under rationing, projects with positive net present values are rejected. This is a situation that violates the firm's goal of shareholder wealth maximization. However, in the real world, capital rationing does exist, and managers must deal with it. Often when firms impose capital constraints, they are recognizing that they do not have the ability to profitably handle more than a certain number of new and/or large projects.

Rationale for Capital Rationing

We first ask why capital rationing exists and whether it is rational. In general, three principal reasons are given for imposing a capital-rationing constraint. First, management may think market conditions are temporarily adverse. In the period surrounding the stock market crash of 1987 this reason was frequently given. At that time interest rates were high and stock prices were depressed, which made the cost of funding projects high. Today, it is used less frequently. Second, there may be a shortage of qualified managers to direct new projects; this can happen when projects are of a highly technical nature. Third, there may be intangible considerations. For example, management may simply fear debt, wishing to avoid interest payments at any cost. Or perhaps issuance of common stock may be limited to maintain a stable dividend policy.

Despite strong evidence that capital rationing exists in practice, the question remains as to its effect on the firm. In brief, the effect is negative, and to what degree depends on the severity of the rationing. If the rationing is minor and short-lived, the firm's share price will not suffer to any great extent. In this case capital rationing can probably be excused, although it should be noted that any capital rationing that rejects projects with positive NPVs is contrary to the firm's goal of maximization of shareholders' wealth. If the capital rationing is a result of the firm's decision to limit dramatically the number of new projects or to limit total investment to internally generated funds, then this policy will eventually have a significantly negative effect on the firm's share price. For example, a lower share price will eventually result from lost competitive advantage if because of a decision to arbitrarily limit its capital budget, a firm fails to upgrade its products and manufacturing processes.

Capital Rationing and Project Selection

If the firm decides to impose a capital constraint on investment projects, the appropriate decision criterion is to select the set of projects with the highest NPV subject to the capital constraint. In effect, we are selecting the projects that increase shareholders' wealth the most because the NPV is the amount of wealth that is created when a project is accepted. This guideline may preclude merely taking the highest-ranked projects in terms of the PI or the IRR. If the projects shown in Figure 10–3 are divisible, the last project accepted may be only partially accepted. Although partial acceptance may be possible in some cases, the indivisibility of most capital investments prevents it. If a project is a sales outlet or a truck, it may be meaningless to purchase half a sales outlet or half a truck.

To illustrate this procedure, consider a firm with a budget constraint of $1 million and five indivisible projects available to it, as given in Table 10–10. If the highest-ranked projects were taken, projects A and B would be taken first. At that point there would not be enough funds available to take project C; hence, projects D and E would be taken. However, a higher total NPV is provided by the combination of projects A and C. Thus, projects A and C should be selected from the set of projects available. This illustrates our guideline: to select the set of projects that maximizes the firm's NPV.

TABLE 10-10	CAPITAL-RATIONING EXAMPLE OF FIVE INDIVISIBLE PROJECTS		
PROJECT	INITIAL OUTLAY	PROFITABILITY INDEX	NET PRESENT VALUE
A	$200,000	2.4	$280,000
B	200,000	2.3	260,000
C	800,000	1.7	560,000
D	300,000	1.3	90,000
E	300,000	1.2	60,000

Project Ranking

In the past, we have proposed that all projects with a positive NPV, a PI greater than 1.0, or an IRR greater than the required rate of return be accepted, assuming there is no capital rationing. However, this acceptance is not always possible. In some cases, when two projects are judged acceptable by the discounted cash flow criteria, it may be necessary to select only one of them because they are mutually exclusive. **Mutually exclusive projects** occur when a *set of investment proposals perform essentially the same task; acceptance of one will necessarily mean rejection of the others.* For example, a company considering the installation of a computer system may evaluate three or four systems, all of which may have positive NPVs; however, the acceptance of one system automatically means rejection of the others. In general, to deal with mutually exclusive projects, we simply rank them by means of the discounted cash flow criteria and select the project with the highest ranking. On occasion, however, problems of conflicting ranking may arise. As we will see, in general the NPV method is the preferred decision-making tool because it leads to the selection of the project that increases shareholder wealth the most.

mutually exclusive projects

CONCEPT CHECK

1. What is capital rationing?
2. How might capital rationing conflict with the goal of maximization of shareholders' wealth?
3. What are mutually exclusive projects? How might they complicate the capital budgeting process?

PROBLEMS IN PROJECT RANKING: CAPITAL RATIONING, MUTUALLY EXCLUSIVE PROJECTS, AND PROBLEMS WITH THE IRR

Objective 4

There are three general types of ranking problems: the size disparity problem, the time disparity problem, and the unequal lives problem. Each involves the possibility of conflict in the ranks yielded by the various discounted cash flow capital-budgeting criteria. As noted previously, when one discounted cash flow criterion gives an accept signal, they will all give an accept signal, but they will not necessarily rank all projects in the same order. In most cases this disparity is not critical; however, for mutually exclusive projects the ranking order is important.

Size Disparity

The size disparity problem occurs when mutually exclusive projects of unequal size are examined. This problem is most easily clarified with an example.

Example

Suppose a firm is considering two mutually exclusive projects, A and B; both with required rates of return of 10 percent. Project A involves a $200 initial outlay and cash inflow of $300 at the end of 1 year, whereas project B involves an initial outlay of $1,500 and a cash inflow of $1,900 at the end of 1 year. The net present values, profitability indexes, and internal rates of return for these projects are given in Table 10–11.

TABLE 10-11 SIZE DISPARITY RANKING PROBLEM

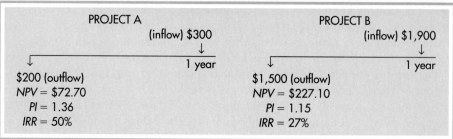

PROJECT A	PROJECT B
(inflow) $300	(inflow) $1,900
1 year	1 year
$200 (outflow)	$1,500 (outflow)
NPV = $72.70	NPV = $227.10
PI = 1.36	PI = 1.15
IRR = 50%	IRR = 27%

In this case, if the NPV criterion is used, project B should be accepted, whereas if the PI or IRR criterion is used, project A should be chosen. The question now becomes, which project is better? The answer depends on whether capital rationing exists. Without capital rationing, project B is better because it provides the largest increase in shareholders' wealth; that is, it has a larger NPV. If there is a capital constraint, the problem then focuses on what can be done with the additional $1,300 that is freed if project A is chosen (costing $200, as opposed to $1,500). If the firm can earn more on project A plus the project financed with the additional $1,300 than it can on project B, then project A and the marginal project should be accepted. In effect, we are attempting to select the set of projects that maximize the firm's NPV. Thus, if the marginal project has an NPV greater than $154.50 ($277.10 − $72.70), selecting it plus project A with an NPV of $72.70 will provide an NPV greater than $277.10, the NPV for project B.

In summary, whenever the size disparity problem results in conflicting rankings between mutually exclusive projects, the project with the largest NPV will be selected, provided there is no capital rationing. When capital rationing exists, the firm should select the set of projects with the largest NPV.

Time Disparity

The time disparity problem and the conflicting rankings that accompany it result from the differing reinvestment assumptions made by the net present value and internal rate of return decision criteria. The NPV criterion assumes that cash flows over the life of the project can be reinvested at the required rate of return or cost of capital, whereas the IRR criterion implicitly assumes that the cash flows over the life of the project can be reinvested at the IRR. Again, this problem may be illustrated through the use of an example.

Example

Suppose a firm with a required rate of return or cost of capital of 10 percent and with no capital constraint is considering the two mutually exclusive projects illustrated in Table 10–12. The NPV and PI indicate that project A is the better of the two, whereas the IRR indicates that project B is the better. Project B receives its cash flows earlier than project A, and the different assumptions made as to how these flows can be reinvested result in the difference in rankings. Which criterion would be followed depends on which reinvestment assumption is used. The NPV criterion is preferred in this case because it makes the most acceptable assumption for the

TABLE 10-12 TIME DISPARITY RANKING PROBLEM

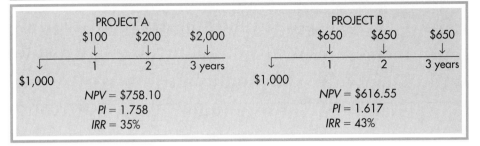

PROJECT A

$100 $200 $2,000
↓   ↓   ↓
|____1____2____3 years
↓
$1,000

NPV = $758.10
PI = 1.758
IRR = 35%

PROJECT B

$650 $650 $650
↓   ↓   ↓
|____1____2____3 years
↓
$1,000

NPV = $616.55
PI = 1.617
IRR = 43%

wealth-maximizing firm. It is certainly the most conservative assumption that can be made, because the required rate of return is the lowest possible reinvestment rate. Moreover, as we have already noted, the NPV method maximizes the value of the firm and the shareholders' wealth. ■

Unequal Lives

The final ranking problem to be examined centers on the question of whether it is appropriate to compare mutually exclusive projects with different life spans.

Example

Suppose a firm with a 10-percent required rate of return is faced with the problem of replacing an aging machine and is considering two replacement machines, one with a 3-year life and one with a 6-year life. The relevant cash flow information for these projects is given in Table 10–13.

Examining the discounted cash flow criteria, we find that the NPV and PI criteria indicate that project B is the better project, whereas the IRR criterion favors project A. This ranking inconsistency is caused by the different life spans of the projects being compared. In this case the decision is a difficult one because the projects are not comparable.

The problem of incomparability of projects with different lives arises because future profitable investment proposals may be rejected without being included in the

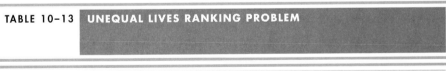

TABLE 10–13 UNEQUAL LIVES RANKING PROBLEM

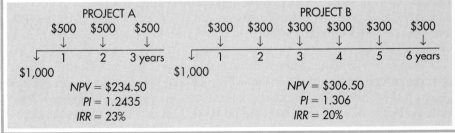

PROJECT A

$500 $500 $500
↓   ↓   ↓
|____1____2____3 years
↓
$1,000

NPV = $234.50
PI = 1.2435
IRR = 23%

PROJECT B

$300 $300 $300 $300 $300 $300
↓   ↓   ↓   ↓   ↓   ↓
|____1____2____3____4____5____6 years
↓
$1,000

NPV = $306.50
PI = 1.306
IRR = 20%

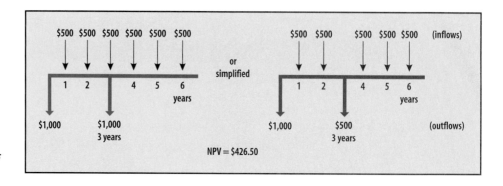

FIGURE 10–4

Replacement Chain Illustration: Two Project A's Back to Back

analysis. This can easily be seen in a replacement problem such as the present example, in which two mutually exclusive machines with different lives are being considered. In this case a comparison of the NPVs alone on each of these projects would be misleading. If the project with the shorter life were taken, at its termination the firm could replace the machine and receive additional benefits, whereas acceptance of the project with the longer life would exclude this possibility, a possibility that is not included in the analysis. The key question thus becomes, does today's investment decision include all future profitable investment proposals in its analysis? If not, the projects are not comparable. In this case, if project B is taken, then the project that could have been taken after 3 years when project A terminates is automatically rejected without being included in the analysis. Thus, acceptance of project B not only forces rejection of project A, but also forces rejection of any replacement machine that might have been considered for years 4 through 6 without including this replacement machine in the analysis.

There are several methods to deal with this situation. The first option is to assume that the cash inflows from the shorter-lived investment will be reinvested at the required rate of return until the termination of the longer-lived asset. Although this approach is the simplest, merely calculating the NPV, it actually ignores the problem at hand—that of allowing for participation in another replacement opportunity with a positive NPV. The proper solution thus becomes the projection of reinvestment opportunities into the future—that is, making assumptions about possible future investment opportunities. Unfortunately, whereas the first method is too simplistic to be of any value, the second is extremely difficult, requiring extensive cash flow forecasts. The final technique for confronting the problem is to assume that reinvestment opportunities in the future will be similar to the current ones. The two most common ways of doing this are by creating a replacement chain to equalize life spans or calculating the project's equivalent annual annuity (EAA). Using a replacement chain, the present example would call for the creation of a two-chain cycle for project A; that is, we assume that project A can be replaced with a similar investment at the end of 3 years. Thus, project A would be viewed as two project A's occurring back to back, as illustrated in Figure 10–4. The NPV on this replacement chain is $426.50, which is comparable with project B's NPV. Therefore, project A should be accepted because the NPV of its replacement chain is greater than the NPV of project B.

One problem with replacement chains is that, depending on the life of each project, it can be quite difficult to come up with equivalent lives. For example, if the two projects had 7- and 13-year lives because the lowest common denominator is 7 × 13 = 91, a 91-year replacement chain would be needed to establish equivalent lives. In this case it is easier to determine the project's **equivalent annual annuity (EAA)**.

equivalent annual annuity (EAA)

Bad Apple for Baby

As we learned in **Axiom 10: Ethical Behavior Is Doing the Right Thing, and Ethical Dilemmas Are Everywhere in Finance,** unethical behavior eliminates trust and the public's confidence. Once this is gone, it is difficult to recover.

It's a widely held but hard to prove belief that a company gains because it is perceived as more socially responsive than its competitors. Over the years, the three major manufacturers of baby food—Gerber Products, Beech-Nut Nutrition and H. J. Heinz—had, with almost equal success, gone out of their way to build an image of respectability.

Theirs is an almost perfect zero-sum business. They know, at any given time, how many babies are being born. They all pay roughly the same price for their commodities, and their manufacturing and distribution costs are almost identical. So how does one company gain a market share edge over another, especially in a stagnant or declining market?

The answer for Beech-Nut was to sell a cheaper, adulterated product. Beginning in 1977, the company began buying a chemical concoction, made up mostly of sugar and water, and labeling it as apple juice. Sales of that product brought Beech-Nut an estimated $60 million between 1977 and 1982, while reducing material costs about $250,000 annually.

When various investigators tried to do something about it, the company stonewalled. Among other things, they shipped the bogus juice out of a plant in New York to Puerto Rico to put it beyond the jurisdiction of federal investigators, and they even offered the juice as a give-away to reduce their stocks after they were finally forced to discontinue selling it.

In the end, the company pleaded guilty to 215 counts of introducing adulterated food into commerce and violating the Federal Food Drug and Cosmetic Act. The FDA fined Beech-Nut $2 million.

In addition, Beech-Nut's president, Neils Hoyvald, and its vice president of operations, John Lavery, were found guilty of similar charges. Each was sentenced to a year and one day in jail and fined $100,000. Both are now out on appeal on a jurisdiction technicality.

Why did they do it? The Fort Washington, Pa.–based company will not comment. But perhaps some portion of motive can be inferred from a report Hoyvald wrote to Nestle, the company that had acquired Beech-Nut in the midst of this coverup. "It is our feeling that we can report safely now that the apple juice recall has been completed. If the recall had been effectuated in early June [when the FDA had first ordered it], over 700,000 cases in inventory would have been affected, due to our many delays, we were only faced with having to destroy 20,000 cases."

One thing is clear. Two executives of a company with an excellent reputation breached a trust and did their company harm.

Since 1987, when the case was brought to a close, Beech-Nut's share of the overall baby food market has fallen from 19.1% to 15.8%. So what was gained in the past has been lost in the present, and perhaps for the future as well.

Source: Stephen Kindel, "Bad Apple for Baby," *Financial World,* June 27, 1989, p. 48, Financial World Partners.

A project's EAA is simply an *annuity cash flow that yields the same present value as the project's NPV.* To calculate a project's EAA we need only calculate a project's NPV and then divide the number by the $PVIF_{i, n}$ to determine the dollar value of an n-year annuity that would produce the same NPV as the project. This can be done in two steps as follows:

Step 1: *Calculate the project's NPV.* In Table 10–13 we determined that project A had an NPV of $234.50, whereas project B had an NPV of $306.50.

Step 2: *Calculate the EAA.* The EAA is determined by dividing each project's NPV by the $PVIFA_{i, n}$ where i is the required rate of return and n is the project's life. This determines the level of an annuity cash flow that would produce the same NPV as the project. For project A the $PVIFA_{10\%, 3\,yr}$ is equal to 2.487, whereas the $PVIFA_{10\%, 6\,yr}$ for project B is equal to 4.355. Dividing each project's NPV by the appropriate $PVIFA_{i, n}$ we determine the EAA for each project:

$$EAA_A = NPV/PVIFA_{i,n}$$
$$= \$234.50/2.487$$
$$= \$94.29$$
$$EAA_B = \$306.50/4.355$$
$$= \$70.38$$

How do we interpret the EAA? For a project with an n-year life, it tells us the dollar value of an n-year annual annuity that would provide the same NPV as the project. Thus, for project A a 3-year annuity of $94.29 given a discount rate of 10 percent would produce an NPV the same as project A's NPV, which is $234.50. We can now directly compare the equivalent annual annuities to determine which project is better. We can do this because we have found the level of annual annuity that produces an NPV equivalent to the project's NPV. Thus, because they are both annual annuities they are comparable. To do this we need only calculate the present value of an infinite stream or perpetuity of equivalent annual annuities. This is done by using the present value of an infinite annuity formula—that is, simply dividing the EAA by the appropriate discount rate. In this case we find:

$$NPV_{\infty,A} = \$94.29/.10$$
$$= \$942.90$$
$$NPV_{\infty,B} = \$70.38/.10$$
$$= \$703.80$$

Here we have calculated the present value of an infinite-life replacement chain. Because the EAA method provides the same results as the infinite-life replacement chain, it really doesn't matter which method you prefer to use. ■

CONCEPT CHECK

1. What are the three general types of ranking problems?
2. In simple terms, what is an equivalent annual annuity (EAA)?

ETHICS IN CAPITAL BUDGETING

Although it may not seem obvious, ethics has a role in capital budgeting. Beech-Nut provides an example of how these rules have been violated in the past and what the consequences can be. No doubt this project appeared to have a positive NPV associated with it, but in fact, it cost Beech-Nut tremendously. The Ethics in Financial Management article, "Bad Apple for Baby" tells what occurred.

BACK TO THE FOUNDATIONS

Ethics and ethical considerations continually crop up when capital-budgeting decisions are being made. This brings us back to **Axiom 10: Ethical Behavior Is Doing the Right Thing, and Ethical Dilemmas Are Everywhere in Finance.** As the Ethics in Financial Management article, "Bad Apple for Baby" points out, the most damaging event a business can experience is a loss of the public's confidence in the business's ethical standards. In making capital-budgeting decisions we must be aware of this, and that ethical behavior is doing the right thing and is the right thing to do.

During the past 40 years, the popularity of each of the capital-budgeting methods has shifted rather dramatically. In the 1950s and 1960s, the payback period method dominated capital budgeting; but through the 1970s and 1980s, the IRR and the NPV techniques slowly gained in popularity until today when they are used by virtually all major corporations in decision making. Table 10–14 provides the results of a 1992 survey of the 100 largest Fortune 500 firms, showing the popularity of the IRR and NPV methods.

Interestingly, although most firms use the NPV and IRR as their primary techniques, most firms also use the payback period as a secondary decision-making method for capital budgeting. In a sense, they are using the payback period to control for risk. The logic behind this is that, because the payback period dramatically emphasizes early cash flows, which are presumably more certain—that is, have less risk—than cash flows occurring later in a project's life, managers believe its use will lead to projects with more certain cash flows.

A reliance on the payback period came out even more dramatically in a study of the capital-budgeting practices of 12 large manufacturing firms.[4] The study also showed that while the discounted cash flow methods are used at most firms, the simple payback criterion was the measure relied on primarily in one-third of the firms examined. The use of the payback period seemed to be even more common for smaller projects, with firms severely simplifying the discounted cash flow analysis or relying primarily on the payback period. Thus, although discounted cash flow decision-making techniques have become more widely accepted, their use depends to an extent on the size of the project and where within the firm the decision is being made.

Without taking on new projects, a company simply wouldn't continue to exist. For example, Smith-Corona's inability to come up with a product to replace the typewriters that it produced resulted in that company going under in 1996. Finding new profitable projects and correctly evaluating them are central to a firm's continued existence—and that's what capital budgeting is all about. It may be your decision to buy a Burger King franchise and open a Burger King restaurant or it may be to

TABLE 10–14	SURVEY OF CAPITAL-BUDGETING PRACTICES OF THE 100 LARGEST FORTUNE 500 INDUSTRIAL FIRMS		
	Percent of Firms		
INVESTMENT EVALUATION METHODS USED:	A PRIMARY METHOD	A SECONDARY METHOD	TOTAL USING THIS METHOD
Internal rate of return	88%	11%	99%
Net present value	63%	22%	85%
Payback period	24%	59%	83%
Profitability index	15%	18%	33%

Source: Harold Bierman, Jr., "Capital Budgeting in 1992: A Survey," *Financial Management* (Autumn 1993):24.

[4]Marc Ross, "Capital Budgeting Practices of Twelve Large Manufacturers," *Financial Management*, 15 (Winter 1986), pp. 15–22.

help in Burger King's decision to introduce the Big King, a new burger that looks an awful lot like the Big Mac. Regardless, when you're making an investment in fixed assets, it's a capital-budgeting decision. It may also involve taking a product that didn't work and trying to redesign it in such a way that it does. That's what 3Com Corporation did with the Palm Pilot electronic datebook and scheduler, which succeeded with small size and simplicity where Apple's Newton and Motorola's Envoy failed.

Much of what is done within a business involves the capital-budgeting process. Many times it's referred to as strategic planning, but it generally involves capital-budgeting decisions. You may be involved in market research dealing with a proposed new product or its marketing plan, or in analyzing its costs—these are all part of the capital-budgeting process. Once all this information has been gathered, it is analyzed using the techniques and tools that we have presented in this chapter. Actually, almost any decision can be analyzed using the framework we presented here. That's because the NPV method "values" the project under consideration. That is, it looks at the present value of its benefits relative to the present value of its costs and if the present value of the benefits outweigh the costs, the project is accepted. That's a pretty good decision rule, and it can be applied to any decision a business faces.

CONCEPT CHECK

1. What capital-budgeting criteria seem to be used most frequently in the real world? Why do you think this is so?

FINANCE AND THE MULTINATIONAL FIRM: CAPITAL BUDGETING

Without question, the key to success in capital budgeting is to identify good projects, and for many companies these good projects are overseas. Just look at the success that Coca-Cola has had in the international markets, with over 80 percent of its beverage profit coming from foreign markets and earning more in Japan than in the United States. This success abroad also holds true for General Motors, which had $146 million in profits in the fourth quarter of 1998 from its GM Europe division alone. Similarly, Exxon earns over half its profits from abroad and is involved in gas and oil exploration projects in West Africa, the Caspian Sea, Russia, the Gulf of Mexico, and South America.

But how do you enter these markets initially? One approach that has been used successfully is through international joint ventures or strategic alliances. Under these arrangements two or more corporations merge their skills and resources on a specific project, trading things like technology and access to marketing channels. For example, in 1998 GM and Suzuki Motors announced a strategic alliance that provides Suzuki with access to Europe, North America, South America, and Africa, where GM has a strong presence, and provides GM with access to the Asia Pacific region, where Suzuki is well established. As John F. Smith, Jr. the GM Chairman and CEO said at the announcement of this joint venture, "Each company has specific competencies and market strengths, which can be better leveraged to the mutual benefit of both parties through this agreement."

An example of a successful market penetration using joint ventures is that of the U.S. oil giant Armco forming a joint venture with Mitsubishi to sell Armco's lightweight plastics in Japan. Similarly, in 1999 Georgia Pacific and Canfor Japan Corporation announced a joint venture in which Georgia Pacific gained access to Canfor's marketing expertise in Japan to sell pulp and paper products in Japan. Likewise, H. J. Heinz Co. announced a joint venture with an Indonesian firm to gain access to its Indonesian marketing channels. Joint ventures also provide a way to get around trade barriers. For example, India and Mexico require joint ventures for entry into their markets. As a result, U.S. firms like Apple Computer and Hewlett-Packard have been forced to enter into Mexican joint ventures in order to be allowed to ship their products into Mexico.

What is the alternative to not looking abroad for projects? It is losing out on potential revenues. Keep in mind that firms like Xerox, Hewlett-Packard, Dow Chemical, IBM, and Gillette all earn more than 50% of their profits from sales abroad. International boundaries no longer apply in finance.

CONCEPT CHECK

1. What methods do corporations use to enter the international markets?

SUMMARY

The process of capital budgeting involves decision making with respect to investment in fixed assets. Before a profitable project can be adopted, it must be identified or found. Unfortunately, coming up with ideas for new products, for ways to improve existing products, or for ways to make existing products more profitable is extremely difficult. In general, the best source of ideas for these new, potentially profitable products is from within the firm. We examine four commonly used criteria for determining the acceptance or rejection of capital-budgeting proposals. The first method, the payback period, does not incorporate the time value of money into its calculations. However, the net present value, profitability index, and internal rate of return do account for the time value of money. These methods are summarized in Table 10–15 on page 316.

Objective 1
Objective 2

This chapter introduces several complications into the capital-budgeting process. First, we examine capital rationing and the problems it can create by imposing a limit on the dollar size of the capital budget. Although capital rationing does not, in general, lead to the goal of maximization of shareholders' wealth, it does exist in practice. We also discuss problems associated with the evaluation of mutually exclusive projects. Mutually exclusive projects occur when a set of investment proposals perform essentially the same task. In general, to deal with mutually exclusive projects, we rank them by means of the discounted cash flow criteria and select the project with the highest ranking. Conflicting rankings may arise because of the size disparity problem, the time disparity problem, and unequal lives. The problem of incomparability of projects with different life spans is not simply a result of the different life spans; rather, it arises because future profitable investment proposals may be rejected without being included in the analysis. Replacement chains and equivalent annual annuities are presented as possible solutions to this problem. Ethics and ethical decisions continuously crop up in capital budgeting. Just as with all other areas of finance, violating ethical considerations results in a loss of public confidence which can have a significant negative effect on shareholder wealth. Over the past 40 years the discounted

Objective 3
Objective 4
Objective 5
Objective 6

TABLE 10-15 CAPITAL-BUDGETING CRITERIA

1. Payback period = number of years required to recapture the initial investment

Accept if payback ≤ maximum acceptable payback period
Reject if payback > maximum acceptable payback period

Advantages:
- Uses cash flows.
- Is easy to calculate and understand.
- May be used as rough screening device.

Disadvantages:
- Ignores the time value of money.
- Ignores cash flows occurring after the payback period.
- Selection of the maximum acceptable payback period is arbitrary.

2. Net present value = present value of the annual after-tax cash flows less the investment's initial outlay

$$NPV = \sum_{t=1}^{n} \frac{ACF_t}{(1 + k)^t} - IO$$

where ACF_t = the annual after-tax cash flow in time period t (this can take on either positive or negative values)

k = the appropriate discount rate; that is, the required rate of return or the cost of capital

IO = the initial cash outlay

n = the project's expected life

Accept if $NPV \geq 0.0$
Reject if $NPV < 0.0$

Advantages:
- Uses cash flows.
- Recognizes the time value of money.
- Is consistent with the firm's goal of shareholder wealth maximization.

Disadvantages:
- Requires detailed long-term forecasts of a project's cash flows.

3. Profitability index = the ratio of the present value of the future net cash flows to the initial outlay

$$PI = \frac{\sum_{t=1}^{n} \frac{ACF_t}{(1+ k)^t}}{IO}$$

Accept if $PI \geq 1.0$
Reject if $PI < 1.0$

Advantages:
- Uses cash flows.
- Recognizes the time value of money.
- Is consistent with the firm's goal of shareholder wealth maximization.

Disadvantages:
- Requires detailed long-term forecasts of a project's cash flows.

4. Internal rate of return = the discount rate that equates the present value of the project's future net cash flows with the project's initial outlay

$$IO = \sum_{t=1}^{n} \frac{ACF_t}{(1 + IRR)^t}$$

where IRR = the project's internal rate of return

TABLE 10-15	CAPITAL-BUDGETING CRITERIA—Cont'd

Accept if *IRR* ≥ required rate of return
Reject if *IRR* < required rate of return

Advantages:
- Uses cash flows.
- Recognizes the time value of money.
- Is, in general, consistent with the firm's goal of shareholder wealth maximization.

Disadvantages:
- Requires detailed long-term forecasts of a project's cash flows.
- Can involve tedious calculations.
- Possibility of multiple IRRs.

capital-budgeting techniques have continued to gain in popularity and today dominate in the decision-making process.

The international markets provide another source for finding good capital-budgeting projects. In fact, many times a new project may simply involve taking an existing product and entering it in a foreign market. One approach that has been successfully used to enter foreign markets is international joint ventures or strategic alliances.

Objective 7

KEY TERMS

benefit-cost ratio (see profitability index), 295

capital budgeting, 290

capital rationing, 305

equivalent annual annuity (EAA), 310

internal rate of return (IRR), 297

mutually exclusive projects, 307

net present value (NPV), 292

net present value profile, 301

payback period, 291

profitability index (PI or benefit-cost ratio), 295

STUDY QUESTIONS

10-1 Why is the capital-budgeting decision such an important process? Why are capital-budgeting errors so costly?

10-2 What are the criticisms of the use of the payback period as a capital-budgeting technique? What are its advantages? Why is it so frequently used?

10-3 In some countries, expropriation of foreign investments is a common practice. If you were considering an investment in one of those countries, would the use of the payback period criterion seem more reasonable than it otherwise might? Why?

10-4 Briefly compare and contrast the NPV, PI, and IRR criteria. What are the advantages and disadvantages of using each of these methods?

10-5 What are mutually exclusive projects? Why might the existence of mutually exclusive projects cause problems in the implementation of the discounted cash flow capital-budgeting criteria?

10-6 What are common reasons for capital rationing? Is capital rationing rational?

10-7 How should managers compare two mutually exclusive projects of unequal size? Would your approach change if capital rationing existed?

10-8 What causes the time disparity ranking problem? What reinvestment rate assumptions are associated with the NPV and IRR capital-budgeting criteria?

10-9 When might two mutually exclusive projects having unequal lives be incomparable? How should managers deal with this problem?

──────────── SELF-TEST PROBLEMS ────────────

ST-1 You are considering a project that will require an initial outlay of $54,200. This project has an expected life of 5 years and will generate after-tax cash flows to the company as a whole of $20,608 at the end of each year over its 5-year life. In addition to the $20,608 cash flow from operations during the fifth and final year, there will be an additional cash inflow of $13,200 at the end of the fifth year associated with the salvage value of the machine, making the cash flow in year 5 equal to $33,808. Thus, the cash flows associated with this project look like this:

	CASH FLOW
Initial outlay	−$54,200
Inflow year 1	20,608
Inflow year 2	20,608
Inflow year 3	20,608
Inflow year 4	20,608
Inflow year 5	33,808

Given a required rate of return of 15 percent, calculate the following:
  a. Payback period
  b. NPV
  c. PI
  d. IRR
Should this project be accepted?

──────────── STUDY PROBLEMS ────────────

10-1 *(IRR Calculation)* Determine the IRR on the following projects:
  a. An initial outlay of $10,000 resulting in a single cash flow of $17,182 after 8 years
  b. An initial outlay of $10,000 resulting in a single cash flow of $48,077 after 10 years
  c. An initial outlay of $10,000 resulting in a single cash flow of $114,943 after 20 years
  d. An initial outlay of $10,000 resulting in a single cash flow of $13,680 after 3 years
10-2 *(IRR Calculation)* Determine the IRR on the following projects:
  a. An initial outlay of $10,000 resulting in a cash flow of $1,993 at the end of each year for the next 10 years
  b. An initial outlay of $10,000 resulting in a cash flow of $2,054 at the end of each year for the next 20 years
  c. An initial outlay of $10,000 resulting in a cash flow of $1,193 at the end of each year for the next 12 years
  d. An initial outlay of $10,000 resulting in a cash flow of $2,843 at the end of each year for the next 5 years
10-3 *(IRR Calculation)* Determine the IRR to the nearest percent on the following projects:
  a. An initial outlay of $10,000 resulting in a cash flow of $2,000 at the end of year 1, $5,000 at the end of year 2, and $8,000 at the end of year 3
  b. An initial outlay of $10,000 resulting in a cash flow of $8,000 at the end of year 1, $5,000 at the end of year 2, and $2,000 at the end of year 3

c. An initial outlay of $10,000 resulting in a cash flow of $2,000 at the end of years 1 through 5 and $5,000 at the end of year 6

10-4 *(NPV, PI, and IRR Calculations)* Fijisawa, Inc., is considering a major expansion of its product line and has estimated the following cash flows associated with such an expansion. The initial outlay associated with the expansion would be $1,950,000 and the project would generate incremental after-tax cash flows of $450,000 per year for 6 years. The appropriate required rate of return is 9 percent.

   a. Calculate the NPV.
   b. Calculate the PI.
   c. Calculate the IRR.
   d. Should this project be accepted?

10-5 *(Payback Period, Net Present Value, Profitability Index, and Internal Rate of Return Calculations)* You are considering a project with an initial cash outlay of $80,000 and expected after-tax cash flows of $20,000 at the end of the year for 6 years. The required rate of return for this project is 10 percent.

   a. What is the project's payback period?
   b. What is the project's NPV?
   c. What is the project's PI?
   d. What is the project's IRR?

10-6 *(Net Present Value, Profitability Index, and Internal Rate of Return Calculations)* You are considering two independent projects, project A and project B. The initial cash outlay associated with project A is $50,000 and the initial cash outlay associated with project B is $70,000. The required rate of return on both projects is 12 percent. The expected annual after-tax cash inflows from each project are as follows:

Calculate the NPV, PI, and IRR for each project and indicate if the project should be accepted.

	PROJECT A	PROJECT B
Initial outlay	−$50,000	−$70,000
Inflow year 1	12,000	13,000
Inflow year 2	12,000	13,000
Inflow year 3	12,000	13,000
Inflow year 4	12,000	13,000
Inflow year 5	12,000	13,000
Inflow year 6	12,000	13,000

10-7 *(Payback Period Calculations)* You are considering three independent projects, project A, project B, and project C. Given the following cash flow information, calculate the payback period for each.

	PROJECT A	PROJECT B	PROJECT C
Initial outlay	−$1,000	−$10,000	−$5,000
Inflow year 1	600	5,000	1,000
Inflow year 2	300	3,000	1,000
Inflow year 3	200	3,000	2,000
Inflow year 4	100	3,000	2,000
Inflow year 5	500	3,000	2,000

If you require a 3-year payback before an investment can be accepted, which project(s) would be accepted?

10-8 *(NPV with Varying Required Rates of Return)* Dowling Sportswear is considering building a new factory to produce aluminum baseball bats. This project would require an initial cash outlay of $5,000,000 and will generate annual after-tax cash inflows of $1,000,000 per year for 8 years. Calculate the project's NPV given:

a. A required rate of return of 9 percent
b. A required rate of return of 11 percent
c. A required rate of return of 13 percent
d. A required rate of return of 15 percent

10-9 *(IRR Calculations)* Given the following cash flows, determine the IRR for the three independent projects A, B, and C.

	PROJECT A	PROJECT B	PROJECT C
Initial outlay	−$50,000	−$100,000	−$450,000
Cash inflows			
Year 1	$10,000	$ 25,000	$200,000
Year 2	15,000	25,000	200,000
Year 3	20,000	25,000	200,000
Year 4	25,000	25,000	—
Year 5	30,000	25,000	—

10-10 *(NPV with Varying Required Rates of Return)* Big Steve's, makers of swizzle sticks, is considering the purchase of a new plastic stamping machine. This investment requires an initial outlay of $100,000 and will generate after-tax cash inflows of $18,000 per year for 10 years. For each of the listed required rates of return, determine the project's net present value.

a. The required rate of return is 10 percent.
b. The required rate of return is 15 percent.
c. Would the project be accepted under part a or b?
d. What is the project's IRR?

10-11 *(Size Disparity Problem)* The D. Dorner Farms Corporation is considering purchasing one of two fertilizer-herbicides for the upcoming year. The more expensive of the two is better and will produce a higher yield. Assume these projects are mutually exclusive and that the required rate of return is 10 percent. Given the following after-tax net cash flows:

	PROJECT A	PROJECT B
Initial outlay	− $500	−$5,000
Inflow year 1	700	6,000

a. Calculate the NPV of each project.
b. Calculate the PI of each project.
c. Calculate the IRR of each project.
d. If there is no capital-rationing constraint, which project should be selected? If there is a capital-rationing constraint, how should the decision be made?

10-12 *(Time Disparity Problem)* The State Spartan Corporation is considering two mutually exclusive projects. The cash flows associated with those projects are as follows:

	PROJECT A	PROJECT B
Initial outlay	−$50,000	−$ 50,000
Inflow year 1	15,625	0
Inflow year 2	15,625	0
Inflow year 3	15,625	0
Inflow year 4	15,625	0
Inflow year 5	15,625	100,000

The required rate of return on these projects is 10 percent.
  a. What is each project's payback period?
  b. What is each project's NPV?
  c. What is each project's IRR?
  d. What has caused the ranking conflict?
  e. Which project should be accepted? Why?

10-13 *(Unequal Lives Problem)* The B. T. Knight Corporation is considering two mutually exclusive pieces of machinery that perform the same task. The two alternatives available provide the following set of after-tax net cash flows:

	EQUIPMENT A	EQUIPMENT B
Initial outflow	−$20,000	−$20,000
Inflow year 1	12,590	6,625
Inflow year 2	12,590	6,625
Inflow year 3	12,590	6,625
Inflow year 4		6,625
Inflow year 5		6,625
Inflow year 6		6,625
Inflow year 7		6,625
Inflow year 8		6,625
Inflow year 9		6,625

Equipment A has an expected life of three years, whereas equipment B has an expected life of 9 years. Assume a required rate of return of 15 percent.
  a. Calculate each project's payback period.
  b. Calculate each project's NPV.
  c. Calculate each project's IRR.
  d. Are these projects comparable?
  e. Compare these projects using replacement chains and EAA. Which project should be selected? Support your recommendation.

10-14 *(Equivalent Annual Annuity)* The Andrzejewski Corporation is considering two mutually exclusive projects, one with a 3-year life and one with a 7-year life. The after-tax cash flows from the two projects are as follows:

	PROJECT A	PROJECT B
Initial outlay	−$50,000	−$50,000
Inflow year 1	20,000	36,000
Inflow year 2	20,000	36,000
Inflow year 3	20,000	36,000
Inflow year 4	20,000	
Inflow year 5	20,000	
Inflow year 6	20,000	
Inflow year 7	20,000	

a. Assuming a 10-percent required rate of return on both projects, calculate each project's EAA. Which project should be selected?
b. Calculate the present value of an infinite-life replacement chain for each project.

10-15 *(Capital Rationing)* The Cowboy Hat Company of Stillwater, Okla., is considering seven capital investment proposals, for which the funds available are limited to a maximum of $12 million. The projects are independent and have the following costs and profitability indexes associated with them:

PROJECT	COST	PROFITABILITY INDEX
A	$4,000,000	1.18
B	3,000,000	1.08
C	5,000,000	1.33
D	6,000,000	1.31
E	4,000,000	1.19
F	6,000,000	1.20
G	4,000,000	1.18

a. Under strict capital rationing, which projects should be selected?
b. What problems are there with capital rationing?

COMPREHENSIVE PROBLEM

Your first assignment in your new position as assistant financial analyst at Caledonia Products is to evaluate two new capital-budgeting proposals. Because this is your first assignment, you have been asked not only to provide a recommendation, but also to respond to a number of questions aimed at judging your understanding of the capital-budgeting process. This is a standard procedure for all new financial analysts at Caledonia, and will serve to determine whether you are moved directly into the capital-budgeting analysis department or are provided with remedial training. The memorandum you received outlining your assignment follows.

TO: The New Financial Analysts
FROM: Mr. V. Morrison, CEO, Caledonia Products
RE: Capital-Budgeting Analysis

Provide an evaluation of two proposed projects, both with 5-year expected lives and identical initial outlays of $110,000. Both of these projects involve additions to Caledonia's highly successful Avalon product line, and as a result, the required rate of return on both projects has been established at 12 percent. The expected after-tax cash flows from each project are as follows:

	PROJECT A	PROJECT B
Initial outlay	−$110,000	−$110,000
Inflow year 1	20,000	40,000
Inflow year 2	30,000	40,000
Inflow year 3	40,000	40,000
Inflow year 4	50,000	40,000
Inflow year 5	70,000	40,000

In evaluating these projects, please respond to the following questions:
  a. Why is the capital-budgeting process so important?
  b. Why is it difficult to find exceptionally profitable projects?
  c. What is the payback period on each project? If Caledonia imposes a 3-year maximum acceptable payback period, which of these projects should be accepted?
  d. What are the criticisms of the payback period?
  e. Determine the NPV for each of these projects. Should they be accepted?
  f. Describe the logic behind the NPV.
  g. Determine the PI for each of these projects. Should they be accepted?
  h. Would you expect the NPV and PI methods to give consistent accept/reject decisions? Why or why not?
  i. What would happen to the NPV and PI for each project if the required rate of return increased? If the required rate of return decreased?
  j. Determine the IRR for each project. Should they be accepted?
  k. How does a change in the required rate of return affect the project's internal rate of return?
  l. What reinvestment rate assumptions are implicity made by the NPV and IRR methods? Which one is better?
You have *also* been asked for your views on three unrelated sets of projects. Each set of projects involves two mutually exclusive projects. These projects follow.
  m. Caledonia is considering two investments with 1-year lives. The more expensive of the two is the better and will produce more savings. Assume these projects are mutually exclusive and that the required rate of return is 10 percent. Given the following after-tax net cash flows:

	PROJECT A	PROJECT B
Initial outlay	−$195,000	−$1,200,000
Inflow year 1	240,000	1,650,000

  1. Calculate the NPV.
  2. Calculate the PI.
  3. Calculate the IRR.

4. If there is no capital-rationing constraint, which project should be selected? If there is a capital-rationing constraint, how should the decision be made?

n. Caledonia is considering two additional mutually exclusive projects. The cash flows associated with these projects are as follows:

	PROJECT A	PROJECT B
Initial outlay	−$10,000	−$100,000
Inflow year 1	32,000	0
Inflow year 2	32,000	0
Inflow year 3	32,000	0
Inflow year 4	32,000	0
Inflow year 5	32,000	200,000

The required rate of return on these projects is 11 percent.
   1. What is each project's payback period?
   2. What is each project's NPV?
   3. What is each project's IRR?
   4. What has caused the ranking conflict?
   5. Which project should be accepted? Why?

o. The final two mutually exclusive projects that Caledonia is considering involves mutually exclusive pieces of machinery that perform the same task. The two alternatives available provide the following set of after-tax net cash flows:

	EQUIPMENT A	EQUIPMENT B
Initial outlay	−$100,000	−$100,000
Inflow year 1	65,000	32,500
Inflow year 2	65,000	32,500
Inflow year 3	65,000	32,500
Inflow year 4		32,500
Inflow year 5		32,500
Inflow year 6		32,500
Inflow year 7		32,500
Inflow year 8		32,500
Inflow year 9		32,500

Equipment A has an expected life of 3 years, whereas equipment B has an expected life of 9 years. Assume a required rate of return of 14 percent.
   1. Calculate each project's payback period.
   2. Calculate each project's NPV.
   3. Calculate each project's IRR.
   4. Are these projects comparable?
   5. Compare these projects using replacement chains and EAAs. Which project should be selected? Support your recommendation.

SS-1

a.
$$\text{Payback period} = \frac{\$54,200}{\$20,608} = 2.630 \text{ years}$$

b.
$$NPV = \sum_{t=1}^{n} \frac{ACF_t}{(1+k)^t} - IO$$

$$= \sum_{t=1}^{4} \frac{\$20,608}{(1+.15)^t} + \frac{\$33,808}{(1+.15)^5} - \$54,200$$
$$= \$20,608(2.855) + \$33,808(.497) - \$54,200$$
$$= \$58,836 + \$16,803 - \$54,200$$
$$= \$21,439$$

c.
$$PI = \frac{\displaystyle\sum_{t=1}^{n} \frac{ACF_t}{(1+k)}}{IO}$$

$$= \frac{\$75,639}{\$54,200}$$

$$= 1.396$$

d.
$$IO = \sum_{t=1}^{n} \frac{ACF_t}{(1+IRR)^t}$$

$$\$54,200 = \$20,608\,(PVIFA_{IRR\%,\ 4\ yr}) + \$33,808\,(PVIF_{IRR\%,\ 5\ yr})$$

Try 29 percent:

$$\$54,200 = \$20,608(2.203) + \$33,808(.280)$$
$$= \$45,399 + \$9,466$$
$$= \$54,865$$

Try 30 percent:

$$\$45,200 = \$20,608(2.166) + \$33,808(.269)$$
$$= \$44,637 + \$9,094$$
$$= \$53,731$$

Thus, the IRR is just below 30 percent and the project should be accepted because the NPV is positive, the PI is greater than 1.0, and the IRR is greater than the required rate of return of 15 percent.

Chapter Eleven

Guidelines for Capital Budgeting • Measuring a
Project's Benefits and Costs • Risk and the
Investment Decision • Incorporating Risk into
Capital Budgeting • Examining a Project's Risk
through Simulation • Finance and the
Multinational Firm: Calculating Cash Flows and
the International Dimension of Risk

CASH FLOWS AND OTHER TOPICS IN CAPITAL BUDGETING

LEARNING OBJECTIVES

AFTER READING THIS CHAPTER, YOU SHOULD BE ABLE TO:

1. Identify guidelines by which we measure cash flows.
2. Explain how a project's benefits and costs—that is, its incremental after-tax cash flows—are calculated.
3. Explain what the appropriate measure of risk is for capital-budgeting purposes.
4. Determine the acceptability of a new project using the risk-adjusted discount method of adjusting for risk.

5. Explain the use of simulation for imitating the performance of a project under evaluation.
6. Explain why a multinational firm faces a more difficult time estimating cash flows along with increased risks.

A major capital-budgeting decision led Universal Studios to build its Islands of Adventure theme park. In Chapter 10, we noted the importance of this $2.6-billion investment by Universal that was targeted directly at taking the first crack at the tourist's dollar in Orlando. Although this capital-budgeting decision may, on the surface, seem like a relatively simple decision, the forecasting of the expected cash flows associated with this theme park were, in fact, quite complicated.

To begin with, Universal was introducing a product that competes directly with itself—the original Universal Studios featuring rides like "Back to the Future" and "Jaws." Are there enough tourists' dollars to support both theme parks, or will the new Islands of Adventure park simply cannibalize ticket sales to the older Universal Studios? In addition, what happens when Disney counters with a new park of its own?

From Universal's point of view, the objective may be threefold: (1) to increase their share of the tourist market; (2) to keep from losing market share as tourists look for the latest in technological rides and entertainment; and (3) to promote Universal's and its parent company, Seagrams', other brands and products. For companies in very competitive markets, the evolution and introduction of new products may serve more to preserve market share than to expand it. Certainly, that's the case in the computer market, where Dell, Compaq, and IBM introduce upgraded models that continually render current models obsolete.

Does competing with yourself just to maintain market share make sense, or is it negative thinking that should be avoided? The answer deals with how we estimate a project's future cash flows. In Chapter 10 we looked at decision criterion, assuming the cash flows were known. In this chapter, we see how difficult and complex estimating cash flows is. We also gain an understanding of what a relevant cash flow is by evaluating projects relative to their base case—that is, what will happen if the project is not carried out? In the case of Universal's Islands of Adventure, we could ask what would happen to attendance at the original Universal Studios if the new park were not opened versus what the attendance would be with the new park. Will tourist traffic through the Islands of Adventure lead to additional sales of the brands and businesses visibly promoted and available in the new park that fall under Universal's and Seagrams' corporate umbrella? Questions like these that lead to an understanding of what qualifies as relevant cash flows are addressed in this chapter. Not only do we try to understand the risks that Universal faced in making this decision, not knowing exactly how Disney would respond, but also try to understand how our capital-budgeting criterion might be modified to deal with this risk.

WHAT'S AHEAD

This chapter continues our discussion of decision-making rules for deciding when to invest in new projects. First, we examine what is a relevant cash flow and how to calculate the relevant cash flow. We then turn our attention to the problem of capital budgeting under uncertainty. In discussing capital-budgeting techniques in the preceding chapter, we implicity assumed the level of risk associated with each investment proposal was the same. In this chapter we lift that assumption and examine various ways in which risk can be incorporated into the capital-budgeting decision.

Objective 1 GUIDELINES FOR CAPITAL BUDGETING

To evaluate investment proposals, we must first set guidelines by which we measure the value of each proposal. In effect, we are deciding what is and what isn't a relevant cash flow.

Use Cash Flows Rather Than Accounting Profits

We use cash flows, not accounting profits, as our measurement tool. The firm receives and is able to reinvest cash flows, whereas accounting profits are shown when they are earned rather than when the money is actually in hand. Unfortunately, a firm's accounting profits and cash flows may not be timed to occur together. For example, capital expenses, such as vehicles and plant and equipment, are depreciated over several years, with their annual depreciation subtracted from profits. Cash flows correctly reflect the timing of benefits and costs—that is, when the money is received, when it can be reinvested, and when it must be paid out.

BACK TO THE FOUNDATIONS

If we are to make intelligent capital-budgeting decisions, we must accurately measure the timing of the benefits and costs, that is, when we receive money and when it leaves our hands. **Axiom 3: Cash—Not Profits—Is King** speaks directly to this. Remember, it is cash inflows that can be reinvested and cash outflows that involve paying out money.

Think Incrementally

Unfortunately, calculating cash flows from a project may not be enough. Decision makers must ask, *What new cash flows will the company as a whole receive if the company takes on a given project?* What if the company does not take on the project? Interestingly, we may find that not all cash flows a firm expects from an investment proposal are incremental in nature. In measuring cash flows, however, the trick is to think incrementally. In doing so, we will see that only **incremental after-tax cash flows** matter. As such, our guiding rule in deciding if a cash flow is incremental is to look at the company with, versus without, the new product. As you will see in the upcoming sections, this may be easier said than done.

> ### BACK TO THE FOUNDATIONS
>
> In order to measure the true effects of our decisions, we analyze the benefits and costs of projects on an incremental basis, which relates directly to **Axiom 4: Incremental Cash Flows—It's Only What Changes That Counts.** In effect, we ask ourselves what the cash flows will be if the project is taken on versus what they will be if the project is not taken on.

Beware of Cash Flows Diverted from Existing Products

Assume for a moment that we are managers of a firm considering a new product line that might compete with one of our existing products and possibly reduce its sales. In determining the cash flows associated with the proposed project, we should consider only the incremental sales brought to the company as a whole. New-product sales achieved at the cost of losing sales of other products in our line are not considered a benefit of adopting the new product. For example, when Quaker Oats introduced Cap'n Crunch's Cozmic Crunch in 1999, the product competed directly with the company's Cap'n Crunch and Crunch Berries cereals. (In fact it was almost identical to Crunch Berries, with the shapes changed to stars and moons along with a packet of orange space dust that turns milk green). Quaker meant to target the market niche held by Post Fruity Pebbles, but there was no question that sales recorded by Cozmic Crunch bit into—literally cannibalized—Quaker's existing product line.

Remember that we are only interested in the sales dollars to the firm if the project were accepted, as opposed to what the sales dollars would be if the project were rejected. Just moving sales from one product line to a new product line does not bring anything new into the company, but if sales are captured from our competitors or if sales that would have been lost to new competing products are retained, then these are relevant incremental cash flows. In each case these are the incremental cash flows to the firm—looking at the firm as a whole, with the new product versus without the new product.

Look for Incidental or Synergistic Effects

Although in some cases a new project may take sales away from a firm's current projects, in other cases a new effort may actually bring new sales to the existing line. For example, when USAir introduced service to Sioux City, Iowa. The new routes connecting this addition to the USAir system not only brought about new ticket sales on those routes, but also fed passengers to connecting routes. If managers were to look at only the revenue from the ticket sales on the Sioux City routes, they would miss the incremental cash flow to USAir as a whole that results from taking on the new route. This is called a synergistic effect. The cash flow comes from any USAir flight that would not have occurred if service to Sioux City had not been available. The bottom line: Any cash flow to any part of the company that may result from the decision at hand must be considered when making that decision.

Work in Working-Capital Requirements

Many times a new project involves additional investment in working capital. This may take the form of new inventory to stock a sales outlet, additional investment in accounts receivable resulting from additional credit sales, or increased investment in cash to operate cash registers, and more. Working-capital requirements are considered a cash flow even though they do not leave the company. How can investment in inventory be considered a cash outflow when the goods are still in the store? Because the firm does not have access to the inventory's cash value, the firm cannot use the money for other investments. Generally, working-capital requirements are tied up over the life of the project. When the project terminates there is usually an offsetting cash inflow as the working capital is recovered, although this offset is not perfect because of the time value of money.

Consider Incremental Expenses

Just as cash inflows from a new project are measured on an incremental basis, expenses should also be measured on an incremental basis. For example, if introducing a new product line necessitates training the sales staff, the after-tax cash flow associated with the training program must be considered a cash outflow and charged against the project. If accepting a new project dictates that a production facility be reengineered, the after-tax cash flows associated with that capital investment should be charged against the project. Again, any incremental after-tax cash flow affecting the company as a whole is a relevant cash flow, whether it is flowing in or flowing out.

For example, shortly after Ford introduced the Windstar, Chrysler came out with redesigned versions of its Caravan and Voyager minivans with sliding doors on both sides, making it easy for passengers to enter and exit the rear seats. In response, Ford spent millions of dollars redesigning the Windstar and retooling its factories so that the driver's seat would fold up and make it easier for its rear passengers to get in and out. Then, 2 years later Ford introduced a redesigned Windstar with sliding doors on both sides. How did Ford make this capital-budgeting decision to redesign the Windstar and retool its factories? It looked at the incremental cash flows. That is, it looked at the cash flows to the company as a whole with this project versus the cash flows to the company as a whole without this project. It then based its decision on the difference in those cash flows—that is, on the incremental cash flows.

Remember That Sunk Costs Are Not Incremental Cash Flows

Only cash flows that are affected by the decision making at the moment are relevant in capital budgeting. The manager asks two questions: (1) Will this cash flow occur if the project is accepted? (2) Will this cash flow occur if the project is rejected? Yes to the first question and no to the second equals an incremental cash flow. For example, let's assume you are considering introducing a new taste treat called Puddin' in a Shoe. You would like to do some test-marketing before production. If you are considering the decision to test-market and have not yet done so, the costs associated with the test-marketing are relevant cash flows. Conversely, if you have already test-marketed, the cash flows involved in test-marketing are no longer relevant in project evaluation. It's a matter of timing. Regardless of what you might decide about future production, the cash flows allocated to marketing have already occurred. Cash flows that have already taken place are often referred to as "sunk costs" because they have been sunk into the project and cannot be undone. As a rule, any cash flows that are not affected by the accept/reject criterion should not be included in capital-budgeting analysis.

Account for Opportunity Costs

Now we will focus on the cash flows that are lost because a given project consumes scarce resources that would have produced cash flows if that project had been rejected. This is the opportunity cost of doing business. For example, a product may use valuable floor space in a production facility. Although the cash flow is not obvious, the real question remains: What else could be done with this space? The space could have been rented out, or another product could have been stored there. The key point is that opportunity-cost cash flows should reflect net cash flows that would have been received if the project under consideration were rejected. Again, we are analyzing the cash flows to the company as a whole, with or without the project.

Decide If Overhead Costs Are Truly Incremental Cash Flows

Although we certainly want to include any incremental cash flows resulting in changes from overhead expenses such as utilities and salaries, we also want to make sure that these are truly incremental cash flows. Many times, overhead expenses—heat, light, rent—would occur whether a given project were accepted or rejected. There is often not a single specific project to which these expenses can be allocated. Thus, the question is not whether the project benefits from overhead items but whether the overhead costs are incremental cash flows associated with the project and relevant to capital budgeting.

Ignore Interest Payments and Financing Flows

In evaluating new projects and determining cash flows, we must separate the investment decision from the financing decision. Interest payments and other financing cash flows that might result from raising funds to finance a project should not be considered incremental cash flows. If accepting a project means we have to raise new funds by issuing bonds, the interest charges associated with raising funds are not a relevant cash outflow. When we discount the incremental cash flows back to the present at the required rate of return, we are implicitly accounting for the cost of raising funds to finance the new project. In essence, the required rate of return reflects the cost of the funds needed to support the project. Managers first determine the desirability of the project and then determine how best to finance it.

CONCEPT CHECK

1. What is an incremental cash flow? What is a sunk cost? What are opportunity costs?
2. If Ford introduces a new auto line, might some of the cash flows from that new car line be diverted from existing product lines? How should you deal with this?

In measuring cash flows, we are interested only in the incremental, or differential, after-tax cash flows that can be attributed to the proposal being evaluated. That is, we focus our attention on the difference in the firm's after-tax cash flows with versus without the project. The worth of our decision depends on the accuracy of our cash flow estimates. For this reason, we first examined the question of what cash flows are relevant. Now we will see that, in general, a project's cash flows fall into one of three categories: (1) the initial outlay, (2) the differential flows over the project's life, and (3) the terminal cash flow.

Initial Outlay

initial outlay

The **initial outlay** involves the *immediate cash outflow necessary to purchase the asset and put it in operating order*. This amount includes the cost of installing the asset (the asset's purchase price plus any expenses associated with shipping or installation) and any nonexpense cash outlays, such as increased working-capital requirements. If we are considering a new sales outlet, there might be additional cash flows associated with investment in working capital in the form of increased inventory and cash necessary to operate the sales outlet. Although these cash flows are not included in the cost of the asset or even expensed on the books, they must be included in our analysis. The after-tax cost of expense items incurred as a result of new investment must also be included as cash outflow—for example, any training expenses or special engineering expenses that would not have been incurred otherwise. Finally, if the investment decision is a replacement decision, the cash inflow associated with the selling price of the old asset, in addition to any tax effects resulting from its sale, must be included.

Determining the initial outlay is a complex matter. Table 11–1 summarizes some of the more common calculations involved in determining the initial outlay. This list is by no means exhaustive, but it should give you a framework for thinking about the initial outlay and help simplify the calculations involved in the example that follows.

PAUSE AND REFLECT

At this point we should realize that the incremental nature of the cash flow is of great importance. In many cases if the project is not accepted, then "status quo" for the firm will simply not continue. In calculating incremental cash flows, we must be realistic in estimating what the cash flows to the company would be if the new project is not accepted. The Financial Management in Practice article "Using the Right Base Case" deals with precisely this question.

TABLE 11–1	SUMMARY OF CALCULATION OF INITIAL OUTLAY

1. Installed cost of asset
2. Additional nonexpense outlays incurred (e.g., working-capital investments)
3. Additional expenses on an after-tax basis (e.g., training expenses)
4. In a replacement decision, the after-tax cash flow associated with the sale of the old machine

Tax Effects—Sale of Old Machine

Potentially one of the most confusing initial outlay calculations is for a replacement project involving the incremental tax payment associated with the sale of an old machine. There are three possible tax situations dealing with the sale of an old asset:

1. The old asset is sold for a price above the depreciated value. Here the difference between the old machine's selling price and its depreciated value is considered a taxable gain and taxed at the marginal corporate tax rate. If, for example, the old machine was originally purchased for $15,000, had a book value of $10,000, and was sold for $17,000, assuming the firm's marginal corporate tax rate is 34 percent, the taxes due from the gain would be ($17,000 − $10,000) × (.34), or $2,380.

2. The old asset is sold for its depreciated (or book) value. In this case no taxes result, as there is neither a gain nor a loss in the asset's sale.

3. The old asset is sold for less than its depreciated value. In this case the difference between the depreciated book value and the salvage value of the asset is a taxable loss and may be used to offset capital gains and thus results in tax savings. For example, if the depreciated book value of the asset is $10,000 and it is sold for $7,000, wc have a $3,000 loss. Assuming the firm's marginal corporate tax rate is 34 percent, the cash inflow from tax savings is ($10,000 − $7,000) × (.34), or $1,020.

Example

To clarify the calculation of the initial outlay, consider an example of a company in the 34-percent marginal tax bracket. This company is considering the purchase of a new machine for $30,000 to be used in manufacturing. It has a 5-year life (according to IRS guidelines) and will be depreciated using the *simplified straight-line method*. (This depreciation method is explained later.) The useful life of this new machine is also 5 years. The new machine will replace an existing machine, originally purchased for $30,000 10 years ago, which currently has 5 more years of expected useful life. The existing machine will generate $2,000 of depreciation expenses for each of the next 5 years, at which time the book value will be equal to zero. To put the new machine in running order, it is necessary to pay after-tax shipping charges of $2,000 and installation charges of $3,000. Because the new machine will work faster than the old one, it will require an increase in goods-in-process inventory of $5,000. Finally, the old machine can be sold to a scrap dealer for $15,000.

The installed cost of the new machine would be the $30,000 cost plus $2,000 shipping and $3,000 installation fees, for a total of $35,000. Additional outflows are associated with taxes incurred on the sale of the old machine and with increased investment in inventory. Although the old machine has a book value of $10,000, it could be sold for $15,000. The increased taxes from the gain on the sale will be equal to the selling price of the old machine less its depreciated book value times the firm's marginal tax rate, or ($15,000 − $10,000) × (.34), or $1,700. The increase in goods-in-process inventory of $5,000 must also be considered part of the initial outlay, with an offsetting inflow of $5,000 corresponding to the recapture of this inventory occurring at the termination of the project. In effect, the firm invests $5,000 in inventory now, resulting in an initial cash outlay, and liquidates this inventory in 5 years, resulting in a cash inflow at the end of the project. The total outlays associated with the new machine are $35,000 for its installed cost, $1,700 in increased taxes, and $5,000 in investment in inventory, for a total of $41,700. This is somewhat offset by the sale of the old machine for $15,000. Thus,

Using the Right Base Case

Finance theory assumes that a project will be evaluated against its base case, that is, what will happen if the project is not carried out. Managers tend to explore fully the implications of adopting the project but usually spend less time considering the likely outcome of not making the investment. Yet unless the base case is realistic, the incremental cash flows—the difference between the "with" and the "without" scenarios—will mislead.

Often companies implicitly assume that the base case is simply a continuation of the status quo, but this assumption ignores market trends and competitor behavior. It also neglects the impact of changes the company might make anyway, like improving operations management.

Using the wrong base case is typical of product launches in which the new product will likely erode the market for the company's existing product line. Take Apple Computer's introduction of the Macintosh SE. The new PC had obvious implications for sales of earlier generation Macintoshes. To analyze the incremental cash flows arising from the new product, Apple would have needed to count the lost contribution from sales of its existing products as a cost of the launch.

Wrongly applied, however, this approach would equate the "without" case to the status quo: It would assume that without the SE, sales of existing Macintoshes would continue at their current level. In the competitive PC market, however, nothing stands still. Competitors like IBM would likely innovate and take market share away from the earlier generation Macintoshes—which a more realistic base case would have

reflected. Sales of existing products would decline even in the base case.

Consider investments in the marketing of existing brands through promotions, media budgets, and the like. They are often sold as if they were likely to lead to ever-increasing market share. But competitors will also be promoting their brands, and market shares across the board still have to add up to 100 percent. Still, such an investment is not necessarily wasted. It may just need a more realistic justification: Although the investment is unlikely to increase sales above existing levels, it may prevent sales from falling. Marketers who like positive thinking may not like this defensive argument, but it is the only argument that makes economic sense in a mature market.

In situations like this, when the investment is needed just to maintain market share, the returns may be high in comparison with the base case, but the company's reported profits may still go down. Senior managers are naturally puzzled at apparently netting only 5 percent return.* Without the investment, however, the profit picture would have looked even worse, especially in the long term.

---

*Joseph L. Bower, *Managing the Resources Allocation Process* (Boston: Harvard Business School Press, 1986), 13.

Source: Reprinted by permission of *Harvard Business Review.* Excerpt from "Must Finance and Strategy Clash?" by P. Barwise, P.R. Marsh, and R. Wensley, *Harvard Business Review* (September—October, 1989). Copyright © 1989 by The President and Fellows of Harvard College. All rights reserved.

the net initial outlay associated with this project is $26,700. These calculations are summarized in Table 11–2.

Differential Flows over Project's Life

The differential cash flows over the project's life involve the incremental after-tax cash flows resulting from increased revenues, plus labor or material savings and reductions in selling expenses. Overhead items, such as utilities, heat, light, and executive salaries, are generally not affected. However, any resultant change in any of these categories must be included. Any increase in interest payments incurred as a result of issuing bonds to finance the project should *not* be included because the costs of funds needed to support the project are implicitly accounted for by discounting the project back to the present using the required rate of return. Finally, an adjustment for the incremental change in taxes should be made, including any increase in taxes

TABLE 11-2	CALCULATION OF INITIAL OUTLAY FOR EXAMPLE PROBLEM

Outflows:		
Purchase price	$30,000	
Shipping fee	2,000	
Installation fee	3,000	
Installed cost of machine		$35,000
Increased taxes from sale of old machine		
$15,000 − $10,000)(.34)		1,700
Increased investment in inventory		5,000
Total outflows		$41,700
Inflows:		
Salvage value of old machine		15,000
Net initial outlay		$26,700

that might result from increased profits or any tax savings from an increase in depreciation expenses. Increased depreciation expenses affect tax-related cash flows by reducing taxable income and thus lowering taxes. Table 11–3 lists some of the factors that might be involved in determining a project's differential cash flows. However, before looking at an example, we briefly examine the calculation of depreciation.

PAUSE AND REFLECT

Depreciation plays an important role in the calculation of cash flows. Although it is not a cash flow item, it lowers profits, which in turn lowers taxes. For students developing a foundation in corporate finance, it is the concept of depreciation, not the calculation of it, that is important. The reason the calculation of depreciation is deemphasized is that it is extremely complicated, and its calculation changes every few years as Congress enacts new tax laws. Through all this bear in mind that although depreciation is not a cash flow item, it does affect cash flows by lowering the level of profits on which taxes are calculated.

The Revenue Reconciliation Act of 1993 largely left intact the modified version of the Accelerated Cost Recovery System introduced in the Tax Reform Act of 1986. Although this was examined in Chapter 1, a review is appropriate here. This modified

TABLE 11-3	SUMMARY OF CALCULATION OF DIFFERENTIAL AFTER-TAX CASH FLOWS BASIS

1. Added revenue offset by increased expenses
2. Labor and material savings
3. Increases in overhead incurred
4. Tax savings from an increase in depreciation expense if the new project is accepted
5. Do *not* include interest expenses if the project is financed by issuing debt because this is accounted for in the required rate of return.

version of the old Accelerated Cost Recovery System (ACRS) is used for most depreciable tangible property placed in service beginning in 1987. Under this method, the life of the asset is determined according to the asset's class life, which is assigned by the IRS; for example, most computer equipment has a 5 year asset life. It also allows for only a half-year's deduction in the first year and a half-year's deduction in the year after the recovery period. The asset is then depreciated using the 200 percent declining balance method or an optional straight-line method.

For our purposes, depreciation is calculated using a simplified straight-line method. This simplified process ignores the half-year convention that allows only a half-year's deduction in the year the project is placed in service and a half-year's deduction in the first year after the recovery period. By ignoring the half-year convention and assuming a zero salvage value, we are able to calculate annual depreciation by taking the project's initial depreciable value and dividing by its depreciable life as follows:

$$\text{annual depreciation using the simplified straight-line method} = \frac{\text{initial depreciable value}}{\text{depreciable life}}$$

The initial depreciable value is equal to the cost of the asset plus any expenses necessary to get the new asset into operating order.

This is not how depreciation would actually be calculated. The reason we have simplified the calculation is to allow you to focus directly on what should and should not be included in the cash flow calculations. Moreover, because the tax laws change rather frequently, we are more interested in recognizing the tax implications of depreciation than in understanding the specific depreciation provisions of the current tax laws.

Our concern with depreciation is to highlight its importance in generating cash flow estimates and to indicate that the financial manager must be aware of the current tax provisions when evaluating capital-budgeting proposals.

Extending the earlier example, which illustrated the calculations of the initial outlay, suppose that purchasing the machine is expected to reduce salaries by $10,000 per year and fringe benefits by $1,000 annually, because it will take only one part-time person to operate, whereas the old machine requires two part-time operators. In addition, the cost of defects will fall from $8,000 per year to $3,000. However, maintenance expenses will increase by $4,000 annually. The annual depreciation on this new machine is $7,000 per year, whereas the depreciation expense lost with the sale of the old machine is $2,000 for each of the next 5 years. Annual depreciation on the new machine is calculated using the simplified straight-line method just described—that is, taking the cost of the new machine plus any expenses necessary to put it in operating order and dividing by its depreciable life. For the new machine these calculations are reflected in Table 11–4.

TABLE 11–4 CALCULATION OF DEPRECIATION FOR EXAMPLE PROBLEM USING SIMPLIFIED STRAIGHT-LINE METHOD

New machine purchase price	$ 30,000
Shipping fee	2,000
Installation fee	3,000
Total depreciable value	$ 35,000
Divided by depreciable life	$35,000/5
Equals: Annual depreciation	$ 7,000

TABLE 11-5	CALCULATION OF DIFFERENTIAL CASH FLOWS FOR EXAMPLE PROBLEM		

		BOOK PROFIT	CASH FLOW
Savings:	Reduced salary	$10,000	$10,000
	Reduced fringe benefits	1,000	1,000
	Reduced defects ($8,000 − $3,000)	5,000	5,000
Costs:	Increased maintenance expense	−4,000	−4,000
	Increased depreciation expense ($7,000 − $2,000)	−5,000	
Net savings before taxes		$ 7,000	$12,000
Taxes (34%)		−2,380 →	−2,380
Net cash flow after taxes			$ 9,620

Because the depreciation on the old machine is $2,000 per year, the increased depreciation will be from $2,000 per year to $7,000 per year, or an increase of $5,000 per year. Although this increase in depreciation expenses is not a cash flow item, it does affect cash flows by reducing book profits, which in turn reduces taxes.

To determine the annual net cash flows resulting from the acceptance of this project, the net savings *before* taxes using both book profit and cash flows must be found. The additional taxes are then calculated based on the before-tax book profit. For this example, Table 11–5 shows the determination of the differential cash flows on an after-tax basis. Thus, the differential cash flows over the project's life are $9,620.

Terminal Cash Flow

The calculation of the terminal cash flow is in general quite a bit simpler than the preceding two calculations. Flows associated with the project's termination generally include the salvage value of the project plus or minus any taxable gains or losses associated with its sales.

Under the current tax laws, in most cases there will be tax payments associated with the salvage value at termination. This is because the current laws allow all projects to be depreciated to zero, and if a project has a book value of zero at termination and a positive salvage value, then that salvage value will be taxed. The tax effects associated with the salvage value of the project at termination are determined exactly like the tax effects on the sale of the old machine associated with the initial outlay. The salvage value proceeds are compared with the depreciated value, in this case zero, to determine the tax.

In addition to the salvage value, there may be a cash outlay associated with the project termination. For example, at the close of a strip-mining operation, the mine must be refilled in an ecologically acceptable manner. Finally, any working-capital outlay required at the initiation of the project—for example, increased inventory needed for the operation of a new plant—will be recaptured at the termination of the project. In effect the increased inventory required by the project can be liquidated when the project expires. Table 11–6 provides a general list of some of the factors that might affect a project's terminal cash flow.

TABLE 11–6	SUMMARY OF CALCULATION OF TERMINAL CASH FLOW ON AFTER-TAX BASIS

1. The after-tax salvage value of the project
2. Cash outlays associated with the project's termination
3. Recapture of nonexpense outlays that occurred at the project's initiation (e.g., working-capital investments)

Extending the example to termination, the depreciated book value and salvage value of the machine at the termination date will be equal to zero. However, there will be a cash flow associated with the recapture of the initial outlay of work-in-process inventory of $5,000 as the inventory is liquidated. Therefore, the expected total terminal cash flow equals $5,000.

If we were to construct a cash flow diagram from this example (Figure 11–1), it would have an initial outlay of $26,700, differential cash flows during years 1 through 5 of $9,620, and an additional terminal cash flow at the end of year 5 of $5,000. The cash flow occurring in year 5 is $14,620: the sum of the differential cash flow in year 5 of $9,620 and the terminal cash flow of $5,000.

Cash flow diagrams similar to Figure 11–1 are used through the remainder of this chapter with arrows above the time line indicating cash inflows and arrows below the time line denoting outflows.

Although the preceding calculations for determining the incremental after-tax net cash flows do not cover all possible cash flows, they do set up a framework in which almost any situation can be handled.

Capital Budgeting: Comprehensive Example

Now let's put what we know about capital budgeting together and look at a manufacturing firm in the electronic components field that is in the 34 percent marginal tax bracket with a 15-percent required rate of return or cost of capital. Management is considering replacing a hand-operated assembly machine with a fully automated assembly operation. Given the information in Table 11–7, we want to determine the cash flows associated with this proposal, the project's net present value (NPV), profitability index (PI), and internal rate of return (IRR), and then to apply the appropriate decision criteria.

The outflows associated with the initial outlay include the cost of the new machine plus the shipping and installation fee, in addition to any taxes on the sale of the old machine. Because the old machine is sold for more than its book value, that

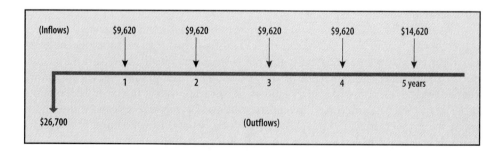

FIGURE 11–1

Example Cash Flow Diagram

TABLE 11-7 COMPREHENSIVE CAPITAL-BUDGETING EXAMPLE

Existing situation:	One part-time operator—salary $12,000
	Variable overtime—$1,000 per year
	Fringe benefits—$1,000 per year
	Cost of defects—$6,000 per year
	Current book value—$10,000
	Expected life—15 years
	Expected salvage value—$0
	Age—10 years
	Annual depreciation—$2,000 per year
	Current salvage value of old machine—$12,000
	Annual maintenance—$0
	Marginal tax rate—34 percent
	Required rate of return—15 percent
Proposed situation:	Fully automated operation—no operator necessary
	Cost of machine—$50,000
	After tax shipping fee—$1,000
	After tax installation costs—$5,000
	Expected economic life—5 years
	Depreciation method—simplified straight-line over 5 years
	Salvage value after 5 years—$0
	Annual maintenance—$1,000
	Cost of defects—$1,000

gain is taxed at the firm's marginal tax rate of 34 percent. The inflows associated with the initial outlay are then subtracted from the outflows to arrive at the net initial outlay of $44,680, as reflected in Table 11–8.

Next, the differential cash flows over the project's life are calculated as shown in Table 11—9, yielding an estimated $15,008 cash flow per annum. In making these computations, the incremental change in depreciation was determined by first calculating the original depreciable value, which is equal to the cost of the new machine ($50,000) plus any after-tax expense charges necessary to get the new machine in operating order (shipping fee of $1,000 plus the installation fee of $5,000). This depreciable amount was then divided by 5 years. The annual

TABLE 11-8 CALCULATION OF INITIAL OUTLAY FOR COMPREHENSIVE EXAMPLE

Outflows:	Cost of new machine	$50,000
	Shipping fee	1,000
	Installation cost	5,000
	Increased taxes on sale of old machine	680
	($12,000 − $10,000)(.34)	
Inflows:	Salvage value—old machine	−12,000
	Net initial outlay	$44,680

		BOOK PROFIT	CASH FLOW
Savings:	Reduced salary	$12,000	$12,000
	Reduced variable overtime	1,000	1,000
	Reduced fringe benefits	1,000	1,000
	Reduced defects ($6,000 − $1,000)	5,000	5,000
Costs:	Increased maintenance expense	−1,000	−1,000
	Increased depreciation expense ($11,200 − $2,000)	−9,200	
	Net savings before taxes	$ 8,800	$18,000
	Taxes (34%)	−2,992 →	−2,992
	Net cash flow after taxes		$15,008

TABLE 11-9 CALCULATION OF DIFFERENTIAL CASH FLOWS FOR COMPREHENSIVE EXAMPLE

depreciation lost with the sale of the old machine was then subtracted out $10,000/5 = $2,000 per year for the old machine's remaining 5 years of life). Once the change in taxes is determined from the incremental change in book profit, it is subtracted from the net cash flow savings before taxes, yielding the $15,008 net cash flow after taxes.

Finally, the terminal cash flow associated with the project has to be determined. In this case, because the new machine is expected to have a zero salvage value, there will be no terminal cash flow. The cash flow diagram associated with this project is shown in Figure 11–2, with cash inflows shown above the time line and the initial outlay below the line.

The net present value for this project is calculated as follows:

$$NPV = \sum_{t=1}^{n} \frac{ACF_t}{(1 + k)^t} - IO \tag{11-1}$$

$$= \sum_{t=1}^{5} \frac{\$15,008}{(1 + .15)^t} - \$44,680$$

$$= \$15,008(PVIFA_{15\%, \, 5 \, yr}) - \$44,680$$
$$= \$15,008(3.352) - \$44,680$$
$$= \$50,307 - \$44,680$$
$$= \$5,627$$

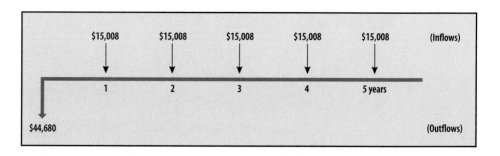

FIGURE 11–2

Cash Flow Diagram for Comprehensive Example

Because its net present value is greater than zero, the project should be accepted. The PI, which gives a measure of relative desirability of a project, is calculated as follows:

$$PI = \sum_{t=1}^{n} \frac{\frac{ACF_t}{(1+k)^t}}{IO} \qquad (11\text{--}2)$$

$$= \frac{\$50,307}{\$44,680}$$

$$= 1.13$$

Because the project's PI is greater than 1.0, the project should be accepted.

The IRR can be determined directly from the PVIFA table, as follows:

$$IO = \sum_{t=1}^{n} \frac{ACF_t}{(1+IRR)^t} \qquad (11\text{--}3)$$

$$\$44,680 = \$15,008 \, (PVIFA_{i,\ 5\ yr})$$

$$2.977 = PVIFA_{i,\ 5\ yr}$$

Looking for the value of the $PVIFA_{i,\ 5\ yr}$ in the 5-year row of the table in Appendix E, we find the value of 2.977 occurs between the 20-percent column (2.991) and the 21-percent column (2.926). As a result, the project's IRR is between 20 percent and 21 percent, and the project should be accepted.

Applying the decision criteria to this example, we find that each of them indicates the project should be accepted because the NPV is positive, the PI is greater than 1.0, and the IRR is greater than the firm's required rate of return of 15 percent.

CONCEPT CHECK

1. In general, a project's cash flows will fall into one of three categories, what are these categories?
2. What is depreciation? Where does it come from?
3. Although depreciation is not a cash flow item, it plays an important role in the calculation of cash flows. How does depreciation affect a project's cash flows?

RISK AND THE INVESTMENT DECISION

Objective 3

Up to this point we have ignored risk in capital budgeting; that is, we have discounted expected cash flows back to the present and ignored any uncertainty that there might be surrounding that estimate. In reality the future cash flows associated with the introduction of a new sales outlet or a new product are estimates of what is *expected* to happen in the future, not necessarily what will happen in the future. For example, when Coca-Cola decided to replace Classic Coke with its "New Coke," you can bet that the expected cash flows it based its decision on were nothing like the cash flows it realized. As a result, it didn't take Coca-Cola long to reintroduce Classic Coke. The cash flows we have discounted back to the present have only been our best estimate of the expected future cash flows. A cash flow diagram based on the

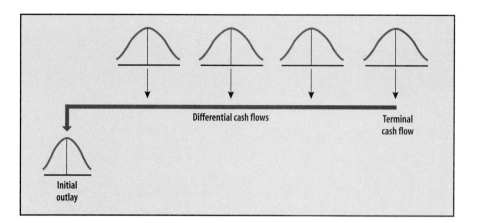

Example Cash Flow Diagram Based on Possible Outcome

Takin' It to the Net
Perhaps the best place to look to find information with respect to capital-budgeting projects currently being developed is the Annual Report Gallery http://www.reportgallery.com/, which provides annual reports on over 1,000 companies.

possible outcomes of an investment proposal rather than the expected values of these outcomes appears in Figure 11–3.

In this section, we assume that under conditions of risk we do not know beforehand what cash flows will actually result from a new project. However, we do have expectations concerning the possible outcomes and are able to assign probabilities to these outcomes. Stated another way, although we do not know what the cash flows resulting from the acceptance of a new project will be, we can formulate the probability distributions from which the flows will be drawn.

As we learned in Chapter 9, risk occurs when there is some question as to the future outcome of an event. We now proceed with an examination of the logic behind this definition. Again, risk is defined as the potential variability in future cash flows.

The fact that variability reflects risk can easily be shown with a coin toss. Consider the possibility of flipping a coin—heads you win, tails you lose—for 25 cents with your finance professor. Most likely you would be willing to take on this game, because the utility gained from winning 25 cents is about equal to the utility lost if you lose 25 cents. Conversely, if the flip is for $1,000, you may be willing to play only if you are offered more than $1,000 if you win—say, you win $1,500 if it turns out heads and lose $1,000 if it turns out tails. In each case the probability of winning and losing is the same; that is, there is an equal chance that the coin will land heads or tails. In each case, however, the width of the dispersion changes, which is why the second coin toss is more risky and why you may not take the chance unless the pay-offs are altered. The key here is the fact that only the dispersion changes; the probability of winning or losing is the same in each case. Thus, the potential variability in future returns reflects the risk.

The final question to be addressed is whether individuals are in fact risk averse. Although, we do see people gambling where the odds of winning are against them, it should be stressed that monetary return is not the only possible return they may receive. A nonmonetary, psychological reward accrues to some gamblers, allowing them to fantasize that they will break the bank, never have to work again, and retire to some offshore island. Actually, the heart of the question is how wealth is measured. Although gamblers appear to be acting as risk seekers, they actually attach an additional nonmonetary return to gambling; the risk is in effect its own reward. When this is considered, their actions seem totally rational. It should also be noted that although gamblers appear to be pursuing risk on one hand, on the other hand, in other endeavors they are eliminating some risk by purchasing insurance and diversifying their investments.

In the remainder of this chapter, we assume that although future cash flows are not known with certainty, the probability distribution from which they come can be estimated. Also, because we have illustrated that the dispersion of possible outcomes reflects risk, we are prepared to use a measure of dispersion or variability later in the chapter when we quantify risk.

In the pages that follow, remember that there are only two basic issues that we address: (1) What is risk in terms of capital-budgeting decisions, and how should it be measured? (2) How should risk be incorporated into capital-budgeting analysis?

What Measure of Risk Is Relevant in Capital Budgeting?

Before we begin our discussion of how to adjust for risk, it is important to determine just what type of risk we are to adjust for. In capital budgeting, a project's risk can be looked at on three levels. First, there is the **project standing alone risk,** which is a *project's risk ignoring the fact that much of this risk will be diversified away as the project is combined with the firm's other projects and assets.* Second, we have the project's **contribution-to-firm risk,** which is the *amount of risk that the project contributes to the firm as a whole; this measure considers the fact that some of the project's risk will be diversified away as the project is combined with the firm's other projects and assets, but ignores the effects of diversification of the firm's shareholders.* Finally, there is **systematic risk,** which is the *risk of the project from the viewpoint of a well-diversified shareholder; this measure takes into account that some of a project's risk will be diversified away as the project is combined with the firm's other projects, and, in addition, some of the remaining risk will be diversified away by shareholders as they combine this stock with other stocks in their portfolios.* Graphically, this is shown in Figure 11–4.

Should we be interested in the project standing alone risk? The answer is no. Perhaps the easiest way to understand why not is to look at an example. Let's take the case of research and design projects at Johnson & Johnson. Each year Johnson &

project standing alone risk

contribution-to-firm risk

systematic risk

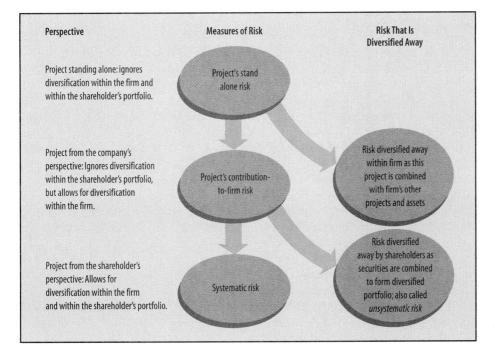

FIGURE 11–4

Looking at Three Measures of a Project's Risk

Johnson takes on hundreds of new R&D projects, knowing that they only have about a 10-percent probability of being successful. If they are successful, the profits can be enormous; if they fail, the investment is lost. If the company has only one project, and it is an R&D project, the company would have a 90 percent chance of failure. Thus, if we look at these R&D projects individually and measure their stand alone risk, we would have to judge them to be enormously risky. However, if we consider the effect of the diversification that comes about from taking on several hundred independent R&D projects a year, all with a 10-percent chance of success, we can see that each R&D project does not add much risk to Johnson & Johnson. In short, because much of a project's risk is diversified away within the firm, the project stand alone risk is an inappropriate measure of the meaningful level of risk of a capital-budgeting project.

Should we be interested in the project's contribution-to-firm risk? Once again, at least in theory the answer is no, provided investors are well diversified and there is no chance of bankruptcy. From our earlier discussion of risk in Chapter 9 we saw that as shareholders, if we combined an individual security with other securities to form a diversified portfolio, much of the risk of the individual security would be diversified away. In short, all that affects the shareholders is the systematic risk of the project and, as such, is all that is theoretically relevant for capital budgeting.

Measuring Risk for Capital-Budgeting Purposes with a Dose of Reality—Is Systematic Risk All There Is?

According to the CAPM, systematic risk is the only relevant risk for capital-budgeting purposes; however, reality complicates this somewhat. In many instances a firm will have undiversified shareholders, including owners of small corporations. Because they are not diversified, for those shareholders the relevant measure of risk is the project's contribution-to-firm risk.

The possibility of bankruptcy also affects our view of what measure of risk is relevant. As you recall in developing the CAPM, we made the assumption that bankruptcy costs were zero. Because the project's contribution-to-firm risk can affect the possibility of bankruptcy, this may be an appropriate measure of risk if there are costs associated with bankruptcy. Quite obviously, in the real world there is a cost associated with bankruptcy. First, if a firm fails, its assets, in general, cannot be sold for their true economic value. Moreover, the amount of money actually available for distribution to stockholders is further reduced by liquidation and legal fees that must be paid. Finally, the opportunity cost associated with the delays related to the legal process further reduces the funds available to the shareholder. Therefore, because costs are associated with bankruptcy, reduction of the chance of bankruptcy has a very real value associated with it.

Indirect costs of bankruptcy also affect other areas of the firm, including production, sales, and the quality and efficiency of management. For example, firms with a higher probability of bankruptcy may have a more difficult time recruiting and retaining quality managers because jobs with that firm are viewed as being less secure. Suppliers also may be less willing to sell on credit. Finally, customers may lose confidence and fear that the firm may not be around to honor the warranty or to supply spare parts for the product in the future. As a result, as the probability of bankruptcy increases, the eventual bankruptcy may become self-fulfilling as potential customers and suppliers flee. The end result is that because the project's contribution-to-firm risk affects the probability of bankruptcy for the firm, it is a relevant risk measure for capital budgeting.

Finally, problems in measuring a project's systematic risk make its implementation extremely difficult. It is much easier talking about a project's systematic risk than it is measuring it.

Given all this, what do we use? The answer is that we will give consideration to both measures. We know in theory systematic risk is correct. We also know that bankruptcy costs and undiversified shareholders violate the assumptions of the theory, which brings us back to the concept of a project's contribution-to-firm risk. Still, the concept of systematic risk holds value for capital-budgeting decisions, because that is the risk that shareholders are compensated for assuming. Therefore, we will concern ourselves with both the project's contribution-to-firm risk and the project's systematic risk, and not try to make any specific allocation of importance between the two for capital-budgeting purposes.

CONCEPT CHECK

1. In capital budgeting, a project's risk can be looked at on three levels, what are they and what are the measures of risk?
2. Is a project's stand alone risk the appropriate level of risk for capital budgeting? Why or why not?
3. What is systematic risk?
4. What problems are there associated with using systematic risk as the measure for risk in capital budgeting?

INCORPORATING RISK INTO CAPITAL BUDGETING

Objective 4

In Chapter 10 we ignored any risk differences between projects. This approach is simple but not valid; different investment projects do in fact contain different levels of risk. We now look at the risk-adjusted discount rate, which is based on the notion that investors require higher rates of return on more risky projects.

BACK TO THE FOUNDATIONS

All the methods used to compensate for risk in capital budgeting find their roots in **Axiom 1: The Risk-Return Trade-off—We Won't Take on Additional Risk Unless We Expect to Be Compensated with Additional Return.** In fact, the risk-adjusted discount method puts this concept directly into play.

Risk-Adjusted Discount Rates

The use of **risk-adjusted discount rates** is based on the concept that investors demand higher returns for more risky projects. This is the basic principle behind **Axiom 1** and the CAPM, and this relationship between risk and return is illustrated graphically in Figure 11–5.

As we know from **Axiom 1,** the expected rate of return on any investment should include compensation for delaying consumption equal to the risk-free rate of return, plus compensation for any risk taken on. Under the risk-adjusted discount

risk-adjusted discount rate

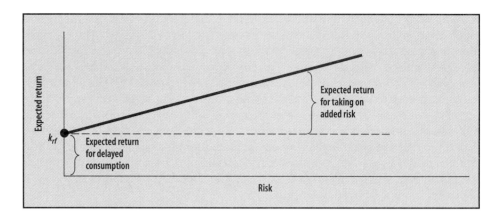

FIGURE 11–5
Risk-Return Relationship

rate approach, if the risk associated with the investment is greater than the risk involved in a typical endeavor, the discount rate is adjusted upward to compensate for this added risk. Once the firm determines the appropriate required rate of return for a project with a given level of risk, the cash flows are discounted back to the present at the risk-adjusted discount rate. Then the normal capital-budgeting criteria are applied, except in the case of the IRR. For the IRR, the hurdle rate with which the project's IRR is compared now becomes the risk-adjusted discount rate. Expressed mathematically, the NPV using the risk-adjusted discount rate becomes

$$NPV = \sum_{t=1}^{n} \frac{ACF_t}{(1 + k^*)^t} - IO \qquad (11-4)$$

where ACF_t = the annual after-tax cash flow expected in time period t
IO = the initial cash outlay
k^* = the risk-adjusted discount rate
n = the project's expected life

The logic behind the risk-adjusted discount rate stems from the idea that if the level of risk in a project is different from that of the typical firm project, then management must incorporate the shareholders' probable reaction to this new endeavor into the decision-making process. If the project has more risk than a typical project, then a higher required rate of return should apply. Otherwise, marginal projects will lower the firm's share price—that is, reduce shareholders' wealth. This will occur as the market raises its required rate of return on the firm to reflect the addition of a more risky project, whereas the incremental cash flows resulting from the acceptance of the new project are not large enough to offset this change fully. By the same logic, if the project has less than normal risk, a reduction in the required rate of return is appropriate. Thus, the risk-adjusted discount method attempts to apply more stringent standards—that is, require a higher rate of return—to projects that will increase the firm's risk level. This is because these projects will lead shareholders to demand a higher required rate of return to compensate them for the higher risk level of the firm. If this adjustment is not made, the marginal projects containing above-average risk could actually lower the firm's share price.

> **Example**

A toy manufacturer is considering the introduction of a line of fishing equipment with an expected life of 5 years. In the past, this firm has been quite conservative in its investment in new products, sticking primarily to standard toys. In this context, the introduction of a line of fishing equipment is considered an abnormally risky project. Management thinks that the normal required rate of return for the firm of 10 percent is not sufficient. Instead, the minimum acceptable rate of return on this project should be 15 percent. The initial outlay would be $110,000, and the expected cash flows from this project are given in the following table:

YEAR	EXPECTED CASH FLOW
1	$30,000
2	30,000
3	30,000
3	30,000
4	30,000
5	30,000

Discounting this annuity back to the present at 15 percent yields a present value of the future cash flows of $100,560. Because the initial outlay on this project is $110,000, the NPV becomes −$9,440, and the project should be rejected. If the normal required rate of return of 10 percent had been used as the discount rate, the project would have been accepted with a NPV of $3,730. ■

In practice, when the risk-adjusted discount rate is used, projects are generally grouped according to purpose, or risk class; then the discount rate preassigned to that purpose or risk class is used. For example, a firm with a required rate of return of 12 percent might use the following rate-of-return categorization:

PROJECT	REQUIRED RATE OF RETURN (%)
Replacement decision	12
Modification or expansion of existing product line	15
Project unrelated to current operations	18
Research and development operations	25

The purpose of this categorization of projects is to make their evaluation easier, but it also introduces a sense of the arbitrary into the calculations that makes the evaluation less meaningful. The trade-offs involved in the preceding classification are obvious; time and effort are minimized, but only at the cost of precision.

Risk-Adjusted Discount Rate and Measurement of a Project's Systematic Risk

When we initially talked about systematic risk or the beta, we were talking about measuring it for the entire firm. As you recall, although we could estimate a firm's beta using historical data, we did not have complete confidence in our results. As we will see, estimating the appropriate level of systematic risk for a single project is even more fraught with difficulties. To truly understand what it is we are trying to do and the difficulties we will encounter, let us step back a bit and examine systematic risk and the risk adjustment for a project.

What we are trying to do is use the CAPM to determine the level of risk and the appropriate risk-return trade-offs for a particular project. We then take the expected return on this project and compare it to the required return suggested by the CAPM to determine whether the project should be accepted. If the project appears to be a typical one for the firm, using the CAPM to determine the appropriate risk-return trade-offs and then judging the project against them may be a warranted approach. But if the project is not a typical project, what do we do? Historical data generally do not exist for a new project. In fact, for some capital investments—for example, a truck or a new building—historical data would not have much meaning. What we need to do is make the best of a bad situation. We either (1) fake it—that is, use historical accounting data, if available, to substitute for historical price data in estimating systematic risk—or (2) we attempt to find a substitute firm in the same industry as the capital-budgeting project and use the substitute firm's estimated systematic risk as a proxy for the project's systematic risk.

Beta Estimation Using Accounting Data

When we are dealing with a project that is identical to the firm's other projects, we need only estimate the level of systematic risk for the firm and use that estimate as a proxy for the project's risk. Unfortunately, when projects are not typical of the firm, this approach does not work. For example, when R. J. Reynolds introduces a new food through one of its food products divisions, this new product most likely carries with it a different level of systematic risk from what is typical for Reynolds as a whole.

To get a better approximation of the systematic risk level on this project, we estimate the level of systematic risk for the food division and use that as a proxy for the project's systematic risk. Unfortunately, historical stock price data are available only for the company as a whole, and as you recall, historical stock return data are generally used to estimate a firm's beta. Thus, we are forced to use accounting return data rather than historical stock return data for the division to estimate the division's systematic risk. To estimate a project's beta using accounting data we need only run a time-series regression of the division's return on assets (net income/total assets) on the market index (the S&P 500). The regression coefficient from this equation would be the project's accounting beta and would serve as an approximation for the project's true beta, or measure of systematic risk. Alternatively, a multiple regression model based on accounting data could be developed to explain betas. The results of this model could then be applied to firms that are not publicly traded to estimate their betas.

How good is the accounting beta technique? It certainly is not as good as a direct calculation of the beta. In fact, the correlation between the accounting beta and the beta calculated on historical stock return data is only about 0.6; however, better luck has been experienced with multiple regression models used to predict betas. Unfortunately, in many cases there may not be any realistic alternative to the calculation of the accounting beta. Owing to the importance of adjusting for a project's risk, the accounting beta method is much preferred to doing nothing.

The Pure Play Method for Estimating a Project's Beta

Whereas the accounting beta method attempts to directly estimate a project or division's beta, the **pure play method** attempts to identify publicly traded firms that are engaged solely in the same business as the project or division. Once the proxy or pure play firm is identified, its systematic risk is determined and then used as a proxy for the project or division's level of systematic risk. What we are doing is *looking for a publicly traded firm on the outside that looks like our project and using that firm's required rate of return to judge our project.* In doing so we are presuming that the systematic risk and the capital structure of the proxy firm are identical to those of the project.

In using the pure play method it should be noted that a firm's capital structure is reflected in its beta. When the capital structure of the proxy firm is different from that of the project's firm, some adjustment must be made for this difference. Although not a perfect approach, it does provide some insights as to the level of systematic risk a project might have.

> ### CONCEPT CHECK
>
> 1. What is the most commonly used method for incorporating risk into the capital budgeting decision? How is this technique related to Axiom 1?
> 2. Describe two methods for estimating a project's systematic risk?

EXAMINING A PROJECT'S RISK THROUGH SIMULATION

Objective 5

Simulation: Explained and Illustrated

Another method for evaluating risk in the investment decision is through the use of **simulation.** The certainty equivalent and risk-adjusted discount rate approaches

pure play method

simulation

provided us with a single value for the risk-adjusted NPV, whereas a simulation approach gives us a probability distribution for the investment's NPV or IRR. Simulation *involves the process of imitating the performance of the project under evaluation. This is done by randomly selecting observations from each of the distributions that affect the outcome of the project, and continuing with this process until a representative record of the project's probable outcome is assembled.*

The easiest way to develop an understanding of the computer simulation process is to follow through an example simulation for an investment project evaluation. Suppose a chemical producer is considering an extension to its processing plant. The simulation process is portrayed in Figure 11–6. First, the probability distributions are determined for all the factors that affect the project's returns; in this case, let us assume there are nine such variables:

1. Market size
2. Selling price
3. Market growth rate
4. Share of market (which results in physical sales volume)
5. Investment required
6. Residual value of investment
7. Operating costs
8. Fixed costs
9. Useful life of facilities

Then the computer randomly selects one observation from each of the probability distributions, according to its chance of actually occurring in the future. These nine observations are combined, and an NPV or IRR figure is calculated. This process is repeated as many times as desired, until a representative distribution of possible future outcomes is assembled. Thus, the inputs to a simulation include all the principal factors affecting the project's profitability, and the simulation output is a probability distribution of net present values or internal rates of return for the project. The decision maker bases the decision on the full range of possible outcomes. The project is accepted if the decision maker feels that enough of the distribution lies above the normal cutoff criteria ($NPV \geq 0$, $IRR \geq$ required rate of return).

Suppose the output from the simulation of a chemical producer's project is as shown in Figure 11–7 on page 352. This output provides the decision maker with the probability of different outcomes occurring in addition to the range of possible outcomes. Sometimes called **scenario analysis,** this *examination identifies the range of possible outcomes under the worst, best, and most likely case.* The firm's management examines the distribution to determine the project's level of risk and then make the appropriate adjustment.

scenario analysis

You'll notice that although the simulation approach helps us to determine the amount of total risk a project has, it does not differentiate between systematic and unsystematic risk. Because systematic risk cannot be diversified away for free, the simulation approach does not provide a complete method of risk assessment. However, it does provide important insights as to the total risk level of a given investment project. Now we will look briefly at how the simulation approach can be used to perform sensitivity analysis.

Sensitivity Analysis through Simulation Approach

sensitivity analysis

Sensitivity analysis involves *determining how the distribution of possible net present values or internal rates of return for a particular project is affected by a change in one particular*

FIGURE 11-6
Capital-Budgeting Simulation

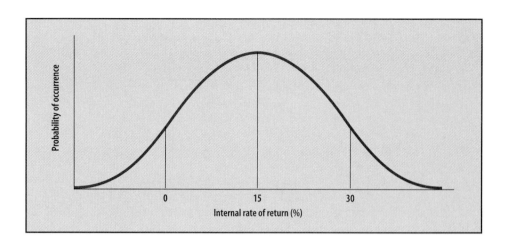

FIGURE 11–7
Output from Simulation

input variable. This is done by changing the value of one input variable while holding all other input variables constant. The distribution of possible net present values or internal rates of return that is generated is then compared with the distribution of possible returns generated before the change was made to determine the effect of the change. For this reason sensitivity analysis is commonly called *what-if analysis.*

For example, the chemical producer that was considering a possible expansion to its plant may wish to determine the effect of a more pessimistic forecast of the anticipated market growth rate. After the more pessimistic forecast replaces the original forecast in the model, the simulation is rerun. The two outputs are then compared to determine how sensitive the results are to the revised estimate of the market growth rate.

CONCEPT CHECK

1. Explain to yourself how simulations work.
2. What is scenario analysis? What is sensitivity analysis? When would you perform sensitivity analysis?

Objective 6

FINANCE AND THE MULTINATIONAL FIRM: CALCULATING CASH FLOWS AND THE INTERNATIONAL DIMENSION OF RISK

The process of measuring the incremental after-tax cash flows to the company as a whole gets a bit more complicated when we are dealing with competition from abroad. One area in which this is certainly true is in calculating the right base case—that is, what the firm's incremental after-tax cash flows would be if the project is not taken on. In determining future cash flows we must always be aware of potential competition from abroad. We need only look to the auto industry to see that competition from abroad can be serious. During the 1970s who would have thought that firms like Toyota, Honda, and Nissan could enter the U.S. markets and actually challenge the likes of Ford and GM? The end result of opening markets to international competition has led not only to increased opportunities, but also to increased risks.

There are also other intangible benefits from investing in countries like Germany and Japan, where cutting-edge technology is making its way into the marketplace. Here investment abroad provides a chance to observe the introduction of new innovations on a first-hand basis, allowing firms like IBM, GE, and 3Com to react more quickly to any technological advances and product innovations that might come out of Germany or Japan.

Along with all the benefits from going multinational come the risks. One of the major risks involves currency fluctuations. For example, in 1998, Boeing introduced the Boeing Business Jet, a new versatile business jet that combines fuel efficiency for short flights with globe-spanning range. Boeing produces these planes in the United States, paying workers and suppliers in U.S. dollars. Boeing then exports them all over the world, with payment received in many different currencies. What if between the time an order was placed and payment was received the value of the foreign currency fell? In fact, on April 1, 1998, the value of the Yugoslav dinar fell by 43% against the U.S. dollar. That means if Boeing had sold a Business Jet to a customer in Yugoslavia for Yugoslav dinars, Boeing would have received the same number of dinar stated in the contract, but they would have been worth 43% less. Risks from economic and currency problems abroad can be devastating. For example, the Asian and Latin American economic crises of 1998 resulted in GM's Latin America/Africa/Mid-East division showing a loss of $161 million in the fourth quarter of 1998 compared with income of $192 million in the fourth quarter of 1997. Also, GM's Asia/Pacific's losses totaled $116 million in the fourth quarter of 1998, compared with a loss of $27 million in the prior-year period.

CONCEPT CHECK

1. In what ways does the process of measuring the incremental after-tax cash flows to the company as a whole get a bit more complicated when we are dealing with competition from abroad?
2. What new risks does a firm face when it enters the international markets?

SUMMARY

In this chapter, we examine the measurement of incremental cash flows associated with a firm's investment proposals and that are used to evaluate those proposals. Relying on **Axiom 3: Cash—Not Profits—Is King,** and **Axiom 4: Incremental Cash Flows—It's Only What Changes That Counts,** we focus only on the incremental or differential after-tax cash flows attributed to the investment proposal. Care is taken to beware of cash flows diverted from existing products, look for incidental or synergistic effects, consider working capital requirements, consider incremental expenses, ignore sunk costs, account for opportunity costs, examine overhead costs carefully, and ignore interest payments and financing flows.

Objective 1

In general, a project's cash flows fall into one of three categories: (1) the initial outlay, (2) the differential flows over the project's life, and (3) the terminal cash flow. A summary of the typical entries in each of these categories appears in Table 11–10.

Objective 2

TABLE 11–10 | SUMMARY OF CALCULATION OF INCREMENTAL AFTER-TAX CASH FLOWS

A. Initial Outlay
   1. Installed cost of asset
   2. Additional nonexpense outlays incurred (e.g., working-capital investment)
   3. Additional expenses, on an after-tax basis (e.g., training expenses)
   4. In a replacement decision, the after-tax flow associated with the sale of the old machine

B. Differential Cash Flows over the Project's Life
   1. Added revenue offset by increased expenses
   2. Labor and material savings
   3. Increase in overhead incurred
   4. Tax savings from an increase in depreciation if the new project is accepted
   5. Do not include interest expenses if the project is financed by issuing debt because this is accounted for in the required rate of return

C. Terminal Cash Flow
   1. The after-tax salvage value of the project
   2. Cash outlays associated with the project's termination
   3. Recapture of nonexpense outlays that occurred at the project's initiation (e.g., working-capital investments)

Objective 3

We also cover the problem of incorporating risk into the capital-budgeting decision. First, we explore just what type of risk to adjust for: the project's stand alone risk, the project's contribution-to-firm risk, or the project's systematic risk. In theory, systematic risk is the appropriate risk measure, but bankruptcy costs and the issue of undiversified shareholders also give weight to considering a project's contribution-to-firm risk as the appropriate risk measure. Both measures of risk are valid, and we avoid making any specific allocation of importance between the two in capital budgeting.

Objective 4
Objective 5

Two commonly used methods for incorporating risk into capital budgeting are (1) risk-adjusted discount rates and (2) simulation. The risk-adjusted discount rate involves an upward adjustment of the discount rate to compensate for risk. This method is based on the concept that investors demand higher returns for riskier projects. The simulation method is used to provide information as to the location and shape of the distribution of possible outcomes. Decisions could be based directly on this method, or it could be used to determine input into either certainty equivalent or risk-adjusted discount rate method approaches.

Objective 6

The process of measuring the incremental after tax cash flows to the company as a whole becomes more complicated when we are dealing with competition from abroad. One area in which this is certainly true is in calculating the right base case—that is, what the firm's incremental after-tax cash flows would be if the project is not taken on. Another complication involves the risks associated with currency fluctuations.

--- **KEY TERMS** ---

contribution-to-firm risk, 343

incremental after-tax cash flows, 329

initial outlay, 332

project standing alone risk, 343

pure play method, 349

risk-adjusted discount rate, 345

scenario analysis, 350

sensitivity analysis, 350

simulation, 349

systematic risk, 343

11-1 Why do we focus on cash flows rather than accounting profits in making our capital-budgeting decisions? Why are we interested only in incremental cash flows rather than total cash flows?

11-2 If depreciation is not a cash flow expense, does it affect the level of cash flows from a project in any way? Why?

11-3 If a project requires additional investment in working capital, how should this be treated in calculating cash flows?

11-4 How do sunk costs affect the determination of cash flows associated with an investment proposal?

11-5 In the preceding chapter we examined the payback period capital-budgeting criterion. Often this capital-budgeting criterion is used as a risk-screening device. Explain the rationale behind its use.

11-6 The use of the risk-adjusted discount rate assumes that risk increases over time. Justify this assumption.

11-7 Explain how simulation works. What is the value in using a simulation approach?

SELF-TEST PROBLEMS

ST-1 The Scotty Gator Corporation of Meadville, Pa., maker of Scotty's electronic components, is considering replacing one of its current hand-operated assembly machines with a new fully automated machine. This replacement would mean the elimination of one employee, generating salary and benefit savings. Given the following information, determine the cash flows associated with this replacement.

Existing situation:	One full-time machine operator—salary and benefits, $25,000 per year
	Cost of maintenance—$2,000 per year
	Cost of defects—$6,000
	Original depreciable value of old machine—$50,000
	Annual depreciation—$5,000 per year
	Expected life—10 years
	Age—five years old
	Expected salvage value in five years—$0
	Current salvage value—$5,000
	Marginal tax rate—34 percent
Proposed situation:	Fully automated machine
	Cost of machine—$60,000
	After tax installation fee—$3,000
	After tax shipping fee—$3,000
	Cost of maintenance—$3,000 per year
	Cost of defects—$3,000 per year
	Expected life—5 years
	Salvage value—$20,000
	Depreciation method—simplified straight-line method over 5 years

11-1 *(Capital Gains Tax)* The J. Harris Corporation is considering selling one of its old assembly machines. The machine, purchased for $30,000 5 years ago, had an expected life of 10 years and an expected salvage value of zero. Assume Harris uses simplified straight-line depreciation, creating deprecation of $3,000 per year, and could sell this old machine for $35,000. Also assume a 34-percent marginal tax rate.
a. What would be the taxes associated with this sale?
b. If the old machine were sold for $25,000, what would be the taxes associated with this sale?
c. If the old machine were sold for $15,000, what would be the taxes associated with this sale?
d. If the old machine were sold for $12,000, what would be the taxes associated with this sale?

11-2 *(Cash Flow Calculations)* The Winky Corporation, maker of cow-grooming equipment, is considering replacing a hand-operated machine used in the manufacturer of grooming components with a new fully automated machine. Given the following information, determine the case flows associated with this replacement.

Existing situation:	Two full-time machine operators—salaries $10,000 each per year
	Cost of maintenance—$5,000 per year
	Cost of defects—$5,000
	Original cost of old machine—$30,000
	Expected life—10 years
	Age—5 years old
	Expected salvage value—$0
	Depreciation method—simplified straight-line over 10 years, $3,000 per year
	Current salvage value—$10,000
	Marginal tax rate—34 percent
Proposed situation:	Fully automated machine
	Cost of machine—$55,000
	After tax installation fee—$5,000
	Cost of maintenance—$6,000 per year
	Cost of defects—$2,000 per year
	Expected life—five years
	Salvage value—$0
	Depreciation method—simplified straight-line method over five years

11-3 *(Capital-Budgeting Calculation)* Given the cash flow information in problem 11-2 and a required rate of return of 15 percent, compute the following for the automated machine:
a. Payback period
b. Net present value
c. Profitability index
d. Internal rate of return
Should this project be accepted?

11-4 *(Cash Flow and New Project Analysis)* The Chung Chemical Corporation is considering the purchase of a chemical analysis machine. Although the machine being considered will not produce any increase in sales revenues, it will result in a before-tax reduction in labor costs of $35,000 per year. The machine has a purchase price of $100,000, and it would cost an additional $5,000 after tax to install this machine properly. In addition, to operate this machine properly, inventory must be increased by $5,000. This machine has an expected life of 10 years, after which it will have no salvage value. Also, assume simplified straight-line depreciation and that this machine is being depreciated down to zero, a 34-percent marginal tax rate, and a required rate of return of 15 percent.

a. What is the initial outlay associated with this project?

b. What are the annual after-tax cash flows associated with this project for years 1 through 9?

c. What is the terminal cash flow in year 10 (i.e., what is the annual after-tax cash flow in year 10 plus any additional cash flows associated with termination of the project)?

d. Should this machine be purchased?

11-5 *(Cash Flow and New Project Analysis)* Raymobile Motors is considering the purchase of a new production machine for $500,000. Although the purchase of this machine will not produce any increase in sales revenues, it will result in a before-tax reduction of labor costs by $150,000 per year. To operate this machine properly, workers would have to go through a brief training session that would cost $25,000 after tax. In addition, it would cost $5,000 after tax to install this machine properly. Also, because this machine is extremely efficient, its purchase would necessitate an increase in inventory of $30,000. This machine has an expected life of 10 years, after which it will have no salvage value. Assume simplified straight-line depreciation and that this machine is being depreciated down to zero, a 34-percent marginal tax rate, and a required rate of return of 15 percent.

a. What is the initial outlay associated with this project?

b. What are the annual after-tax cash flows associated with this project for years 1 through 9?

c. What is the terminal cash flow in year 10 (i.e., what is the annual after-tax cash flow in year 10 plus any additional cash flows associated with termination of the project)?

d. Should this machine be purchased?

11-6 *(Cash Flow and Capital-Budgeting Calculation)* The Jabot Cosmetics Corporation is considering replacing a 10-year-old machine that originally cost $30,000, has a current book value of $10,000 with 5 years of expected life left, and is being depreciated using the simplified straight-line method over its 15-year expected life down to a terminal value of zero in 5 years, generating depreciation of $2,000 per year. The replacement machine being considered would cost $80,000 and have a 5-year expected life over which it would be depreciated using the simplified straight-line method down to zero. At termination in 5 years the new machine would have a salvage value of $40,000. Material efficiencies resulting from the replacement would result in savings of $30,000 per year before depreciation and taxes. Currently, the old machine could be sold for $15,000. Assuming simplified straight-line depreciation, a 34-percent marginal tax rate, and a required rate of return of 20 percent, calculate

a. The payback period

b. The net present value

c. The profitability index

d. The internal rate of return

11-7 *(Risk-Adjusted NPV)* The Hokie Corporation is considering two mutually exclusive projects. Both require an initial outlay of $10,000 and will operate for 5 years. Project A will produce expected cash flows of $5,000 per year for years 1 through 5, while Project B will produce expected cash flows of $6,000 per year for years 1 through 5. Because project B is the riskier of the two projects, the management of Hokie Corporation has decided to apply a required rate of return of 15 percent to its evaluation but only a 12-percent required rate of return to project A. Determine each project's risk-adjusted net present value.

11-8 *(Risk-Adjusted Discount Rates and Risk Classes)* The G. Wolfe Corporation is examining two capital-budgeting projects with 5-year lives. The first, project A, is a replacement project; the second, project B, is a project unrelated to current operations. The G. Wolfe Corporation uses the risk-adjusted discount rate method and groups projects according to purpose, and then uses a required rate of return or discount rate that has been preassigned to that purpose or risk class. The expected cash flows for these projects are given below:

	PROJECT A	PROJECT B
Initial investment:	−$250,000	−$400,000
Cash inflows:		
Year 1	$ 30,000	$135,000
Year 2	40,000	135,000
Year 3	50,000	135,000
Year 4	90,000	135,000
Year 5	130,000	135,000

The purpose/risk classes and preassigned required rates of return are as follows:

PURPOSE	REQUIRED RATE OF RETURN
Replacement decision	12%
Modification or expansion of existing product line	15
Project unrelated to current operations	18
Research and development operations	20

Determine the project's risk-adjusted net present value.

COMPREHENSIVE PROBLEM

It's been 2 months since you took a position as an assistant financial analyst at Caledonia Products. While your boss has been pleased with your work, he is still a bit hesitant about unleashing you without supervision. Your next assignment involves both the calculation of the cash flows associated with a new investment under consideration and the evaluation of several risky projects. Given your lack of tenure at Caledonia, you have been asked not only to provide a recommendation, but also to respond to a number of questions aimed at judging your understanding of the capital-budgeting process. The memorandum you received outlining your assignment follows:

TO: The Financial Analyst

FROM: Mr. V. Morrison, CEO, Caledonia Products

RE: Cash Flow Analysis and Capital Budgeting

We are currently considering the purchase of a new fully automated machine to replace an older, manually operated one. The machine being replaced, now 5 years old, originally had an expected life of 10 years. It was being depreciated using the simplified straight-line method from $20,000 down to zero, thus generating $2,000 in depreciation per year, and could be sold for $25,000. The old machine took one operator, who earned $15,000 per year in salary and $2,000 per year in fringe benefits. Since the new machine is fully automated, this worker would no longer be needed. The annual costs of maintenance and defects associated with the old machine were $7,000 and $3,000, respectively. The replacement machine being considered has a purchase price of $50,000, a salvage value after 5 years of

$10,000, and would be depreciated over 5 years using the simplified straight-line depreciation method down to zero. To get the automated machine in running order, there would be a $2,000 shipping fee and a $2,000 installation charge, both on an after-tax basis. In addition, because the new machine would work faster than the old one, investment in raw materials and goods-in-process inventories would need to be increased by a total of $5,000. The annual costs of maintenance and defects on the new machine would be $2,000 and $4,000, respectively. The new machine also requires maintenance workers to be specially trained; fortunately, a similar machine was purchased 3 months ago, and at that time the maintenance workers went through the $5,000 after tax training program needed to familiarize themselves with the new equipment. Caledonia's management is uncertain whether or not to charge half of this $5,000 after tax training fee toward the new project. Finally, to purchase the new machine, it appears the firm would have to borrow an additional $20,000 at 10 percent interest from its local bank, resulting in additional interest payments of $2,000 per year. The required rate of return on projects of this kind is 20 percent and Caledonia is in the 34-percent marginal tax bracket. Please provide a written response to the following questions:

a. Should Caledonia focus on cash flows or accounting profits in making our capital-budgeting decisions? Should we be interested in incremental cash flows, incremental profits, total cash flows, or total profits?

b. How does depreciation affect cash flows?

c. How do sunk costs affect the determination of cash flows?

d. What is the project's initial outlay?

e. What are the differential cash flows over the project's life?

f. What is the terminal cash flow?

g. Draw a cash flow diagram for this project.

h. What is its NPV?

i. What is its IRR?

j. Should the project be accepted? Why or why not?

k. In capital budgeting, risk can be measured from three perspectives. What are those three measures of a project's risk?

l. According to the CAPM, which measurement of a project's risk is relevant? What complications does reality introduce into the CAPM view of risk, and what does that mean for our view of the relevant measure of a project's risk?

m. Explain how simulation works. What is the value in using a simulation approach?

n. What is sensitivity analysis and what is its purpose?

SELF-TEST SOLUTIONS

SS-1

Step 1: First calculate the initial outlay.

Initial outlay	
Outflows:	
Cost of machine	$60,000
Installation fee	3,000
Shipping fee	3,000
Inflows:	
Salvage value—old machine	−5,000
Tax savings on sale of old machine	
($25,000 − $5,000)(.34)	−6,800
	$54,200

Step 2: Calculate the differential cash flows over the project's life.

		BOOK PROFIT	CASH FLOW
Savings:	Reduced salary	$25,000	$25,000
	Reduced defects	3,000	3,000
Costs:	Increased maintenance	−1,000	−1,000
	Increased depreciation		
	($13,200 − $5,000)ᵃ	−8,200	
Net savings before taxes		$18,800	$27,000
Taxes (.34)		−6,392	−6,392
Annual net cash flow after taxes			$20,608

ᵃAnnual depreciation on the new machine is equal to the cost of the new machine ($60,000) plus any expenses necessary to get it in operating order (the shipping fee of $3,000 plus the installation fee of $3,000) divided by the depreciable life (5 years).

Step 3: Calculate the terminal cash flow.

Salvage value—new machine	$20,000
Less: Taxes—recapture of depreciation ($20,000 × .34)	− 6,800
	$13,200

Thus, the cash flow in the final year will be equal to the annual net cash flow in that year of $20,608 plus the terminal cash flow of $13,200 for a total of $33,808.

COST OF CAPITAL

LEARNING OBJECTIVES

AFTER READING THIS CHAPTER, YOU SHOULD BE ABLE TO:

1. Describe the concepts underlying the firm's cost of capital (technically, its weighted average cost of capital) and the purpose for its calculation.
2. Calculate the after-tax cost of debt, preferred stock, and common equity.
3. Calculate a firm's weighted average cost of capital
4. Describe the procedure used by PepsiCo to estimate the cost of capital for a multiple division firm.
5. Use the cost of capital to evaluate new investment opportunities.
6. Compute the economic profit earned by the firm and use this quantity to calculate incentive-based compensation.
7. Calculate equivalent interest rates for different countries.

Encore, Inc. and H&L Manufacturing are both faced with the need to assess financial performance. In one case, it is the anticipated performance of a new capital investment, and in the other, it is the performance of the firm as a whole. Consider the following scenarios:

- The Morristown division of Encore, Inc. is faced with an investment opportunity that requires the investment of $75 million to construct a new shipping and distribution facility. The new facility will free up existing factory space for additional productive capacity that the firm needs to meet growing demand.
- The management of H&L Manufacturing Company is trying to come to grips with the company's overall performance. Profits have grown by more than 20 percent per year over the past 5 years, but the firm's stock price has not kept pace with those of competitor firms.

Encore needs a benchmark return that can be used to evaluate whether the anticipated return from the new shipping and distribution investment is going to create or destroy shareholder wealth. H&L, on the other hand, needs a benchmark return to compare against the performance of the entire firm.

In this chapter, we learn that the benchmark return that is appropriate in both instances is the firm's cost of capital. We recognize the first problem as the capital-budgeting

Having studied the connection between risk and rates of return for securities (Chapter 9) and the valuation of bonds and stocks (Chapters 7 and 8), we are prepared to consider the firm's cost of capital. A firm's cost of capital serves as the link between the firm's financing decisions and its investment decisions. The cost of capital becomes the hurdle rate that must be achieved by an investment before it will increase shareholder wealth. The term *cost of capital* is commonly used interchangeably with the firm's *required rate of return,* the *hurdle rate for new investments,* the *discount rate for evaluating a new investment,* and the firm's *opportunity costs of funds.* Regardless of the term used, the basic concept is the same. The cost of capital is the rate that must be earned on an investment project if the project is to increase the value of the common stockholders' investment in the project.

The cost of capital is also the appropriate basis for evaluating the performance of a division or even an entire firm. In this case, the cost of capital becomes the key determinant of the capital cost associated with a firm's investments. We use economic profit to provide such a measure of performance.

In this chapter, we discuss the fundamental determinants of a firm's cost of capital and the rationale for its calculation and use. This entails developing the logic for estimating the cost of debt capital, preferred stock, and common stock. Chapter 13 takes up consideration of the impact of the firm's financing mix on the cost of capital.

This chapter emphasizes Axioms 1, 2, 3, 6, 7, 8, and 9: **Axiom 1: The Risk-Return Trade-Off—We Won't Take on Additional Risk Unless We Expect to Be Compensated with Additional Return; Axiom 2: The Time Value of Money—A Dollar Received Today Is Worth More Than a Dollar Received in the Future; Axiom 3: Cash—Not Profits—Is King. Axiom 6: Efficient Capital Markets—The Markets Are Quick and the Prices Are Right; Axiom 7: The Agency Problem—Managers Won't Work for the Owners Unless It's in Their Best Interest; Axiom 8: Taxes Bias Business Decisions; Axiom 9: All Risk Is Not Equal—Some Risk Can Be Diversified Away, and Some Cannot.**

problem introduced earlier in Chapter 10. The second problem is the focal point of shareholder value-based management (SVBM).

In July 1994, Boise Cascade adopted economic value added or EVA®, a very popular method for implementing shareholder value–based management, as its key measure of financial performance. Their description of why they did so tells us a lot about the role of the cost of capital in managing a firm to create value for shareholders[1]:

> "Economic value is created by earning a return greater than investors require and is destroyed by earning a return less than they require. The EVA measurement process encourages management to make business decisions that create economic value through improved operating efficiency, better asset utilization, and growth that generates returns which exceed the cost of capital."

But shareholder value–based management is about more than using the cost of capital as the standard for making financial choices. It is also about rewarding the firm's employees in

---

[1] 1994 Boise Cascade Annual Report.

ways that continually encourage them to seek out new ways to create shareholder value. Thus, the EVA system also involves rewarding employees for creating shareholder values as captured in the EVA performance metric. As we see in the following quote, Boise Cascade saw the need to connect EVA performance to compensation following the old adage that what you measure and reward gets done[2]:

> "We believe our emphasis on EVA will more closely align the interest of employees and shareholders. Therefore, we are also using EVA to determine incentive compensation for management. The compensation of plan participants, including corporate officers, will be tied directly to improvement in the EVA of their operations and the corporation as a whole. We believe this measurement, and the fact that incentive compensation is linked to it, will effectively encourage management decisions that maximize the market value of the capital contributed by investors."

Note: Stern Stewart & Co. have trademarked the term Economic Value Added or EVA® to refer to their particular method for calculating a firm's economic profit using accounting statement results.

THE COST OF CAPITAL: KEY DEFINITIONS AND CONCEPTS

Objective 1

Investor Opportunity Costs, Required Rates of Return, and the Cost of Capital

In Chapter 10, we referred to the discount rate used in calculating net present value (NPV) simply as the appropriate discount rate. In this chapter, we define what we mean by this term. Specifically, the appropriate discount rate primarily reflects the **investor's required rate of return.** In Chapter 9, we defined the investor's required rate of return for a security as the *minimum rate of return necessary to attract an investor to purchase or hold a security.* This rate of return considers the investor's opportunity cost of making an investment; that is, if an investment is made, the investor must forgo the return available on the next-best investment. This forgone return is the opportunity cost of undertaking the investment and, consequently, is the investor's required rate of return.

investor's required rate of return

Is the investor's required rate of return the same thing as the cost of capital? Not exactly. Two basic considerations drive a wedge between the investor's required rate of return and the cost of capital to the firm. First, there are taxes. When a firm borrows money to finance the purchase of an asset, the interest expense is deductible for federal income tax calculations. Consider a firm that borrows at 9 percent and then deducts its interest expense from its revenues before paying taxes at a rate of 34 percent. For each dollar of interest it pays, the firm reduces its taxes by $.34. Consequently, the actual cost of borrowing to the firm is only 5.94% ($.09 - (.34 \times .09) = .09(1 - .34) = 0.0594 = 5.94\%$). The second thing that causes the firm's cost of capital to differ from the investor's required rate of return is *any transaction costs incurred when a firm raises funds by issuing a particular type of security,* sometimes called **flotation costs.** For example, if a firm sells new shares for $25 per share but incurs transaction costs of $5 per share, then the cost of capital for the new common equity is increased. Assume that the investor's required rate of return is 15 percent for each $25 share, then $.15 \times \$25 = \$3.75$ must be earned each year to satisfy the investor's

flotation costs

---

[2]1994 Boise Cascade Annual Report.

required return. However, the firm has only $20 to invest, so the cost of capital (k) is calculated as the rate of return that must be earned on the $20 net proceeds, which will produce a dollar return of $3.75; that is,

$$\$20k = \$25 \times .15 = \$3.75$$

$$k = \frac{\$3.75}{\$20.00} = .1875 = 18.75\%$$

We have more to say about both these considerations as we discuss the costs of the individual sources of capital to the firm.

Financial Policy and the Cost of Capital

financial policy

A firm's **financial policy**—that is, *the policies regarding the sources of finances it plans to use and the particular mix (proportions) in which they will be used*, governs its use of debt and equity financing. The particular mixture of debt and equity that the firm utilizes can impact the firm's cost of capital. However, in this chapter, we assume that the firm maintains a fixed financial policy that is reflected in a fixed debt-equity ratio. Determination of the target mix of debt and equity financing is the subject of Chapter 13.

weighted average cost of capital

The firm's overall cost of capital reflects the combined costs of all the sources of financing used by the firm. We refer to this overall cost of capital as the firm's **weighted average cost of capital.** The weighted average cost of capital is *the weighted average of the after-tax costs of each of the sources of capital used by a firm to finance a project where the weights reflect the proportion of total financing raised from each source.* Consequently, the weighted average cost of capital is the rate of return that the firm must earn on its investments so that it can compensate both its creditors and stockholders with their individual required rates of return. Let's now turn to a discussion of how the costs of debt and equity can be estimated.

CONCEPT CHECK

1. Define the concept of an investor's required rate of return.
2. How do flotation costs impact the investor's required rate of return?

DETERMINING INDIVIDUAL COSTS OF CAPITAL

In order to attract new investors, companies have created a wide variety of financing instruments or securities. In this chapter, we stick to three basic types of financing instruments: debt, preferred stock, and common stock. In calculating the respective cost of financing from each of these types of financing instruments, we estimate the investor's required rate of return properly adjusted for any transaction or flotation costs associated with each funding source. In addition, because we will be discounting after-tax cash flows, we should adjust our cost of capital for any influence of corporate taxes. In summary, the cost of a particular source of capital is equal to the investor's required rate of return after adjusting for the effects of both flotation costs and corporate taxes.

The Cost of Debt

The investor's required rate of return on debt is simply the return that creditors demand on new borrowing. In Chapter 7, we estimated this required rate of return by solving the following bond valuation equation:

$$P_d = \sum_{t=1}^{n} \frac{\text{interest paid in period } t(\$I_t)}{(1 + \text{bondholder's required rate of return } (k_d)^t} +$$

$$\frac{\text{maturity value of the debt } (\$M)}{(1 + \text{bondholder's required rate of return } (k_d)^n} \qquad (12\text{--}1)$$

where P_d is the market price of the debt security and n is the number of periods to maturity. Should the firm incur flotation costs such as brokerage commissions and legal and accounting fees in issuing the debt, then the cost of debt capital, k_d, is found as follows:

$$\frac{\text{net proceeds}}{\text{per bond} (NP_d)} = \sum_{t=1}^{n} \frac{\$I_t}{(1 + \$k_d)^t} + \frac{\$M}{(1 + k_d)^n} \qquad (12\text{--}2)$$

The adjustment for flotation costs simply involves replacing the market price of the bond with the net proceeds per bond (NP_d) received by the firm after paying these costs. The result of this adjustment is that the discount rate that solves equation (12–2) is now the firm's cost of debt financing before adjusting for the effect of corporate taxes—that is, the before-tax cost of debt (k_d). The final adjustment we make is to account for the fact that interest is tax deductible. Thus the after-tax cost of debt capital is simply $k_d(1 - T_c)$, where T_c is the corporate tax rate.

As we learned in Chapter 7, the interest payments on bonds are generally the same for each period. Under these conditions, equation (12–2) can be restated using the interest factors in the present value tables found inside the back cover of the book as follows:

$$NP_d = \$I_t(PVIFA_{k_d,n}) + \$M(PVIF_{k_d,n}) \qquad (12\text{--}2a)$$

BACK TO THE FOUNDATIONS

When we calculate the bondholder's required rate of return, we are discounting the interest and principal payments to the bondholder back to the present using a discount rate that makes this present value equal the current price of the firm's bonds. In essence, we are valuing the bond, which relies on two basic axioms of finance: **Axiom 1: The Risk-Return Trade-Off—We Won't Take an Additional Risk Unless We Expect to Be Compensated with Additional Return,** and **Axiom 2: The Time Value of Money—A Dollar Received Today Is Worth More Than a Dollar Received in the Future.**

In addition, the calculation of the bondholder's required rate of return relies on the observed market price of the firm's bonds to be an accurate reflection of their worth. Buyers and sellers only stop trading when they are convinced that the price properly reflects all available information. **Axiom 6: Efficient Capital Markets—The Markets Are Quick and the Prices Are Right.** What we mean here, very simply, is that investors are ever vigilant and quickly act on information that affects the riskiness and, consequently, the price of a firm's bonds and other securities.

Example

Synopticom, Inc. plans a bond issue for the near future and wants to estimate its current cost of debt capital. After talking with the firm's investment banker, the firm's chief financial officer has determined that a 20-year maturity bond with a $1,000 face value and 8 percent coupon (paying 8% × $1,000 = $80 per year in interest) can be sold to investors for $908.32. Equation (12–1) can be used to solve for the investor's required rate of return as we illustrated in Chapter 7. In this case, Synopticom's creditors require a 9-percent rate of return. The cost of capital to the firm is higher than 9 percent, however, because the firm will have to pay flotation costs of $58.32 per bond when it issues the securities. The flotation costs reduce the net proceeds to Synopticom to $850. Substituting into equation (12–2), we find that the before-tax cost of capital for the bond issue is 9.75 percent. Once again, we can solve equation (12–2) using a financial calculator as we illustrate in the margin.

One final adjustment is necessary to obtain the firm's after-tax cost of debt capital. Assuming that Synopticom is in the 34-percent corporate income tax (T_c) bracket, we estimate the after-tax cost of debt capital as follows:

$$\text{after-tax cost of debt} = k_d(1 - T_c)$$

$$\text{after-tax cost of debt} = 9.75\%(1 - .34) = 6.435\%$$

CALCULATOR SOLUTION

Data Input	Function Key
20	N
850	+/– PV
80	PMT
1000	FV
Function Key	Answer
CPT I/Y	9.73*

*The difference between 9.75 percent and 9.73 percent is simply the result of rounding.

BACK TO THE FOUNDATIONS

The tax deductibility of interest expense makes debt financing less costly to the firm. This is an example of **Axiom 8: Taxes Bias Business Decisions.** The tax deductibility of interest, other things remaining constant, serves to encourage firms to use more debt in their capital structure than they might otherwise use.

The Cost of Preferred Stock

Determining the cost of preferred stock is very straightforward because of the simple nature of the cash flows paid to the holders of preferred shares. You will recall from Chapter 8 that the value of a preferred stock is simply

$$\begin{array}{c}\text{price of preferred}\\\text{stock } (P_{ps})\end{array} = \frac{\text{preferred stock dividend}}{\text{required rate of return for preferred stockholder}} \quad (12\text{–}3)$$

where P_{ps} is the current market price of the preferred shares. Solving for the preferred stockholder's required rate of return, we get the following:

$$\begin{array}{c}\text{required rate of return}\\\text{for preferred stockholder}\end{array} = \frac{\text{preferred stock dividend}}{\text{price of preferred stock}} \quad (12\text{–}4)$$

Once again, where flotation costs are incurred when new preferred shares are sold, the investor's required rate of return is less than the cost of preferred capital to the firm. To calculate the cost of preferred stock, we must adjust the required rate of return to reflect these flotation costs. We replace the price of a preferred share in equation (12–4) with the net proceeds per share from the sale of new preferred shares (NP_{ps}). The resulting formula can be used to calculate the cost of preferred stock to the firm.

$$\text{cost of preferred stock } (k_{ps}) = \frac{\text{preferred stock dividend}}{\text{net proceeds per preferred share}} \quad (12\text{–}5)$$

What about corporate taxes? In the case of preferred stock, no tax adjustment must be made because preferred dividends are not tax deductible.

Example

On January 10, 1996, AmaxGold had an issue of preferred stock that traded on the NYSE. The issue paid an annual dividend of $3.75 per share and the preferred stock price closed at $60.375. Assume that if the firm were to sell an issue of preferred stock with the same characteristics as its outstanding issue, it would incur flotation costs of $2.375 per share and the shares would sell for their January 10, 1996 closing price. What is AmaxGold's cost of preferred stock?

Substituting into equation (12–5), we get the following cost of preferred stock for AmaxGold:

$$k_{ps} = \frac{\$3.75}{(\$60.375 - \$2.375)} = .06465 \text{ or } 6.465\%$$

Note that there is no adjustment for taxes because preferred dividends are not tax deductible—that is, preferred dividends are paid after corporate taxes, unlike bond interest, which is paid with before-tax dollars.

The Cost of Common Equity

Common equity is unique in two respects. First, the cost of common equity is more difficult to estimate than the cost of debt or preferred stock because the common stockholder's required rate of return is not observable. This results from the fact that common stockholders are the residual owners of the firm, which means that their return is equal to what is left of the firm's earnings after paying the firm's bondholders their contractually set interest and principal payments and the preferred stockholders their promised dividends. Second, common equity can be obtained from either the retention of firm earnings or through the sale of new shares. The cost associated with each of these sources is different from one another because the firm does not incur any flotation costs when it retains earnings but does when it sells new common shares.

We discuss two methods for estimating the common stockholder's required rate of return, which is the foundation for our estimate of the firm's cost of equity capital. These methods are based on the dividend growth model and the capital asset pricing model, which were both discussed earlier in Chapter 8 when we discussed stock valuation.

The Dividend Growth Model

Recall from Chapter 8 that the value of a firm's common stock is equal to the present value of all future dividends. Where dividends are expected to grow at a rate g forever and rate g is less than the investor's required rate of return, k_{cs}, then the value of a share of common stock, P_{cs}, can be written as:

$$P_{cs} = \frac{D_1}{k_{cs} - g} \tag{12–6}$$

where D_1 is the dividend expected to be received by the firm's common shareholders 1 year hence. The expected dividend is simply equal to the current dividend multiplied by 1 plus the annual rate of growth in dividends (i.e., $D_1 = D_0(1 + g)$). The investor's required rate of return then is found by solving equation (12–6) for k_{cs}.

$$k_{cs} = \frac{D_1}{P_{cs}} + g \qquad \text{(12-7)}$$

Note that k_{cs} is the investor's required rate of return for investing in the firm's stock. It also serves as our estimate of the cost of equity capital, where new equity capital is obtained by retaining a part of the firm's current period earnings. Recall that common equity financing can come from one of two sources: the retention of earnings (i.e., earnings not paid out in dividends to the common stockholders) or from the sale of new common shares. When the firm retains earnings, it doesn't incur any flotation costs, thus the investor's required rate of return is the same as the firm's cost of new equity capital in this instance.

If the firm issues new shares to raise equity capital, then it incurs flotation costs. Once again we adjust the investor's required rate of return for flotation costs by substituting the net proceeds per share, NP_{cs}, for the stock price, P_{cs}, in equation (12-7) to estimate the cost of new common stock, k_{ncs}.

$$k_{ncs} = \frac{D_1}{NP_{cs}} + g \qquad \text{(12-8)}$$

Example

The Talbot Corporation's common shareholders anticipate receiving a $2.20 per share dividend next year based on the fact that they received $2 last year and expect dividends to grow 10 percent next year. Furthermore, analysts predict that dividends will continue to grow at a rate of 10 percent into the foreseeable future. Given that the firm's stock is trading for $50 per share, we can calculate the investor's required rate of return (and the cost of retained earnings) as follows:

$$k_{cs} = \frac{D_1}{P_{cs}} + g = \frac{\$2.20}{\$50.00} + .10 = .144 \text{ or } 14.4\%$$

Should Talbot decide to issue new common stock, then it would incur a cost of $7.50 per share, or 15 percent of the current stock price. The resulting cost of new common equity capital would be:

$$k_{ncs} = \frac{D_1}{NP_{cs}} + g = \frac{\$2.20}{\$50 - 7.50} + .10 = .1518 \text{ or } 15.18\%$$

Thus Talbot faces two costs of capital with respect to common equity. If it retains earnings, then the cost of capital to the firm is 14.4 percent, and if it issues new common stock, the corresponding cost is 15.18 percent. This difference will prove to be important later when we calculate the overall or weighted average cost of capital for the firm. ▪

BACK TO THE FOUNDATIONS

The dividend growth model for common stock valuation relies on three of the fundamental axioms of finance. First, stock value is equal to the present value of expected future dividends. This reflects **Axiom 2: The Time Value of Money—A Dollar Received Today Is Worth More Than a Dollar Received in the Future.** Furthermore, dividends represent actual cash receipts to stockholders and are incorporated into the valuation model in a manner that reflects the timing of their receipt. This attribute of the dividend growth model reflect **Axiom 3: Cash—Not Profits—Is King.** Finally, the rate used to discount the expected future dividends back to the present reflects the riskiness of the dividends. The higher the riskiness of the dividend payments, the higher the investor's required rate of return. This reflects **Axiom 1: The Risk-Return Trade-Off—We Won't Take on Additional Risk Unless We Expect to Be Compensated with Additional Return.**

Issues in Implementing the Dividend Growth Model

The principal advantage of the dividend growth model is its simplicity. To estimate an investor's required rate of return, the analyst needs only to observe the current dividend and stock price and to estimate the rate of growth in future dividends. The primary drawback relates to the applicability or appropriateness of the valuation model. That is, the dividend growth model is based on the fundamental assumption that dividends are expected to grow at a constant rate g forever. To avoid this assumption, analysts frequently utilize more complex valuation models in which dividends are expected to grow for, say, 5 years at one rate and then grow at a lower rate from year 6 forward. We do not consider these more complex models here.

Even if the constant growth rate assumption is acceptable, we must arrive at an estimate of that growth rate. We could estimate the rate of growth in historical dividends ourselves or go to published sources of growth rate expectations. Investment advisory services such as Value Line provide their own analysts' estimates of earnings growth rates (generally spanning up to 5 years), and the Institutional Brokers' Estimate System (I/B/E/S) collects and publishes earnings per share forecasts made by over 1,000 analysts for a broad list of stocks. These estimates are helpful but still require the careful judgment of the analyst in their use because they relate to earnings (not dividends) and only extend 5 years into the future (not forever, as required) by the dividend growth model. Nonetheless, these estimates provide a useful guide to making your initial dividend growth rate estimate.

The Capital Asset Pricing Model

Recall from Chapter 9 that the **capital asset pricing model (CAPM)** provides a basis for determining the investor's expected or required rate of return from investing in common stock. The model depends on three things:

capital asset pricing model

1. the risk-free rate, k_{rf};
2. the systematic risk of the common stock's returns relative to the market as a whole or the stock's beta coefficient, β; and
3. the market risk premium, which is equal to the difference in the expected rate of return for the market as a whole; that is, the expected rate of return for the "average security" minus the risk-free rate, or in symbols, $k_m - k_{rf}$.

Using the CAPM, the investor's required rate of return can be written as follows:

$$k_c = k_{rf} + \beta \ (k_m - k_{rf}) \tag{12–9}$$

The Talbot Corporation's common stock has a beta coefficient of 0.82. Furthermore, the risk-free rate is currently 7 percent, and the expected rate of return on the market portfolio of all risky assets is 16 percent. Using the CAPM from equation (12–9), we can estimate Talbot's cost of capital as follows:

$$k_c = k_{rf} + \beta \ (k_m - k_{rf})$$
$$= 7\% + .82 \ (.16 - .07) = .144 \text{ or } 14.4\%$$

Note that the required rate of return we have estimated is the cost of internal common equity, because no transaction costs are considered. ∎

Issues in Implementing the CAPM

The CAPM approach has two primary advantages. First, the model is simple and easy to understand and implement. The model variables are readily available from

IPOs: Should a Firm Go Public?

When a privately owned company decides to distribute its shares to the general public, it goes through a process known as an initial public offering (IPO). There are a number of advantages to having a firm's shares traded in the public equity market, including the following:

- **New capital is raised.** When the firm sells its shares to the public, it acquires new capital that can be invested in the firm.
- **The firm's owners gain liquidity of their share holdings.** Publicly traded shares are more easily bought and sold so that the owners can more easily liquidate all or a part of their investment in the firm.
- **The firm gains future access to the public capital market.** Once a firm has raised capital in the public markets, it is easier to go back a second and third time.
- **Being a publicly traded firm may benefit the firm's business.** Public firms tend to enjoy a higher profile than their privately-held counterparts. This may make it easier to make sales and attract vendors to supply goods and services to the firm.

However, all is not rosy as a publicly-held firm. There are a number of potential disadvantages, including the following:

- **Reporting requirements can be onerous.** Publicly-held firms are required to file periodic reports with the Securities and Exchange Commission (SEC). This is not only onerous in terms of the time and effort required, but some business owners feel they must reveal information to their competitors that could be potentially damaging.

- **Private equity investors now must share any new wealth with the new public investors.** Now that the firm is a publicly held company, the new shareholders share on an equal footing with the company founders in the good (and bad) fortune of the firm.
- **The private investors lose a degree of control of the organization.** Outsiders gain voting control over the firm to the extent that they own its shares.
- **An IPO is expensive.** A typical firm may spend 15 to 25 percent of the money raised on expenses directly connected to the IPO. This cost is increased further if we consider the cost of lost management time and disruption of business associated with the IPO process.
- **Exit of company owners is usually limited.** The company founders may want to sell their shares through the IPO, but this is not allowed for an extended period of time. Therefore, the IPO is not usually a good mechanism for cashing out the company founders.
- **Everyone involved faces legal liability.** The IPO participants are jointly and severally liable for each others' actions. This means that they can be sued for any omissions from the IPO prospectus should the public market valuation fall below the IPO offering price.

A careful weighing of the financial consequences of each of these advantages and disadvantages can provide a company's owners (and management) with some basis for answering the question of whether they want to become a public corporation.

Other sources: Professor Ivo Welch's Web site http://welch.som.yale.edu provides a wealth of information concerning IPOs.

public sources with the possible exception of beta coefficients for small and/or non–publicly traded firms. Second, because the model does not rely on dividends or any assumption about the growth rate in dividends, it can be applied to companies that do not currently pay dividends or are not expected to experience a constant rate of growth in dividends.

Using the CAPM requires that we obtain estimates of each of the three model variables—k_{rf}, β, and $(k_m - k_{rf})$. Let's consider each in turn. First, the analyst has a wide range of U.S. government securities upon which to base an estimate of the risk-free rate. Treasury securities with maturities from 30 days to 20 years are readily available, but the CAPM offers no guidance as to the appropriate choice. In fact, the model itself assumes that there is but one risk-free rate, and it corresponds to a one-period return (the length of the period is not specified, however). Consequently, we are left to our own judgment as to which maturity we should use to represent the risk-free rate. For applications of the cost of capital involving long-term capital expenditure decisions, it seems reasonable to select a risk-free rate of comparable maturity. So, if we are calculating the cost of capital to be used as the basis for evaluating investments that will provide returns over the next 20 years, it seems appropriate to use a risk-free rate corresponding to a U.S. Treasury bond of comparable maturity.

Second, estimates of security beta coefficients are available from a wide variety of investment advisory services, including Merrill Lynch and Value Line, among others. Alternatively, we could collect historical stock market returns for the company of interest as well as a general market index (such as the Standard and Poor's 500 Index) and estimate the stock's beta as the slope of the relationship between the two return series—as we did in Chapter 9. However, because beta estimates are widely available for a large majority of publicly traded firms, analysts frequently rely on published sources for betas.

Finally, estimation of the market risk premium can be accomplished by looking at the history of stock returns and the premium earned over (under) the risk-free rate of interest. In Chapter 9, we reported a summary of the historical returns earned on risk-free securities and common stocks in Figure 9–2. We saw that on average over the last 70 years, common stocks have earned a premium of roughly 7 percent over long-term government bonds. Thus, for our purposes, we will utilize this estimate of the market risk premium $(k_m - k_{rf})$ when estimating the investor's required rate of return on equity using the CAPM.

Takin' It to the Net
Ibbotson Associates maintains a historical database on rates of return earned on stocks and bonds, as well as the market risk premium. See their site http://www.ibbotson.com.

BACK TO THE FOUNDATIONS

The capital asset pricing model, or CAPM, is a formal representation of **Axiom 1: The Risk-Return Trade-Off—We Won't Take on Additional Risk Unless We Expect to Be Compensated with Additional Return.** By "formal" we mean that the specific method of calculating the additional returns needed to compensate for additional risk is specified in the form of an equation—the CAPM. The CAPM's recognition of systematic or nondiversifiable risk as the source of risk that is rewarded in the capital market is a reflection of **Axiom 9: All Risk Is Not Equal—Some Risk Can Be Diversified Away, and Some Cannot.**

CONCEPT CHECK

1. Define the cost of debt financing, preferred equity, and common equity.
2. The cost of common equity financing is more difficult to estimate than the cost of debt and preferred equity. Explain why.
3. What is the dividend growth model, and how is it used to estimate the cost of common equity financing?
4. Describe the capital asset pricing model and how it can be used to estimate the cost of common equity financing.
5. What practical problems are encountered in using the CAPM to estimate common equity capital cost?

THE WEIGHTED AVERAGE COST OF CAPITAL

capital structure

Now that we have calculated the individual costs of capital for each of the sources of financing the firm might use, we now turn to the combination of these capital costs into a single weighted average cost of capital. To estimate the weighted average cost of capital, we need to know the cost of each of the sources of capital used and the capital structure mix. We use the term **capital structure** to refer to *the proportions of each source of financing used by the firm.* Although a firm's capital structure can be quite complex, we focus our examples on the three basic sources of capital: bonds, preferred stock, and common equity.

In words, we calculate the weighted average cost of capital for a firm that uses only debt and common equity using the following equation:

$$\begin{matrix} \text{weighted} \\ \text{average cost} \\ \text{of capital} \end{matrix} = \left(\begin{matrix} \text{after-tax} \\ \text{cost of} \\ \text{debt} \end{matrix} \times \begin{matrix} \text{proportion} \\ \text{of debt} \\ \text{financing} \end{matrix} \right) + \left(\begin{matrix} \text{cost of} \\ \text{equity} \end{matrix} \times \begin{matrix} \text{proportion} \\ \text{of equity} \\ \text{financing} \end{matrix} \right)$$

For example, if a firm borrows money at 6 percent after taxes, pays 10 percent for equity, and raises its capital in equal proportions from debt and equity, its weighted average cost of capital is 8 percent—that is,

$$\begin{matrix} \text{weighted} \\ \text{average cost} \\ \text{of capital} \end{matrix} = [.06 \times .5] + [.10 \times .5] = .08 \text{ or } 8\%$$

In practice, the calculation of the cost of capital is generally more complex than this example. For one thing, firms often have multiple debt issues with different required rates of return, and they also use preferred equity as well as common equity financing. Furthermore, when new common equity capital is raised, it is sometimes the result of retaining and reinvesting the firm's current period earnings and, at other times, it involves a new stock offering. In the case of retained earnings, the firm does not incur the costs associated with selling new common stock. This means that equity from retained earnings is less costly than a new stock offering. In the examples that follow, we address each of these complications.

Capital Structure Weights

We opened this chapter with a description of an investment opportunity faced by the Morristown division of Encore, Inc. A critical element in the analysis of that investment was an estimate of the cost of capital—the discount rate—to be used to calculate the NPV for the project. The reason we calculate a cost of capital is that it enables us to evaluate one or more of the firm's investment opportunities. Remember that the cost of capital should reflect the riskiness of the project being evaluated, so a firm may calculate multiple costs of capital where it makes investments in multiple divisions or business units having different risk characteristics. Thus for the calculated cost of capital to be meaningful, it must correspond directly to the riskiness of the particular project being analyzed. That is, in theory the cost of capital should reflect the particular way in which the funds are raised (the capital structure used) and the systemic risk characteristics of the project. Consequently, the correct way to calculate capital structure weights is to use

Innovative Management
of a Growth Firm's Capital Structure

A classic problem growth firms face is the balancing of the use of debt and equity such that its capital costs are not adversely affected by the way it finances its growing needs for assets. The Enron Corporation, led by CFO Andy Fastow, has walked a delicate balancing act over the last decade as the total value of the firm's common equity (i.e., its market capitalization or simply market cap) has increased from $3.5 billion in 1990 to around $35 billion in 1999.

The fundamental problem is that firms like Enron make very large investments that only begin to provide returns after several years. Thus, if the firm issues debt to finance the investments, investors may think the company is unduly risky in which case the firm's debt rating may fall. On the other hand, with no earnings to show for the investment an equity issue may lead to a drop in the firm's stock price. What's a nice growth firm to do? Enron's approach to its financing dilemma has been as innovative as its approach to developing energy-based derivatives based on everything from natural gas prices to the weather. For example, faced with the prospect of financing the acquisition of its first water company (a $2.2 billion purchase of Wessex Water Pic, a U.K.-based water company), Enron issued contingent equity that was used as collateral for a nonrecourse debt issue.

What does this finance lingo mean? Basically Enron borrowed the money for the purchase but with the proviso that only Wessex stood behind the debt (i.e., the debt holders could not turn to Enron in the event that Wessex defaulted on the bonds—thus the nonrecourse language). To get the lenders to loan the money, however, Enron had to issue equity to a trust that was set aside to repay the creditors in the event of default by Wessex. Furthermore, Enron promised its shareholders that the acquisition financing for Wessex would be replaced with permanent financing on terms that would maintain the company's capital structure. What this did for Enron was allow the firm to finance the Wessex acquisition entirely with borrowed funds to which the lenders had recourse only to the Wessex assets being purchased and the Enron shares placed in the trust. Within 6 months Enron announced an IPO to replace the debt financing. Thus, Enron achieved debt-like financing on an equity issue that did not dilute Enron's stock. This all resulted from deferring the equity issue and using nonrecourse debt.

Source: Russ Banham, "The Finest in Finance: How Enron Financed its Amazing Transformation from Pipelines to Piping Hot," *CFO Magazine* (October 1999): 62–65.

the actual dollar amounts of the various sources of capital actually used by the firm.[3]

In practice, *the mixture of financing sources used by a firm will vary from year to year.* For this reason, many firms find it expedient to use target capital structure proportions in calculating the firm's weighted average cost of capital. For example, a firm might use its target mix of 40 percent debt and 60 percent equity to calculate its weighted average cost of capital even though, in that particular year, it raised the majority of its financing requirements by borrowing. Similarly, it would continue to use the target proportions in the subsequent year when it might raise the majority of its financing needs by reinvesting earnings or through a new stock offering.

---

[3]There are instances when we will want to calculate the cost of capital for the firm as a whole. In this case, the appropriate weights to use are based upon the market value of the various capital sources used by the firm. Market values rather than book values properly reflect the sources of financing used by a firm at any particular point in time. However, where a firm is privately owned, it is not possible to get market values of its securities, and book values are often used.

	TABLE 12-1	CALCULATING THE WEIGHTED AVERAGE COST OF CAPITAL

Panel A: Common equity raised by retaining earnings

SOURCE OF CAPITAL	CAPITAL STRUCTURE WEIGHTS	× COST OF CAPITAL	= PRODUCT
Bonds	w_d	$k_d(1 - T_c)$	$w_d \cdot k_d(1 - T_c)$
Preferred stock	w_{ps}	k_{ps}	$w_{ps} \cdot k_{ps}$
Common equity			
Retained earnings	w_{cs}	k_{cs}	$w_{cs} \cdot k_{cs}$
Sum =	100%		Sum = k_{wacc}

Panel B: Common equity raised by selling new common stock

SOURCE OF CAPITAL	CAPITAL STRUCTURE WEIGHTS	× COST OF CAPITAL	= PRODUCT
Bonds	w_d	$k_d(1 - T_c)$	$w_d \cdot k_d(1 - T_c)$
Preferred stock	w_{ps}	k_{ps}	$w_{ps} \cdot k_{ps}$
Common equity			
Common stock	w_{ncs}	k_{ncs}	$w_{ncs} \cdot k_{cs}$
Sum =	100%		Sum = k_{wacc}

Calculating the Weighted Average Cost of Capital

The weighted average cost of capital, k_{wacc}, is simply a weighted average of all the capital costs incurred by the firm. Table 12–1 illustrates the procedure used to estimate k_{wacc} for a firm that has debt, preferred stock, and common equity in its target capital structure mix. Note that in Panel A, the firm is able to finance all its target capital structure requirements for common equity through the retention of firm earnings, and in Panel B, it utilizes a new equity offering. For example, if the firm targets 75 percent equity financing and has current earnings of $750,000, then it can raise up to $750,000/.75 = $1,000,000 in new financing before it has to sell new equity. For $1,000,000 or less in capital spending, the firm's weighted average cost of capital would be calculated using the cost of equity from retained earnings (following Panel A of Table 12–1). For more than $1,000,00 in new capital, the cost of capital would rise to reflect the impact of the higher cost of using new common stock (following Panel B of Table 12–1).

Takin' It to the Net

Takin' It to the Net
The Alcar corporation provides a cost of capital calculator at the Web site http://www.alcar.net/web/homepage.nsf/WebPages/CostOfCapital.

Example

Ash, Inc.'s capital structure and estimated capital costs are found in Table 12–2. Note that sum of the capital structure weights must sum to 100 percent if we have properly accounted for all sources of financing and in the correct amounts. For example, Ash plans to invest a total of $3 million in common equity into the $5 million investment. Because Ash has earnings equal to the $3,000,000 it needs in new equity financing, the entire amount of new equity will be raised by retaining earnings.

We calculate the weighted average cost of capital following the procedure described in Panel A of Table 12–1 and using the information found in Table 12–2. The resulting calculations are found in Panel A of Table 12–3, in which Ash, Inc.'s weighted average cost of capital for up to $5,000,000 in new financing is found to be 12.7 percent.

TABLE 12-2 CAPITAL STRUCTURE AND CAPITAL COSTS FOR ASH, INC.

SOURCE OF CAPITAL	AMOUNT OF FUNDS RAISED ($)	PERCENTAGE OF TOTAL	AFTER-TAX COST OF CAPITAL
Bonds	$1,750,000	35%	7%
Preferred stock	250,000	5%	13%
Common equity			
Retained earnings	3,000,000	60%	16%
	$5,000,000	100%	

If Ash needs more than $5,000,000 then it will not have any retained earnings to provide the additional equity capital. Thus, to maintain its desired 60 percent equity financing proportion, Ash will now have to issue new equity that costs 18 percent.

Panel B of Table 12–3 contains the calculation of Ash's weighted average cost of capital for more than $5,000,000. The resulting cost is 13.9 percent.

In practice, many firms calculate only one cost of capital using a cost of equity capital that ignores the transaction costs associated with raising new equity capital. In essence, they would use the capital cost calculated for Ash in Panel A Table 12–3 regardless of the level of new financing for the year. Although this is technically incorrect, it is understandable given the difficulties involved in estimating equity capital cost.[4]

TABLE 12-3 WEIGHTED AVERAGE COST OF CAPITAL FOR ASH, INC.

Panel A: Cost of capital for $0 to $5,000,000 in new capital

CAPITAL STRUCTURE

SOURCE OF CAPITAL	WEIGHTS	COST OF CAPITAL	PRODUCT
Bonds	35%	7%	2.45%
Preferred stock	5%	13%	0.65%
Common equity			
Retained earnings	60%	16%	9.60%
	100%	k_{wacc}	= 12.70%

Panel B: Cost of capital for more than $5,000,000

CAPITAL STRUCTURE

SOURCE OF CAPITAL	WEIGHTS	COST OF CAPITAL	PRODUCT
Bonds	35%	7%	2.45%
Preferred stock	5%	13%	0.65%
Common equity			
Common stock	60%	18%	10.80%
	100%	k_{wacc}	= 13.90%

---

[4]For a discussion of the imprecise nature of equity capital cost estimates, see Eugene F. Fama and Kenneth R. French, 1997 "Industry costs of equity," *Journal of Financial Economics 43*, 153–193.

How Do Managers Resolve Ethical Decisions?

What makes a managerial choice an ethical one? Brief et al.[a] (1991) suggest that if the decision entails reflection on the moral significance of the choice, then the choice is an ethical one. How do managers resolve ethical dilemmas? There is some evidence suggesting that two factors come to bear on ethical choices: values and accountability.

We will consider two social value systems that are present in Western society, which are particularly relevant to the study of finance. These are the Smithian and Humanitarian value systems. The Smithian system is derived from the writings of the 19th-century moral philosopher and political economist Adam Smith. This value system is reflected in the current-day teachings of economists such as Milton Friedman[b] (1962). Briefly, this system holds that when individuals pursue their own self-interest in the marketplace, they contribute to the good of society. At the firm level, this system provides the basis for the market system and is used as the basis for corporate self-interest. In contrast, the Humanitarian system is based on the fundamental premise of the equality of individuals in society. This system seeks to protect individuals from the harshness of the market system and to promote equality of opportunity.

Personal value systems are not the only influence on managerial decisions that have ethical implications. Managers are influenced by their perception of the value systems of the individuals to whom they are held accountable. That is, ethical choices made by managers are influenced by the values they believe are held by the person to whom they are accountable.[c]

Arendt (1951, 1977) provides evidence that suggests that the effects of accountability may be more profound than those of the individual manager's values. Consequently, the potentially overpowering effects of hierarchical accountability may lead individual managers not to construe the moral significance attached to the choices they make. They may see no choice but to comply with the higher authority. Brief et al. (1991) provide empirical evidence bearing on the question of the relative importance of personal values versus accountability in the choices made by individuals. Using a set of experiments involving 135 M.B.A. students, they concluded that personal values may not be related to how an individual chooses to resolve ethical dilemmas when the choices (values) of the higher authority are known explicitly.

Note that we have not addressed the normative issue: How should ethical dilemmas be resolved? Instead, we have addressed the question, How do managers actually deal with ethical choices? The principal finding of the studies we have reviewed is that the *perceived values of one's superiors* have a profound impact on the way in which a subordinate resolves ethical dilemmas. So choose your superior carefully.

Sources:[a] A. Brief, J. M. Dukerich, and L. I. Doran, "Resolving Ethical Dilemmas in Management: Experimental Investigations of Values, Accountability and Choice," *Journal of Applied Social Psychology* 21 (1991):380–96;[b] M. Friedman, *Capitalism and Freedom* (Chicago: University of Chicago Press, 1962);[c] H. Arendt, *The Origins of Totalitarianism* (New York: Harcourt Brace, 1951); H. Arendt, *Eichmann in Jerusalem* (New York: Penguin Books, 1977).

CONCEPT CHECK

1. A firm's capital structure and its target capital structure proportions are important determinants of a firm's weighted average cost of capital. Explain.
2. Explain in words the calculation of a firm's weighted average cost of capital. What exactly are we averaging and what do the weights represent?

Objective 4

CALCULATING DIVISIONAL COSTS OF CAPITAL: PEPSICO, INC.

If a firm operates in multiple industries, each with its own particular risk characteristics, should it use different capital costs for each division? **Axiom 1** suggests that the financial manager should recognize these risk differences in estimating the cost of

TABLE 12-4 — ESTIMATING PEPSICO'S COST OF DEBT

	PRETAX COST OF DEBT	×	(1 − TAX RATE)	=	AFTER-TAX COST OF DEBT
Restaurants	8.93%	×	.62		5.54%
Snack foods	8.43%	×	.62		5.23%
Beverages	8.51%	×	.62		5.28%

capital to use in each division. This is exactly what PepsiCo did before February 1997, when it operated in three basic industries.

PepsiCo went to great lengths to estimate the cost of capital for each of its three major operating divisions (restaurants, snack foods, and beverages).[5] We briefly summarize the basic elements of the calculations involved in these estimates, including the cost of debt financing, the cost of common equity, the target capital structure weights, and the weighted average cost of capital.

Table 12–4 contains the estimates of the after-tax cost of debt for each of PepsiCo's three divisions. Tables 12–5 contains the estimates of the cost of equity capital for each of PepsiCo's three operating divisions using the CAPM. We will not explain the intricacies of their method for estimating divisional betas, except to say that they make use of beta estimates for a number of competitor firms from each of the operating divisions, which involves making appropriate adjustments for differences in the use of financial leverage across the competitor firms used in the analysis.[6]

The weighted average cost of capital for each of the divisions is estimated in Table 12–6 using the capital costs estimated in Tables 12–4 and 12–5 and using PepsiCo's target capital structure weights for each operating division. Note that the weighted average costs of capital for all three divisions fall within a very narrow range, between 10.08 percent and 10.29 percent.

TABLE 12-5 — COST OF EQUITY CAPITAL FOR PEPSICO'S OPERATING DIVISIONS

	RISK-FREE RATE	+	BETA	[EXPECTED MARKET RETURN	−	RISK-FREE RATE]	=	COST OF EQUITY
Restaurants	7.28%	+	1.17	(11.48%	−	7.28%)	=	12.20%
Snack foods	7.28%	+	1.02	(11.48%	−	7.28%)	=	11.56%
Beverages	7.28%	+	1.07	(11.48%	−	7.28%)	=	11.77%

---

[5]PepsiCo spun off its restaurants division in February 1997. However, the example used here was based on the pre-spinoff company.

[6]This method of using betas from comparable firms is sometimes referred to as the pure play method, because the analyst seeks independent beta estimates for firms engaged in only one business (i.e., restaurants or beverages). The betas for these pure play companies are then used to estimate the beta for a business or division.

TABLE 12-6 | **PEPSICO'S WEIGHTED AVERAGE COST OF CAPITAL FOR EACH OF ITS OPERATING DIVISIONS**

	COST OF EQUITY TIMES THE TARGET EQUITY RATIO	+	COST OF DEBT TIMES THE TARGET DEBT RATIO	=	WEIGHTED AVERAGE COST OF CAPITAL
Restaurants	(12.20%) (0.70)	+	(5.54%) (0.30)	=	10.20%
Snack foods	(11.56%) (0.80)	+	(5.23%) (0.20)	=	10.29%
Beverages	(11.77%) (0.74)	+	(5.28%) (0.26)	=	10.08%

CONCEPT CHECK

1. Why should firms that own and operate multiple businesses with very different risk characteristics use business specific or divisional costs of capital?
2. Describe the process used to estimate the divisional costs of capital for PepsiCo.

Table 12–7 contains a summary of the formulas involved in estimating the weighted average cost of capital. If divisional costs of capital are to be estimated, then we must apply these formulas individually to each division where the opportunity costs of capital sources and the financing mix (proportions) used can differ as we have just seen in the PepsiCo example.

Objective 5 | **USING A FIRM'S COST OF CAPITAL TO EVALUATE NEW CAPITAL INVESTMENTS**

If a firm has traditionally used a single cost of capital for all projects undertaken within each of several operating divisions (or companies) that have very different risk characteristics then it will encounter resistance to the change from the high-risk divisions. Consider the case of the hypothetical firm Global Energy whose divisional costs of capital are illustrated in Figure 12–1 on page 380. Global Energy is an integrated oil company that engages in a wide range of hydrocarbon-related businesses, including exploration and development, pipelines, and refining. Each of these businesses has its unique set of risks. In Figure 12–1 we see that the overall or enterprise-wide cost of capital for Global Energy is 11 percent, reflecting an average of the firm's divisional costs of capital ranging from a low of 8 percent for pipelines up to 18 percent for exploration and production.

At present Global Energy is using 11 percent to evaluate new investment proposals from all three operating divisions. This means that exploration and production projects earning as little as 11 percent are being accepted even though the capital market dictates that projects of this risk should earn 18 percent. Thus, Global Energy overinvests in high-risk projects. Similarly the company will underinvest in its two lower-risk divisions where the company-wide cost of capital is used.

TABLE 12–7   SUMMARY OF COST OF CAPITAL FORMULAS

1. The After-Tax Cost of Debt, $k_d(1 - T_c)$
   a. Calculate the before-tax cost of debt, k_d, as follows:

$$NP_d = \sum_{t=1}^{n} \frac{\$I_t}{(1 + k_d)^t} + \frac{\$M}{(1 + k_d)^n} \qquad (12\text{–}2)$$

   where NP_d is the net proceeds received by the firm from the sale of each bond; $\$I_t$ is the dollar amount of interest paid to the investor in period t for each bond; $\$M$ is the maturity value of each bond paid in period n; k_d is the before-tax cost of debt to the firm; and n is the number of periods to maturity.

   b. Calculate the after-tax cost of debt as follows:

   after-tax cost of debt $= k_d(1 - T_c)$
   where T_c is the corporate tax rate.

2. The Cost of Preferred Stock, k_p

$$k_{ps} = \frac{\text{preferred stock dividend}}{NP_{ps}} \qquad (12\text{–}5)$$

   where NP_{ps} is the net proceeds per share of new preferred stock sold after flotation costs.

3. The Cost of Common Equity
   a. Method 1: dividend growth model
      Calculate the cost of internal common equity (retained earnings), k_{cs}, as follows:

$$k_{cs} = \frac{D_1}{P_{cs}} + g \qquad (12\text{–}7)$$

   where D_1 is the expected dividend for the next year, P_{cs} is the current price of the firm's common stock, and g is the rate of growth in dividends per year. Calculate the cost of external common equity (new stock offering), k_{ncs}, as follows:

$$k_{ncs} = \frac{D_1}{NP_{cs}} + g \qquad (12\text{–}8)$$

   where NP_{cs} is the net proceeds to the firm after flotation costs per share of stock sold.

   b. Method 2: capital asset pricing model, k_c

$$k_c = k_{rf} + \beta(k_m - k_{rf}) \qquad (12\text{–}9)$$

   where the risk-free rate is k_{rf}; the systemic risk of the common stock's returns relative to the market as a whole, or the stock's beta coefficient, is β; and the market risk premium, which is equal to the difference in the expected rate of return for the market as a whole (i.e., the expected rate of return for the "average security") minus the risk-free rate, is $k_m - k_{rf}$

4. The Weighted Average Cost of Capital

$$k_{wacc} = w_d\, k_d(1 - T_c) + w_{ps}\, k_{ps} + w_{cs}\, k_{cs} + w_{ncs}\, k_{ncs} \qquad (12\text{–}10)$$

   where the w_i terms represent the market value weights associated with the firm's use of each of its sources of financing. Note that we are simply calculating a weighted average of the costs of each of the firm's sources of capital where the weights reflect the firm's relative use of each source.

FIGURE 12–1

*Global Energy Divisional
Costs of Capital*

Using a company-wide cost
of capital for a multidivision
firm results in systematic
overinvestment in high-risk
projects and underinvestment
in low-risk projects.

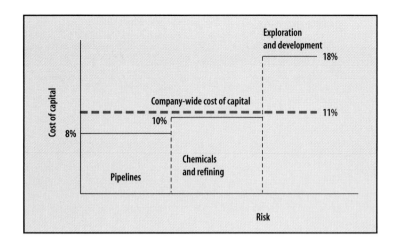

Now consider the prospect of moving to division costs of capital and the implications this might have for the three divisions. Specifically, the exploration and development division is likely to see this as an adverse move for them because it will surely cut the level of new investment capital flowing into their operations. In contrast, the management of the remaining two divisions will see the change as good news because under the company-wide cost of capital system they have been rejecting projects earning more than their market-based costs of capital (8 percent and 10 percent for pipelines and refining, respectively) but less than the company's 11 percent cost of capital.

BACK TO THE FOUNDATIONS

The firm's weighted average cost of capital provides the appropriate discount rate for evaluating new projects only where the projects offer the same riskiness as the firm as a whole. This limitation of the usefulness of the firm's weighted average cost of capital is a direct extension of **Axiom 1: The Risk-Return Trade-Off—We Won't Take on Additional Risk Unless We Expect to Be Compensated with Additional Return.** If project risk differs from that of the firm, then the firm's cost of capital (which reflects the risk of the firm's investment portfolio) is no longer the appropriate cost of capital for the project. For this reason, firms that invest in multiple divisions or business units that have different risk characteristics should calculate a different cost of capital for each division. In theory, each individual investment opportunity has its own unique risk attributes and correspondingly should have a unique cost of capital. However, given the impreciseness with which we estimate the cost of capital, we generally calculate the cost of capital for each operating division of the firm, not each project.

CONCEPT CHECK

1. What are the implications for a firm's capital investment decisions of using a company-wide cost of capital when the firm has multiple operating divisions that each have unique risk attributes and capital costs?
2. If a firm has decided to move from a situation in which it uses a company-wide cost of capital to divisional costs of capital, what are the behavioral problems it is likely to encounter?

New Users Explain Their Goals and Objectives in Adopting EVA

The following excerpts taken from company annual reports and press releases document the rationale underlying the adoption of EVA as a system for implementing shareholder value-based management. The fundamental element throughout all the excerpts is the recognition of the need to place top priority on shareholder interests by considering the impact of all the firm's decisions on share value. In addition, we see the importance of tying compensation to EVA such that value creation is reinforced and rewarded.

OLIN CORPORATION (501 MERRITT 7, P.O. BOX 4500, NORWALK, CT 06856-4500)

The primary goal of any company is to manage its operations to create long-term value for shareholders and employees alike. Economic Value Added, or EVA, is a business management system that clearly shows how well a company is meeting that goal. EVA can help Olin to realize the sustained growth needed to meet the company's full potential.

We are using EVA to tie everything we do—investing in core businesses, financing activities, streamlining our business mix—to the goal of enhancing value for you, our shareholders. In fact, we are using EVA measures to tie compensation of our key managers to the achievement of tough multiyear goals. (Excerpts from "EVA: The Meaning of our Success," and the 1995 Annual Report. Olin Corp., used with permission.)

BOISE CASCADE CORPORATION (1111 WEST JEFFERSON STREET, P.O. BOX 50, BOISE, IDAHO 83728-0001)

In July 1994, Boise Cascade adopted EVA as its key financial measure. Economic value is created by earning a return greater than investors require and is destroyed by earning a return less than they require. The EVA measurement process encourages management to make business decisions that create economic value through improved operating efficiency, better asset utilization, and growth that generates returns which exceed the cost of capital.

We believe our emphasis on EVA will more closely align the interests of employees and shareholders. Therefore, we are also using EVA to determine incentive compensation for management. The compensation of plan participants, including corporate officers, will be tied directly to improvement in the EVA of their operations and the corporation as a whole. We believe this measurement, and the fact that incentive compensation is linked to it, will effectively encourage management decisions that maximize the market value of the capital contributed by investors. (Excerpt from 1994 Annual Report, Boise Cascade, used with permission.)

EQUIFAX, INC. (1600 PEACHTREE STREET, NW, ATLANTA, GA 30309)

Our financial strategy is centered on creating shareholder value by maximizing Economic Value Added (EVA). The EVA framework helps us identify which "value drivers" will be the most effective in increasing the total return on capital employed in each of our operating units. These drivers fall within the general classifications of margin improvements, revenue growth and capital efficiency. (Excerpt from 1992 Annual Report, Equifax, Inc., used with permission.)

JOHNSON WORLDWIDE ASSOCIATES, INC. (1326 WILLOW ROAD, STURTEVANT, WISCONSIN 53177)

Why was EVA chosen as a new financial measure at JWA?

We wanted a single concept to which all employees could relate. We reviewed many options and decided that EVA would provide the simplest, yet most comprehensive way to look at all aspects of managing our business, from inventory levels to sales programs and operating expenses.

How will the adoption of EVA change the financial environment of JWA?

We haven't managed the balance sheet as well as we should. EVA requires us to manage not only sales and profitability, but weighs these against what we invest in the business—its "capital." We will be focusing on earning an adequate return on that capital. That's what shareholders expect when they purchase our stock. If we don't earn the return investors expect, they will put their money elsewhere. As managers, we will be scrutinizing each of our business units to see that they are adding value.

What exactly do you mean by "adding value?"

Each business unit must cover the cost of operating—labor, materials, advertising and wear and tear on its equipment, for example. What remains after those costs are subtracted from sales revenue is the unit's operating profit. Each business unit will also deduct a charge for its cost of capital from its operating profit. The remainder is value created, or EVA. Over the long-term, a business unit will not be successful unless its operating profits recover the cost of capital. Today, that is not always the case. Going forward, we want each unit to achieve net positive EVA, and to grow it every year. (Excerpt from 1996 Annual Report, Johnson Worldwide Association, used with permission.)

Continued.

New Users Explain Their Goals and Objectives in Adopting EVA—Cont'd.

SPX CORPORATION (700 TERRACE POINT DRIVE, MUSKEGON, MI 49443)

SPX adopted EVA because it:

- is easily understood and applied;
- fits into operational improvement efforts, because success requires continuous improvement in EVA,
- correlates closer to market value than any other operating performance measure;
- links directly to investor expectations through EVA improvement targets;
- focuses on long-term performance by using a bonus bank and predetermined improvement targets; and
- provides a common language for performance measurement, decision support, compensation and communication.

Today, people throughout SPX are making operating and strategic decisions using EVA decision support tools. We have trained our managers so they understand the link between daily operating decisions and shareholder value. Our recent restructuring of an operation in Germany was supported by EVA analysis. We chose the strategy that created the greatest EVA. (Excerpt from *1995 Annual Report*, SPX Corp., used with permission.)

BALL CORPORATION (345 SOUTH HIGH STREET, P.O. BOX 2407, MUNCIE, IN 47307-0407)

Ball joins a growing list of successful Fortune 500 companies, which are focusing on EVA instead of exclusively monitoring more common measures such as earnings per share. Coca-Cola Co., a major customer of Ball, is among them.

A more in-depth explanation of the Economic Value Added concept begins with the understanding that investors require a minimum rate of return on their investment in the equity of a corporation to compensate them for the risk they assume. In turn, the corporation's management must earn at least this same rate of return to meet these investor expectations. When management earns a higher rate of return than the minimum required by investors, value has been created. The magnitude of that value depends on the amount of capital invested and the extent to which return on that capital exceeds investor expectations; this is economic value added. (Joan D. LaGuardia, "Adding Value: Ball Measures Up with a New Market Standard," *Ball Line Magazine*, No. 4, 1991, pp. 4–6.)

Objective 6	SHAREHOLDER VALUE–BASED MANAGEMENT

How do you know whether you are creating or destroying shareholder value? Asked somewhat differently, "how can you tell how much wealth a firm has created for its shareholders?" In recent years a whole host of systems have been developed that purport to answer these questions and in so doing provide guidance to the firm's management for use in making decisions that are expected to have the greatest positive impact on shareholder wealth. We refer to this cadre of methods as shareholder value–based management or simply value–based management tools. We focus on one very popular method in our discussion that is based on the concept of economic profit.

How Much Value Has a Firm Created for Its Owners?

In the introduction we described a firm, H&L Manufacturing, that was trying to come to grips with why its stock price was not growing as rapidly as its competitors'. In essence, H&L needs to know whether it is creating or destroying shareholder

market value added

wealth. How can we tell? The answer is **market value added (MVA).** MVA is a very simple concept. It represents *the difference in the current market value of the firm and the sum of all the funds that have been invested in the firm over its entire operating life*. If the market value of the firm exceeds the investment made in the firm, then the firm has created shareholder wealth. MVA is calculated as follows:

$$\text{MVA} = \text{total market value of the firm} - \text{invested capital} \quad (12\text{-}10)$$

Total market value of the firm is simply the sum of the market value of the firm's outstanding shares of stock (current share price times the number of shares outstanding) plus the market value of the firm's debt (book value is frequently substituted). Invested capital is basically the sum total of the money invested in the firm to date. Invested capital is estimated by adjusting the firm's book value of total assets for things such as R&D expense and allowances for doubtful accounts receivable, which are not included in the total assets of the firm but, nonetheless, represent dollars that have been invested in the firm[7]:

In essence, MVA is the NPV of all the firm's investments. A firm that is using its investments to produce what investors perceive to be positive NPVs will have a positive MVA. Similarly, a firm that is using its invested capital in ways that investors feel destroys value will have a negative MVA. Note that because the market value of the firm's securities is based on expected future cash flows, MVA is a reflection of the expected NPV. Because MVA is not a measure of historical performance but instead reflects anticipated future performance, it can change dramatically as a firm's fortunes change. For example, in 1988, IBM's MVA was the largest of any U.S. company. By 1990, the fortunes of IBM had changed dramatically as the personal computer became the computer of the future. In 1991, IBM ranked thirty-first and by 1993 its rank slipped to 1000th. However, changes in the perceived fortunes of the company in 1997 resulted in a dramatic turnaround in investors' perceptions of IBM's future and raised its rank to sixteenth. Not every firm experiences this degree of volatility from year to year. The sources of the volatility in MVA are the market

TABLE 12-8	THE TOP AND BOTTOM FIVE FIRMS IN THE 1998 STERN STEWART PERFORMANCE 1000

Firm ranking is based on market value added (MVA) in 1997. MVA = firm market value − invested capital.

1997 RANK	1996 RANK	1992 RANK	COMPANY NAME	MARKET VALUE ADDED (MVA) ($ MILLIONS)	ECONOMIC VALUE ADDED (EVA) ($ MILLIONS)	INVESTED CAPITAL ($ MILLIONS)	RETURN ON INVESTED CAPITAL (%)	COST OF CAPITAL (%)
1	2	5	General Electric	$195,830	$1,917	$59,251	17.34	13.76
2	1	2	Coca-Cola	158,247	2,615	10,957	30.33	12.13
3	3	12	Microsoft	143,740	2,781	8,676	52.94	14.20
4	5	4	Merck	107,418	1,921	23,112	23.15	14.51
5	4	24	Intel	90,010	4,821	21,436	42.71	15.14
996	996	992	St. Paul Companies	−2,614	−282	9,478	7.69	10.74
997	995	995	Digital Equipment	−3,916	−1,321	10,561	0.22	11.27
998	999	994	RJR Nabisco	−9,530	−1,140	35,410	5.42	8.67
999	997	996	Loews Corporation	−10,081	−1,350	22,285	4.66	10.91
1000	1000	999	General Motors	−13,876	−4,120	75,354	4.38	9.36

Source: Irwin Ross, "The Stern Stewart Performance 1000," *The Bank of America Journal of Applied Corporate Finance,* (Winter 1999), pp. 122–134.

[7]We will not go into the adjustments that are made to a firm's book assets to measure invested capital. The adjustments add equity equivalent reserves to capital and periodic changes in those reserves to after-tax operating profits. For example, equivalent reserves include such items as the deferred income tax reserve, LIFO reserve, cumulative amortization of goodwill, capitalized intangibles (including R&D), allowance for doubtful accounts and warranty claim reserves.

value of the firm's equity and adjustments the firm makes to its invested capital through acquisitions and sales of assets.

Table 12–8 contains the top and bottom five firms in terms of MVA for 1998. With the exception of Intel and Microsoft, all the top five wealth creators were ranked in the top 10 in 1992 which suggests that there is some stability among the top performers. Furthermore, all of the bottom five performers were in the bottom ten in 1992.

Did the Firm Create Shareholder Value This Year?

economic profit

MVA measures the wealth created by a firm at a particular point in time. However, the financial manager needs to evaluate the performance of the firm over a specific interval of time, say 1 year. For this purpose, we calculate the firm's **economic profit.** Economic profit is defined as follows:

$$\text{economic profit} = \left(\begin{array}{c} \text{net operating} \\ \text{profit after-tax} \\ \text{(NOPAT)} \end{array} \right) - \left(\begin{array}{c} \text{invested} \\ \text{capital} \end{array} \times \begin{array}{c} \text{cost of} \\ \text{capital} \end{array} \right) \quad (12\text{–}11)$$

Note that the distinction between economic and accounting profit (net operating profit) is the deduction of a return to the firm's invested capital. The product of the firm's invested capital (the total dollar investment made in the firm by its creditors and owners) and the cost of capital constitutes a capital charge. This capital charge is not a recognized accounting expense but it is a very real expense from the perspective of the firm's bondholders and stockholders. The firm's accounting profits must not only be positive but also must cover the required rate of return on the firm's investment (the cost of capital) before shareholder value has been created. Thus economic profit is simply accounting profit (net operating profit or income) less a charge for the use of capital.

So what? How does the use of economic profit help the financial manager? The answer is surprisingly simple. Most firms manage to earn positive profits. However, earning positive profits is no assurance that the firm is creating shareholder wealth because profits fail to incorporate any opportunity cost for the dollars that investors have tied up in the business. Economic profit, on the other hand, includes an explicit charge in the form of the capital charge, which recognizes the size of the investment made in the firm and the opportunity cost of that investment.

Consider the case of Kmart Corporation, which ranked 995th in the MVA rankings. Kmart's economic profit for 1997 can be calculated as follows:

$$\text{economic profit} = \text{NOPAT} - \left(\begin{array}{c} \text{invested} \\ \text{capital} \end{array} \times \begin{array}{c} \text{cost of} \\ \text{capital} \end{array} \right) \quad (12\text{–}11)$$

$$(\$166.449 \text{ M}) = \$944.193 \text{ M} - (\$14{,}730 \text{ M} \times .0754)$$

How can this be? Kmart earned a positive NOPAT of $944.193 million. The answer lies in the size of Kmart's NOPAT relative to its assets. Compared to the firm's $14,730 million invested capital, its NOPAT represents a return of only 6.41 percent, which is less than the firm's 7.54 percent cost of capital. So long as Kmart continues to earn a return on its invested capital that is lower than its cost of capital it will continue to destroy shareholder value no matter how large its profits.

How Can the Firm Increase Its Economic Profits?

What can a firm do to improve its performance such that it creates more shareholder value for its owners? The answer can be found by reviewing the variables that are found on the right hand side of equation (12–11). These variables include the level of NOPAT, the cost of capital and the amount of invested capital (often referred to as value drivers). One way to create additional value is by seeking ways to increase NOPAT without a corresponding increase in the firm's invested capital. This can be accomplished by increasing revenues and/or driving down expenses. There are a number of ways that a firm might reduce costs and increase profits without the need to spend additional capital. For example, the Domtar Corporation (a forest management company that deals in paper, pulp, and wood products) adopted an economic profit–based system and notes the following ways in which it can improve its economic profit by identifying operating efficiencies:

- cutting down on waste and damaged products,
- operating machinery and equipment more efficiently,
- improving product mix, devising methods to save on the purchase of raw materials,
- improve health and safety performance, attract and retain customers,
- make better use of time in the office and plant, implement or improve preventative maintenance programs, and
- develop links with suppliers.

A second way to improve economic profit is by growing the firm's investments in projects that earn returns in excess of the firm's costs of capital. For example, the firm might introduce new marketing plans that improve customer satisfaction and sales and profits, expand existing businesses that offer the potential to earn positive NPVs, or introduce new information systems to better track customer buying habits and correspondingly increase firm sales.

The third and final approach to improving economic profits involves reducing the firm's capital charge (cost of capital × invested capital). This can be accomplished in either of two ways. If the firm is not using its minimum cost of capital financing mix, then restructuring its financing sources might lead to a lowering of the firm's cost of capital and a corresponding decrease in the firm's dollar cost of capital. Alternatively, the firm might consider withdrawing capital from its operations through the sale of underutilized assets (e.g., excess plant capacity, underperforming operating units, or real estate).

How Can a Firm Link Pay for Performance to Reinforce Wealth Creation?

Economic profit has become an important tool for aligning shareholder and manager interests in the running of the company. This is accomplished by basing management's incentive compensation on economic profit. A very simple version of such a compensation scheme is illustrated in equation (12–12).

$$\text{incentive compensation} = \text{base pay} \times \text{percent incentive compensation} \times \frac{\text{actual economic profit}}{\text{target economic profit}} \quad (12\text{–}12)$$

For example, consider the case of the assistant treasurer for NewCo Oil, Inc. The assistant treasurer's base pay is $80,000 a year and 20 percent of the total compensation for this position is designated by the company to be incentive based. If in a particular year, NewCo set a target economic profit of $1 million and earned $1.2

Takin' It to the Net

There are a wide array of vendors for value-based management systems, including Alcar http://www.Alcar.com/, Holt Valuation http://www.holtvalue.com/, Marakon http://www.Marakon.com/, and Stern Stewart http://www.SternStewart.com/.

million, then the assistant treasurer's incentive compensation would be calculated as follows using equation (12–12):

$$\begin{matrix} \text{incentive} \\ \text{compensation} \end{matrix} = \text{base pay} \times \begin{matrix} \text{percent} \\ \text{incentive} \\ \text{compensation} \end{matrix} \times \frac{\text{actual economic profit}}{\text{target economic profit}}$$

$$= \$80{,}000 \times .20 \times (\$1.2 \text{ million}/\$1 \text{ million})$$

$$= \$19{,}200$$

In this case, the assistant treasurer's total annual compensation would be $99,200 = $80,000 + $19,200. If NewCo earned only $800,000 in economic profit, then the incentive compensation paid to the assistant treasurer would be $12,800 = $80,000 × .20 × ($800,000/$1,000,000).

Clearly, with this type of incentive compensation plan, the firm's managers will be very careful to manage for increased net operating profits while holding down the firm's invested capital and maintaining the lowest possible cost of capital. If they do this, then they will maximize the contribution to shareholder wealth and also maximize their own year-end bonuses.

CONCEPT CHECK

1. What is market value added (MVA)?
2. Define economic profit and its determinants.
3. How is economic profit related to MVA?

Objective 7

FINANCE AND THE MULTINATIONAL FIRM: WHY DO INTEREST RATES DIFFER BETWEEN COUNTRIES?[8]

If borrowers and lenders can freely obtain money in one country and invest it in another, why are interest rates not the same the world over? Stated somewhat differently, if capital markets are fully integrated and money flows to the highest rate of interest, it would seem that the forces of competition would make interest rates the same for a given risk borrower.

Let's consider a hypothetical example to see how this might work. Assume that a U.S. borrower can borrow 1,000 yen in Japan for a 5 percent interest paying back 1,050 yen in 1 year. Alternatively, the U.S. firm can borrow an equivalent amount in the United States and pay 15.5 percent interest. Why the big difference? Is capital 10.5 percent cheaper in Japan, and if so, why don't U.S. firms simply switch to the Japanese capital market for their funds? The answer, as we will now illustrate, lies in the differences in the anticipated rates of inflation for Japan versus the United States.

Although it was not obvious in the preceding example, we assumed a zero rate of inflation for the Japanese economy and a 10 percent rate of inflation for the U.S. economy. With a zero anticipated rate of inflation, the nominal rate of interest in Japan is equal to the real rate of 5 percent. Under these assumptions, the nominal rate in the United States can be calculated using the Fisher model as follows:

$$\begin{matrix} \text{U.S. nominal} \\ \text{rate of interest} \end{matrix} = (1 + \text{real rate, U.S.})\,(1 + \text{inflation rate, U.S.}) - 1$$

$$= (1 + .05)\,(1.10) - 1 = .155 \text{ or } 15.5\%$$

---

[8]This section is from W. Carl Kester and Timothy A. Luehrman, "What Makes You Think U.S. Capital Is So Expensive?" *Journal of Applied Corporate Finance* (Summer 1992): 29–41. Reprinted with permission.

To understand the reason for the different interest rate in Japan and the United States, we must extend the Fisher model to its international counterpart.

The International Fisher Effect

In an international context, we must recognize that there can be different rates of inflation among the different countries of the world. For example, the Fisher model for the nominal rate in the home or domestic country ($r_{n,h}$) is a function of the real interest rate in the home country ($r_{r,h}$) and the anticipated rate of inflation in the home country (i_h). For the domestic economy, the Fisher relationship can be described as follows:

$$r_{n,h} = [(1 + r_{r,h})(1 + i_h)] - 1 = r_{r,h} + (i_h)(r_{r,h}) + i_h \qquad \text{(12-13a)}$$

Using "f" as a subscript to denote a foreign country, we can define a similar relationship for any foreign country (Japan in our previous example):

$$r_{n,f} = [(1 + r_{r,f})(1 + i_f)] - 1 = r_{r,f} + (i_f)(r_{rf}) + i_f \qquad \text{(12-13b)}$$

The international version of the Fisher model prescribes that real returns will be equalized across countries through arbitrage—that is,

$$r_{r,h} = r_{r,f}$$

Solving for the real rates of interest in (1a) and (1b) and equating the results produces the international version of the Fisher model—that is,

$$r_{n,h} - (i_h)(r_{r,h}) - i_h = r_{n,f} - (i_f)(r_{r,f}) - i_f \qquad \text{(12-14)}$$

For simplicity analysts frequently ignore the intermediate product terms on both sides of equation (3) such that equation (2) reduces to the following:

$$r_{n,h} - i_h = r_{n,f} - i_f$$

Rearranging terms, we get the following relationship between nominal interest rates in the domestic and foreign country and the differences in anticipated inflation in the two countries:

$$r_{n,h} - r_{n,f} = i_h - i_f \qquad \text{(12-15)}$$

Thus differences in observed nominal rates of interest should equal differences in the expected rates of inflation between the two countries. This means that when we compare the interest rates for similar loans in two countries and they are not the same, we should immediately suspect that the expected rates of inflation for the two economies differs by an amount roughly equal to the interest rate differential.

Interest Rates and Currency Exchange Rates: Interest Rate Parity

Economists have formalized the relationship between interest rates of different countries in the interest rate parity theorem. This theorem is as follows:

$$\frac{(1 + r_{n,h})}{(1 + r_{n,f})} = \frac{E_1}{E_0} \qquad \text{(12-16)}$$

where $r_{n,h}$ is the domestic one-period rate of interest, $r_{n,f}$ is the corresponding rate of interest in a foreign country and the E_j are exchange rates corresponding to the current period (i.e., the spot rate, E_0) and one-period hence (i.e., the one-period forward rate, E_1).

Tying Incentive Compensation to Economic Value Added

In the following excerpts from company press releases, annual reports, proxy statements, and publications we see evidence of the age-old adage, "What you measure and reward gets done." Specifically, these companies explicitly tie company incentive compensation to the creation of shareholder value as measured by EVA. Note that because EVA is a single–period of performance metric, many firms do not pay out the full EVA bonus in a single payment, but rather pay it into a bonus bank that gets paid out over several years. This payment practice is designed to encourage long-term value creation (i.e., multiple-year positive improvements in EVA) and to discourage gaming by managers that would increase one year's EVA at the expense of future years' EVA.

MATTHEWS INTERNATIONAL CORPORATION (TWO NORTHSHORE CENTER, PITTSBURGH, PA 15212-5851)

Annual incentive payments paid to officers in 1998 were based upon the improvement in economic value added over the prior two years' base. Economic value added is defined for this purpose as operating profit less associated capital costs of operating assets.

The incentive pools are determined based upon a percentage of absolute economic value added plus a percentage of the incremental economic value added over a two-year base. The incentive pools are distributed to individuals based upon each participant's target incentive and performance relative to achievement of personal goals.

Earned incentive awards that exceed target levels are deferred and paid in the subsequent two fiscal years. In 1998, certain executive officers received a payout of fifty percent of incentive reward amounts earned and deferred from fiscal 1997. The remaining fifty percent is payable in 1999. In fiscal 1998, certain executive officers earned incentive awards in excess of target levels. Amounts in excess of target have been deferred and are payable contingent upon economic value added performance and continued employment during fiscal 1999 and fiscal 2000. (*1999 Matthews International Corporation Notice of Annual Meeting and Proxy Statement*, pp. 24–25)

SPX CORPORATION (700 TERRACE POINT DRIVE, MUSKEGON, MI 49443)

In an EVA incentive compensation plan, managers and shareholders face similar risks. With EVA, compensation is tied to meeting investor expectations, not to meeting plan or budget. By disconnecting incentive compensation from planning and budgeting, and connecting it to investor expectations, managers focus on creating value, and not on negotiating performance targets.

Our EVA incentive compensation plan rewards managers only for continuous permanent improvement in EVA; failure to do so inflicts a cost. Meeting the EVA improvement target equates to meeting investor expectations and results in a competitive bonus. Exceeding the EVA improvement target results in a higher than competitive bonus. And falling short of the EVA improvement target produces a bonus that is less than competitive and can even be negative. Two-thirds of all bonuses above target are set aside in a "bonus bank," which is carried forward, payable only upon achieving EVA targets in subsequent years. Managers must earn back any negative bonuses accumulated in the bank before any bonus payment can be made.

The EVA incentive system simulates long-term ownership by tying bonuses to improvements in EVA over time. EVA improvement targets have been set for the next four years to provide strong incentives for management to increase long-term investor value.

The strong correlation between changes in EVA and in market value also means that the EVA compensation system is effectively "self-financing." That is, managers win only when the shareholders are winning. (*1995 SPX Annual Report*, p. 5)

BALL CORPORATION (345 SOUTH HIGH STREET, P.O. BOX 2407, MUNCIE, IN 47307-0407)

Effective January 1, 1992, the Corporation has established a new incentive compensation plan, entitled the "Ball Corporation 1992 Economic Value Added Incentive Compensation Plan for Key Members of Management." Referred to as the EVA Plan, it applies to all officers and key employees. The EVA Plan establishes a direct link between incentive compensation and the return earned on capital relative to a minimum required rate of return and historic actual performance. The EVA Plan establishes a specific target incentive amount for each participant based on a percentage of salary. (Ball Corporation *Notice of Annual Meeting and Proxy Statement*, 1992)

To illustrate, let's consider the previous example where the domestic one-period interest rate $(r_{n,b})$ is 15.5 percent, the Japanese rate of interest $(r_{n,f})$ is 5 percent, the spot exchange ratio (E_0) is \$1 to 1 yen and the forward exchange rate (E_1) is \$1.10 to 1 yen. Substituting into equation (1) produces the following result:

$$\frac{(1 + .155)}{(1 + .05)} = \frac{1.1}{1} = 1.10$$

The key thing to note here is that nominal interest rates are tied to exchange rates, and, as we learned earlier, differences in nominal rates of interest are tied to expected rates of inflation.

Why would we expect the interest rate parity relationship to hold? The answer lies in the greed of investors who stand ready to engage in arbitrage (trading) to enforce this relationship (within the bounds of transaction costs). Formally, we rely on the fundamental dictum of an efficient market (the law of one price). Very simply, the exchange-adjusted prices of identical loans must be within transaction costs of equality or the opportunity exists for traders to buy the low cost loan and sell the higher priced loan for a profit.

SUMMARY

The cost capital: definitions and concepts

Objective 1

We opened our discussion of this chapter by discussing the investment opportunity facing Encore, Inc. The investment required that the firm invest \$75 million to renovate a production facility that will provide after-tax savings to the firm of \$25 million per year over the next 5 years. In Chapter 9, we learned that the proper way to evaluate whether or not to undertake the investment involves calculating its net present value (NPV). To calculate NPV, we must estimate both project cash flows and an appropriate discount rate. In this chapter, we have learned that the proper discount rate is a weighted average of the after-tax costs of all the firm's sources of financing. In addition, we have learned that the cost of capital for any source of financing is estimated by first calculating the investor's required rate of return, then making appropriate adjustments for flotation costs and corporate taxes (where appropriate). If Encore's weighted average cost of capital is 10 percent, then the NPV of the plant renovation is \$4,250 and the investment should be made. The reason is that the project is expected to increase the wealth of Encore's shareholders by \$4,250. Very simply, the project is expected to return a present value amount of \$4,250 more than Encore's sources of capital require, and because the common stockholders get any residual value left after returning the promised return to each of the other sources of capital, they receive the NPV.

Determining individual costs of capital

Objective 2

To calculate the after-tax cost of debt capital, we must first calculate the before-tax cost of debt capital using the following formula:

$$NP_d = \sum_{t=1}^{n} \frac{\$I_t}{(1 + k_d)^t} + \frac{\$M}{(1 + k_d)^n} \qquad (12\text{--}2)$$

where NP_d = the net proceeds received by the firm from the sale of each bond

$\$I_t$ = the dollar amount of interest paid to the investor in period t for each bond

$\$M$ = the maturity value of each bond paid in period n

k_d = the before-tax cost of debt to the firm

n = the number of periods to maturity

Next, we adjust for the effects of corporate taxes because the bond interest is deducted from the firm's taxable income.

$$\text{after-tax cost of debt} = k_d(1 - \text{corporate tax rate})$$

The cost of preferred stock is relatively easy to calculate. Below we calculate the dividend yield on the preferred issue using net proceeds from the sale of each new share as follows:

$$\text{cost of preferred stock } (k_{ps}) = \frac{\text{preferred stock dividend}}{\text{net proceeds per preferred share}} \quad \text{(12–5)}$$

Note that no adjustment is made for corporate taxes because preferred stock dividends, unlike bond interest, are paid with after-tax earnings.

Common equity can be obtained by the firm in one of two ways. First, the firm can retain a portion of its net income after paying common dividends. The retention of earnings constitutes a means of raising common-equity financing internally—that is, no capital market issuance of securities is involved. Second, the firm can also raise equity capital through the sale of a new issue of common stock.

We discussed two methods for estimating the cost of common equity. The first involved using the dividend growth model:

$$k_{cs} = \frac{D_1}{P_{cs}} + g \quad \text{(12–7)}$$

where g is the rate at which dividends are expected to grow forever, k_{cs} is the investor's required rate of return, and P_{cs} is the current price of a share of common stock. When a new issue of common shares is issued, the firm incurs flotation costs. These costs reduce the amount of funds the firm receives per share. Consequently, the cost of external common equity using the dividend growth model requires that we substitute the net proceeds per share, NP_{cs}, for share price:

$$k_{ncs} = \frac{D_1}{NP_{cs}} + g \quad \text{(12–8)}$$

The second method for estimating the cost of common equity involves the use of capital asset pricing model (CAPM), which we first discussed in Chapter 9. There we learned that the CAPM provides a basis for evaluating investor's required rates of return on common equity, k_c, using three variables:

1. the risk-free rate, k_{rf},
2. the systematic risk of the common stock's returns relative to the market as a whole or the stock's beta coefficient, β; and
3. the market risk premium which is equal to the difference in the expected rate of return for the market as a whole—that is, the expected rate of return for the "average security" minus the risk-free rate, $k_m - k_{rf}$.

The CAPM is written as follows:

$$k_c = k_{rf} + \beta(k_m - k_{rf}) \quad \text{(12–9)}$$

We found that all of the variables on the right side of equation (12–9) could be obtained from public sources for larger, publicly traded firms. However, for non–publicly traded firms, the CAPM is more difficult to apply in the estimation of investor-required rates of return.

Objective 3

The weighted average cost of capital

The firm's weighted average cost of capital, k_{wacc}, can be defined as follows:

$$k_{wacc} = w_d\, k_d(1 - T_c) + w_{ps}\, k_{ps} + w_{cs}k_{cs} + w_{ncs}k_{ncs} \quad \text{(12–10)}$$

where the w terms represent the market value weights associated with the firm's use of each of its sources of financing. Note that we are simply calculating a weighted average of the costs of each of the firm's sources of capital where the weights reflect the firm's relative use of each source.

The weights used to calculate k_{wacc} should theoretically reflect the market values of each capital source as a fraction of the total market value of all capital sources (i.e., the market value of the firm). However, the analyst frequently finds the use of market value weights is impractical, either because the firm's securities are not publicly traded or because all capital sources are not used in proportion to their makeup of the firm's target capital structure in every financing episode. In these instances, we found that the weights should be the firm's long-term target financial mix.

Calculating divisional costs of capital and using a firm's cost of capital to evaluate new investments

Objectives 4, 5

The firm's weighted average cost of capital will reflect the operating or business risk of the firm's present set of investments and the financial risk attendant upon the way in which those assets are financed. Therefore, this cost of capital estimate is useful only for evaluating new investment opportunities that have similar business and financial risks. Remember that the primary determinant of the cost of capital for a particular investment is the risk of the investment itself, not the source of the capital. Multidivision firms such as PepsiCo resolve this problem by calculating a different cost of capital for each of their major operating divisions.

Shareholder value-based management

Objective 6

How can we tell whether a firm's management is creating or destroying wealth? We found that a very common-sense measure known as market value added, or MVA, can be used for this purpose. MVA is simply the difference in the market value of the firm's securities (debt and equity) and the sum total of the funds that have been invested in the firm since its creation. If the market value of the firm's investments exceeds the total capital invested in the firm, then shareholder wealth has been created to the extent of this difference. Likewise, where the difference is negative, then shareholder wealth has been destroyed.

MVA measures the total shareholder wealth created by the firm at a particular point in time. How do we know whether shareholder wealth was created last year or last month? The answer is found in calculating the firm's economic profit, defined as follows:

$$\text{economic profit} = \begin{pmatrix} \text{net operating} \\ \text{profit after-tax} \\ \text{(NOPAT)} \end{pmatrix} - \begin{pmatrix} \text{invested} \\ \text{capital} \end{pmatrix} \times \begin{pmatrix} \text{cost of} \\ \text{capital} \end{pmatrix} \quad \text{(12-11)}$$

Thus a firm's management has successfully created shareholder wealth when its after-tax net operating profits are sufficient to cover the opportunity cost of its invested capital.

Firms are increasingly using the concept of economic profit to link employee compensation to shareholder interests. The following general model can be used for this purpose:

$$\begin{matrix} \text{incentive} \\ \text{compensation} \end{matrix} = \text{base pay} \times \begin{matrix} \text{percent} \\ \text{incentive} \\ \text{compensation} \end{matrix} \times \frac{\text{actual economic profit}}{\text{target economic profit}} \quad \text{(12-12)}$$

If the firm manages to earn higher economic profits than was targeted for the period, then employee incentive compensation rises. Similarly, higher economic profits lead to greater shareholder value being created.

Calculating equivalent interest rates between countries

Objective 7

If borrowers and lenders can freely choose where they borrow and lend money, why aren't interest rates the same all over the world? The answer lies in differences in the anticipated rates of inflation between countries. In fact, the international Fisher Effect states that the differences in the rates of interest charged for the same loan in two different countries is equal to the difference in the anticipated rates of inflation in the countries. So, rates of interest are equal around the world only after we account for differences in rates of inflation between countries. Of course, the international Fisher Effect does not hold exactly due to political and other risk considerations that can serve to restrict capital flow between countries. However, the Fisher Effect does provide a useful starting point for understanding why there are differences in interest rates throughout the world.

Cost of Capital   391

capital asset pricing model, 369

capital structure, 372

economic profit, 384

financial policy, 364

flotation costs, 363

investor's required rate of return, 363

market value added, 382

weighted average cost of capital, 364

STUDY QUESTIONS

12-1 Define the term *cost of capital.*

12-2 Why do we calculate a firm's weighted average cost of capital?

12-3 In computing the cost of capital, which sources of capital do we consider?

12-4 How does a firm's tax rate affect its cost of capital? What is the effect of the flotation costs associated with a new security issue?

12-5 **a.** Distinguish between internal common equity and new common stock.
b. Why is a cost associated with internal common equity?
c. Describe the two approaches that could be used in computing the cost of common equity.

12-6 What might we expect to see in practice in the relative costs of different sources of capital?

SELF-TEST PROBLEMS

ST-1 *(Individual or Component Costs of Capital)* Compute the cost for the following sources of financing:
a. A $1,000 par value bond with a market price of $970 and a coupon interest rate of 10 percent. Flotation costs for a new issue would be approximately 5 percent. The bonds mature in 10 years and the corporate tax rate is 34 percent.
b. A preferred stock selling for $100 with an annual dividend payment of $8. If the company sells a new issue, the flotation cost will be $9 per share. The company's marginal tax rate is 30 percent.
c. Internally generated common stock totaling $4.8 million. The price of the common stock is $75 per share, and the dividend per share was $9.80 last year. The dividend is not expected to change in the future.
d. New common stock where the most recent dividend was $2.80. The company's dividends per share should continue to increase at an 8-percent growth rate into the indefinite future. The market price of the stock is currently $53; however, flotation costs of $6 per share are expected if the new stock is issued.

ST-2 *(Weighted Average Cost of Capital)* The capital structure for the Carion Corporation is provided below. The company plans to maintain its debt structure in the future. If the firm has a 5.5-percent after-tax cost of debt, a 13.5-percent cost of preferred stock, and an 18-percent cost of common stock, what is the firm's weighted average cost of capital?

CAPITAL STRUCTURE ($000)	
Bonds	$1,083
Preferred stock	268
Common stock	3,681
	$5,032

12-1 *(Individual or Component Costs of Capital)* Compute the cost of the following:

   a. A bond that has a $1,000 par value (face value) and a contract or coupon interest rate of 11 percent. A new issue would have a flotation cost of 5 percent of the $1,125 market value. The bonds mature in 10 years. The firm's average tax rate is 30 percent and its marginal tax rate is 34 percent.

   b. A new common stock issue that paid a $1.80 dividend last year. The par value of the stock is $15, and earnings per share have grown at a rate of 7 percent per year. This growth rate is expected to continue into the foreseeable future. The company maintains a constant dividend-earnings ratio of 30 percent. The price of this stock is now $27.50, but 5-percent flotation costs are anticipated.

   c. Internal common equity where the current market price of the common stock is $43. The expected dividend this coming year should be $3.50, increasing thereafter at a 7-percent annual growth rate. The corporation's tax rate is 34 percent.

   d. A preferred stock paying a 9-percent dividend on a $150 par value. If a new issue is offered, flotation costs will be 12 percent of the current price of $175.

   e. A bond selling to yield 12 percent after flotation costs, but before adjusting for the marginal corporate tax rate of 34 percent. In other words, 12 percent is the rate that equates the net proceeds from the bond with the present value of the future cash flows (principal and interest).

12-2 *(Individual or Component Costs of Capital)* Compute the cost of the following:

   a. A bond selling to yield 8 percent after flotation costs, but before adjusting for the marginal corporate tax rate of 34 percent. In other words, 8 percent is the rate that equates the net proceeds from the bond with the present value of the future cash flows (principal and interest).

   b. A new common stock issue that paid a $1.05 dividend last year. The par value of the stock is $2, and the earnings per share have grown at a rate of 5 percent per year. This growth rate is expected to continue into the foreseeable future. The company maintains a constant dividend-earnings ratio of 40 percent. The price of this stock is now $25, but 9-percent flotation costs are anticipated.

   c. A bond that has a $1,000 par value and a contract or coupon interest rate of 12 percent. A new issue would net the company 90 percent of the $1,150 market value. The bonds mature in 20 years, the firm's average tax rate is 30 percent, and its marginal tax rate is 34 percent.

   d. A preferred stock paying a 7-percent dividend on a $100 par value. If a new issue is offered, the company can expect to net $85 per share.

   e. Internal common equity where the current market price of the common stock is $38. The expected dividend this forthcoming year should be $3, increasing thereafter at a 4-percent annual growth rate. The corporation's tax rate is 34 percent.

12-3 *(Cost of Equity)* Salte Corporation is issuing new common stock at a market price of $27. Dividends last year were $1.45 and are expected to grow at an annual rate of 6 percent forever. Flotation costs will be 6 percent of market price. What is Salte's cost of equity?

12-4 *(Cost of Debt)* Belton is issuing a $1,000 par value bond that pays 7 percent annual interest and matures in 15 years. Investors are willing to pay $958 for the bond. Flotation costs will be 11 percent of market value. The company is in an 18-percent tax bracket. What will be the firm's after-tax cost of debt on the bond?

12-5 *(Cost of Preferred Stock)* The preferred stock of Walter Industries sells for $36 and pays $2.50 in dividends. The net price of the security after issuance costs is $32.50. What is the cost of capital for the preferred stock?

12-6 *(Cost of Debt)* The Zephyr Corporation is contemplating a new investment to be financed 33 percent from debt. The firm could sell new $1,000 par value bonds at a net price of $945. The coupon interest rate is 12 percent, and the bonds would mature in 15 years. If the company is in a 34-percent tax bracket, what is the after-tax cost of capital to Zephyr for bonds?

12-7 *(Cost of Preferred Stock)* Your firm is planning to issue preferred stock. The stock sells for $115; however, if new stock is issued, the company would receive only $98. The par value of the stock is $100 and the dividend rate is 14 percent. What is the cost of capital for the stock to your firm?

12-8 *(Cost of Internal Equity)* Pathos Co.'s common stock is currently selling for $21.50. Dividends paid last year were $.70. Flotation costs on issuing stock will be 10 percent of market price. The dividends and earnings per share are projected to have an annual growth rate of 15 percent. What is the cost of internal common equity for Pathos?

12-9 *(Cost of Equity)* The common stock for the Bestsold Corporation sells for $58. If a new issue is sold, the flotation costs are estimated to be 8 percent. The company pays 50 percent of its earnings in dividends, and a $4 dividend was recently paid. Earnings per share 5 years ago were $5. Earnings are expected to continue to grow at the same annual rate in the future as during the past 5 years. The firm's marginal tax rate is 34 percent. Calculate the cost of (a) internal common and (b) external common.

12-10 *(Cost of Debt)* Sincere Stationery Corporation needs to raise $500,000 to improve its manufacturing plant. It has decided to issue a $1,000 par value bond with a 14 percent annual coupon rate and a 10-year maturity. The investors require a 9-percent rate of return.
  a. Compute the market value of the bonds.
  b. What will the net price be if flotation costs are 10.5 percent of the market price?
  c. How many bonds will the firm have to issue to receive the needed funds?
  d. What is the firm's after-tax cost of debt if its average tax rate is 25 percent and its marginal tax rate is 34 percent?

12-11 *(Cost of Debt)*
  a. Rework problem 12-10 as follows: assume a 10-percent coupon rate. What effect does changing the coupon rate have on the firm's after-tax cost of capital?
  b. Why is there a change?

12-12 *(Economic profit)* The following table below contains the firm market value (sum of debt and equity), invested capital, cost of capital, and return on invested capital for three prominent firms measured at year-end 1997:

	MARKET VALUE ($ MILLIONS)	INVESTED CAPITAL ($ MILLIONS)	NET OPERATING PROFIT AFTER TAX (NOPAT)	COST OF CAPITAL (k_{wacc}) (%)
Wal-Mart Stores	103,568.00	33,890.00	4,578.54	10.55
Walt Disney	79,576.00	32,707.00	2,956.71	12.00
Novell	1,884.00	1,895.00	(28.05)	12.51

  a. Based on the data presented here, which of these firms created value for its stockholders during 1997 based on their economic profit?
  b. What is the MVA for each of these firms and what does it tell you about the firm's success or failure to create wealth for its stockholders?

12-13 *(Incentive Compensation)* The Navasar Manufacturing Company is implementing a new incentive compensation program for its top four executives that puts a portion of each executive's compensation "at risk" as an incentive to improve their performance on the job. The chief financial officer is now estimating the total compensation (base pay plus the incentive portion) for each of these executives in an effort to determine whether the total is reasonable given the historical compensation paid to them. The following table contains the necessary information for evaluating compensation under the proposed plan, as well as the total compensation paid to each executive during the last calendar year:

EMPLOYEE TITLE	LAST YEAR'S COMPENSATION	% INCENTIVE PAY	Proposed TARGET PERFORMANCE	BASE COMPENSATION
Chief Executive Officer	$750,000	90%	$5,000,000	$ 75,000
Chief Operating Officer	500,000	80%	5,000,000	100,000
Chief Financial Officer	425,000	50%	5,000,000	212,500
Controller	275,000	30%	5,000,000	192,500

a. Calculate incentive and total compensation that will be paid to each of these officers of the firm when actual firm performance is 80%, 100%, and 120% of targeted performance. To calculate incentive pay use the following relationship:

$$\frac{\text{incentive}}{\text{compensation}} = \text{base pay} \times \left(\begin{array}{c} \text{percent} \\ \text{incentive} \\ \text{compensation} \end{array} \right) \times \left(\frac{\text{actual performance}}{\text{target performance}} \right)$$

b. The chief financial officer is also considering a recommendation that incentive compensation be capped based upon the firm's performance. For example, incentive pay would only begin when the firm's actual performance reaches 60% of target performance and no additional incentive compensation would be paid once actual performance passed 150% of target performance. Under this plan, what is the minimum and maximum compensation that would be paid to each of the officers?

12-14 (*Divisional Costs of Capital*) HPH, Inc. is an integrated oil company headquartered in Houston, Texas. The company has three operating divisions: oil exploration and production (commonly referred to as E&P), pipelines, and refining. Historically, HPH had not spent a great deal of time thinking about the opportunity costs of capital for each of its divisions and had used a company-wide weighted average cost of capital of 14% for all new capital investment projects. Recent changes in its businesses have made it abundantly clear to HPH's management that is not a reasonable approach. For example, investors demand a much higher expected rate of return for exploration and production ventures than they do for pipeline investment. Although HPH's management agrees, in principle at least, that different operating divisions should face an opportunity cost of capital that reflects their individual risk characteristics, they are not in agreement as to whether a move toward divisional costs of capital is a good idea based on practical considerations.

a. Pete Jennings is the chief operating officer for the E&P division, and he is concerned that going to a system of divisional costs of capital may restrain his ability to undertake very promising exploration opportunities. He argued that the firm really should be concerned about finding those opportunities that offer the highest possible rate of return on invested capital. Pete contended that using the firm's scarce capital to take on the most promising projects would lead to the greatest increase in shareholder value. Do you agree with Pete? Why or why not?

b. The pipeline division manager, Donna Selma, had long argued that charging her division the company-wide cost of capital of 14% severely penalized her opportunities to increase shareholder value. Do you agree with Donna? Explain.

c. "There is also the matter of the firm's EVA-based incentive compensation system," remarked Bill Simon, the firm's CEO. "If we move to divisional opportunity costs of capital, it seems to me that we should also define the divisional EVAs using a different cost of capital for each operating division." This, Bill contends, might make it seem as if the managers in the less risky divisions (those that carried a lower cost of capital) would have an easier time earning EVA-based bonuses. Is Bill correct in his contention that the firm will have to move toward the use of multiple EVA formulas in which the cost of capital varies across divisions?

The capital structure for Nealon, Inc., follows. Flotation costs are (a) 15 percent of market value for a new bond issue, (b) $1.21 per share for common stock, and (c) $2.01 per share for preferred stock. The dividends for common stock were $2.50 last year and are projected to have an annual grown rate of 6 percent. The firm is in a 34-percent tax bracket. What is the weighted average cost of capital if the firm finances are in the following proportions?

NEALON, INC., BALANCE SHEET

TYPE OF FINANCING	PERCENTAGE OF FUTURE FINANCING
Bonds (8%, $1,000 par, 16-year maturity)	38%
Preferred stock (5,000 shares outstanding, $50 par, $1.50 dividend)	15%
Common equity	47%
Total	100%

Market prices are $1,035 for bonds, $19 for preferred stock, and $35 for common stock. There will be sufficient internal common equity funding (i.e., retained earnings) available such that the firm does not plan to issue new common stock.

SELF-TEST SOLUTIONS

The following notations are used in this group of problems:

k_d = the before-tax cost of debt
k_{ps} = the cost of preferred stock
k_{cs} = the cost of internal common stock
k_{ncs} = the cost of new common stock
t = the marginal tax rate
D_t = the dollar dividend per share, where D_0 is the most recently paid dividend and D_1 is the forthcoming dividend
P_0 = the value (present value) of a security
NP_0 = the value of a security less any flotation costs incurred in issuing the security

SS-1

a. $\$921.50 = \sum_{t=1}^{n} \dfrac{\$100}{(1 + k_d)^t} + \dfrac{\$1,000}{(1 + k_d)^{10}}$

RATE	VALUE		
11%	$940.90	} $19.40	
k_d%	$921.50		} $53.90
12%	$887.00		

$$k_d = 0.11 + \left(\frac{\$19.40}{\$53.90} \right) 0.01 = .1136 = 11.36\%$$

$$k_{d\,(1\,-\,t)} = 11.36\% \,(1 - 0.34) = 7.50\%$$

b. $k_{ps} = \dfrac{D}{NP_0}$

$$k_{ps} = \frac{\$8}{\$100 - \$9} = .0879 = 8.79\%$$

c. $k_{cs} = \dfrac{D_1}{P_0} + g$

$$k_{cs} = \frac{\$9.80}{\$75} + 0\% = .1307 = 13.07\%$$

d. $k_{ncs} = \dfrac{D_1}{NP_0} + g$

$$k_{ncs} = \frac{\$2.80(1 + 0.08)}{\$53 - \$6} + 0.08 = .1443 = 14.43\%$$

SS-2

Carion Corporation—Weighted Cost of Capital

	CAPITAL STRUCTURE	WEIGHTS	INDIVIDUAL COSTS	WEIGHTED COSTS
Bonds	$1,083	0.2152	5.5%	1.18%
Preferred stock	268	0.0533	13.5%	0.72%
Common stock	3,681	0.7315	18.0%	13.17%
	$5,032	1.0000		15.07%

Business and Financial Risk • Break-Even
Analysis • Operating Leverage • Financial
Leverage • Combination of Operating and
Financial Leverage • Planning the Financing
Mix • A Quick Look at Capital Structure Theory
• Basic Tools of Capital Structure Management
• A Glance at Actual Capital Structure
Management • Finance and the Multinational
Firm: Business Risk and Global Sales

DETERMINING THE FINANCING MIX

LEARNING OBJECTIVES

AFTER READING THIS CHAPTER, YOU SHOULD BE ABLE TO:

1. Understand the difference between business risk and financial risk.
2. Use the technique of break-even analysis in a variety of analytical settings.
3. Distinguish among the financial concepts of operating leverage, financial leverage, and combined leverage.
4. Calculate the firm's degree of operating leverage, financial leverage, and combined leverage.
5. Understand the concept of an optimal capital structure.
6. Explain the main underpinnings of capital structure theory.
7. Understand and be able to graph the moderate position on capital structure importance.
8. Incorporate the concepts of agency costs and free cash flow into a discussion on capital structure management.
9. Use the basic tools of capital structure management.
10. Understand how business risk and global sales impact the multinational firm.

In 1997, the Coca-Cola Company posted only a moderate sales increase of 1.7 percent over the level of reported sales for 1996. The firm's change in net income, however, rose by a pleasant 18.2 percent over the same 1-year period. Thus the relative change in net income was 10.7 times the relative fluctuation in sales (i.e., 18.2 percent/1.7 percent). Such disparity in the relationship between sales fluctuations and net income fluctuations is not peculiar to Coca-Cola.

Consider that in 1993 Phillips Petroleum saw its sales rise by only 3.2 percent, yet its net income rose by a whopping 35 percent. Further, in 1998 Home Depot enjoyed a 25.1 percent sales rise while its net income increased by a larger 39.1 percent.

We know that sales fluctuations are not always in the positive direction. International business conditions affected Coca-Cola's sales during 1998 and the company endured a 0.3 percent contraction in revenues. Importantly, Coke's net income contracted by a larger and more painful 14.4 percent.

What is it about the nature of business that causes changes in sales revenues to translate into larger variations in net income and finally the earnings available to the common shareholders? It would actually be a good planning tool for management to be able to decompose such fluctuations into those policies associated with the operating side of the business as distinct from those policies associated with the financing side of the business.

WHAT'S AHEAD

Our work in Chapters 7, 8, 9, and 12 allowed us to develop an understanding of how financial assets are valued in the marketplace. Drawing on the tenets of valuation theory, we presented various approaches to measuring the cost of funds to the business organization. This chapter presents concepts that relate to the valuation process and the cost of capital; it also discusses the crucial problem of planning the firm's financing mix.

The cost of capital provides a direct link between the formulation of the firm's asset structure and its financial structure. This is illustrated in Figure 13–1. Recall that the cost of capital is a basic input to the time-adjusted capital-budgeting models. It therefore affects the capital-budgeting, or asset-selection, process. The cost of capital is affected, in turn, by the composition of the right-hand side of the firm's balance sheet—that is, its financial structure.

This chapter examines tools that can be useful aids to the financial manager in determining the firm's proper financial structure. First, we review the technique of break-even analysis, which provides the foundation for the relationships to be highlighted in the remainder of the chapter. We then examine the concept of operating leverage, some consequences of the firm's use of financial leverage, and the impact on the firm's earnings stream when operating and financial leverage are combined in various patterns. With this foundation to effectively analyze the variability in the firm's earnings streams, we move on to a discussion of capital structure theory and the basic tools of capital structure management. Actual capital structure practices are also placed in perspective. We close with a discussion involving the multinational firm and its relationship to both the business risk concept and global sales opportunities. Our immediate tasks are to distinguish two types of risk that confront the firm and to clarify some key terminology that is used throughout this chapter.

This chapter shows you how to do just that—and more. Consider that the United States was recession free from November 1982 until July 1990. Then a general business contraction did occur that officially lasted until the end of February 1991. The nation's labor markets never regained full speed until the first half of 1994. Essentially, business enterprises were going through a once-in-a-lifetime global realignment. This time period was an essentially challenging one for many American business firms that had loaded their balance sheets with debt over the "good times."

Financial executives had to delicately manage cash flows to service existing debt contracts or face bankruptcy. These same executives had to give considerable thought as to how to finance the next (i.e., incremental) capital project.

Along these lines one company that pays explicit attention to managing its financing mix is the Georgia-Pacific Corporation. This firm is one of the world's leaders in the manufacturing and distributing of building products, pulp, and paper. The firm employs about 46,500 individuals and ranked exactly 122nd among the Fortune 500 largest domestic corporations at the end of 1998. Georgia-Pacific posted sales revenues of $13.2 billion for 1998 and possessed $11.5 billion in assets.

Georgia-Pacific's *1996 Annual Report* contained a separate section on "Financial Strategy." On that subject, the management of the firm said: "Georgia-Pacific's objective is to provide superior returns to our shareholders. To achieve this goal, our financial strategy must complement our operating strategy. We must maintain a capital structure that mini-

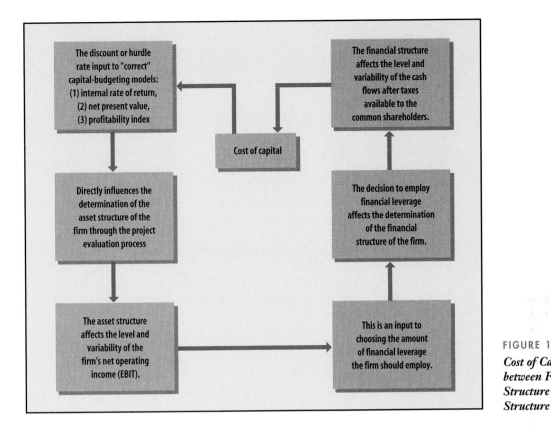

FIGURE 13-1

Cost of Capital As a Link between Firm's Asset Structure and Financial Structure

mizes our cost of capital while providing flexibility in financing our capital (expenditure) requirements."

If you understand the material and analytical processes in this chapter, you will be able to make positive contributions to company strategies that deal with the firm's financing mix. You will be able to formulate a defensible answer to the question, Should we finance the next capital project with a new issue of bonds or a new issue of common stock? You can also help a lot of firms avoid making serious financial errors, the consequences of which last for several years, because financing decisions typically impact the firm for several years.

BUSINESS AND FINANCIAL RISK

Objective 1

In studying capital-budgeting techniques we referred to **risk** as the *likely variability associated with expected revenue or income streams.* Because our attention is now focused on the firm's financing decision rather than its investment decision, it is useful to separate the income stream variations attributable to (1) the company's exposure to business risk and (2) its decision to incur financial risk.

risk

Business risk refers to the *relative dispersion (variability) in the firm's expected earnings before interest and taxes* **(EBIT)**[1] Figure 13–2 shows a subjectively estimated probability distribution of net year's EBIT for the Pierce Grain Company and the

business risk

---

[1]If what accountants call "other income" and "other expenses" are equal to zero, then EBIT is equal to net operating income. These terms are used interchangeably.

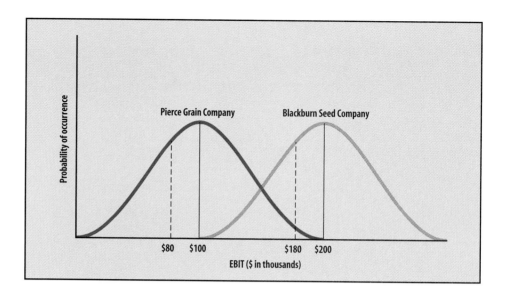

FIGURE 13–2
Subjective Probability Distribution of Next Year's EBIT

same type of projection for Pierce's larger competitor, the Blackburn Seed Company. The expected value of EBIT for Pierce is $100,000, with an associated standard deviation of $20,000. If next year's EBIT for Pierce fell one standard deviation short of the expected $100,000, the actual EBIT would equal $80,000. Blackburn's expected EBIT is $200,000, and the size of the associated standard deviation is $20,000. The standard deviation for the expected level of EBIT is the same for both firms. We would say that Pierce's degree of business risk exceeds Blackburn's because of its larger coefficient of variation of expected EBIT, as follows:

$$\text{Pierce's coefficient of variation of expected } EBIT = \frac{\$20,000}{\$100,000} = .20$$

$$\text{Blackburn's coefficient of variation of expected } EBIT = \frac{\$20,000}{\$200,000} = .10$$

The relative dispersion in the firm's EBIT stream, measured here by its expected coefficient of variation, is the *residual* effect of several causal influences. Dispersion in operating income does not *cause* business risk; rather, this dispersion, which we call business risk, is the *result* of several influences. The company's cost structure, product demand characteristics and intraindustry competitive position all affect its business risk exposure. Such business risk is a direct result of the firm's investment decision. It is the firm's asset structure, after all, that gives rise to both the level and variability of its operating profits.

financial risk

Financial risk, conversely, is a direct result of the firm's financing decision. In the context of selecting a proper financing mix, this risk applies to *(1) the additional variability in earnings available to the firm's common shareholders and (2) the additional chance of insolvency borne by the common shareholder caused by the use of financial leverage.*[2]

financial leverage

Financial leverage means *financing a portion of the firm's assets with securities bearing a fixed (limited) rate of return* in hopes of increasing the ultimate return to the common stockholders. The decision to use debt or preferred stock in the financial structure of

[2]Note that the concept of financial risk used here differs from that used in our examination of cash and marketable securities management in Chapter 16.

the corporation means that those who own the common shares of the firm are exposed to financial risk. Any given level of variability in EBIT is magnified by the firm's use of financial leverage, and such additional variability is embodied in the variability of earnings available to the common stockholder and earnings per share. If these magnifications are negative, the common stockholder has a higher chance of insolvency than would have existed had the use of fixed-charge securities (debt and preferred stock) been avoided.

In the rest of this chapter we study techniques that permit a precise assessment of the earnings stream variability caused by (1) operating leverage and (2) financial leverage. **Operating leverage** refers to the *incurrence of fixed operating costs in the firm's income stream.* To understand the nature and importance of operating leverage, we need to draw on the basics of cost-volume-profit analysis, or *break-even analysis.*

operating leverage

CONCEPT CHECK

1. Explain the concept of business risk within the context of financial structure management.
2. Explain the concept of financial risk within the context of financial structure management.
3. Distinguish between financial leverage and operating leverage.

BREAK-EVEN ANALYSIS

Objective 2

The technique of break-even analysis is familiar to legions of business people. It is usefully applied in a wide array of business settings, including both small and large organizations. This tool is widely accepted by the business community for two reasons: It is based on straightforward assumptions, and companies have found that the information gained from the break-even model is beneficial in decision-making situations.

Objective and Uses

The objective of break-even analysis is to determine the break-even quantity of output by studying the relationships among the firm's cost structure, volume of output, and profit. Alternatively, the firm ascertains the break-even level of sales dollars that corresponds to the break-even quantity of output. We develop the fundamental relationships by concentrating on units of output and then extend the procedure to permit direct calculation of the break-even sales level.

What is meant by the break-even quantity of output? It is that quantity of output, denominated in units, that results in an EBIT level equal to zero. Use of the break-even model, therefore, enables the financial officer (1) to determine the quantity of output that must be sold to cover all operating costs, as distinct from financial costs, and (2) to calculate the EBIT that will be achieved at various output levels.

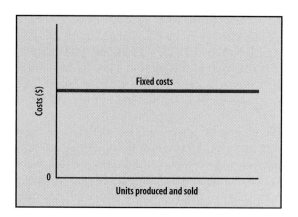

FIGURE 13-3
Fixed-Cost Behavior over Relevant Range of Output

Essential Elements of the Break-Even Model

To implement the break-even model, we must separate the production costs of the company into two mutually exclusive categories: fixed costs and variable costs. You will recall from your study of basic economics that in the long run all costs are variable. Break-even analysis, therefore, is a short-run concept.

Assumed Behavior of Costs

Fixed Costs

fixed costs
indirect costs

Fixed costs, also referred to as **indirect costs,** *do not vary in total amount as sales volume or the quantity of output changes* over some relevant range of output. Total fixed costs are independent of the quantity of product produced and equal some constant dollar amount. As production volume increases, fixed cost per unit of product falls, as fixed costs are spread over larger and larger quantities of output. Figure 13–3 graphs the behavior of total fixed costs with respect to the company's relevant range of output. This total is shown to be unaffected by the quantity of product that is manufactured and sold. Over some other relevant output range, the amount of total fixed costs might be higher or lower for the same company.

In a manufacturing setting, some specific examples of fixed costs are

1. Administrative salaries
2. Depreciation
3. Insurance
4. Lump sums spent on intermittent advertising programs
5. Property taxes
6. Rent

Variable Costs

variable costs
direct costs

Variable costs are sometimes referred to as **direct costs.** Variable costs are *fixed per unit of output but vary in total as output changes.* Total variable costs are computed by taking the variable cost per unit and multiplying it by the quantity produced and sold. The break-even model assumes proportionality between total variable costs and sales. Thus, if sales rise by 10 percent, it is assumed that variable costs will rise by 10 percent. Figure 13–4 graphs the behavior of total variable costs with respect to the company's relevant range of output. Total variable costs are seen to depend on the quantity of product that is manufactured and sold. Notice that if zero units of the product are manufactured, then variable costs are zero, but fixed costs are greater

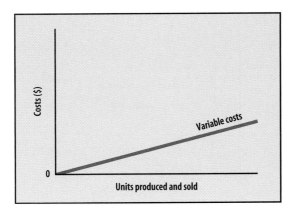

FIGURE 13-4

Variable-Cost Behavior over Relevant Range of Output

than zero. This implies that some contribution to the coverage of fixed costs occurs as long as the selling price per unit exceeds the variable costs per unit. This helps explain why some firms will operate a plant even when sales are temporarily depressed—that is, to provide some increment of revenue toward the coverage of fixed costs.

For a manufacturing operation, some examples of variable costs include

1. Direct labor
2. Direct materials
3. Energy costs (fuel, electricity, natural gas) associated with the production area
4. Freight costs for products leaving the plant
5. Packaging
6. Sales commissions

More on Behavior of Costs

No one really believes that *all* costs behave as neatly as we have illustrated the fixed and variable costs in Figures 13–3 and 13–4. Nor does any law or accounting principle dictate that a certain element of the firm's total costs always be classified as fixed or variable. This depends on each firm's specific circumstances. In one firm energy costs may be predominantly fixed, whereas in another they may vary with output.[3]

Furthermore, some costs may be fixed for a while, then rise sharply to a higher level as a higher output is reached, remain fixed, and then rise again with further increases in production. Such costs may be termed either (1) *semivariable*, or (2) *semifixed*. The label is your choice, because both are used in industrial practice. An example might be the salaries paid to production supervisors. Should output be cut back by 15 percent for a short period, the management of the organization is not likely to lay off 15 percent of the supervisors. Similarly, commissions paid to salespeople often follow a stepwise pattern over wide ranges of success. This sort of cost behavior is shown in Figure 13–5.

To implement the break-even model and deal with such a complex cost structure, the financial manager must (1) identify the most relevant output range for planning purposes and then (2) approximate the cost effect of semivariable items

---

[3]In a greenhouse operation, where plants are grown (manufactured) under strictly controlled temperatures, heat costs will tend to be fixed whether the building is fully or only half full of seedlings. In a metal stamping operation, where levers are being produced, there is no need to heat the plant to as high a temperature when the machines are stopped and the workers are not there. In this latter case, the heat costs will tend to be variable.

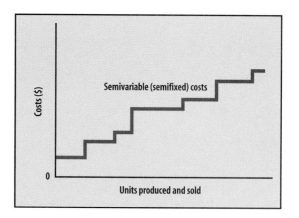

FIGURE 13-5

Semivariable Cost Behavior over the Relevant Range of Output

over this range by segregating a portion of them to fixed costs and a portion to variable costs. In the actual business setting this procedure is not fun. It is not unusual for the analyst who deals with the figures to spend considerably more time allocating costs to fixed and variable categories than in carrying out the actual break-even calculations.

Total Revenue and Volume of Output

total revenue

volume of output

Besides fixed and variable costs, the essential elements of the break-even model include total revenue from sales and volume of output. **Total revenue** means *total sales dollars* and is equal to the selling price per unit multiplied by the quantity sold. The **volume of output** refers to the *firm's level of operations* and may be *indicated either as a unit quantity or as sales dollars.*

Finding the Break-Even Point

Finding the break-even point in terms of units of production can be accomplished in several ways. All approaches require the essential elements of the break-even model just described. The break-even model is a simple adaptation of the firm's income statement expressed in the following analytical format:

$$\text{sales} - (\text{total variable cost} + \text{total fixed cost}) = \text{profit} \quad \text{(13-1)}$$

On a units-of-production basis, it is necessary to introduce (1) the price at which each unit is sold and (2) the variable cost per unit of output. Because the profit item studied in break-even analysis is EBIT, we use the acronym instead of the word "profit." In terms of units, the income statement shown in equation (13–1) becomes the break-even model by setting EBIT equal to zero:

$$\left(\begin{matrix}\text{sales price} \\ \text{per unit}\end{matrix}\right)\left(\begin{matrix}\text{units} \\ \text{sold}\end{matrix}\right) - \left[\left(\begin{matrix}\text{variable cost} \\ \text{per unit}\end{matrix}\right)\left(\begin{matrix}\text{units} \\ \text{sold}\end{matrix}\right)\right.$$
$$\left. + \left(\begin{matrix}\text{total fixed} \\ \text{cost}\end{matrix}\right)\right] = EBIT = \$0 \quad \text{(13-2)}$$

Our task now becomes finding the number of units that must be produced and sold in order to satisfy equation (13–2)—that is, to arrive at EBIT = $0. This can be done by (1) contribution margin analysis or (2) algebraic analysis. Each approach is illustrated using the same set of circumstances.

Problem Situation

Even though the Pierce Grain Company manufactures several different products, it has observed over a lengthy period that its product mix is rather constant. This allows management to conduct its financial planning by use of a "normal" sales price per unit and "normal" variable cost per unit. The "normal" sales price and variable cost per unit are calculated from the constant product mix. It is like assuming that the product mix is one big product. The selling price is $10 and the variable cost is $6. Total fixed costs for the firm are $100,000 per year. What is the break-even point in units produced and sold for the company during the coming year?

Contribution Margin Analysis

The contribution margin technique permits direct computation of the break-even quantity of output. The **contribution margin** is the *difference between the unit selling price and unit variable costs*, as follows:

contribution margin

$$
\begin{array}{rl}
& \text{unit sales price} \\
- & \underline{\text{unit variable cost}} \\
= & \underline{\text{unit contribution margin}}
\end{array}
$$

The use of the word *contribution* in the present context means contribution to the coverage of fixed operating costs. For the Pierce Grain Company, the unit contribution margin is

unit sales price	$10
unit variable cost	−6
unit contribution margin	$ 4

If the annual fixed costs of $100,000 are divided by the unit contribution margin of $4, we find the break-even quantity of output for Pierce Grain is 25,000 units. Figure 13–6 portrays the contribution-margin technique for finding the break-even point.

Algebraic Analysis

To explain the algebraic method for finding the break-even output level, we need to adopt some notation.

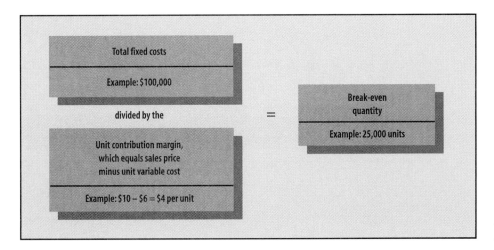

FIGURE 13–6

Contribution Margin Approach to Break-even Analysis

Let

$$Q = \text{the number of units sold}$$
$$Q_B = \text{the break-even level of } Q$$
$$P = \text{the unit sales price}$$
$$F = \text{total fixed costs anticipated over the planning period}$$
$$V = \text{the unit variable cost}$$

Equation (13–2), the break-even model, is repeated on the following pages as equation (13–2a) with the model symbols used in place of words. The break-even model is then solved for Q, the number of units that must be sold so that EBIT equals $0. We label the break-even point quantity Q_B.

$$(P \cdot Q) - [(V \cdot Q) + (F)] = EBIT = \$0$$
$$(P \cdot Q) - (V \cdot Q) - F = \$0 \qquad (13\text{–}2a)$$
$$Q(P - V) = F$$

$$Q_B = \frac{F}{P - V} \qquad (13\text{–}3)$$

Observe that equation (13–3) says: Divide total fixed operating costs, F, by the unit contribution margin, $P - V$, and the break-even level of output, Q_B, will be obtained. The contribution margin analysis is nothing more than equation (13–3) in different garb.

Application of equation (13–3) permits direct calculation of Pierce Grain's break-even point, as follows:

$$Q_B = \frac{F}{P - V} = \frac{\$100,000}{\$10 - \$6} = 25,000 \text{ units}$$

Break-Even Point in Sales Dollars

In dealing with the multiproduct firm, it is convenient to compute the break-even point in terms of sales dollars rather than units of output. Sales, in effect, become a common denominator associated with a particular product mix. Furthermore, an outside analyst may not have access to internal unit cost data. He or she may, however, be able to obtain annual reports for the firm. If the analyst can separate the firm's total costs as identified from its annual reports into their fixed and variable components, he or she can calculate a general break-even point in sales dollars.

We illustrate this procedure using the Pierce Grain Company's cost structure. Suppose that the reported financial information is arranged in the format shown in Table 13–1. We refer to this type of financial statement as an *analytical income statement*. This distinguishes it from audited income statements published, for example,

TABLE 13–1	PIERCE GRAIN COMPANY ANALYTICAL INCOME STATEMENT
Sales	$300,000
Less: Total variable costs	180,000
Revenue before fixed costs	$120,000
Less: Total fixed costs	100,000
EBIT	$ 20,000

in the annual reports of public corporations. If we are aware of the simple mathematical relationships on which cost-volume-profit analysis is based, we can use Table 13–1 to find the break-even point in sales dollars for the Pierce Grain Company.

First, let us explore the logic of the process. Recall from equation (13–1) that

$$\text{sales} - (\text{total variable cost} + \text{total fixed cost}) = EBIT$$

If we let total sales = S, total variable cost = VC, and total fixed cost = F, the preceding relationship becomes

$$S - (VC + F) = EBIT$$

Because variable cost per unit of output and selling price per unit are *assumed* constant over the relevant output range in break-even analysis, the ratio of total variable costs to sales, VC/S, is a constant for any level of sales. This permits us to rewrite the previous expression as

$$S - \left[\left(\frac{VC}{S} \right) S \right] - F = EBIT$$

and

$$S \left(1 - \frac{VC}{S} \right) - F = EBIT$$

At the break-even point, however, EBIT = 0, and the corresponding break-even level of sales can be represented as S^*. At the break-even level of sales, we have

$$S^* \left(1 - \frac{VC}{S} \right) - F = 0$$

or

$$S^* \left(1 - \frac{VC}{S} \right) = F$$

Therefore,

$$S^* = \frac{F}{1 - \dfrac{VC}{S}} \tag{13–4}$$

The application of equation (13–4) to Pierce Grain's analytical income statement in Table 13–1 permits the break-even sales level for the firm to be directly computed, as follows:

$$S^* = \frac{\$100,000}{1 - \dfrac{\$180,000}{\$300,000}}$$

$$= \frac{\$100,000}{1 - .60} = \$250,000$$

CONCEPT CHECK

1. Distinguish among fixed costs, variable costs, and semivariable costs.
2. Define the term *contribution margin*.
3. When is it useful or necessary to compute the break-even point in terms of sales dollars rather than units of output?

If *fixed* operating costs are present in the firm's cost structure, so is operating leverage. Fixed operating costs do *not* include interest charge incurred from the firm's use of debt financing. Those costs will be incorporated into the analysis when financial leverage is discussed.

So operating leverage arises from the firm's use of fixed operating costs. But what is operating leverage? *Operating leverage* is the responsiveness of the firm's EBIT to fluctuations in sales. By continuing to draw on our data for the Pierce Grain Company, we can illustrate the concept of operating leverage. Table 13–2 contains data for a study of a possible fluctuation in the firm's sales level. It is assumed that Pierce Grain is currently operating at an annual sales level of $300,000. This is referred to in the tabulation as the base sales level at t (time period zero). The question is, How will Pierce Grain's EBIT level respond to a positive 20 percent change in sales? A sales volume of $360,000, referred to as the forecast sales level at $t + 1$, reflects the 20-percent sales rise anticipated over the planning period. Assume that the planning period is 1 year.

Operating leverage relationships are derived within the mathematical assumptions of cost-volume-profit analysis. In the present example, this means that Pierce Grain's variable cost-to-sales ratio of .6 will continue to hold during time period $t + 1$, and the fixed costs will hold steady at $100,000.

Given the forecasted sales level for Pierce Grain and its cost structure, we can measure the responsiveness of EBIT to the upswing in volume. Notice in Table 13–2 that EBIT is expected to be $44,000 at the end of the planning period. The percentage change in EBIT from t to $t + 1$ can be measured as follows:

$$\text{percentage change in } EBIT = \frac{\$44,000_{t+1} - \$20,000_t}{\$20,000_t}$$

$$= \frac{\$24,000}{\$20,000}$$

$$= 120\%$$

We know that the projected fluctuation in sales amounts to 20 percent of the base period, t, sales level. This is verified below:

$$\text{percentage change in sales} = \frac{\$360,000_{t+1} - \$300,000_t}{\$300,000_t}$$

$$= \frac{\$60,000}{\$300,000}$$

$$= 20\%$$

TABLE 13–2	CONCEPT OF OPERATING LEVERAGE: INCREASE IN PIERCE GRAIN COMPANY SALES

ITEM	BASE SALES LEVEL, t	FORECAST SALES LEVEL, $t + 1$
Sales	$300,000	$360,000
Less: Total variable costs	180,000	216,000
Revenue before fixed costs	$120,000	$144,000
Less: Total fixed costs	100,000	100,000
EBIT	$ 20,000	$ 44,000

	BASE SALES	FORECAST SALES
TABLE 13-3	**CONCEPT OF OPERATING LEVERAGE: DECREASE IN PIERCE GRAIN COMPANY SALES**	

ITEM	BASE SALES LEVEL, t	FORECAST SALES LEVEL, $t+1$
Sales	$ 300,000	$ 240,000
Less: Total variable costs	180,000	144,000
Revenue before fixed costs	$ 120,000	$ 96,000
Less: Total fixed costs	100,000	100,000
EBIT	$ 20,000	$ −4,000

By relating the percentage fluctuation in EBIT to the percentage fluctuation in sales, we can calculate a specific measure of operating leverage. Thus, we have

$$\begin{matrix} \text{degree of operating} \\ \text{leverage} \\ \text{from the base sales level(s)} \end{matrix} = DOL_s = \frac{\text{percentage change in } EBIT}{\text{percentage change in sales}} \quad (13\text{–}5)$$

Applying equation (13–5) to our Pierce Grain data gives

$$DOL_{\$300,000} = \frac{120\%}{20\%} = 6 \text{ times}$$

Unless we understand what the specific measures of operating leverage tell us, the fact that we may know it is equal to six times is nothing more than sterile information. For Pierce Grain, the inference is that for *any* percentage fluctuation in sales from the base level, the percentage fluctuation in EBIT will be six times as great. If Pierce Grain expected only a 5-percent rise in sales over the coming period, a 30-percent rise in EBIT would be anticipated as follows:

$$\begin{matrix} (\text{percentage change in sales}) \times (DOL_s) = \text{percentage change in } EBIT \\ (5\%) \times (6) = 30\% \end{matrix}$$

We will now return to the postulated 20-percent change in sales. What if the direction of the fluctuation is expected to be negative rather than positive? What is in store for Pierce Grain? Unfortunately for Pierce Grain, but fortunately for the analytical process, will see that the operating leverage measure holds in the negative direction as well. This situation is displayed in Table 13–3.

At the $240,000 sales level, which represents the 20-percent decrease from the base period, Pierce Grain's EBIT is expected to be −$4,000. How sensitive is EBIT to this sales change? The magnitude of the EBIT fluctuation is calculated as

$$\text{percentage change in } EBIT = \frac{-\$4,000_{t+1} - \$20,000_t}{\$20,000_t}$$

$$= \frac{-\$24,000}{\$20,000}$$

$$= -120\%$$

Making use of our knowledge that the sales change was equal to −20 percent permits us to compute the specific measure of operating leverage as

$$DOL_{\$300,000} = \frac{-120\%}{-20\%} = 6 \text{ times}$$

What we have seen, then, is that the degree of operating leverage measure works in the positive or negative direction. A negative change in production volume and sales can be magnified severalfold when the effect on EBIT is calculated.

To this point our calculations of the degree of operating leverage have required two analytical income statements: one for the base period and a second for the subsequent period that incorporates the possible sales alteration. This cumbersome process can be simplified. If unit cost data are available to the financial manager, the relationship can be expressed directly in the following manner:

$$DOL_s = \frac{Q\,(P - V)}{Q\,(P - V) - F} \qquad (13\text{--}6)$$

Observe in equation (13–6) that the variables were all previously defined in our algebraic analysis of the break-even model. Recall that Pierce sells its product at $10 per unit, the unit variable cost is $6, and total fixed costs over the planning horizon are $100,000. Still assuming that Pierce is operating at a $300,000 sales volume, which means output (Q) is 30,000 units, we can find the degree of operating leverage by application of equation (13–6):

$$DOL_{\$300,000} = \frac{30,000\,(\$10 - \$6)}{30,000\,(\$10 - \$6) - \$100,000} = \frac{\$120,000}{\$20,000} = 6 \text{ times}$$

Whereas equation (13–6) requires us to know unit cost data to carry out the computations, the next formulation we examine does not. If we have an analytical income statement for the base period, then equation (13–7) can be employed to find the firm's degree of operating leverage:

$$DOL_s = \frac{\text{revenue before fixed costs}}{EBIT} = \frac{S - VC}{S - VC - F} \qquad (13\text{--}7)$$

Using equation (13–7) in conjunction with the base period data for Pierce Grain shown in Table 13–3 gives

$$DOL_{\$300,000} = \frac{\$120,000}{\$20,000} = 6 \text{ times}$$

The three versions of the operating leverage measure all produce the same result. Data availability will sometimes dictate which formulation can be applied. The crucial consideration, though, is that you grasp what the measurement tells you. For Pierce Grain, a 1-percent change in sales will produce a 6-percent change in EBIT.

Before we complete this discussion of operating leverage and move on to the subject of financial leverage, ask yourself, "Which type of leverage is more under the control of management?" You will probably (and correctly) come to the conclusion that the firm's managers have less control over the operating cost structure and almost complete control over its financial structure. What the firm actually produces, for example, will determine to a significant degree the division between fixed and variable costs. There is more room for substitution among the various sources of financial capital than there is among the labor and real capital inputs that enable the firm to meet its production requirements. Thus, you can anticipate more arguments over the choice to use a given degree of financial leverage than the corresponding choice over operating leverage use.

Implications

As the firm's scale of operations moves in a favorable manner above the break-even point, the degree of operating leverage at each subsequent (higher) sales base will decline. In short, the greater the sales level, the lower the degree of operating leverage. As long as some fixed operating costs are present in the firm's cost structure, however, operating leverage exists, and the degree of operating leverage (DOL$_s$) will exceed 1.00. Operating leverage is present, then, whenever the firm faces the following situation:

$$\frac{\text{percentage change in } EBIT}{\text{percentage change in sales}} > 1.00$$

The greater the firm's degree of operating leverage, the more its profits will vary with a given percentage change in sales. Thus, operating leverage is definitely an attribute of the business risk that confronts the company. We know that the degree of operating leverage falls as sales increase past the firm's break-even point. The sheer size and operating profitability of the firm, therefore, affect and can lessen its business risk exposure.

The manager considering an alteration in the firm's cost structure will benefit from an understanding of the operating leverage concept. It might be possible to replace part of the labor force with capital equipment (machinery). A possible result is an increase in fixed costs associated with the new machinery and a reduction in variable costs attributable to a lower labor bill. This conceivably could raise the firm's degree of operating leverage at a specific sales base. If the prospects for future sales increases are high, then increasing the degree of operating leverage might be a prudent decision. The opposite conclusion will be reached if sales prospects are unattractive.

CONCEPT CHECK

1. If a firm's degree of operating leverage happens to be six times, what precisely does that mean?
2. What does the degree of operating leverage concept suggest when a negative shock in production volume and sales occurs?
3. When is operating leverage present in the firm's cost structure? What condition is necessary for operating leverage not to be present in the firm's cost structure?

FINANCIAL LEVERAGE

We have defined *financial leverage* as the practice of financing a portion of the firm's assets with securities bearing a fixed rate of return in hope of increasing the ultimate return to the common shareholders. In the present discussion we focus on the responsiveness of the company's earnings per share to changes in its EBIT. For the time being, then, the return to the common stockholder being concentrated on is earnings per share. We are *not* saying that earnings per share is the appropriate criterion for all financing decisions. In fact, the weakness of such a contention is examined later. Rather, the use of financial leverage produces a certain type of *effect*. This effect can be illustrated clearly by concentrating on an earnings-per-share criterion.

Let us assume that the Pierce Grain Company is in the process of getting started as a going concern. The firm's potential owners have calculated that $200,000 is

TABLE 13-4	PIERCE GRAIN COMPANY POSSIBLE CAPITAL STRUCTURES

Plan A: 0% Debt

		Total debt	$ 0
		Common equity	200,000^a
Total assets	$200,000	Total liabilities and equity	$200,000

Plan B: 25% Debt at 8% Interest Rate

		Total debt	$ 50,000
		Common equity	150,000^b
Total assets	$200,000	Total liabilities and equity	$200,000

Plan C: 40% Debt at 8% Interest Rate

		Total debt	$ 80,000
		Common equity	120,000^c
Total assets	$200,000	Total liabilities and equity	$200,000

[a]2,000 common shares outstanding.
[b]1,500 common shares outstanding.
[c]1,200 common shares outstanding.

needed to purchase the necessary assets to conduct the business. Three possible financing plans have been identified for raising the $200,000; they are presented in Table 13–4. In plan A no financial risk is assumed: The entire $200,000 is raised by selling 2,000 common shares, each with a $100 par value. In plan B a moderate amount of financial risk is assumed: 25 percent of the assets are financed with a debt issue that carries an 8-percent annual interest rate. Plan C would use the most financial leverage: 40 percent of the assets would be financed with a debt issue costing 8 percent.

Table 13–5 presents the impact of financial leverage on earnings per share associated with each fund-raising alternative. If EBIT should increase from $20,000 to $40,000, then earnings per share would rise by 100 percent under plan A. The same positive fluctuation in EBIT would occasion an earnings-per-share rise of 125 percent under plan B, and 147 percent under plan C. In plans B and C the 100 percent increase in EBIT (from $20,000 to $40,000) is magnified to a greater than 100-percent increase in earnings per share. The firm is employing financial leverage and exposing its owners to financial risk when the following situation exists:

$$\frac{\text{percentage change in earnings per share}}{\text{percentage change in } EBIT} > 1.00$$

By following the same general procedures that allowed us to analyze the firm's use of operating leverage, we can lay out a precise measure of financial leverage. Such a measure deals with the sensitivity of earnings per share to EBIT fluctuations. The relationship can be expressed as

$$\begin{array}{c}\text{degree of financial} \\ \text{leverage } (DFL) \text{ from} \\ \text{base } EBIT \text{ level}\end{array} = DFL_{EBIT} = \frac{\begin{array}{c}\text{percentage change} \\ \text{in earnings per share}\end{array}}{\text{percentage change in } EBIT} \quad (13\text{–}8)$$

Using equation (13–8) with each of the financing choices outlined for Pierce Grain yields the following. The base EBIT level is $20,000 in each case.

TABLE 13–5

(1) EBIT	(2) INTEREST	(3) = (1) − (2) EBT	(4) = (3) × .5 TAXES	(5) = (3) − (4) NET INCOME TO COMMON	(6) EARNINGS PER SHARE	
\multicolumn{7}{c}{Plan A: 0% Debt; $200,000 Common Equity; 2,000 Shares}
$ 0	$ 0	$ 0	$ 0	$ 0	$ 0	
20,000	0	20,000	10,000	10,000	5.00	} 100%
40,000	0	40,000	20,000	20,000	10.00	
60,000	0	60,000	30,000	30,000	15.00	
80,000	0	80,000	40,000	40,000	20.00	
\multicolumn{7}{c}{Plan B: 25% Debt; 8% Interest Rate; $150,000 Common Equity; 1,500 Shares}
$ 0	$4,000	$ (4,000)	$ (2,000)[a]	$ (2,000)	$ (1.33)	
20,000	4,000	16,000	8,000	8,000	5.33	} 125%
40,000	4,000	36,000	18,000	18,000	12.00	
60,000	4,000	56,000	28,000	28,000	18.67	
80,000	4,000	76,000	38,000	38,000	25.33	
\multicolumn{7}{c}{Plan C: 40% Debt; 8% Interest Rate; $120,000 Common Equity; 1,200 Shares}
$ 0	$6,400	$ (6,400)	$ (3,200)[a]	$ (3,200)	$ (2.67)	
20,000	6,400	13,600	6,800	6,800	5.67	} 147%
40,000	6,400	33,600	16,800	16,800	14.00	
60,000	6,400	53,600	26,800	26,800	22.33	
80,000	6,400	73,600	36,800	36,800	30.67	

[a]The negative tax bill recognizes the credit arising from the carryback and carryforward provision of the tax code.

$$\text{Plan A:} \quad DFL_{\$20,000} = \frac{100\%}{100\%} = 1.00 \text{ time}$$

$$\text{Plan B:} \quad DFL_{\$20,000} = \frac{125\%}{100\%} = 1.25 \text{ times}$$

$$\text{Plan C:} \quad DFL_{\$20,000} = \frac{147\%}{100\%} = 1.47 \text{ times}$$

Like operating leverage, the *degree of financial leverage* concept performs in the negative direction as well as the positive. Should EBIT fall by 10 percent, the Pierce Grain Company would suffer a 12.5-percent decline in earnings per share under plan B. If plan C were chosen to raise the necessary financial capital, the decline in earnings would be 14.7 percent. Observe that the greater the DFL, the greater the fluctuations (positive or negative) in earnings per share. The common shareholder is required to endure greater variations in returns when the firm's management chooses to use more financial leverage rather than less. The DFL measure allows the variation to be quantified.

Rather than take the time to compute percentage changes in EBIT and earnings per share, the DFL can be found directly, as follows:

$$DFL_{EBIT} = \frac{EBIT}{EBIT - I} \tag{13–9}$$

In equation (13–9) the variable I represents the total interest expense incurred on *all* the firm's contractual debt obligations. If six bonds are outstanding, I is the sum of the interest expense on all six bonds. If the firm has preferred stock in its financial structure, the dividend on such issues must be inflated to a before-tax basis and included in the computation of I.[4] In this latter instance, I is in reality the sum of all fixed financing costs.

Equation (13–9) has been applied to each of Pierce Grain's financing plans (Table 13–5) at a base EBIT level of $20,000. The results are as follows:

$$\text{Plan A:} \quad DFL_{\$20,000} = \frac{\$20,000}{\$20,000 - 0} = 1.00 \text{ time}$$

$$\text{Plan B:} \quad DFL_{\$20,000} = \frac{\$20,000}{\$20,000 - \$4,000} = 1.25 \text{ times}$$

$$\text{Plan C:} \quad DFL_{\$20,000} = \frac{\$20,000}{\$20,000 - \$6,400} = 1.47 \text{ times}$$

As you probably suspected, the measures of financial leverage shown previously are identical to those obtained by use of equation (13–8). This will always be the case.

CONCEPT CHECK

1. If a firm's degree of financial leverage happens to be 1.25 times, what precisely does that mean?
2. What does the degree of financial leverage concept suggest when a negative shock in earnings before interest and taxes (EBIT) occurs?
3. From the viewpoint of the company's shareholders explain the difference between enduring a degree of financial leverage of five times versus two times.

Objective 4

COMBINATION OF OPERATING AND FINANCIAL LEVERAGE

Changes in sales revenues cause greater changes in EBIT. Additionally, changes in EBIT translate into larger variations in both earnings per share (EPS) and total earnings available to the common shareholders (EAC), if the firm chooses to use financial leverage. It should be no surprise, then, to find out that combining operating and financial leverage causes rather large variations in earnings per share. This entire process is visually displayed in Figure 13–7.

Because the risk associated with possible earnings per share is affected by the use of combined or total leverage, it is useful to quantify the effect. To illustrate, we refer once more to the Pierce Grain Company. The cost structure identified for Pierce Grain in our discussion of break-even analysis still holds. Furthermore, assume that

---

[4]Suppose (1) preferred dividends of $4,000 are paid annually by the firm and (2) it faces a 40-percent marginal tax rate. How much must the firm earn *before taxes* to make the $4,000 payment out of after-tax earnings? Because preferred dividends are not tax deductible to the paying company, we have $4,000/(1 − .40) = $6,666.67.

FINANCIAL MANAGEMENT IN PRACTICE

Coca-Cola Financial Policies

Because financial leverage effects can be measured, management has the opportunity to formally shape corporate policy around the decision to use or avoid the use of leverage-inducing financial instruments (primarily debt issues). One company with very specific policies on the use of financial leverage is the Coca-Cola Company. The following discussion is from that firm's 1990 *Annual Report*.

Note how several of the key concepts and techniques presented throughout this book are mentioned in this excerpt. For example, mention is made of (1) the firm's primary objective, (2) its weighted average cost of capital, (3) investment risk characteristics, (4) the prudent use of debt capital, and (5) borrowing capacity.

> Management's primary objective is to increase shareholder value over time. To accomplish this objective, the Coca-Cola Company and subsidiaries (the Company) have developed a comprehensive business strategy that emphasizes maximizing long-term cash flow by expanding its global business systems, increasing gallon sales, improving margins, investing in areas offering attractive returns and maintaining an appropriate capital structure.

> Management seeks investments that strategically enhance existing operations and offer long-term cash returns that exceed the Company's weighted average cost of capital. For investments with risk characteristics similar to the soft drink industry and assuming a net-debt-to-capital ratio ceiling of 35 percent, that cost of capital is estimated by management to be approximately 12 percent after taxes.

> The Company utilizes prudent amounts of debt to lower its overall cost of capital and increase its total return to shareholders. The Company has established a net-debt-to-net-capital ratio ceiling of 35 percent. Net debt is defined as total debt less excess cash, cash equivalents, and current marketable securities. Excluding the Company's finance subsidiary, net debt represented 22.8 percent of net capital at December 31, 1990.

> Additional borrowing capacity within the 35 percent debt ceiling was approximately $940 million at December 31, 1990, excluding the Company's finance subsidiary. The Company anticipates using this additional borrowing capacity principally to fund investment opportunities that meet its strategic and financial objectives and, as a second priority, to fund the share repurchase program.

Source: Excerpt from *1990 Annual Report*, The Coca-Cola Company, pp. 32–34, used with permission.

plan B, which carried a 25-percent debt ratio, was chosen to finance the company's assets. Turn your attention to Table 13–6.

In Table 13–6 an increase in output for Pierce Grain from 30,000 to 36,000 units is analyzed. This increase represents a 20-percent rise in sales revenues. From our earlier discussion of operating leverage and the data in Table 13–6, we can see that this 20-percent increase in sales is magnified into a 120-percent rise in EBIT. From this base sales level of $300,000 the degree of operating leverage is 6 times.

The 120-percent rise in EBIT induces a change in earnings per share and earnings available to the common shareholders of 150 percent. The degree of financial leverage is therefore 1.25 times.

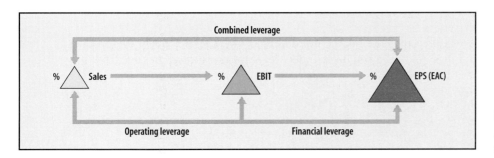

FIGURE 13–7

Leverage and Earnings Fluctuations

TABLE 13-6

TABLE 13-6 PIERCE GRAIN COMPANY COMBINED LEVERAGE ANALYSIS

ITEM	BASE SALES LEVEL, t	FORECAST SALES LEVEL, $t+1$	SELECTED PERCENTAGE CHANGES
Sales	$300,000	$360,000	+ 20
Less: Total variable costs	180,000	216,000	
Revenue before fixed costs	$120,000	$144,000	
Less: Total fixed costs	100,000	100,000	
EBIT	$ 20,000	$ 44,000	+120
Less: Interest expense	4,000	4,000	
Earnings before taxes (EBT)	$ 16,000	$ 40,000	
Less: Taxes at 50%	8,000	20,000	
Net income	$ 8,000	$ 20,000	+150
Less: Preferred dividends	0	0	
Earnings available to common (EAC)	$ 8,000	$ 20,000	+150
Number of common shares	1,500	1,500	
Earnings per share (EPS)	$ 5.33	$ 13.33	+150

$$\text{Degree of operating leverage} = DOL_{\$300,000} = \frac{120\%}{20\%} = 6 \text{ times}$$

$$\text{Degree of financial leverage} = DFL_{\$20,000} = \frac{150\%}{120\%} = 1.25 \text{ times}$$

$$\text{Degree of combined leverage} = DCL_{\$300,000} = \frac{150\%}{20\%} = 7.50 \text{ times}$$

The upshot of the analysis is that the 20-percent rise in sales has been magnified to 150 percent, as reflected by the percentage change in earnings per share. The formal measure of combined leverage can be expressed as follows:

$$\left(\begin{array}{c} \text{degree of combined} \\ \text{leverage from the} \\ \text{base sales level} \end{array} \right) = DCL_s = \left(\frac{\text{percentage change in earnings per share}}{\text{percentage change in sales}} \right) \quad (13\text{--}10)$$

This equation was used in the bottom portion of Table 13–6 to determine that the degree of combined leverage from the base sales level of $300,000 is 7.50 times. Pierce Grain's use of both operating and financial leverage will cause any percentage change in sales (from the specific base level) to be magnified by a factor of 7.50 when the effect on earnings per share is computed. A 1-percent change in sales, for example, will result in a 7.50 percent change in earnings per share.

Notice that the degree of combined leverage is actually the product (not the simple sum) of the two independent leverage measures. Thus, we have

$$(DOL_s) \times (DFL_{EBIT}) = DCL_s \quad (13\text{--}11)$$

or

$$(6) \times (1.25) = 7.50 \text{ times}$$

It is possible to ascertain the degree of combined leverage in a direct fashion, without determining any percentage fluctuations or the separate leverage values. We need only substitute the appropriate values into equation (13–12):[5]

$$DCL_s = \frac{Q(P - V)}{Q(P - V) - F - I} \qquad (13\text{–}12)$$

The variable definitions in equation (13–12) are the same ones that have been employed throughout this chapter. Use of equation (13–12) with the information in Table 13–6 gives

$$DCL_{\$300,000} = \frac{30,000(\$10 - \$6)}{30,000(\$10 - \$6) - \$100,000 - \$4,000}$$

$$= \frac{\$120,000}{\$16,000}$$

$$= 7.5 \text{ times}$$

Implications

The total risk exposure the firm assumes can be managed by combining operating and financial leverage in different degrees. Knowledge of the various leverage measures helps the financial officer determine the proper level of overall risk that should be accepted. If a high degree of business risk is inherent in the specific line of commercial activity, then a low posture regarding financial risk would minimize additional earnings fluctuations stemming from sales changes. Conversely, the firm that by its very nature incurs a low level of fixed operating costs might choose to use a high degree of financial leverage in the hope of increasing earnings per share and the rate of return on the common equity investment. Table 13–7 summarizes the salient concepts and calculation formats discussed thus far in this chapter.

CONCEPT CHECK

1. Explain the degree of combined leverage concept.
2. When would the degree of operating leverage and the degree of combined leverage be equal?

PLANNING THE FINANCING MIX

Objective 5

Given our understanding of both operating and financial leverage we now direct our attention to the determination of an appropriate financing mix for the firm. First, we must distinguish between financial structure and capital structure. **Financial structure** is the *mix of all items that appear on the right-handed side of the company's balance sheet.*

financial structure

---

[5]As was the case with the degree of financial leverage metric, the variable I in the combined leverage measure must include the before-tax equivalent of any preferred dividend payments when preferred stock is in the financial structure.

TABLE 13–7 — SUMMARY OF LEVERAGE CONCEPTS AND CALCULATIONS

TECHNIQUE	DESCRIPTION OR CONCEPT	CALCULATION	TEXT REFERENCE
	Break-even Analysis		
1. Break-even point quantity	Total fixed costs divided by the unit contribution margin	$Q_B = \dfrac{F}{P - V}$	(13–3)
2. Break-even sales level	Total fixed costs divided by 1 minus the ratio of total variable costs to the associated level of sales	$S^* = \dfrac{F}{1 - \dfrac{VC}{S}}$	(13–4)
	Operating Leverage		
3. Degree of operating leverage	Percentage change in EBIT divided by the percentage change in sales; or revenue before fixed costs divided by revenue after fixed costs	$DOL_S = \dfrac{Q\,(P - V)}{Q\,(P - V) - F}$	(13–6)
	Financial Leverage		
4. Degree of financial leverage	Percentage change in earnings per share divided by the percentage change in EBIT; or EBIT divided by EBT[a]	$DFL_{EBIT} = \dfrac{EBIT}{EBIT - I}$	(13–9)
	Combined Leverage		
5. Degree of combined leverage	Percentage change in earnings per share divided by the percentage change in sales; or revenue before fixed costs divided by EBT[a]	$DCL_S = \dfrac{Q\,(P - V)}{Q\,(P - V) - F - I}$	(13–12)

[a]The use of EBT here presumes no preferred dividend payments. In the presence of preferred dividend payments replace EBT with earnings available to common stock (EAC).

---

capital structure

Capital structure is the *mix of the long-term sources of funds used by the firm.* The relationship between financial and capital structure can be expressed in equation form:

$$(\text{financial structure}) - (\text{current liabilities}) = \text{capital structure} \quad (13\text{–}13)$$

Prudent financial structure design requires answers to the following two questions:

1. What should be the maturity composition of the firm's sources of funds; in other words, how should a firm best divide its total fund sources between short- and long-term components?
2. In what proportions relative to the total should the various forms of permanent financing be utilized?

The major influence on the maturity structure of the financing plans is the nature of the assets owned by the firm. A company heavily committed to real capital investment, represented primarily by fixed assets on its balance sheet, should finance those assets with permanent (long-term) types of financial capital. Furthermore, the permanent portion of the firm's investment in current assets should likewise be financed with permanent capital. Alternatively, assets held on a temporary basis are to be financed with temporary sources. The present discussion assumes that the bulk of the company's current liabilities are comprised of temporary capital.

This hedging concept is discussed in Chapter 15. Accordingly, our focus in this chapter is on answering the second of the two questions noted previously—this process is usually called *capital structure management.*

TABLE 13-8	BALANCE SHEET

The objective of capital-structure management is to mix the permanent sources of funds used by the firm in a manner that will maximize the company's common stock price. Alternatively, this objective may be viewed as a search for the *funds mix that will minimize the firm's composite cost of capital.* We can call this proper mix of funds sources the **optimal capital structure.**

optimal capital structure

Table 13–8 looks at equation (13–13) in terms of a simplified balance sheet format. It helps us visualize the overriding problem of capital structure management. The sources of funds that give rise to financing fixed costs (long-term debt and preferred equity) must be combined with common equity in the proportions most suitable to the investment marketplace. If that mix can be found, then holding all other factors constant, the firm's common stock price will be maximized.

Although equation (13–13) quite accurately indicates that the corporate capital structure may be viewed as an absolute dollar amount, the real capital structure problem is one of balancing the array of funds sources in a proper manner. Our use of the term *capital structure* emphasizes this latter problem of relative magnitude, or proportions.

It pays to understand the essential components of capital structure theory. The assumption of excessive financial risk can put the firm into bankruptcy proceedings. Some argue that the decision to use little financial leverage results in an undervaluation of the firm's shares in the marketplace. The effective financial manager must know how to find the area of optimum financial leverage use—this will enhance share value, all other considerations held constant. Thus, grasping the theory will make you better able to formulate a sound financial structure policy.

The rest of this chapter covers three main areas. First, we briefly discuss the theory of capital structure to provide a perspective. Second, we examine the basic tools of capital structure management. We conclude with a real-world look at actual capital structure management.

CONCEPT CHECK

1. What is the objective of capital structure management?
2. What is the main attribute of a firm's optimal capital structure?

An enduring controversy within financial theory concerns the effect of financial leverage on the overall cost of capital to the enterprise. The heart of the argument may be stated in the form of a question:

> Can the firm affect its overall cost of funds, either favorably or unfavorably, by varying the mixture of financing sources used?

This controversy has taken many elegant forms in the finance literature. Most of these presentations appeal more to academics than financial management practitioners. To emphasize the ingredients of capital structure theory that have practical applications for business financial management, we will pursue an intuitive, or non-mathematical, approach to reach a better understanding of the underpinnings of this cost of capital–capital structure argument.

Importance of Capital Structure

It makes economic sense for the firm to strive to minimize the cost of using financial capital. Both capital costs and other costs, such as manufacturing costs, share a common characteristic in that they potentially reduce the size of the cash dividend that could be paid to common stockholders.

We saw in Chapters 8 and 9 that the ultimate value of a share of common stock depends in part on the returns investors expect to receive from holding the stock. Cash dividends comprise all (in the case of an infinite holding period) or part (in the case of a holding period less than infinity) of these expected returns. Now, hold constant all factors that could affect share price except capital costs. If these capital costs could be kept at a minimum, the dividend stream flowing to the common stockholders would be maximized. This, in turn, would maximize the firm's common stock price.

If the firm's cost of capital can be affected by its capital structure, then capital structure management is clearly an important subset of business financial management.

Analytical Setting

The essentials of the capital structure controversy are best highlighted within a framework that economists would call a "partial equilibrium analysis." In a partial equilibrium analysis changes that do occur in several factors and have an impact on a certain key item are ignored to study the effect of changes in a main factor on that same item of interest. Here, two items are simultaneously of interest: (1) K_0, the firm's composite cost of capital, and (2) P_0, the market price of the firm's common stock. The firm's use of financial leverage is the main factor that is allowed to vary in the analysis. This means that important financial decisions, such as investing policy and dividend policy, are held constant throughout the discussion. We are only concerned with the effect of changes in the financing mix on share price and capital costs.

Consider a rarified economic world where

1. corporate income is not subject to taxation;
2. capital structures consist only of stock and bonds;
3. investors make homogeneous forecasts of net operating income (what we earlier called "EBIT"); and
4. securities are traded in perfect or efficient markets.

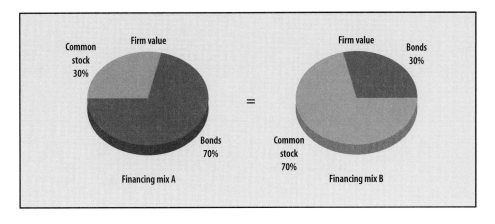

FIGURE 13-8
Firm Value and Capital Structure Design

In this market setting the direct answer to our question, "Can the firm affect its overall cost of funds, either favorably or unfavorably, by varying the mixture of financing sources used?" would be no. This view of capital structure importance was put into rather elegant form back in 1958 by two well-known financial economists, Franco Modigliani and Merton Miller, both of whom have been awarded the Nobel Prize in economics.

The Modigliani and Miller hypothesis, or the MM view, puts forth that within the perfect economic world previously described, the total market value of the firm's outstanding securities will be *unaffected* by the manner in which the right-hand side of the balance sheet is arranged. This means the sum of the market value of outstanding common stock plus outstanding debt will always be the same regardless of how much or little debt is actually used by the company. This MM view is sometimes called the *independence hypothesis*, as firm value is independent of capital structure design.[6]

The crux of this position on financing choice is illustrated in Figure 13–8. Here the firm's asset mix (i.e., the left-hand side of the balance sheet) is held constant. All that is different is the way the assets are financed. Under financing mix A, the firm funds 30 percent of its assets with common stock and the other 70 percent with bonds. Under financing mix B, the firm reverses this mix and funds 70 percent of the assets with common stock and only 30 percent with bonds. From our earlier discussions we know that financing mix A is the more heavily levered plan.

Notice, however, that the size of each "pie" in Figure 13–8 is exactly the same. The pie represents firm value—the total market value of the firm's outstanding securities. Thus, total firm value associated with financing mix A equals that associated with financing mix B. Firm value is *independent* of the actual financing mix that has been chosen.

This implication is taken further in Figures 13–9 and 13–10. They display how (1) the firm's cost of funds and (2) common stock price, P_0, relate to the firm's financing mix. In Figure 13–9 we see that the firm's overall cost of capital, K_0, is unaffected by an increased use of financial leverage. If more debt is used with a cost of K_d in the

[6]See Franco Modigliani and Merton H. Miller, "The Cost of Capital, Corporation Finance, and the Theory of Investment," *American Economic Review* 48 (June 1958): 261–97; Modigliani and Miller, "Corporate Income Taxes and the Cost of Capital: A Correction," *American Economic Review* 53 (June 1963): 433–43; and Merton H. Miller, "Debt and Taxes," *Journal of Finance* 32 (May 1977): 261–75. The Modigliani-Miller capital structure theories and positions are put into a longer and broader perspective in Merton H. Miller, "The Modigliani-Miller Propositions After Thirty Years," in Joel Stern and Donald Chew, eds., *The Revolution in Corporate Finance*, 3rd Ed, (Malden, Mass: Blackwell Publishers Ltd, 1998): 99–110.

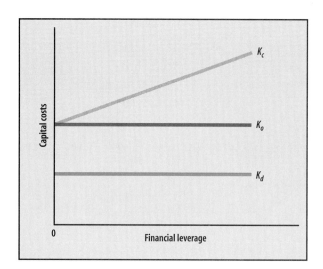

capital structure, the cost of common equity, k_c, will rise at the same rate additional earnings are generated. This will keep the composite cost of capital to the corporation unchanged. Figure 13–10 shows that because the overall cost of capital will not change with the leverage use, neither will the firm's common stock price.

The lesson of this view on financing choices is that debt financing is not as cheap as it first appears to be. This will keep the composite cost of funds constant over the full range of financial leverage use. The stark implication for financial officers is that one capital structure is just as good as any other.

Recall, though, the strict economic world in which this viewpoint was developed. We next turn to a market and legal environment that relaxes the extreme assumptions.

BACK TO THE FOUNDATIONS

The suggestion from capital structure theory that one capital structure is just as good as any other within a perfect ("pure") market framework relies directly on **Axiom 1: The Risk-Return Trade-off—We Won't Take On Added Risk Unless We Expect to Be Compensated with Additional Return.** This means that using more debt in the capital structure will not be ignored by investors in the financial markets. These rational investors will require a higher return on common stock investments in the firm that uses more leverage (rather than less), to compensate for the increased uncertainty stemming from the addition of the debt securities in the capital structure.

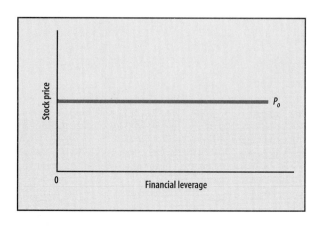

Moderate Position: Corporate Income Is Taxed and Firms May Fail

We turn now to a description of the cost of capital–capital structure relationship that has rather wide appeal to both business practitioners and academics. This moderate view (1) admits to the fact that interest expense is tax deductible and (2) acknowledges that the probability of the firm's suffering bankruptcy costs is directly related to the company's use of financial leverage.

Tax Deductibility of Interest Expense

This portion of the analysis recognizes that corporate income is subject to taxation. Furthermore, we assume that interest expense is tax deductible for purposes of computing the firm's tax bill. In this environment the use of debt financing should result in a higher total market value for the firm's outstanding securities. We see why subsequently.

Table 13–9 illustrates this important element of the U.S. system of corporate taxation. It is assumed that Skip's Camper Manufacturing Company has an expected level of net operating income (EBIT) of $2 million and faces a corporate tax rate (made simple for example purposes) of 50 percent. Two financing plans are analyzed. The first is an unlevered capital structure. The other assumes that Skip's Camper has $8 million of bonds outstanding that carry an interest rate of 6 percent per year.

Notice that if corporate income is *not* taxed, then earnings before taxes of $2 million per year could be paid to shareholders in the form of cash dividends or to bond investors in the form of interest payments, or any combination of the two. This means that the *sum* of the cash flows that Skip's Camper could pay to its contributors of debt or equity is *not* affected by its financing mix.

When corporate income is taxed by the government, however, the sum of the cash flows made to all contributors of financial capital *is affected* by the firm's financing mix. Table 13–9 illustrates this point.

If Skip's Camper chooses the levered capital structure, the total payments to equity and debt holders will be $240,000 *greater* than under the all-common-equity capitalization. Where does this $240,000 come from? The government's take, through taxes collected, is lower by that amount. This *difference, which flows to the* Skip's Camper *security holders*, is called the **tax shield** on interest. In general, it may be calculated by equation (13–14), where r_d is the interest rate paid on the debt, M is the principal amount of the debt, and t is the firm's marginal tax rate:

tax shield

$$\text{tax shield} = r_d (M) (t) \qquad (13\text{–}14)$$

TABLE 13-9	SKIP'S CAMPER CASH FLOWS TO ALL INVESTORS— THE CASE OF TAXES	
	UNLEVERED CAPITAL STRUCTURE	LEVERED CAPITAL STRUCTURE
Expected level of net operating income	$2,000,000	$2,000,000
Less: Interest expense	0	480,000
Earnings before taxes	$2,000,000	$1,520,000
Less: Taxes at 50%	1,000,000	760,000
Earnings available to common stockholders	$1,000,000	$ 760,000
Expected payments to *all* security holders	$1,000,000	$1,240,000

The moderate position on the importance of capital structure presumes that the tax shield must have value in the marketplace. Accordingly, this tax benefit will increase the total market value of the firm's outstanding securities relative to the all-equity capitalization. Financial leverage does affect firm value. Because the cost of capital is just the other side of the valuation coin, financial leverage also affects the firm's composite cost of capital. Can the firm increase firm value indefinitely and lower its cost of capital continuously by using more and more financial leverage? Common sense would tell us no! So would most financial managers and academicians. The acknowledgment of bankruptcy costs provides one possible rationale.

BACK TO THE FOUNDATIONS

The section above on the "Tax Deductibility of Interest Expense" is a compelling example of **Axiom 8: Taxes Bias Business Decisions.** We have just seen that corporations have an important incentive provided by the tax code to finance projects with debt securities rather than new issues of common stock. The interest expense on the debt tissue is tax deductible. The common stock dividends are not tax deductible. So firms can indeed increase their total after-tax cash flows available to all investors in their securities by using financial leverage. This element of the U.S. tax code should also remind you of **Axiom 3: Cash—Not Profits—Is King.**

The Likelihood of Firm Failure

The probability that the firm will be unable to meet the financial obligations identified in its debt contracts increases as more debt is employed. The highest costs would be incurred if the firm actually went into bankruptcy proceedings. Here, assets would be liquidated. If we admit that these assets might sell for something less than their perceived market values, both equity investors and debt holders could suffer losses. Other problems accompany bankruptcy proceedings. Lawyers and accountants have to be hired and paid. Managers must spend time preparing lengthy reports for those involved in the legal action.

Milder forms of financial distress also have their costs. As their firm's financial condition weakens, creditors may take action to restrict normal business activity. Suppliers may not deliver materials on credit. Profitable capital investments may have to be forgone, and dividend payments may even be interrupted. At some point the expected cost of default will be large enough to outweigh the tax shield advantage of debt financing. The firm will turn to other sources of financing, mainly common equity. At this point the real cost of debt is thought to be higher than the real cost of common equity.

Objective 7 | ## Moderate View: Saucer-Shaped Cost of Capital Curve

This moderate view of the relationship between financing mix and the firm's cost of capital is depicted in Figure 13–11. The result is a saucer-shaped (or U-shaped) average cost of capital curve, K_0. The firm's average cost of equity, K_c, is seen to rise over all positive degrees of financial leverage use. For a while the firm can borrow funds at a relatively low after-tax cost of debt, K_d. Even though the cost of equity is rising, it does not rise at a fast enough rate to offset the use of the less expensive debt financing. Thus, between points 0 and A on the financial-leverage axis, the average cost of capital declines and stock price rises.

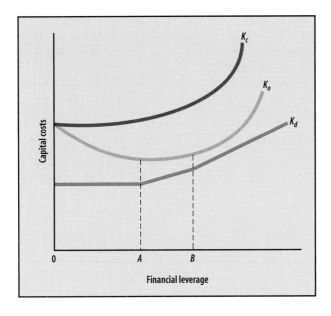

FIGURE 13-11

Capital Costs and Financial Leverage: The Moderate View, Considering Taxes and Financial Distress

Eventually, the threat of financial distress causes the cost of debt to rise. In Figure 13–11 this increase in the cost of debt shows up in the after-tax average cost of debt curve, K_d, at point A. Between points A and B, mixing debt and equity funds produces an average cost of capital that is (relatively) flat. The firm's **optimal range of financial leverage** lies between points A and B. *All capital structures between these two points are optimal because they produce the lowest composite cost of capital.* As we said earlier in this chapter, finding this optimal range of financing mixes is the objective of capital structure management.

optimal range of financial leverage

Point B signifies the firm's debt capacity. **Debt capacity** is the *maximum proportion of debt the firm can include in its capital structure and still maintain its lowest composite cost of capital.* Beyond point B, additional fixed-charge capital can be attracted only at very costly interest rates. At the same time, this excessive use of financial leverage would cause the firm's cost of equity to rise at a faster rate than previously. The composite cost of capital would then rise quite rapidly, and the firm's stock price would decline.

debt capacity

Firm Value and Agency Costs

Objective 8

In Chapter 1 we mentioned the agency problem. Recall that the agency problem gives rise to agency costs, which tend to occur in business organizations because ownership and management control are often separate. Thus, the firm's managers can properly be thought of as agents for the firm's stockholders.[7] To ensure that agent-managers act in the stockholders' best interests requires that (1) they have

---

[7]Economists have studied the problems associated with control of the corporation for decades. An early, classic work on this topic was A. A. Berle, Jr., and G. C. Means, *The Modern Corporation and Private Property* (New York: Macmillan, 1932). The recent emphasis in corporate finance and financial economics stems from the important contribution of Michael C. Jensen and William H. Meckling, "Theory of the Firm: Managerial Behavior, Agency Costs, and Ownership Structure," *Journal of Financial Economics* 3 (October 1976): 305–60. Professors Jensen and Clifford Smith have analyzed the bondholder–stockholder conflict in a very clear style. See Michael C. Jensen and Clifford W. Smith, Jr., "Stockholder, Manager, and Creditor Interests: Applications of Agency Theory," in Edward I. Altman and Marti G. Subrahmanyam, eds., *Recent Advances in Corporate Finance* (Homewood, Ill: Irwin, 1985); 93–131.

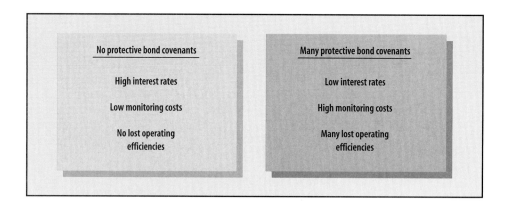

FIGURE 13–12

Agency Costs of Debt:
Trade-offs

proper incentives to do so and (2) their decisions are monitored. The incentives usually take the form of executive compensation plans and perquisites. The perquisites, though, might be a bloated support staff, country club memberships, luxurious corporate planes, or other amenities. Monitoring requires that certain costs be borne by the stockholders, such as (1) bonding the managers, (2) auditing financial statements, (3) structuring the organization in unique ways that limit useful managerial decisions, and (4) reviewing the costs and benefits of management perquisites. This list is indicative, not exhaustive. The main point is that monitoring costs are ultimately covered by the owners of the company—its common stockholders.

Capital structure management also gives rise to agency costs. Agency problems stem from conflicts of interest, and capital structure management encompasses a natural conflict between stockholders and bondholders. Acting in the stockholders' best interests might cause management to invest in extremely risky projects. Existing investors in the firm's bonds could logically take a dim view of such an investment policy. A change in the risk structure of the firm's assets would change the business risk exposure of the firm. This could lead to a downward revision of the bond rating the firm currently enjoys. A lowered bond rating in turn would lower the current market value of the firm's bonds. Clearly, bondholders would be unhappy with this result.

To reduce this conflict of interest, the creditors (bond investors) and stockholders may agree to include several protective covenants in the bond contract. These bond convenants are discussed in more detail in Chapter 7, but essentially they may be thought of as restrictions on managerial decision making. Typical covenants restrict payment of cash dividends on common stock, limit the acquisition or sale of assets or limit further debt financing. To make sure management complies with the protective covenants means that monitoring costs are incurred. Like all monitoring costs, they are borne by common stockholders. Furthermore, like many costs, they involve the analysis of an important trade-off.

Figure 13–12 displays some of the trade-offs involved with the use of protective bond convenants. Note (in the left panel of Figure 13–12) that the firm might be able to sell bonds that carry no protective covenants only by incurring very high interest rates. With no protective convenants, there are no associated monitoring costs. Also, there are no lost operating efficiencies, such as being able to move quickly to acquire a particular company in the acquisitions market. Conversely, the willingness to submit to several covenants could reduce the explicit cost of the debt contract, but would involve incurring significant monitoring costs and losing some operating efficiencies (which also translates into higher costs). When the debt issue

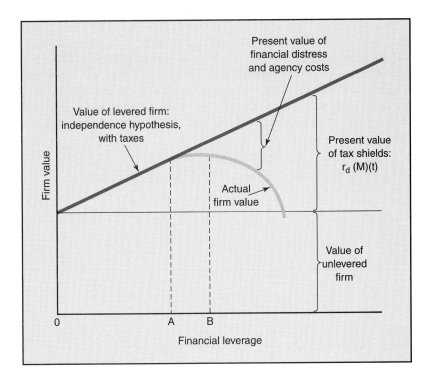

is first sold, then a trade-off will be arrived at among incurring monitoring costs, losing operating efficiencies, and enjoying a lower explicit interest cost.

Next, we have to consider the presence of monitoring costs at low and higher levels of leverage. When the firm operates at a low debt-to-equity ratio, there is little need for creditors to insist on a long list of bond covenants. The financial risk is just not there to require that type of activity. The firm will likewise benefit from low explicit interest rates when leverage is low. When the debt-to-equity ratio is high, however, it is logical for creditors to demand a great deal of monitoring. This increase in agency costs will raise the implicit cost (the true total cost) of debt financing. It seems logical, then, to suggest that monitoring costs will rise as the firm's use of financial leverage increases. Just as the likelihood of firm failure (financial distress) raises a company's overall cost of capital (K_0), so do agency costs. On the other side of the coin, this means that total firm value (the total market value of the firm's securities) will be *lower* because of agency costs. Taken together, the agency costs and the costs associated with financial distress argue in favor of the concept of an *optimal* capital structure for the individual firm.

This discussion can be summarized by introducing equation (13–15) for the market value of the levered firm.

$$\begin{array}{c} \text{market value of} \\ \text{levered firm} \end{array} = \begin{array}{c} \text{market value of} \\ \text{unlevered firm} \end{array} + \begin{array}{c} \text{present value} \\ \text{of tax shields} \end{array}$$

$$- \left(\begin{array}{c} \text{present value} \\ \text{of financial} \\ \text{distress costs} \end{array} + \begin{array}{c} \text{present value} \\ \text{of agency} \\ \text{costs} \end{array} \right) \quad (13\text{–}15)$$

The relationship expressed in equation (13–15) is presented graphically in Figure 13–13. There we see that the tax shield effect is dominant until point *A* is reached. After point *A*, the rising costs of the likelihood of firm failure (financial distress) and agency costs cause the market value of the levered firm to decline. The objective for the financial manager here is to find point B by using all of his or her analytical skill; this must also include a good dose of seasoned judgment. At point B the actual market value of the levered firm is maximized, and its composite cost of capital (K_0) is at a minimum. The implementation problem is that the precise costs of financial distress and monitoring can only be estimated by subjective means; a definite mathematical solution is not available. Thus, planning the firm's financing mix always requires good decision-making and management judgment.

Agency Costs, Free Cash Flow, and Capital Structure

In 1986, Professor Michael C. Jensen further extended the concept of agency costs into the area of capital structure management. The contribution revolves around a concept that Jensen labels "free cash flow," which he defines as follows:

> Free cash flow is cash flow in excess of that required to fund all projects that have positive net present values when discounted at the relevant cost of capital.[8]

Jensen then proposes that substantial free cash flow can lead to misbehavior by managers and poor decisions that are not in the best interests of the firm's common stockholders. In other words, managers have an incentive to hold on to the free cash flow and have "fun" with it, rather than "disgorge" it, say, in the form of higher cash dividend payments.

But all is not lost. This leads to what Jensen calls his "control hypothesis" for debt creation. This means that by levering up, the firm's shareholders will enjoy increased control over their management team. For example, if the firm issues new debt and uses the proceeds to retire outstanding common stock, then management is obligated to pay out cash to service the debt—this simultaneously reduces the amount of free cash flow available to management to have fun with.

We can also refer to this motive for financial leverage use as the "threat hypothesis." Management works under the threat of financial failure; therefore, according to the "free cash flow theory of capital structure," it works more efficiently. This is supposed to reduce the agency costs of free cash flow, which will in turn be recognized by the marketplace in the form of greater returns on the common stock.

BACK TO THE FOUNDATIONS

The discussions on agency costs, free cash flow, and the control hypothesis for debt creation return us to **Axiom 7: The Agency Problem—Managers Won't Work for the Owners Unless It's in Their Best Interest.** The control hypothesis put forth by Jensen suggests that managers will work harder for shareholder interests when they have to "sweat it out" to meet contractual interest payments on debt securities. But we also learned that managers and bond investors can have a conflict that leads to agency costs associated with using debt capital. Thus, the theoretical benefits that flow from minimizing the agency costs of free cash flow by using more debt will cease when the rising agency costs of debt exactly offset those benefits. You can see how very difficult it is, then, for financial managers to identify precisely their true optimal capital structure.

---

[8]Michael C. Jensen, "Agency Costs of Free Cash Flow, Corporate Finance, and Takeovers," *American Economic Review* 76 (May 1986): 323–29.

Note that the free cash flow theory of capital structure does not give a theoretical solution to the question of just how much financial leverage is enough. Nor does it suggest how much leverage is too much leverage. It is a way of thinking about why shareholders and their boards of directors might use more debt to control management behavior and decisions. The basic decision tools of capital structure management still have to be utilized. They are presented later in this chapter.

Managerial Implications

Where does our examination of capital structure theory leave us? The upshot is that the determination of the firm's financing mix is centrally important to the financial manager. The firm's stockholders are affected by capital structure decisions.

At the very least, and before bankruptcy costs and agency costs become detrimental, the tax shield effect will cause the shares of a levered firm to sell at a higher price than they would if the company had avoided debt financing. Because both the risk of failure and agency costs accompany the excessive use of leverage, the financial manager must exercise caution in the use of fixed-charge capital. This problem of searching for the optimal range of use of financial leverage is our next task.[9]

You have now developed a workable knowledge of capital structure theory. This makes you better equipped to search for your firm's optimal capital structure. Several tools are available to help you in this search process and simultaneously help you make prudent financing choices. These tools are decision oriented. They help us answer the question, The next time we need $20 million, should we issue common stock or sell long-term bonds?

CONCEPT CHECK

1. What is the enduring controversy within the subject of capital structure theory?
2. Name the two financial economists, both of whom have won the Nobel Prize in economics, who back in 1958 challenged the importance of capital structure management.
3. Explain the independence hypothesis as it relates to capital structure management.
4. Explain the moderate view of the relationship between a firm's financing mix and its average cost of capital.
5. How do agency costs and free cash flow relate to capital structure management?

---

[9]The relationship between capital structure and enterprise valuation by the marketplace continues to stimulate considerable research output. The complexity of the topic is reviewed in Stewart C. Myers, "The Capital Structure Puzzle," *Journal of Finance* 39 (July 1984): 575–92. Ten useful papers are contained in Benjamin M. Friedman, ed., *Corporate Capital Structures in the United States* (Chicago: National Bureau of Economic Research and The University of Chicago, Press, 1985). A more recent treatment is Stewart C. Myers, "Still Searching for Optimal Capital Structure," in Joel Stern and Donald Chew, eds., *The Revolution in Corporate Finance*, 3rd ed (Malden, Mass: Blackwell Publishers Ltd, 1998): 120–130.

Georgia-Pacific on Capital Structure

The *Introduction* to this chapter referred to the Georgia-Pacific Corporation's financial strategies and management of its capital structure. The discussion below further illustrates the care that this firm's key officers place on managing its financing mix.

As you read the discussion notice that (1) Georgia-Pacific actually uses the weighted average cost of capital concept that you studied in Chapter 12; (2) the firm subscribes to what we called the "moderate view" of the relationship between financing mix and the company's average cost of capital [see Learning Objective 7]; and (3) the firm's management directly relates the stage of the aggregate business cycle to its capital structure planning process.

> Georgia-Pacific tries to balance the mix of debt and equity in a way that will benefit our shareholders, by keeping our weighted average cost of capital low, while retaining the flexibility needed to finance attractive internal projects or acquisitions. Risk factors that contribute to the volatility of our cash flows include economic cycles, changes in industry capacity, environmental regulations and litigation.

> On a market-value basis, our debt-to-capital ratio was 47 percent (year-end 1996). By employing this capital structure, we believe that our weighted average cost of capital is nearly optimized at approximately 10 percent. Although reducing debt significantly would somewhat reduce the marginal cost of debt, significant debt reduction would likely increase our weighted average cost of capital by raising the proportion of higher-cost equity.

> Considering Georgia-Pacific's ability to generate strong cash flow—even at the bottom of the cycle—we believe the current debt structure is quite manageable. In fact, combining the lowest full-year cash flows from building products and pulp and paper operations over recent business cycles would still provide enough cash to pay taxes, cover interest on $5.5 billion of debt, pay dividends, and fund several hundred million dollars of reinvestment needed to maintain our facilities in competitive condition.

Source: Georgia-Pacific, *1996 Annual Report*, 15.

Objective 9   ## BASIC TOOLS OF CAPITAL STRUCTURE MANAGEMENT

Recall from our earlier work that the use of financial leverage has two effects on the earnings stream flowing to the firm's common stockholders. For clarity Tables 13–4 and 13–5 are repeated here as Tables 13–10 and 13–11. Three possible financing mixes for the Pierce Grain Company are contained in Table 13–10, and an analysis for the corresponding financial leverage effects is displayed in Table 13–11.

The first financial leverage effect is the added variability in the earnings-per-share stream that accompanies the use of fixed-charge securities in the company's capital structure. By means of the degree-of-financial-leverage measure (DFL_{EBIT}) we explained how this variability can be quantified. The firm that uses more financial leverage (rather than less) will experience larger relative changes in its earnings per share (rather than smaller) following EBIT fluctuations. Assume that Pierce Grain elected financing plan C rather than plan A. Plan C is highly levered and plan A is unlevered. A 100-percent increase in EBIT from $20,000 to $40,000 would cause earnings per share to rise by 147 percent under plan C, but only 100 percent under plan A. Unfortunately, the effect would operate in the negative direction as well. A given change in EBIT is *magnified* by the use of financial leverage. This magnification is reflected in the variability of the firm's earnings per share.

The second financial leverage effect concerns the level of earnings per share at a given EBIT under a given capital structure. Refer to Table 13–11. At the EBIT level of $20,000, earnings per share would be $5, $5.33, and $5.67 under financing

TABLE 13-10 | **PIERCE GRAIN COMPANY POSSIBLE CAPITAL STRUCTURES**

Plan A: 0% Debt

		Total debt	$ 0
		Common equity	200,000[a]
Total assets	$200,000	Total liabilities and equity	$200,000

Plan B: 25% Debt at 8% Interest Rate

		Total debt	$ 50,000
		Common equity	150,000[b]
Total assets	$200,000	Total liabilities and equity	$200,000

Plan C: 40% Debt at 8% Interest Rate

		Total debt	$ 80,000
		Common equity	120,000[c]
Total assets	$200,000	Total liabilities and equity	$200,000

[a] 2,000 common shares outstanding.
[b] 1,500 common shares outstanding.
[c] 1,200 common shares outstanding.

TABLE 13-11 | **PIERCE GRAIN COMPANY ANALYSIS OF FINANCIAL LEVERAGE AT DIFFERENT EBIT LEVELS**

(1) EBIT	(2) INTEREST	(3) = (1) − (2) EBT	(4) = (3) × .5 TAXES	(5) = (3) − (4) NET INCOME TO COMMON	(6) EARNINGS PER SHARE	
Plan A: 0 debt; $200,000 common equity; 2,000 shares					
$ 0	$ 0	$ 0	$ 0	$ 0	$ 0	
20,000	0	20,000	10,000	10,000	5.00	100%
40,000	0	40,000	20,000	20,000	10.00	
60,000	0	60,000	30,000	30,000	15.00	
80,000	0	80,000	40,000	40,000	20.00	
Plan B: 25% debt; 8% interest rate; $150,000 common equity; 1,500 shares					
$ 0	$4,000	$(4,000)	$(2,000)[a]	$(2,000)	$(1.33)	
20,000	4,000	16,000	8,000	8,000	5.33	125%
40,000	4,000	36,000	18,000	18,000	12.00	
60,000	4,000	56,000	28,000	28,000	18.67	
80,000	4,000	76,000	38,000	38,000	25.33	
Plan C: 40% debt; 8% interest rate; $120,000 common equity; 1,200 shares					
$ 0	$6,400	$(6,400)	$(3,200)[a]	$(3,200)	$(2.67)	
20,000	6,400	13,600	6,800	6,800	5.67	147%
40,000	6,400	33,600	16,800	16,800	14.00	
60,000	6,400	53,600	26,800	26,800	22.33	
80,000	6,400	73,600	36,800	36,800	30.67	

[a] The negative tax bill recognizes the credit arising from the carryback and carryforward provision of the tax code.

arrangements A, B, and C, respectively. Above a critical level of EBIT, the firm's earnings per share will be higher if greater degrees of financial leverage are employed. Conversely, below some critical level of EBIT, earnings per share will suffer at greater degrees of financial leverage. Whereas the first financial-leverage effect is quantified by the degree-of-financial-leverage measure (DFL_{EBIT}), the second is quantified by what is generally referred to as EBIT-EPS analysis. (EPS refers, of course, to earnings per share.) The rationale underlying this sort of analysis is simple. Earnings is one of the key variables that influences the market value of the firm's common stock. The effect of a financing decision on EPS, then, should be understood because the decision will probably affect the value of the stockholder's investment.

EBIT-EPS Analysis

Example

Assume that plan B in Table 13–11 is the existing capital structure for the Pierce Grain Company. Furthermore, the asset structure of the firm is such that EBIT is expected to be $20,000 per year for a very long time. A capital investment is available to Pierce Grain that will cost $50,000. Acquisition of this asset is expected to raise the projected EBIT level to $30,000, permanently. The firm can raise the needed cash by (1) selling 500 shares of common stock at $100 each or (2) selling new bonds that will net the firm $50,000 and carry an interest rate of 8.5 percent. These capital structures and corresponding EPS amounts are summarized in Table 13–12.

At the projected EBIT level of $30,000, the EPS for the common stock and debt alternatives are $6.50 and $7.25, respectively. Both are considerably above the $5.33

TABLE 13–12 PIERCE GRAIN COMPANY ANALYSIS OF FINANCING CHOICES

Part A: Capital Structures

EXISTING CAPITAL STRUCTURE		WITH NEW COMMON STOCK FINANCING		WITH NEW DEBT FINANCING	
Long-term debt at 8%	$ 50,000	Long-term debt at 8%	$ 50,000	Long-term debt at 8%	$ 50,000
Common stock	150,000	Common stock	200,000	Long-term debt at 8.5%	50,000
				Common stock	150,000
Total liabilities and equity	$200,000	Total liabilities and equity	$250,000	Total liabilities and equity	$250,000
Common shares		Common shares		Common shares	
outstanding	1,500	outstanding	2,000	outstanding	1,500

Part B: Projected EPS Levels

	EXISTING CAPITAL STRUCTURE	WITH NEW COMMON STOCK FINANCING	WITH NEW DEBT FINANCING
EBIT	$20,000	$30,000	$30,000
Less: Interest expense	4,000	4,000	8,250
Earnings before taxes (EBT)	$16,000	$26,000	$21,750
Less: Taxes at 50%	8,000	13,000	10,875
Net income	$ 8,000	$13,000	$10,875
Less: Preferred dividends	0	0	0
Earnings available to common	$ 8,000	$13,000	$10,875
EPS	$ 5.33	$ 6.50	$ 7.25

that would occur if the new project were rejected and the additional financial capital were not raised. Based on a criterion of selecting the financing plan that will provide the highest EPS, the bond alternative is favored. But what if the basic business risk to which the firm is exposed causes the EBIT level to vary over a considerable range? Can we be sure that the bond alternative will *always* have the higher EPS associated with it? The answer, of course, is no. When the EBIT level is subject to uncertainty, a graphic analysis of the proposed financing plans can provide useful information to the financial manager. ■

Graphic Analysis

The EBIT-EPS analysis chart allows the decision maker to visualize the impact of different financing plans on EPS over a range of EBIT levels. The relationship between EPS and EBIT is linear. All we need, therefore, to construct the chart is two points for each alternative. Part B of Table 13–12 already provides us with one of these points. The answer to the following question for each choice gives us the second point: At what EBIT level will the EPS for the plan be exactly zero? If the EBIT level *just covers* the plan's financing costs (on a before-tax basis), then EPS will be zero. For the stock plan, an EPS of zero is associated with an EBIT of $4,000. The $4,000 is the interest expense incurred under the existing capital structure. If the bond plan is elected, the interest costs will be the present $4,000 plus $4,250 per year arising from the new debt issue. An EBIT level of $8,250, then, is necessary to provide a zero EPS with the bond plan.

The EBIT-EPS analysis chart representing the financing choices available to the Pierce Grain Company is shown as Figure 13–14. EBIT is charted on the horizontal axis and EPS on the vertical axis. The intercepts on the horizontal axis represent the before-tax equivalent financing charges related to each plan. The straight lines for each plan tell us the EPS amounts that will occur at different EBIT amounts.

Notice that the bond-plan line has a *steeper slope* than the stock-plan line. This ensures that the lines for each financing choice will *intersect*. Above the intersection point, EPS for the plan with greater leverage will exceed that for the plan with lesser

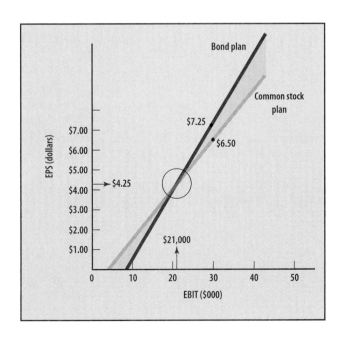

FIGURE 13–14
EBIT-EPS Analysis Chart

leverage. The intersection point, encircled in Figure 13–14, occurs at an EBIT level of $21,000 and produces EPS of $4.25 for each plan. When EBIT is $30,000, notice that the bond plan produces EPS of $7.25, and the stock plan, $6.50. Below the intersection point, EPS with the stock plan will *exceed* that with the more highly levered bond plan. The steeper slope of the bond-plan line indicates that with greater leverage, EPS is more sensitive to EBIT changes.

Computing Indifference Points

EBIT-EPS indifference point

The point of intersection in Figure 13–14 is called the **EBIT-EPS indifference point.** It identifies the *EBIT level at which the EPS will be the same regardless of the financing plan chosen by the financial manager.* This indifference point, sometimes called the break-even point, has major implications for financial planning. At EBIT amounts in excess of the EBIT indifference level, the more heavily levered financing plan will generate a higher EPS. At EBIT amounts below the EBIT indifference level, the financing plan involving less leverage will generate a higher EPS. It is important, then, to know the EBIT indifference level.

We can find it graphically, as in Figure 13–14. At times it may be more efficient, though, to calculate the indifference point directly. This can be done by using the following equation:

$$\underset{\text{EPS: Stock Plan}}{\underbrace{\frac{(EBIT - I)\,(1 - t) - P}{S_s}}} = \underset{\text{EPS: Bond Plan}}{\underbrace{\frac{(EBIT - I)\,(1 - t) - P}{S_b}}} \qquad (13\text{–}16)$$

where S_s and S_b are the number of common shares outstanding under the stock and bond plans, respectively; I is interest expense; t is the firm's income tax rate; and P is preferred dividends paid. In the present case P is zero, because there is no preferred stock outstanding. If preferred stock is associated with one of the financing alternatives, keep in mind that the preferred dividends, P, are not tax deductible. Equation (13–16) does take this fact into consideration.

For the present example, we calculate the indifference level of EBIT as

$$\frac{(EBIT - \$4,000)\,(1 - 0.5) - 0}{2,000} = \frac{(EBIT - \$8,250)\,(1 - 0.5) - 0}{1,500}$$

When the expression above is solved for EBIT, we obtain $21,000. If EBIT turns out to be $21,000, then EPS will be $4.25 under both plans.

Word of Caution

Above the EBIT-EPS indifference point, a more heavily levered financial plan promises to deliver a larger EPS. Strict application of the criterion of selecting the financing plan that produces the highest EPS might have the firm issuing debt most of the time it raised external capital. Our discussion of capital structure theory taught us the dangers of that sort of action.

The primary weakness of EBIT-EPS analysis is that it disregards the implicit costs of debt financing. The effect of the specific financing decision on the firm's cost of common equity capital is totally ignored. Investors should be concerned with both the level and variability of the firm's expected earnings stream. EBIT-EPS analysis considers only the level of the earnings stream and ignores the variability (riskiness) inherent in it. Thus, this type of analysis must be used in conjunction with other basic tools in reaching the objective of capital structure management.

Comparative Leverage Ratios

In Chapter 4 we explored the overall usefulness of financial ratio analysis. Leverage ratios, one of the categories of financial ratios, are identified in that chapter. We emphasize here that the computation of leverage ratios is one of the basic tools of capital structure management.

Two types of leverage ratios must be computed when a financing decision faces the firm. We call these *balance-sheet leverage ratios* and *coverage ratios*. The firm's balance sheet supplies inputs for computing the balance sheet leverage ratios. In various forms these balance sheet metrics compare the firm's use of funds supplied by creditors with those supplied by owners.

Inputs to the coverage ratios generally come from the firm's income statement. At times the external analyst may have to consult balance sheet information to construct some of these needed estimates. On a privately placed debt issue, for example, some fraction of the current portion of the firm's long-term debt might have to be used as an estimate of that issue's sinking fund. Coverage ratios provide estimates of the firm's ability to service its financing contracts. High coverage ratios, compared with a standard, imply unused debt capacity.

In reality we know that EBIT might be expected to vary over a considerable range of outcomes. For this reason the coverage ratios should be calculated several times, each at a different level of EBIT. If this is accomplished over all possible values of EBIT, a probability distribution for each coverage ratio can be constructed. This provides the financial manager with much more information than simply calculating the coverage ratios based on the expected value of EBIT.

Industry Norms

The comparative leverage ratios calculated have additional utility to the decision maker if they can be compared with some standard. Generally, corporate financial analysts, investment bankers, commercial bank loan officers, and bond-rating agencies rely on industry classes from which to compute "normal" ratios. Although industry groupings may actually contain firms whose basic business risk exposure differs widely, the practice is entrenched in American business behavior. At the very least, then, the financial officer must be interested in industry standards because almost everybody else is.

Several published studies indicate that capital structure ratios vary in a significant manner among industry classes.[10] For example, random samplings of the common equity ratios of large retail firms seem to differ statistically from those of major steel producers. The major steel producers use financial leverage to a lesser degree then do the large retail organizations. On the whole, firms operating in the *same* industry tend to exhibit capital structure ratios that cluster around a central value that we call a norm. Business risk varies from industry to industry. As a consequence, the capital structure norms vary from industry to industry.

This is not to say that all companies in the industry will maintain leverage ratios "close" to the norm. For instance, firms that are very profitable may display

An efficient way to calculate various (1) balance-sheet leverage ratios and (2) coverage ratios for actual firms is to go to http://www.quicken.com/investments. Once there, type in the stock market ticker symbol of the firm you are analyzing (e.g., for Disney it would be DIS). Once the stock quote comes up, click on "financial statements." The balance sheets and income statements for recent years will be displayed. Then you can calculate your own leverage ratios (e.g., total debt to total assets and the times-interest-earned ratio) and compare them with other firms.

Takin' It to the Net

---

[10]See, for example, Eli Schwartz and J. Richard Aronson, "Some Surrogate Evidence in Support of the Concept of Optimal Financial Structure," *Journal of Finance* 22 (March 1967): 10–18; David F. Scott, Jr., "Evidence on the Importance of Financial Structure," *Financial Management 1* (Summer 1972): 45–50; and David F. Scott, Jr., and John D. Martin, "Industry Influence on Financial Structure," *Financial Management* 4 (Spring 1975): 67–73.

The Walt Disney Company on Capital Costs and Capital Structure

At the end of fiscal year 1998, the Walt Disney Company had a total market capitalization of $65 billion; this placed it among the 40 largest corporations in the United States, while its sales revenues of $23.0 billion placed it fifty-third on the 1999 Fortune 500 list. This multinational giant with 117,000 employees provides several real examples of the capital structure concepts presented in this chapter.

In the following discussion from Disney management, notice how the firm (1) relates capital costs to shareholder value; (2) believes in the "prudent degree of leverage" concept; (3) is concerned with its interest coverage ratio—measured as earnings before net interest, taxes, depreciation, and amortization or EBITDA divided by net interest expense; and (4) strives to maintain a minimum desired or target bond rating. Within the accompanying graph you see that Disney's coverage ratio for fiscal year 1998 of EBITDA to net interest expense is 8.1 times (i.e., $5,019 million/$622 million).

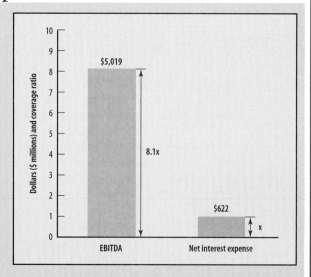

Disney's solid balance sheet allows the company to borrow at attractive rates, helping to reduce the overall cost of capital and thereby creating value for shareholders. As of year end, Disney maintained total borrowings of approximately $12 billion and a debt-to-total-capital ratio of 38%. The company believes that this level of debt represents a prudent degree of leverage, which provides for substantial financial flexibility to borrow should sound business opportunities present themselves. As measured by the ratio of earnings before net interest, taxes, depreciation and amortization (EBITDA) to net interest expense, the company covered its interest costs by a factor of more than eight times for the year ended September 30.

The company monitors its cash flow, interest coverage and its debt-to-total-capital ratio with the long-term goal of maintaining a strong single-A or better credit rating.

Source: The Walt Disney Company, 1998 Annual Report, p. 12.

high coverage ratios and high balance-sheet leverage ratios. The moderately profitable firm, though, might find such a posture unduly risky. Here the usefulness of industry-normal leverage ratios is clear. If the firm chooses to deviate in a material manner from the accepted values for the key ratios, it must have a sound reason.

CONCEPT CHECK

1. Explain the meaning of the EBIT-EPS indifference point.
2. How are various leverage ratios and industry norms used in capital structure management?

A GLANCE AT ACTUAL CAPITAL STRUCTURE MANAGEMENT

We now examine some opinions and practices of financial executives that reinforce an emphasis on the importance of capital structure management.

Target Debt Ratios

Selected comments from financial executives point to the widespread use of target debt ratios. A vice-president and treasurer of the American Telephone and Telegraph Company (AT&T) described his firm's debt ratio policy in terms of a range:

> All of the foregoing considerations led us to conclude, and reaffirm for a period of many years, that the proper range of our debt was 30% to 40% of total capital. Reasonable success in meeting financial needs under the diverse market and economic conditions that we have faced attests to the appropriateness of this conclusion.[11]

A frequently mentioned influence on the level of the target debt ratio is ability to meet financing charges. Other factors identified by executives as affecting the target are (1) maintaining a desired bond rating, (2) providing an adequate borrowing reserve, and (3) exploiting the advantages of financial leverage.

Who Sets Target Debt Ratios?

We know that firms do use target debt ratios in arriving at financing decisions. But who sets or influences these target ratios? This and other questions concerning corporate financing policy were investigated in one study published in 1982.[12] This survey of the 1,000 largest industrial firms in the United States (as ranked by total sales dollars) involved responses from 212 financial executives.

Takin' It to the Net

The Coca-Cola Company maintains an extensive and useful Internet site, where you can read about the firm's financial strategies in its latest annual report. Go to http://Cocacola.com/annualreport/1998/. For the most recent report, type in the latest year where 1998 appears in this address. Once you access the annual report, click on "quick index" and then "financial strategies." Now you can review Coke's debt policy, bond ratings, and various measures of leverage use (e.g., the interest coverage ratio). Many of the concepts discussed in this chapter are touched upon by Coke management's elaboration on "debt management policies."

TABLE 13-13 — SETTING TARGET FINANCIAL STRUCTURE RATIOS

| | Rank | |
TYPE OF INFLUENCE	1	2
Internal management and staff analysts	85%	7%
Investment bankers	3	39
Commercial bankers	0	9
Trade creditors	1	0
Security analysts	1	4
Comparative industry ratios	3	23
Other	7	18
Total	100%	100%

Source: David F. Scott, Jr., "Financing Policies and Practices in Large Corporations." *Financial Management*, Vol 11, No 2, 1982, Summer. Used with permission of Financial Management Association International, University of South Florida, Tampa, Florida.

---

[11]John J. Scanlon, "Bell System Financial Policies," *Financial Management* 1 (Summer 1972): 16–26.

[12]David F. Scott, Jr., and Dana J. Johnson, "Financing Policies and Practices in Large Corporations," *Financial Management* 11 (Summer 1982): 51–59.

In one portion of this study the participants were asked to rank several possible influences on their target leverage (debt) ratios. Table 13–13 displays the percentage of responses ranked either number 1 or number 2 in importance. Ranks past the second are omitted in that they were not very significant. Notice that the most important influence is the firm's own management group and staff of analysts. This item accounted for 85 percent of the responses ranked number 1. Of the responses ranked number 2 in importance, investment bankers dominated the outcomes and accounted for 39 percent of such replies. Also notice that comparisons with ratios of industry competitors and commercial bankers have some impact on the determination of leverage targets.

Debt Capacity

Previously in this chapter we noted that the firm's debt capacity is the maximum proportion of debt that it can include in its capital structure and still maintain its lowest composite cost of capital. But how do financial executives make the concept of debt capacity operational? Table 13–14 is derived from the same 1982 survey, involving 212 executives, previously mentioned. These executives defined debt capacity in a wide variety of ways. The most popular approach was as a target percentage of total capitalization. Twenty-seven percent of the respondents thought of debt capacity in this manner. Forty-three percent of the participating executives remarked that debt capacity is defined in terms of some balance sheet–based financial ratio (see the first three items in Table 13–14). Maintaining a specific bond rating was also indicated to be a popular approach to implementing the debt capacity concept.

Business Risk

The single most important factor that should affect the firm's financing mix is the underlying nature of the business in which it operates. In this chapter we defined

Takin' It to the Net
We learned that one method used by financial executives to implement the debt capacity concept is to maintain a specific bond rating. This means the firm will issue new debt only as long as the desired (target) bond rating is not impaired. Now, suppose your firm wishes to maintain a bond rating of Aaa in the Moody's system of ratings. We want to know what the likely before-tax cost of debt of a bond rated Aaa is today. Such information is available at http://www.federalreserve.gov. At this site you can retrieve the H.15 (for daily data) and G.13 (for weekly data) reports called "Selected Interest Rates." Towards the bottom of those reports you will find the current yields on Aaa- and Baa-rated corporate bonds.

TABLE 13–14	DEFINITIONS OF DEBT CAPACITY IN PRACTICE

STANDARD OR METHOD	1,000 LARGEST CORPORATIONS (PERCENT USING)
Target percent of total capitalization (long-term debt to total capitalization)	27%
Long-term debt to net worth ratio (or its inverse)	14
Long-term debt to total assets	2
Interest (or fixed charge) coverage ratio	6
Maintain bond ratings	14
Restrictive debt covenants	4
Most adverse cash flow	4
Industry standard	3
Other	10
No response	16
Total	100%

Source: David F. Scott, Jr., "Financing Policies and Practices in Large Corporations." *Financial Management,* Vol 11, No 2, 1982, Summer. Used with permission of Financial Management Association International, University of South Florida, Tampa, Florida.

business risk as the relative dispersion in the firm's expected stream of EBIT. If the nature of the firm's business is such that the variability inherent in its EBIT stream is high, then it would be unwise to impose a high degree of financial risk on top of this already uncertain earnings stream.

The AT&T financial officer referred to earlier has commented on the relationship between business risk and financial risk:

> In determining how much debt a firm can safely carry, it is necessary to consider the basic risks inherent in that business. This varies considerably among industries and is related essentially to the nature and demand for an industry's product, the operating characteristics of the industry, and its ability to earn an adequate return in an unknown future.[13]

CONCEPT CHECK

1. Identify several factors that influence target debt ratios in actual business practice.
2. Identify several methods used by executives to make the concept of debt capacity operational.

It appears clear that the firm's capital structure cannot be properly designed without a thorough understanding of its commercial strategy.

FINANCE AND THE MULTINATIONAL FIRM: BUSINESS RISK AND GLOBAL SALES

Objective 10

Early in this chapter we defined business risk as the relative dispersion (variability) in the firm's expected earnings before interest and taxes (EBIT). And when we discussed operating leverage and the degree of operating leverage concept, we learned that changes or shocks to the firm's overall sales level will cause a greater percentage change in EBIT if fixed operating costs are present in the firm's cost structure. Thus, any event that induces a fluctuation in measured sales will impact a firm's business risk and its resulting EBIT.

Business risk is multidimensional and international. It is directly affected by several factors including (1) the sensitivity of the firm's product demand to general economic conditions, (2) the degree of competition to which the firm is exposed, (3) product diversification, (4) growth prospects, and (5) global sales volume and production output. The latter factor is especially important to the multinational firm, and such firms are aware of it. Some seek to take advantage of it in an aggressive manner.

Consider the Coca-Cola Company. In his statement to shareholders published in 1998, Mr. M. Douglas Ivester, CEO and chairman of Coke's Board, commented on the firm's commercial strategy in both China and Russia.[14] He said, "In China, the world's largest market, our volume soared another 30 percent in 1997. But the average resident of China still drinks just six of our products a year—certainly a business in its infancy." Notice that although Coke's presence in China increases its total

---

[13]Scanlon, "Bell System Financial Policies," p. 19.
[14]The Coca-Cola Company, *Annual Report*, 1997, pp. 5–6.

business risk exposure, Mr. Ivester views this exposure as a commercial opportunity for the firm.

In his discussion of the Russian market Mr. Ivester offered, "In Russia, where we took the lead over our largest competitor in 1996, we widened that lead to 3-to-1 in 1997; we opened four more plants there on October 1, bringing our system's Russian investment to $650 million and pointing to strong future growth." Here we see that Coke is both cultivating the Russian consumer and simultaneously investing in plant and equipment there. Thus, Coke's broad commercial strategy, which impacts business risk, also encompasses the capital budgeting decision discussed earlier in this text.

CONCEPT CHECK

1. Identify several factors that directly affect a firm's business risk.
2. How might a firm's commercial strategy be influenced by its presence in foreign markets?

SUMMARY

In this chapter we study the process of arriving at an appropriate financial structure for the firm and examine tools that can assist the financial manager in this task. We are concerned with assessing the variability in the firm's residual earnings stream (either earnings per share or earnings available to the common shareholders) induced by the use of operating and financial leverage. This assessment builds on the tenets of break-even analysis.

Objective 1

We then deal with the design of the firm's financing mix, particularly emphasizing management of the firm's permanent sources of funds—that is, its capital structure. The objective of capital structure management is to arrange the company's sources of funds so that its common stock price is maximized, all other factors held constant.

Objective 2

Break-even analysis

Break-even analysis permits the financial manager to determine the quantity of output or the level of sales that will result in an EBIT level of zero. This means the firm has neither a profit nor a loss before any tax considerations. The effect of price changes, cost structure changes, or volume changes on profits (EBIT) can be studied. To make the technique operational, it is necessary that the firm's costs be classified as fixed or variable. Not all costs fit neatly into one of these two categories. Over short planning horizons, though, the preponderance of costs can be assigned to either the fixed or variable classification. Once the cost structure has been identified, the break-even point can be found by use of contribution margin analysis or algebraic analysis.

Objective 3

Operating leverage

Operating leverage is the responsiveness of the firm's EBIT to changes in sales revenues. It arises from the firm's use of fixed operating costs. When fixed operating costs are present in the company's cost structure, changes in sales are magnified into even greater changes in EBIT. The firm's degree of operating leverage from a base sales level is the percentage change in EBIT divided by the percentage change in sales. All types of leverage are two-edged swords. When sales decrease by some percentage, the negative impact on EBIT is even larger.

Objective 4

Financial leverage

A firm employs financial leverage when it finances a portion of its assets with securities bearing a fixed rate of return. The presence of debt and/or preferred stock in the company's financial structure means that it is using financial leverage. When financial leverage is used, changes in EBIT translate into larger changes in earnings per share. The concept of the degree of financial leverage dwells on the sensitivity of earnings per share to changes in EBIT. The DFL from a base EBIT level is defined as the percentage change in earnings per share divided by the percentage change in EBIT. All other things equal, the more fixed-charge securities the firm employs in its financial structure, the greater its degree of financial leverage. Clearly, EBIT can rise or fall. If it falls, and financial leverage is used, the firm's shareholders endure negative changes in earnings per share that are larger than the relative decline in EBIT. Again, leverage is a two-edged sword.

Combining operating and financial leverage

Firms use operating and financial leverage in various degrees. The joint use of operating and financial leverage can be measured by computing the degree of combined leverage, defined as the percentage change in earnings per share divided by the percentage change in sales. This measure allows the financial manager to ascertain the effect on total leverage caused by adding financial leverage on top of operating leverage. Effects can be dramatic, because the degree of combined leverage is the product of the degrees of operating and financial leverage.

Capital structure theory

Can the firm affect its composite cost of capital by altering its financing mix? Attempts to answer this question have comprised a significant portion of capital structure theory for over three decades. Extreme positions show that the firm's stock price is either unaffected or continually affected as the firm increases its reliance on leverage-inducing funds. In the real world, an operating environment where interest expense is tax deductible and market imperfections operate to restrict the amount of fixed-income obligations a firm can issue, most financial officers and financial academics subscribe to the concept of an optimal capital structure. The optimal capital structure minimizes the firm's composite cost of capital. Searching for a proper range of financial leverage, then, is an important financial management activity.

Complicating the manager's search for an optimal capital structure are conflicts that lead to agency costs. A natural conflict exists between stockholders and bondholders (the agency costs of debt). To reduce excessive risk taking by management on behalf of stockholders, it may be necessary to include several protective covenants in bond contracts that serve to restrict managerial decision making.

Another type of agency cost is related to "free cash flow." Managers, for example, have an incentive to hold on to free cash flow and enjoy it, rather than pay it out in the form of higher cash-dividend payments. This conflict between managers and stockholders leads to the concept of the *free cash flow theory of capital structure*. This same theory is also known as the *control hypothesis* and the *threat hypothesis*. The ultimate resolution of these agency costs affects the specific form of the firm's capital structure.

Tools of capital structure management

The decision to use senior securities in the firm's capitalization causes two types of financial leverage effects. The first is the added variability in the earnings-per-share stream that accompanies the use of fixed-charge securities. We explain how this can be quantified by the use of the degree of financial leverage metric. The second financial leverage effect relates to the level of earnings per share (EPS) at a given EBIT under a specific capital structure. We rely on EBIT-EPS analysis to measure this second effect. Through EBIT-EPS analysis the decision maker can inspect the impact of alternative financing plans on EPS over a full range of EBIT levels.

A second tool of capital structure management is the calculation of comparative leverage ratios. Balance-sheet leverage ratios and coverage ratios can be computed according to the contractual stipulations of the proposed financing plans. Comparison of these ratios with industry standards enables the financial officer to determine if the firm's key ratios are materially out of line with accepted practice.

Capital structure practices

Surveys indicate that most financial officers in large firms believe in the concept of an optimal capital structure. The optimal capital structure is approximated by the identification of target

Objective 5
Objective 6
Objective 7

Objective 8

Objective 9

debt ratios. The targets reflect the firm's ability to service fixed financing costs and also consider the business risk to which the firm is exposed.

Survey studies have provided information on who sets or influences the firm's target leverage ratios. The firm's own management group and staff of analysts are the major influence, followed in importance by investment bankers. Studies also show that executives put the concept of debt capacity in operation in many ways. The most popular approach is to define debt capacity in terms of a target long-term debt to total capitalization ratio. Maintaining a specific bond rating (such as Aa or A) is also a popular approach to implementing the debt capacity concept.

Objective 10

The multinational firm: business risk and global sales

Business risk is both multidimensional and international. It is directly affected by several factors including (1) the sensitivity of the firm's product demand to general economic conditions, (2) the degree of competition to which the firm is exposed, (3) product diversification, (4) growth prospects, and (5) global sales. On the last factor, we explored how the Coca-Cola Company related the firm's commercial strategy to include sales prospects in the huge markets of China and Russia.

KEY TERMS

business risk, 401

capital structure, 420

contribution margin, 407

debt capacity, 427

direct costs (see variable costs), 404

EBIT-EPS indifference point, 436

financial leverage, 402

financial risk, 402

financial structure, 419

fixed costs, 404

indirect costs (see fixed costs), 404

operating leverage, 403

optimal capital structure, 421

optimal range of financial leverage, 427

risk, 401

tax shield, 425

total revenue, 406

variable costs, 404

volume of output, 406

STUDY QUESTIONS

13-1 Distinguish between business risk and financial risk. What gives rise to, or causes, each type of risk?

13-2 Define the term *financial leverage*. Does the firm use financial leverage if preferred stock is present in the capital structure?

13-3 Define the term *operating leverage*. What type of effect occurs when the firm uses operating leverage?

13-4 A manager in your firm decides to employ break-even analysis. Of what shortcomings should this manager be aware?

13-5 If a firm has a degree of combined leverage of 3.0 times, what does a negative sales fluctuation of 15 percent portend for the earnings available to the firm's common stock investors?

13-6 Break-even analysis assumes linear revenue and cost functions. In reality these linear functions over large output and sales levels are highly improbable. Why?

13-7 Define the following terms:
   a. Financial structure
   b. Capital structure
   c. Optimal capital structure
   d. Debt capacity

13-8 What is the primary weakness of EBIT-EPS analysis as a financing decision tool?

13-9 What is the objective of capital structure management?

13-10 Distinguish between (a) balance-sheet leverage ratios and (b) coverage ratios. Give two examples of each and indicate how they would be computed.

13-11 Why might firms whose sales levels change drastically over time choose to use debt only sparingly in their capital structures?

13-12 What condition would cause capital structure management to be a meaningless activity?

13-13 What does the term *independence hypothesis* mean as it applies to capital structure theory?

13-14 Who have been the foremost advocates of the independence hypothesis?

13-15 A financial manager might say that the firm's composite cost of capital is saucer-shaped or U-shaped. What does this mean?

13-16 Define the EBIT-EPS indifference point.

13-17 Explain how industry norms might be used by the financial manager in the design of the company's financing mix.

13-18 Define the term *free cash flow*.

13-19 What is meant by the *free cash flow theory of capital structure?*

13-20 In almost every instance, what funds source do managers use first in the financing of their capital budgets?

SELF-TEST PROBLEM

ST-1 *(Fixed Costs and the Break-even Point)* Bonaventure Manufacturing expects to earn $210,000 next year after taxes. Sales will be $4 million. The firm's single plant is located on the outskirts of Olean, N.Y. The firm manufactures a combined bookshelf and desk unit used extensively in college dormitories. These units sell for $200 each and have a variable cost per unit of $150. Bonaventure experiences a 30-percent tax rate.

a. What are the firm's fixed costs expected to be next year?

b. Calculate the firm's break-even point in both units and dollars.

STUDY PROBLEMS

13-1 *(Leverage Analysis)* You have developed the following analytical income statement for the Hugo Boss Corporation. It represents the most recent year's operations, which ended yesterday.

Sales	$ 50,439,375
Variable costs	(25,137,000)
Revenue before fixed costs	$ 25,302,375
Fixed costs	(10,143,000)
EBIT	$ 15,159,375
Interest expense	(1,488,375)
Earnings before taxes	$ 13,671,000
Taxes at 50%	(6,835,500)
Net income	$ 6,835,500

Your supervisor in the controller's office has just handed you a memorandum asking for written responses to the following questions:

a. At this level of output, what is the degree of operating leverage?

b. What is the degree of financial leverage?

c. What is the degree of combined leverage?

d. What is the firm's break-even point in sales dollars?

e. If sales should increase by 30 percent, by what percent would earnings before taxes (and net income) increase?

13-2 *(EBIT-EPS Analysis)* Four recent liberal arts graduates have interested a group of venture capitalists in backing a new business enterprise. The proposed operation would consist of a series of retail outlets to distribute and service a full line of vacuum cleaners and accessories. These stores would be located in Dallas, Houston, and San Antonio. Two financing plans have been proposed by the graduates. Plan A is an all-common-equity structure. Two million dollars would be raised by selling 100,000 shares of common stock. Plan B would involve the use of long-term debt financing. One million dollars would be raised by marketing bonds with an effective interest rate of 8 percent. Under this alternative, another $1 million would be raised by selling 50,000 shares of common stock. With both plans, then, $2 million is needed to launch the new firm's operations. The debt funds raised under plan B are considered to have no fixed maturity date, in that this portion of financial leverage is thought to be a permanent part of the company's capital structure. The fledgling executives have decided to use a 30-percent tax rate in their analysis, and they have hired you on a consulting basis to do the following:

a. Find the EBIT indifference level associated with the two financing proposals.

b. Prepare an analytical income statement that proves EPS will be the same regardless of the plan chosen at the EBIT level found in part a above.

13-3 *(Leverage Analysis)* You have developed the following analytical income statement for your corporation. It represents the most recent year's operations, which ended yesterday.

Sales	$45,750,000
Variable costs	22,800,000
Revenue before fixed costs	$22,950,000
Fixed costs	9,200,000
EBIT	$13,750,000
Interest expense	1,350,000
Earnings before taxes	$12,400,000
Taxes at 50%	6,200,000
Net income	$ 6,200,000

Your supervisor in the controller's office has just handed you a memorandum asking for written responses to the following questions:

a. At this level of output, what is the degree of operating leverage?

b. What is the degree of financial leverage?

c. What is the degree of combined leverage?

d. What is the firm's break-even point in sales dollars?

e. If sales should increase by 25 percent, by what percent would earnings before taxes (and net income) increase?

13-4 *(Break-even Point and Operating Leverage)* Footwear, Inc., manufacturers a complete line of men's and women's dress shoes for independent merchants. The average selling price of its finished product is $85 per pair. The variable cost for this same pair of shoes is $58. Footwear, Inc., incurs fixed costs of $170,000 per year.

a. What is the break-even point in pairs of shoes for the company?

b. What is the dollar sales volume the firm must achieve to reach the break-even point?

c. What would be the firm's profit or loss at the following units of production sold: 7,000 pairs of shoes? 9,000 pairs of shoes? 15,000 pairs of shoes?

d. Find the degree of operating leverage for the production and sales levels given in part c above.

13-5 *(Break-even Point and Profit Margin)* Mary Clark, a recent graduate of Clarion South University, is planning to open a new wholesaling operation. Her target operating profit margin is 26 percent. Her unit contribution margin will be 50 percent of sales. Average annual sales are forecast to be $3,250,000.

    a. How large can fixed costs be for the wholesaling operation and still allow the 26-percent operating profit margin to be achieved?

    b. What is the break-even point in dollars for the firm?

13-6 *(Leverage Analysis)* You have developed the following analytical income statement for your corporation. It represents the most recent year's operations, which ended yesterday.

Sales	$30,000,000
Variable costs	13,500,000
Revenue before fixed costs	$16,500,000
Fixed costs	8,000,000
EBIT	$ 8,500,000
Interest expense	1,000,000
Earnings before taxes	$ 7,500,000
Taxes at 50%	3,750,000
Net income	$ 3,750,000

Your supervisor in the controller's office has just handed you a memorandum asking for written responses to the following questions:

    a. At this level of output, what is the degree of operating leverage?

    b. What is the degree of financial leverage?

    c. What is the degree of combined leverage?

    d. What is the firm's break-even point in sales dollars?

    e. If sales should increase by 25 percent, by what percent would earnings before taxes (and net income) increase?

13-7 *(Break-even Point and Selling Price)* Parks Castings, Inc., will manufacture and sell 200,000 units next year. Fixed costs will total $300,000, and variable costs will be 60 percent of sales.

    a. The firm wants to achieve an earnings before interest and taxes level of $250,000. What selling price per unit is necessary to achieve this result?

    b. Set up an analytical income statement to verify your solution to part a.

13-8 *(Operating Leverage)* Rocky Mount Metals Company manufactures an assortment of woodburning stoves. The average selling price for the various units is $500. The associated variable cost is $350 per unit. Fixed costs for the firm average $180,000 annually.

    a. What is the break-even point in units for the company?

    b. What is the dollar sales volume the firm must achieve to reach the break-even point?

    c. What is the degree of operating leverage for a production and sales level of 5,000 units for the firm? (Calculate to three decimal places.)

    d. What will be the projected effect on earnings before interest and taxes if the firm's sales level should increase by 20 percent from the volume noted in part c above?

13-9 *(Sales Mix and Break-even Point)* Toledo Components produces four lines of auto accessories for the major Detroit automobile manufacturers. The lines are known by the code letters A, B, C, and D. The current sales mix for Toledo and the contribution margin ratio (unit contribution margin divided by unit sales price) for these product lines are as follows:

PRODUCT LINE	PERCENT OF TOTAL SALES	CONTRIBUTION MARGIN RATIO
A	$33^1/_3$	40%
B	$41^2/_3$	32
C	$16^2/_3$	20
D	$8^1/_3$	60

Total sales for next year are forecast to be $120,000. Total fixed costs will be $29,400.

    a. Prepare a table showing (1) sales, (2) total variable costs, and (3) the total contribution margin associated with each product line.

    b. What is the aggregate contribution margin ratio indicative of this sales mix?

    c. At this sales mix, what is the break-even point in dollars?

13-10 *(Sales Mix and Break-even Point)* Because of production constraints, Toledo Components (see problem 13–9) may have to adhere to a different sales mix for next year. The alternative plan is outlined below.

PRODUCT LINE	PERCENT OF TOTAL SALES
A	25
B	$36^2/_3$
C	$33^1/_3$
D	5

    a. Assuming all other facts in problem 13—9 remain the same, what effect will this different sales mix have on Toledo's break-even point in dollars?

    b. Which sales mix will Toledo's management prefer?

13-11 *(EBIT-EPS Analysis)* A group of retired college professors has decided to form a small manufacturing corporation. The company will produce a full line of traditional office furniture. Two financing plans have been proposed by the investors. Plan A is an all-common-equity alternative. Under this agreement, 1 million common shares will be sold to net the firm $20 per share. Plan B involves the use of financial leverage. A debt issue with a 20-year maturity period will be privately placed. The debt issue will carry an interest rate of 10 percent, and the principal borrowed will amount to $6 million. The corporate tax rate is 50 percent.

    a. Find the EBIT indifference level associated with the two financing proposals.

    b. Prepare an analytical income statement that proves EPS will be the same regardless of the plan chosen at the EBIT level found in part a.

    c. Prepare an EBIT-EPS analysis chart for this situation.

    d. If a detailed financial analysis projects that long-term EBIT will always be close to $2.4 million annually, which plan will provide for the higher EPS?

13-12 *(EBIT-EPS Analysis)* Four recent liberal arts graduates have interested a group of venture capitalists in backing a new business enterprise. The proposed operation would consist of a series of retail outlets to distribute and service a full line of vacuum cleaners and accessories. These stores would be located in Dallas, Houston, and San Antonio. Two financing plans have been proposed by the graduates. Plan A is an all-common-equity structure. Two million dollars would be raised by selling 80,000 shares of common stock. Plan B would involve the use of long-term debt financing. One million dollars would be raised by marketing bonds with an effective interest rate of 12 percent. Under the alternative, another $1 million would be raised by selling 40,000 shares of common stock. With both plans, then, $2 million is needed to launch the new firm's operations. The debt funds raised under plan B are considered to have no fixed maturity date, in that this portion of financial leverage is thought to be a permanent part of the company's capital structure. The fledging executives have decided to use a 40-percent tax rate in their analysis, and they have hired you on a consulting basis to do the following:

a. Find the EBIT indifference level associated with the two financing proposals.

b. Prepare an analytical income statement that proves EPS will be the same regardless of the plan chosen at the EBIT level found in part a.

13-13 (*Assessing Leverage Use*) Some financial data for three corporations are displayed below.

MEASURE	FIRM A	FIRM B	FIRM C	INDUSTRY NORM
Debt ratio	20%	25%	40%	20%
Times burden covered	8 times	10 times	7 times	9 times
Price-earnings ratio	9 times	11 times	6 times	10 times

a. Which firm appears to be excessively levered?

b. Which firm appears to be employing financial leverage to the most appropriate degree?

c. What explanation can you provide for the higher price-earnings ratio enjoyed by firm B as compared with firm A?

——————— COMPREHENSIVE PROBLEM ———————

Imagine that you were hired recently as a financial analyst for a relatively new, highly leveraged ski manufacturer located in the foothills of Colorado's Rocky Mountains. Your firm manufacturers only one product, a state-of-the-art snow ski. The company has been operating up to this point without much quantitative knowledge of the business and financial risks it faces.

Ski season just ended, however, so the president of the company has started to focus more on the financial aspects of managing the business. He has set up a meeting for next week with the CFO, Maria Sanchez, to discuss matters such as the business and financial risks faced by the company. Accordingly, Maria has asked you to prepare an analysis to assist her in her discussions with the president.

As a first step in your work, you compiled the following information regarding the cost structure of the company:

Output level	80,000 units
Operating assets	$4,000,000
Operating asset turnover	8 times
Return on operating assets	32%
Degree of operating leverage	6 times
Interest expense	$600,000
Tax rate	35%

As the next step, you need to determine the break-even point in units of output for the company. One of your strong points has been that you always prepare supporting work papers, which show how you arrive at your conclusions. You know Maria would like to see such work papers for this analysis to facilitate her review of your work.

Therefore, you will have the information you require to prepare an analytical income statement for the company. You are sure that Maria would like to see this statement; in addition, you know that you need it to be able to answer the following questions. You also know Maria expects you to prepare, in a format that is presentable to the president, answers to the following questions to serve as a basis for her discussions with the president.

a. What is the degree of financial leverage?

b. What is the degree of combined leverage?

c. What is the firm's break-even point in sales dollars?

d. If sales should increase by 30 percent (as the president expects), by what percent would EBT (earnings before taxes) and net income increase?

e. Prepare another analytical income statement, this time to verify the calculations from part d above.

―――――――――― **SELF-TEST SOLUTION** ――――――――――

SS-1

a.

$$
\begin{aligned}
[(P \cdot Q) - [(V \cdot Q) + (F)]] \,(1 - T) &= \$210{,}000 \\
[(\$4{,}000{,}000) - (\$3{,}000{,}000) - F]\,(.7) &= \$210{,}000 \\
(\$1{,}000{,}000 - F)\,(.7) &= \$210{,}000 \\
\$700{,}000 - .7F &= \$210{,}000 \\
.7F &= \$490{,}000 \\
F &= \underline{\underline{\$700{,}000}}
\end{aligned}
$$

Fixed costs next year, then, are expected to be $700,000.

b.

$$
Q_B = \frac{F}{P - V} = \frac{\$700{,}000}{\$50} = \underline{\underline{14{,}000}} \; units
$$

$$
S^* = \frac{F}{1 - \dfrac{VC}{S}} = \frac{\$700{,}000}{1 - .75} = \frac{\$700{,}000}{.25} = \underline{\underline{\$2{,}800{,}000}}
$$

The firm will break even (EBIT = 0) when it sells 14,000 units. With a selling price of $200 per unit, the break-even sales level is $2,800,000.

DIVIDEND POLICY AND INTERNAL FINANCING

LEARNING OBJECTIVES

AFTER READING THIS CHAPTER, YOU SHOULD BE ABLE TO:

1. Describe the trade-off between paying dividends and retaining the profits within the company.
2. Explain the relationship between a corporation's dividend policy and the market price of its common stock.
3. Describe practical considerations that may be important to the firm's dividend policy.
4. Distinguish among the types of dividend policies corporations frequently use.
5. Specify the procedures a company follows in administering the dividend payment.
6. Describe why and how a firm might pay non-cash dividends (stock dividends and stock splits) instead of cash dividends.
7. Explain the purpose and procedures related to stock repurchases.
8. Understand the relationship between a policy of low dividend payments and international capital budgeting opportunities that confront the multinational firm.

The corporate choice to pay or not to pay a cash dividend to stockholders and the further choice to increase the dividend, reduce the dividend, or keep it at the same dollar amount represents one of the most challenging and perplexing areas of corporate financial policy. Because stockholder returns only come in two forms—stock price change and cash dividends received—it follows that the dividend decision directly impacts shareholder wealth.

We know that rational investors would rather be more wealthy than less wealthy. Accordingly, corporate boards of directors face a daunting decision every time the question of dividend policy and the possibility of changing the cash dividend is on the agenda.

In the simplest form, increasing the cash dividend simultaneously reduces the stock of internal financial capital (cash) available for capital expenditures. Thus, the firm's stockholders find themselves smack in the middle of **Axiom 1: The Risk-Return Trade-off—We Won't Take on Additional Risk Unless We Expect to Be Compensated with Additional Return.** The cash dividend, after all, is in your hand to be spent today; the proposed capital expenditure is made based on the valuation of its expected, incremental net cash flows. Recall Axiom 4.

The expected net present value (NPV) of the proposed capital project will be reflected into the firm's stock price. But, the arrival of new information over time about the success (or lack of success) of the capital project will be digested by the capital market and subsequently reflected in its stock price. So to be better off in a wealth context, the investor needs the firm to earn a higher rate of return on a dollar that is retained in the firm than that same investor could earn by investing that dollar elsewhere, given all economic considerations such as having to pay a personal tax on the dollar of cash dividends received. It is indeed a perplexing corporate choice.

Over the years 1995 to 1998, the total return on the S&P 500 stock index equaled 37.4, 23.1, 33.4, and 28.6 percent respectively.[1] These 4 years of abnormally high nominal returns followed 3 consecutive years, 1992 to 1994, during which the total return on this same stock index never exceeded 10.0 percent. The recent history of lofty total returns on equity investments induced corporate executives and their boards of directors to reign in their dividend payout policies.

For example in 1997, fewer firms increased their cash dividends from the previous year than had occurred since 1990. This tendency reflected widespread corporate sentiment that firms could increase shareholder wealth by retaining a larger proportion of earnings per share. Along these same lines, the management of The Coca-Cola Company said, "In 1996, our dividend payout ratio was approximately 36 percent of our net income. To free up additional cash for reinvestment in our high-return beverages business, our Board of Directors intends to gradually reduce our dividend payout ratio to 30 percent over time."[2] This explicit statement describes the Coca-Cola's dividend policy. The firm's dividend policy is the focus of this chapter.

Objective 1   **KEY TERMS**

Before taking up the particular issues relating to dividend policy, we must understand several key terms and interrelationships.

dividend payout ratio

A firm's dividend policy includes two basic components. First, the **dividend payout ratio** indicates the *amount of dividends paid relative to the company's earnings.* For instance, if the dividend per share is $2 and the earnings per share is $4, the payout ratio is 50 percent ($2/$4). The second component is the stability of the divi-

---

[1]*Wall Street Journal* (January 4, 1999): R14.

[2]The Coca-Cola Company, *Annual Report*, 1996, p. 42.

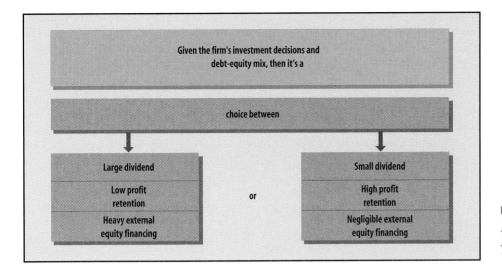

FIGURE 14–1
*Dividend vs.
Retention/Financing
Trade-offs*

dends over time. As we observe later in the chapter, dividend stability may be almost as important to the investor as the amount of dividends received.

In formulating a dividend policy, the financial manager faces trade-offs. Assuming that management has already decided how much to invest and chosen its debt-equity mix for financing these investments, the decision to pay a large dividend means simultaneously deciding to retain little, if any, profits; this in turn results in a greater reliance on external equity financing. Conversely, given the firm's investment and financing decisions, a small dividend payment corresponds to high profit retention with less need for externally generated equity funds. These trade-offs, which are fundamental to our discussion, are illustrated in Figure 14–1.

CONCEPT CHECK

1. Provide a financial executive a useful definition of the term dividend payout ratio.
2. How does the firm's actual dividend policy affect its need for externally generated financial capital?

DOES DIVIDEND POLICY AFFECT STOCK PRICE?[3]

Objective 2

The fundamental question to be resolved in our study of the firm's dividend policy may be stated simply as, What is a sound rationale or motivation for dividend payments? If we believe our objective should be to maximize the value of the common

---

[3]The concepts of this section draw heavily from Donald H. Chew, Jr., ed., "Do Dividends Matter? A Discussion of Corporate Dividend Policy," in *Six Roundtable Discussions of Corporate Finance with Joel Stern* (New York: Quorum Books, 1986), 67–101; and a book of readings edited by Joel M. Stern and Donald H. Chew, Jr., *The Revolution in Corporate Finance* (New York: Basil Blackwell, 1986). For a more recent discussion on the firm's dividend policy, but with the same conclusions as the other articles just listed, see Michael J. Barclay, Clifford W. Smith, and Ross L. Watts, "The Determinants of Corporate Leverage and Dividend Policies," *Journal of Applied Corporate Finance* 7, no. 4 (Winter 1995): 4–19.

stock, we may restate the question as, Given the firm's capital-budgeting and borrowing decisions, what is the effect of the firm's dividend policies on the stock price? *Does a high dividend payment decrease stock value, increase it, or make no real difference?*

At first glance, we might reasonably conclude that a firm's dividend policy is important. We have already (Chapter 8) defined the value of a stock to be equal to the present value of future dividends. How can we now suggest that dividends are not important? Why do so many companies pay dividends, and why is a page in the *Wall Street Journal* devoted to dividend announcements? Based on intuition, we could quickly conclude that dividend policy is important. However, we might be surprised to learn that the dividend question has been a controversial issue for well over three decades. Fischer Black, some 25 years ago, called it the "dividend puzzle." In his words:

> Why do corporations pay dividends? Why do investors pay attention to dividends? Perhaps the answers to these questions are obvious. Perhaps the answers are not so obvious. I claim the answers to these questions are not obvious at all. The harder we look at the dividend picture, the more it seems like a puzzle, with pieces that just don't fit together. What should the individual investor do about dividends in his portfolio? We don't know. What should the corporation do about dividend policy? We don't know.[4]

Twenty years later, in 1996 Peter Bernstein reexamined the "puzzle that fascinated Fischer Black."[5] He concluded the role of dividend policy in creating shareholder value is still very much a puzzle.

Three Basic Views

Some would argue that the amount of the dividend is irrelevant and any time spent on the decision is a waste of energy. Others contend that a high dividend results in a high stock price. Still others take the view that dividends actually hurt the stock value. Let us look at these three views in turn.

View 1: Dividend Policy Is Irrelevant

Much of the controversy about the dividend issue is based in the time-honored disagreements between the academic and professional communities. Experienced practitioners perceive stock price changes as resulting from dividend announcements and therefore see dividends as important. Professors who argue that dividends are irrelevant see a failure to carefully define dividend policy and argue that the relationship between dividends and stock price may be an illusion.[6]

The position that dividends are not important rests on two preconditions. First, we assume that investment and borrowing decisions have already been made and that these decisions will not be altered by the amount of any dividend payments. **perfect capital markets** Second, **perfect capital markets** are assumed to exist, which means that *(1) investors can buy and sell stocks without incurring any transaction costs, such as brokerage commissions; (2) companies can issue stocks without any cost of doing so; (3) there are no corporate or*

---

[4]Fischer Black, "The Dividend Puzzle," *Journal of Portfolio Management* 2 (Winter 1976): 5–8.

[5]Peter L. Bernstein, "Dividends: The Puzzle," *Journal of Applied Corporate Finance* 9, no. 1 (Spring 1996): 16–22.

[6]For an excellent presentation of this issue, see Merton Miller, "Can Management Use Dividends to Influence the Value of the Firm?" in Stern and Chew, eds., *The Revolution in Corporate Finance* (New York: Basil Blackwell, 1986), pp. 299–305.

personal taxes; (4) complete information about the firm is readily available; (5) there are no conflicts of interest between managements and stockholders; and (6) financial distress and bankruptcy costs are nonexistent.

The first assumption—that we have already made the investment and financing decisions—simply keeps us from confusing the issues. We want to know the effect of dividend decisions on a stand-alone basis, without mixing in other decisions. The second assumption, that of perfect markets, also allows us to study the effect of dividend decisions in isolation, much as a physicist studies motion in a vacuum to avoid the influence of friction.

Given these assumptions, the effect of a dividend decision on share price may be stated unequivocally: *There is no relationship between dividend policy and stock value.* One dividend policy is as good as another. In the aggregate, investors are concerned only with *total* returns from investment decisions; they are indifferent whether these returns come from capital gains or dividend income. They also recognize that the dividend decision, given the investment policy, is really a choice of financing strategy. That is, to finance growth, the firm (a) may choose to issue stock, allowing internally generated funds (profits) to be used to pay dividends; or (b) it may use internally generated funds to finance its growth, while paying less in dividends but not having to issue stock. In the first case, shareholders receive dividend income; in the second case, the value of their stock should increase, providing capital gains. The nature of the return is the only difference; total returns should be about the same. Thus, to argue that paying dividends can make shareholders better off is to argue that paying out cash with one hand and taking it back with the other hand is a worthwhile activity for management.

The firm's dividend payout could affect stock price if the shareholder has no other way to receive income from the investment. However, assuming the capital markets are relatively efficient, a stockholder who needs current income could always sell shares. If the firm pays a dividend, the investor could eliminate any dividend received, in whole or in part, by using the dividend to purchase stock. The investor can thus personally create any desired dividend stream, no matter what dividend policy is in effect.

View 2: High Dividends Increase Stock Value

The belief that a firm's dividend policy is unimportant implicitly assumes that an investor is indifferent as to whether income comes through capital gains or through dividends. However, dividends are more predictable than capital gains; management can control dividends, but it cannot dictate the price of the stock. Investors are less certain of receiving income from capital gains than from dividends. The incremental risk associated with capital gains relative to dividend income implies a higher required rate for discounting a dollar of capital gains than for discounting a dollar of dividends. In other words, we would value a dollar of expected dividends more highly than a dollar of expected capital gains. We might, for example, require a 14-percent rate of return for a stock that pays its entire return from dividends, but a 20-percent return for a high-growth stock that pays no dividend. In so doing, we would give a higher value to the dividend income than we would to the capital gains. This view, which says *dividends are more certain than capital gains*, has been called the **bird-in-the-hand dividend theory.**

bird-in-the-hand dividend theory

The position that dividends are less risky than capital gains, and should therefore be valued differently, is not without its critics. If we hold to our basic decision not to let the firm's dividend policy influence its investment and capital-mix decisions, the company's operating cash flows, both in expected amount and variability, are unaffected by its dividend policy. Because the dividend policy has no impact on the volatility of the company's overall cash flows, it has no impact on the riskiness of the firm.

Increasing a firm's dividend does not reduce the basic riskiness of the stock; rather, if a dividend payment requires management to issue new stock, it only transfers risk *and* ownership from the current owners to new owners. We would have to acknowledge that the current investors who receive the dividend trade an uncertain capital gain for a "safe" asset (the cash dividend). However, if risk reduction is the only goal, the investor could have kept the money in the bank and not bought the stock in the first place.

We might find fault with this bird-in-the-hand dividend theory, but there is still a strong perception among many investors and professional investment advisers that dividends are important. They frequently argue their case based on their own personal experience, as expressed by one investment adviser:

> In advising companies on dividend policy, we're absolutely sure on one side that the investors in companies like the utilities and the suburban banks want dividends. We're absolutely sure on the other side that . . . the high-technology companies should have no dividends. For the high earners—the ones that have a high rate of return like 20 percent or more than their cost of capital—we think they should have a low payout ratio. We think a typical industrial company which earns its cost of capital—just earns its cost of capital—probably should be in the average [dividend payout] range of 40 to 50 percent.[7]

BACK TO THE FOUNDATIONS

The previous discussion specifying the "bird-in-the-hand" theory between the relationship of stock price and the firm's dividend policy, relates directly to **Axiom 2: The Time Value of Money—A Dollar Received Today is Worth More Than a Dollar Received in the Future.** This theory suggests that because the dollar of dividends is received today it *should* be valued more highly than an uncertain capital gain that *might* be received in the future. The fundamental premise of this position is that the cash dividend in your hand (placed there today by the firm's payout policy) is more certain (less risky) than a possible capital gain. Many practitioners adhere to this theory; but many also adhere to the theory that is advanced in the next section. If nothing else, because it is controversial, dividend policy is important to the firm and its stockholders. And, in reality, many companies do pay cash dividends. Cash dividends are ubiquitous, so they are discussed in depth.

View 3: Low Dividends Increase Stock Value

The third view of how dividends affect stock price argues that dividends actually hurt the investor. This belief has largely been based on the difference in tax treatment for dividend income and capital gains. Contrary to the perfect-markets assumption of no taxes, most investors do pay income taxes. For these taxpayers, the objective is to maximize the *after-tax* return on investment relative to the risk assumed. This objective is realized by *minimizing* the effective tax rate on the income and, whenever possible, by *deferring* the payment of taxes.

---

[7]From a discussion by John Childs, an investment adviser at Kidder Peabody, in Chew, ed., "Do Dividends Matter?" in *Six Roundtable Discussions of Corporate Finance with Joel Stern* (New York: Quorum Books, 1986), 83–84.

Like most tax code complexities, Congress over the years has altered the outcome of whether capital gains are taxed at either (1) a lower or (2) similar rate as "earned income." Think of a water faucet being randomly turned on and then off. From 1987 through 1992, no federal tax advantage was provided for capital gains income relative to dividend income. A revision in the tax code that took effect beginning in 1993 did provide a preference for capital gains income. Then, the Taxpayer Relief Act of 1997 made the difference (preference) even more favorable for capital gains as opposed to cash dividend income. For some taxpayers if a minimum holding period has been reached, the tax rate applied to capital gains was reduced to 20 percent from the previous level of 28 percent. As a result, investors in the higher income tax brackets are taxed at a lower rate on a dollar of capital gains than on a dollar of dividend income. Also, taxes on dividend income are paid when the dividend is received, while taxes on price appreciation (capital gains) are deferred until the stock is actually sold. Thus, when it comes to tax considerations, most investors would prefer the retention of a firm's earnings as opposed to the payment of cash dividends. If earnings are retained within the firm, the stock price increases, but the increase is not taxed until the stock is sold.

Although the majority of investors are subject to taxes, certain investment companies, trusts, and pension plans are exempt on their dividend income. Also, for tax purposes a corporation may generally exclude 70 percent of the dividend income received from another corporation. In these cases, and unlike the above situations, investors may prefer dividends over capital gains.

To summarize, when it comes to taxes, we want to maximize our *after*-tax return, as opposed to the *before*-tax return. Investors try to defer taxes whenever possible. Stocks that allow tax deferral (low dividends–high capital gains) will possibly sell at a premium relative to stocks that require current taxation (high dividends-low capital gains). In this way, the two stocks may provide comparable *after-tax* returns. This suggests that a policy of paying low dividends will result in a higher stock price. Again, we are reminded of the fundamental **Axiom 8: Taxes Bias Business Decisions** with the tax benefits associated with capital gains as opposed to dividend income supporting a low-dividend policy.

BACK TO THE FOUNDATIONS

The presentation here of the argument that low cash dividends might increase common stock prices depends prominently on **Axiom 8: Taxes Bias Business Decisions.** For most individual economic units, income received in the form of cash dividends is subject to taxation at the relevant personal income tax rate. But, the amount received from the sale of common stock that represents a "capital gain" is subject to a lower and, thus, more favorable tax rate. So the argument suggests that taxpayers (investors) who find themselves in higher personal tax brackets will actually prefer to invest in companies that have dividend policies calling for low or no cash dividends being paid. Not only is the ultimate tax deferred until the gain is realized, but it enjoys a lower tax rate, leaving a larger residual gain for the investor who actually assumed the risk of the financial investment. Axiom 8 is also an important underpinning of something called "the clientele effect," discussed a bit later in this chapter.

Improving Our Thinking

We have now looked at three views on dividend policy. Which is right? The argument that dividends are irrelevant is difficult to refute, given the perfect market assumptions. However, in the real world, it is not always easy to feel comfortable with such an argument. Conversely, the high-dividend philosophy, which measures risk by how we split the firm's cash flows between dividends and retention, is not particularly appealing when studied carefully. The third view, which is essentially a tax argument against high dividends, is persuasive. Even today, although the preferential tax rate for capital gains is limited, its "deferral advantage" is still alive and well. However, if low dividends are so advantageous and generous dividends are so hurtful, why do companies continue to pay dividends? It is difficult to believe that managers would forgo such an easy opportunity to benefit their stockholders. What are we missing?

The need to find the missing elements in our "dividend puzzle" has not been ignored. When we need to better understand an issue or phenomenon, we can either improve our thinking or gather more evidence about the topic. Scholars and practitioners have taken both approaches. Although no single definitive answer has yet been found that is acceptable to all, several plausible extensions have been developed. Some of the more popular additions include (1) the residual dividend theory, (2) the clientele effect, (3) the information effect, (4) agency costs, and (5) expectations theory.

The Residual Dividend Theory

In perfect markets, we assume there is no cost to the firm when it issues new securities. However, in reality the process is quite expensive, and the flotation costs associated with a new offering may be as much as 20 percent of the dollar issue size. Thus, if management chooses to issue stock rather than retain profits to finance new investments, a larger amount of securities is required to receive the amount needed for the investment. For example, if $300,000 is needed to finance proposed investments, an amount exceeding the $300,000 will have to be issued to offset flotation costs incurred in the sale of the new stock issue. This means, very simply, that new equity capital raised through the sale of common stock will be more expensive than capital raised through the retention of earnings.

residual dividend theory

In effect, flotation costs eliminate our indifference between financing by internal capital and by new common stock. Given these costs, *dividends would be paid only if profits are not completely used for investment purposes;* that is, only when there are "residual earnings" after the financing of new investments. This policy is called the **residual dividend theory.**[8]

Given the existence of flotation costs, the firm's dividend policy should now be as follows:

1. Accept an investment if the NPV is positive; that is, the expected rate of return exceeds the cost of capital.
2. Finance the equity portion of new investments *first* by internally generated funds. Only after this capital is fully utilized should the firm issue new common shares.
3. If any internally generated funds still remain after making all investments, pay dividends to the investors. However, if all internal capital is needed for financing the equity portion of proposed investments, pay no dividend.

Thus, dividend policy is influenced by (1) the company's investment opportunities, and (2) the availability of internally generated capital, where dividends are paid

---

[8]The residual dividend theory is consistent with the "pecking order" theory of finance as described by Stewart Myers, "The Capital Structure Puzzle," *The Journal of Finance* (July 1984): 575–92.

only after all acceptable investments have been financed. According to this concept, dividend policy is totally passive in nature, having by itself no direct influence on the market price of the common stock.

The Clientele Effect

What if the investors do not like the dividend policy chosen by management? In perfect markets, where we have no costs in buying or selling stock, there is no problem. The investors may simply satisfy their personal income preferences by purchasing or selling securities when the dividends received do not satisfy their current needs for income. If an investor does not view the dividends received in any given year to be sufficient, he or she can simply sell a portion of stock, thereby "creating a dividend." In addition, if the dividend is larger than the investor desired, he or she will purchase stock with the "excess cash" created by the dividend. However, once we remove the assumption of perfect markets, we find that buying or selling stock is not cost free. Brokerage fees are incurred, ranging approximately from 1 percent to 10 percent. Even more costly is that the investor who buys the stock with cash received from a dividend will have to pay taxes before reinvesting the cash. And when a stock is bought or sold, it must first be reevaluated. Acquisition of the information for decision making also may be time-consuming and costly. Finally, aside from the cost of buying or selling part of the stock, some institutional investors, such as university endowment funds, are precluded from selling stock and "spending" the proceeds.

As a result of these considerations, investors may not be too inclined to buy stocks that require them to "create" a dividend stream more suitable to their purposes. Rather, if investors do in fact have a preference between dividends and capital gains, we could expect them to seek firms that have a dividend policy consistent with these preferences. They would, in essence, "sort themselves out" by buying stocks that satisfy their preferences for dividends and capital gains. Individuals and institutions that need current income would be drawn to companies that have high dividend payouts. Other investors, such as wealthy individuals, would much prefer to avoid taxes by holding securities that offer no or small dividend income but large capital gains. In other words, there would be a **clientele effect:** *Firms draw a given clientele, given their stated dividend policy.*

clientele effect

The possibility that clienteles of investors exist might lead us to believe that the firm's dividend policy matters. However, unless there is a greater aggregate demand for a particular policy than the market can satisfy, dividend policy is still unimportant; one policy is as good as the other. The clientele effect only warns firms to avoid making capricious changes in their dividend policy. Given that the firm's investment decisions are already made, the level of the dividend is still unimportant. The change in the policy matters only when it requires clientele to shift to another company.

The Information Effect

The investor in the world of perfect markets would argue with considerable persuasion that a firm's value is determined strictly by its investment and financing decisions and that the dividend policy has no impact on value. Yet we know from experience that a large, unexpected change in dividends can have a significant impact on the stock price. For instance, in November 1990 Occidental Petroleum cut its dividend from $2 to $1. In response, the firm's stock price went from about $32 to $17. How can we suggest that dividend policy matters little, when we can cite numerous such examples of a change in dividend affecting the stock price, especially when the change is negative?

Despite such "evidence," we are not looking at the real cause and effect. It may be that investors use a change in dividend policy as a *signal* about the firm's financial condition, especially its earning power. Thus, a dividend increase that is larger than expected might signal to investors that management expects significantly higher earnings in the future. Conversely, a dividend decrease, or even a less than expected increase, might signal that management is forecasting less favorable future earnings.

Some would claim that management frequently has inside information about the firm that it cannot make available to investors. This *difference in accessibility to information between management and investors*, called **information asymmetry,** *may result in a lower stock price than would occur under conditions of certainty*. This reasoning says that, by regularly increasing dividends, management is making a commitment to continue these cash flows to the stockholders for the foreseeable future. So in a risky marketplace, dividends become a means to minimize any "drag" on the stock price that might come from differences in the level of information available to managers and investors.

Dividends may therefore be important only as a communication tool; management may have no other credible way to inform investors about future earnings, or at least no convincing way that is less costly.

Agency Costs

Up to this point, we have not allowed for separation between management and owners. However, with only a superficial look at the real world, we know that managers and investors are typically not the same people. Moreover, they do not have access to the same information about the firm; nor at times do they even have the same incentives.

If the two groups are not the same, we must then assume that management is dedicated to the same goals as its owners. That is, we are making a presupposition that the behavior of companies with separate owners and managers will not differ from the behavior of owner-managed firms.

BACK TO THE FOUNDATIONS

Axiom 7 warned us there may be a conflict between management and owners, especially in large firms where managers and owners have different incentives. That is, **Managers Won't Work for the Owners Unless It Is in Their Best Interest** to do so. As we shall see in this section, the dividend policy may be one way to reduce this problem.

In reality, however, conflicts may still exist, and the stock price of a company owned by investors who are separate from management may be less than the stock value of a closely held firm. This potential difference in price is the *cost of the conflict to the owners*, which has come to be called **agency costs.**[9]

Recognizing the possible problem, management, acting independently or at the insistence of the board of directors, frequently takes action to minimize the cost associated with the separation of ownership and management control. Such action, which in itself is costly, includes auditing by independent accountants, assigning supervisory functions to the company's board of directors, creating covenants in lending agreements that restrict management's powers, and providing

---

[9]See M. C. Jensen and W. H. Meckling, "Theory of the Firm: Managerial Behavior, Agency Costs, and Ownership Structure," *Journal of Financial Economics* (October 1976): 305–60.

incentive compensation plans for management that help "bond" management with the owners.

A firm's dividend policy may be perceived by owners as a tool to minimize agency costs. Assuming that the payment of a dividend requires management to issue stock to finance new investments, new investors may be attracted to the company only if management provides convincing information that the capital will be used profitably. Thus, the payment of dividends indirectly results in a closer monitoring of management's investment activities. In this case, dividends may make a meaningful contribution to the value of the firm.

Expectations Theory[10]

A common thread through much of our discussion of dividend policy, particularly as it relates to information effects, is the word *expected*. We should not overlook the significance of this word when we are making any financial decision within the firm. *No matter what the decision area, how the market price responds to management's actions is not determined entirely by the action itself; it is also affected by investors' expectations about the ultimate decision to be made by management.* This concept or idea is called the **expectations theory.**

As the time approaches for management to announce the amount of the next dividend, investors form expectations as to how much that dividend will be. These expectations are based on several factors internal to the firm, such as past dividend decisions, current and expected earnings, investment strategies, and financing decisions. They also consider such things as the condition of the general economy, the strength or weakness of the industry at the time, and possible changes in government policies.

When the actual dividend decision is announced, the investor compares the actual decision with the expected decision. If the amount of the dividend is as expected, even if it represents an increase from prior years, the market price of the stock will remain unchanged. However, if the dividend is higher or lower than expected, investors will reassess their perceptions of the firm. They will question the meaning of the *unexpected* change in the dividend. They may use the unexpected dividend decision as a clue about unexpected changes in earnings; that is, the unexpected dividend change has information content about the firm's earnings and other important factors. In short, management's actual decision about the firm's dividend policy may not be terribly significant, unless it departs from investors' expectations. If there is a difference between actual and expected dividends, we will more than likely see a movement in the stock price.

expectations theory

The Empirical Evidence

Our search for an answer to the question of dividend relevance has been less than successful. We have given it our best thinking, but still no single definitive position has emerged. Maybe we could gather evidence to show the relationship between dividend practices and security prices. We might also inquire into the perceptions of financial managers who make decisions about dividend policies, with the idea that their beliefs affect their decision making. Then we could truly know that dividend policy is important or that it does not matter.

---

[10]Much of the thinking in this section came from Miller, "Can Management Use Dividends to Influence the Value of the Firm?" in Stern and Chew, eds., *The Revolution in Corporate Finance* (New York: Basil Blackwell, 1986), pp. 299–303.

To test the relationship between dividend payments and security prices, we could compare a firm's dividend yield (dividend/stock price) and the stock's total return. The question is, Do stocks that pay high dividends provide higher or lower returns to investors? Such tests have been conducted with the use of highly sophisticated statistical techniques. Despite the use of these extremely powerful analytical tools, which involve intricate and complicated procedures, the results have been mixed.[11] However, over long periods, the results have given a slight advantage to the low-dividend stocks; that is, stocks that pay lower dividends appear to have higher prices. More recently, researchers have found some modest relationships between a firm's dividend policy and share price, but still nothing convincing either way.[12] Thus, the findings are far from conclusive, however, owing to the relatively large standard errors of the estimates. (The apparent differences may be the result of random sampling error and not real differences). We simply have been unable to disentangle the effect of dividend policy from other influences.

Several reasons may be given for our inability to arrive at conclusive results. First, to be accurate, we would need to know the amount of dividends investors *expected* to receive. Because these expectations cannot be observed, we can only use historical data, which may or may not relate to current expectations. Second, most empirical studies have assumed a linear relationship between dividend payments and stock prices. The actual relationship may be nonlinear, possibly even discontinuous. Whatever the reasons, the evidence to date is inconclusive and the jury is still out.

Because our statistical prowess does not provide any conclusive evidence, let's turn to our last hope. What do the financial managers of the world believe about the relevance of dividend policy? Although we may not conclude that a manager's opinion is necessarily the "final word on the matter," having these insights is helpful. If financial managers believe that dividends matter and act consistently in accordance with that conviction, they could influence the relationship between stock value and dividend policy. As stated by one group of researchers[13]:

> In the matter of dividend policy, designing broad-based tests of actual corporate decision-making that would allow us to distinguish among these theories has proven to be quite difficult. The dearth of reliable empirical evidence on this topic has forced proponents of each theory to rely largely on anecdotes to buttress their arguments.

To help us gain some understanding of managements' perceptions, let's turn to a study by Baker, Farrelly, and Edelman, that surveyed financial executives at 318 firms listed on the New York Stock Exchange.[14] The study favors the relevance of dividend policy, but not overwhelmingly so. For the most part, managers are divided between (a) believing that dividends are important or (b) having no opinion about the matter.

Regarding the question about the price-dividend relationship, Baker et al. asked the financial managers straight up, "Does the firm's dividend policy affect the price

[11]See F. Black and M. Scholes, "The Effects of Dividend Yield and Dividend Policy on Common Stock Prices and Returns," *Journal of Financial Economics*, 1 (May 1974): 1–22; and M. H. Miller and M. Scholes, "Dividends and Taxes: Some Empirical Evidence," *Journal of Political Economy*, 90 (1982): 1118–41.

[12]Clifford Smith and Ross Watts, "The Investment Opportunity Set and Corporate Financing, Dividend, and Compensation Policies," *Journal of Financial Economics* 32 (1992): 263–92.

[13]Barclay, Smith, and Watts, "The Determinants of Corporate Leverage and Dividend Policies," *Journal of Corporate Finance* 7, no. 4 (Winter 1995): 4.

[14]H. Kent Baker, Gail E. Farrelly, and Richard B. Edelman, "A Survey of Management Views on Dividend Policy," *Financial Management* 14 (Autumn 1985): 78–84.

of the common stock?" Slightly more than 60 percent of the responses were affirmative, which is significant, but there were still almost 40 percent who had no opinion or disagreed. Thus, we could conclude that most managers think that dividends matter, but they have no mandate. Similarly, when asked if dividends provide informational content about the firm's future, the managers are basically split between no opinion and agreement. When asked about the trade-off between dividends and capital gains, almost two-thirds of the managers thought stockholders have a preference either for dividends or capital gains, with a lesser number (56 percent) believing that investors perceive the relative riskiness of capital gains and dividends to be different. Interestingly enough, though, almost half of the managers felt no clear responsibility to be responsive to stockholders' preferences.

What Are We to Conclude?

We have now looked carefully at the importance of a firm's dividend policy as management seeks to increase the shareholders' wealth. We have gone to great lengths to gain insight and understanding from our best thinking. We have even drawn from the empirical evidence on hand to see what the findings suggest.

A reasonable person cannot reach a definitive conclusion; nevertheless, management is left with no choice. A firm must develop a dividend policy, based, it is hoped, on the best available knowledge. Although we can give advice with some reservation, the following conclusions would appear reasonable:

1. As a firm's investment opportunities increase, the dividend payout ratio should decrease. In other words, an inverse relationship should exist between the amount of investments with an expected rate of return that exceeds the cost of capital (positive *NPVS*s) and the dividends remitted to investors. Because of flotation costs associated with raising external capital, the retention of internally generated equity financing is preferable to selling stock (in terms of the wealth of the current common shareholders).

2. The firm's dividend policy appears to be important; however, appearances may be deceptive. The real issue may be the firm's *expected* earning power and the riskiness of these earnings. Investors may be using the dividend payment as a source of information about the company's *expected* earnings. Management's actions regarding dividends may carry greater weight than a statement by management that earnings will be increasing.

3. If dividends influence stock price, this is probably based on the investor's desire to minimize and defer taxes, and from the role of dividends in minimizing agency costs.

4. If the expectations theory has merit, which we believe it does, management should avoid surprising investors when it comes to the firm's dividends decision. The firm's dividend policy might effectively be treated as a *long-term residual*. Rather than project investment requirements for a single year, management could anticipate financing needs for several years. Based on the expected investment opportunities during the planning horizon, the firm's debt-equity mix, and the funds generated from operations, a *target* dividend payout ratio could be established. If internal funds remained after projection of the necessary equity financing, dividends would be paid. However, the planned dividend stream should distribute residual capital evenly to investors over the planning period. Conversely, if over the long term the entire amount of internally generated capital is needed for reinvestment in the company, then no dividend should be paid.

THE DIVIDEND DECISION IN PRACTICE

In setting a firm's dividend policy, financial managers must work in the world of reality with the concepts we have set forth so far in this chapter. Again, although these concepts do not provide an equation that explains the key relationships, they certainly give us a more complete view of the finance world, which can only help us make better decisions. Other considerations of a more practical nature also appear as part of the firm's decision making about its dividend policy.

Other Practical Considerations

Many considerations may influence a firm's decision about its dividends, some of them unique to that company. Some of the more general considerations are given here.

Legal Restrictions

Certain legal restrictions may limit the amount of dividends a firm may pay. These legal constraints fall into two categories. First, *statutory restrictions* may prevent a company from paying dividends. While specific limitations vary by state, generally a corporation may not pay a dividend (1) if the firm's liabilities exceed its assets, (2) if the amount of the dividend exceeds the accumulated profits (retained earnings), and (3) if the dividend is being paid from capital invested in the firm.

The second type of legal restriction is unique to each firm and results from restrictions in debt and preferred stock contracts. To minimize their risk, investors frequently impose restrictive provisions on management as a condition to their investment in the company. These constraints may include the provision that dividends may not be declared before the debt is repaid. Also, the corporation may be required to maintain a given amount of working capital. Preferred stockholders may stipulate that common dividends may not be paid when any preferred dividends are delinquent.

Liquidity Position

Contrary to common opinion, the mere fact that a company shows a large amount of retained earnings in the balance sheet does not indicate that cash is available for the payment of dividends. The firm's current position in liquid assets, including cash, is basically independent of the retained earnings account. Historically, a company with sizable retained earnings has been successful in generating cash from operations. Yet these funds are typically either reinvested in the company within a short period or used to pay maturing debt. Thus, a firm may be extremely profitable and still be *cash poor*. Because dividends are paid with cash, *and not with retained earnings*, the firm must have a cash available for dividends to be paid. Hence, the firm's liquidity position has a direct bearing on its ability to pay dividends.

Absence or Lack of Other Sources of Financing

As already noted, a firm may (1) retain profits for investment purposes or (2) pay dividends and issue new debt or equity securities to finance investments. For many small or new companies, this second option is not realistic. These firms do not have access to the capital markets, so they must rely more heavily on internally generated funds. As a consequence, the dividend payout ratio is generally much lower for a small or newly established firm than for a large, publicly owned corporation.

Earnings Predictability

A company's dividend payout ratio depends to some extent on the predictability of a firm's profits over time. If earnings fluctuate significantly, management cannot rely on internally generated funds to meet future needs. When profits are realized, the firm may retain larger amounts to ensure that money is available when needed. Conversely, a firm with a stable earnings trend will typically pay out a larger portion of its earnings in dividends. This company has less concern about the availability of profits to meet future capital requirements.

Ownership Control

For many large corporations, control through the ownership of common stock is not an issue. However, for many small and medium-sized companies, maintaining voting control takes a high priority. If the current common stockholders are unable to participate in a new offering, issuing new stock is unattractive, in that the control of the current stockholder is diluted. The owners might prefer that management finance new investments with debt and through profits rather than by issuing new common stock. This firm's growth is then constrained by the amount of debt capital available and by the company's ability to generate profits.

Inflation

Before the late 1970s, inflationary pressures had not been a significant problem for either consumers or businesses. However, during much of the 1980s, the deterioration of the dollar's purchasing power had a direct impact on the replacement of fixed assets. In a period of inflation, as fixed assets become worn and obsolete, the funds generated from depreciation ideally are used to finance the replacements. As the cost of equivalent equipment continues to increase, the depreciation funds become insufficient. This requires a greater retention of profits, which implies that dividends have to be adversely affected.

Alternative Dividend Policies

Objective 4

Regardless of a firm's long-term dividend policy, most firms choose one of several year-to-year dividend payment patterns.

1. **Constant dividend payout ratio.** In this policy, the *percentage of earnings paid out in dividends is held constant*. Although the dividend-to-earnings ratio is stable, the dollar amount of the dividend naturally fluctuates from year to year as profits vary.

constant dividend payout ratio

2. Stable dollar dividend per share. This policy *maintains a relatively stable dollar dividend over time*. An increase in the dollar dividend usually does not occur until management is convinced that the higher dividend level can be maintained in the future. Management also will not reduce the dollar dividend until the evidence clearly indicates that a continuation of the current dividend cannot be supported.

3. Small, regular dividend plus a year-end extra. A corporation following this policy *pays a small regular dollar dividend plus a year-end extra dividend in prosperous years*. The extra dividend is declared toward the end of the fiscal year, when the company's profits for the period can be estimated. Management's objective is *to avoid the connotation of a permanent dividend*. However, this purpose may be defeated if *recurring* extra dividends come to be expected by investors.

Of the three dividend policies, the stable dollar dividend is by far the most common. In one study, corporate managers were found to be reluctant to change the dollar amount of the dividend in response to temporary fluctuations in earnings from year to year. This aversion was particularly evident when it came to decreasing the amount of the dividend from the previous level.[15] One explanation for the stable dividend is the **increasing-stream hypothesis of dividend policy** which suggests that *dividend stability is essentially a smoothing of the dividend stream to minimize the effect of other types of company reversals.*[16] Thus, corporate managers make every effort to avoid a dividend cut, attempting instead to develop a gradually increasing dividend series over the long-term future. However, if a dividend reduction is absolutely necessary, the cut should be large enough to reduce the probability of future cuts.

Dividend Policy and Corporate Strategy: Things Will Change— Even Dividend Policy

The recession of 1990 to 1991 induced a large number of American corporations to revisit their broadest corporate strategies that directly impact shareholder wealth. Today, the results of that "rethinking" are evident in many aspects of corporate behavior, including adjusted dividend policies.

One firm that altered its dividend policy in response to new strategies was the W.R. Grace & Co., headquartered in Boca Raton, Florida. The firm's core businesses include packaging, catalysts and silica products, and construction products. Grace & Co. ranked number 271 within the 1997 *Fortune 500* list of the largest U.S. corporations with sales of $5.26 billion. The new corporate plans involved (1) divesting or discontinuing several product lines and (2) initiating a significant repurchase program of its own common stock. (Stock repurchase programs are discussed in depth later in this chapter.)

As a result, both the firm's payout ratio and actual cash dividend paid per share declined in significant fashion. The change in observed dividend policy is evident in Table 14–1. Notice that over the 1992 to 1994 period, Grace & Co. provided a good example of what we have called a "stable dividend policy." During this period the firm maintained a stable dollar dividend of $1.40 per share, while the payout ratio varied from 80.5 percent to 101.0 percent.

---

[15]John Lintner, "Distribution of Income of Corporations among Dividends, Retained Earnings, and Taxes," *American Economic Review* 46 (May 1956): 97–113.

[16]Keith V. Smith, "Increasing-Stream Hypothesis of Corporate Dividend Policy," *California Management Review* 15 (Fall 1971): 56–64.

TABLE 14-1

TABLE 14-1	EARNINGS PER SHARE, DIVIDENDS PER SHARE AND THE DIVIDEND PAYOUT RATIO: W.R. GRACE & COMPANY, 1992–1996		
YEAR	EARNINGS PER SHARE[a]	DIVIDENDS PER SHARE	PAYOUT RATIO
1992	$1.70	$1.40	82.3%
1993	1.39	1.40	101.0
1994	1.74	1.40	80.5
1995	2.14	1.175	54.9
1996	2.41	0.50	20.7

[a]This series represents earnings from continuing operations, but before special items.
Source: Basic data from W.R. Grace & Co., *Annual Report,* 1996, p. 55.

But, when company policies changed dramatically, so did the associated dividend variables. The absolute dollar amount of the cash dividend per share was lowered to $0.50 in 1996 and the accompanying payout ratio fell to 20.7 percent. Importantly, the firm's total return to investors was a robust 30.9 percent during 1996 compared to its 10-year average of 16.4 percent. The market liked the change in dividend policy. So, although firms may be reluctant to change their dividend policies, it is possible with good planning and proper information dissemination to convince the financial markets that such a new direction might be good for investors.

CONCEPT CHECK

1. Identify some practical considerations that affect a firm's payout policy.
2. Identify and explain three different dividend policies. *Hint:* One of these is a constant dividend payout ratio.
3. What is the increasing-stream hypothesis of dividend policy?

DIVIDEND PAYMENT PROCEDURES

Objective 5

After the firm's dividend policy has been structured, several procedural details must be arranged. For instance, how frequently are dividend payments to be made? If a stockholder sells the shares during the year, who is entitled to the dividend? To answer these questions, we need to understand dividend payment procedures.

Generally, companies pay dividends on a quarterly basis. To illustrate, General Electric pays $6.72 per share in annual dividends. However, the firm actually issues a $1.68 quarterly dividend for a total yearly dividend of $6.72 ($1.68 × 4 quarters).

The final approval of a dividend payment comes from the board of directors. As an example, Emerson Electric on August 5, 1996, announced that holders of record as of August 16 would receive a $.49 dividend. The dividend payment was to be made on September 10. August 5 is the **declaration date**—the *date when the dividend is formally declared by the board of directors.* The **date of record,** August 16, designates

declaration date
date of record

when the stock transfer books are to be closed. Investors shown to own the stock on this date receive the dividend. If a notification of a transfer is recorded subsequent to August 16, the new owner is not entitled to the dividend. However, a problem could develop if the stock were sold on August 15, one day prior to the record date. Time would not permit the sale to be reflected on the stockholder list by the August 16 date of record. To avoid this problem, *stock brokerage companies have uniformly decided to terminate the right of ownership to the dividend 2 working days before the date of record.* This prior date is the **ex-dividend date.** Therefore, any acquirer of Emerson Electric stock on August 14 or thereafter does not receive the dividend. Finally, the *company mails the dividend check to each investor* on September 10, the **payment date.** These events may be diagrammed as follows:

ex-dividend date
payment date

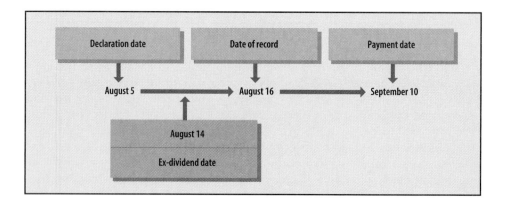

CONCEPT CHECK

1. What is the typical frequency with which cash dividends are paid to investors?
2. Distinguish among the (a) declaration date, (b) date of record, and (c) ex-dividend date.

Objective 6   ## STOCK DIVIDENDS AND STOCK SPLITS

An integral part of dividend policy is the use of stock dividends and stock splits. Both involve issuing new shares of stock on a pro rata basis to the current shareholders, while the firm's assets, its earnings, the risk assumed, and the investors' percentage of ownership in the company remain unchanged. The only definite result from either a stock dividend or a stock split is the increase in the number of shares of stock outstanding.

To illustrate the effect of a stock dividend, assume that the Katie Corporation has 100,000 shares outstanding. The firm's after-tax profits are $500,000, or $5 in earnings per share. Currently, the company's stock is selling at a price-earnings multiple of 10, or $50 per share. Management is planning to issue a 20-percent stock dividend, so that a stockholder owning 10 shares would receive two additional shares. We might immediately conclude that this investor is being given an asset (two shares of stock) worth $100; consequently, his or her personal worth should increase by $100. This conclusion is erroneous. The firm will be issuing 20,000 new shares

(100,000 shares × 20 percent). Because the $500,000 in after-tax profits does not change, the new earnings per share will be $4.167 ($500,000/120,000 shares). If the price-earnings multiple remains at 10, the market price of the stock after the dividend should fall to $41.67 ($4.167 earnings per share × 10). The investor now owns 12 shares worth $41.67, which provides a $500 total value; thus, he or she is neither better nor worse off than before the stock dividend.

This example may make us wonder why a corporation would even bother with a stock dividend or stock split if no one benefits. However, before we study the rationale for such distributions, we should understand the differences between a stock split and a stock dividend.

Stock Dividend versus Split

The only difference between a stock dividend and a stock split relates to their respective accounting treatment. Stated differently, *there is absolutely no difference on an economic basis between a stock dividend and a stock split.* Both represent a proportionate distribution of additional shares to the current stockholders. However, *for accounting purposes* the **stock split** has been defined as a *stock dividend exceeding 25 percent.* Thus, a **stock dividend** is conventionally defined as a *distribution of shares up to 25 percent of the number of shares currently outstanding.*

stock split
stock dividend

The accounting treatment for a stock dividend requires the issuing firms to capitalize the "market value" of the dividend. In other words, the dollar amount of the dividend is transferred from retained earnings to the capital accounts (par and paid-in capital). This procedure may best be explained by an example. Assume that the L. Bernard Corporation is preparing to issue a 15-percent stock dividend. Table 14–2 presents the equity portion of the firm's balance sheet before the distribution. The market price for the stock has been $14. Thus, the 15-percent stock dividend increases the number of shares by 150,000 (1,000,000 shares × 15 percent). The "market value" of this increase is $2,100,000 (150,000 shares × $14 market price). To record this transaction, $2,100,000 would be transferred from retained earnings, resulting in an $300,000 increase in total par value (150,000 shares × $2 par value) and a $1,800,000 increment to paid-in capital. The $1,800,000 is the residual difference between $2,100,000 and $300,000. Table 14–3 shows the revised balance sheet.

What if the management of L. Bernard Corporation changed the plan and decided to split the stock two for one? In other words, a 100-percent increase in the number of shares would result. In accounting for the split, the changes to be recorded are (1) an increase in the number of shares and (2) a decrease in the per-share par value from $2 to $1. The dollar amounts of each account do not change. Table 14–4 reveals the new balance sheet.

TABLE 14–2	L. BERNARD CORPORATION BALANCE SHEET BEFORE STOCK DIVIDEND

Common stock	
Par value (1,000,000 shares outstanding; $2 par value)	$ 2,000,000
Paid-in capital	8,000,000
Retained earnings	15,000,000
Total equity	$25,000,000

TABLE 14–3	L. BERNARD CORPORATION BALANCE SHEET AFTER STOCK DIVIDEND

Common stock	
Par value (1,150,000 shares outstanding; $2 par value)	$ 2,300,000
Paid-in capital	9,800,000
Retained earnings	12,900,000
Total equity	$25,000,000

Thus, for a stock dividend, an amount equal to the market value of the stock dividend is transferred from retained earnings to the capital stock accounts. When stock is split, only the number of shares changes, and the par value of each share is decreased proportionately. Despite this dissimilarity in accounting treatment, remember that no real economic difference exists between a split and a dividend.

Rationale for a Stock Dividend or Split

Although *stock* dividends and splits occur far less frequently than *cash* dividends, a significant number of companies choose to use these share distributions either with or in lieu of cash dividends. The extent of stock splits and stock dividends over the years can be made clear by a little price comparison. In 1926, a ticket to the movies cost 25¢—and even much less in the rural communities. At the same time, the average share price on the New York Stock Exchange was $35. Today, if we want to go to a new movie, we can pay $7 or more. However, the average share price is still about $35. The relatively constant share price is the result of the shares being split over and over again. We can only conclude that investors apparently like it that way. But why do they, if no economic benefit results to the investor from doing so?

Proponents of stock dividends and splits frequently maintain that stockholders receive a key benefit because the price of the stock will not fall precisely in proportion to the share increase. For a two-for-one split, the price of the stock might not decrease a full 50 percent, and the stockholder is left with a higher total value. There are two reasons for this disequilibrium. First, many financial executives believe that an optimal price range exists. Within this range the total market value of the common stockholders is thought to be maximized. As the price exceeds this range, fewer investors can purchase the stock, thereby restraining the demand. Consequently, downward pressure is placed on its price. For instance, Hershey Foods Corporation in 1996 announced a two-for-one split on its shares that were trading for $80. The

TABLE 14–4	L. BERNARD CORPORATION BALANCE SHEET AFTER STOCK SPLIT

Common stock	
Par value (2,000,000 shares outstanding; $1 par value)	$ 2,000,000
Paid-in capital	8,000,000
Retained earnings	15,000,000
Total equity	$25,000,000

reason given: The split would put it "in a more popular price range and should enhance trading liquidity." ("Liquidity") in this context means that more shares would be bought and sold by investors.)

The second explanation relates to the *informational content* of the dividend-split announcement. Stock dividends and splits have generally been associated with companies with growing earnings. The announcement of a stock dividend or split has therefore been perceived as favorable news. The empirical evidence, however, fails to verify these conclusions. Most studies indicate that investors are perceptive in identifying the true meaning of a share distribution. If the stock dividend or split is not accompanied by a positive trend in earnings and increases in cash dividends, price increases surrounding the stock dividend or split are insignificant.[17] Therefore, we should be suspicious of the assertion that a stock dividend or split can help increase investors' net worth.

A second reason for stock dividends or splits is the conservation of corporate cash. If a company is encountering cash problems, it may substitute a stock dividend for a cash dividend. However, as before, investors will probably look beyond the dividend to ascertain the underlying reason for conserving cash. If the stock dividend is an effort to conserve cash for attractive investment opportunities, the shareholder may bid up the stock price. If the move to conserve cash relates to financial difficulties within the firm, the market price will most likely react adversely.

CONCEPT CHECK

1. From an economic standpoint, is there any meaningful difference between a stock split and a stock dividend?
2. What managerial logic might lie behind a stock split or stock dividend?

STOCK REPURCHASES

Objective 7

A **stock repurchase (stock buyback)** is when *a firm repurchases its own stock, resulting in a reduction in the number of shares outstanding.* For well over three decades, corporate managements have been active in repurchasing their own equity securities. Also, if you were to look at the balance sheet of a firm like the McDonald's Corporation, you would see that the firm's treasury stock—the amount paid for repurchasing its own stock—is severalfold the amount of the total amount originally invested by the stockholders. This situation is not unusual for many large companies. Several reasons have been given for *stock repurchases.* Examples of such benefits include

1. Means for providing an internal investment opportunity
2. Approach for modifying the firm's capital structure
3. Favorable impact on earnings per share
4. Elimination of a minority ownership group of stockholders

stock repurchase (stock buyback)

---

[17]See James A. Millar and Bruce D. Fielitz, "Stock Split and Stock-Dividend Decisions," *Financial Management 2* (Winter 1973): 35–45; and Eugene Fama, Lawrence Fisher, Michael Jensen, and Richard Roll, "The Adjustment of Stock Prices to New Information," *International Economic Review* (February 1969); 1–21.

5. Minimization of the dilution in earnings per share associated with mergers

6. Reduction in the firm's costs associated with servicing small stockholders

Also, from the shareholders' perspective, a stock repurchase, as opposed to a cash dividend, has a potential tax advantage.

Share Repurchase as a Dividend Decision

Clearly, the payment of a common stock dividend is the conventional method for distributing a firm's profits to its owners. However, it need not be the only way. Another approach is to repurchase the firm's stock. The concept may best be explained by an example.

Example

Telink, Inc. is planning to pay $4 million ($4 per share) in dividends to its common stockholders. The following earnings and market price information is provided for Telink:

Net income	$7,500,000
Number of shares	1,000,000
Earnings per share	$7.50
Price-earnings ratio	8
Expected market price per share after dividend payment	$60

In a recent meeting several board members, who are also major stockholders, question the need for a dividend payment. They maintain that they do not need the income, so why not allow the firm to retain the funds for future investments? In response, management contends that the available investments are not sufficiently profitable to justify retention of the income. That is, the investor's required rates of return exceed the expected rates of return that could be earned with the additional $4 million in investments.

Because management opposes the idea of retaining the profits for investment purposes, one of the firm's directors has suggested that the $4 million be used to repurchase the company's stock. In this way, the value of the stock should increase. This result may be demonstrated as follows:

1. Assume that shares are repurchased by the firm at the $60 market price (ex-dividend price) plus the contemplated $4 dividend per share, or for $64 per share.

2. Given a $64 price, 62,500 shares would be repurchased ($4 million ÷ $64 price).

3. If net income is not reduced, but the number of shares declines as a result of the share repurchase, earnings per share would increase from $7.50 to $8, computed as follows:

$$\begin{align} \text{earnings per share} &= \text{net income/outstanding shares} \\ \text{(before repurchase)} &= \$7,500,000/1,000,000 \\ &= \$7.50 \\ \text{(after repurchase)} &= \$7,500,000/(1,000,000 - 62,500) \\ &= \$8 \end{align}$$

"Many Concerns Use Excess Cash to Repurchase Their Shares"

Mattel, Inc. and General Dynamics are two firms, among many, who are repurchasing their own shares. These events, along with the rationale for the decision to repurchase their shares, are told in this *Wall Street Journal* article.

Stock buybacks are back. Faced with the prospect of only modest economic growth, many companies are using excess cash to buy their own shares rather than build new plants.

Consider the case of Mattel Inc., the El Segundo, Calif., toy maker. It just announced plans to buy 10 million shares during the next four years, even though its stock, priced at $24, is selling at a healthy 16.6 times its past 12-month earnings. The reason: Plant capacity is sufficient to handle current sales growth of 10% to 12% yearly and excess cash is building up at the rate of $200 million a year.

"We don't need the cash to grow so we've decided to give it back," says James Eskridge, Mattel's chief financial officer. Actually, Mattel plans to use about half of the $200 million each year for buybacks and dividends and the rest for growth.

The effect [of a stock repurchase] on individual stocks can be significant, says Robert Giordano, director of economic research at Goldman Sachs & Co. A case in point is General Dynamics Corp., which last summer began selling some divisions and using the proceeds to buy its stock when shares were trading at about $65 each. After nearly $1 billion in buybacks, the stock has gained about 37% closing yesterday at $89 \frac{1}{2}$.

"The market reacts positively to purchases, and it appreciates a firm that does not squander excess cash," says Columbia Business School professor Gailen Hite.

Some of the buybacks have come from companies whose stock prices have been hurt. Drug makers, for example, have seen their stocks pummeled by fears that healthcare reform will sap profits. As a result, pharmaceutical companies have been big players in the buyback game.

But economists and analysts are much more intrigued by companies that are awash in cash, thanks to improving sales and several years of cost-cutting and debt reduction. At this stage of an economic recovery, many such companies would be investing heavily in plant and equipment. Not this time.

"Companies are throwing off more cash than they can ever hope to invest in plant, equipment or inventories.'" says Charles Clough, chief investment strategist for Merrill Lynch Capital Markets. Companies already have pared down debt, and now they're turning to equity, he says. His prediction: "He who shrinks his balance sheet the fastest wins in the '90s."

4. Assuming that the price-earnings ratio remains at 8, the new price after the repurchase would be $64, up from $60, where the increase exactly equals the amount of the forgone dividend.

In this example, Telink's stockholders are essentially provided the same value, whether a dividend is paid or stock is repurchased. If management pays a dividend, the investor will have a stock valued at $60 plus $4 received from the dividend. Conversely, if stock is repurchased in lieu of the dividend, the stock will be worth $64. These results were based on assuming (1) the stock is being repurchased at the exact $64 price, (2) the $7,500,000 net income is unaffected by the repurchase, and (3) the price-earnings ratio of 8 does not change after the repurchase. Given these assumptions, however, the stock repurchase serves as a perfect substitute for the dividend payment to the stockholders.

The Investor's Choice

Given the choice between a stock repurchase and a dividend payment, which would an investor prefer? In perfect markets, where there are no taxes, no commissions when buying and selling stock, and no informational content assigned to a dividend, the investor would be indifferent with regard to the choices. The investor could create a dividend stream by selling stock when income is needed.

If market imperfections exist, the investor may have a preference for one of the two methods of distributing the corporate income. First, the firm may have to pay too high a price for the repurchase stock, which is to the detriment of the remaining stockholders. If a relatively large number of shares are being bought, the price may be bid up too high, only to fall after the repurchase operation. Second, as a result of the repurchase the market may perceive the riskiness of the corporation as increasing, which would lower the price-earnings ratio and the value of the stock.

Financing or Investment Decision

Repurchasing stock when the firm has excess cash may be regarded as a dividend decision. However, a stock repurchase may also be viewed as a financing decision. By issuing debt and then repurchasing stock, a firm can immediately alter its debt-equity mix toward a higher proportion of debt. Rather than choose how to distribute cash to the stockholders, management is using stock repurchase as a means to change the corporation's capital structure.

In addition to dividend and financing decisions, many managers consider stock repurchase an investment decision. When equity prices are depressed in the marketplace, management may view the firm's own stock as being materially undervalued and representing a good investment opportunity. While the firm's management may be wise to repurchase stock at unusually low prices, this decision cannot and should not be viewed in the context of an investment decision. Buying its own stock cannot provide expected returns as other investments do. No company can survive, much less prosper, by investing only in its own stock.

The Repurchase Procedure

If management intends to repurchase a block of the firm's outstanding shares, it should make this information public. All investors should be given the opportunity to work with complete information. They should be told the purpose of the repurchase, as well as the method to be used to acquire the stock.

Three methods for stock repurchase are available. First, the shares could be bought in the open market. Here the firm acquires the stock through a stockbroker at the going market price. This approach may place upward pressure on the stock price until the stock is acquired. Also, commissions must be paid to the stockbrokers as a fee for their services.

tender offer

The second method is to make a tender offer to the firm's shareholders. A **tender offer** is a *formal offer by the company to buy a specified number of shares at a predetermined and stated price. The tender price is set above the current market price in order to attract sellers.* A tender offer is best when a relatively large number of shares are to be bought because the company's intentions are clearly known and each shareholder has the opportunity to sell the stock at the tendered price.

The third and final method for repurchasing stock entails the purchase of the stock from one or more major stockholders. These purchases are made on a negotiated basis. Care should be taken to ensure a fair and equitable price. Otherwise, the remaining stockholders may be hurt as a result of the sale.

CONCEPT CHECK

1. Identify three reasons why a firm might buy back its own common stock shares.
2. What financial relationships must hold for a stock repurchase to be a perfect substitute for a cash dividend payment to stockholders?
3. Within the context of a stock repurchase, what is meant by a tender offer?

FINANCE AND THE MULTINATIONAL FIRM: THE CASE OF LOW DIVIDEND PAYMENTS; SO WHERE DO WE INVEST?

Objective 8

During late 1999, the U.S. economy continued an outstanding period of aggregate expansion that placed it among the longest in business cycle history. When such periods of relative prosperity occur, financially strong firms tend to focus their business strategies on growth; as a direct result corporate dividend yields (i.e., cash dividends divided by common stock price) tend to decline. Firms retain more cash dollars for internal investment opportunities and disgorge less cash to investors. For growth-seeking companies, the capital-budgeting decision takes on greater importance, while the consequence of the dividend decision relative to both firm value and cash outflows shrinks. This might properly remind you of what we called the *residual dividend theory* earlier in this chapter.

During general economic prosperity, the multinational firm logically looks to international markets for prospectively high NPV projects. There are at least two solid reasons for such investing behavior: (1) to spread or dilute country-related economic risks by diversifying geographically and (2) to achieve a cost advantage over competitors. These two reasons for U.S. direct investment abroad should remind you of **Axiom 9: All Risk is Not Equal—Some Risk Can Be Diversified Away and Some Cannot;** and **Axiom 5: The Curse of Competitive Markets—Why It's Hard to Find Exceptionally Profitable Projects.**

Table 14–5 identifies those countries, apart from the United States, that make up the so-called Group of Seven Industrialized Nations. Just think of them as the most advanced economies on the globe. They are referred to in the popular business press as the "G-7" countries. Government finance officials from the G-7 and sometimes their chief executive officers (like the President of the United States) usually meet twice a year to discuss multinational economic policy. In Table 14–5 we can observe the historical dollar amounts where U.S. multinational firms have invested internationally.

Notice that when corporate cash is available, U.S. multinational firms favor (1) the United Kingdom and (2) Canada as domiciles for direct investment. A full 67.6 percent of U.S. firms' investment in other G-7 countries is placed in those two countries. Also notice that the capital projects chosen by U.S. multinational firms tend to be concentrated in various manufacturing industries. For instance in Italy, a full 58.5-percent of the U.S. investment lies within the manufacturing sector. These relationships and the dominance of international manufacturing projects are displayed in Figure 14–2. A perceived cost advantage associated with overseas manufacturing,

	AMOUNT	PERCENT	PERCENT IN
COUNTRY	($ BILLIONS)	OF TOTAL	MANUFACTURING
Canada	$103.9	24.8%	44.7
France	$ 39.2	9.4	48.4
Germany	$ 42.9	10.3	51.9
Italy	$ 14.6	3.5	58.5
Japan	$ 38.2	9.2	37.2
United Kingdom	$178.6	42.8	26.0
Total	**$417.4**	**100.0%**	

TABLE 14-5 U.S. DIRECT INVESTMENT ABROAD, 1998 GROUP OF SEVEN INDUSTRIALIZED NATIONS

Source: U.S. Net International Position at Year-end, 1998. U.S. Department of Commerce (June 30, 1999), p. 10.

usually related to lower labor costs, explains the bias towards manufacturing-oriented projects by U.S. multinational firms. The competitive nature of a capitalist-based economy induces U.S. firms to seek low-cost labor inputs from their direct international investments.

CONCEPT CHECK

1. Identify two reasons why multinational firms might turn to international markets in search of high NPV projects.
2. Among the Group of Seven countries, which two are most favored with direct investment by U.S. companies?

FIGURE 14-2

U.S. Direct Investment Abroad, 1998 Group of Seven Industrialized Nations

Source: U.S. Net International Position at Year-end, 1998. U.S. Department of Commerce (June 30, 1999), p. 10.

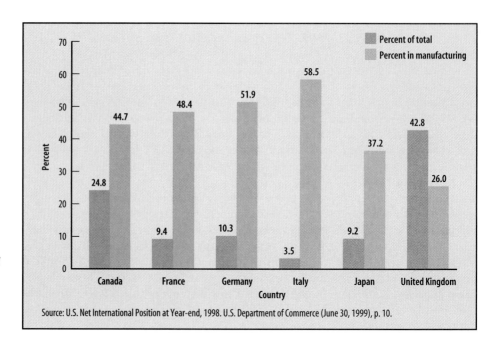

Source: U.S. Net International Position at Year-end, 1998. U.S. Department of Commerce (June 30, 1999), p. 10.

SUMMARY

Describe the trade-off between paying dividends and retaining the profits within the company

Objective 1

A company's dividend decision has an immediate impact upon the firm's financial mix. If the dividend payment is increased, less funds are available internally for financing investments. Consequently, if additional equity capital is needed, the company has to issue new common stock.

Explain the relationship between a corporation's dividend policy and the market price of its common stock

Objective 2

In trying to understand the effect of the dividend policy on a firm's stock price, we must realize the following:

- In perfect markets, the choice between paying or not paying a dividend does not matter. However, when we realize in the real world that there are costs of issuing stock, we have a preference to use internal equity to finance our investment opportunities. Here the dividend decision is simply a residual factor, where the dividend payment should equal the remaining internal capital after financing the equity portion of investments.
- Other market imperfections that may cause a company's dividend policy to affect the firm's stock price include (1) the tax benefit of capital gains, (2) agency costs, (3) the clientele effect, and (4) the informational content of a given policy.

Describe practical considerations that may be important to the firm's dividend policy

Objective 3

Other practical considerations that may affect a firm's dividend payment decision include

- Legal restrictions
- The firm's liquidity position
- The company's accessibility to capital markets
- The stability of earnings
- The desire of investors to maintain control of the company
- Inflation rates

Distinguish among the types of dividend policies corporations frequently use

Objective 4

In practice, managers have generally followed one of three dividend policies:

- Constant dividend payout ratio, where the percentage of dividends to earnings is held constant
- Stable dollar dividend per share, where a relatively stable dollar dividend is maintained over time
- Small, regular dividend plus a year-end extra, where the firm pays a small, regular dollar dividend plus a year-end extra dividend in prosperous years

Of the three dividend policies, the stable dollar dividend is by far the most common.

Specify the procedures a company follows in administering the dividend payment

Objective 5

Generally, companies pay dividends on a quarterly basis. The final approval of a dividend payment comes from the board of directors. The critical dates in this process are as follows:

- Declaration date—the date when the dividend is formally declared by the board of directors
- Date of record—the date when the stock transfer books are closed to determine who owns the stock
- Ex-dividend date—two working days before the date of record, after which the right to receive the dividend no longer goes with the stock
- Payment date—the date the dividend check is mailed to the stockholders

Describe why and how a firm might pay noncash dividends (stock dividends and stock splits) instead of cash dividends

Objective 6

Stock dividends and stock splits have been used by corporations either in lieu of or to supplement cash dividends. At the present, no empirical evidence identifies a relationship between stock dividends and splits and the market price of the stock. Yet a stock dividend or split could

Dividend Policy and Internal Financing 477

conceivably be used to keep the stock price within an optimal trading range. Also, if investors perceive that the stock dividend contains favorable information about the firm's operations, the price of the stock could increase.

Objective 7

Explain the purpose and procedures related to stock repurchases

As an alternative to paying a dividend, management can repurchase stock. In perfect markets, an investor would be indifferent between receiving a dividend or a share repurchase. The investor could simply create a dividend stream by selling stock when income is needed. If, however, market imperfections exist, the investor may have a preference for one of the two methods of distributing the corporate income. A stock repurchase may also be viewed as a financing decision. By issuing debt and then repurchasing stock, a firm can immediately alter its debt-equity mix toward a higher proportion of debt. Also, many managers consider a stock repurchase an investment decision—buying the stock when they believe it to be undervalued.

Objective 8

The multinational firm: the case of low dividend payments; so where do we invest?

During periods of general economic prosperity, financially strong firms tend to focus their business strategies on growth. As a result, dividend yields and cash dividend payments can decline. With internally generated cash to invest, the multinational firm will look to international markets for prospectively high NPV projects. This may allow the firm to (1) spread country-related economic risks by diversifying geographically and (2) achieve a cost advantage over competitors.

KEY TERMS

agency costs, 460

bird-in-the-hand dividend theory, 455

clientele effect, 459

constant dividend payout ratio, 465

date of record, 467

declaration date, 467

dividend payout ratio, 452

ex-dividend date, 468

expectations theory, 461

increasing-stream hypothesis of dividend policy, 466

information asymmetry, 460

payment date, 468

perfect capital markets, 454

residual dividend theory, 458

small, regular dividend plus a year-end extra, 466

stable dollar dividend per share, 466

stock dividend, 469

stock repurchase (stock buyback), 471

stock split, 469

tender offer, 474

STUDY QUESTIONS

14-1 What is meant by the term *dividend payout ratio?*

14-2 Explain the trade-off between retaining internally generated funds and paying cash dividends.

14-3 **a.** What are the assumptions of a perfect market?
   b. What effect does dividend policy have on the share price in a perfect market?

14-4 What is the impact of flotation costs on the financing decision?

14-5 **a.** What is the *residual dividend theory?*
   b. Why is this theory operational only in the long term?

14-6 Why might investors prefer capital gains to the same amount of dividend income?

14-7 What legal restrictions may limit the amount of dividends to be paid?

14-8 How does a firm's liquidity position affect the payment of dividends?

14-9 How can ownership control constrain the growth of a firm?

14-10 **a.** Why is a stable dollar dividend policy popular from the viewpoint of the corporation?
    b. Is it also popular with investors? Why?

14-11 Explain declaration date, date of record, and ex-dividend date.

14-12 What are the advantages of a stock split or dividend over a cash dividend?

14-13 Why would a firm repurchase its own stock?

SELF-TEST PROBLEMS

ST-1 *(Dividend Growth Rate)* Schulz, Inc. maintains a constant dividend payout ratio of 35 percent. Earnings per share last year were $8.20 and are expected to grow indefinitely at a rate of 12 percent. What will be the dividend per share this year? In 5 years?

ST-2 *(Stock Split)* The debt and equity section of the Robson Corporation balance sheet is shown below. The current market price of the common shares is $20. Reconstruct the financial statement assuming that (a) a 15-percent stock dividend is issued and (b) a two-for-one stock split is declared.

Debt	$1,800,000
Common	
Par ($2; 100,000 shares)	200,000
Paid-in capital	400,000
Retained earnings	900,000
	$3,300,000

STUDY PROBLEMS

14-1 *(Flotation Costs and Issue Size)* Your firm needs to raise $10 million. Assuming that flotation costs are expected to be $15 per share and that the market price of the stock is $120, how many shares would have to be issued? What is the dollar size of the issue?

14-2 *(Flotation Costs and Issue Size)* If flotation costs for common stock issue are 18 percent, how large must the issue be so that the firm will net $5,800,000? If the stock sells for $85 per share, how many shares must be issued?

14-3 *(Stock Dividend)* RCB has 2 million shares of common stock outstanding. Net income is $550,000, and the P/E ratio for the stock is 10. Management is planning a 20-percent stock dividend.
    a. What will be the price of the stock after the stock dividend?
    b. If an investor owns 100 shares before the stock dividend, does the total value of his or her shares change? Explain.

14-4 *(Stock Split)* You own 5 percent of Trexco Corporation's common stock, which most recently sold for $98 before a planned two-for-one stock split announcement. Before the split there are 25,000 shares of common stock outstanding.
    a. Relative to now, what will be your financial position after the stock split? (Assume the stock price falls proportionately.)
    b. The executive vice-president in charge of finance believes the price will only fall 40 percent after the split because she feels the price is above the optimal price range. If she is correct, what will be your net gain?

14-5 *(Dividend Policies)* The earnings for Crystal Cargo, Inc. have been predicted for the next 5 years and are as follows. There are 1 million shares outstanding. Determine the yearly dividend per share to be paid if the following policies are enacted:
    a. Constant dividend payout ratio of 50 percent.

b. Stable dollar dividend targeted at 50 percent of the earnings over the 5-year period.

c. Small, regular dividend of $.50 per share plus a year-end extra when the profits in any year exceed $1,500,000. The year-end extra dividend will equal 50 percent of profits exceeding $1,500,000.

YEAR	PROFITS AFTER TAXES
1	$1,400,000
2	2,000,000
3	1,860,000
4	900,000
5	2,800,000

14-6 *(Repurchase of Stock)* The Dunn Corporation is planning to pay dividends of $500,000. There are 250,000 shares outstanding, with an earnings per share of $5. The stock should sell for $50 after the ex-dividend date. If instead of paying a dividend, management decides to repurchase stock

a. What should be the repurchase price?

b. How many shares should be repurchased?

c. What if the repurchase price is set below or above your suggested price in part a?

d. If you own 100 shares, would you prefer that the company pay the dividend or repurchase stock?

14-7 *(Flotation Costs and Issue Size)* D. Butler, Inc. needs to raise $14 million. Assuming that the market price of the firm's stock is $95 and flotation costs are 10 percent of the market price, how many shares would have to be issued? What is the dollar size of the issue?

14-8 *(Stock Split)* You own 20 percent of Rainy Corp., which recently sold for $86 before a planned two-for-one split announcement. Before the split there are 80,000 shares of common stock outstanding.

a. What is your financial position before the split, and what will it be after the stock split? (Assume the stock price falls proportionately.)

b. Your stockbroker believes the market will react positively to the split and that the price will fall only 45 percent after the split. If she is correct, what will be your net gain?

--- **COMPREHENSIVE PROBLEM** ---

The following article appeared in the July 2, 1995, issue of the *Dallas Morning News*. Scott Burns, the author, argues the case for the importance of dividends.

Let us now praise the lowly dividend.

Insignificant to some. Small potatoes to others. An irksome sign of tax liability to many. However characterized, dividends are experiencing yet another round of defamation on Wall Street.

Why pay out dividends, the current argument goes, when a dollar of dividend can be retained as a dollar of book value that the market will value at two, three, or four dollars? With the average stock now selling at more than three times book value, investors should prefer companies that retain earnings rather than pay them out, even if they do nothing more with the money than repurchase shares.

The New Wisdom

Instead, the New Wisdom says, the investor should go for companies that retain earnings, reinvest them, and try to maximize shareholder value. Dividends should be avoided in the pursuit of long-term capital gains.

The only problem with this reasoning is that we've heard it before. And always at market tops.

- We heard it in the late 1960s as stock prices soared and dividend yields fell.
- We heard it again in the early '70s as investors fixated on the "Nifty Fifty" and analysts calmly projected that with growth companies yielding 1 percent or less, the most important part of the return was the certainty of 20 percent annual earnings growth.
- And we're hearing it now, with stock prices hitting new highs each day. The Standard & Poor's 500 Index, for instance, is up 19.7 percent since Dec. 31, the equivalent of more than seven years of dividends at the current yield of 2.6 percent.

Tilting the Yield

Significantly, we didn't hear that dividends were irrelevant in the late '70s, as stock valuations moved to new lows. At that time, portfolio managers talked about "yield tilt"—running a portfolio with a bias toward dividend return to offset some of the risk of continuing stock market decline. Indeed, many of the best performing funds in the late '70s were Equity-Income funds, the funds that seek above-average dividend income.

You can understand how much dividends contribute to long-term returns by taking a look at the performance of a major index, with and without dividend reinvestment. If you had invested $10,000 in the S&P's 500 Index in January 1982 and taken all dividends in cash, your original investment would have grown to $37,475 by the end of 1994.

It doesn't get much better than that.

The gain clocks a compound annual return of 10.7 percent, and total gain of $27,475. During the same period you would have collected an additional $14,244 in dividends.

Not a trivial sum, either.

In other words, during one of the biggest bull markets in history, unreinvested dividend income accounted for more than one-third of your total return.

If you had reinvested those dividends in additional stock, the final score would be even better: $60,303. The appreciation of your original investment would have been $27,475 while the growth from reinvested dividends would have been $22,828. Nearly half—45 percent—of your total return came from reinvested dividends. And this happened during a stellar period of rising stock prices.

Now consider the same investment during a period of misery. If you had invested $10,000 in the S&P's Index stocks in January 1968, your investment would have grown to only $14,073 over the next 13 years, a gain of only $4,073. During much of that time, the value of your original investment would have been less than $10,000. Dividends during the period would have totaled $7,088—substantially more than stock appreciation. Reinvested, the same dividends would have grown to $9,705, helping your original investment growth to $23,778.

In a period of major ups and downs that many investors don't like to remember, dividends accounted for 70 percent of total return (see accompanying chart).

We could fiddle with these figures any number of ways. We could reduce the value of dividends by calculating income taxes. We could raise it by starting with the Dow Jones industrial average stocks, which tend to have higher dividends. But the point here is very simple: Whether you spend them or reinvest them, dividends are always an important part of the return on common stock.

Source: Scott Burns, "Those Lowly Dividends," *Dallas Morning News,* July 2, 1995, p. 1H. Reprinted with permission of the *Dallas Morning News.*

Anatomy of the bull market of 1982–1994

Original investment		$10,000
Gain on original investment		$27,475
Total dividends	$14,244	
Gain on reinvested dividends	$ 8,584	
Total gain from dividends		$22,828
Total		$60,303

Compound annualized return equals 14.8%;
45% from dividends.

Anatomy of a bear market, 1968–1980

Original investment		$10,000
Gain on original investment		$ 4,073
Total dividends	$ 7,088	
Gain on reinvested dividends	$ 2,617	
Total gain from dividends		$ 9,705
Total		$23,778

Compound annualized return equals 6.9%; 70%
from dividends.

Source: Franklin/Templeton Group Hypothetical Illustration Program.

Based on your reading of this chapter, evaluate what Burns is saying. Do you agree or disagree with him? Why?

SELF-TEST SOLUTIONS

SS-1

$$\text{Dividend per share} = 35\% \times \$8.20$$
$$= \$2.87$$

Dividends:

$$1 \text{ year} = \$2.87 \, (1 + 0.12)$$
$$= \$3.21$$
$$5 \text{ years} = \$2.87 \, (1 + 0.12)^5$$
$$= \$2.87 \, (1.762)$$
$$= \$5.06$$

a. If a 15-percent stock dividend is issued, the financial statement would appear as follows:

Debt	$1,800,000
Common	
Par ($2 par; 115,000 shares)	230,000
Paid-in capital	670,000
Retained earnings	600,000
	$3,300,000

b. A two-for-one split would result in a 100-percent increase in the number of shares. Because the total par value remains at $200,000, the new par value per share is $1 ($200,000/200,000 shares). The new financial statement would be as follows:

Debt	$1,800,000
Common	
Par ($1 par; 200,000 shares)	200,000
Paid-in capital	400,000
Retained earnings	900,000
	$3,300,000

Chapter Fifteen

Managing Current Assets and Liabilities •
Appropriate Level of Working Capital • Using
the Cash Conversion Cycle to Evaluate Working-
Capital Management • Estimation of the Cost
of Short-Term Credit • Sources of Short-Term
Credit

INTRODUCTION TO WORKING-CAPITAL MANAGEMENT

LEARNING OBJECTIVES

AFTER READING THIS CHAPTER, YOU SHOULD BE ABLE TO:

1. Describe the risk-return trade-off involved in managing a firm's working capital.
2. Explain the determinants of net working capital.
3. Use the cash conversion cycle to evaluate the efficiency of a firm's management of its working capital.
4. Calculate the effective cost of short-term credit.
5. List and describe the basic sources of short-term credit.

On average, U.S. companies invest more than 15¢ in working capital from each $1 of sales. In 1990, American Standard fit this mold very well with over $735 million invested in working capital. By the mid-1990s American Standard had revenues totaling $4.2 billion but had reduced its net working capital roughly by half.

In 1990, American Standard had three primary product lines: plumbing supplies, air conditioners, and brakes for trucks and buses. The firm faced static sales and huge interest payments (the result of a $3.1 billion junk bond issue used to stave off a hostile takeover attempt by Black and Decker in 1989). To improve the firm's operating performance, its chairman, Emmanuel Kampouris, introduced a strategy aimed at reducing the firm's $735 million in net working capital to zero by the late 1990s. This was feasible if the company could reduce its inventories so low that they could be financed without borrowing. The ideas was to deliver goods and bill customers more rapidly so that customer payments were sufficient to pay for minimal stocks of inventories. Kampouris sought to accomplish this ambitious goal through implementation of a lean manufacturing system known as *demand flow technology*. Under this system, plants manufacture products as customers order them. Suppliers deliver straight to the assembly line, thus reducing stocks of parts, and plants ship the products as soon as they are completed. The system dramatically reduces inventories of both parts and finished goods. To date, American Standard has

working capital
net working capital

reduced its inventories by more than one-half, down to $326 million since 1990. Thus, American Standard invests only 5¢ out of each sales dollar in working capital, compared to the norm of 15¢. By saving interest payments on supplies, the company has increased its cash flow by $60 million a year.

Objective 1 ═══ **MANAGING CURRENT ASSETS AND LIABILITIES**

Other things remaining the same, the greater the firm's investment in current assets, the greater its liquidity. As a means of increasing its liquidity, the firm may choose to invest additional funds in cash or marketable securities. Such action involves a trade-off, however, because such assets earn little or no return. The firm thus finds that it can reduce its risk of illiquidity only by reducing its overall return on invested funds, and vice versa.

Working-Capital Management and the Risk-Return Trade-off

The risk-return trade-off involved in managing the firm's working capital involves a trade-off between the firm's liquidity and its profitability. By maintaining a large investment in current assets like cash and inventory, the firm reduces the chance of production stoppages and lost sales from inventory shortages and the inability to pay bills on time, which might in turn result in credit-rating problems. However, as the firm increases its investment in working capital, there is not a corresponding increase in its returns. This means that the firm's return on investment drops because profits are unchanged, while the investment in assets increases.

The Decision to Move Manufacturing Offshore Has Hidden Costs

Throughout the last two decades manufacturing firms have moved larger and larger portions of their manufacturing and assembly operations offshore to locations where labor costs are substantially lower than in the United States. All too often the decision to do so has been based solely on a comparison of relative labor costs without giving due consideration to the opportunity costs associated with the added funds that must be tied up in inventories in transit.

Consider the case of Cypress Semiconductor. Cypress manufactures integrated circuits (computer chips) that sell for $8 each. The firm estimated that it could save $0.032 per chip in labor costs by manufacturing them overseas. However, the labor cost savings do not capture the full cost implications of the decision to manufacture offshore. Cypress would incur shipping and customs duties of $0.025 per chip. Combining the labor cost savings with the added out-of-pocket costs, it appears that the firm can net $0.007 per chip in savings if it moves production offshore. However, this analysis ignores a hidden cost of the decision. Specifically, if production is moved offshore it will add an additional 5 weeks to the total production time because of the special problems associated with shipping the component parts offshore and shipping the finished product back. This additional 5 weeks is costly, because Cypress will have invested $8 in production that cannot be recouped until the chip is available for sale. In financial terms this added time produces an additional opportunity cost of $0.154 per chip where Cypress requires a 20-percent return on the funds invested in the business. That is,

$$\begin{matrix} \text{added} \\ \text{interest} \\ \text{expense} \end{matrix} = \begin{matrix} \text{opportunity} \\ \text{cost of} \\ \text{funds} \end{matrix} \times \begin{matrix} \text{additional} \\ \text{transit} \\ \text{time} \end{matrix} \times \begin{matrix} \text{cost} \\ \text{per} \\ \text{part} \end{matrix}$$

$$= 20\% \times 5/52 \times \$8 = \$0.154$$

Consequently, the $0.032/chip cost savings or benefit of moving offshore was more than offset by the $0.179/chip in added shipping, customs, and opportunity costs, i.e., $0.154 + 0.025.

Source: Joel Kotkin, "The Case for Manufacturing in America," Inc., March 1985, p. 54. Reprinted with permission of the Goldhirsch Group.

BACK TO THE FOUNDATIONS

Many of the working-capital decisions made by financial managers involve risk-return trade-offs between liquidity and profitability. The principles that guide these decisions are the same ones set out in **Axiom 1: The Risk-Return Trade-off—We Won't Take On Additional Risk Unless We Expect to Be Compensated with Additional Return.** The more current assets held and the more long-term financing used, the less the risk and the less the return.

The firm's use of current versus long-term debt also involves a risk-return trade-off. *Other things remaining the same, the greater the firm's reliance on short-term debt or current liabilities in financing its asset investments, the greater the risk of illiquidity.* On the other hand, the use of current liabilities offers some very real advantages in that they can be less costly than long-term financing, and they provide the firm with a flexible means of financing its fluctuating needs for assets. However, if for some reason the firm has problems raising short-term funds or needs funds for longer than expected, there can be real trouble. Thus, a firm can reduce its risk of illiquidity through the use of long-term debt at the expense of a reduction in its return on invested funds. Once again we see that the risk-return trade-off involves an increased risk of illiquidity versus increased profitability.

Advantages of Current Liabilities: The Return

Flexibility

Current liabilities offer the firm a flexible source of financing. They can be used to match the timing of a firm's needs for short-term financing. If, for example, a firm needs funds for a 3-month period during each year to finance a seasonal expansion in inventories, then a 3-month loan can provide substantial cost savings over a long-term loan (even if the interest rate on short-term financing should be higher). The use of long-term debt in this situation involves borrowing for the entire year rather than for the period when the funds are needed, which increases the amount of interest the firm must pay. This brings us to the second advantage generally associated with the use of short-term financing.

Interest Cost

In general, interest rates on short-term debt are lower than on long-term debt for a given borrower. This relationship was introduced in Chapter 2 and is referred to as the term structure of interest rates. For a given firm, the term structure might appear as follows.

LOAN MATURITY	INTEREST RATE
3 months	4.00%
6 months	4.60
1 year	5.30
3 years	5.90
5 years	6.75
10 years	7.50
30 years	8.25

Note that this term structure reflects the rates of interest applicable to a given borrower at a particular time. It would not, for example, describe the rates of interest available to another borrower or even those applicable to the same borrower at a different time.

Disadvantages of Current Liabilities: The Risk

The use of current liabilities or short-term debt as opposed to long-term debt subjects the firm to a greater risk of illiquidity for two reasons. First, short-term debt, because of its very nature, must be repaid or rolled over more often, and so it increases the possibility that the firm's financial condition might deteriorate to a point where the needed funds might not be available.[1]

A second disadvantage of short-term debt is the uncertainty of interest costs from year to year. For example, a firm borrowing during a 6-month period each year to finance a seasonal expansion in current assets might incur a different rate of interest each year. This rate reflects the current rate of interest at the time of the

---

[1]The dangers of such a policy are readily apparent in the experiences of firms that have been forced into bankruptcy. Penn Central, for example, went bankrupt when it had $80 million in short-term debt that it was unable to refinance (roll over).

loan, as well as the lender's perception of the firm's riskiness. If fixed-rate long-term debt were used, the interest cost would be known for the entire period of the loan agreement.

CONCEPT CHECK

1. How does investing more heavily in current assets while not increasing the firm's current liabilities decrease both the firm's risk and its expected return on its investment?
2. How does the use of current liabilities enhance firm profitability and also increase the firm's risk of default on its financial obligations?

APPROPRIATE LEVEL OF WORKING CAPITAL

Objective 2

Managing the firm's net working capital (its liquidity) has been shown to involve simultaneous and interrelated decisions regarding investments in current assets and use of current liabilities. Fortunately, a guiding principle exists that can be used as a benchmark for the firm's working-capital policies: the hedging principle, or principle of self-liquidating debt. This principle provides a guide to the maintenance of a level of liquidity sufficient for the firm to meet its maturing obligations on time.[2]

In Chapter 13 we discussed the firm's financing decision in terms of the choice between debt and equity sources of financing. There is, however, yet another critical dimension of the firm's financing decision. This relates to the maturity structure of the firm's debt. How should the decision be made as to whether to use short-term or current debt or longer-maturity debt? This is one of the fundamental questions addressed in this chapter and one that is critically important to the financial success of the firm. Basically, the hedging principle is one rule of thumb for guiding a firm's debt-maturity financing decisions. This principle states that financing maturity should follow the cash flow–producing characteristics of the asset being financed. For example, an asset that is expected to provide cash flows over an extended period such as 5 years should, in accordance with the hedging principle, be financed with debt with a pattern of similar cash flow requirements. Note that when the hedging principle is followed, the firm's debt will "self-liquidate" because the assets being financed will generate sufficient cash to retire the debt as it comes due.

Takin' It to the Net
Working capital management is such a significant problem that specialized consulting firms have developed that devote significant parts of their practice to helping firms improve their working capital management practices. See http://www.metapraxis.com/.

Hedging Principle

Very simply, the **hedging principle,** or **principle of self-liquidating debt,** involves *matching the cash flow–generating characteristics of an asset with the maturity of the source of financing used to finance its acquisition.* For example, a seasonal expansion in inventories,

hedging principle
principle of self-liquidating debt

---

[2]A value-maximizing approach to the management of the firm's liquidity involves assessing the value of the benefits derived from increasing the firm's investment in liquid assets and weighing them against the added costs to the firm's owners resulting from investing in low-yield current assets. Unfortunately, the benefits derived from increased liquidity relate to the expected costs of bankruptcy to the firm's owners, and these costs are "unmeasurable" by existing technology. Thus, a "valuation" approach to liquidity management exists only in the theoretical realm.

according to the hedging principle, should be financed with a short-term loan or current liability. The rationale underlying the rule is straightforward. Funds are needed for a limited period, and when that time has passed, the cash needed to repay the loan will be generated by the sale of the extra inventory items. Obtaining the needed funds from a long-term source (longer than 1 year) would mean that the firm would still have the funds after the inventories they helped finance had been sold. In this case the firm would have "excess" liquidity, which it either holds in cash or invests in low-yield marketable securities until the seasonal increase in inventories occurs again and the funds are needed. The result of all this would be an overall lowering of firm profits.

Consider an example in which a firm purchases a new conveyor belt system, which is expected to produce cash savings to the firm by eliminating the need for two laborers and, consequently, their salaries. This amounts to an annual savings of $24,000, whereas the conveyor belt costs $250,000 to install and will last 20 years. If the firm chooses to finance this asset with a 1-year note, then it will not be able to repay the loan from the $24,000 cash flow generated by the asset. In accordance with the hedging principle, the firm should finance the asset with a source of financing that more nearly matches the expected life and cash flow—generating characteristics of the asset. In this case, a 15- to 20-year loan would be more appropriate.

Permanent and Temporary Assets

The notion of maturity matching in the hedging principle can be most easily understood when we think in terms of the distinction between permanent and temporary investments in assets, as opposed to the more traditional fixed and current asset categories. **Permanent investments** in an asset are *investments that the firm expected to hold for a period longer than 1 year.* Note that we are referring to the period the firm plans to hold an investment, not the useful life of the asset. For example, permanent investments are made in the firm's minimum level of current assets, as well as in its fixed assets. **Temporary investments,** on the other hand, are composed of *current assets that will be liquidated and not replaced within the current year.* Thus, some part of the firm's current assets is permanent and the remainder is temporary. For example, a seasonal increase in level of inventories is a temporary investment; the buildup in inventories will be eliminated when it is no longer needed.

permanent investments

temporary investments

Temporary, Permanent, and Spontaneous Sources of Financing

Because total assets must always equal the sum of temporary, permanent, and spontaneous sources of financing, the hedging approach provides the financial manager with the basis for determining the sources of financing to use at any point.

Now, what constitutes a temporary, permanent, or spontaneous source of financing? Temporary sources of financing consist of current liabilities. Short-term notes payable constitute the most common example of a temporary source of financing. Examples of notes payable include unsecured bank loans, commercial paper, and loans secured by accounts receivable and inventories. Permanent sources of financing include intermediate-term loans, long-term debt, preferred stock, and common equity.

Spontaneous sources of financing consist of trade credit and other accounts payable that arise *spontaneously* in the firm's day-to-day operations. For example, as the firm acquires materials for its inventories, **trade credit** is often *made available spontaneously or on demand from the firm's suppliers. Trade credit appears on the firm's balance sheet as accounts payable,* and the size of the accounts-payable balance varies directly with the firm's purchases of inventory items. In turn, inventory purchases are related to anticipated sales. Thus, part of the financing needed by the firm is spontaneously provided in the form of trade credit.

trade credit

In addition to trade credit, wages and salaries payable, accrued interest, and accrued taxes also provide valuable sources of spontaneous financing. These

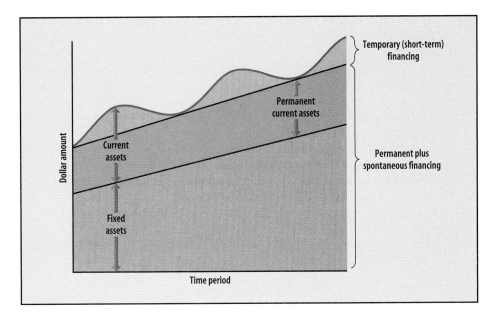

FIGURE 15–1
Hedging Principle

expenses accrue throughout the period until they are paid. For example, if a firm has a wage expense of $10,000 a week and pays its employees monthly, then its employees effectively provide financing equal to $10,000 by the end of the first week following a payday, $20,000 by the end of the second week, and so forth, until the workers are paid. Because these expenses generally arise in direct conjunction with the firm's ongoing operations, they too are referred to as spontaneous.

Hedging Principle: Graphic Illustration

The hedging principle can now be stated very succinctly: *Asset needs of the firm not financed by spontaneous sources should be financed in accordance with this rule: Permanent asset investments are financed with permanent sources, and temporary investments are financed with temporary sources.*

The hedging principle is depicted in Figure 15–1. Total assets are broken down into temporary and permanent asset investment categories. The firm's permanent investment in assets is financed by the use of permanent sources of financing (intermediate- and long-term debt, preferred stock, and common equity) or spontaneous sources (trade credit and other accounts payable). For illustration purposes spontaneous sources of financing are treated as if their amount were fixed. In practice, of course, spontaneous sources of financing fluctuate with the firm's purchases and its expenditures for wages, salaries, taxes, and other items that are paid on a delayed basis. Its temporary investment in assets is financed with temporary (short-term) debt.

CONCEPT CHECK

1. What is the hedging principle or principle of self-liquidating debt?
2. What are some examples of permanent and temporary investments in current assets?
3. Is trade credit a permanent, temporary or spontaneous source of financing? Explain.

USING THE CASH CONVERSION CYCLE TO EVALUATE WORKING-CAPITAL MANAGEMENT

Firms vary widely in their ability to manage their new working capital, and an overall measure of effectiveness is needed. An increasingly popular method to evaluate a firm's effective working-capital management takes the approach that the firm's objective should be to minimize working capital subject to the constraint that it has sufficient working capital to support the firm's operations.

Minimizing working capital is accomplished by speeding up the collection of cash from sales, increasing inventory turns, and slowing down the disbursement of cash. We can incorporate all of these factors in a single measure called the cash conversion cycle.

Measuring Working-Capital Efficiency

cash conversion cycle

The **cash conversion cycle (CCC)** is simply *the sum of days of sales outstanding (DSO) and days of sales in inventory (DSI) less days of payables outstanding (DPO):*

$$\begin{array}{c} \text{cash} \\ \text{conversion} \\ \text{cycle} \end{array} (CCC) = \begin{array}{c} \text{days of} \\ \text{sales} \\ \text{outstanding} \end{array} (DSO) + \begin{array}{c} \text{days of} \\ \text{sales in} \\ \text{inventor} \end{array} (DSI) - \begin{array}{c} \text{days of} \\ \text{payables} \\ \text{outstanding} \end{array} (DPO)$$

15–2

We calculate days of sales outstanding as follows:

$$DSO = \frac{\text{accounts receivable}}{\text{sales}/365}$$

days of sales outstanding

Recall from Chapter 4 that **days of sales outstanding (DSO)** can also be thought of as *the average age of the firm's accounts receivable or the average collection period.*

days of sales in inventory

Days of sales in inventory is defined as follows:

$$DSI = \frac{\text{inventories}}{\text{sales}/365}$$

Note that DSI can also be thought of as the *average age of the firm's inventory*—that is, *the average number of days that a dollar of inventory is held by the firm.*

days of payables outstanding

Days of payables outstanding is defined as follows:

$$DPO = \frac{\text{accounts payable}}{\text{sales}/365}$$

This ratio indicates *the average age, in days, of the firm's accounts payable.*

To illustrate the use of the CCC metric, consider Dell Computer Corporation. In 1989 Dell was a fledgling start-up whose CCC was 121.88 days (Table 15–1); by 1998, Dell had reduced this number to −18.12 days. How, you might ask, does a firm reduce its CCC below zero? The answer is through very aggressive management of its working capital. As Table 15–1 indicates, Dell achieved this phenomenal reduction in CCC primarily through very effective management of inventories (DSI dropped from 132.04 in 1989 to 9.13 in 1998) and more favorable trade credit payment practices (DPO increased from 47.46 in 1989 to 62.13 in 1998). Specifically, Dell is a direct marketer of personal computers who does not build your computer until the order is received and then purchases its supplies using trade credit. This business model results in minimal investment in inventories. Dell has obviously improved its working capital management practices over the 1989–1998 period as is evidenced in Figure 15–2, where we compare Dell with

TABLE 15-1	DETERMINANTS OF DELL COMPUTER CORPORATION'S CASH CONVERSION CYCLE FOR 1989-1998									

cash conversion cycle (CCC) = days of sales outstanding (DSO) + days of sales in inventory (DSI) − days of payables outstanding (DPO)

	JAN '89	JAN '90	JAN '91	JAN '92	JAN '93	JAN '94	JAN '95	JAN '96	JAN '97	JAN '98
Days of sales outstanding (DSO)	37.30	44.66	49.34	51.51	48.17	49.17	49.14	42.96	37.79	34.88
Days of sales in inventory (DSI)	132.04	113.82	79.17	65.16	50.08	40.28	34.16	31.01	20.25	9.13
Days of payables outstanding (DPO)	47.46	78.31	74.49	55.47	61.72	45.10	57.96	38.77	63.80	62.13
Cash conversion cycle (CCC)	121.88	80.17	54.02	61.20	36.53	44.35	25.35	35.20	−5.76	−18.12

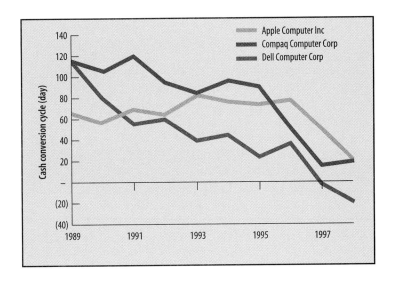

FIGURE 15-2
Cash Conversion Cycles for Apple, Compaq, and Dell: 1989–1998.

Compaq and Apple. The dramatic differences in CCC reflect both differences in business models (direct seller versus the use of more traditional channels of distribution involving the use of resellers such as CompUSA, Best Buy, and Computer City) and the relative efficiency of the firms in managing inventories, receivables, and payables.

ESTIMATION OF THE COST OF SHORT-TERM CREDIT

Objective 4

Approximate Cost-of-Credit Formula

The procedure for estimating the cost of short-term credit is a very simple one and relies on the basic interest equation:

$$\text{interest} = \text{principal} \times \text{rate} \times \text{time} \qquad (15\text{-}3)$$

where *interest* is the dollar amount of interest on a *principal* that is borrowed at some annual *rate* for a fraction of a year (represented by *time*). For example, a 6-month loan for $1,000 at 8 percent interest would require an interest payment of $40.

$$interest = \$1,000 \times .08 \times \frac{1}{2} = \$40$$

Takin' It to the Net
As we have just seen, the Dell Computer Corporation is a leader in the use of electronic commerce to support its computer sales. To see how this works visit their site at http://www.dell.com/.

We use this basic relationship to solve for the cost of a source of short-term financing or the annual percentage rate (APR) where the interest amount, the principal sum, and the time period for financing are known. Thus, solving the basic interest equation for APR produces[3]

$$APR = \frac{interest}{principal \times time} \tag{15-4}$$

or

$$APR = \frac{interest}{principal} \times \frac{1}{time} \tag{15-4a}$$

This equation, called the APR calculation, is clarified by the following example.

Example

The SKC Corporation plan to borrow $1,000 for a 90-day period. At maturity the firm will repay the $1,000 principal amount plus $30 interest. The effective annual rate of interest for the loan can be estimated using the APR equation, as follows:

$$APR = \frac{\$30}{\$1,000} \times \frac{1}{90/360}$$

$$= .03 \times \frac{360}{90} = .12 = 12\%$$

The effective annual cost of funds provided by the loan is therefore 12 percent.

Annual Percentage Yield Formula

The simple APR calculation does not consider compound interest. To account for the influence of compounding, we can use the following equation:

$$APY = \left(1 + \frac{i}{m} \right)^m - 1 \tag{15-5}$$

where *APY* is the annual percentage yield, *i* is the nominal rate of interest per year (12 percent in the above example), and *m* is the number of compounding periods within a year [$m = 1/time = 1/(90/360) = 4$ in the preceding example]. Thus, the effective rate of interest on the loan in the example problem, considering compounding, is

$$APY = \left(1 + \frac{.12}{4} \right)^4 - 1 = .126 = 12.6\%$$

---

[3]For ease of computation we assume a 30-day month and 360-day year in this chapter.

Managing Working Capital by Trimming Receivables

LaFarge Corporation is located in Reston, Virginia and operates in the building materials industry. Last year LaFarge was able to dramatically improve its management of accounts receivable. This improvement is reflected in a decrease in the days of sales outstanding ratio (DSO), that is,

$$DSO = \frac{accounts\ receivable}{sales/365}$$

After reviewing this formula, you may recall that we referred to DSO in Chapter 4 as the average collection period. The company's success is due in large part to the fact that it ties incentive pay to the return on net assets (RONA) as defined below:

$$RONA = \frac{Earnings\ before\ interest\ and\ taxes}{net\ assets}$$

Note that improvements in accounts receivable management that result in a decrease in DSO also lead to a reduction in the firm's net assets and a corresponding increase in RONA. Of course, this presumes that the reduction in DSO does not have an adverse impact on firm revenues and, consequently, earnings.

How Did They Do It?

Pete Sacripanti, vice president and controller of LaFarge's Calgary-based construction materials business, credits the firm's improved collections to 12 fundamental steps:[a]

1. **Focusing on customers and collections,** which involves all layers of management, and is not just a finance responsibility.
2. **Building a base of preferred customers** that confer a competitive advantage.
3. **Delineating clear ownership of customer accounts** among the sales staff, which prevents passing the buck on delinquent accounts.
4. **Fixing clear guidelines** that govern LaFarge's commitments and responsibilities to customers.
5. **Articulating standard sales terms and conditions,** stipulating terms that are negotiable and those that are never negotiable.
6. **Establishing monthly collection targets by salesperson and division,** with collection targets based on the prior month's sales plus past-due accounts.
7. **Training salespeople on customer profitability,** with particular attention to (1) the link between past-due accounts and increased risk of bad debt write-offs,

(2) the volume of business required to recover the cost of bad debts, and (3) higher borrowing costs for the company.
8. **Engaging in regular (weekly) credit and collections meetings** with the sales team, the credit manager, and the general manager.
9. **Encouraging constant "in-your face" executive management,** featuring weekly status updates of collections by salespeople, including key account information.
10. **Facilitating collections through advance phone calls** to establish expected payment amount and availability, and provide a courier to pick up the payments.
11. **Developing collection skills.** These include partial hold-back releases; offsetting balances owed for services or equipment; use of construction liens, guarantees, letters of credit, payment bonds; negotiation techniques for securing extras in lieu of write-offs; and better knowledge of the company's products, its industry, and its customers.
12. **Developing unique value** by building stronger relationships with customers, such as air miles loyalty programs, engineered solutions, quality assurance, and new-product development.

The key thing to note in this list is that each item represents a managerial action aimed at improving the firm's success in collecting its receivables. The DSO metric captures the success of these actions but it is these 12 steps that actually brought about the improvements.

Measuring Success

LaFarge engaged in a 3-year program aimed at reducing its investment in working capital. The success of the program is most clearly evident in the company's western Canadian construction-materials operation based in Calgary. This unit slashed its working capital by 38 percent to around $36 million while increasing sales by 10 percent to $425 million. The effect on RONA was dramatic because the firm simultaneously increased earnings (the numerator of the ratio) and decreased net assets (the denominator).

---

[a]From S. L. Mintz, "The 1999 Working Capital Survey: Dollars in the Details," *CFO Magazine* (July 1999): 58.

Compounding effectively raises the cost of short-term credit. Because the differences between APR and APY are usually small, we use the simple interest values of APR to compute the cost of short-term credit.

CONCEPT CHECK

1. What is the fundamental interest equation that underlies the calculation of the approximate cost of credit formula?
2. What is the annual percentage yield (APY) and why is it preferred to the annual percentage rate (APR)?

| Objective 5 | **SOURCES OF SHORT-TERM CREDIT** |

unsecured loans

secured loans

Short-term credit sources can be classified into two basic groups: unsecured and secured. **Unsecured loans** include all those *sources that have as their security only the lender's faith in the ability of the borrower to repay the funds when due.* Major sources of unsecured short-term credit include accrued wages and taxes, trade credit, unsecured bank loans, and commercial paper. **Secured loans** involve the *pledge of specific assets as collateral in the event the borrower defaults in payment of principal or interest.* Commercial banks, finance companies, and factors are the primary suppliers of secured credit. The principal sources of collateral include accounts receivable and inventories.

Unsecured Sources: Accrued Wages and Taxes

Because most business pay their employees only periodically (weekly, biweekly, or monthly), firms accrue a wages-payable account that is, in essence, a loan from their employees. For example, if the wage expense for the Appleton Manufacturing Company is $450,000 per week and it pays its employees monthly, then by the end of a 4-week month the firm will owe its employees $1.8 million in wages for services they have already performed during the month. Consequently, the employees finance their own efforts through waiting a full month for payment.

Similarly, firms generally make quarterly income tax payments for their estimated quarterly tax liability. This means that the firm has the use of the tax moneys it owes based on quarterly profits up through the end of the quarter. In addition, the firm pays sales taxes and withholding (income) taxes for its employees on a deferred basis. The longer the period that the firm holds the tax payments, the greater the amount of financing they provide.

Note that these sources of financing *rise and fall spontaneously* with the level of firm sales. That is, as the firm's sales increase, so do its labor expense, sales taxes collected, and income tax. Consequently, these accrued expense items provide the firm with automatic or spontaneous sources of financing.

Unsecured Sources: Trade Credit

Trade credit provides one of the most flexible sources of short-term financing available to the firm. We previously noted that trade credit is a primary source of spontaneous, or on-demand, financing. That is, trade credit arises spontaneously with the firm's purchases. To arrange for credit the firm need only place an order with

TABLE 15–2	EFFECTIVE RATES OF INTEREST ON SELECTED TRADE CREDIT TERMS	

Credit Terms	Effective Rates
2/10, net 60	14.69%
2/10, net 90	9.18
3/20, net 60	27.84
6/10, net 90	28.72

one of its suppliers. The supplier checks the firm's credit and, if it is good, sends the merchandise. The purchasing firm then pays for the goods in accordance with the supplier's credit terms.

Credit Terms and Cash Discounts

Very often the credit terms offered with trade credit involve a cash discount for early payment. For example, a supplier might offer terms of 2/10, net 30, which means that a 2 percent discount is offered for payment within 10 days or the full amount is due in 30 days. Thus, a 2-percent penalty is involved for not paying within 10 days, or for delaying payment from the tenth to the thirtieth day (i.e., for 20 days). The effective annual cost of not taking the cash discount can be quite severe. Using a $1 invoice amount, the effective cost of passing up the discount period using the preceding credit terms and our APR equation can be estimated.

$$APR = \frac{\$.02}{\$.98} \times \frac{1}{20/360} = .3673 = 36.73\%$$

Note that the 2-percent cash discount is the *interest* cost of extending the payment period an *additional* 20 days. Note also that the principal amount of the credit is $.98. This amount constitutes the full principal amount as of the tenth day of the credit period, after which time the cash discount is lost. The effective cost of passing up the 2-percent discount for 20 days is quite expensive: 36.73 percent. Furthermore, once the discount period has passed, there is no reason to pay before the final due date (the thirtieth day). Table 15–2 lists the effective annual cost of a number of alternative credit terms. Note that the cost of trade credit varies directly with the size of the cash discount and inversely with the length of time between the end of the discount period and the final due date.

Stretching of Trade Credit

Some firms that use trade credit engage in a practice called *stretching of trade accounts*. This practice involves delaying payments beyond the prescribed credit period. For example, a firm might purchase materials under credit terms of 3/10, net 60; however, when faced with a shortage of cash, the firm might extend payment to the eightieth day. Continued violation of trade terms can eventually lead to a loss of credit. However, for short periods, and at infrequent intervals, stretching offers the firm an emergency source of short-term credit.

Advantages of Trade Credit

As a source of short-term financing, trade credit has a number of advantages. First, trade credit is conveniently obtained as a normal part of the firm's operations.

Second, no formal agreements are generally involved in extending credit. Furthermore, the amount of credit extended expands and contracts with the needs of the firm; this is why it is classified as a spontaneous, or on-demand, source of financing.

Unsecured Sources: Bank Credit

Commercial banks provide unsecured short-term credit in two basic forms: lines of credit and transaction loans (notes payable). Maturities of both types of loans are usually 1 year or less, with rates of interest depending on the creditworthiness of the borrower and the level of interest rates in the economy as a whole.

Line of Credit

line of credit

A **line of credit** is *generally an informal agreement or understanding between the borrower and the bank as to the maximum amount of credit that the bank will provide the borrower at any one time.* Under this type of agreement there is no *legal commitment on the part of the bank to provide the stated credit.* In a **revolving credit agreement,** which is a variant of this form of financing, a *legal obligation is involved.* The line of credit agreement generally covers a period of 1 year corresponding to the borrower's *fiscal* year. Thus, if the borrower is on a July 31 fiscal year, its lines of credit are based on the same annual period.

revolving credit agreement

Credit Terms Lines of credit generally do not involve fixed rates of interest; instead they state that credit will be extended at $^1/_2$ *percent over prime* or some other spread over the bank's prime rate.[4] Furthermore, the agreement usually does not spell out the specific use that will be made of the funds beyond a general statement, such as *for working-capital purposes.*

compensating balance

Lines of credit usually require that the borrower maintain a *minimum balance in the bank throughout the loan period,* called a **compensating balance.** This required balance (which can be stated as a percent of the line of credit or the loan amount) increases the effective cost of the loan to the borrower, unless a deposit balance equal to or greater than this balance requirement is ordinarily maintained in the bank.

The effective cost of short-term bank credit can be estimated using the APR equation. Consider the following example.

Example

M&M Beverage Company has a $300,000 line of credit that requires a compensating balance equal to 10 percent of the loan amount. The rate paid on the loan is 12 percent per annum, $200,000 is borrowed for a 6-month period, and the firm does not currently have a deposit with the lending bank. The dollar cost of the loan includes the interest expense and, in addition, the opportunity cost of maintaining an idle cash balance equal to the 10 percent compensating balance. To accommodate the cost of the compensating-balance requirement, assume that the added funds will have to be borrowed and simply left idle in the firm's checking accounts. Thus, the amount actually borrowed (B) will be larger than the $200,000 needed. In fact, the needed $200,000 will constitute 90 percent of the total borrowed funds because of the 10 percent compensating-balance requirement, hence $.90B = \$200,000$, such that $B = \$222,222$. Thus, interest is paid on a

---

[4]The *prime rate of interest* is the rate that a bank charges its most creditworthy borrowers.

$222,222 loan ($222,222 × .12 × $\frac{1}{2}$ = $13,333.32), of which only $200,000 is available for use by the firm.[5] The effective annual cost of credit, therefore, is

$$APR = \frac{\$13,333.32}{\$200,000} \times \frac{1}{180/360} = .1333 = 13.33\%$$

In the M&M Beverage Company example, the loan required the payment of principal ($222,222) plus interest ($13,333.32) at the end of the 6-month loan period. Frequently, bank loans will be made on a discount basis. That is, the loan interest will be deducted from the loan amount before the funds are transferred to the borrower. Extending the M&M Beverage Company example to consider discounted interest involves reducing the loan proceeds ($200,000) in the previous example by the amount of interest for the full 6-months ($13,333.32). The effective rate of interest on the loan is now

$$APR = \frac{\$13,333.32}{\$200,000 - \$13,333.32} \times \frac{1}{180/360}$$

$$= .1429 = 14.29\%$$

The effect of discounting interest was to raise the cost of the loan from 13.33 percent to 14.29 percent. This results from the fact that the firm pays interest on the same amount of funds as before ($222,222); however, this time it gets the use of $13,333.32 less, or $200,000 − $13,333.32 = $186,666.68.[6] ∎

Transaction Loans

Still another form of unsecured short-term bank credit can be obtained in the form of **transaction loans.** Here the loan is *made for a specific purpose.* This is the type of loan that most individuals associate with bank credit and is obtained by signing a promissory note.

transaction loans

---

[5]The same answer would have been obtained by assuming a total loan of $200,000, of which only 90 percent, or $180,000, was available for use by the firm; that is,

$$APR = \frac{\$12,000}{\$180,000} \times \frac{1}{180/360} = 13.3$$

Interest is now calculated on the $200,000 loan amount ($12,000 = $200,000 × .12 × $\frac{1}{2}$).

[6]If M&M needs the use of a full $200,000, then it will have to borrow more than $222,222 to cover both the compensating-balance requirement *and* the discounted interest. In fact, the firm will have to borrow some amount B such that

$$B - .10B - (.12 \times \frac{1}{2})B = \$200,000$$

$$.84B = \$200,000$$

$$B = \frac{\$200,000}{.84} = \$238,095$$

The cost of credit remains the same at 14.29 percent, as we see below:

$$APR = \frac{\$14,285.70}{\$238.095 - \$23,810 - \$14,285.70} \times \frac{1}{180/360}$$

$$= .1429 = 14.29\%$$

Unsecured transaction loans are very similar to a line of credit regarding cost, term to maturity, and compensating-balance requirements. In both instances commercial banks often require that the borrower *clean up* its short-term loans for a 30- to 45-day period during the year. This means, very simply, that the borrower must be free of any bank debt for the stated period. The purpose of such a requirement is to ensure that the borrower is not using short-term bank credit to finance a part of its permanent needs for funds.

Unsecured Sources: Commercial Paper

commercial paper

Only the largest and most creditworthy companies are able to use **commercial paper,** which is simply a *short-term promise to pay that is sold in the market for short-term debt securities.*

Credit Terms

The maturity of the credit source is generally 6 months or less, although some issues carry 270-day maturities. The interest rate on commercial paper is generally slightly lower ($\frac{1}{2}$ to 1 percent) than the prime rate on commercial bank loans. Also, interest is usually discounted, although sometimes interest-bearing commercial paper is available.

New issues of commercial paper are either placed directly (sold by the issuing firm directly to the investing public) or dealer placed. Dealer placement involves the use of a commercial paper dealer, who sells the issue for the issuing firm. Many major finance companies, such as General Motors Acceptance Corporation, place their commercial paper directly. The volume of direct versus dealer placements is roughly 4 to 1 in favor of direct placements. Dealers are used primarily by industrial firms that either make only infrequent use of commercial paper market or, owing to their small size, would have difficulty placing the issue without the help of a dealer.

Commercial Paper as a Source of Short-Term Credit

Several advantages accrue to the user of commercial paper.

1. **Interest rate.** Commercial paper rates are generally lower than rates on bank loans and comparable sources of short-term financing.
2. **Compensating-balance requirement.** No minimum balance requirements are associated with commercial paper. However, issuing firms usually find it desirable to maintain line-of-credit agreements sufficient to back up their short-term financing needs in the event that a new issue of commercial paper cannot be sold or an outstanding issue cannot be repaid when due.
3. **Amount of credit.** Commercial paper offers the firm with very large credit needs a single source for all its short-term financing. Because of loan restrictions placed on the banks by the regulatory authorities, obtaining the necessary funds from a commercial bank might require dealing with a number of institutions.[7]
4. **Prestige.** Because it is widely recognized that only the most creditworthy borrowers have access to the commercial paper market, its use signifies a firm's credit status.

---

[7]Member banks of the Federal Reserve System are limited to 10 percent of their total capital, surplus, and undivided profits when making loans to a single borrower. Thus, when a corporate borrower's needs for financing are very large, it may have to deal with a group of participating banks to raise the needed funds.

Using commercial paper for short-term financing, however, involves a very important risk. That is, the commercial paper market is highly impersonal and denies even the most creditworthy borrower any flexibility in terms of repayment. When bank credit is used, the borrower has someone with whom he or she can work out any temporary difficulties that might be encountered in meeting a loan deadline. This flexibility simply does not exist for the user of commercial paper.

Estimation of the Cost of Commercial Paper

The cost of commercial paper can be estimated using the simple effective cost-of-credit equation (APR). The key points to remember are that commercial paper interest is usually discounted and that if a dealer is used to place the issue, a fee is charged. Even if a dealer is not used, the issuing firm will incur costs associated with preparing and placing the issue, and these costs must be included in estimating the cost of credit.

Example

The EPG Manufacturing Company uses commercial paper regularly to support its needs for short-term financing. The firm plans to sell $100 million in 270-day-maturity paper on which it expects to have to pay discounted interest at a rate of 12 percent per annum ($9 million). In addition, EPG expects to incur a cost of approximately $100,000 in dealer placement fees and other expenses of issuing the paper. The effective cost of credit to EPG can be calculated as follows:

$$APR = \frac{\$9,000,000 + \$100,000}{\$100,000,000 - \$100,000 - \$9,000,000} \times \frac{1}{270/360}$$

$$= .1335 = 13.35\%$$

where the interest cost is calculated as $\$100,000,000 \times .12 \times [270/360] = \$9,000,000$ plus the $100,000 dealer placement fee. Thus, the effective cost of credit to EPG is 13.35 percent.

Secured Sources: Accounts-Receivable Loans

Secured sources of short-term credit have certain assets of the firm pledged as collateral to secure the loan. Upon default of the loan agreement, the lender has first claim to the pledged assets in addition to its claim as a general creditor of the firm. Hence, the secured credit agreement offers an added margin of safety to the lender.

Generally, a firm's receivables are among its most liquid assets. For this reason they are considered by many lenders to be prime collateral for a secured loan. Two basic procedures can be used in arranging for financing based on receivables: pledging and factoring.

Pledging Accounts Receivable

Under the **pledging accounts receivable** arrangement, the *borrower simply pledges accounts receivable as collateral for a loan obtained from either a commercial bank or a finance company.* The amount of the loan is stated as a percent of the face value of the receivables pledged. If the firm provides the lender with a *general line* on its receivables, then all of the borrower's accounts are pledged as security for the loan. This method of pledging is simple and inexpensive. However, because the lender has no control over the quality of the receivables being pledged, it will set the maximum loan at a relatively low percent of the total face value of the accounts, generally ranging downward from a maximum of around 75 percent.

pledging accounts receivable

Still another approach to pledging involves the borrower's presenting specific invoices to the lender as collateral for a loan. This method is somewhat more expensive because the lender must assess the creditworthiness of each individual account pledged; however, given this added knowledge the lender should be willing to increase the loan as a percent of the face value of the invoices. In this case the loan might reach as high as 85 or 90 percent of the face value of the pledged receivables.

Credit Terms Accounts-receivable loans generally carry an interest rate 2 to 5 percent higher than the bank's prime lending rate. Finance companies charge an even higher rate. In addition, the lender usually charges a handling fee stated as a percent of the face value of the receivables processed, which may be as much as 1 to 2 percent of the face value.

Example

The A. B. Good Company sells electrical supplies to building contractors on terms of net 60. The firm's average monthly sales are $100,000; thus, given the firm's 2-month credit terms, its average receivables balance is $200,000. The firm pledges all its receivables to a local bank, which in turn advances up to 70 percent of the face value of the receivables at 3 percent over prime and with a 1 percent processing charge on *all* receivables pledged. A. B. Good follows a practice of borrowing the maximum amount possible, and the current prime rate is 10 percent.

The APR of using this source of financing for a full year is computed as follows:

$$APR = \frac{\$18,200 + \$12,000}{\$140,000} \times \frac{1}{360/360} = .2157 = 21.57\%$$

where the total dollar cost of the loan consists of both the annual interest expense (.13 × .70 × $200,000 = $18,200) and the annual processing fee (.01 × $100,000 × 12 months = $12,000). The amount of credit extended is .70 × $200,000 = $140,000. Note that the processing charge applies to *all* receivables pledged. Thus, the A. B. Good Company pledges $100,000 each month, or $1,200,000 during the year, on which a 1 percent fee must be paid, for a total annual charge of $12,000.

One more point: The lender, in addition to making advances or loans, may be providing certain credit services to the borrower. For example, the lender may provide billing and collection services. The value of these services should be considered in computing the cost of credit. In the preceding example, A. B. Good Company may *save* credit department expenses of $10,000 per year by pledging all its accounts and letting the lender provide those services. In this case, the cost of short-term credit is only

$$APR = \frac{\$18,200 + \$12,000 - \$10,000}{\$140,000} \times \frac{1}{360/360} = \$.1443 = 14.43\%$$

Advantages and Disadvantages of Pledging The primary advantage of pledging as a source of short-term credit is the flexibility it provides the borrower. Financing is available on a continuous basis. The new accounts created through credit sales provide the collateral for the financing of new production. Furthermore, the lender may provide credit services that eliminate or at least reduce the need for similar services within the firm. The primary disadvantage associated with this method of financing is its cost, which can be relatively high compared with other sources of short-term credit, owing to the level of the interest rate charged on loans and the processing fee on pledged accounts.

Factoring Accounts Receivable

Factoring accounts receivable involves the *outright sale of a firm's accounts to a financial institution called a factor.* A **factor** is *a firm that acquires the receivables of other firms.* The factoring institution may be a commercial finance company that engages solely in the factoring of receivables (known as an *old-line factor*) or it may be a commercial bank. The factor, in turn, bears the risk of collection and, for a fee, services the accounts. The fee is stated as a percent of the face value of all receivables factored (usually 1 to 3 percent).

factoring accounts receivable
factor

The factor firm typically does *not* make payment for factored accounts until the accounts have been collected or the credit terms have been met. Should the firm wish to receive immediate payment for its factored accounts, it can borrow from the factor, using the factored accounts as collateral. The maximum loan the firm can obtain is equal to the face value of its factored accounts less the factor's fee (1 to 3 percent) less a reserve (6 to 10 percent) less the interest on the loan. For example, if $100,000 in receivables is factored, carrying 60-day credit terms, a 2-percent factor's fee, a 6-percent reserve, and interest at 1 percent per month on advances, then the maximum loan or advance the firm can receive is computed as follows:

Face amount of receivables factored	$100,000
Less: Fee (.02 × $100,000)	(2,000)
Reserve (.06 × $100,000)	(6,000)
Interest (.01 × $92,000 × 2 months)	(1,840)
Maximum advance	$90,160

Note that interest is discounted and calculated based on a maximum amount of funds available for advance ($92,000 = $100,000 − $2,000 − $6,000). Thus, the effective cost of credit can be calculated as follows:

$$APR = \frac{\$1,840 + \$2,000}{\$90,160} \times \frac{1}{60/360}$$

$$= .2555 = 25.55\%$$

Secured Sources: Inventory Loans

Inventory loans, or *loans secured by inventories*, provide a second source of security for short-term credit. The amount of the loan that can be obtained depends on both the marketability and perishability of the inventory. Some items, such as raw materials (grains, oil, lumber, and chemicals), are excellent sources of collateral, because they can easily be liquidated. Other items, such as work-in-process inventories, provide very poor collateral because of their lack of marketability.

inventory loans

There are several methods by which inventory can be used to secure short-term financing. These include a floating or blanket lien, chattel mortgage, field warehouse receipt, and terminal warehouse receipt.

Under a **floating lien agreement,** the *borrower gives the lender a lien against all its inventories.* This provides the simplest but least secure form of inventory collateral. The borrowing firm maintains full control of the inventories and continues to sell and replace them as it sees fit. Obviously, this lack of control over the collateral greatly dilutes the value of this type of security to the lender.

floating lien agreement

Under a **chattel mortgage agreement,** the *inventory is identified* (by serial number or otherwise) *in the security agreement and the borrower retains title to the inventory but cannot sell the items without the lender's consent.*

Under a **field warehouse–financing agreement,** *inventories used as collateral are physically separated from the firm's other inventories and placed under the control of a third-party field-warehousing firm.*

The **terminal warehouse agreement** differs from the field warehouse agreement in only one respect. Here the *inventories pledged as collateral are transported to a public warehouse that is physically removed from the borrower's premises.* The lender has an added degree of safety or security because the inventory is totally removed from the borrower's control. Once again the cost of this type of arrangement is increased because the warehouse firm must be paid by the borrower; in addition, the inventory must be transported to and, eventually, from the public warehouse.

CONCEPT CHECK

1. What are some examples of unsecured and secured sources of short-term credit?
2. What is the difference between a line of credit and revolving credit agreement?
3. What are the types of credit agreements a firm can get that are secured by its accounts receivable as collateral?
4. What are some examples of loans secured by a firm's inventories?

SUMMARY

Objective 1

Managing current assets and current liabilities
Working-capital management involves managing the firm's liquidity, which in turn involves managing (1) the firm's investment in current assets and (2) its use of current liabilities. Each of these problems involves risk-return trade-offs. Investing in current assets reduces the firm's risk of illiquidity at the expense of lowering its overall rate of return on its investment in assets. Furthermore, the use of long-term sources of financing enhances the firm's liquidity while reducing its rate of return on assets.

Objective 2

Appropriate level of working capital
The hedging principle, or principle of self-liquidating debt, is a benchmark for working-capital decisions. Basically, this principle involves matching the cash flow–generating characteristics of an asset with the cash flow requirements of the source of funds used to finance its acquisition.

Objective 3

Using the cash conversion cycle to evaluate working capital management
The cash conversion cycle is a very useful measure of the overall effectiveness with which a firm is managing its working capital. It is calculated as the sum of the average number of days sales outstanding in both accounts receivable and inventories less the average number of days sales represented by the firm's accounts payable. Thus, a cash conversion cycle of 30 implies that the firm has tied up 30 times its average daily sales in accounts receivable and inventories after netting out the firm's use of trade credit or accounts payable.

Objective 4

Estimating the cost of short-term credit
Three basic factors provide the key considerations in selecting a source of short-term financing: (1) the effective cost of credit, (2) the availability of financing in the amount and for the time needed, and (3) the effect of the use of credit from a particular source on the cost and availability of other sources of credit.

Sources of short-term credit

The various sources of short-term credit can be categorized into two groups: unsecured and secured. Unsecured credit offers no specific assets as security for the loan agreement. The primary sources include trade credit, lines of credit, unsecured transaction loans from commercial banks, and commercial paper. Secured credit is generally provided to business firms by commercial banks, finance companies, and factors. The most popular sources of security involve the use of accounts receivable and inventories. Loans secured by accounts receivable include pledging agreements, in which a firm pledges its receivables as security for a loan, and factoring agreements, in which the firm sells the receivables to a factor. A primary difference in these two arrangements relates to the ability of the lender to seek payment from the borrower in the event the accounts used as collateral become uncollectible. In a pledging arrangement the lender retains the right of recourse in the event of default, whereas in factoring, a lender is generally without recourse.

Loans secured by inventories can be made using one of several types of security arrangements. Among the most widely used are the floating lien, chattel mortgage, field warehouse financing, and terminal warehouse agreement. The form of agreement used depends on the type of inventories pledged as collateral and the degree of control the lender wishes to exercise over the loan collateral.

KEY TERMS

cash conversion cycle, 492

chattel mortgage agreement, 504

commercial paper, 500

compensating balance, 498

days of sales outstanding, 492

days of sales in inventory, 492

days of payables outstanding, 492

factor, 503

factoring accounts receivable, 503

field warehouse–financing agreement, 504

floating lien agreement, 503

hedging principle, 489

inventory loans, 503

line of credit, 498

net working capital, 486

permanent investments, 490

pledging accounts receivable, 501

principle of self-liquidating debt (see hedging principle), 489

revolving credit agreement, 498

secured loans, 496

temporary investments, 490

terminal warehouse agreement, 504

trade credit, 490

transaction loans, 499

unsecured loans, 496

working capital, 486

STUDY QUESTIONS

15-1 Define and contrast the terms *working capital* and *net working capital.*

15-2 Discuss the risk-return relationship involved in the firm's asset investment decisions as that relationship pertains to working-capital management.

15-3 What advantages and disadvantages are generally associated with the use of short-term debt? Discuss.

15-4 Explain what is meant by the statement "The use of current liabilities as opposed to long-term debt subjects the firm to a greater risk of illiquidity."

15-5 Define the hedging principle. How can this principle be used in the management of working capital?

15-6 Define the following terms:
  a. Permanent asset investments

b. Temporary asset investments

c. Permanent sources of financing

d. Temporary sources of financing

e. Spontaneous sources of financing

15-7 What distinguishes short-term, intermediate-term, and long-term debt?

15-8 What considerations should be used in selecting a source of short-term credit? Discuss each.

15-9 How can the formula "interest = principal × rate × time" be used to estimate the effective cost of short-term credit?

15-10 How can we accommodate the effects of compounding in our calculation of the effective cost of short-term credit?

15-11 There are three major sources of unsecured short-term credit other than accrued wages and taxes. List and discuss the distinguishing characteristics of each.

15-12 What is meant by the following trade credit terms: 2/10, net 30? 4/20, net 60? 3/15, net 45?

15-13 Define the following:

a. Line of credit

b. Commercial paper

c. Compensating balance

d. Prime rate

15-14 List and discuss four advantages of the use of commercial paper.

15-15 What risk is involved in the firm's use of commercial paper as a source of short-term credit? Discuss.

15-16 List and discuss the distinguishing features of the principal sources of secured credit based on accounts receivable.

SELF-TEST PROBLEMS

ST-1 *(Analyzing the Cost of a Commercial Paper Offering)* The Marilyn Sales Company is a wholesale machine tool broker that has gone through a recent expansion of its activities, resulting in doubling of its sales. The company has determined that it needs an additional $200 million in short-term funds to finance peak season sales during roughly 6 months of the year. Marilyn's treasurer has recommended that the firm use a commercial paper offering to raise the needed funds. Specifically, he has determined that a $200 million offering would require 10 percent interest (paid in advance or discounted) plus a $125,000 placement fee. The paper would carry a 6-month (180-day) maturity. What is the effective cost of credit?

ST-2 *(Analyzing the Cost of Short-Term Credit)* The treasurer of the Lights-a-Lot Manufacturing Company is faced with three alternative bank loans. The firm wishes to select the one that minimizes its cost of credit on a $200,000 note that it plans to issue in the next 10 days. Relevant information for the three loan configurations is found below:

a. An 18-percent rate of interest with interest paid at year-end and no compensating-balance requirement.

b. A 16-percent rate of interest but carrying a 20-percent compensating-balance requirement. This loan also calls for interest to be paid at year-end.

c. A 14-percent rate of interest that is discounted, plus a 20-percent compensating-balance requirement.

Analyze the cost of each of these alternatives. You may assume the firm would not normally maintain any bank balance that might be used to meet the 20 percent compensating-balance requirements of alternatives (b) and (c).

15-1 *(Estimating the Cost of Bank Credit)* Paymaster Enterprises has arranged to finance its seasonal working-capital needs with a short-term bank loan. The loan will carry a rate of 12-percent per annum with interest paid in advance (discounted). In addition, Paymaster must maintain a minimum demand deposit with the bank of 10 percent of the loan balance throughout the term of the loan. If Paymaster plans to borrow $100,000 for a period of 3 months, what is the effective cost of the banking loan?

15-2 *(Estimating the Cost of Commercial Paper)* On February 3, 2000, the Burlington Western Company plans a commercial paper issue of $20 million. The firm has never used commercial paper before but has been assured by the firm placing the issue that it will have no difficulty raising the funds. The commercial paper will carry a 270-day maturity and require interest based on a rate of 11 percent per annum. In addition, the firm will have to pay fees totaling $200,000 to bring the issue to market and place it. What is the effective cost of the commercial paper to Burlington Western?

15-3 *(Cost of Trade Credit)* Calculate the effective cost of the following trade credit terms where payment is made on the net due date.

a. 2/10, net 30
b. 3/15, net 30
c. 3/15, net 45
d. 2/15, net 60

15-4 *(Annual Percentage Yield)* Compute the cost of the trade credit terms in problem 15–3 using the compounding formula, or annual percentage yield.

15-5 *(Cost of Short-Term Financing)* The R. Morin Construction Company needs to borrow $100,000 to help finance the cost of a new $150,000 hydraulic crane used in the firm's commercial construction business. The crane will pay for itself in one year, and the firm is considering the following alternatives for financing its purchase:

Alternative A—The firm's bank has agreed to lend the $100,000 at a rate of 14 percent. Interest would be discounted, and a 15-percent compensating-balance would be required. However, the compensating balance requirement would not be binding on R. Morin because the firm normally maintains a minimum demand deposit (checking account) balance of $25,000 in the bank.

Alternative B—The equipment dealer has agreed to finance the equipment with a 1-year loan. The $100,000 loan would require payment of principal and interest totaling $116,300.

a. Which alternative should R. Morin select?
b. If the bank's compensating-balance requirement were to necessitate idle demand deposits equal to 15 percent of the loan, what effect would this have on the cost of the bank loan alternative?

15-6 *(Cost of Short-term Bank Loan)* On July 1, 2000, the Southwest Forging Corporation arranged for a line of credit with the First National Bank of Dallas. The terms of the agreement called for $100,000 maximum loan with interest set at 1 percent over prime. In addition, the firm has to maintain a 20-percent compensating balance in its demand deposit account throughout the year. The prime rate is currently 12 percent.

a. If Southwest normally maintains a $20,000 to $30,000 balance in its checking account with FNB of Dallas, what is the effective cost of credit through the line-of-credit agreement where the maximum loan amount is used for a full year?
b. Recompute the effective cost of trade to Southwest if the firm will have to borrow the compensating balance and it borrows the maximum possible under the loan agreement. Again, assume the full amount of the loan is outstanding for a whole year.

15-7 *(Cost of Commercial Paper)* Tri-State Enterprises plans to issue commercial paper for the first time in the firm's 35-year history. The firm plans to issue $500,000 in 180-day maturity notes. The paper will carry a $10\frac{1}{4}$ percent rate with discounted interest and will cost Tri-State $12,000 (paid in advance) to issue.

a. What is the effective cost of credit to Tri-State?

b. What other factors should the company consider in analyzing whether to issue the commercial paper?

15-8 *(Cost of Accounts Receivable)* Johnson Enterprises, Inc., is involved in the manufacture and sale of electronic components used in small AM/FM radios. The firm needs $300,000 to finance an anticipated expansion in receivables due to increased sales. Johnson's credit terms are net 60, and its average monthly credit sales are $200,000. In general, the firm's customers pay within the credit period; thus the firm's average account receivable balance is $400,000. Chuck Idol, Johnson's comptroller, approached the firm's bank with a request for a loan for the $300,000, using the firm's accounts receivable as collateral. The bank offered to make a loan at a rate of 2 percent over prime plus a 1-percent processing charge on all receivables pledged ($200,000 per month). Furthermore, the bank agreed to lend up to 75 percent of the face value of the receivables pledged.

a. Estimate the cost of the receivables loan to Johnson where the firm borrows the $300,000. The prime rate is currently 11 percent.

b. Idol also requested a line of credit for $300,000 from the bank. The bank agreed to grant the necessary line of credit at a rate of 3 percent over prime and required a 15-percent compensating balance. Johnson currently maintains an average demand deposit of $80,000. Estimate the cost of the line of credit to Johnson.

c. Which source of credit should Johnson select? Why?

15-9 *(Cost of Factoring)* MDM, Inc., is considering factoring its receivables. The firm has credit sales of $400,000 per month and has an average receivables balance of $800,000 with 60-day credit terms. The factor has offered to extend credit equal to 90 percent of the receivables factored less interest on the loan at a rate of $1\frac{1}{2}$ percent per month. The 10 percent difference in the advance and the face value of all receivables factored consists of a 1-percent factoring fee plus a 9-percent reserve, which the factor maintains. In addition, if MDM, Inc., decides to factor its receivables, it will sell them all, so that it can reduce its credit department costs by $1,500 a month.

a. What is the cost of borrowing the maximum amount of credit available to MDM, Inc., through the factoring agreement?

b. What considerations other than cost should be accounted for by MDM, Inc., in determining whether to enter the factoring agreement?

15-10 *(Cost of Secured Short-Term Credit)* The Sean-Janeow Import Co. needs $500,000 for the 3-month period ending September 30, 2000. The firm has explored two possible sources of credit.

1. S-J has arranged with its bank for a $500,000 loan secured by accounts receivable. The bank has agreed to advance S-J 80 percent of the value of its pledged receivables at a rate of 11 percent plus a 1-percent fee based on all receivables pledged. S-J's receivables average a total of $1 million year-round.

2. An insurance company has agreed to lend the $500,000 at a rate of 9 percent per annum, using a loan secured by S-J's inventory of salad oil. A field warehouse agreement would be used, which would cost S-J $2,000 a month. Which source of credit should S-J select? Explain.

15-11 *(Cost of Short-Term Financing)* You plan to borrow $20,000 from the bank to pay for inventories for a gift shop you have just opened. The bank offers to lend you the money at 10 percent annual interest for the 6 months the funds will be needed.

a. Calculate the effective rate of interest on the loan.

b. In addition, the bank requires you to maintain a 15-percent compensating balance in the bank. Because you are just opening your business, you do not have a demand deposit account at the bank that can be used to meet the compensating balance requirement. This means that you will have to put 15 percent of the loan amount from your own personal money (which you had planned to use to help finance the business) in a checking account. What is the cost of the loan now?

c. In addition to the compensating-balance requirement in part (b), you are told that interest will be discounted. What is the effective rate of interest on the loan now?

15-12 *(Cost of Factoring)* A factor has agreed to lend the JVC Corporation working capital on the following terms. JVC's receivables average $100,000 per month and have a 90-day average collection period. (Note that JVC's credit terms call for payment in 90 days, and accounts receivable average $300,000 because of the 90-day average collection period.) The factor will charge 12 percent interest on any advance (1 percent per month paid in advance), will charge a 2-percent processing fee on all receivables factored, and will maintain a 20-percent reserve. If JVC undertakes the loan, it will reduce its own credit department expenses by $2,000 per month. What is the annual effective rate of interest to JVC on the factoring arrangement? Assume that the maximum advance is taken.

15-13 *(Cash Conversion Cycle)* Mega PC, Inc. has been striving for the last five years to improve its management of working capital. Historical data for the firm's sales, accounts receivable, inventories and accounts payable follow:

	JAN '96	JAN '97	JAN '98	JAN '99	JAN '00
Sales—Net	2,873	3,475	5,296	7,759	12,327
Receivables—Total	411	538	726	903	1,486
Accounts Payable	283	447	466	1,040	1,643
Inventories—Total	220	293	429	251	233

a. Calculate Mega's DSO and DSI for each of the 5 years' data provided above. What has Mega accomplished in its attempts to better manage its investments in accounts receivable and inventory?

b. Calculate Mega's cash conversion cycle for each of the above 5 years. Evaluate Mega's overall management of its working capital.

SELF-TEST SOLUTIONS

SS-1

The discounted interest cost of the commercial paper issue is calculated as follows:

$$\text{interest expense} = .10 \times \$200,000,000 \times 180/360 = \$10,000,000$$

The effective cost of credit can now be calculated as follows:

$$APR = \frac{\$10,000,000 + \$125,000}{\$200,000,000 - \$125,000 - \$10,000,000} \times \frac{1}{180/360}$$

$$= .1066 = 10.66\%$$

SS-2

a.
$$APR = \frac{.18 \times \$200{,}000}{\$200{,}000} \times \frac{1}{1}$$

$$= .18 = 18\%$$

b.
$$APR = \frac{.16 \times \$200{,}000}{\$200{,}000 - (.20 \times \$200{,}000)} \times \frac{1}{1}$$

$$= .20 = 20\%$$

c.
$$APR = \frac{.14 \times \$200{,}000}{\$200{,}000 - (.14 \times \$200{,}000) - (.2 \times \$200{,}000)} \times \frac{1}{1}$$

$$= .2121 = 21.21\%$$

Alternative (a) offers the lowest-cost service of financing, although it carries the highest stated rate of interest. The reason for this is that there is no compensating-balance requirement, nor is interest discounted for this alternative.

Chapter Sixteen

LIQUID ASSET MANAGEMENT

16

LEARNING OBJECTIVES

AFTER READING THIS CHAPTER, YOU SHOULD BE ABLE TO:

1. Understand why a firm holds cash.
2. Explain various cash management objectives and decisions.
3. Describe and analyze the different mechanisms for managing the firm's cash collection and disbursement procedures.
4. Be able to quantitatively evaluate the expected costs and benefits of cash management services.
5. Determine a prudent composition for the firm's marketable-securities portfolio.

6. Discuss the determinants of the firm's investment in accounts receivable and learn how decisions regarding changes in credit policy are determined.
7. Discuss the reasons for both carrying inventory and how inventory management decisions are made.

At the end of fiscal year 1998 the Walt Disney Company held 0.3 percent of its total assets in the form of cash and short-term marketable securities. During 1998 Disney generated sales revenues of $22.976 billion. Based on a 365-day year, this means Disney "produced" $62,947,945 in sales revenues each day.

If Disney could have freed up only 1 day's worth of sales and invested it in 3-month U.S. Treasury bills in 1998 yielding 4.61 percent, the firm's before-tax profits would have jumped by $2,901,900. That is a tidy sum and demonstrates why firms like to have efficient treasury management departments in place. Shareholders enjoy the added profits.

Now, if Disney's management felt it could bear a little more risk, then the freed-up cash might be invested in bank certificates of deposit (CDs) of a similar 3-month maturity. At the same time in September 1998, the CDs of major money center banks were yielding 5.41 percent to investors.

That difference of 80 basis points (i.e., 5.41–4.61) may not seem like much, but when put to work on an investment of over $62 million, it produces a considerable income. In this case, the increased before-tax profits would total $3.41 million. So by investing the excess cash in CDs rather than in Treasury bills, Disney's before-tax profits would be $500,000 greater (i.e., $3.41 million–$2.90 million).

Managing the cash and marketable-securities portfolio are important tasks for the financial executive. This chapter teaches you about sophisticated cash management systems

WHAT'S AHEAD

Chapter 15 provided an introduction and overview of the concept of working-capital management. In this chapter, we explore in more depth management of the asset components of the working-capital equation. Accordingly, we focus on the alternatives available to managers for increasing shareholder wealth with respect to the most important types of current assets: (1) cash, (2) marketable securities, (3) accounts receivable, and (4) inventory. These are listed in order of declining liquidity.

Such alternatives include (1) techniques available to management for favorably influencing cash receipt and disbursement patterns, (2) investments that allow a firm to employ excess cash balances productively, (3) critical decision formulas for determining the appropriate amount of investment in accounts receivable, and (4) methods, such as those pertaining to order quantity and order point issues, for evaluating most suitable levels of inventory.

These issues are important to the financial manager for several reasons. For example, judicious management of cash and near-cash assets allows the firm to hold the minimum amount of cash necessary to meet the firm's obligations in a timely manner. As a result, the firm is able to take advantage of the opportunity to earn a return on its liquid assets and increase its profitability.

Wise management of accounts receivable and inventory is important because these two classes of assets generally constitute a large portion of a firm's total assets. Using Disney as an example, taken together, this firm's investment in accounts receivable and inventory represented 19.62 percent of its total assets at the end of 1998. On an absolute basis, Disney held $8.1 billion in receivables and inventory at that time. This is a major challenge to the organization and its financial management abilities. Any changes in assets of such magnitude to the firm will affect its profitability. An increase in accounts receivable, for example, not only results in higher sales through extension of additional trade credit, but also increases the need for financing to support the additional investment. The costs of credit investigation and collection also are increased, as could be bad debt expense. Likewise, a larger investment in inventory, by allowing more efficient production and speedier delivery to customers, leads to increased sales. At the same time, additional financing is required to support the increased level of inventory and the concomitant handling and carrying costs.

With such significance in mind, we begin the study of current asset management by exploring the various aspects of the management of cash and marketable securities. Afterward, we turn to an analysis of the important issues related to the management of accounts receivable and inventory.

Before proceeding to our discussion of cash management, it will be helpful to distinguish among several terms. **Cash** is the *currency and coin the firm has on hand in petty cash drawers, in cash registers, or in checking accounts (i.e, demand deposit accounts) at the various commercial banks.* **Marketable securities,** also called near cash or near-cash assets, are *security investments that the firm can quickly convert into cash balances.* Generally, firms hold marketable securities with very short maturity periods—less than 1 year. Together, cash and marketable securities constitute the most liquid assets of a firm.

cash

marketable securities

and about prudent places to "park" the firm's excess cash balances so they earn a positive rate of return and are liquid at the same time. We also explore sound management techniques that relate to the other asset components of the firm's working capital—accounts receivable and inventory.

WHY A COMPANY HOLDS CASH

Objective 1

A thorough understanding of why and how a firm holds cash requires an accurate conception of how cash flows into and through the enterprise. Figure 16–1 depicts the process of cash generation and disposition in a typical manufacturing setting. The arrows designate the direction of the flow—that is, whether the cash balance increases or decreases.

Cash Flow Process

The irregular increases in the firm's cash holdings can come from several external sources. Funds can be obtained in the financial markets from the sale of securities such as bonds, preferred stock, and common stock, or the firm can enter into non-marketable-debt contracts with lenders such as commercial banks. These irregular cash inflows do not occur on a daily basis. The reason is that external financing contracts or arrangements usually involve huge sums of money stemming from a major need identified by the company's management, and these needs do not occur every day. For example, a new product might be in the launching process, or a plant expansion might be required to provide added productive capacity.

In most organizations the financial officer responsible for cash management also controls the transactions that affect the firm's investment in marketable securities. As excess cash becomes temporarily available, marketable securities are purchased. When cash is in short supply, a portion of the marketable-securities portfolio is liquidated.

Whereas the irregular cash inflows are from external sources, the other main sources of cash arise from internal operations and occur on a more regular basis. Over long periods, the largest receipts come from accounts-receivable collections and to a lesser extent from direct cash sales of finished goods. Many manufacturing

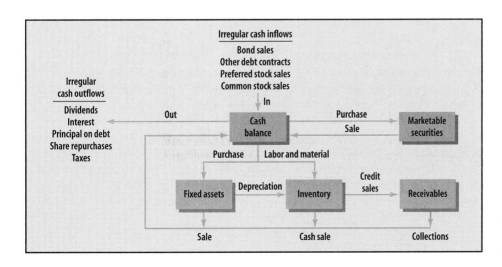

FIGURE 16–1

The Cash Generation and Disposition Process

concerns also generate cash on a regular basis through the liquidation of scrap or obsolete inventory. At various times fixed assets may also be sold, thereby generating some cash inflow.

Apart from the investment of excess cash in near-cash assets, the cash balance experiences reductions for three key reasons. First, on an irregular basis, withdrawals are made to (1) pay cash dividends on preferred and common stock shares, (2) meet interest requirements on debt contracts, (3) repay the principal borrowed from creditors, (4) buy the firm's own shares in the financial markets for use in executive compensation plans or as an alternative to paying a cash dividend, and (5) pay tax bills. Again, by an *irregular basis* we mean items *not* occurring on a daily or frequent schedule. Second, the company's capital expenditure program designates that fixed assets be acquired at various intervals. Third, inventories are purchased on a regular basis to ensure a steady flow of finished goods off the production line. Note that the arrow linking the investment in fixed assets with the inventory account is labeled *depreciation*. This indicates that a portion of the cost of fixed assets is charged against the products coming off the assembly line. This cost is subsequently recovered through the sale of the finished-goods inventory, because the product's selling price will be set by management to cover all the costs of production, including depreciation.

Motives for Holding Cash

The influences described above that affect the firm's cash balance can be classified in terms of the three motives put forth by John Maynard Keynes: (1) the transactions motive, (2) the precautionary motive, and (3) the speculative motive.[1]

The Transactions Motive

Balances held for transaction purposes allow the firm to meet cash needs that arise in the ordinary course of doing business. In Figure 16–1, transaction balances would be used to meet the irregular outflows as well as the planned acquisition of fixed assets and inventories.

The relative amount of cash needed to satisfy transaction requirements is affected by a number of factors, including the industry in which the firm operates. It is well known that utilities can forecast cash receipts quite accurately, because of stable demand for their services. Computer software firms, however, have a more difficult time predicting their cash flows. New products are brought to market at a rapid pace, thereby making it difficult to project cash flows and balances precisely.

Precautionary Motive

Precautionary balances are a buffer stock of liquid assets. This motive for holding cash relates to the maintenance of balances to be used to satisfy possible, but as yet unknown, needs.

Cash flow predictability also has a material influence on the firm's demand for cash through this precautionary motive. The airline industry provides a typical illustration. Air passenger carriers are plagued with a high degree of cash flow uncertainty. The weather, rising fuel costs, and continual strikes by operating personnel make cash forecasting difficult for any airline. The upshot of this problem is that

---

[1]John Maynard Keynes, *The General Theory of Employment, Interest, and Money* (New York: Harcourt Brace Jovanovich, 1936).

because of all the things that *might* happen, the minimum cash balances desired by the management of the air carriers tend to be large.

In actual business practice, the precautionary motive is met to a large extent by the holding of a portfolio of *liquid assets*, not just cash. Notice in Figure 16–1 the two-way flow of funds between the company's holdings of cash and marketable securities. In large corporate organizations, funds may flow either into or out of the marketable-securities portfolio on a daily basis.

Speculative Motive

Cash is held for speculative purposes in order to take advantage of potential profit-making situations. Construction firms that build private dwellings will at times accumulate cash in anticipation of a significant drop in lumber costs. If the price of building supplies does drop, the companies that built up their cash balances stand to profit by purchasing materials in large quantities. This will reduce their cost of goods sold and increase their net profit margin. Generally, the speculative motive is the least important component of a firm's preference for liquidity. The transactions and precautionary motives account for most of the reasons why a company holds cash balances.

CONCEPT CHECK

1. Describe the typical cash flow cycle for a firm.
2. What are the three motives for holding cash?

CASH MANAGEMENT OBJECTIVES AND DECISIONS

Objective 2

Risk-Return Trade-off

A companywide cash management program must be concerned with minimizing the firm's risk of insolvency. In the context of cash management, the term **insolvency** describes the *situation where the firm is unable to meet its maturing liabilities on time.* In such a case the company is *technically insolvent* in that it lacks the necessary liquidity to make prompt payment on its current debt obligations. A firm could avoid this problem by carrying large cash balances to pay the bills that come due.

insolvency

The financial manager must strike an acceptable balance between holding too much cash and too little cash. This is the focal point of the risk-return trade-off. A large cash investment minimizes the chances of insolvency, but penalizes company profitability. A small cash investment frees excess balances for investment in both marketable securities and longer-lived assets; this enhances company profitability and the value of the firm's common shares, but increases the chances of running out of cash.

BACK TO THE FOUNDATIONS

The dilemma faced by the financial manager is a clear application of **Axiom 1: The Risk-Return Trade-off—We Won't Take On Additional Risk Unless We Expect to Be Compensated with Additional Return.** To accept the risk of not having sufficient cash on hand, the firm must be compensated with a return on the cash that is invested. Moreover, the greater the risk of the investment in which the cash is placed, the greater the return the firm demands.

Objectives

The risk-return trade-off can be reduced to two prime objectives for the firm's cash management system.

1. Enough cash must be on hand to meet the disbursal needs that arise in the course of doing business.
2. Investment in idle cash balances must be reduced to a minimum.

Evaluation of these operational objectives, and a conscious attempt on the part of management to meet them, gives rise to the need for some typical cash management decisions.

Decisions

Two conditions or ideals would allow the firm to operate for extended periods with cash balances near or at a level of zero: (1) a completely accurate forecast of net cash flows over the planning horizon and (2) perfect synchronization of cash receipts and disbursements.

Cash flow forecasting is the initial step in any effective cash management program. Given that the firm will, as a matter of necessity, invest in some cash balances, certain types of decisions related to the size of those balances dominate the cash management process. These include decisions that answer the following questions:

1. What can be done to speed up cash collections and slow down or better control cash outflows?
2. What should be the composition of a marketable-securities portfolio?

CONCEPT CHECK

1. Describe the relationship between the firm's cash management program and the firm's risk of insolvency.
2. What are the fundamental decisions that the financial manager must make with respect to cash management?

COLLECTION AND DISBURSEMENT PROCEDURES

The efficiency of the firm's cash management program can be enhanced by knowledge and use of various procedures aimed at (1) accelerating cash receipts and (2) improving the methods used to disburse cash. We will see that greater opportunity for corporate profit improvements lies with the cash receipts side of the funds flow process, although it would be unwise to ignore opportunities for favorably affecting cash disbursement practices.

Managing the Cash Inflow

float

The reduction of float lies at the center of the many approaches employed to speed up cash receipts. **Float** (or total float), which is *the length of time from when a check is written until the actual recipient can draw upon or use the "good funds,"* has the following four elements:

1. **Mail float** is caused by the time lapse from the moment a customer mails a remittance check until the firm begins to process it.
2. **Processing float** is caused by the time required for the firm to process remittance checks before they can be deposited in the bank.
3. **Transit float** is caused by the time necessary for a deposited check to clear through the commercial banking system and become usable funds to the company. Credit is deferred for a maximum of two business days on checks that are cleared through the Federal Reserve System.
4. **Disbursing float** derives from the fact that funds are available in the company's bank account until its payment check has cleared through the banking system.

We use the term *float* to refer to the total of its four elements just described. Float reduction can yield considerable benefits in terms of usable funds released for company use and returns produced on such freed-up balances. As an example, for 1998 General Motors (GM) reported total revenues of $158.514 billion. The amount of usable funds that would be released if GM could achieve a 1-day reduction in float can be approximated by dividing annual revenues (sales) by the number of days in a year. In this case one day's freed-up balances would be

$$\frac{\text{annual revenues}}{\text{days in year}} = \frac{\$158,514,000,000}{365} = \$434,284,932$$

If these released funds, which represent 1 day's sales of approximately $434 million, could be invested to return 6 percent a year, then the annual value of the one-day float reduction would be

$$(\text{sales per day}) \times (\text{assumed yield}) = \$434,284,932 \times .06 = \$26,057,070$$

It is clear that effective cash management can yield impressive opportunities for profit improvement. Let us look now at specific techniques for reducing float.

Example

The positive operating profit effects that stem from the use of wise cash management techniques that result in float reduction can be dramatic when large total revenues are involved. Our previous analysis showed that the value of 1-day float reductions for GM could yield $26 million for the year when money market yields are in the vicinity of 6 percent annually.

Suppose now that we want to estimate the value of a 1-day float reduction for Wal-Mart. Wal-Mart's 1998 sales revenues were reported at $137.63 billion. Again, let's assume that prudent investment in money-market securities will earn 6 percent annually. We ask, What is the estimated value of a 1-day float reduction to Wal-Mart? Following the procedures previously outlined, you will find that 1-day's freed-up balances for Wal-Mart will be $377,079,500 or in excess of $377 million. Then we find the annual (before-tax) value of the float reduction as

$$(\text{sales per day}) \times (\text{assumed yield}) = \$377,079,500 \times .06 = \$22,624,770$$

Such prospective gains in operating profits make it worthwhile for the firm and its treasury management function to closely evaluate the cash management services offered by commercial banks—even when the bank fees can also be quite costly. We learn how to make decisions of this nature later in the chapter. ∎

Lockbox Arrangement

The lockbox system is the most widely used commercial banking service for expediting cash gathering. Banks have offered this service since 1946. Such a system speeds up the conversion of receipts into usable funds by reducing both mail and processing float. In addition, it is possible to reduce transit float if lockboxes are located near Federal Reserve Banks and their branches. For large corporations that receive checks from all parts of the country, float reductions of 2 to 4 days are not unusual.

Figure 16–2 illustrates an elementary, but typical, cash collection system for a hypothetical firm. It also shows the origin of mail float, processing float, and transit float. The numbers represent the steps in this system. First, the customer places his or her remittance check in the U.S. mail, which is then delivered to the firm's headquarters. This causes the mail float. On the check's arrival at the firm's headquarters (or local collection center), general accounting personnel must go through the bookkeeping procedures needed to prepare them for local deposit. The checks are then deposited. This causes the processing float. The checks are then forwarded for payment through the commercial bank clearing mechanism. The checks will be charged against the customer's own bank account. At this point the checks are said to be "paid" and become "good" funds available for use by the company that received them. This bank clearing procedure represents transit float and, as we said earlier, can amount to a delay of up to 2 business days.

The lockbox arrangement shown in Figure 16–3 is based on a simple procedure. The firm's customers are instructed to mail their remittance checks not to company headquarters or regional offices, but to a numbered post office box. The bank that is providing the lockbox service is authorized to open the box, collect the mail, process the checks, and deposit the checks directly into the company's account.

Typically a large bank will collect payments from the lockbox at 1- to 2-hour intervals, 365 days of the year. During peak business hours, the bank may pick up mail every 30 minutes.

Once the mail is received at the bank, the checks are examined, totaled, photocopied, and microfilmed. A deposit form is then prepared by the bank, and each batch of processed checks is forwarded to the collection department for clearance. Funds deposited in this manner are usually available for company use in 1 business day or less.

Takin' It to the Net
The Internet is revolutionizing the banking business as well as retail distribution. For an example of the type of firm offering banking services to e-commerce firms see http://www.magnetbanking.com/.

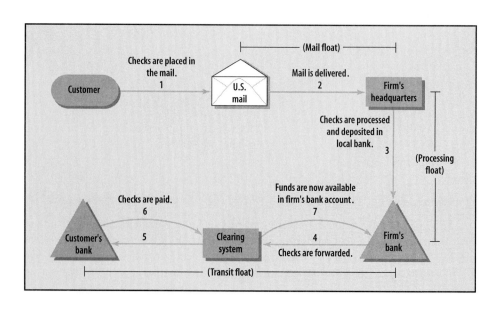

FIGURE 16–2

Ordinary Cash Collection System

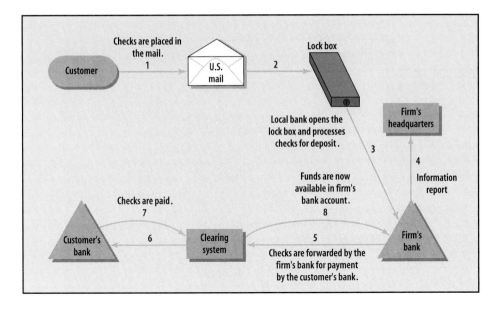

FIGURE 16-3
Simple Lockbox System

The bank can notify the firm via some type of telecommunications system the same day deposits are made about their amount. At the conclusion of each day, all check photocopies, invoices, deposit slips, and any other documents included with the remittances are mailed to the firm.

Note that the firm that receives checks from all over the country will have to use several lockboxes to take full advantage of a reduction in mail float. The firm's major bank should be able to offer as a service a detailed lockbox study, analyzing the company's receipt patterns to determine the proper number and location of lockbox receiving points.

The two systems described by Figures 16–2 and 16–3 are summarized in Table 16–1. There, the step numbers refer to those shown in Figure 16–2 (the ordinary system). Furthermore, Table 16–1 assumes that the customer and the firm's headquarters or its collection center are located in different cities. This causes the lag of 2 working days before the firm actually receives the remittance check. We notice at the bottom of Table 16–1 that the installation of the lockbox system can result in funds being credited to the firm's bank account a full *4* working days *faster* than is possible under the ordinary collection system.

Previously in this chapter we calculated the 1998 sales per day for Disney to be $63 million and assumed the firm could invest its excess cash in marketable securities to yield 6 percent annually. If Disney could speed up its cash collections by four days, as the hypothetical firm did in Table 16–1, the results would be startling. The gross annual savings to Disney (apart from operating the lockbox system) would amount to $15.11 million, as follows:

$$\text{(sales per day)} \times \text{(days of float reduction)} \times \text{(assumed yield)}$$
$$= \$62,947,945 \times 4 \times .06 = \$15,107,507$$

As you might guess, the prospects for generating revenues of this magnitude are important not only to the firms involved, but also to commercial banks that offer lockbox services.

In summary, the benefits of a lockbox arrangement are

1. **Increased working cash.** The time required for converting receivables into available funds is reduced. This frees up cash for use elsewhere in the enterprise.

TABLE 16-1

TABLE 16-1 COMPARISON OF ORDINARY CASH COLLECTION SYSTEM WITH SIMPLE LOCKBOX SYSTEM

STEPS	ORDINARY SYSTEM AND TIME		ADVANTAGE OF LOCKBOX
1	Customer writes check and places it in the mail.	1 day	
2	Mail is delivered to firm's headquarters.	2 days	Mail will not have to travel as far. Result: Save 1 day.
3	Accounting personnel process the checks and deposit them in the firm's local bank.	2 days	Bank personnel prepare checks for deposit. Result: Save 2 days.
4 and 5	Checks are forwarded for payment through the clearing mechanism.	1 day	Because the lockboxes are located near Federal Reserve Banks or branches, transit float can be reduced.
6 and 7	The firm receives notice from its bank that the checks have cleared and the funds are now "good."	1 day	Result: Save 1 day.
	Total working days	7 days	Overall result: Save 4 working days.

2. Elimination of clerical functions. The bank takes over the tasks of receiving, endorsing, totaling, and depositing checks. With less handling of receipts by employees, better audit control is achieved and the chance of documents becoming lost is reduced.

3. Early knowledge of dishonored checks. Should a customer's check be uncollectible because of lack of funds, it is returned, usually by special handling, to the firm.

These benefits are not free. Usually, the bank levies a charge for each check processed through the system. The benefits derived from the acceleration of receipts must exceed the incremental costs of the lockbox system, or the firm would be better off without it. Later in this chapter a straightforward method for assessing the desirability of a specific cash management service, such as the lockbox arrangement, is illustrated.

Preauthorized Checks

Whereas the lockbox arrangement can often reduce total float by 2 to 4 days, for some firms the use of preauthorized checks (PACs) can be an even more effective way of converting receipts into working cash. A PAC resembles the ordinary check, but it does not contain or require the signature of the person on whose account it is being drawn. A PAC is created only with the individual's legal authorization.

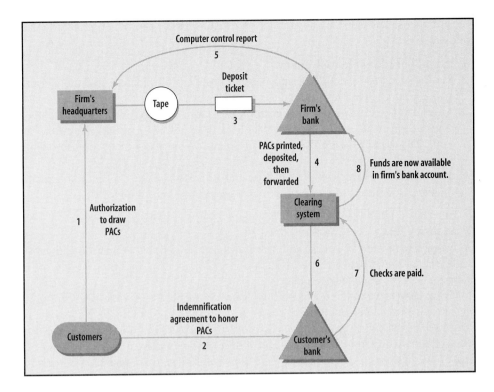

Preauthorized Check (PAC)
System

The PAC system is advantageous when the firm regularly receives a large volume of payments of a fixed amount from the same customers. This type of cash management service has proved useful to insurance companies, savings and loan associations, consumer credit firms, leasing enterprises, and charitable and religious organizations. The objective of this system is to reduce both mail and processing float. Notice, in relation to either the typical cash collection system (Figure 16–2) or the lockbox system (Figure 16–3), that the customer no longer (1) physically writes his or her own check nor (2) deposits such check in the mail.

The operation of a PAC system is illustrated in Figure 16–4. It involves the following sequence of events:

1. The firm's customers authorize it to draw checks on their respective demand deposit accounts.
2. Indemnification agreements are signed by the customers and forwarded to the banks where they maintain their demand deposit accounts. These agreements authorize the banks to honor the PACs when they are presented for payment through the commercial bank clearing system.
3. The firm prepares a magnetic tape that contains all appropriate information about the regular payments.
4. At each processing cycle (monthly, weekly, semimonthly) the corporation retains a hard-copy listing of all tape data for control purposes. Usually, the checks that are about to be printed will be deposited in the firm's demand deposit account, so a deposit ticket will also be forwarded to the bank.
5. Upon receipt of the tape the bank will produce the PACs, deposit them to the firm's account, forward them for clearing through the commercial banking system, and return a control report to the firm.

Liquid Asset Management   **521**

For firms that can take advantage of a PAC system, the benefits include the following:

1. **Highly predictable cash flows.**
2. **Reduced expenses.** Billing and postage costs are eliminated, and the clerical processing of customer payments is significantly reduced.
3. **Customer preference.** Many customers prefer not to be bothered with a regular billing. With a PAC system the check is actually written for the customer and the payment made even if he or she is on vacation or otherwise out of town.
4. **Increased working cash.** Mail float and processing float can be dramatically reduced in comparison with other payment-processing systems.

Depository Transfer Checks (DTCs)

concentration banking

Both depository transfer checks and wire transfers are used in conjunction with what is known as **concentration banking.** A concentration bank is one *where the firm maintains a major disbursing account.*

In an effort to accelerate collections, many companies have established multiple collection centers. Regional lockbox networks are one type of approach to strategically located collection points. Even without lockboxes, firms may have numerous sales outlets throughout the country and collect cash over the counter. This requires many local bank accounts to handle daily deposits. Rather than have funds sitting in these multiple bank accounts in different geographic regions of the country, most firms regularly transfer the surplus balances to one or more concentration banks. Centralizing the firm's pool of cash provides the following benefits:

1. **Lower levels of excess cash.** Desired cash-balance target levels are set for each regional bank. These target levels consider both compensating balance requirements and necessary working levels of cash. Cash in excess of the target levels can be transferred regularly to concentration banks for deployment by the firm's top-level management.
2. **Better control.** With more cash held in fewer accounts, stricter control over available cash is achieved. Quite simply, there are fewer problems. The concentration banks can prepare sophisticated reports that detail corporatewide movements of funds into and out of the central cash pool.
3. **More efficient investments in near-cash assets.** The coupling of information from the firm's cash forecast with data on available funds supplied by the concentration banks allows the firm quickly to transfer cash to the marketable-securities portfolio.

depository transfer checks
(DTCs)

Depository transfer checks (DTCs) provide a *means for moving funds from local bank accounts to concentration bank accounts.* The depository transfer check itself is an *unsigned, nonnegotiable instrument.* It is payable only to the bank of deposit (the concentration bank) for credit to the firm's specific account. The firm files an authorization form with each bank from which it might withdraw funds. This form instructs the bank to pay the DTC without any signature. The movement of cash through the use of DTC can operate with a conventional mail system or an automated system.

When the mail system is used, a company employee deposits the day's receipts in a local bank and fills out a preprinted depository transfer check for the exact amount of the deposit. The company then mails the depository transfer check to the firms' concentration bank. While this document is traveling in the mails, the checks just deposited at the local bank are being cleared. As soon as the concentration bank

522   **Chapter Sixteen**

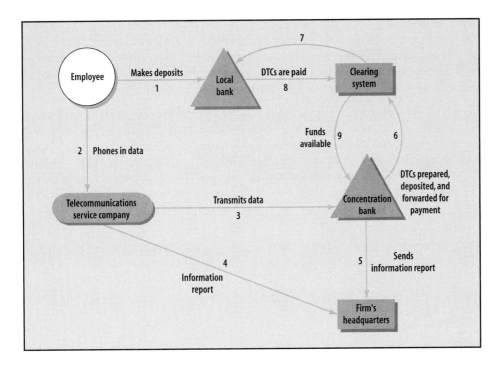

*Automated Depository
Transfer Check (DTC)
System*

receives the depository transfer check, the firm's account is credited for the designated amount. The funds credited to the concentration account are not available for the firm's use, of course, until the document has been cleared with the local depository bank for payment.

If the firm's depository banks are geographically dispersed so that the mail will take several days to reach the concentration bank, then *no* float reduction might be achieved through the system. In an attempt to reduce the mail float associated with conventional depository transfer check systems, some banks have initiated a type of special mail handling of these instruments that can cut as much as 1 full day off regular mail delivery schedules.

An innovation in sending cash into concentration bank accounts is the **automated depository transfer check (DTC) system.** In this system the *mail float involved in moving the transfer document from the local bank to the concentration bank is eliminated.* This system is depicted in Figure 16–5.

automated depository
transfer check (DTC) system

The local company employee makes the daily deposit as usual. This employee does *not*, however, manually fill out the preprinted DTC; instead, he or she telephones the deposit information to a regional data collection center. Usually, the center is operated for a fee by a firm, such as National Data Corporation. Various data collection centers accumulate information throughout the day on the firm's regional deposits. Then, at specified cutoff times the deposit information from all local offices is transmitted to the concentration bank.

At this point the concentration bank prepares the DTC and credits it to the company's account. The transfer checks are placed into the commercial bank check-clearing process and presented to the firm's local bank for payment. When paid by the local bank, the funds become available in the concentration bank account for company use. Major banks claim that funds transferred by use of the automated depository transfer check system can become available for company use in 1 business day or less.

Wire Transfers

wire transfers

The fastest way to move cash between banks is by use of **wire transfers,** which *eliminate transit float.* Funds moved in this manner, then, immediately become usable funds or "good funds" to the firm at the receiving bank. The following two major communication facilities are used to accommodate wire transfers:

1. **Bank Wire.** Bank Wire is a private wire service used and supported by approximately 250 banks in the United States for transferring funds, exchanging credit information, or effecting securities transactions.
2. **Federal Reserve Wire System.** The Fed Wire is directly accessible to commercial banks that are members of the Federal Reserve System. A commercial bank that is not on the Bank Wire or is not a member of the Federal Reserve System can use the wire transfer through its correspondent bank.

Wire transfers are often initiated on a standing-order basis. By means of a written authorization from company headquarters, a local depository bank might be instructed to transfer funds regularly to the firm's concentration bank.

As might be expected, wire transfers are a relatively expensive method of marshaling funds through a firm's money management system. Generally, the movement of small amounts does not justify the use of wire transfers.

Management of Cash Outflow

Significant techniques and systems for improving the firm's management of cash disbursements include (1) zero balance accounts, (2) payable-through drafts, and (3) remote disbursing. The first two offer significantly better control over companywide payments, and as a secondary benefit they *may* increase disbursement float. The last technique, remote disbursing, aims solely to increase disbursement float.

Zero Balance Accounts

Large corporations that operate multiple branches, divisions, or subsidiaries often maintain numerous bank accounts (in different banks) for the purpose of making timely operating disbursements. It does make good business sense for payments for purchased parts that go into, say, an automobile transmission to be made by the Transmission and Chassis Division of the auto manufacturer rather than its central office. The Transmission and Chassis Division originates such purchase orders, receives and inspects the shipment when it arrives at the plant, authorizes payment, and writes the appropriate check. To have the central office involved in these matters would be a waste of company time.

What tends to happen, however, is that with several divisions utilizing their own disbursal accounts, excess cash balances build up in outlying banks and rob the firm of earning assets. Zero balance accounts are used to alleviate this problem. The objectives of a zero balance account system for the firm are (1) to achieve better control over its cash payments, (2) to reduce excess cash balances held in regional banks for disbursing purposes, and (3) to increase disbursing float.

zero balance accounts (ZBAs)

Zero balance accounts (ZBAs) *permit centralized control (at the headquarters level) over cash outflows while maintaining divisional disbursing authority.* Under this system the firm's authorized employees, representing their various divisions, continue to write checks on their individual accounts. Note that the numerous individual disbursing accounts are now *all* located in the same concentration bank. Actually these separate accounts contain no funds at all, thus their appropriate label, "zero balance." These accounts have all the characteristics of regular demand deposit accounts including separate titles, numbers, and statements.

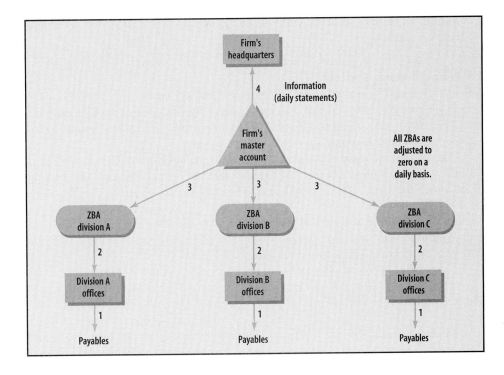

FIGURE 16-6
Zero Balance Account (ZBA) Cash Disbursement System

Figure 16–6 presents a schematic of a zero balance account (ZBA) cash disbursement system. The firm is assumed to have three operating divisions, each with its own ZBA. The system works as follows: The firm's authorized agents write their payment checks as usual against their specific accounts. These checks clear through the banking system in the usual way. On a daily basis checks are presented to the firm's concentration bank (the drawee bank) for payment. As the checks are paid by the bank, negative (debit) balances build up in the proper disbursing accounts. At the end of each day the negative balances are restored to a zero level by means of credits to the ZBAs; a corresponding reduction of funds is made against the firm's concentration (master) demand deposit account. Each morning a report is electronically forwarded to corporate headquarters reflecting the balance in the master account as well as the previous day's activity in each ZBA. Using the report, the financial officer in charge of near-cash investments is ready to initiate appropriate transactions.

Managing the cash outflow through use of a ZBA system offers the following benefits to the firm with many operating units:

1. Centralized control over disbursements is achieved, even though payment and authority continues to rest with operating units.
2. Management time spent on superficial cash management activities is reduced. Exercises such as observing the balances held in numerous bank accounts, transferring funds to those accounts short of cash, and reconciling the accounts demand less attention.
3. Excess balances held in outlying accounts can be reduced.
4. The costs of cash management can be reduced, as wire transfers to build up funds in outlying disbursement accounts are eliminated.
5. Funds may be made available for company use through an increase in disbursement float. When local bank accounts are used to pay nearby suppliers, the checks clear rapidly. The same checks, if drawn on a ZBA located in a more

distant concentration bank, will take more time to clear against the disbursing firm's account.

Payable-Through Drafts

payable-through drafts (PTDs)

Payable-through drafts (PTDs) are *legal instruments that have the physical appearance of ordinary checks but are not drawn on a bank. Instead, payable-through drafts are drawn on and payment is authorized by the issuing firm against its demand deposit account.* Figure 16–7 illustrates a payable-through draft system.

Like checks, the drafts are cleared through the banking system and are presented to the issuing firm's bank. The bank serves as a collection point and passes the drafts on to the firm. The corporate issuer usually has to return by the following business day all drafts it does not wish to cover (pay). Those documents not returned to the bank are automatically paid. The firm inspects the drafts for validity by checking signatures, amounts, and dates. Stop-payment orders can be initiated by the company on any drafts considered inappropriate.

The main purpose of using a payable-through draft system is *to provide for effective control over field payments.* Central office control over payments begun by regional units is provided as the drafts are reviewed in advance of final payment. Payable-through drafts, for example, are used extensively in the insurance industry. The claims agent does not typically have check-signing authority against a corporate disbursement account. This agent can issue a draft, however, for quick settlement of a claim.

The Federal Reserve System requires transfer of available or "good" funds upon presentation of drafts to the payable-through bank. The payable-through bank will cover drafts but will be reluctant to absorb the float that would occur until the issuing firm authorizes payment the next business day. Therefore, the drafts presented for payment will usually be charged *in total* against the corporate master demand deposit account. That is, this process allows the firm to measure its usable funds available on that day. Legal payment of the *individual drafts* will still take place after their review and approval by the firm.

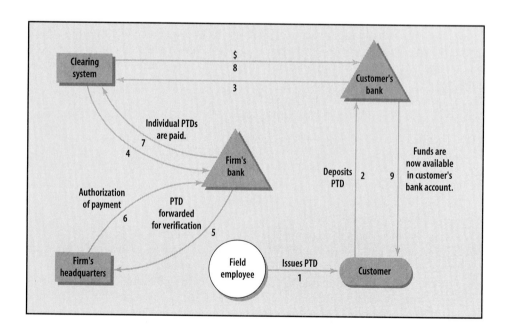

FIGURE 16–7

Payable-Through Draft (PTD) Cash Disbursement System

Remote Disbursing

A few banks will provide the corporate customer with a cash management service specifically designed to extend disbursing float. The firm's concentration bank may have a correspondent relationship with a smaller bank located in a distant city. In that remote city the Federal Reserve System is unable to maintain frequent clearings of checks drawn on local banks. For example, a firm that is located in Dallas and maintains its master account there may open an account with a bank situated in, say, Amarillo, Texas. The firm will write the bulk of its payment checks against the account in the Amarillo bank. The checks will probably take at least 1 business day longer to clear, so the firm can "play the float" to its advantage.

A firm must use this technique of remote disbursing with extreme care. If a key supplier of raw materials located in Dallas has to wait the extra day for funds drawn on the Amarillo account, the possibility of incurring ill will might outweigh the apparent gain from an increase in the disbursing float. The impact on the firm's reputation of using remote disbursing should be explicitly evaluated. The practice of remote disbursing is discouraged by the Federal Reserve System.

BACK TO THE FOUNDATIONS

These collection and disbursement procedures are an illustration of **Axiom 2: The Time Value of Money—A Dollar Received Today Is Worth More Than a Dollar Received in the Future.** The faster the firm can take possession of the money to which it is entitled, the sooner the firm can put the money to work generating a return. Similarly, the longer the firm can hold on to the liquid assets in its possession, the greater the return the firm can receive on such funds.

CONCEPT CHECK

1. Define "float" and its origins in the cash management process (i.e., mail, processing, transit, and disbursing).
2. What is a lockbox arrangement and how does its use reduce float?
3. Describe the following methods for managing cash outflow: zero balance accounts, payable-through drafts, and remote disbursing.

EVALUATION OF COSTS OF CASH MANAGEMENT SERVICES

Objective 4

A form of breakeven analysis can help the financial officer decide whether a particular collection of disbursement service will provide an economic benefit to the firm. The evaluation process involves a very basic relationship in microeconomics:

$$\text{added costs} = \text{added benefits} \qquad (16\text{--}1)$$

If equation (16–1) holds exactly, then the firm is no better or worse off for having adopted the given service. We will illustrate this procedure in terms of the desirability of installing an additional lockbox. Equation (16–1) can be restated on a per unit basis as follows:

$$P = (D)(S)(i) \tag{16–2}$$

where P = increases in per check processing cost if the new system is adopted
D = days saved in the collection process (float reduction)
S = average check size in dollars
i = the daily, before-tax opportunity cost (rate of return) of carrying cash

Assume that check processing cost P will rise by $.18 a check if the lockbox is used. The firm has determined that the average check size, S, that will be mailed to the lockbox location will be $900. If funds are freed by use of the lockbox, they will be invested in marketable securities to yield an *annual* before-tax return of 6 percent. With these data it is possible to determine the reduction in check collection time D required to justify the use of the lockbox. That level of D is found to be

$$\$.18 = (D)(\$900)\left(\frac{.06}{365}\right)$$
$$1.217 \text{ days} = D$$

TABLE 16–2 **FEATURES OF SELECTED CASH COLLECTION AND DISBURSAL TECHNIQUES: A SUMMARY**

TECHNIQUE	OBJECTIVE	HOW ACCOMPLISHED
Cash Collection Techniques		
1. Lockbox system	Reduce (1) mail float, (2) processing float, and (3) transit float.	Strategic location of lockboxes to reduce mail float and transit float. Firm's commercial bank has access to lockbox to reduce processing float.
2. Preauthorized checks	Reduce (1) mail float and (2) processing float.	The firm writes the checks (the PACs) *for* its customers to be charged against their demand deposit accounts.
3. (Ordinary) Depository transfer checks	Eliminate excess funds in regional banks.	Used in conjunction with concentration banking whereby the firm maintains several collection centers. The transfer check authorizes movement of funds from a local bank to the concentration bank.
4. Automated depository transfer checks	Eliminate the mail float associated with the ordinary transfer check.	Telecommunications company transmits deposit data to the firm's concentration bank.
5. Wire transfers	Move funds immediately between banks. This eliminates transit float in that only "good funds" are transferred.	Use of Bank Wire or the Federal Reserve Wire System.
Cash Disbursal Techniques		
1. Zero balance accounts	(1) Achieve better control over cash payments, (2) reduce excess cash balances held in regional banks, and, possibly, (3) increase disbursing float.	Establish zero balance accounts for all of the firm's disbursing units. These accounts are all in the same concentration bank. Checks are drawn against these accounts, with the balance in each account never exceeding $0. Divisional disbursing authority is thereby maintained at the local level of management.
2. Payable-through drafts	Achieve effective central-office control over field-authorized payments.	Field office issues drafts rather than checks to settle up payables.
3. Remote disbursing	Extend disbursing float.	Write checks against demand deposit accounts held in distant banks.

Thus, the lockbox is justified if the firm can speed up its collections by *more* than 1.217 days. This same style of analysis can be adapted to analyze the other tools of cash management.

Before moving on to a discussion of the firm's marketable-securities portfolio, it will be helpful to draw together the preceding material. Table 16–2 summarizes the salient features of the cash collection and disbursal techniques we have considered here.

CONCEPT CHECK

1. Describe the use of the breakeven concept with respect to the management of cash.
2. How would you estimate the financial benefits of using a lockbox system?

COMPOSITION OF MARKETABLE-SECURITIES PORTFOLIO

Objective 5

Once the design of the firm's cash receipts and payments system has been determined, the financial manager faces the task of selecting appropriate financial assets for inclusion in the firm's marketable-securities portfolio.

General Selection Criteria

Certain criteria can provide a financial manager with a useful framework for selecting a proper marketable-securities mix. These considerations include evaluation of the (1) financial risk, (2) interest rate risk, (3) liquidity, (4) taxability, and (5) yields among different financial assets. The following sections briefly delineate these criteria from the investor's viewpoint.

Financial Risk

Financial risk here refers to the uncertainty of expected returns from a security attributable to possible changes in the financial capacity of the security issuer to make future payments to the security owner. If the chance of default on the terms of the instrument is high (or low), then the financial risk is said to be high (or low).

In both financial practice and research, when estimates of risk-free returns are desired, the yields available on Treasury securities are consulted and the safety of other financial instruments is weighed against them.

Interest Rate Risk

Interest rate risk refers to the uncertainty of expected returns from a financial instrument attributable to changes in interest rates. Of particular concern to the corporate treasurer is the price volatility associated with instruments that have long, as opposed to short, terms to maturity. An illustration can help clarify this point.

Suppose the financial officer is weighing the merits of investing temporarily available corporate cash in a new offering of U.S. Treasury obligations that will mature in either (1) 3 years or (2) 20 years from the date of issue. The purchase price

TABLE 16-3	MARKET PRICE EFFECT OF RISE IN INTEREST RATES	

ITEM	THREE-YEAR INSTRUMENT	TWENTY-YEAR INSTRUMENT
Original price	$1,000.00	$1,000.00
Price after one year	964.84	821.01
Decline in price	$ 35.16	$ 178.99

of the 3-year notes or 20-year bonds is at their par value of $1,000 per security. The maturity value of either class of security is equal to par, $1,000, and the coupon rate (stated interest rate) is set at 7 percent, compounded annually.

If after 1 year from the date of purchase prevailing interest rates rise to 9 percent, the market prices of these currently outstanding Treasury securities will fail to bring their yields to maturity in line with what investors could obtain by buying a new issue of a given instrument. The market prices of *both* the 3-year and 20-year obligations will decline. The price of the 20-year instrument will decline by a greater dollar amount, however, than that of the 3-year instrument.

One year from the date of issue the price obtainable in the marketplace for the original 20-year instrument, which now has 19 years to go to maturity, can be found by computing P as follows:

$$P = \sum_{t=1}^{19} \frac{\$70}{(1 + .09)^t} + \frac{\$1,000}{(1 + .09)^{19}} = \$821.01$$

In the previous expression (1) t is the year in which the particular return, either interest or principal amount, is received; (2) $70 is the annual interest payment; and (3) $1,000 is the contractual maturity value of the bond. The rise in interest rates has forced the market price of the bond down to $821.01.

What will happen to the price of the note that has 2 years remaining to maturity? In a similar manner, we can compute its price, P:

$$P = \sum_{t=1}^{2} \frac{\$70}{(1 + .09)^t} + \frac{\$1,000}{(1 + .09)^{2}} = \$964.84$$

The market price of the shorter-term note will decline to $964.84. Table 16–3 shows that the market value of the shorter-term security was penalized much less by the given rise in the general level of interest rates.

If we extended the illustration, we would see that, in terms of market price, a 1-year security would be affected less than a 2-year security, a 91-day security less than a 182-day security, and so on. Equity securities would exhibit the largest price changes because of their infinite maturity periods. To hedge against the price volatility caused by interest rate risk, the firm's marketable-securities portfolio will tend to be composed of instruments that mature over short periods.

Liquidity

In the present context of managing the marketable-securities portfolio, *liquidity* refers to the ability to transform a security into cash. Should an unforeseen event require that a significant amount of cash be immediately available, then a sizable portion of the portfolio might have to be sold. The financial manager will want the

TABLE 16–4 | **COMPARISON OF AFTER-TAX YIELDS**

	TAX-EXEMPT DEBT ISSUE (6% COUPON)	TAXABLE DEBT ISSUE (8% COUPON)
Interest income	$ 60.00	$ 80.00
Income tax (.34)	0.00	27.20
After-tax interest income	$ 60.00	$ 52.80
After-tax yield	$ 60.00 = 6% $1,000.00	$ 52.80 = 5.28% $1,000.00

Derivation of equivalent before-tax yield on a taxable debt issue:

$$r = \frac{r^*}{1 - T} = \frac{.06}{1 - .34} = 9.091\%$$

where r = equivalent before-tax yield
r^* = after-tax yield on tax-exempt security
T = firm's marginal income tax rate

Proof: Interest income [$1,000 × .09091]	$90.91
Income tax (.34)	$30.91
After-tax interest income	$60.00

cash quickly and will not want to accept a large price concession in order to convert the securities. Thus, in the formulation of preferences for the inclusion of particular instruments in the portfolio, the manager must consider (1) the period needed to sell the security and (2) the likelihood that the security can be sold at or near its prevailing market price.

Taxability

The tax treatment of the income a firm receives from its security investments does not affect the ultimate mix of the marketable-securities portfolio as much as the criteria mentioned earlier. This is because the interest income from most instruments suitable for inclusion in the portfolio is taxable at the federal level. Still, some corporate treasurers seriously evaluate the taxability of interest income and capital gains.

The interest income from only one class of securities escapes the federal income tax. That class of securities is generally referred to as *municipal obligations*, or more simply as *municipals.* Because of the tax-exempt feature of interest income from state and local government securities, municipals sell at lower yields to maturity in the market than do securities that pay taxable interest. The after-tax yield on a municipal obligation, however, could be higher than the yield from a non–tax-exempt security. This would depend mainly on the purchasing firm's tax situation.

Consider Table 16–4. A firm is assumed to be analyzing whether to invest in a 1-year tax-free debt issue yielding 6 percent on a $1,000 outlay or a 1-year taxable issue that yields 8 percent on a $1,000 outlay. The firm pays federal taxes at the rate of 34 percent. The yields quoted in the financial press and in the prospectuses that describe debt issues are *before-tax* returns. The actual *after-tax* return enjoyed by the investor depends on his or her tax bracket. Notice that the actual after-tax yield received by the firm is only 5.28 percent on the taxable issue versus 6 percent on the

FIGURE 16–8

Designing the Marketable Securities Portfolio

Considerations →	Influence →	Focus upon →	Determine
Financial risk Interest rate risk Liquidity Taxability	Yields	Risk vs. return preferences	Marketable- securities mix

tax-exempt obligation. The lower portion of Table 16–4 shows that the fully taxed bond must yield 9.091 percent to make it comparable with the tax-exempt issue.

Yields

The final selection criterion that we mention is a significant one—the yields that are available on the different financial assets suitable for inclusion in the near-cash portfolio. By now it is probably obvious that the factors of (1) financial risk, (2) interest rate risk, (3) liquidity, and (4) taxability all influence the available yields on financial instruments. The yield criterion involves an evaluation of the risks and benefits inherent in all of these factors. If a given risk is assumed, such as lack of liquidity, a higher-yield may be expected on the nonliquid instrument.

Figure 16–8 summarizes our framework for designing the firm's marketable-securities portfolio. The four basic considerations are shown to influence the yields available on securities. The financial manager must focus on the risk-return trade-offs identified through analysis. Coming to grips with these trade-offs will enable the financial manager to determine the proper marketable-securities mix for the company. Let us look now at the marketable securities prominent in firms' near-cash portfolios.

Marketable-Security Alternatives

U.S. Treasury Bills

U.S. Treasury bills are the best-known and most popular short-term investment outlet among firms. A Treasury bill is a direct obligation of the U.S. government sold on a regular basis by the U.S. Treasury. New Treasury bills are issued in denominations of $10,000, $15,000, $50,000, $100,000, $500,000, and $1 million. In effect, therefore, one can buy bills in multiples of $5,000 above the smallest purchase price of $10,000 by combining $10,000 bills and $15,000 bills to reach the desired sum.

Bills currently are regularly offered with maturities of 91, 182, and 365 days. The 3-month and 6-month bills are auctioned weekly by the Treasury, and the 1-year bills are offered every 4 weeks. Bids (orders to purchase) are accepted by the various Federal Reserve Banks and their branches, which perform the role of agents for the Treasury. Each Monday, bids are received until 1:30 P.M.; after that time they are opened, tabulated, and forwarded to the Treasury for allocation (filling the purchase orders).

Treasury bills are sold on a discount basis; for that reason the investor does not receive an actual interest payment. The return is the difference between the purchase price and the face (par) value of the bill.

Of prime importance to the corporate treasurer is the fact that a very active secondary market exists for bills. After a bill has been acquired by the firm, should the need arise to turn it into cash, a group of securities dealers stand ready to purchase it. This highly developed secondary market for bills not only makes them extremely liquid, but also allows the firm to buy bills with maturities of a week or even less.

Because bills have the full financial backing of the U.S. government, they are, for all practical purposes, risk free. This negligible financial risk and high degree of liquidity makes the yields lower than those obtainable on other marketable securities. The income from Treasury bills is subject to federal income taxes, but *not* to state and local income taxes.

Federal Agency Securities

Federal agency securities are debt obligations of corporations and agencies that have been created to effect the various lending programs of the U.S. government. Five such government-sponsored corporations account for the majority of outstanding agency debt. The "big five" agencies are

1. The Federal National Mortgage Association (FNMA)
2. The Federal Home Loan Banks (FHLB)
3. The Federal Land Banks
4. The Federal Intermediate Credit Banks
5. The Banks for Cooperatives

It is not true that the "big five" federally sponsored agencies are owned by the U.S. government and that the securities they issue are fully guaranteed by the government. The "big five" agencies are now entirely owned by their member associations or the general public. In addition, the issuing agency, not the federal government, stands behind its promises to pay.

These agencies sell their securities in a variety of denominations. The entry barrier caused by the absolute dollar size of the smallest available Treasury bill—$10,000—is not as severe in the market for agencies. A wide range of maturities is also available. Obligations can at times be purchased with maturities as short as 30 days or as long as 15 years.

Agency debt usually sells on a coupon basis and pays interest to the owner on a semiannual schedule, although there are exceptions. Some issues have been sold on a discount basis, and some have paid interest only once a year.

The income from agency debt that the investor receives is subject to taxation at the federal level. Of the "big five" agencies, only the income from FNMA issues is taxed at the state and local level.

The yields available on agency obligations will always exceed those of Treasury securities of similar maturity. This yield differential is attributable to lesser marketability and greater default risk. The financial officer might keep in mind, however, that none of these agency issues has ever gone into default.

Bankers' Acceptances

Bankers' acceptances are one of the least-understood instruments suitable for inclusion in the firm's marketable-securities portfolio. Their part in U.S. commerce today is largely concentrated in the financing of foreign transactions. Generally, an acceptance is a draft (order to pay) drawn on a specific bank by an exporter in order to obtain payment for goods shipped to a customer, who maintains an account with that specific bank.

Because acceptances are used to finance the acquisition of goods by one party, the document is not "issued" in specialized denominations; its dollar size is determined by the cost of the goods being purchased. Usual sizes, however, range from $25,000 to $1 million. The maturities on acceptances run from 30 to 180 days, although longer periods are available from time to time. The most common period is 90 days.

Acceptances, like Treasury bills, are sold on a discount basis and are payable to the bearer of the paper. A secondary market for the acceptances of large banks does exist.

The income generated from investing in acceptances is fully taxable at the federal, state, and local levels. Because of their greater financial risk and lesser liquidity, acceptances provide investors a yield advantage over Treasury bills and agency obligations. In fact, the acceptances of major banks are a very safe investment, making the yield advantage over Treasuries worth looking at from the firm's vantage point.

Negotiable Certificates of Deposit

A *negotiable certificate of deposit (CD)* is a marketable receipt for funds that have been deposited in a bank for a fixed period. The deposited funds earn a fixed rate of interest. These are not to be confused with ordinary passbook savings accounts or nonmarketable time deposits offered by all commercial banks. CDs are offered by major money-center banks. We are talking here about "corporate" CDs—not those offered to individuals.

CDs are offered by key banks in a variety of denominations running from $25,000 to $10 million. The popular sizes are $100,000, $500,000, and $1 million. The original maturities on CDs can range from 1 to 18 months.

CDs are offered by banks on a basis different from Treasury bills; that is, they are not sold at a discount. Rather, when the certificate matures, the owner receives the full amount deposited plus the earned interest.

A secondary market for CDs does exist, the heart of which is found in New York City. Whereas CDs may be issued in registered or bearer form, the latter facilitates transactions in the secondary market and thus is the more common.

Even though the secondary market for CDs of large banks is well organized, it does not operate as smoothly as the aftermarket in Treasuries. CDs are more heterogeneous than Treasury bills, Treasury bills have similar rates, maturity periods, and denominations; more variety is found in CDs. This makes it harder to liquidate large blocks of CDs, because a more specialized investor must be found. The securities dealers who "make" the secondary market in CDs mainly trade in $1 million units. Smaller denominations can be traded, but they will bring a relatively lower price.

The income received from an investment in CDs is subject to taxation at all government levels. In recent years CD yields have been above those available on bankers' acceptances.

Commercial Paper

Commercial paper refers to short-term, unsecured promissory notes sold by large businesses to raise cash. These are sometimes described in the popular financial press as short-term corporate IOUs. Because they are unsecured, the issuing side of the market is dominated by large corporations, which typically maintain sound credit ratings. The issuing (borrowing) firm can sell the paper to a dealer who will in turn sell it to the investing public; if the firm's reputation is solid, the paper can be sold directly to the ultimate investor.

The denominations in which commercial paper can be bought vary over a wide range. At times paper can be obtained in sizes from $5,000 to $5 million, or even more.

Commercial paper can be purchased with maturities that range from 3 to 270 days. Notes with maturities exceeding 270 days are very rare, because they would have to be registered with the Securities and Exchange Commission—a task firms avoid, when possible, because it is time-consuming and costly.

These notes are *generally* sold on a discount basis in bearer form, although sometimes paper that is interest bearing and made payable to the order of the investor is available.

The next point is of considerable interest to the financial officer responsible for management of the firm's near-cash portfolio. For practical purposes, there is *no* active trading in a secondary market for commercial paper. This distinguishes commercial paper from all the previously discussed short-term investment vehicles. On occasion, a dealer or finance company (the borrower) will redeem a note before its contract maturity date, but this is not a regular procedure. Thus, when the corporation evaluates commercial paper for possible inclusion in its marketable securities portfolio, it should plan to hold it to maturity.

The return on commercial paper is fully taxable to the investor at all levels of government. Because of its lack of marketability, commercial paper in past years consistently provided a yield advantage over other near-cash assets of comparable maturity. The lifting of interest rate ceilings in 1973 by the Federal Reserve Board on certain large CDs, however, allowed commercial banks to make CD rates fully competitive in the attempt to attract funds. Over any time period, then, CD yields *may* be slightly above the rates available on commercial paper.

Repurchase Agreements

Repurchase agreements (repos) are legal contracts that involve the actual sale of securities by a *borrower* to the *lender*, with a commitment on the part of the borrower to *repurchase* the securities at the contract price plus a stated interest charge. The securities sold to the lender are U.S. government issues or other instruments of the money market such as those described above. The borrower is either a major financial institution—most often a commercial bank—or a dealer in U.S. government securities.

Why might the corporation with excess cash prefer to buy repurchase agreements rather than a given marketable security? There are two major reasons. First, the original maturities of the instruments being sold can, in effect, be adjusted to suit the particular needs of the investing corporation. Funds available for very short periods, such as 1 or 2 days, can be productively employed. The second reason is closely related to the first. The firm could, of course, buy a Treasury bill and then resell it in the market in a few days when cash is required. The drawback here would be the risk involved in liquidating the bill at a price equal to its earlier cost to the firm. The purchase of a repo removes this risk. The contract price of the securities that make up the arrangement is *fixed* for the duration of the transaction. The corporation that buys a repurchase agreement, then, is protected against market price fluctuations throughout the contract period. This makes it a sound alternative investment for funds that are freed up for only very short periods.

These agreements are usually executed in sizes of $1 million or more. The maturities may be for a specified time period or may have no fixed maturity date. In the latter case either lender or borrower may terminate the contract without advance notice.

The returns the lender receives on repurchase agreements are taxed at all government levels. Because the interest rates are set by direct negotiation between lender and borrower, no regular published series of yields is available for direct comparison with the other short-term investments. The rates available on repurchase agreements, however, are closely related to, but generally *less* than, Treasury bill rates of comparable maturities.

Money-Market Mutual Funds

The money-market mutual funds sell their shares to raise cash, and by pooling the funds of large numbers of small savers, they can build their liquid-asset portfolios. Many of these funds allow the investor to start an account with as little as $1,000. This small initial investment, coupled with the fact that some liquid-asset funds permit subsequent investments in amounts as small as $100, makes this type of outlet for excess cash suited to the small firm and even the individual. Furthermore, the management of a small

Takin' It to the Net
To get economywide data on business interest rates, and a wide range of economic time series see http://www.stls,frb.org/fred/. Frequently there are historical sales data for specific industries. For example, historical industry sales for semiconductors can be found at http://www.eb-mag.com.

enterprise may not be highly versed in the details of short-term investments. By purchasing shares in a liquid-asset fund, the investor is also buying managerial expertise.

Money-market mutual funds typically invest in a diversified portfolio of short-term, high-grade debt instruments such as those described previously. Some such funds, however, will accept more interest rate risk in their portfolios and acquire some corporate bonds and notes. Money-market mutual funds offer the investing firm a high degree of liquidity. By redeeming (selling) shares, the investor can obtain cash quickly. Procedures for liquidation vary among the funds, but shares can usually be redeemed by means of (1) special redemption checks supplied by the fund, (2) telephone instructions, (3) wire instructions, or (4) a letter. When liquidation is ordered by telephone or wire, the mutual fund can remit to the investor by the next business day.

The returns earned from owning shares in a money-market mutual fund are taxable at all government levels. The yields follow the returns the investor could receive by purchasing the marketable securities directly.

The Yield Structure of Marketable Securities

What type of return can the financial manager expect on a marketable securities portfolio? This is a reasonable question. Some insight can be obtained by looking at the past, although we must realize that future returns are not guided by past experience. It is also useful to have some understanding of how the returns on one type of instrument stack up against another. The behavior of yields on short-term debt instruments over the 1980–1999 period is shown in Table 16–5.

TABLE 16–5	ANNUAL YIELDS (PERCENT) ON SELECTED THREE-MONTH MARKETABLE SECURITIES		

YEAR	T-BILLS	ACCEPTANCES	COMMERCIAL PAPER	CDs
1980	11.51	12.72	12.66	13.07
1981	14.03	15.32	15.32	15.91
1982	10.69	11.89	11.89	12.27
1983	8.61	8.90	8.88	9.07
1984	9.52	10.14	10.10	10.37
1985	7.48	7.92	7.95	8.05
1986	5.98	6.38	6.49	6.51
1987	5.82	6.75	6.82	6.87
1988	6.68	7.56	7.66	7.73
1989	8.12	8.87	8.99	9.09
1990	7.51	7.93	8.06	8.15
1991	5.42	5.70	5.87	5.83
1992	3.45	3.62	3.75	3.68
1993	3.02	3.13	3.22	3.17
1994	4.29	4.56	4.66	4.63
1995	5.51	5.81	5.93	5.92
1996	5.01	5.31	5.42	5.39
1997	5.06	5.54	5.60	5.62
1998	4.78	5.39	5.37	5.47
1999	4.72	5.30	5.28	5.41

Source: Federal Reserve Statistical Release G.13 (415), various issues.

The discussion in this chapter on designing the firm's marketable-securities portfolio touched on the essential elements of several near-cash assets. At times it is difficult to sort out the distinguishing features among these short-term investments. To alleviate that problem, Table 16–6 draws together their principal characteristics.

TABLE 16–6	FEATURES OF SELECTED MONEY-MARKET INSTRUMENTS

INSTRUMENTS	DENOMINATIONS	MATURITIES	BASIS	LIQUIDITY	TAXABILITY
U.S. Treasury bills— direct obligations of the U.S. government	$ 10,000 15,000 50,000 100,000 500,000 1,000,000	91 days 182 days 365 days 9-month not presently issued	Discount	Excellent secondary market	Exempt from state and local income tax
Federal agency securities—obligations of corporations and agencies created to effect the federal government's lending programs	Wide variation; from $1,000 to $1 million	5 days (Farm Credit consolidated discount notes) to more than 10 years	Discount or coupon; usually on coupon	Good for issues of "big five" agencies	Generally exempt at local level; FNMA issues are *not* exempt
Bankers' acceptances— drafts accepted for future payment by commercial banks	No set size; typically range from $25,000 to $1 million	Predominantly from 30 to 180 days	Discount	Good for acceptances of large "money-market" banks	Taxed at all levels of government
Negotiable certificates of deposit—marketable receipts for funds deposited in a bank for a fixed time period	$25,000 to $10 million	1 to 18 months	Accrued interest	Fair to good	Taxed at all levels of government
Commercial paper— short-term unsecured promissory notes	$5,000 to $5 million; $1,000 and $5,000 multiples above the initial offering size are sometimes available.	3 to 270 days	Discount	Poor; no active secondary market in usual sense	Taxed at all levels of government
Repurchase agreements—legal contracts between a borrower (security seller) and lender (security buyer). The borrower will repurchase at the contract price plus an interest charge.	Typical sizes are $500,000 or more.	According to terms of contract	Not applicable	Fixed by the agreement; that is, borrower will repurchase	Taxed at all levels of government
Money-market mutual funds—holders of diversified portfolios of short-term, high-grade debt instruments	Some require an initial investment as small as $1,000.	Shares can be sold at any time	Net asset value	Good; provided by the fund itself	Taxed at all levels of government

Objective 6 | ACCOUNTS-RECEIVABLE MANAGEMENT

We now turn from the most liquid of the firm's currents assets (cash and marketable securities) to those which are less liquid—accounts receivable and inventories. All firms by their very nature are involved in selling either goods or services. Although some of these sales will be for cash, a large portion will involve credit. Whenever a sale is made on credit, it increases the firm's accounts receivable. Thus, the importance of how a firm manages its accounts receivable depends on the degree to which the firm sells on credit.

Accounts receivable typically comprise over 25 percent of a firm's assets. In effect, when we discuss management of accounts receivable, we are discussing the management of one-quarter of the firm's assets. Moreover, because cash flows from a sale cannot be invested until the account is collected, control of receivables takes on added importance; efficient collection determines both profitability and liquidity of the firm.

Size of Investment in Accounts Receivable

The size of the investment in accounts receivable is determined by several factors. First, the percentage of credit sales to total sales affects the level of accounts receivable held. Although this factor certainly plays a major role in determining a firm's investment in accounts receivable, it generally is not within the control of the financial manager. The nature of the business tends to determine the blend between credit sales and cash sales. A large grocery store tends to sell exclusively on a cash basis, whereas most construction-lumber supply firms make their sales primarily with credit.

The level of sales is also a factor in determining the size of the investment in accounts receivable. Very simply, the more sales, the greater accounts receivable. It is not a decision variable for the financial manager, however.

The final determinants of the level of investment in accounts receivable are the credit and collection policies—more specifically, the terms of sale, the quality of customer, and collection efforts. These policies *are* under the control of the financial manager. The terms of sale specify both the time period during which the customer must pay and the terms, such as penalties for late payments or discounts for early payments. The type of customer or credit policy also affects the level of investment in accounts receivable. For example, the acceptance of poorer credit risks and their subsequent delinquent payments may lead to an increase in accounts receivable. The strength and timing of the collection efforts can affect the period for which past-due accounts remain delinquent, which in turn affects the level of accounts receivable. Collection and credit policy decisions may further affect the level of investment in

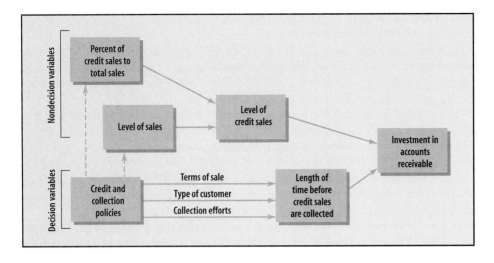

FIGURE 16–9

*Determinants of Investment
in Accounts Receivable*

accounts receivable by causing changes in the sales level and the ratio of credit sales to total sales. The factors that determine the level of investment in accounts receivable are displayed in Figure 16–9.

Terms of Sales—Decision Variable

The **terms of sale** *identify the possible discount for early payment, the discount period, and the total credit period.* They are generally stated in the form *a/b* net *c*, indicating that the customer can deduct *a* percent if the account is paid within *b* days; otherwise, the account must be paid within *c* days. Thus, for example, trade credit terms of 2/10, net 30, indicate that a 2-percent discount can be taken if the account is paid within 10 days; otherwise it must be paid within 30 days. Failure to take the discount represents a cost to the customer. For instance, if the terms are 2/10, net 30, the annualized opportunity cost of passing up this 2-percent discount in order to withhold payment for an additional 20 days is 36.73 percent. This is determined as follows:

terms of sale

$$\left(\begin{array}{c} \text{annualized opportunity cost} \\ \text{of forgoing the discount} \end{array} \right) = \frac{a}{1-a} \times \frac{360}{c-b} \qquad (16\text{–}3)$$

Substituting the values from the example, we get

$$36.73\% = \frac{.02}{1-.02} \times \frac{360}{30-10}$$

In industry the typical discount ranges anywhere from 1/2 to 10 percent, whereas the discount period is generally 10 days and the total credit period varies from 30 to 90 days. Although the terms of credit vary radically from industry to industry, they tend to remain relatively uniform within any particular industry. Moreover, the terms tend to remain relatively constant over time, and they do not appear to be used frequently as a decision variable.

Type of Customer—Decision Variable

A second decision variable involves determining the *type of customer* who is to qualify for trade credit. Several costs always are associated with extending credit to less creditworthy customers. First, as the probability of default increases, it becomes more important to identify which of the possible new customers would be a poor risk. When more time is spent investigating the less creditworthy customer, the costs of credit investigation increase.

Default costs also vary directly with the quality of the customer. As the customer's credit rating declines, the chance that the account will not be paid on time increases. In the extreme case, payment never occurs. Thus, taking on less-creditworthy customers results in increases in default costs.

Collection costs also increase as the quality of the customer declines. More delinquent accounts force the firm to spend more time and money collecting them. Overall, the decline in customer quality results in increased costs of credit investigation, collection, and default.

In determining whether to grant credit to an individual customer, we are primarily interested in the customer's short-run welfare. Thus, liquidity ratios, other obligations, and the overall profitability of the firm become the focal point in this analysis. Credit-rating services, such as Dun & Bradstreet, provide information on the financial status, operations, and payment history for most firms. Other possible sources of information would include credit bureaus, trade associations, Chambers of Commerce, competitors, bank references, public financial statements, and, of course, the firm's past relationship with the customer.

credit scoring One way in which both individuals and firms are often evaluated as credit risks is through the use of credit scoring. **Credit scoring** involves the *numerical evaluation of each applicant*. An applicant receives a score based on his or her answers to a simple set of questions. This score is then evaluated according to a predetermined standard, its level relative to the standard determining whether credit should be extended. The major advantage of credit scoring is that it is inexpensive and easy to perform. For example, once the standards are set, a computer or clerical worker without any specialized training could easily evaluate any applicant.

The techniques used for constructing credit-scoring indexes range from the simple approach of adding up default rates associated with the answers given to each question, to sophisticated evaluations using multiple discriminate analysis (MDA). MDA is a statistical technique for calculating the appropriate importance to assign each question used in evaluating the applicant.

Another model that could be used for credit scoring has been provided by Edward Altman, who used multiple discriminant analysis to identify businesses that might go bankrupt. In his landmark study Altman used financial ratios to predict which firms would go bankrupt over the period 1946–1965. Using multiple discriminant analysis, Altman came up with the following index:

$$Z = 3.3 \left(\frac{\text{EBIT}}{\text{total assets}} \right) + 1.0 \left(\frac{\text{sales}}{\text{total assets}} \right) + .06 \left(\frac{\text{market value of equity}}{\text{book value of debt}} \right)$$
$$+ 1.4 \left(\frac{\text{retained earnings}}{\text{total assets}} \right) + 1.2 \left(\frac{\text{working capital}}{\text{total assets}} \right) \quad \text{(16–4)}$$

Altman found that of the firms that went bankrupt over this time period, 94 percent had Z scores of less than 2.7 one year before bankruptcy and only 6 percent had scores above 2.7 percent. Conversely, of those firms that did not go bankrupt, only 3 percent had Z scores below 2.7 and 97 percent had scores above 2.7.

Collection Efforts—Decision Variable

The key to maintaining control over collection of accounts receivable is the fact that the probability of default increases with the age of the account. Thus, control of accounts receivable focuses on the control and elimination of past-due receivables.

One common way of evaluating the current situation is *ratio analysis*. The financial manager can determine whether accounts receivables are under control by examining the average collection period, the ratio of receivables to assets, the ratio of credit sales to receivables (called the accounts-receivable turnover ratio), and the amount of bad debts relative to sales over time. In addition, the manager can perform what is called an aging of accounts receivable to provide a breakdown in both dollars and percentages of the proportion of receivables that are past due. Comparing the current aging of receivables with past data offers even more control.

Once the delinquent accounts have been identified, the firm's accounts-receivable group makes an effort to collect them. For example, a past-due letter, called a *dunning letter*, is sent if payment is not received on time, followed by an additional dunning letter in a more serious tone if the account becomes 3 weeks past due, followed after 6 weeks by a telephone call. Finally, if the account becomes 12 weeks past due, it might be turned over to a collection agency. Again, a direct trade-off exists between collection expenses and lost goodwill on one hand and noncollection of accounts on the other, and this trade-off is always part of making the decision.

INVENTORY MANAGEMENT

Objective 7

Inventory management involves the *control of the assets that are produced to be sold in the normal course of the firm's operations.* The general categories of inventory include raw-materials inventory, work-in-process inventory, and finished-goods inventory. The importance of the inventory management to the firm depends on the extent of the inventory investment. For an average firm, approximately 4.88 percent of all assets are in the form of inventory. However, the percentage varies widely from industry to industry. Thus, the importance of inventory management and control varies from industry to industry also. For example, it is much more important in the automotive dealer and service station trade, where inventories make up 49.72 percent of total assets, than in the hotel business, where the average investment in inventory is only 1.56 percent of total assets.

inventory management

Purposes and Types of Inventory

The purpose of carrying inventories is to uncouple the operations of the firm—that is, to make each function of the business independent of each other function—so that delays or shutdowns in one area do not affect the production and sale of the final product. Because production shutdowns result in increased costs, and because delays in delivery can lose customers, the management and control of inventory are important duties of the financial manager.

Decision making in investment in inventory involves a basic trade-off between risk and return. The risk is that if the level of inventory is too low, the various functions of business do not operate independently, and delays in product and customer delivery can result. The return results because reduced inventory investment saves money. As the size of inventory increases, storage and handling costs as well as the required return on capital invested in inventory rise. Therefore, as the inventory a firm holds is increased, the risk of running out of inventory is lessened, but inventory expenses rise.

Raw-Materials Inventory
Raw-materials inventory consists of *basic materials purchased from other firms to be used in the firm's production operations.* These goods may include steel, lumber, petroleum,

raw-materials inventory

or manufactured items such as wire, ball bearings, or tires that the firm does not produce itself. Regardless of the specific form of the raw-materials inventory, all manufacturing firms by definition maintain a raw-materials inventory. Its purpose is to uncouple the production function from the purchasing function—that is, to make these two functions independent of each other—so that delays in shipment of raw materials do not cause production delays. In the event of a delay in shipment, the firm can satisfy its need for raw materials by liquidating its inventory.

Work-in-Process Inventory

Work-in-process inventory consists of *partially finished goods requiring additional work before they become finished goods.* The more complex and lengthy the production process, the larger the investment in work-in-process inventory. The purpose of work-in-process inventory is to uncouple the various operations in the production process so that machine failures and work stoppages in one operation will not affect the other operations. Assume, for example, there are 10 different production operations, each one involving the piece of work produced in the previous operation. If the machine performing the first production operation breaks down, a firm with no work-in-process inventory will have to shut down all 10 production operations. Yet if a firm has such inventory, the remaining 9 operations can continue by drawing the input for the second operation from inventory.

work-in-process inventory (margin)

Finished-Goods Inventory

Finished-goods inventory consists of *goods on which production has been completed but that are not yet sold.* The purpose of a finished-goods inventory is to uncouple the production and sales functions so that it is not necessary to produce the goods before a sale can occur—sales can be made directly out of inventory. In the auto industry, for example, people would not buy from a dealer who made them wait weeks or months when another dealer could fill the order immediately.

finished-goods inventory (margin)

Stock of Cash

Although we have already discussed cash management at some length, it is worthwhile to mention cash again in the light of inventory management. This is because the *stock of cash* carried by a firm is simply a special type of inventory. In terms of uncoupling the various operations of the firm, the purpose of holding a stock of cash is to make the payment of bills independent of the collection of accounts due. When cash is kept on hand, bills can be paid without prior collection of accounts.

Inventory Management Techniques

The importance of effective inventory management is directly related to the size of the investment in inventory. Effective management of these assets is essential to the goal of maximizing shareholder wealth. To control the investment in inventory, management must solve two problems: the order quantity problem and the order point problem.

Order Quantity Problem

The **order quantity problem** involves *determining the optimal order size for an inventory item given its expected usage, carrying costs, and ordering costs.*

The economic order quantity (EOQ) model attempts to determine the order size that will minimize total inventory costs. It assumes that

order quantity problem (margin)

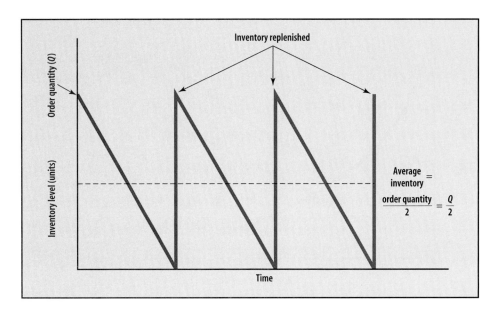

FIGURE 16–10

Inventory Level and the Replenishment Cycle

$$\text{total inventory costs} = \text{total carrying costs} + \text{total ordering costs} \qquad (16\text{–}5)$$

Assuming the inventory is allowed to fall to zero and then is immediately replenished (this assumption will be lifted when we discuss the order point problem), the average inventory becomes $Q/2$, where Q is inventory order size in units. This can be seen graphically in Figure 16–10.

If the average inventory is $Q/2$ and the carrying cost per unit is C, then carrying costs become

$$\text{total carrying costs} = \left(\text{average inventory} \right) \left(\text{carrying cost per unit} \right) \qquad (16\text{–}6)$$

$$= \left(\frac{Q}{2} \right) C$$

where Q = the inventory order size in units
C = carrying costs per unit

The carrying costs on inventory include the required rate of return on investment in inventory, in addition to warehouse or storage costs, wages for those who operate the warehouse, and costs associated with inventory shrinkage. Thus, carrying costs include both real cash flows and opportunity costs associated with having funds tied up in inventory.

The ordering costs incurred are equal to the ordering costs per order times the number of orders. If we assume total demand over the planning period is S, we order in lots sizes of Q, then S/Q represents the number of orders over the planning period. If the ordering cost per order is O, then

$$\text{total ordering costs} = \left(\text{number of orders} \right) \left(\text{ordering cost per order} \right) \qquad (16\text{–}7)$$

$$= \left(\frac{S}{Q} \right) O \qquad (16\text{–}7a)$$

Takin' It to the Net

Inventory management is critical to many firms, and a whole host of software companies offers tools for managing all aspects of a firm's inventories. For an example of the breadth of areas in which software is available check out http:// www.accurateid.com and http://www.dstm.com/.

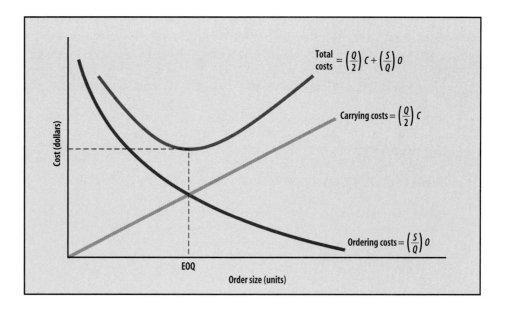

FIGURE 16–11

Total Cost and EOQ Determination

where S = total demand in units over the planning period
O = ordering cost per order

Thus, total costs in equation (16–5) become

$$\text{total costs} = \left(\frac{Q}{2}\right) C + \left(\frac{S}{Q}\right) O \qquad (16\text{–}8)$$

Figure 16–11 illustrates this equation graphically.

What we are looking for is the ordering size Q^*, which provides the minimum total costs. By manipulating equation (16–8), we find that the optimal value of Q—that is, the economic ordering quantity (EOQ)—is

$$Q^* = \sqrt{\frac{2SO}{C}} \qquad (16\text{–}9)$$

The use of EOQ model can best be illustrated through an example.

Example

Suppose a firm expects total demand (S) for its product over the planning period to be 5,000 units, whereas the ordering cost per order (O) is \$200 and the carrying cost per unit (C) is \$2. Substituting these values into equation (16–9) yields

$$Q^* = \sqrt{\frac{2 \cdot 5{,}000 \cdot 200}{2}} = \sqrt{1{,}000{,}000} = 1{,}000 \text{ units}$$

Thus, if this firm orders in 1,000-unit lot sizes, it will minimize its total inventory costs. ■

Examination of EOQ Assumptions

Despite the fact that the EOQ model tends to yield quite good results, there are weaknesses associated with several of its assumptions. When its assumptions have been dramatically violated, the EOQ model can generally be modified to accommodate the situation. The model's assumptions are as follows:

1. **Constant or uniform demand.** Although the EOQ model assumes constant demand, demand may vary from day to day. If demand is stochastic—that is, not known in advance—the model must be modified through the inclusion of a safety stock.
2. **Constant unit price.** The inclusion of variable prices resulting from quantity discounts can be handled quite easily through a modification of the original EOQ model, redefining total costs and solving for the optimum order quantity.
3. **Constant carrying costs.** Unit carrying costs may vary substantially as the size of the inventory rises, perhaps decreasing because of economies of scale or storage efficiency or increasing as storage space runs out and new warehouses have to be rented. This situation can be handled through a modification in the original model similar to the one used for variable unit price.
4. **Constant ordering costs.** Although this assumption is generally valid, its violation can be accommodated by modifying the original EOQ model in a manner similar to the one used for variable unit price.
5. **Instantaneous delivery.** If delivery is not instantaneous, which is generally the case, the original EOQ model must be modified through the inclusion of a safety stock, that is, the inventory held to accommodate any unusually large and unexpected usage during the delivery time.
6. **Independent orders.** If multiple orders result in cost savings by reducing paperwork and transportation cost, the original EOQ model must be further modified. Although this modification is somewhat complicated, special EOQ models have been developed to deal with it.

These assumptions illustrate the limitations of the basic EOQ model and the ways in which it can be modified to compensate for them. An understanding of the limitations and assumptions of the EOQ model provides the financial manager with more of a base for making inventory decisions.

Order Point Problem

The two most limiting assumptions—those of constant or uniform demand and instantaneous delivery—are dealt with through the inclusion of **safety stock,** which is the *inventory held to accommodate any unusually large and unexpected usage during delivery time.* The *decision on how much safety stock to hold* is generally referred to as the **order point problem;** that is, how low should inventory be depleted before it is reordered?

Two factors go into the determination of the appropriate order point: (1) the procurement or delivery-time stock and (2) the safety stock desired. Figure 16–12 graphs the process involved in order point determination. We observe that the order point problem can be decomposed into its two components, the **delivery-time stock**—that is, the *inventory needed between the order date and the receipt of the inventory ordered*—and the safety stock. Thus, the order point is reached when inventory falls to a level equal to the delivery-time stock plus the safety stock.

$$\begin{bmatrix} \text{inventory order point} \\ \text{[order new inventory} \\ \text{when the level of inventory} \\ \text{falls to this level]} \end{bmatrix} = \begin{pmatrix} \text{delivery-time} \\ \text{stock} \end{pmatrix} + \begin{pmatrix} \text{safety} \\ \text{stock} \end{pmatrix} \quad \text{(16–10)}$$

safety stock

order point problem

delivery-time stock

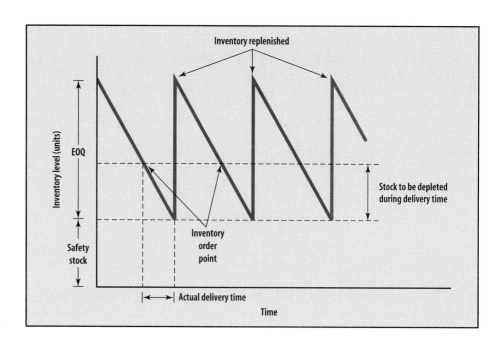

FIGURE 16–12
Order point Determination

As a result of constantly carrying safety stock, the average level of inventory increases. Whereas before the inclusion of safety stock the average level of inventory was equal to EOQ/2, now it will be

$$\text{average inventory} = \frac{\text{EOQ}}{2} + \text{safety stock} \qquad (16\text{-}11)$$

In general, several factors simultaneously determine how much delivery-time stock and safety stock should be held. First, the efficiency of the replenishment system affects how much delivery-time stock is needed. Because the delivery-time stock is the expected inventory usage between ordering and receiving inventory, efficient replenishment of inventory would reduce the need for delivery-time stock.

The uncertainty surrounding both the delivery time and the demand for the product affects the level of safety stock needed. The more certain the patterns of these inflows and outflows from the inventory, the less safety stock required. In effect, if these inflows and outflows are highly predictable, then there is little chance of any stock-out occurring. However, if they are unpredictable, it becomes necessary to carry additional safety stock to prevent unexpected stock-outs.

The safety margin desired also affects the level of safety stock held. If it is a costly experience to run out of inventory, the safety stock held will be larger than it would be otherwise. If running out of inventory and the subsequent delay in supplying customers result in strong customer dissatisfaction and the possibility of lost future sales, then additional safety stock is necessary. A final determinant is the cost of carrying additional inventory, in terms of both the handling and storage costs and the opportunity cost associated with the investment in additional inventory. Very simply, the greater the costs, the smaller the safety stock.

Over the past decade or so, a different technique aimed at reducing the firm's investment in inventory has been adopted by numerous companies. It is known as the **just-in-time inventory control system.** The aim is to operate with the *lowest average level of inventory possible*. Within the EOQ model the basics are to reduce (1) ordering costs and (2) safety stocks. This is achieved by attempting to receive an

just-in-time inventory control
system

almost continuous flow of deliveries of component parts. The result is to actually have about two to four hours' worth of inventory on hand. In effect, trucks, railroads, and airplanes become the firm's warehouses. This system has spawned a new emphasis on the dual relationship between the firm and its suppliers.

Inflation and EOQ

Inflation affects the EOQ model in two major ways. First, although the EOQ model can be modified to assume constant price increases, often major price increases occur only once or twice a year and are announced ahead of time. If this is the case, the EOQ model may lose its applicability and may be replaced with **anticipatory buying**—that is, *buying in anticipation of a price increase to secure the goods at a lower cost.* Of course, as with most decisions, there are trade-offs. The costs are the added carrying costs associated with the inventory. The benefits, of course, come from buying at a lower price. The second way inflation affects the EOQ model is through increased carrying costs. As inflation pushes interest rates up, the cost of carrying inventory increases. In our EOQ model this means that C increases, which results in a decline in Q^*, the optimal economic order quantity.

anticipatory buying

$$\downarrow Q^* = \sqrt{\frac{2SO}{C\uparrow}} \qquad (16\text{--}12)$$

CONCEPT CHECK

1. Describe the types of inventory that firms have.
2. What is the fundamental objective of the economic order quantity (EOQ) formula?
3. What assumptions underlie the EOQ formula?

SUMMARY

As you recall, several of the axioms that form the foundations of financial management relate to the importance of cash and cash flows. In this chapter, we have developed many of the tools that a financial manager needs to manage the firm's cash and other current assets with the overall objective of ensuring that the firm has an appropriate level of liquidity or net working capital to carry out the goal of maximizing shareholder wealth.

Why a company holds cash

Objective 1

The firm experiences both regular and irregular cash flows. Once cash is obtained, the firm has three motives for holding cash rather than investing it: to satisfy transactions, precautionary, and speculative liquidity needs. To a certain extent, such needs can be satisfied by holding readily marketable securities rather than cash. A significant challenge of cash management, then, is dealing with the trade-off between the firm's need to have cash on hand to pay liabilities that arise in the course of doing business and the objective of maximizing wealth by minimizing idle cash balances that earn no return.

Cash management objectives and decisions

Objective 2

Collection and disbursement procedures

Objective 3

Various procedures exist to improve the efficiency of a firm's cash management. Such procedures focus not only (although primarily) on accelerating the firm's cash receipts, but also on improving the methods for disbursing cash. Generally, at the heart of attempts to accelerate cash receipts is a significant effort to reduce the mail, processing, and transit elements of the float. Often used in conjunction with concentration banking and a lockbox arrangement are depository transfer checks and wire transfers.

On the cash disbursements side, firms try to prolong time cash stays in their own accounts by increasing the disbursement float through the use of zero balance accounts; payable-through drafts; and, especially, remote disbursing. The first two methods also offer much better central-office control over disbursements. Before any collection or disbursement procedure is introduced, however, a careful analysis should be performed to ensure that expected benefits outweigh the expected costs of such procedures.

Objective 4   **Evaluation of costs of cash management services**
Objective 5   **Composition of marketable securities portfolio**

Because idle cash earns no return, a financial manager looks for opportunities to invest such cash until it is required in the operations of the company. A variety of different readily marketable securities, described in the chapter, are available in the market today. The yields on such securities vary depending on four factors: the (1) financial risk, (2) interest rate risk, (3) liquidity, and (4) taxability of the security. By simultaneously taking into account these factors and the desired rate of return, the financial manager is able to determine the most suitable mix of cash and marketable securities for the firm.

Objective 6   **Accounts receivable management**

When we consider that accounts receivable constitute approximately 25 percent of total assets for the typical firm, the importance of accounts-receivable management becomes even more apparent. The size of a firm's investment in accounts receivable depends on three factors: the percentage of credit sales to total sales, the level of sales, and the credit and collection policies of the firm. The financial manager, however, generally only has control over the terms of sale, the quality of the customer, and the collection efforts.

Objective 7   **Inventory management**

Although the level of investment in inventories by the typical firm is less than the investment in accounts receivable, inventory management and control remains an important function of the financial manager because inventories play a significant role in the operations of the firm. The purpose of holding inventory is to make each function of the business independent of the other functions. The primary issues related to inventory management are (1) How much inventory should be ordered? and (2) When should the order be placed? The EOQ model is used to answer the first of these questions. The order point model, which depends on the desired levels of delivery-time stock and safety stock, is applied to answer the second question. The relatively new just-in-time approach to inventory control is growing in popularity as an attempt to obtain additional cost savings by reducing the level of inventory a firm needs to have on hand. Instead of depending solely on its own inventories, the firm relies on its vendors to furnish supplies "just in time" to satisfy the firm's production requirements.

KEY TERMS

---

anticipatory buying, 547

automated depository transfer check (DTC) system, 523

cash, 512

concentration banking, 522

credit scoring, 540

delivery-time stock, 545

depository transfer checks (DTCs), 522

finished-goods inventory, 542

float, 516

insolvency, 515

inventory management, 541

just-in-time inventory control system, 546

marketable securities, 512

order point problem, 545

order quantity problem, 542

payable-through drafts (PTDs), 526

raw-materials inventory, 541

safety stock, 545

terms of sale, 539

wire transfers, 524

work-in-process inventory, 542

zero balance accounts (ZBAs), 524

STUDY QUESTIONS

16-1 What is meant by the cash flow process?

16-2 Identify the principal motives for holding cash and near-cash assets. Explain the purpose of each motive.

16-3 What is concentration banking and how may it be of value to the firm?

16-4 What are the two major objectives of the firm's cash management system?

16-5 What three decisions dominate the cash management process?

16-6 Within the context of cash management, what are the key elements of (total) float? Briefly define each element.

16-7 Distinguish between financial risk and interest rate risk as these terms are commonly used in discussions of cash management.

16-8 Your firm invests in only three different classes of marketable securities: commercial paper, Treasury bills, and federal agency securities. Recently, yields on these money-market instruments of 3 months' maturity were quoted at 6.10, 6.25, and 5.90 percent. Match the available yields with the types of instruments your firm purchases.

16-9 What key factors might induce a firm to invest in repurchase agreements rather than a specific security of the money market?

16-10 What factors determine the size of the investment a firm makes in accounts receivable? Which of these factors are under the control of the financial manager?

16-11 If a credit manager experienced no bad debt losses over the past year, would this be an indication of proper credit management? Why or why not?

16-12 What are the risk-return trade-offs associated with adopting a more liberal trade credit policy?

16-13 What is the purpose of holding inventory? Name several types of inventory and describe their purpose.

16-14 Can cash be considered a special type of inventory? If so, what functions does it attempt to uncouple?

16-15 What are the major assumptions made by the EOQ model?

16-16 How might inflation affect the EOQ model?

SELF-TEST PROBLEMS

ST-1 *(Buying and Selling Marketable Securities)* Mountaineer Outfitters has $2 million in excess cash that it might invest in marketable securities. To buy and sell the securities, however, the firm must pay a transaction fee of $45,000.

    a. Would you recommend purchasing the securities if they yield 12 percent annually and are held for

      1. One month?

      2. Two months?

      3. Three months?

      4. Six months?

      5. One year?

    b. What minimum required yield would the securities have to return for the firm to hold them for 3 months? (What is the break-even yield for a 3-month holding period?)

ST-2 *(EOQ Calculations)* Consider the following inventory information and relationships for the F. Beamer Corporation:

1. Orders can be placed only in multiples of 100 units.
2. Annual unit usage is 300,000. (Assume a 50-week year in your calculations.)
3. The carrying cost is 30 percent of the purchase price of the goods.
4. The purchase price is $10 per unit.
5. The ordering cost is $50 per order.
6. The desired safety stock is 1,000 units. (This does not include delivery-time stock.)
7. Delivery time is 2 weeks.

Give this information

a. What is the optimal EOQ level?
b. How many orders will be placed annually?
c. At what inventory level should a reorder be made?

STUDY PROBLEMS

16-1 *(Concentration Banking)* Byron Sporting Goods operates in Miami, Florida. The firm produces and distributes a full line of athletic equipment on a nationwide basis. The firm currently uses a centralized billing system. Byron Sporting Goods has annual credit sales of $438 million. Austin National Bank has presented an offer to operate a concentration-banking system for the company. Byron already has an established line of credit with Austin. Austin says it will operate the system on a flat-fee basis of $200,000 per year. The analysis done by the bank's cash-management services division suggests that 3 days in mail float and 1 day in processing float can be eliminated.

Because Byron borrows almost continuously from Austin National, the value of the float reduction would be applied against the line of credit. The borrowing rate on the line of credit is set at an annual rate of 8 percent. Furthermore, because of the reduction in clerical help, the new system will save the firm $66,000 in processing costs. Byron uses a 365-day year in analyses of this sort. Should Byron accept the bank's offer to install the new system?

16-2 *(Concentration Banking)* Treemont Shops operates in Naples, Florida. The firm distributes specialty gardening supplies nationwide. The firm currently uses a centralized billing system. Treemont has annual credit sales of $362 million. Lasdon National Bank has presented an offer to operate a concentration banking system for the company. Treemont already has an established line of credit with Lasdon. The bank says it will operate the system on a flat-fee basis of $175,000 per year. The analysis done by the bank's cash-management services division suggests that 3 days in mail float and 1 day in processing float can be eliminated.

Because Treemont borrows almost continuously, the value of the float reduction would be applied against the line of credit. The borrowing rate on the line of credit is set at an annual rate of 7 percent. Furthermore, because of the reduction in clerical help, the new system will save the firm $57,500 in processing costs. Treemont uses a 365-day year in analyses of this sort. Should Treemont's management accept the bank's offer to install the new system?

16-3 *(Buying and Selling Marketable Securities)* Miami Dice & Card Company has generated $800,000 in excess cash that it could invest in marketable securities. In order to buy and sell the securities, the firm will pay total transaction fees of $20,000.

a. Would you recommend purchasing the securities if they yield 10.5 percent annually and are held for

1 One month?
2. Two months?
3. Three months?
4. Six months?
5. One year?

b. What minimum required yield would the securities have to return for the firm to hold them for 2 months? (What is the break-even yield for a two-month holding period?)

16-4 *(Costs of Services)* Mustang Ski-Wear, Inc., is investigating the possibility of adopting a lockbox system as a cash receipts acceleration device. In a typical year this firm receives remittances totaling $12 million by check. The firm will record and process 6,000 checks over this same period. The Colorado Springs Second National Bank has informed the management of Mustang that it will expedite checks and associated documents through the lockbox system for a unit cost of $.20 per check. Mustang's financial manager has projected that cash freed up by adoption of the system can be invested in a portfolio of near-cash assets that will yield an annual before-tax return of 7 percent. Mustang financial analysts use a 365-day year in their procedures.

  a. What reduction in check collection time is necessary for Mustang to be neither better nor worse off for having adopted the proposed system?

  b. How would your solution to part a be affected if Mustang could invest the freed-up balances at an expected annual return of only 4.5 percent?

  c. What is the logical explanation for the difference in your answers to part a and part b?

16-5 *(Lockbox System)* Penn Steelworks is a distributor of cold-rolled steel products to the automobile industry. All its sales are on a credit basis, net 30 days. Sales are evenly distributed over its 10 sales regions throughout the United States. Delinquent accounts are no problem. The company has recently undertaken an analysis aimed at improving its cash management procedures. Penn determined that it takes an average of 3.2 days for customers' payments to reach the head office in Pittsburgh from the time they are mailed. It takes another full day in processing time prior to depositing the checks with a local bank. Annual sales average $4.8 million for each regional office. Reasonable investment opportunities can be found yielding 7 percent per year. To alleviate the float problem confronting the firm, the use of a lockbox system in each of the 10 regions is being considered. This would reduce mail float by 1.2 days. One day in processing float would also be eliminated, plus a full day in transit float. The lockbox arrangement would cost each region $250 per month.

  a. What is the opportunity cost to Penn Steelworks of the funds tied up in mailing and processing? Use a 365-day year.

  b. What would the net cost or savings be from use of the proposed cash acceleration technique? Should Penn adopt the system?

16-6 *(Cash Receipts Acceleration System)* Peggy Pierce Designs, Inc., is a vertically integrated, national manufacturer and retailer of women's clothing. Currently, the firm has no coordinated cash management system. A proposal, however, from the First Pennsylvania Bank aimed at speeding up cash collections is being examined by several of Pierce's corporate executives.

The firm currently uses a centralized billing procedure, which requires that all checks be mailed to the Philadelphia head office for processing and eventual deposit. Under this arrangement all the customers' remittance checks take an average of 5 business days to reach the head office. Once in Philadelphia, another 2 days are required to process the checks for ultimate deposit at the First Pennsylvania Bank.

The firm's daily remittances average $1 million. The average check size is $2,000. Pierce Designs currently earns 6 percent annually on its marketable-securities portfolio.

The cash acceleration plan proposed by officers of First Pennsylvania involves both a lockbox system and concentration banking. First Pennsylvania would be the firm's only concentration bank. Lockboxes would be established in (1) San Francisco, (2) Dallas, (3) Chicago, and (4) Philadelphia. This would reduce funds tied up by mail float to 3 days, and processing float will be eliminated. Funds would then be transferred twice each business day by means of automated depository transfer checks from local banks in San Francisco, Dallas, and Chicago to the First Pennsylvania Bank. Each DTC costs $15. These transfers will occur all 270 business days of the year. Each check processed through the lockbox system will cost $.18.

a. What amount of cash balances will be freed-up if Peggy Pierce Designs, Inc., adopts the system suggested by First Pennsylvania?

b. What is the opportunity cost of maintaining the current banking setup?

c. What is the projected annual cost of operating the proposed system?

d. Should Pierce adopt the new system? Compute the net annual gain or loss associated with adopting the system.

16-7 *(Marketable-Securities Portfolio)* The Alex Daniel Shoe Manufacturing Company currently pays its employees on a weekly basis. The weekly wage bill is $500,000. This means that on average the firm has accrued wages payable of ($500,000 + $0)/2 = $250,000.

Alex Daniel, Jr., works as the firm's senior financial analyst and reports directly to his father, who owns all of the firm's common stock. Alex Daniel, Jr., wants to move to a monthly wage payment system. Employees would be paid at the end of every fourth week. The younger Daniel is fully aware that the labor union representing the company's workers will not permit the monthly payments system to take effect unless the workers are given some type of fringe benefit compensation. A plan has been worked out whereby the firm will make a contribution to the cost of life insurance coverage for each employee. This will cost the firm $35,000 annually. Alex Daniel, Jr., expects the firm to earn 7 percent annually on its marketable-securities portfolio.

a. Based on the projected information, should Daniel Shoe Manufacturing move to the monthly wage-payment system?

b. What annual rate of return on the marketable-securities portfolio would enable the firm to just break even on this proposal?

16-8 *(Valuing Float Reduction)* The Cowboy Bottling Company will generate $12 million in credit sales next year. Collection of these credit sales will occur evenly over this period. The firm's employees work 270 days a year. Currently, the firm's processing system ties up four days' worth of remittance checks. A recent report from a financial consultant indicated procedures that will enable Cowboy Bottling to reduce processing float by two full days. If Cowboy invests the released funds to earn 6 percent, what will be the annual savings?

16-9 *(Accounts Payable Policy and Cash Management)* Bradford Construction Supply Company is suffering from a prolonged decline in new construction in its sales area. In an attempt to improve its cash position, the firm is considering changes in its accounts-payable policy. After careful study it has determined that the only alternative available is to slow disbursements. Purchases for the coming year are expected to be $37.5 million. Sales will be $65 million, which represents about a 20 percent drop from the current year. Currently, Bradford discounts approximately 25 percent of its payments at 3 percent, 10 days, net 30, and the balance of accounts is paid in 30 days. If Bradford adopts a policy of payment in 45 days or 60 days, how much can the firm gain if the annual opportunity cost of investment is 12 percent? What will be the result if this action causes Bradford Construction suppliers to increase their prices to the company by $\frac{1}{2}$ percent to compensate for the 60-day extended term of payment? In your calculations use a 365-day year and ignore any compounding effects related to expected returns.

16-10 *(Interest Rate Risk)* Two years ago your corporate treasurer purchased for the firm a 20-year bond at its par value of $1,000. The coupon rate on this security is 8 percent. Interest payments are made to bondholders once a year. Currently, bonds of this particular risk class are yielding investors 9 percent. A cash shortage has forced you to instruct your treasurer to liquidate his bond.

a. At what price will your bond be sold? Assume annual compounding.

b. What will be the amount of your gain or loss over the original purchase price?

c. What would be the amount of your gain or loss had the treasurer originally purchased a bond with a 4-year rather than a 20-year maturity? (Assume all characteristics of the bonds are identical except their maturity periods.)

d. What do we call this type of risk assumed by your corporate treasurer?

16-11 *(Comparison of After-Tax Yields)* The corporate treasurer of Aggieland Fireworks is considering the purchase of a BBB-rated bond that carries a 9 percent coupon. The BBB-rated security is taxable, and the firm is in the 46 percent marginal tax bracket. The face value of this bond is $1,000. A financial analyst who reports to the corporate treasurer has alerted him to the fact that a municipal obligation is coming to the market with a $5\frac{1}{2}$ percent coupon. The par value of this security is also $1,000.

  a. Which one of the two securities do you recommend the firm purchase? Why?

  b. What must the fully taxed bond yield before tax to make it comparable with the municipal offering?

16-12 *(Trade Credit Discounts)* Determine the effective annualized cost of forgoing the trade credit discount on the following terms:

  a. 1/10, net 20

  b. 2/10, net 30

  c. 3/10, net 30

  d. 3/10, net 60

  e. 3/10, net 90

  f. 5/10, net 60

16-13 *(Altman Model)* The following ratios were supplied by six loan applicants. Given this information and the credit-scoring model developed by Altman (equation [16-4]), which loans have a high probability of defaulting next year?

	EBIT ÷ TOTAL ASSETS	SALES ÷ TOTAL ASSETS	MARKET VALUE OF EQUITY ÷ BOOK VALUE OF DEBT	RETAINED EARNINGS ÷ TOTAL ASSETS	WORKING CAPITAL ÷ TOTAL ASSETS
Applicant 1	.2	.2	1.2	.3	.5
Applicant 2	.2	.8	1.0	.3	.8
Applicant 3	.2	.7	.6	.3	.4
Applicant 4	.1	.4	1.2	.4	.4
Applicant 5	.3	.7	.5	.4	.7
Applicant 6	.2	.5	.5	.4	.4

16-14 *(Ratio Analysis)* Assuming a 360-day year, calculate what the average investment in inventory would be for a firm, given the following information in each case.

  a. The firm has sales of $600,000, a gross profit margin of 10 percent, and an inventory turnover ratio of 6.

  b. The firm has a cost-of-goods-sold figure of $480,000 and an average age of inventory of 40 days.

  c. The firm has a cost-of-goods-sold figure of $1.15 million and an inventory turnover rate of 5.

  d. The firm has a sales figure of $25 million, a gross profit margin of 14 percent, and an average age of inventory of 45 days.

16-15 *(EOQ Calculations)* A downtown bookstore is trying to determine the optimal order quantity for a popular novel just printed in paperback. The store feels that the book will sell at four times its hardback figures. It would therefore sell approximately 3,000 copies in the next year at a price of $1.50. The store buys the book at a wholesale figure of $1. Costs for carrying the book are estimated at $.10 a copy per year, and it costs $10 to order more books.

  a. Determine the EOQ.

  b. What would be the total costs for ordering the books 1, 4, 5, 10, and 15 times a year?

  c. What questionable assumptions are being made by the EOQ model?

16-16 (*Comprehensive EOQ Calculations*) Knutson Products, Inc., is involved in the production of airplane parts and has the following inventory, carrying, and storage costs:

1. Orders must be placed in round lots of 100 units.
2. Annual unit usage is 250,000. (Assume a 50-week year in your calculations.)
3. The carrying cost is 10 percent of the purchase price.
4. The purchase price is $10 per unit.
5. The ordering cost is $100 per order.
6. The desired safety stock is 5,000 units. (This does not include delivery-time stock.)
7. The delivery time is 1 week.

Given the above information:

a. Determine the optimal EOQ level.
b. How many orders will be placed annually?
c. What is the inventory order point? (That is, at what level of inventory should a new order be placed?)
d. What is the average inventory level?
e. What would happen to the EOQ if annual unit sales doubled (all other unit costs and safety stocks remaining constant)? What is the elasticity of EOQ with respect to sales? (That is, what is the percent change in EOQ divided by the percent change in sales?)
f. If carrying costs double, what would happen to the EOQ level? (Assume the original sales level of 250,000 units.) What is the elasticity of EOQ with respect to carrying costs?
g. If the ordering costs double, what would happen to the level of EOQ? (Again assume original levels of sales and carrying costs.) What is the elasticity of EOQ with respect to ordering costs?
h. If the selling price doubles, what would happen to EOQ? What is the elasticity of EOQ with respect to selling price?

COMPREHENSIVE PROBLEM

New Wave Surfing Stuff, Inc. is a manufacturer of surfboards and related gear that sells to exclusive surf shops located in several Atlantic and Pacific mainland coastal towns as well as several Hawaiian locations. The company's headquarters are located in Carlsbad, California, a small southern California coastal town. True to form, the company's officers, all veteran surfers, have been somewhat laid back about various critical areas of financial management. With an economic downturn in California adversely affecting their business, however, the officers of the company have decided to focus intently on ways to improve New Wave's cash flows. The CFO, Willy Bonik, has been requested to forgo any more daytime surfing jaunts until he has wrapped up a plan to accelerate New Wave's cash flows.

In an effort to ensure his quick return to the surf, Willy has decided to focus on what he believes is one of the easiest methods of improving New Wave's cash collections, namely, adoption of a cash receipts acceleration system that includes a lockbox system and concentration banking. Willy is well aware that New Wave's current system leaves much room for improvement. The company's accounts-receivable system currently requires that remittances from customers be mailed to the headquarters office for processing and then deposited in the local branch of the Bank of the U.S. Such an arrangement takes a considerable amount of time. The checks take an average of 5 days to reach the Carlsbad headquarters. Then, depending on the surf conditions, processing within the company takes anywhere from 2 to 4 days, with the average from the day of receipt by the company to the day of deposit at the bank being 3 days.

Willy feels pretty certain that such delays are costly. After all, New Wave's average daily collections are $150,000. The average remittance size is $750. If Willy could get these funds into his marketable-securities account more quickly, he could earn an annual rate of 5 percent on such funds. In addition, if he could arrange for someone else to do the processing, Willy could save $55,000 per year in costs related to clerical staffing.

New Wave's banker was pleased to provide Willy with a proposal for a combination of a lockbox system and a concentration-banking system. Bank of the U.S. would be New Wave's concentration bank. Lockboxes would be established in Honolulu, Newport Beach, and Daytona Beach. Each check processed through the lockbox system would cost New Wave $0.30. This arrangement, however, would reduce mail float by an average 2.5 days. The funds so collected would be transferred twice each day, 270 days a year, using automated depository transfer checks (DTCs) from each of the local lockbox banks to Bank of the U.S. Each DTC would cost $0.35. The combination of lockbox system and concentration banking would eliminate the time it takes the company to process cash collections, thereby making the funds available for short-term investment.

   a. What would be the average amount of cash made available if New Wave were to adopt the system proposed by Bank of the U.S.?

   b. What is the annual opportunity cost of maintaining the current cash collection and deposit system?

   d. What is the expected annual cost of the complete system proposed by Bank of the U.S.?

   d. What is the net gain or loss that is expected to result from the proposed new system? Should New Wave adopt the new system?

SELF-TEST SOLUTIONS

SS-1

a. Here we must calculate the dollar value of the estimated return for each holding period and compare it with the transaction fee to determine if a gain can be made by investing in the securities. Those calculations and the resultant recommendations follow.

b. Let (%) be the required yield. With $2 million to invest for 3 months we have

				RECOMMENDATION
1. $2,000,000 (.12) $\left(\frac{1}{12}\right)$	=	$20,000	< $45,000	No
2. $2,000,000 (.12) $\left(\frac{2}{12}\right)$	=	$40,000	< $45,000	No
3. $2,000,000 (.12) $\left(\frac{3}{12}\right)$	=	$60,000	> $45,000	Yes
4. $2,000,000 (.12) $\left(\frac{6}{12}\right)$	=	$120,000	> $45,000	Yes
5. $2,000,000 (.12) $\left(\frac{12}{12}\right)$	=	$240,000	> $45,000	Yes

$2,000,000(\%)(3/12) = $45,000$

$2,000,000(\%) \quad\quad = $180,000$

$\quad\quad\quad\quad\quad\quad = $180,000/2,000,000 = 9\%$

The break-even yield, therefore, is 9%.

SS-2

a.

$$EOQ = \sqrt{\frac{2SO}{C}}$$

$$= \sqrt{\frac{2(300,000)(50)}{3}}$$

= 3,162 units, but because orders must be placed in 100-unit lots, the effective EOQ becomes 3,200 units

b.

$$\frac{\text{total usage}}{\text{EOQ}} = \frac{300{,}000}{3{,}200} = 93.75 \text{ orders per year}$$

c. Inventory order point = delivery time + safety stock

$$= \frac{2}{50} \times 300{,}000 + 1{,}000$$

$$= 12{,}000 + 1{,}000$$
$$= 13{,}000 \text{ units}$$

Chapter Seventeen

INTERNATIONAL BUSINESS FINANCE

The Globalization of Product and Financial Markets • Exchange Rates • Interest-Rate Parity Theory • Purchasing-Power Parity Theory • Exposure to Exchange Rate Risk • Multinational Working-Capital Management • International Financing and Capital Structure Decisions • Direct Foreign Investment

LEARNING OBJECTIVES

AFTER READING THIS CHAPTER, YOU SHOULD BE ABLE TO:

1. Discuss the internationalization of business.
2. Explain why foreign exchange rates in two different countries must be in line with each other.
3. Discuss the concept of interest rate parity.
4. Explain the purchasing-power parity theory and the law of one price.
5. Explain what exchange rate risk is and how it can be controlled.
6. Identify working-capital management techniques that are useful for international businesses to reduce exchange rate risk and potentially increase profits.
7. Explain how the financing sources available to multinational corporations differ from those available to domestic firms.
8. Discuss the risks involved in direct foreign investment.

F inding new projects doesn't necessarily mean coming up with a new product; it may mean taking an existing product and applying it to a new market. That's certainly been the direction that McDonald's has taken in recent years. Today, McDonald's operates in over 70 countries with more than 20,000 restaurants. One of the biggest is a 700-seat McDonald's in Moscow. Was this an expensive venture? It certainly was. In fact, the food plant that McDonald's built to supply burgers, buns, fries, and everything else sold there cost over $60 million.

In addition to the costs, a number of other factors make opening an outlet outside of the United States both different and challenging. First, in order to keep the quality of what McDonald's sells identical to what is served at any McDonald's anywhere in the world, McDonald's spent 6 years putting together a supply chain that would provide the necessary raw materials at the quality level McDonald's demands. On top of that, the risks associated with the Russian economy and its currency are well beyond the scope of what is experienced in the United States.

These risks all materialized in 1998 when the Russian economy, along with their currency, the ruble, went in the tank. In an attempt to shore up their economy, the Russian government cut their exchange rate from 6,000 rubles for each U.S. dollar to a new rate of 6 rubles per U.S. dollar—in effect, they cut off 3 zeros. Unfortunately, that didn't solve the problems the Russian economy faced. In May of 1998 the

This chapter highlights the complications that an international business faces when it deals in multiple currencies. Effective strategies for the reduction of foreign exchange risk are discussed. Working-capital management and capital structure decisions in the international context are also covered. For the international firm, direct foreign investment is a capital-budgeting decision—with some additional complexities.

first Russian bank crashed and the value of the ruble started to drop. Then in the summer of 1998, the Russian economy lost control, and in August the entire banking system failed. When it was all over, by the end of 1998, the exchange rate had fallen to 23 rubles per dollar, a drop of over 280 percent.

Because McDonald's sells its burgers for rubles, when it comes time to trade the rubles in for U.S. dollars, McDonald's won't be worth nearly as much as it was a year earlier. In spite of all this, the Moscow McDonald's has proven to be enormously successful. It all goes to show that not all capital budgeting projects have to be new products; they can be existing domestic products that are introduced into the international markets.

Objective 1

THE GLOBALIZATION OF PRODUCT AND FINANCIAL MARKETS

Takin' It to the Net
If you run across any terms you're not familiar with you might want to try the International Financial Encyclopedia http://www/euro.net/innovation/Finance_Base/Fin_encyc.html.

World trade has grown much faster over the last few decades than world aggregate output (global gross national product [GNP]). The dollar value of world exports has grown from $129.5 billion in 1962 to $5.5 *trillion* in 1998. This remarkable increase in international trade is reflected in the increased openness of almost all national economies to international influences. For example, the proportion of U.S. GNP accounted for by exports and imports (about one-fifth) is now double what it was two decades ago, and is even higher for manufactured goods. The U.S. Department of Commerce estimates that the United States exports about one-fifth of its industrial production and that about 70 percent of all U.S. goods compete directly with foreign goods.

Some industries and states are highly dependent on the international economy. For example, the electronic consumer products and automobile industries are widely considered to be global industries. Ohio ranks fourth in terms of manufactured exports, and more than half of Ohio workers are employed by firms that depend to some extent on exports.

There has also been a rise in the global level of international portfolio and direct investment. Both direct and portfolio investment in the United States have been increasing faster than U.S. investment overseas. Direct investment occurs when the **multinational corporation (MNC),** *a corporation with holdings and/or operations in more than one country*, has control over the investment, such as when it builds an offshore manufacturing facility. Portfolio investment involves financial assets with maturities greater than 1 year, such as the purchase of foreign stocks and bonds. Total foreign investment in the U.S. now exceeds such U.S. investment overseas.

multinational corporation (MNC)

A major reason for long-run overseas investments of United States companies is the high rates of return obtainable from these investments. The amount of U.S. *direct foreign investment (DFI)* abroad is large and growing. Significant amounts of the total assets, sales, and profits of American MNCs are attributable to foreign investments and foreign operations. Direct foreign investment is not limited to American firms. Many European and Japanese firms have operations abroad, too. During the last decade, these firms have been increasing their sales and setting up production facilities abroad, especially in the United States.

Capital flows between countries for international financial investment have also been increasing. Many firms, investment companies, and individuals invest in the capital markets in foreign countries. The motivation is twofold; to obtain returns higher than those obtainable in the domestic capital markets, and to reduce portfolio risk through international diversification. The increase in world trade and investment activity is reflected in the recent globalization of financial markets. The Eurodollar market is larger than any domestic financial market. U.S. companies are increasingly turning to this market for funds. Even companies and public entities that have no overseas presence are beginning to rely on this market for financing.

In addition, most national financial markets are becoming more integrated with global markets because of the rapid increase in the volume of interest rate and currency swaps. Because of the widespread availability of these swaps, the currency denomination and the source country of financing for many globally integrated companies are dictated by accessibility and relative cost consideration regardless of the currency ultimately needed by the firm.

The foreign exchange markets have also grown rapidly, and the weekly trading volume in these globally integrated markets, between $4 and $7 trillion, exceeds the annual trading volume on the world's securities markets. Even a *purely domestic firm* that buys all its inputs and sells all its output in its home country is not immune to foreign competition, nor can it totally ignore the workings of the international financial markets.

CONCEPT CHECK

1. Why do U.S. companies invest overseas?

EXCHANGE RATES

Objective 2

Recent History of Exchange Rates

Between 1949 and 1970, the exchange rates between the major currencies were fixed. All countries were required to set a specific *parity rate* for their currency vis-à-vis the U.S. dollar. For example, consider the German currency, the deutsche Mark (DM). In 1949, the parity rate was set at DM 4.0 per dollar (DM 4.0/$). The actual exchange rate prevailing on any day was allowed to lie within a narrow band around the parity rate. The DM was allowed to fluctuate between DM 4.04 and DM 3.96/$. A country could effect a major adjustment in the exchange rate by changing its parity rate with respect to the dollar. When the currency was made cheaper with respect to the dollar, this adjustment was called a *devaluation. A revaluation* resulted when a currency became more expensive with respect to the dollar. In 1969, the DM parity rate was adjusted to DM 3.66/$. This adjustment was a revaluation of the DM parity by 9.3 percent. The new bands around the parity were DM 3.7010 and DM 3.6188/$. The DM strengthened against the dollar because fewer DM were needed to buy a dollar.

Takin' It to the Net
If you'd like to learn more on how to effectively trade overseas, take a look at the Trade Facilitation Information Exchange site http://www.unece.org/trade/facil/tf_home.htm.

Since 1973, a **floating-rate international currency system,** *a system in which exchange rates between different national currencies are allowed to fluctuate with supply and demand conditions,* has been operating. For most currencies, there are no parity rates and no bands within which the currencies fluctuate.[1] Most major currencies, including the U.S. dollar, fluctuate freely, depending on their values as perceived by the traders in foreign exchange markets. The country's relative economic strengths, its level of exports and imports, the level of monetary activity, and the deficits or surpluses in its balance of payments (BOP) are all important factors in the determination of exchange rates.[2] Short-term, day-to-day fluctuations in exchange rates are caused by changing supply and demand conditions in the foreign exchange market.

The Euro: The New Currency of Europe

Beginning January 1, 1999, 11 countries in the European Union introduced a new, single currency—the Euro. These countries, often referred to as Euroland, include Germany, France, Italy, Spain, Portugal, Belgium, Netherlands, Luxembourg, Ireland, Finland, and Austria. Without question, Germany and France are the big players, accounting for over 50 percent of Euroland's output. Eventually, the Euro will replace the existing national currencies in those countries. The timetable is:

- January 1, 1999: The Euro is introduced in principle only. The foreign exchange rates of the participating national currencies are fixed against each other and the Euro. Even though the currency doesn't exist, consumers and businesses can borrow money, open bank accounts, and write checks in Euros.
- January 1, 2002: Euro currency, both coins and notes, begins circulation.
- July 1, 2002: The national currencies in the 11 countries using the Euro will disappear.

Why has the European Union gone to a single currency? For several reasons: First, it will make it easier for goods, people, and services to travel across national borders. As a result, the economies of the European Union should flourish. A common currency eliminates the exchange costs that occur when you have to trade your German marks for French francs. It also eliminates the uncertainty associated with exchange rate fluctuations. It should also help to eliminate cost differences for goods in different countries. For example, when the Euro was introduced in 1999, "The Classics" Swatch watch was selling for 39.2 Euros ($45.97) in Belgium and only 25.7 Euros ($30.14) in Italy. With the introduction of the Euro, it should be easier to compare prices and eliminate the discrepancies.

What does all this mean for the United States? First, it means the competition from abroad will be stronger. It also makes the exchange rate between the Euro and the U.S. dollar a very important exchange rate. If the Euro is strong, it should help U.S. exports by making them cheaper. On the other hand, if the Euro is weak, U.S. exports may suffer. Fortunately, many U.S. multinational firms appear to be in good shape to cash in on any economic surge that may hit Euroland. For example, look at Wal-Mart, which has 21 stores in Germany. In Germany, Wal-Mart is doing just what it does here in the United States—it is wiping out the competition. For the Germans, this is their first sight of wide aisles—(bigger than some of the local streets)—and discount shopping. The Euro will allow Wal-Mart both to offer even

---

[1]The system of floating rates is referred to as the "floating-rate regime."

[2]The balance of payments for the United States reflects the difference between the import and export of goods (the trade balance) and services. Capital inflows and outflows are tabulated in the capital account.

more bargains from all over Euroland and to provide a much more diverse selection of goods. That's because in Europe, because of all the exchange rate uncertainties, most goods are regional in nature. That's the bottom line, the Euro should introduce greater choice and greater competition—both good for the consumer.

The Foreign Exchange Market

The foreign exchange market provides a mechanism for the transfer of purchasing power from one currency to another. This market is not a physical entity like the New York Stock Exchange; it is a network of telephone and computer connections among banks, foreign exchange dealers, and brokers. The market operates simultaneously at three levels. At the first level, customers buy and sell foreign exchange (i.e., foreign currency) through their banks. At the second level, banks buy and sell foreign exchange from other banks in the same commercial center. At the last level, banks buy and sell foreign exchange from banks in commercial centers in other countries. Some important commercial centers for foreign exchange trading are New York, London, Zurich, Frankfurt, Hong Kong, Singapore, and Tokyo.

Takin' It to the Net
The Ohio State University provides an outstanding listing of Web sites dealing with international financial management http://www.cob. ohio-state.edu/~fin/cern/ world.htm. You'll find links to all kinds of excellent sites, all dealing with international finance.

An example illustrates this multilevel trading. A trader in Texas may buy foreign exchange (pounds) from a bank in Houston for payment to a British supplier against some purchase made. The Houston bank, in turn, may purchase the foreign currency (pounds) from a New York bank. The New York bank may buy the pounds from another bank in New York or from a bank in London.

Because this market provides transactions in a continuous manner for a very large volume of sales and purchases, the currency markets are efficient: In other words, it is difficult to make a profit by shopping around from one bank to another. Minute differences in the quotes from different banks are quickly eliminated. Because of the arbitrage mechanism, simultaneous quotes to different buyers in London and New York are likely to be the same.

Two major types of transactions are carried out in the foreign exchange markets: spot and forward transactions.

Spot Exchange Rates

A typical spot transaction involves an American firm buying foreign currency from its bank and paying for it in dollars. *The price of foreign currency in terms of the domestic currency* is the **exchange rate.** Another type of spot transaction is when an American firm receives foreign currency from abroad. The firm typically would sell the foreign currency to its bank for dollars. These are both **spot transactions** because *one currency is traded for another currency today.* The actual exchange rate quotes are expressed in several different ways, as discussed later. To allow time for the transfer of funds, the *value date* when the currencies are actually exchanged is two days after the spot transaction occurs. Four banks could easily be involved in the transactions: the local banks of the buyer and seller of the foreign exchange, and the money-center banks that handle the purchase and sale in the interbank market. Perhaps the buyer or seller will have to move the funds from one of its local banks to another, bringing even more banks into the transaction. A forward transaction entails an agreement today to deliver a specified number of units of a currency on a future date in return for a specified number of units of another currency.

exchange rate

spot transactions

On the spot exchange market, contrasted with the over-the-counter market, the quoted exchange rate is typically called a direct quote. A **direct quote** *indicates the number of units of the home currency required to buy one unit of the foreign currency.* That is, in New York the typical exchange-rate quote indicates the number of dollars

direct quote

needed to buy one unit of a foreign currency: dollars per pound, dollars per mark, and so on. The spot rates in column 1 of Table 17–1 are the direct exchange quotes taken from the *Wall Street Journal*. Thus, according to Table 17–1, to buy 1 British pound (£1), $1.6458 was needed. To buy French francs and German marks, $.1763 and $.5912 were needed, respectively.

indirect quote

An **indirect quote** *indicates the number of units of a foreign currency that can be bought for one unit of the home currency.* This reads as francs per dollar, marks per dollar, and so forth. An indirect quote is the general method used in the over-the-counter market. Exceptions to this rule include British pounds, Irish punts, Australian dollars, and New Zealand dollars, which are quoted via direct quote for historical reasons. Indirect quotes are given in the last column of Table 17–1.

In summary, a direct quote is the dollar/foreign currency rate (FC/$), and an indirect quote is the foreign currency/dollar (FC/$). Therefore, an indirect quote is the reciprocal of a direct quote and vice versa. The following example illustrates the computation of an indirect quote from a given direct quote.

Example

Suppose you want to compute the indirect quote from the direct quote of the spot rate for pounds given in column 1 of Table 17–1. The direct quote for the pound is $1.6458. The related indirect quote is calculated as the *reciprocal* of the direct quote as follows:

$$\text{indirect quote} = \frac{1}{\text{direct quote}}$$

Thus,

$$\frac{1}{\$1.6458} = \pounds.6076/\$$$

Notice that the previous direct quote and indirect quote are identical to those shown in Table 17–1.

Direct and indirect quote are useful in conducting international transactions, as the following examples show.

Example

An American business must pay DM 1,000 to a German firm on January 20, 1999. How many dollars will be required for this transaction?

$$\$.5912 \text{ DM} \times \text{DM } 1,000 = \$591.20$$

Example

An American business must pay $2,000 to a British resident on January 20, 1999. How many pounds will the British resident receive?

$$\pounds.6076 \times \$2,000 = \pounds1,215.20$$

Exchange Rates and Arbitrage

The foreign exchange quotes in two different countries must be in line with each other. The direct quote for U.S. dollars in London is given in pounds per dollar. Because the foreign exchange markets are efficient, the direct quotes for the per U.S. dollar in London, on January 20, 1999, must be very close to the indirect rate of £.6603/$ prevailing in New York on that date.

If the exchange rate quotations between the London and New York spot exchange markets were *out of line*, then an *enterprising trader could make a profit by buy-*

TABLE 17–1   FOREIGN EXCHANGE RATES

CURRENCY TRADING

Wednesday, January 20, 1999

EXCHANGE RATES

The New York foreign exchange mid-range rates below apply to trading among banks in amounts of $1 million and more, as quoted at 4 p.m. Eastern time by Telerate and other sources. Retail transactions provide fewer units of foreign currency per dollar. Rates for the 11 Euro currency countries are derived from the latest dollar-euro rate using the exchange ratios set 1/1/99.

Country	U.S. $ equiv.	Currency per U.S. $
Argentina (Peso)	1.0002	.9998
Australia (Dollar)	.6393	1.5642
Austria (Schilling)	.08402	11.901
Bahrain (Dinar)	2.6525	.3770
Belgium (Franc)	.02866	34.890
Brazil (Real)	.6329	1.5800
Britain (Pound)	1.6458	.6076
1-month forward	1.6444	.6081
3-months forward	1.6429	.6087
6-months forward	1.6416	.6092
Canada (Dollar)	.6572	1.5215
1-month forward	.6564	1.5235
3-months forward	.6566	1.5230
6-months forward	.6560	1.5245
Chile (Peso)	.002093	477.75
China (Renminbi)	.1208	8.2787
Colombia (Peso)	.0006300	1587.18
Czech. Rep. (Koruna)..	- - - -	- - - -
Commercial rate	.03180	31.450
Denmark (Krone)	.1552	6.4425
Ecuador (Sucre)	- - - -	- - - -
Floating rate	.0001406	7113.00
Finland (Markka)	.1945	5.1425
France (Franc)	.1763	5.6734
1-month forward	.1765	5.6644
3-months forward	.1771	5.6465
6-months forward	.1780	5.6185
Germany (Mark)	.5912	1.6916
1-month forward	.5921	1.6889
3-months forward	.5940	1.6836
6-months forward	.5969	1.6753
Greece (Drachma)	.003584	279.00
Hong Kong (Dollar)	.1291	7.7483
Hungary (Forint)	.004631	215.93
India (Rupee)	.02353	42.505
Indonesia (Rupiah)	.0001183	8450.00
Ireland (Punt)	1.4656	.6823
Israel (Shekel)	.2467	4.0543
Italy (Lira)	.0005971	1674.68

Country	U.S. $ equiv.	Currency per U.S. $
Japan (Yen)	.008853	112.96
1-month forward	.008853	112.96
3-months forward	.008854	112.95
6-months forward	.008855	112.93
Jordan (Dinar)	1.4114	.7085
Kuwait (Dinar)	3.3124	.3019
Lebanon (Pound)	.0006631	1508.00
Malaysia (Ringgit-b)	.2632	3.8000
Malta (Lira)	2.6378	.3791
Mexico (Peso)	- - - -	- - - -
Floating rate	.09799	10.205
Netherland (Guilder)	.5247	1.9060
New Zealand (Dollar)..	.5396	1.8532
Norway (Krone)	.1343	7.4443
Pakistan (Rupee)	.02004	49.910
Peru (new Sol)	.3078	3.2485
Philippines (Peso)	.02606	38.370
Poland (Zloty)	.2857	3.5006
Portugal (Escudo)	.005767	173.40
Russia (Ruble) (a)	.04466	22.390
Saudi Arabia (Riyal)	.2665	3.7518
Singapore (Dollar)	.5959	1.6780
Slovak Rep. (Koruna)..	.02712	36.869
South Africa (Rand)	.1670	5.9880
South Korea (Won)	.0008573	1166.50
Spain (Peseta)	.006949	143.91
Sweden (Krona)	.1294	7.7253
Switzerland (Franc)	.7201	1.3887
1-month forward	.7224	1.3842
3-months forward	.7267	1.3762
6-months forward	.7332	1.3639
Taiwan (Dollar)	.03100	32.263
Thailand (Baht)	.02738	36.520
Turkey (Lira)	.00000311	321253.00
United Arab (Dirham)..	.2723	3.6730
Uruguay (New Peso)	- - - -	- - - - - -
Financial	.09066	11.030
Venezuela (Bolivar)	.001751	571.00
SDR	1.4021	.7132
Euro	1.1562	.8649

Special Drawing Rights (SDR) are based on exchange rates for the U.S., German, British, French, and Japanese currencies. Source: International Monetary Fund.

a-Russian Central Bank rate. Trading band lowered on 8/17/98. b-Government rate.

The Wall Street Journal daily foreign exchange data from 1996 forward may be purchased through the Readers' Reference Service (413) 592-3600.

ing in the market where the currency was cheaper and selling it in the other. Such a buy-and-sell strategy would involve a zero net investment of funds and no risk bearing yet would provide a sure profit. Such a person is called an **arbitrageur,** and the process of buying and selling in more than one market to make a riskless profit is called arbitrage. Spot exchange markets are efficient in the sense that arbitrage opportunities do not persist for any length of time. That is, the exchange rates between two different markets are quickly brought *in line,* aided by the arbitrage process. **Simple arbitrage** *eliminates exchange rate differentials across the markets for a single currency,* as in the preceding example for the New York and London quotes. **Triangular arbitrage** does the *same across the markets for all currencies.* **Covered-interest arbitrage** *eliminates differentials across currency and interest rate markets.*

Suppose that London quotes £.6200/$ instead of £.6076/$. If you simultaneously bought a pound in New York for £.6076/$ and sold a pound in London for £.6200/$, you would have (1) taken a zero net investment position since you bought £1 and sold £1, (2) locked in a sure profit of £.0124/$ *no matter which way* the pound subsequently moves, and (3) set in motion the forces that will eliminate the different quotes in New York and London. As others in the marketplace learn of your transaction, they will attempt to make the same transaction. The increased demand to buy pounds in New York will lead to a higher quote there and the increased supply of pounds will lead to a lower quote in London. The workings of the market will produce a new spot rate that lies between £.6076/$ and £.6200/$ and is the same in New York and in London.

Asked and Bid Rates

Two types of rates are quoted in the spot exchange market: the asked and the bid rates. The **asked rate** is the *rate the bank or the foreign exchange trader "asks" the customer to pay in home currency for foreign currency when the bank is selling and the customer is buying.* The asked rate is also known as the **selling rate** or the *offer rate.* The **bid rate** is *the rate at which the bank buys the foreign currency from the customer by paying in home currency.* The bid rate is also known as the **buying rate.** Note that Table 17–1 contains only the selling, offer, or asked rates, not the buying rate.

The bank sells a unit of foreign currency for more than it pays for it. Therefore, the direct asked quote ($/FC) is greater than the direct bid quote. *The difference between the asked quote and the bid quote* is known as the **bid-asked spread.** When there is a large volume of transactions and the trading is continuous, the spread is small and can be less than −1% (.01) for the major currencies. The spread is much higher for infrequently traded currencies. The spread exists to compensate the banks for holding the risky foreign currency and for providing the service of converting currencies.

Cross Rates

A **cross rate** is *the computation of an exchange rate for a currency from the exchange rates of two other currencies.* The following example illustrates how this works.

Example

Taking the dollar/pound and the mark/dollar rates from column 1 and 2 of Table 17–1, determine the mark/pound and pound/mark exchange rates. We see that

$$(\$/£) \times (DM/\$) = (DM/£)$$

or

$$1.6458 \times 1.6916 = DM\ 2.7840/£$$

Thus, the pound/mark exchange rate is

$$1/2.7840 = £.3592/DM$$

Cross-rate computations make it possible to use quotations in New York to compute the exchange rate between pounds, marks, and francs. Arbitrage conditions hold in cross rates, too. For example, the pound exchange rate in Frankfurt (the direct quote marks/pound) must be 2.7840. The mark exchange rate in London must be .3592 pounds/mark. If the rates prevailing in Frankfurt and London were different from the computed cross rates, using quotes from New York, a trader could use three different currencies to lock in arbitrage profits through a process called triangular arbitrage.

Forward Exchange Rates

A **forward exchange contract** *requires delivery, at a specified future date, of one currency for a specified amount of another currency.* The exchange rate for the forward transaction is agreed on today; the actual payment of one currency and the receipt of another currency take place at the future date. For example, a 30-day contract on March 1 is for delivery on March 31. Note that the forward rate is not the same as the spot rate that will prevail in the future. The actual spot rate that will prevail is not known today; only the forward rate is known. The actual spot rate will depend on the market conditions at that time; it may be more or less than today's forward rate. **Exchange rate risk** is the *risk that tomorrow's exchange rate will differ from today's rate.*

forward-exchange contract

exchange rate risk

As indicated earlier, it is extremely unlikely that the future spot rate will be exactly the same as the forward rate quoted today. Assume that you are going to receive a payment denominated in pounds from a British customer in 30 days. If you wait for 30 days and exchange the pounds at the spot rate, you will receive a dollar amount reflecting the exchange rate 30 days hence (i.e., the future spot rate). As of today, you have no way of knowing the exact dollar value of your future pound receipts. Consequently, you cannot make precise plans about the use of these dollars. If, conversely, you buy a future contract, then you know the exact dollar value of your future receipts, and you can make precise plans concerning their use. The forward contract, therefore, can reduce your uncertainty about the future, and the major advantage of the forward market is that of risk reduction.

Forward contracts are usually quoted for periods of 30, 90, and 180 days. A contract for any intermediate date can be obtained, usually with the payment of a small premium. Forward contracts for periods longer than 180 days can be obtained by special negotiations with banks. Contracts for periods greater than 1 year can be costly.

Forward rates, like spot rates, are quoted in both direct and indirect form. The direct quotes for the 30-day and 90-day forward contracts on pounds, francs, and marks are given in column 1 of Table 17–1. The indirect quotes are indicated in column 2 of Table 17–1. The direct quotes are the dollar/foreign currency rate, and the indirect quotes are the foreign currency/dollar rate similar to the spot exchange quotes.

In Table 17–1 the 30-day forward quote for pounds is $1.6444 per pound. This means that the bank is contractually bound to deliver £1 at this price, and the buyer of the contract is legally obligated to buy it at this price in 30 days. Therefore, this is the price the customer must pay regardless of the actual spot rate prevailing in 30 days. If the spot price of the pound is less than 1.6444 discount, then the customer pays *more* than the spot price. If the spot price is greater than $1.6444, then the customer pays *less* than the spot price.

The forward rate is often quoted at a premium or a discount from the existing spot rate. For example, the 30-day forward rate for the pound may be quoted as a .0014 discount (1.6444 forward rate − 1.6458 spot rate). If the British pound is more expensive in the future than it is today, it is said to be selling at a premium relative to the dollar, and the dollar is said to be selling at a discount to the British pound. Notice in Table 17–1 that while the British pound is selling at a discount relative to the dollar, both the French franc and German mark are selling at a premium relative to the dollar. This premium or discount is also called the **forward-spot differential**.

forward-spot differential

Notationally, the relationship may be written

$$F - S = \text{premium } (F > S) \text{ or discount } (S > F) \qquad (17\text{–}1)$$

where
F = the forward rate, direct quote
S = the spot rate, direct quote

The premium or discount can also be expressed as an annual percentage rate, computed as follows:

$$\frac{F - S}{S} \times \frac{12}{n} \times 100 = \text{annualized percentage} \qquad (17\text{–}2)$$

$$\text{premium } (F > S) \text{ or discount } (S > F)$$

where
n = the number of months of the forward contract

Example

Compute the percent-per-annum premium on the 30-day pound.
Step 1: Identify F, S, and n.

$$F = 1.6444, \ S = 1.6458, \ n = 1 \text{ month}$$

Step 2: Because S is greater than F we compute the annualized percentage discount:

$$D = \frac{1.6444 - 1.6458}{1.6458} \times \frac{12 \text{ months}}{1 \text{ month}} \times 100$$

$$= -1.02\%$$

The percent-per-annum discount on the 30-day pound is 1.02%. The percent-per-annum discount on the 30-day and 90-day pound and franc contracts are computed similarly. The results are given in Table 17–2.

Examples of Exchange Rate Risk

The concept of exchange rate risk applies to all types of international business. The measurement of these risks, and the type of risk, may differ among businesses. Let us

TABLE 17–2	PERCENT-PER-ANNUM (DISCOUNT)	
	30-DAY	90-DAY
British pound	−1.02%	−2.11%
French franc	+1.36%	+5.45%

see how exchange rate risk affects international trade contracts, international portfolio investments, and direct foreign investments.

Exchange Rate Risk in International Trade Contracts

The idea of exchange rate risk in trade contracts is illustrated in the following situations.

Case I. An American automobile distributor agrees to buy a car from the manufacturer in Detroit. The distributor agrees to pay $15,000 on delivery of the car, which is expected to be 30 days from today. The car is delivered on the thirtieth day and the distributor pays $15,000. Notice that from the day this contract was written until the day the car was delivered, the buyer knew the *exact dollar amount* of the liability. There was, in other words, *no uncertainty* about the value of the contract.

Case II. An American automobile distributor enters into a contract with a British supplier to buy a car from Britain for £8,800. The amount is payable on the delivery of the car, 30 days from today. From Figure 17–1 we see the range of spot rates that we believe can occur on the date the contract is consummated. On the thirtieth day, the American importer will pay some amount in the range of $13,699.84 (8,800 × 1.5568) to $15,087.60 (8,800 × 1.7145) for the car. Today, the American firm is not certain what its future dollar outflow will be 30 days hence. That is, the *dollar value of the contract is uncertain.*

These two examples help illustrate the idea of foreign exchange risk in international trade contracts. In the domestic trade contract (Case I), the exact dollar amount of the future dollar payment is known today with certainty. In the case of the international trade contract (Case II), where the *contract is written in the foreign currency*, the exact dollar amount of the contract is not known. The variability of the exchange rate induces variability in the future cash flow.

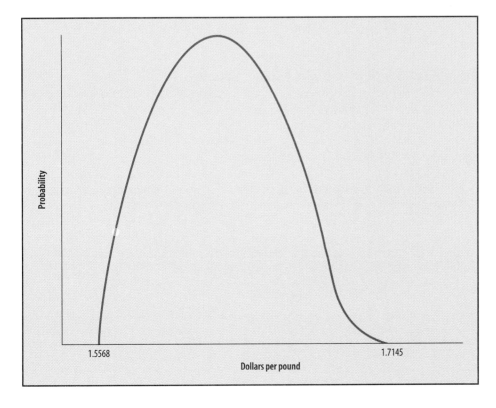

FIGURE 17–1

A Subjective Probability Distribution of the Pound Exchange Rate, 30 Days in the Future

Exchange rate risk exists when the contract is written in terms of the foreign currency or *denominated* in foreign currency. There is no direct exchange rate risk if the international trade contract is written in terms of the domestic currency. That is, in Case II, if the contract were written in dollars, the American importer would face *no* direct exchange rate risk. With the contract written in dollars, the British exporter would bear *all* the exchange rate risk because the British exporter's future pound receipts would be uncertain. That is, the British exporter would receive payment in dollars, which would have to be converted into pounds at an unknown (as of today) pound/dollar exchange rate. In international trade contracts of the type discussed here, at least one of the two parties to the contract *always* bears the exchange rate risk.

Certain types of international trade contracts are denominated in a third currency, different from either the importer's or the exporter's domestic currency. In Case II, the contract might have been denominated in, say, the deutsche mark. With a mark contract, both importer and exporter would be subject to exchange rate risk.

Exchange rate risk is not limited to the two-party trade contracts; it exists also in foreign portfolio investments and direct foreign investments.

Exchange Rate Risk in Foreign Portfolio Investments

Let us look at an example of exchange rate risk in the context of portfolio investments. An American investor buys a German security. The exact return on the investment in the security is unknown. Thus, the security is a risky investment. The investment return in the holding period of, say, 3 months stated in marks could be anything from -2 to $+8$ percent. In addition, the mark/dollar exchange rate may depreciate by 4 percent or appreciate by 6 percent in the 3-month period during which the investment is held. The return to the American investor, in dollars, will therefore be in the range of -6 to $+14$ percent.[3] Notice that the return to a German investor, in marks, is in the range of -2 to $+8$ percent. Clearly, for the American investor, the exchange factor induces a greater variability in the dollar rate of return. Hence, the exchange rate fluctuations may increase the riskiness of the investments.

Exchange Rate Risk in Direct Foreign Investment

The exchange rate risk of a direct foreign investment (DFI) is more complicated. In a DFI, the parent company invests in assets denominated in a foreign currency. That is, the balance sheet and the income statement of the subsidiary are written in terms of the foreign currency. The parent company receives the repatriated profit stream in dollars. Thus, the exchange rate risk concept applies to fluctuations in the dollar value of the assets located abroad as well as to the fluctuations in the home currency–denominated profit stream. Exchange risk not only affects immediate profits, it may affect the future profit stream as well.

Although exchange rate risk can be a serious complication in international business activity, remember the principle of the risk-return trade-off: Traders and corporations find numerous reasons that the returns from international transactions outweigh the risks.

---

[3]Example: Assume the spot exchange rate is $.50/DM. In 3 months, the exchange rate would be $.50 \times (1 - .04) = .48$ to $.50 \times (1 + .06) = .53$. A $50 investment today is equivalent to a DM 100 investment. The DM 100 investment would return DM 98 to DM 108 in 3 months. The return, in the worst case, is DM $98 \times .48 = \$47.04$. The return, in the best case, is DM $108 \times .53 = \$57.24$. The holding-period return, on the $50 investment, will be between -6 percent $((\$47.04 - \$50)/\$50)$ and $+14$ percent $((\$57.24 - \$50)/\$50)$.

CONCEPT CHECK

1. What is a spot transaction? What is a direct quote? An indirect quote?
2. What is an arbitrageur? How does an arbitrageur make money?
3. What is a forward exchange rate?
4. Describe exchange rate risk in direct foreign investment.

INTEREST-RATE PARITY THEORY

Objective 3

Forward rates generally entail a premium or a discount relative to current spot rates. However, these forward premiums and discounts differ between currencies and maturities (see Table 17–2). These differences depend solely on the difference in the level of interest rates between the two countries, called the *interest rate differential.* The value of the premium or discount can be theoretically computed from the **interest-rate parity (IRP) theory.** This theory states that *(except for the effects of small transaction costs) the forward premium or discount should be equal and opposite in size to the difference in the national interest rates for securities of the same maturity.*

interest-rate parity (IRP) theory

Stated very simply, what does all this mean? It means that because of arbitrage, the interest rate differential between two countries must be equal to the difference between the forward and spot exchange rates. If this were not true, arbitrageurs would buy in the forward market and sell in the spot market (or vice versa) until prices were back in line and there were no profits left to be made. For example, if prices in the forward market were too low, arbitrageurs would enter the market, increase the demand for the forward foreign currency, and drive up the prices in the forward market until those prices obeyed the interest-rate parity theory.

Takin' It to the Net
Export Today Magazine
http://www.exporttoday.com/index.htm provides great ideas that help readers sort through the mire of international transactions and keep them ahead of the pack. For example, on the Tools of the Trade page, short articles appear to guide traders to the latest products and services available for global business.

CONCEPT CHECK

1. In simple terms, what does the interest-rate parity theory mean?

Objective 4

PURCHASING-POWER PARITY THEORY

Long-run changes in exchange rates are influenced by international differences in inflation rates and the purchasing power of each nation's currency. Exchange rates of countries with high rates of inflation will tend to decline. According to the **purchasing-power parity (PPP) theory,** *in the long run, exchange rates adjust so that the purchasing power of each currency tends to be the same. Thus, exchange rate changes tend to reflect international differences in inflation rates. Countries with high rates of inflation tend to experience declines in the value of their currency.* Thus, if Britain experiences a 10-percent rate of inflation in a year that Germany experiences only a 6-percent rate, the UK currency (the pound) will be expected to decline in value approximately by 3.77 percent (1.10/1.06) against the German currency (the deutsche Mark). More accurately, according to the PPP theory

expected spot rate = current spot rate × expected difference in inflation rate

$$\begin{pmatrix} \text{expected spot rate} \\ \text{(domestic currency} \\ \text{per unit of foreign} \\ \text{currency)} \end{pmatrix} = \begin{pmatrix} \text{current spot rate} \\ \text{(domestic currency} \\ \text{per unit of foreign} \\ \text{currency)} \end{pmatrix} \times \frac{(1 + \text{expected domestic} \\ \text{inflation rate})}{(1 + \text{expected foreign} \\ \text{inflation rate})}$$

purchasing-power parity (PPP) theory

Thus, if the beginning value of the mark were £.40, with a 6-percent inflation rate in Germany and a 10-percent inflation rate in Britain, according to the PPP, the expected value of the deutsche Mark at the end of that year will be £.40 × [1.10/1.06], or £.4151.

Stated very simply, what does this mean? It means that a dollar should have the same purchasing power anywhere in the world—well, at least on average. Obviously, this is not quite true. However, what the PPP theory tells us is that we should expect, on average, that differences in inflation rates between two countries should be reflected in changes in the exchange rates. In effect, the best forecast of the difference in inflation rates between two countries should also be the best forecast of the change in the spot rate of exchange.

The Law of One Price

Underlying the PPP relationship is the **law of one price.** This law is actually *a proposition that in competitive markets where there are no transportation costs or barriers to trade, the same goods sold in different countries sells for the same price if all the different prices are expressed in terms of the same currency.* The idea is that the worth, in terms of marginal utility, of a good does not depend on where it is bought or sold. Because inflation will erode the purchasing power of any currency, its exchange rate must adhere to the PPP relationship if the law of one price is to hold over time.

law of one price

There are enough obvious exceptions to the concept of purchasing-power parity that it may, at first glance, seem difficult to accept. For example, recently a Big Mac cost $2.36 in the United States, and given the then existing exchange rates, it cost an equivalent of $2.02 in Mexico, $2.70 in Japan, and $3.22 in Germany. On the surface this might appear to violate the PPP theory and the law of one price; however, we must remember that this theory is based upon the concept of arbitrage. In the case of a Big Mac, it's pretty hard to imagine buying Big Macs in Mexico for $2.02, shipping them to Germany, and reselling them for $3.22. But for commodities like gold and other items that are relatively inexpensive to ship and do not have to be consumed immediately, the law of one price holds much better.

International Fisher Effect

According to the domestic Fisher effect (FE), nominal interest rates reflect the expected inflation rate and a real rate of return. In other words,

$$\frac{\text{nominal}}{\text{interest rate}} = \frac{\text{expected}}{\text{inflation rate}} + \frac{\text{real rate}}{\text{of interest}}$$

Although there is mixed empirical support for the international Fisher effect (IFE), it is widely thought that, for the major industrial countries, the real rate of interest is about 3 percent when a long-term period is considered. In such a case, with the previous assumption regarding inflation rates, interest rates in Britain and Germany would be (.10 + .03 + .003) or 13.3 percent and (.06 + .03 + .0018) or 9.18 percent, respectively.

In effect, the IFE states that the real interest rate should be the same all over the world, with the difference in nominal or stated interest rates simply resulting from the differences in expected inflation rates. As we look at interest rates around the world, this tells us that we should not necessarily send our money to a bank account in the country with the highest interest rates. That course of action might only result in sending our money to a bank in the country with the highest expected level of inflation.

| Objective 5 | **EXPOSURE TO EXCHANGE RATE RISK** |

An asset denominated or valued in terms of foreign-currency cash flows will lose value if that foreign currency declines in value. It can be said that such an asset is exposed to exchange rate risk. However, this possible decline in asset value may be offset by the decline in value of any liability that is also denominated or valued in terms of that foreign currency. Thus, a firm would normally be interested in its net exposed position (exposed assets − exposed liabilities) for each period in each currency.

While expected changes in exchange rates can often be included in the cost-benefit analysis relating to such transactions, in most cases there is an unexpected component in exchange rate changes and often the cost-benefit analysis for such transactions does not fully capture even the expected change in the exchange rate. For example, price increases for the foreign operations of many MNCs often have to be less than those necessary to fully offset exchange rate changes, owing to the competitive pressures generated by local businesses, as the Japanese automakers found in 1988 for their U.S. sales.

Three measures of foreign exchange exposure are translation exposure, transactions exposure, and economic exposure. Translation exposure arises because the foreign operations of MNCs have accounting statements denominated in the local currency of the country in which the operation is located. For U.S. MNCs, the *reporting currency* for its consolidated financial statements is the dollar, so the assets, liabilities, revenues, and expenses of the foreign operations must be translated into dollars. International transactions often require a payment to be made or received in a foreign currency in the future, so these transactions are exposed to exchange rate risk. Economic exposure exists over the long term because the value of future cash flows in the reporting currency (that is, the dollar) from foreign operations are exposed to exchange rate risk. Indeed, the whole stream of future cash flows is exposed. The Japanese automaker situation highlights the effect of economic exposure on an MNC's revenue stream. The three measures of exposure now are examined more closely.

Translation Exposure

Foreign currency assets and liabilities are considered exposed if their foreign currency value for accounting purposes is to be translated into the domestic currency using the currency exchange rate—the exchange rate in effect on the balance sheet date. Other assets and liabilities and equity amounts that are translated at the historic exchange rate—the rate in effect when these items were first recognized in the company's accounts—are not considered to be exposed. The rate (current or historic) used to translate various accounts depends on the translation procedure used.

While transaction exposure can result in exchange rate change–related losses and gains that are realized and have an impact on both reported and taxable income, translation exposure results in exchange rate losses and gains that are reflected in the company's accounting books, but are unrealized and have little or no impact on taxable income. Thus, if financial markets are efficient and managerial goals are consistent with owner wealth maximization, a firm should not have to waste real resources hedging against possible paper losses caused by translation exposure. However, if there are significant agency or information costs or if markets are not efficient, a firm may indeed find it economical to hedge against translation losses or gains.

Transaction Exposure

Receivables, payables, and fixed-price sales or purchase contracts are examples of foreign currency transactions whose monetary value was fixed at a time different from the time when these transactions are actually completed. **Transaction exposure** is a term that *describes the net contracted foreign currency transactions for which the settlement amounts are subject to changing exchange rates.* A company normally must set up an additional reporting system to track transaction exposure, because several of these amounts are not recognized in the accounting books of the firm.

transaction exposure

Exchange rate risk may be neutralized or hedged by a change in the asset and liability position in the foreign currency. An exposed asset position (such as an account receivable) can be hedged or covered by creating a liability of the same amount and maturity denominated in the foreign currency (such as a forward contract to sell the foreign currency). An exposed liability position (such as an account payable) can be covered by acquiring assets of the same amount and maturity in the foreign currency (such as a forward contract to buy the foreign currency). The objective is to have a zero net asset position in the foreign currency. This eliminates exchange rate risk because the loss (gain) in the liability (asset) is exactly offset by the gain (loss) in the value of the asset (liability) when the foreign currency appreciates (depreciates). Two popular forms of hedge are the money-market hedge and the exchange-market or forward-market hedge. In both types of hedge the amount and the duration of the asset (liability) positions are matched. Note as you read the next two subsections how IRP theory assures that each hedge provides the same cover.

Money-Market Hedge

In a money-market hedge, the exposed position in a foreign currency is offset by borrowing or lending in the money market. Consider the case of the American firm with a net liability position (i.e., the amount it owes) of £3,000. The firm knows the exact amount of its pound liability in 30 days, but it does not know the liability in dollars. Assume that the 30-day money-market rates in both the United States and Britain are, respectively, 1 percent for lending and 1.5 percent for borrowing. The American business can take the following steps:

Step 1: Calculate the present value of the foreign currency liability (£3,000) that is due in 30 days. Use the money-market rate applicable for the foreign country (1 percent in the United Kingdom). The present value of £3,000 is £2,970.30, computed as follows: 3,000/(1 + .01).

Step 2: Exchange dollars on today's spot market to obtain the £2,970.30. The dollar amount needed today is $4,888.52 (2,970.30 × 1.6458).

Step 3: Invest £2,970.30 in a United Kingdom 1-month money-market instrument. This investment will compound to exactly £3,000 in 1 month. The future liability of £3,000 is covered by the £2,970.30 investment.[4]

---

[4]Observe that £2,970.30 × (1 + .01) = £3,000.

Note: If the American business does not own this amount today, it can borrow 4,888.52 from the U.S. money market at the going rate of 1.5 percent. In 30 days the American business will need to repay $4961.85 [$4,888.52 $\times$ (1 + .015)].

Assuming that the American business borrows the money, its management may base its calculations on the knowledge that the British goods, on delivery in 30 days, will cost it 4961.85. The British business will receive £3,000. The American business need not wait for the future spot exchange rate to be revealed. On today's date, the future dollar payment of the contract is known with certainty. This certainty helps the American business in making its pricing and financing decisions.

Many businesses hedge in the money market. The firm needs to borrow (creating a liability) in one market, lend or invest in the other money market, and use the spot exchange market on today's date. The mechanics of covering a net asset position in the foreign currency are the exact reverse of the mechanics of covering the liability position. With a net asset positioning pounds: Borrow in the United Kingdom money market in pounds, convert to dollars on the spot exchange market, invest in the U.S. money market. When the net assets are converted into pounds (i.e., when the firm receives what it is owed), pay off the loan and the interest. The cost of hedging in the money market is the cost of doing business in three different markets. Information about the three markets is needed, and analytical calculations of the type indicated here must be made.

Many small and infrequent traders find the cost of the money-market hedge prohibitive, especially because of the need for information about the market. These traders use exchange-market or forward-market hedge, which has very similar hedging benefits.

The Forward-Market Hedge

The forward market provides a second possible hedging mechanism. It works as follows: A net asset (liability) position is covered by a liability (asset) in the forward market. Consider again the case of the American firm with a liability of £3,000 that must be paid in 30 days. The firm may take the following steps to cover its liability position:

Step 1: Buy a forward contract today to purchase £3,000 in 30 days. The 30-day forward rate is $1.6444/£.

Step 2: On the thirtieth day pay the banker $4,933.20 (3,000 $\times$ $1.6444) and collect £3,000. Pay these pounds to the British supplier.

By the use of the forward contract the American business knows the exact worth of the future payment in dollars ($4,933.20). The exchange rate risk in pounds is totally eliminated by the net asset position in the forward pounds. In the case of a net asset exposure, the steps open to the American firm are the exact opposite: Sell the pounds forward, and on the future day receive and deliver the pounds to collect the agreed-on dollar amount.

The use of the forward market as a hedge against exchange rate risk is simple and direct—that is, match the liability or asset position against an offsetting position in the forward market. The forward-market hedge is relatively easy to implement. The firm directs its banker that it needs to buy or sell a foreign currency on a future date, and the banker gives a forward quote.

The forward-market hedge and the money-market hedge give an identical future dollar payment (or receipt) if the forward contracts are priced according to the interest-rate parity theory. The alert student may have noticed that the dollar payments in the money-market hedge and the forward-market hedge examples were, respectively, $4888.52 and $4,933.20. Recall from our previous discussions that in efficient markets, the forward contracts do indeed conform to IRP theory. However, the numbers in our example are not identical because the forward rate used in the forward-market hedge is not exactly equal to the interest rates in the money-market hedge.

Currency-Futures Contracts and Options

The forward-market hedge is not adequate for some types of exposure. If the foreign currency asset or liability position occurs on a date for which forward quotes are not available, the forward-market hedge cannot be accomplished. In certain cases the forward-market hedge may cost more than the money-market hedge. In these cases, a corporation with a large amount of exposure may prefer the money-market hedge. In addition to forward-market and money-market hedges, a company can also hedge its exposure by buying (or selling) some relatively new instruments—foreign currency futures contracts and foreign currency options. Although futures contracts are similar to forward contracts in that they provide fixed prices for the required delivery of foreign currency at maturity, exchange traded options permit fixed (strike) price foreign currency transactions anytime before maturity. Futures contracts and options differ from forward contracts in that, unlike forward contracts, which are customized regarding amount and maturity date, futures and options are traded in standard amounts with standard maturity dates. In addition, although forward contracts are written by banks, futures and options are traded on organized exchanges, and individual traders deal with the exchange-based clearing organization rather than with each other. The purchase of futures requires the fulfillment of margin requirements (about 5 to 10 percent of the face amount), whereas the purchase of forward contracts requires only good credit standing with a bank. The purchase of options requires an immediate outlay that reflects a premium above the strike price and an outlay equal to the strike price when and if the option is executed.

Economic Exposure

The economic value of a company can vary in response to exchange rate changes. This change in value may be caused by a rate change–induced decline in the level of expected cash flows and/or by an increase in the riskiness of these cash flows. *Economic exposure* refers to the overall impact of exchange rate changes on the value of the firm and includes not only the strategic impact of changes in competitive relationships that arise from exchange rate changes, but also the economic impact of transactions exposure, and if any, translation exposure.

Economic exposure to exchange rate changes depends on the competitive structure of the markets for a firm's inputs and outputs and how these markets are influenced by changes in exchange rates. This influence, in turn, depends on several economic factors, including price elasticities of the products, the degree of competition from foreign markets, and direct (through prices) and indirect (through incomes) impact of exchange rate changes on these markets. Assessing, the economic exposure faced by a particular firm thus depends on the ability to understand and model the structure of the markets for its major inputs (purchases) and outputs (sales).

A company need not engage in any cross-border business activity to be exposed to exchange rate changes, because product and financial markets in most countries are related and influenced to a large extent by the same global forces. The output of a company engaged in business activity only within one country may be competing with imported products, or it may be competing for its inputs with other domestic and foreign purchasers. For example, a Canadian chemical company that did no cross-border business nevertheless found that its profit margin depended directly on the U.S. dollar/Japanese yen exchange rate. The company used coal as an input in its production process, and the Canadian price of coal was heavily influenced by the extent to which the Japanese bought U.S. coal, which in turn depended on the dollar/yen exchange rate.

Although translation exposure need not be managed, it might be useful for a firm to manage its transaction and economic exposures because they affect firm value directly. In most companies, transaction exposure is generally tracked and managed by the office of the corporate treasurer. Economic exposure is difficult to define in operating terms, and very few companies manage it actively. In most companies, economic exposure is generally considered part of the strategic planning process, rather than a treasurer's or finance function.

CONCEPT CHECK

1. Give a simple explanation of translation exposure.
2. Give a simple explanation of transaction exposure.
3. Give a simple explanation of economic exposure.

Objective 6

MULTINATIONAL WORKING-CAPITAL MANAGEMENT

The basic principles of working-capital management for a multinational corporation are similar to those for a domestic firm. However, tax and exchange rate factors are additional considerations for the MNC. For an MNC with subsidiaries in many countries, the optimal decisions in the management of working capital are made by considering the market as a whole. The global or centralized financial decisions for an MNC is superior to the set of independent optimal decisions for the subsidiaries. This is the control problem of the MNC. If the individual subsidiaries make decisions that are best for them individually, the consolidation of such decisions may not be best for the MNC as a whole. To effect global management, sophisticated computerized models—incorporating many variables for each subsidiary—are solved to provide the best overall decision for the MNC.

Before considering the components of working-capital management, we examine two techniques that are useful in the management of a wide variety of working-capital components.

Leading and Lagging

Two important risk-reduction techniques for many working-capital problems are called leading and lagging. Often forward-market and money-market hedges are not available to eliminate exchange risk. Under such circumstances, leading and lagging may be used to reduce exchange risk.

Recall that a net asset (long) position is not desirable in a weak or potentially depreciating currency. If a firm has a net asset position in such a currency, it should expedite the disposal of the asset. The firm should get rid of the asset earlier than it otherwise would have, or *lead*, and convert the funds into assets in a relatively stronger currency. By the same reasoning, the firm should *lag*, or delay the collection against a net asset position in a strong currency. If the firm has a net liability (short) position in the weak currency, then it should delay the payment against the liability, or lag, until the currency depreciates. In the case of an appreciating or strong foreign currency and a net liability position, the firm should lead the payments—that is, reduce the liabilities earlier than it would otherwise have.

These principles are useful in the management of working capital of an MNC. They cannot, however, eliminate the foreign exchange risk. When exchange rates change continuously, it is almost impossible to guess whether or when the currency will depreciate or appreciate. This is why the risk of exchange rate changes cannot be eliminated. Nevertheless, the reduction of risk, or the increased gain from exchange rate changes, via the lead and lag is useful for cash management, accounts-receivable management, and short-term liability management.

Cash Management and Positioning of Funds

Positioning of funds takes on an added importance in the international context. Funds may be transferred from a subsidiary of the MNC in country A to another subsidiary in country B such that the foreign exchange exposure and the tax liability of the MNC as a whole are minimized. It bears repeating that because of the global strategy of the MNC, the tax liability of the subsidiary in country A may be greater than it would otherwise have been, but the overall tax payment for all units of the MNC is minimized.

The transfer of funds among subsidiaries and the parent company is done by royalties, fees, and transfer pricing. A **transfer price** is the *price a subsidiary or a parent company charges other companies that are part of the MNC for its good or services.* A parent that wishes to transfer funds from a subsidiary in a depreciating-currency country may charge a higher price on the goods and services sold to this subsidiary by the parent or by subsidiaries from strong-currency countries.

transfer price

CONCEPT CHECK

1. Describe the risk reduction techniques of leading and lagging.
2. How can a parent company use the concept of transfer pricing to move funds from a subsidiary in a depreciating-currency country to a strong-currency country?

INTERNATIONAL FINANCING AND CAPITAL STRUCTURE DECISIONS

Objective 7

An MNC has access to many more financing sources than a domestic firm. It can tap not only the financing sources in its home country that are available to its domestic counterparts, but also sources in the foreign countries in which it operates. Host countries often provide access to low-cost subsidized financing to attract foreign investment. In addition, the MNC may enjoy preferential credit standards because of its size and investor preference for its home currency. An MNC may be able to access third-country capital markets—countries in which it does not operate but which may have large, well-functioning capital markets. Finally, an MNC can also access external currency markets: Eurodollar,

Eurocurrency, or Asian dollar markets. These external markets are unregulated, and because of their lower spread, can offer very attractive rates for financing *and* for investments. With the increasing availability of interest rate and currency swaps, a firm can raise funds in the lowest-cost maturities and currencies and swap them into funds with the maturity and currency denomination it requires. Because of its ability to tap a larger number of financial markets, the MNC may have a lower cost of capital; and because it may be better able to avoid the problems or limitations of any one financial market, it may have a more continuous access to external finance compared to a domestic company.

Access to national financial markets is regulated by governments. For example, in the United States, access to capital markets is governed by SEC regulations. Access to Japanese capital markets is governed by regulations issued by the Ministry of Finance. Some countries have extensive regulations; other countries have relatively open markets. These regulations may differ depending on the legal residency terms of the company raising funds. A company that cannot use its local subsidiary to raise funds in a given market will be treated as foreign. In order to increase their visibility in a foreign capital market, a number of MNCs are now listing their equities on the stock exchanges of many of these countries.

The external currency markets are predominantly centered in Europe, and about 80 percent of their value is denominated in terms of the U.S. dollar. Thus most external currency markets can be characterized as Eurodollar markets. Such markets consist of an active short-term money market and an intermediate-term capital market with maturities ranging up to 15 years and averaging about 7 to 9 years. The intermediate-term market consists of the Eurobond and the Syndicated Eurocredit markets. Eurobonds are usually issued as unregistered bearer bonds and generally tend to have higher flotation costs but lower coupon rates compared to similar bonds issued in the United States. A Syndicated Eurocredit loan is simply a large-term loan that involves contributions by a number of lending banks.

In arriving at its capital structure decisions, an MNC has to consider a number of factors. First, the capital structure of its local affiliates is influenced by local norms regarding capital structure in that industry and in that country. Local norms for companies in the same industry can differ considerably from country to country. Second, the local affiliate capital structure must also reflect corporate attitudes toward exchange rate and political risk in that country, which would normally lead to higher levels of local debt and other local capital. Third, local affiliate capital structure must reflect home country requirements with regard to the company's consolidated capital structure. Finally, the optimal MNC capital structure should reflect its wider access to financial markets, its ability to diversify economic and political risks, and its other advantages over domestic companies.

BACK TO THE FOUNDATIONS

Investment across international boundaries gives rise to special risks not encountered when investing domestically. Specifically, political risks and exchange rate risk are unique to international investing. Once again, **Axiom 1: The Risk-Return Trade-off—We Won't Take On Additional Risk Unless We Expect to Be Compensated with Additional Return** provides a rationale for evaluating these considerations. Where added risks are present, added rewards are necessary to induce investment.

CONCEPT CHECK

1. What factors might an MNC consider in making a capital structure decision?

DIRECT FOREIGN INVESTMENT

Objective 8

An MNC often makes direct foreign investments abroad in the form of plants and equipment. The decision process for this type of investment is very similar to the capital-budgeting decision in the domestic context—with some additional twists. Most real-world capital-budgeting decisions are made with uncertain future outcomes. Recall that a capital-budgeting decision has three major components: the estimation of the future cash flows (including the initial cost of the proposed investment), the estimation of the risk in these cash flows, and the choice of the proper discount rate. We will assume that the NPV criterion is appropriate as we examine (1) the risks associated with direct foreign investment and (2) factors to be considered in making the investment decision that may be unique to the international scene.

Risks in Direct Foreign Investment

Risks in domestic capital budgeting arise from two sources: business risk and financial risk. The international capital-budgeting problem incorporates these risks as well as political risk and exchange risk.

Business Risk and Financial Risk

International business risk is due to the response of business to economic conditions in the foreign country. Thus the U.S. MNC needs to be aware of the business climate in both the United States and the foreign country. Additional business risk is due to competition from other MNCs, local businesses, and imported goods. Financial risk refers to the risks introduced in the profit stream by the firm's financial structure. The financial risks of foreign operations are not very different from those of domestic operations.

Political Risk

Political risk arises because the foreign subsidiary conducts its business in a political system different from that of the home country. Many foreign governments, especially those in the Third World, are less stable than the U.S. government. A change in a country's political setup frequently brings a change in policies with respect to businesses—and especially with respect to foreign businesses. An extreme change in policy might involve nationalization or even outright expropriation of certain businesses. These are the political risks of conducting business abroad. A business with no investment in plant and equipment is less susceptible to these risks. Some examples of political risk are listed below:

1. Expropriation of plant and equipment without compensation.
2. Expropriation with minimal compensation that is below actual market value.
3. Nonconvertibility of the subsidiary's foreign earnings into the parent's currency—the problem of *blocked funds*.
4. Substantial changes in the laws governing taxation.

Takin' It to the Net
If you'd like information on Japan, try Japan Information Network Web site http://www.jinjapan.org/stat/index.html, which includes all Japanese direct investments abroad and inwards of direct investments by region, major country, and business categories. This site also provides statistics on other aspects of Japan: major macroeconomics, financial, and international transactions, including balance of payments, gold and foreign exchange reserves, trade in goods and services, and international investments.

"Ukraine: Not for the Fainthearted"

KIEV, UKRAINE—S.C. Johnson & Son Inc., the $3 billion family-owned company that makes clothes, floor wax, furniture cleaners, bug killers, and air fresheners, has traditionally been challenged by new frontiers.

When the company opened a plant in Britain 80 years ago, it was one of the first American corporations to go abroad. At the end of the cold war, it trailblazed again this time into the uncertain precincts of the Ukraine.

Johnson Wax's experience since 1990—when the company started to make and bottle detergents and furniture polish in a renovated corner of a ramshackle factory on the outskirts of Kiev—helps explain the reluctance of other consumer-products companies to jump in.

A few months after Ukraine joined Russia and Belarus in leaving the crumbling Soviet Union, it introduced a coupon currency to replace the ruble. In relatively short order, the coupons become all but worthless. By late last year, inflation had reached about 100 percent a month, from almost zero two years before. A fierce credit squeeze by the government left wholesalers little money to buy Johnson's products. And a government that had initially promised to create a friendly environment for Western investors became encrusted with old style—many say corrupt—former Communists.

Last year, Johnson Wax halved its production from that of 1992. And almost half of 1993's 10 million bottles that came off the assembly line had to be sold in Russia, where the economy, however turbulent, is far stronger than Ukraine's.

A major attraction for Western manufacturers here is low wages. Johnson would like to raise the pay of some workers above the monthly $150 that the best get, but a 92 percent tax rate on earned income above $150 makes it impossible to do so.

Some improvements in everyday life make the difficulty of doing business here a little easier. To make an overseas telephone call took two days several years ago. Now they can be made on the spot. And there are more flights in and out of the country.

But unpredictability prevails. In the last six months, the Ukrainian government has raised or lowered the value-added tax rate three times. Now there are worries that the government might impose an excise tax on supplies coming across the border from Russia. And still another currency is expected, prompting further headaches.

Source: From Jane Perex: "Ukraine: Not for the Fainthearted," *The New York Times,* June 1, 1994, D1, 5. Copyright © 1994 by *The New York Times.* All rights reserved.

5. Governmental controls in the foreign country regarding the sale price of the products, wages, and compensation to personnel, hiring of personnel, making of transfer payments to the parent, and local borrowing.
6. Some governments require certain amounts of local equity participation in the business. Some require that the majority of the equity participation belong to their country.

All these controls and governmental actions introduce risks in the cash flows of the investment to the parent company. These risks must be considered before making the foreign investment decision. The MNC may decide against investing in countries with risks of types 1 and 2. Other risks can be borne—provided that the returns from the foreign investments are high enough to compensate for them. Insurance against some types of political risks may be purchased from private insurance companies or from the U.S. government Overseas Private Investment Corporation. It should be noted that although an MNC cannot protect itself against all foreign political risks, political risks are also present in domestic business.

Exchange Rate Risk

The exposure of the fixed assets is best measured by the effects of the exchange rate changes on the firm's future earnings stream: that being economic exposure rather than translation exposure. For instance, changes in the exchange rate may adversely affect sales by making competing imported goods cheaper. Changes in the cost of goods sold may result if some components are imported and their price in the foreign currency changes because of exchange rate fluctuations. The thrust of these examples is that the effect of exchange rate changes on income statement items should be properly measured to evaluate exchange rate risk. Finally, exchange rate risk affects the dollar-denominated profit stream of the parent company, whether or not it affects the foreign-currency profits.

CONCEPT CHECK

1. What are some of the risks associated with direct foreign investments?

SUMMARY

The growth of our global economy, the increasing number of multinational corporations, and the increase in foreign trade itself underscore the importance of the study of international finance.

Objective 1

Exchange rate mechanics are discussed in the context of the prevailing floating rates. Under this system, exchange rates between currencies vary in an apparently random fashion in accordance with the supply and demand conditions in the exchange market. Important economic factors affecting the level of exchange rates include the relative economic strengths of the countries involved, the balance-of-payments mechanism, and the countries' monetary policies. Several important exchange rate terms are introduced. These include the asked and the bid rates, which represent the selling and buying rates of currencies. The direct quote is the units of home currency per unit of foreign currency, and the indirect quote is the reciprocal of the direct quote. Cross-rate computations reflect the exchange rate between two foreign currencies.

Objective 2

The forward exchange market provides a valuable service by quoting rates for the delivery of foreign currencies in the future. The foreign currency is said to sell at a discount (premium) forward from the spot rate when the forward rate is greater (less) than the spot rate, in direct quotation. In addition, the influences of purchasing-power parity (PPP) and the international Fisher effect (IFE) in determining the exchange rate are discussed. In rational and efficient markets, forward rates are unbiased forecasts of future spot rates that are consistent with the PPP.

Objective 3
Objective 4

Exchange rate risk exists because the exact spot rate that prevails on a future date is not known with certainty today. The concept of exchange rate risk is applicable to a wide variety of businesses, including export-import firms and firms involved in making direct foreign investments or international investments in securities. Exchange exposure is a measure of exchange rate risk. There are different ways of measuring the foreign exposure, including the net asset (net liability) measurement. Different strategies are open to businesses to counter the exposure to this risk, including the money-market hedge, the forward-market hedge, futures contracts, and options. Each involves different costs.

Objective 5

In discussing working-capital management in an international environment, we find leading and lagging techniques useful in minimizing exchange rate risk and increasing profitability. In addition, funds positioning is a useful tool for reducing exchange rate risk exposure. The MNC may have a lower cost of capital because it has access to a larger set of

Objective 6

financial markets than a domestic company. In addition to the home, host, and third-country financial markets, the MNC can tap the rapidly growing external currency markets. In making capital structure decisions, the MNC must consider political and exchange rate risks and host and home country capital structure norms.

Objective 7
Objective 8
The complexities encountered in the direct foreign investment decision include the usual sources of risk—business and financial—and additional risks associated with fluctuating exchange rates and political factors. Political risk is due to differences in political climates, institutions, and processes between the home country and abroad. Under these conditions, the estimation of future cash flows and the choice of the proper discount rates are more complicated than for the domestic investment situation.

KEY TERMS

arbitrageur, 564

asked rate, 564

bid-rate, 564

bid-asked spread, 564

buying rate, 564

covered-interest arbitrage, 564

cross rate, 564

direct quote, 561

exchange rate, 561

exchange rate risk, 565

floating-rate international currency system, 560

forward exchange contract, 565

forward-spot differential, 566

indirect quote, 562

interest-rate parity theory, 569

law of one price, 571

multinational corporation (MNC), 558

purchasing-power parity theory, 570

selling rate, 564

simple arbitrage, 564

spot transactions, 561

transaction exposure, 573

transfer price, 577

triangular arbitrage, 564

STUDY QUESTIONS

17-1 What additional factors are encountered in international as compared with domestic financial management? Discuss each briefly.

17-2 What different types of businesses operate in the international environment? Why are the techniques and strategies available to these firms different?

17-3 What is meant by arbitrage profits?

17-4 What are the markets and mechanics involved in generating (a) simple arbitrage profits, (b) triangular arbitrage profits?

17-5 How do the purchasing power parity, interest rate parity, and the Fisher effect explain the relationships among the current spot rate, the future spot rate, and the forward rate?

17-6 What is meant by (a) exchange risk, (b) political risk?

17-7 How can exchange risk be measured?

17-8 What are the differences between transaction, translation, and economic exposures? Should all of them be ideally reduced to zero?

17-9 What steps can a firm take to reduce exchange risk? Indicate at least two different techniques.

17-10 How are the forward market and the money market hedges affected? What are the major differences between these two types of hedges?

17-11 In the New York exchange market, the forward rate for the Indian currency, the rupee, is not quoted. If you were exposed to exchange risk in rupees, how could you cover your position?

17-12 Compare and contrast the use of forward contracts, futures contracts, and options to reduce foreign exchange exposure. When is each instrument most appropriate?

17-13 Indicate two rocking-capital management techniques that are useful for international businesses to reduce exchange risk and potentially increase profits.

17-14 How do the financing sources available to an MNC differ from those available to a domestic firm? What do these differences mean for the company's cost of capital?

17-15 What risks are associated with direct foreign investment? How do these risks differ from those encountered in domestic investment?

17-16 How is the direct foreign investment decision made? What are the inputs to this decision process? Are the inputs more complicated than those to the domestic investment problem? If so, why?

17-17 A corporation desires to enter a particular foreign market. The DFI analysis indicates that a direct investment in the plant in the foreign country is not profitable. What other course of action can the company take to enter the foreign market? What are the important considerations?

17-18 What are the reasons for the acceptance of a sales office or licensing arrangement when the DFI itself is not profitable?

SELF-TEST PROBLEMS

The data for Self-Test Problem ST-1 are given in the following table:

COUNTRY	CONTRACT	$/FOREIGN CURRENCY
Germany—mark	Spot	.3893
	30-day	.3910
	90-day	.3958

ST-1 You own $10,000. The dollar rate on the German mark is 2.5823 DM/$. The German mark rate is given in the table above. Are arbitrage profits possible? Set up an arbitrage scheme with your capital. What is the gain (loss) in dollars?

STUDY PROBLEM

The data for Study Problems 17-1 through 17-6 are given in the following table:

COUNTRY	CONTRACT	$/FOREIGN CURRENCY
Canada—dollar	Spot	.8437
	30-day	.8417
	90-day	.8395
Japan—yen	Spot	.004684
	30-day	.004717
	90-day	.004781
Switzerland—franc	Spot	.5139
	30-day	.5169
	90-day	.5315

17-1 An American business needs to pay (a) 10,000 Canadian dollars, (b) 2 million yen, and (c) 50,000 Swiss francs to businesses abroad. What are the dollar payments to the respective countries?

17-2 An American business pays $10,000, $15,000, and $20,000 to suppliers in, respectively, Japan, Switzerland, and Canada. How much, in local currencies, do the suppliers receive?

17-3 Compute the indirect quote for the spot and forward Canadian dollar, yen, and Swiss franc contracts.

17-4 The spreads on the contracts as a percent of the asked rates are 2 percent for yen, 3 percent for Canadian dollars, and 5 percent for Swiss francs. Show, in a table similar to the one above, the bid rates for the different spot and forward rates.

17-5 You own $10,000. The dollar rate in Tokyo is 216.6743. The yen rate in New York is given in the previous table. Are arbitrage profits possible? Set up an arbitrage scheme with your capital. What is the gain (loss) in dollars?

17-6 Compute the Canadian dollar/yen and the yen/Swiss franc spot rate from the data in the table above.

COMPREHENSIVE PROBLEM

For your job as the business reporter for a local newspaper, you are given the assignment of putting together a series of articles on the multinational finance and the international currency markets for your readers. Much recent local press coverage has been given to losses in the foreign exchange markets by JGAR, a local firm that is the subsidiary of Daedlufetarg, a large German manufacturing firm. Your editor would like you to address several specific questions dealing with multinational finance. Prepare a response to the following memorandum from your editor:

TO: Business Reporter

FROM: Perry White, Editor, *Daily Planet*

RE: Upcoming Series on Multinational Finance

In your upcoming series on multinational finance, I would like to make sure you cover several specific points. In addition, before you begin this assignment, I want to make sure we are all reading from the same script because accuracy has always been the cornerstone of the *Daily Planet*. I'd like a response to the following questions before we proceed:

    a. What new problems and factors are encountered in international as opposed to domestic financial management?

    b. What does the term *arbitrage profits* mean?

    c. What can a firm do to reduce exchange risk?

    d. What are the differences between a forward contract, a futures contract, and options?

Use the following data in your response to the remaining questions:

e. An American business needs to pay (a) 15,000 Canadian dollars, (b) 1.5 million yen, and (c) 55,000 Swiss francs to businesses abroad. What are the dollar payments to the respective countries?

f. An American business pays $20,000, $5,000, and $15,000 to suppliers in, respectively, Japan, Switzerland, and Canada. How much, in local currencies, do the suppliers receive?

g. Compute the indirect quote for the spot and forward Canadian dollar contract.

h. You own $10,000. The dollar rate in Tokyo is 216.6752. The yen rate in New York is given in the table above. Are arbitrage profits possible? Set up an arbitrage scheme with your capital. What is the gain (loss) in dollars?

i. Compute the Canadian dollar/yen spot rate from the data in the table above.

SELF-TEST SOLUTIONS

ST-1

The German rate is 2.5823 marks/$1, while the (indirect) New York rate is 1/.3893 = 2.5687 marks/$.

Assuming no transaction costs, the rates between Germany and New York are out of line. Thus, arbitrage profits are possible.

Step 1: Because the mark is cheaper in Germany, buy $10,000 worth of marks in Germany. The number of marks purchased would be $10,000 × 2.5823 = 25,823 marks

Step 2: Simultaneously sell the marks in New York at the prevailing rate. The amount received upon the sale of the marks would be:

$$25,823 \text{ marks} \times \$.3893/\text{mark} = \$10,052.89$$

net gain is $10,052.89 − $10,000 = $52.89

USING A CALCULATOR

As you prepare for a career in business, the ability to use a financial calculator is essential, whether you are in the finance division or the marketing department. For most positions, it will be assumed that you can use a calculator in making computations that at one time were simply not possible without extensive time and effort. The following examples let us see what is possible, but they represent only the beginning of using the calculator in finance.

With just a little time and effort, you will be surprised at how much you can do with the calculator, such as calculating a stock's beta, or determining the value of a bond on a specific day given the exact date of maturity, or finding net present values and internal rates of return, or calculating the standard deviation. The list is almost endless.

In demonstrating how calculators may make our work easier, we must first decide which calculator to use. The options are numerous and largely depend on personal preference. We have chosen the Texas Instruments BAII Plus.

We will limit our discussion to the following issues:

    I. Introductory Comments
   II. An Important Starting Point
  III. Calculating Table Values for:
      A. Appendix B (Compound sum of $1)
      B. Appendix C (Present value of $1)
      C. Appendix D (Sum of an annuity of $1 for n periods)
      D. Appendix E (Present value of an annuity of $1 for n periods)
   IV. Calculating Present Values
    V. Calculating Future Values (Compound sum)
   VI. Calculating the Number of Payments or Receipts
  VII. Calculating the Payment Amount
 VIII. Calculating the Interest Rate
   IX. Bond Valuation
      A. Computing the value of a bond
      B. Calculating the yield to maturity of a bond
    X. Computing the Net Present Value and Internal Rate of Return
      A. Where future cash flows are equal amounts in each period (annuity)
      B. Where future cash flows are unequal amounts in each period

I. Introductory Comments

In the examples that follow, you are told (1) which keystrokes to use, (2) the resulting appearance of the calculator display, and (3) a supporting explanation.

The keystrokes column tells you which keys to press. The keystrokes shown in a white box tell you to use one of the calculator's dedicated or "hard" keys. For example, if +/− is shown in the keystrokes instruction column, press that key on the keyboard of the calculator. To use a function printed in a shaded box above a dedicated key, always press the shaded key 2nd first, then the function key.

II. An Important Starting Point

Example: You want to display four numbers to the right of the decimal.

Keystrokes	Display	Explanation
2nd FORMAT 4 ENTER	DEC= DEC= 4.0000	Sets display to show four numbers to the right of the decimal
CE/C CE/C	0.0000	Clears display

Example: You want to display two payments per year to be paid at the end of each period.

Keystrokes	Display	Explanation
2nd P/Y 2 ENTER 2nd	P/Y = P/Y = 2.0000	Sets number of payments per year at 2
BGN	END	Sets timing of payment at the end of each period
CE/C CE/C	0.0000	Clears display

III. Calculating Table Values

A. The compound sum of $1 (Appendix B)

Example: What is the table value for the compound sum of $1 for 5 years at a 12 percent annual interest rate?

Keystrokes	Display	Explanation
2nd P/Y 1 ENTER 2nd	P/Y = P/Y = 1.0000	Sets number of payments per year at 1
BGN	END	Sets timing of payment at the end of each period
CE/C CE/C	0.0000	Clears display
2nd CLR TVM	0.0000	Clears TVM variables
1 +/- PV	PV = −1.0000	Stores initial $1 as a negative present value. Otherwise the answer will appear as negative.
5 N	N = 5.0000	Stores number of periods
12 I/Y	I/Y = 12.0000	Stores interest rate
CPT FV	FV = 1.7623	Table value

III. Calculating Table Values (continued)

B. The present value of $1 (Appendix C)

Example: What is the table value for the present value of $1 for 8 years at a 10 percent annual interest rate?

Keystrokes	Display	Explanation
2nd P/Y 1 ENTER	P/Y = P/Y = 1.0000	Sets number of payments per year at 1
2nd BGN	END	Sets timing of payment at the end of each period
CE/C CE/C	0.0000	Clears display
2nd CLR TVM	0.0000	Clears TVM variables
1 +/− FV	FV = −1.0000	Stores future amount as negative value
8 N	N = 8.0000	Stores number of periods
10 I/Y	I/Y = 10.0000	Stores interest rate
CPT PV	PV = 0.4665	Table value

C. The sum of an annuity of $1 for *n* periods (Appendix D)

Example: What is the table value for the compound sum of an annuity of $1 for 6 years at a 14 percent annual interest rate?

Keystrokes	Display	Explanation
2nd P/Y 1 ENTER	P/Y = P/Y = 1.0000	Sets number of payments per year at 1
2nd BGN	END	Sets timing of payment at the end of each period
CE/C CE/C	0.0000	Clears display
2nd CLR TVM	0.0000	Clears TVM variables
1 +/− PMT	PMT = −1.0000	Stores annual payment (annuity) as a negative number. Otherwise the answer will appear as a negative.
6 N	N = 6.0000	Stores number of periods
14 I/Y	I/Y = 14.0000	Stores interest rate
CPT FV	FV = 8.5355	Table value

III. Calculating Table Values (continued)

D. The present value of an annuity of $1 for *n* periods (Appendix E)

Example: What is the table value for the present value of an annuity of $1 for 12 years at 9 percent annual interest rate?

Keystrokes	Display	Explanation
2nd P/Y 1 ENTER	P/Y = P/Y = 1.0000	Sets number of payments per year at 1
2nd BGN	END	Sets timing of payment at the end of each period
CE/C CE/C	0.0000	Clears display
2nd CLR TVM	0.0000	Clears TVM variables
1 +/− PMT	PMT = −1.0000	Stores annual payment (annuity) as a negative number. Otherwise the answer will appear as a negative.
12 N	N = 12.0000	Stores number of periods
9 I/Y	I/Y = 9.0000	Stores interest rate
CPT PV	PV = 7.1607	Table value

IV. Calculating Present Values

Example: You are considering the purchase of a franchise of quick oil-change locations, which you believe will provide an annual cash flow of $50,000. At the end of 10 years, you believe that you will be able to sell the franchise for an estimated $900,000. Calculate the maximum amount you should pay for the franchise (present value) in order to realize at least an 18 percent annual yield.

Keystrokes	Display	Explanation
2nd BGN	END	Sets timing of payment at the end of each period
CE/C CE/C	0.0000	Clears display
2nd CLR TVM	0.0000	Clears TVM variables
10 N	N = 10.0000	Stores *n*, the holding period
18 I/Y	I/Y = 18.0000	Stores *i*, the required rate of return
50,000 PMT	PMT = 50,000.0000	Stores PMT, the annual cash flow to be received
900,000 FV	FV = 900,000.0000	Stores FV, the cash flow to be received at the end of the project

IV. Calculating Present Values (continued)

CPT PV	PV = −396,662.3350	The present value, given a required rate of return of 18 percent. (Note: The present value is displayed with a minus sign since it represents cash paid out.)

V. Calculating Future Values (Compound Sum)

Example: If you deposit $300 a month (at the beginning of each month) into a new account that pays 6.25 percent annual interest compounded monthly, how much will you have in the account after 5 years?

Keystrokes	Display	Explanation
2nd BGN	END	Sets timing of payment at the end of each period
2nd SET	BGN	Sets timing of payments to beginning of each period
2nd P/Y 12 ENTER	P/Y = P/Y = 12.0000	Sets 12 payments per year
CE/C CE/C	0.0000	Clears display
2nd CLR TVM	0.0000	Clears TVM variables
60 N	N = 60.0000	Stores n, the number of months for the investment
6.25 I/Y	I/Y = 6.2500	Stores i, the annual rate
300 +/− PMT	PMT = −300.0000	Stores PMT, the monthly amount invested (with a minus sign for cash paid out)
CPT FV	FV = 21,175.7613	The future value after 5 years

VI. Calculating the Number of Payments or Receipts

Example: If you wish to retire with $500,000 saved, and can only afford payments of $500 each month, how long will you have to contribute toward your retirement if you can earn a 10 percent return on your contributions?

Keystrokes	Display	Explanation
2nd BGN	BGN	Verifies timing of payment at the beginning of each period
2nd P/Y 12 ENTER	P/Y = 12.0000 P/Y = 12.0000	Sets 12 payments per year

VI. Calculating the Number of Payments or Receipts (continued)

Keystrokes	Display	Explanation
CE/C CE/C	0.0000	Clears display
2nd CLR TVM	0.0000	Clears TVM variables
10 I/Y	I/Y = 10.0000	Stores i, the interest rate
500 +/− PMT	PMT = −2500.0000	Stores PMT, the monthly amount invested (with a minus sign for cash paid out)
500,000 FV	FV = 500,000.0000	The value we want to achieve
CPT N	N = 268.2539	Number of months (since we considered monthly payments) required to achieve our goal

VII. Calculating the Payment Amount

Example: Suppose your retirement needs were $750,000. If you are currently 25 years old and plan to retire at age 65, how much will you have to contribute each month for retirement if you can earn 12.5 percent on your savings?

Keystrokes	Display	Explanation
2nd BGN	BGN	Verifies timing of payment at the beginning of each period
2nd P/Y 12 ENTER	P/Y = 12.0000 P/Y = 12.0000	Sets 12 payments per year
CE/C CE/C	0.0000	Clears display
2nd CLR TVM	0.0000	Clears TVM variables
12.5 I/Y	I/Y = 12.5000	Stores i, the interest rate
480 N	N = 480.0000	Stores n, the number of periods until we stop contributing (40 years × 12 months/year = 480 months)
750,000 FV	FV = 750,000.0000	The value we want to achieve
CPT PMT	PMT = −53.8347	Monthly contribution required to achieve our ultimate goal (shown as negative since it represents cash paid out)

VIII. Calculating the Interest Rate

Example: If you invest $300 at the end of each month for 6 years (72 months) for a promised $30,000 return at the end, what interest rate are you earning on your investment?

Keystrokes	Display	Explanation
2nd BGN	BGN	Sets timing of payments to beginning of each period
2nd SET	END	Sets timing of payments to end of each period
2nd P/Y 12 ENTER	P/Y = 12.0000 P/Y = 12.0000	Sets 12 payments per year
CE/C CE/C	0.0000	Clears display
2nd CLR TVM	0.0000	Clears TVM variables
72 N	N = 72.0000	Stores n, the number of deposits (investments)
300 +/− PMT	PMT = −300.0000	Stores PMT, the monthly amount invested (with a minus sign for cash paid out)
30,000 FV	FV = 30,000.0000	Stores the future value to be received in 6 years
CPT I/Y	I/Y = 10.5892	The annual interest rate earned on the investment

IX. Bond Valuation

A. Computing the value of a bond

Example: Assume the current date is January 1, 1993, and that you want to know the value of a bond that matures in 10 years and has a coupon rate of 9 percent (4.5 percent semiannually). Your required rate of return is 12 percent.

Keystrokes	Display	Explanation
2nd BGN	END	Verifies timing of payments to end of each period
2nd P/Y 2 ENTER	P/Y = 12.0000 P/Y = 2.0000	Sets 2 payments per year; end mode (END) assumes cash flows are at the end of each 6-month period
CE/C CE/C	0.0000	Clears display
2nd CLR TVM	0.0000	Clears TVM variables
20 N	N = 20.0000	Stores the number of semiannual periods (10 years × 2)

IX. Bond Valuation (continued)

12 I/Y	I/Y = 12.0000	Stores annual rate of return
45 PMT	PMT = 45.0000	Stores the semiannual interest payment
1,000 FV	FV = 1,000.0000	Stores the bond's maturity or par value
CPT PV	PV = −827.9512	Value of the bond, expressed as a negative number

Solution Using the Bond Feature:

CE/C CE/C 2nd	0.0000	Clears display
BOND 2nd	STD = 1-01-1970	(This will be the last date entered)
CLR WORK	STD = 1-01-1970	Clears BOND variables
1.01.93 ENTER	STD = 1-01-1993	Stores the current date (month, date, year)
↓	CPN = 0.0000	
9 ENTER	CPN = 9.0000	Stores the coupon interest rate
↓	RDT = 12-31-1990	(This will be the last date entered)
1.01.03 ENTER	RDT = 1-01-2003	Stores the maturity date in 10 years
↓	RV = 100.0000	Verifies bond maturity or par value
↓ 2nd	ACT	
SET	360	Sets calculations to be based on 360-day year
↓	2/Y	Verifies semiannual compounding rate
↓	YLD = 0.0000	
12 ENTER	YLD = 12.0000	Stores the investor's required rate of return
↓	PRI = 0.0000	
CPT	PRI = 82.7951	Value of bond as a percent of par value; i.e., value of bond is $827.95

IX. Bond Valuation

B. Computing the yield to maturity of a bond

Example: Assume the current date is January 1, 1994, and that you want to know your yield to maturity on a bond that matures in 8 years and has a coupon rate of 12 percent (6 percent semiannually). The bond is selling for $1,100.

Keystrokes	Display	Explanation
2nd BGN	END	Verifies timing of payments to end of each period

IX. Bond Valuation (continued)

2nd P/Y 2 ENTER	P/Y = 12.0000 P/Y = 2.0000	Sets 2 payments per year; end mode (END) assumes cash flows are at the end of each 6-month period
CE/C CE/C	0.0000	Clears display
2nd CLR TVM	0.0000	Clears TVM variables
16 N	N = 16.0000	Stores the number of semiannual periods (8 years × 2)
1100 +/− PV	PV = −1,100.0000	Value of the bond, expressed as a negative number
60 PMT	PMT = 60.0000	Stores the semiannual interest payments
1,000 FV	FV = 1,000.0000	Stores the bond's maturity or par value
CPT I/Y	I/Y = 10.1451	The yield to maturity, expressed on an annual basis

Solution Using the Bond Feature:

CE/C CE/C 2nd Bond 2nd CLR WORK 1.03.94 ENTER	0.0000 STD = 1-01-1993 STD = 1-01-1993 STD = 1-03-1994	Clears display (This will be the last date entered) Clears BOND variables Stores the current date (month, date, year)
↓ 12 ENTER	CPN = 0.0000 CPN = 12.0000	 Stores the coupon interest rate
↓ 1.03.02 ENTER ↓ ↓ 2nd SET ↓ ↓ ↓	RDT = 1-01-2003 RDT = 1-03-2002 RV = 100.0000 ACT 360 2/Y YLD = 0.0000 PRI = 0.0000	(This will be the last date entered) Stores the maturity date in 8 years Verifies bonds maturity or par value Sets calculations to be based on 360-day year Verifies semiannual compounding rate
110 ENTER	PRI = 110.0000	Stores the bond value as a percentage of par value
↑ CPT	YLD = 0.0000 YLD = 10.1451	 Bond's yield to maturity

X. Computing the Net Present Value and Internal Rate of Return

A. Where future cash flows are equal amounts in each period (annuity)

Example: The firm is considering a capital project that would cost $80,000. The firm's cost of capital is 12 percent. The project life is 10 years, during which time the firm expects to receive $15,000 per year. Calculate the NPV and the IRR.

Keystrokes	Display	Explanation
2nd BGN	END	Verifies timing of payments to end of each period
2nd P/Y 1 ENTER	P/Y = 12.0000 P/Y = 1.0000	Sets 1 payment per year; end mode (END) assumes cash flows are at the end of each year
CE/C CE/C	0.0000	Clears display
2nd CLR TVM	0.0000	Clears TVM variables
15,000 PMT	PMT = 15.0000	Stores the annual cash flows of $15,000
10 N	N = 10.0000	Stores the life of the project
12 I/Y	I/Y = 12.0000	Stores the cost of capital
CPT PV +/−	PV = −84,753.3454 PV = 84,753.3454	Calculates present value Changes PV to positive
−80,000 =	4,753.3454	Calculates net present value by subtracting the cost of the project
80,000 +/− PV CPT I/Y	−80,000.0000 PV = −80,000.0000 I/Y = 13.4344	Calculates the IRR

B. Where future cash flows are unequal amounts in each period

Example: The firm is considering a capital project that would cost $110,000. The firm's cost of capital is 15 percent. The project life is 5 years, with the following expected cash flows: $−25,000, $50,000, $60,000, $60,000 and $70,000. In addition, you expect to receive $30,000 in the last year from the salvage value of the equipment. Calculate the NPV and IRR.

Keystrokes	Display	Explanation
CE/C CE/C CF 2nd	0.0000 CF$_0$ = 0.0000	Clears display
CLR WORK	CF$_0$ = 0.0000	Clears cash flow variables
110,000 +/− ENTER	CF$_0$ = −10,000.0000	Stores CF$_0$, the initial investment (with a minus sign for a negative cash flow)

X. Computing the Net Present Value and Internal Rate of Return (continued)

↓ 25,000 +/− ENTER	CO1 = 0.0000 CO1 = 25,000.0000	Stores CF_1, the first year's cash flow (with a minus sign for a negative cash flow)
↓ ENTER	FO1 = 1.0000	Stores the number of years CF_1 is repeated (in this case, 1 year only)
↓ 50,000 ENTER	CO2 = 0.0000 CO2 = 50,000.0000	Stores CF_2
↓ ENTER	FO2 = 1.0000 FO2 = 1.0000	Stores the number of years CF_2 is repeated
↓ 60,000 ENTER	CO3 = 0.0000 CO3 = 60,000.0000	Stores CF_3
↓ 2 ENTER	FO3 = 2.0000	Stores the number of years CF_3 is repeated (here, 2 years, so our response is 2 to the FO_3 prompt)
↓ 100,000 ENTER	CO4 = 0.0000 CO4 = 100,000.0000	Stores CF_4, $70,000 plus expected $30,000
↓ ENTER	FO4 = 1.0000	Stores the number CF_4
2nd QUIT	0.0000	Ends storage of individual cash flows
NPV 15 ENTER	I = 0.0000 I = 15.0000	Stores interest rate
↓ CPT	NPV = 0.0000 NPV = 29,541.8951	Calculates the project's NPV at the stated interest rate
IRR CPT	IRR = 0.0000 IRR = 22.0633	Calculates the project's IRR

APPENDIX B

COMPOUND SUM OF $1

n	1%	2%	3%	4%	5%	6%	7%	8%	9%	10%
1	1.010	1.020	1.030	1.040	1.050	1.060	1.070	1.080	1.090	1.100
2	1.020	1.040	1.061	1.082	1.102	1.124	1.145	1.166	1.188	1.210
3	1.030	1.061	1.093	1.125	1.158	1.191	1.225	1.260	1.295	1.331
4	1.041	1.082	1.126	1.170	1.216	1.262	1.311	1.360	1.412	1.464
5	1.051	1.104	1.159	1.217	1.276	1.338	1.403	1.469	1.539	1.611
6	1.062	1.126	1.194	1.265	1.340	1.419	1.501	1.587	1.677	1.772
7	1.072	1.149	1.230	1.316	1.407	1.504	1.606	1.714	1.828	1.949
8	1.083	1.172	1.267	1.369	1.477	1.594	1.718	1.851	1.993	2.144
9	1.094	1.195	1.305	1.423	1.551	1.689	1.838	1.999	2.172	2.358
10	1.105	1.219	1.344	1.480	1.629	1.791	1.967	2.159	2.367	2.594
11	1.116	1.243	1.384	1.539	1.710	1.898	2.105	2.332	2.580	2.853
12	1.127	1.268	1.426	1.601	1.796	2.012	2.252	2.518	2.813	3.138
13	1.138	1.294	1.469	1.665	1.886	2.133	2.410	2.720	3.066	3.452
14	1.149	1.319	1.513	1.732	1.980	2.261	2.579	2.937	3.342	3.797
15	1.161	1.346	1.558	1.801	2.079	2.397	2.759	3.172	3.642	4.177
16	1.173	1.373	1.605	1.873	2.183	2.540	2.952	3.426	3.970	4.595
17	1.184	1.400	1.653	1.948	2.292	2.693	3.159	3.700	4.328	5.054
18	1.196	1.428	1.702	2.026	2.407	2.854	3.380	3.996	4.717	5.560
19	1.208	1.457	1.753	2.107	2.527	3.026	3.616	4.316	5.142	6.116
20	1.220	1.486	1.806	2.191	2.653	3.207	3.870	4.661	5.604	6.727
21	1.232	1.516	1.860	2.279	2.786	3.399	4.140	5.034	6.109	7.400
22	1.245	1.546	1.916	2.370	2.925	3.603	4.430	5.436	6.658	8.140
23	1.257	1.577	1.974	2.465	3.071	3.820	4.740	5.871	7.258	8.954
24	1.270	1.608	2.033	2.563	3.225	4.049	5.072	6.341	7.911	9.850
25	1.282	1.641	2.094	2.666	3.386	4.292	5.427	6.848	8.623	10.834
30	1.348	1.811	2.427	3.243	4.322	5.743	7.612	10.062	13.267	17.449
40	1.489	2.208	3.262	4.801	7.040	10.285	14.974	21.724	31.408	45.258
50	1.645	2.691	4.384	7.106	11.467	18.419	29.456	46.900	74.354	117.386

n	11%	12%	13%	14%	15%	16%	17%	18%	19%	20%
1	1.110	1.120	1.130	1.140	1.150	1.160	1.170	1.180	1.190	1.200
2	1.232	1.254	1.277	1.300	1.322	1.346	1.369	1.392	1.416	1.440
3	1.368	1.405	1.443	1.482	1.521	1.561	1.602	1.643	1.685	1.728
4	1.518	1.574	1.630	1.689	1.749	1.811	1.874	1.939	2.005	2.074
5	1.685	1.762	1.842	1.925	2.011	2.100	2.192	2.288	2.386	2.488
6	1.870	1.974	2.082	2.195	2.313	2.436	2.565	2.700	2.840	2.986
7	2.076	2.211	2.353	2.502	2.660	2.826	3.001	3.185	3.379	3.583
8	2.305	2.476	2.658	2.853	3.059	3.278	3.511	3.759	4.021	4.300
9	2.558	2.773	3.004	3.252	3.518	3.803	4.108	4.435	4.785	5.160
10	2.839	3.106	3.395	3.707	4.046	4.411	4.807	5.234	5.695	6.192
11	3.152	3.479	3.836	4.226	4.652	5.117	5.624	6.176	6.777	7.430
12	3.498	3.896	4.334	4.818	5.350	5.936	6.580	7.288	8.064	8.916
13	3.883	4.363	4.898	5.492	6.153	6.886	7.699	8.599	9.596	10.699
14	4.310	4.887	5.535	6.261	7.076	7.987	9.007	10.147	11.420	12.839
15	4.785	5.474	6.254	7.138	8.137	9.265	10.539	11.974	13.589	15.407
16	5.311	6.130	7.067	8.137	9.358	10.748	12.330	14.129	16.171	18.488
17	5.895	6.866	7.986	9.276	10.761	12.468	14.426	16.672	19.244	22.186
18	6.543	7.690	9.024	10.575	12.375	14.462	16.879	19.673	22.900	26.623

COMPOUND SUM OF $1 (continued)

n	11%	12%	13%	14%	15%	16%	17%	18%	19%	20%
19	7.263	8.613	10.197	12.055	14.232	16.776	19.748	23.214	27.251	31.948
20	8.062	9.646	11.523	13.743	16.366	19.461	23.105	27.393	32.429	38.337
21	8.949	10.804	13.021	15.667	18.821	22.574	27.033	32.323	38.591	46.005
22	9.933	12.100	14.713	17.861	21.644	26.186	31.629	38.141	45.923	55.205
23	11.026	13.552	16.626	20.361	24.891	30.376	37.005	45.007	54.648	66.247
24	12.239	15.178	18.788	23.212	28.625	35.236	43.296	53.108	65.031	79.496
25	13.585	17.000	21.230	26.461	32.918	40.874	50.656	62.667	77.387	95.395
30	22.892	29.960	39.115	50.949	66.210	85.849	111.061	143.367	184.672	237.373
40	64.999	93.049	132.776	188.876	267.856	378.715	533.846	750.353	1051.642	1469.740
50	184.559	288.996	450.711	700.197	1083.619	1670.669	2566.080	3927.189	5988.730	9100.191

n	21%	22%	23%	24%	25%	26%	27%	28%	29%	30%
1	1.210	1.220	1.230	1.240	1.250	1.260	1.270	1.280	1.290	1.300
2	1.464	1.488	1.513	1.538	1.562	1.588	1.613	1.638	1.664	1.690
3	1.772	1.816	1.861	1.907	1.953	2.000	2.048	2.097	2.147	2.197
4	2.144	2.215	2.289	2.364	2.441	2.520	2.601	2.684	2.769	2.856
5	2.594	2.703	2.815	2.932	3.052	3.176	3.304	3.436	3.572	3.713
6	3.138	3.297	3.463	3.635	3.815	4.001	4.196	4.398	4.608	4.827
7	3.797	4.023	4.259	4.508	4.768	5.042	5.329	5.629	5.945	6.275
8	4.595	4.908	5.239	5.589	5.960	6.353	6.767	7.206	7.669	8.157
9	5.560	5.987	6.444	6.931	7.451	8.004	8.595	9.223	9.893	10.604
10	6.727	7.305	7.926	8.594	9.313	10.086	10.915	11.806	12.761	13.786
11	8.140	8.912	9.749	10.657	11.642	12.708	13.862	15.112	16.462	17.921
12	9.850	10.872	11.991	13.215	14.552	16.012	17.605	19.343	21.236	23.298
13	11.918	13.264	14.749	16.386	18.190	20.175	22.359	24.759	27.395	30.287
14	14.421	16.182	18.141	20.319	22.737	25.420	28.395	31.691	35.339	39.373
15	17.449	19.742	22.314	25.195	28.422	32.030	36.062	40.565	45.587	51.185
16	21.113	24.085	27.446	31.242	35.527	40.357	45.799	51.923	58.808	66.541
17	25.547	29.384	33.758	38.740	44.409	50.850	58.165	66.461	75.862	86.503
18	30.912	35.848	41.523	48.038	55.511	64.071	73.869	85.070	97.862	112.454
19	37.404	43.735	51.073	59.567	69.389	80.730	93.813	108.890	126.242	146.190
20	45.258	53.357	62.820	73.863	86.736	101.720	119.143	139.379	162.852	190.047
21	54.762	65.095	77.268	91.591	108.420	128.167	151.312	178.405	210.079	247.061
22	66.262	79.416	95.040	113.572	135.525	161.490	192.165	228.358	271.002	321.178
23	80.178	96.887	116.899	140.829	169.407	203.477	244.050	292.298	349.592	417.531
24	97.015	118.203	143.786	174.628	211.758	256.381	309.943	374.141	450.974	542.791
25	117.388	144.207	176.857	216.539	264.698	323.040	393.628	478.901	581.756	705.627
30	304.471	389.748	497.904	634.810	807.793	1025.904	1300.477	1645.488	2078.208	2619.936
40	2048.309	2846.941	3946.340	5455.797	7523.156	10346.879	14195.051	19426.418	26520.723	36117.754
50	13779.844	20795.680	31278.301	46889.207	70064.812	104354.562	154942.687	229345.875	338440.000	497910.125

n	31%	32%	33%	34%	35%	36%	37%	38%	39%	40%
1	1.310	1.320	1.330	1.340	1.350	1.360	1.370	1.380	1.390	1.400
2	1.716	1.742	1.769	1.796	1.822	1.850	1.877	1.904	1.932	1.960
3	2.248	2.300	2.353	2.406	2.460	2.515	2.571	2.628	2.686	2.744
4	2.945	3.036	3.129	3.224	3.321	3.421	3.523	3.627	3.733	3.842
5	3.858	4.007	4.162	4.320	4.484	4.653	4.826	5.005	5.189	5.378
6	5.054	5.290	5.535	5.789	6.053	6.328	6.612	6.907	7.213	7.530
7	6.621	6.983	7.361	7.758	8.172	8.605	9.058	9.531	10.025	10.541
8	8.673	9.217	9.791	10.395	11.032	11.703	12.410	13.153	13.935	14.758
9	11.362	12.166	13.022	13.930	14.894	15.917	17.001	18.151	19.370	20.661
10	14.884	16.060	17.319	18.666	20.106	21.646	23.292	25.049	26.924	28.925
11	19.498	21.199	23.034	25.012	27.144	29.439	31.910	34.567	37.425	40.495
12	25.542	27.982	30.635	33.516	36.644	40.037	43.716	47.703	52.020	56.694
13	33.460	36.937	40.745	44.912	49.469	54.451	59.892	65.830	72.308	79.371
14	43.832	49.756	54.190	60.181	66.784	74.053	82.051	90.845	100.509	111.190

COMPOUND SUM OF $1 (continued)

n	31%	32%	33%	34%	35%	36%	37%	38%	39%	40%
15	57.420	64.358	72.073	80.643	90.158	100.712	112.410	125.366	139.707	155.567
16	75.220	84.953	95.857	108.061	121.713	136.968	154.002	173.005	194.192	217.793
17	98.539	112.138	127.490	144.802	164.312	186.277	210.983	238.747	269.927	304.911
18	129.086	148.022	169.561	194.035	221.822	253.337	289.046	329.471	375.198	426.875
19	169.102	195.389	225.517	260.006	299.459	344.537	395.993	454.669	521.525	597.625
20	221.523	257.913	299.937	348.408	404.270	468.571	542.511	627.443	724.919	836.674
21	290.196	340.446	398.916	466.867	545.764	637.256	743.240	865.871	1007.637	1171.343
22	380.156	449.388	530.558	625.601	736.781	865.668	1018.238	1194.900	1400.615	1639.878
23	498.004	593.192	705.642	838.305	994.653	1178.668	1394.986	1648.961	1946.854	2295.829
24	652.385	783.013	938.504	1123.328	1342.781	1602.988	1911.129	2275.564	2706.125	3214.158
25	854.623	1033.577	1248.210	1505.258	1812.754	2180.063	2618.245	3140.275	3761.511	4499.816
30	3297.081	4142.008	5194.516	6503.285	8128.426	10142.914	12636.086	15716.703	19517.969	24201.043
40	49072.621	66519.313	89962.188	121388.437	163433.875	219558.625	294317.937	393684.687	525508.312	700022.688

APPENDIX C

PRESENT VALUE OF OF $1

n	1%	2%	3%	4%	5%	6%	7%	8%	9%	10%
1	.990	.980	.971	.962	.952	.943	.935	.926	.917	.909
2	.980	.961	.943	.925	.907	.890	.873	.857	.842	.826
3	.971	.942	.915	.889	.864	.840	.816	.794	.772	.751
4	.961	.924	.888	.855	.823	.792	.763	.735	.708	.683
5	.951	.906	.863	.822	.784	.747	.713	.681	.650	.621
6	.942	.888	.837	.790	.746	.705	.666	.630	.596	.564
7	.933	.871	.813	.760	.711	.665	.623	.583	.547	.513
8	.923	.853	.789	.731	.677	.627	.582	.540	.502	.467
9	.914	.837	.766	.703	.645	.592	.544	.500	.460	.424
10	.905	.820	.744	.676	.614	.558	.508	.463	.422	.386
11	.896	.804	.722	.650	.585	.527	.475	.429	.388	.350
12	.887	.789	.701	.625	.557	.497	.444	.397	.356	.319
13	.879	.773	.681	.601	.530	.469	.415	.368	.326	.290
14	.870	.758	.661	.577	.505	.442	.388	.340	.299	.263
15	.861	.743	.642	.555	.481	.417	.362	.315	.275	.239
16	.853	.728	.623	.534	.458	.394	.339	.292	.252	.218
17	.844	.714	.605	.513	.436	.371	.317	.270	.231	.198
18	.836	.700	.587	.494	.416	.350	.296	.250	.212	.180
19	.828	.686	.570	.475	.396	.331	.277	.232	.194	.164
20	.820	.673	.554	.456	.377	.312	.258	.215	.178	.149
21	.811	.660	.538	.439	.359	.294	.242	.199	.164	.135
22	.803	.647	.522	.422	.342	.278	.226	.184	.150	.123
23	.795	.634	.507	.406	.326	.262	.211	.170	.138	.112
24	.788	.622	.492	.390	.310	.247	.197	.158	.126	.102
25	.780	.610	.478	.375	.295	.233	.184	.146	.116	.092
30	.742	.552	.412	.308	.231	.174	.131	.099	.075	.057
40	.672	.453	.307	.208	.142	.097	.067	.046	.032	.022
50	.608	.372	.228	.141	.087	.054	.034	.021	.013	.009

n	11%	12%	13%	14%	15%	16%	17%	18%	19%	20%
1	.901	.893	.885	.877	.870	.862	.855	.847	.840	.833
2	.812	.797	.783	.769	.756	.743	.731	.718	.706	.694
3	.731	.712	.693	.675	.658	.641	.624	.609	.593	.579
4	.659	.636	.613	.592	.572	.552	.534	.516	.499	.482
5	.593	.567	.543	.519	.497	.476	.456	.437	.419	.402
6	.535	.507	.480	.456	.432	.410	.390	.370	.352	.335
7	.482	.452	.425	.400	.376	.354	.333	.314	.296	.279
8	.434	.404	.376	.351	.327	.305	.285	.266	.249	.233
9	.391	.361	.333	.308	.284	.263	.243	.225	.209	.194
10	.352	.322	.295	.270	.247	.227	.208	.191	.176	.162
11	.317	.287	.261	.237	.215	.195	.178	.162	.148	.135
12	.286	.257	.231	.208	.187	.168	.152	.137	.124	.112
13	.258	.229	.204	.182	.163	.145	.130	.116	.104	.093
14	.232	.205	.181	.160	.141	.125	.111	.099	.088	.078
15	.209	.183	.160	.140	.123	.108	.095	.084	.074	.065
16	.188	.163	.141	.123	.107	.093	.081	.071	.062	.054

n	11%	12%	13%	14%	15%	16%	17%	18%	19%	20%
17	.170	.146	.125	.108	.093	.080	.069	.060	.052	.045
18	.153	.130	.111	.095	.081	.069	.059	.051	.044	.038
19	.138	.116	.098	.083	.070	.060	.051	.043	.037	.031
20	.124	.104	.087	.073	.061	.051	.043	.037	.031	.026
21	.112	.093	.077	.064	.053	.044	.037	.031	.026	.022
22	.101	.083	.068	.056	.046	.038	.032	.026	.022	.018
23	.091	.074	.060	.049	.040	.033	.027	.022	.018	.015
24	.082	.066	.053	.043	.035	.028	.023	.019	.015	.013
25	.074	.059	.047	.038	.030	.024	.020	.016	.013	.010
30	.044	.033	.026	.020	.015	.012	.009	.007	.005	.004
40	.015	.011	.008	.005	.004	.003	.002	.001	.001	.001
50	.005	.003	.002	.001	.001	.001	.000	.000	.000	.000

n	21%	22%	23%	24%	25%	26%	27%	28%	29%	30%
1	.826	.820	.813	.806	.800	.794	.787	.781	.775	.769
2	.683	.672	.661	.650	.640	.630	.620	.610	.601	.592
3	.564	.551	.537	.524	.512	.500	.488	.477	.466	.455
4	.467	.451	.437	.423	.410	.397	.384	.373	.361	.350
5	.386	.370	.355	.341	.328	.315	.303	.291	.280	.269
6	.319	.303	.289	.275	.262	.250	.238	.227	.217	.207
7	.263	.249	.235	.222	.210	.198	.188	.178	.168	.159
8	.218	.204	.191	.179	.168	.157	.148	.139	.130	.123
9	.180	.167	.155	.144	.134	.125	.116	.108	.101	.094
10	.149	.137	.126	.116	.107	.099	.092	.085	.078	.073
11	.123	.112	.103	.094	.086	.079	.072	.066	.061	.056
12	.102	.092	.083	.076	.069	.062	.057	.052	.047	.043
13	.084	.075	.068	.061	.055	.050	.045	.040	.037	.033
14	.069	.062	.055	.049	.044	.039	.035	.032	.028	.025
15	.057	.051	.045	.040	.035	.031	.028	.025	.022	.020
16	.047	.042	.036	.032	.028	.025	.022	.019	.017	.015
17	.039	.034	.030	.026	.023	.020	.017	.015	.013	.012
18	.032	.028	.024	.021	.018	.016	.014	.012	010	.009
19	.027	.023	.020	.017	.014	.012	.011	.009	.008	.007
20	.022	.019	.016	.014	.012	.010	.008	.007	.006	.005
21	.018	.015	.013	.011	.009	.008	.007	.006	.005	.004
22	.015	.013	.011	.009	.007	.006	.005	.004	.004	.003
23	.012	.010	.009	.007	.006	.005	.004	.003	.003	.002
24	.010	.008	.007	.006	.005	.004	.003	.003	.002	.002
25	.009	.007	.006	.005	.004	.003	.003	.002	.002	.001
30	.003	.003	.002	.002	.001	.001	.001	.001	.000	.000
40	.000	.000	.000	.000	.000	.000	.000	.000	.000	.000
50	.000	.000	.000	.000	.000	.000	.000	.000	.000	.000

n	31%	32%	33%	34%	35%	36%	37%	38%	39%	40%
1	.763	.758	.752	.746	.741	.735	.730	.725	.719	.714
2	.583	.574	.565	.557	.549	.541	.533	.525	.518	.510
3	.445	.435	.425	.416	.406	.398	.389	.381	.372	.364
4	.340	.329	.320	.310	.301	.292	.284	.276	.268	.260
5	.259	.250	.240	.231	.223	.215	.207	.200	.193	.186
6	.198	.189	.181	.173	.165	.158	.151	.145	.139	.133
7	.151	.143	.136	.129	.122	.116	.110	.105	.100	.095
8	.115	.108	.102	.096	.091	.085	.081	.076	.072	.068
9	.088	.082	.077	.072	.067	.063	.059	.055	.052	.048

n	31%	32%	33%	34%	35%	36%	37%	38%	39%	40%
10	.067	.062	.058	.054	.050	.046	.043	.040	.037	.035
11	.051	.047	.043	.040	.037	.034	.031	.029	.027	.025
12	.039	.036	.033	.030	.027	.025	.023	.021	.019	.018
13	.030	.027	.025	.022	.020	.018	.017	.015	.014	.013
14	.023	.021	.018	.017	.015	.014	.012	.011	.010	.009
15	.017	.016	.014	.012	.011	.010	.009	.008	.007	.006
16	.013	.012	.010	.009	.008	.007	.006	.006	.005	.005
17	.010	.009	.008	.007	.006	.005	.005	.004	.004	.003
18	.008	.007	.006	.005	.005	.004	.003	.003	.003	.002
19	.006	.005	.004	.004	.003	.003	.003	.002	.002	.002
20	.005	.004	.003	.003	.002	.002	.002	.002	.001	.001
21	.003	.003	.003	.002	.002	.002	.001	.001	.001	.001
22	.003	.002	.002	.002	.001	.001	.001	.001	.001	.001
23	.002	.002	.001	.001	.001	.001	.001	.001	.001	.000
24	.002	.001	.001	.001	.001	.001	.001	.000	.000	.000
25	.001	.001	.001	.001	.001	.000	.000	.000	.000	.000
30	.000	.000	.000	.000	.000	.000	.000	.000	.000	.000
40	.000	.000	.000	.000	.000	.000	.000	.000	.000	.000

APPENDIX D

SUM OF AN ANNUITY OF $1 FOR n PERIODS

n	1%	2%	3%	4%	5%	6%	7%	8%	9%	10%
1	1.000	1.000	1.000	1.000	1.000	1.000	1.000	1.000	1.000	1.000
2	2.010	2.020	2.030	2.040	2.050	2.060	2.070	2.080	2.090	2.100
3	3.030	3.060	3.091	3.122	3.152	3.184	3.215	3.246	3.278	3.310
4	4.060	4.122	4.184	4.246	4.310	4.375	4.440	4.506	4.573	4.641
5	5.101	5.204	5.309	5.416	5.526	5.637	5.751	5.867	5.985	6.105
6	6.152	6.308	6.468	6.633	6.802	6.975	7.153	7.336	7.523	7.716
7	7.214	7.434	7.662	7.898	8.142	8.394	8.654	8.923	9.200	9.487
8	8.286	8.583	8.892	9.214	9.549	9.897	10.260	10.637	11.028	11.436
9	9.368	9.755	10.159	10.583	11.027	11.491	11.978	12.488	13.021	13.579
10	10.462	10.950	11.464	12.006	12.578	13.181	13.816	14.487	15.193	15.937
11	11.567	12.169	12.808	13.486	14.207	14.972	15.784	16.645	17.560	18.531
12	12.682	13.412	14.192	15.026	15.917	16.870	17.888	18.977	20.141	21.384
13	13.809	14.680	15.618	16.627	17.713	18.882	20.141	21.495	22.953	24.523
14	14.947	15.974	17.086	18.292	19.598	21.015	22.550	24.215	26.019	27.975
15	16.097	17.293	18.599	20.023	21.578	23.276	25.129	27.152	29.361	31.772
16	17.258	18.639	20.157	21.824	23.657	25.672	27.888	30.324	33.003	35.949
17	18.430	20.012	21.761	23.697	25.840	28.213	30.840	33.750	36.973	40.544
18	19.614	21.412	23.414	25.645	28.132	30.905	33.999	37.450	41.301	45.599
19	20.811	22.840	25.117	27.671	30.539	33.760	37.379	41.446	46.018	51.158
20	22.019	24.297	26.870	29.778	33.066	36.785	40.995	45.762	51.159	57.274
21	23.239	25.783	28.676	31.969	35.719	39.992	44.865	50.422	56.764	64.002
22	24.471	27.299	30.536	34.248	38.505	43.392	49.005	55.456	62.872	71.402
23	25.716	28.845	32.452	36.618	41.430	46.995	53.435	60.893	69.531	79.542
24	26.973	30.421	34.426	39.082	44.501	50.815	58.176	66.764	76.789	88.496
25	28.243	32.030	36.459	41.645	47.726	54.864	63.248	73.105	84.699	98.346
30	34.784	40.567	47.575	56.084	66.438	79.057	94.459	113.282	136.305	164.491
40	48.885	60.401	75.400	95.024	120.797	154.758	199.630	295.052	337.872	442.580
50	64.461	84.577	112.794	152.664	209.341	290.325	406.516	573.756	815.051	1163.865

n	11%	12%	13%	14%	15%	16%	17%	18%	19%	20%
1	1.000	1.000	1.000	1.000	1.000	1.000	1.000	1.000	1.000	1.000
2	2.110	2.120	2.130	2.140	2.150	2.160	2.170	2.180	2.190	2.200
3	3.342	3.374	3.407	3.440	3.472	3.506	3.539	3.572	3.606	3.640
4	4.710	4.779	4.850	4.921	4.993	5.066	5.141	5.215	5.291	5.368
5	6.228	6.353	6.480	6.610	6.742	6.877	7.014	7.154	7.297	7.442
6	7.913	8.115	8.323	8.535	8.754	8.977	9.207	9.442	9.683	9.930
7	9.783	10.089	10.405	10.730	11.067	11.414	11.772	12.141	12.523	12.916
8	11.859	12.300	12.757	13.233	13.727	14.240	14.773	15.327	15.902	16.499
9	14.164	14.776	15.416	16.085	16.786	17.518	18.285	19.086	19.923	20.799
10	16.722	17.549	18.420	19.337	20.304	21.321	22.393	23.521	24.709	25.959
11	19.561	20.655	21.814	23.044	24.349	25.733	27.200	28.755	30.403	32.150
12	22.713	24.133	25.650	27.271	29.001	30.850	32.824	34.931	37.180	39.580
13	26.211	28.029	29.984	32.088	34.352	36.786	39.404	42.218	45.244	48.496
14	30.095	32.392	34.882	37.581	40.504	43.672	47.102	50.818	54.841	59.196
15	34.405	37.280	40.417	43.842	47.580	51.659	56.109	60.965	66.260	72.035
16	39.190	42.753	46.671	50.980	55.717	60.925	66.648	72.938	79.850	87.442
17	44.500	48.883	53.738	59.117	65.075	71.673	78.978	87.067	96.021	105.930
18	50.396	55.749	61.724	68.393	75.836	84.140	93.404	103.739	115.265	128.116

n	11%	12%	13%	14%	15%	16%	17%	18%	19%	20%
19	56.939	63.439	70.748	78.968	88.211	98.603	110.283	123.412	138.165	154.739
20	64.202	72.052	80.946	91.024	102.443	115.379	130.031	146.626	165.417	186.687
21	72.264	81.698	92.468	104.767	118.809	134.840	153.136	174.019	197.846	225.024
22	81.213	92.502	105.489	120.434	137.630	157.414	180.169	206.342	236.436	271.028
23	91.147	104.602	120.203	138.295	159.274	183.600	211.798	244.483	282.359	326.234
24	102.173	118.154	136.829	158.656	184.166	213.976	248.803	289.490	337.007	392.480
25	114.412	133.333	155.616	181.867	212.790	249.212	292.099	342.598	402.038	471.976
30	199.018	241.330	293.192	356.778	434.738	530.306	647.423	790.932	966.698	1181.865
40	581.812	767.080	1013.667	1341.979	1779.048	2360.724	3134.412	4163.094	5529.711	7343.715
50	1668.723	2399.975	3459.344	4994.301	7217.488	10435.449	15088.805	21812.273	31514.492	45496.094

n	21%	22%	23%	24%	25%	26%	27%	28%	29%	30%
1	1.000	1.000	1.000	1.000	1.000	1.000	1.000	1.000	1.000	1.000
2	2.210	2.220	2.230	2.240	2.250	2.260	2.270	2.280	2.290	2.300
3	3.674	3.708	3.743	3.778	3.813	3.848	3.883	3.918	3.954	3.990
4	5.446	5.524	5.604	5.684	5.766	5.848	5.931	6.016	6.101	6.187
5	7.589	7.740	7.893	8.048	8.207	8.368	8.533	8.700	8.870	9.043
6	10.183	10.442	10.708	10.980	11.259	11.544	11.837	12.136	12.442	12.756
7	13.321	13.740	14.171	14.615	15.073	15.546	16.032	16.534	17.051	17.583
8	17.119	17.762	18.430	19.123	19.842	20.588	21.361	22.163	22.995	23.858
9	21.714	22.670	23.669	24.712	25.802	26.940	28.129	29.369	30.664	32.015
10	27.274	28.657	30.113	31.643	33.253	34.945	36.723	38.592	40.556	42.619
11	34.001	35.962	38.039	40.238	42.566	45.030	47.639	50.398	53.318	56.405
12	42.141	44.873	47.787	50.895	54.208	57.738	61.501	65.510	69.780	74.326
13	51.991	55.745	59.778	64.109	68.760	73.750	79.106	84.853	91.016	97.624
14	63.909	69.009	74.528	80.496	86.949	93.925	101.465	109.611	118.411	127.912
15	78.330	85.191	92.669	100.815	109.687	119.346	129.860	141.302	153.750	167.285
16	95.779	104.933	114.983	126.010	138.109	151.375	165.922	181.867	199.337	218.470
17	116.892	129.019	142.428	157.252	173.636	191.733	211.721	233.790	258.145	285.011
18	142.439	158.403	176.187	195.993	218.045	242.583	269.885	300.250	334.006	371.514
19	173.351	194.251	217.710	244.031	273.556	306.654	343.754	385.321	431.868	483.968
20	210.755	237.986	268.783	303.598	342.945	387.384	437.568	494.210	558.110	630.157
21	256.013	291.343	331.603	377.461	429.681	489.104	556.710	633.589	720.962	820.204
22	310.775	356.438	408.871	469.052	538.101	617.270	708.022	811.993	931.040	1067.265
23	377.038	435.854	503.911	582.624	673.626	778.760	990.187	1040.351	1202.042	1388.443
24	457.215	532.741	620.810	723.453	843.032	982.237	1144.237	1332.649	1551.634	1805.975
25	554.230	650.944	764.596	898.082	1054.791	1238.617	1454.180	1706.790	2002.608	2348.765
30	1445.111	1767.044	2160.459	2640.881	3227.172	3941.953	4812.891	5873.172	7162.785	8729.805
40	9749.141	12936.141	17153.691	22728.367	30088.621	39791.957	52570.707	69376.562	91447.375	120389.375

n	31%	32%	33%	34%	35%	36%	37%	38%	39%	40%
1	1.000	1.000	1.000	1.000	1.000	1.000	1.000	1.000	1.000	1.000
2	2.310	2.320	2.330	2.340	2.350	2.360	2.370	2.380	2.390	2.400
3	4.026	4.062	4.099	4.136	4.172	4.210	4.247	4.284	4.322	4.360
4	6.274	6.362	6.452	6.542	6.633	6.725	6.818	6.912	7.008	7.104
5	9.219	9.398	9.581	9.766	9.954	10.146	10.341	10.539	10.741	10.946
6	13.077	13.406	13.742	14.086	14.438	14.799	15.167	15.544	15.930	16.324
7	18.131	18.696	19.277	19.876	20.492	21.126	21.779	22.451	23.142	23.853
8	24.752	25.678	26.638	27.633	28.664	29.732	30.837	31.982	33.167	34.395
9	33.425	34.895	36.429	38.028	39.696	41.435	43.247	45.135	47.103	49.152
10	44.786	47.062	49.451	51.958	54.590	57.351	60.248	63.287	66.473	69.813
11	59.670	63.121	66.769	70.624	74.696	78.998	83.540	88.335	93.397	98.739
12	79.167	84.320	89.803	95.636	101.840	108.437	115.450	122.903	130.822	139.234
13	104.709	112.302	120.438	129.152	138.484	148.474	159.166	170.606	182.842	195.928
14	138.169	149.239	161.183	174.063	187.953	202.925	219.058	236.435	255.151	275.299

SUM OF AN ANNUITY OF $1 FOR n PERIODS (continued)

n	31%	32%	33%	34%	35%	36%	37%	38%	39%	40%
15	182.001	197.996	215.373	234.245	254.737	276.978	301.109	327.281	355.659	386.418
16	239.421	262.354	287.446	314.888	344.895	377.690	413.520	452.647	495.366	541.985
17	314.642	347.307	383.303	422.949	466.608	514.658	567.521	625.652	689.558	759.778
18	413.180	459.445	510.792	567.751	630.920	700.935	778.504	864.399	959.485	1064.689
19	542.266	607.467	680.354	761.786	852.741	954.271	1067.551	1193.870	1334.683	1491.563
20	711.368	802.856	905.870	1021.792	1152.200	1298.809	1463.544	1648.539	1856.208	2089.188
21	932.891	1060.769	1205.807	1370.201	1556.470	1767.380	2006.055	2275.982	2581.128	2925.862
22	1223.087	1401.215	1604.724	1837.068	2102.234	2404.636	2749.294	3141.852	3588.765	4097.203
23	1603.243	1850.603	2135.282	2462.669	2839.014	3271.304	3767.532	4336.750	4989.379	5737.078
24	2101.247	2443.795	2840.924	3300.974	3833.667	4449.969	5162.516	5985.711	6936.230	8032.906
25	2753.631	3226.808	3779.428	4424.301	5176.445	6052.957	7073.645	8261.273	9642.352	11247.062
30	10632.543	12940.672	15737.945	19124.434	23221.258	28172.016	34148.906	41357.227	50043.625	60500.207

APPENDIX E

PRESENT VALUE OF AN ANNUITY OF $1 FOR n PERIODS

n	1%	2%	3%	4%	5%	6%	7%	8%	9%	10%
1	.990	.980	.971	.962	.952	.943	.935	.926	.917	.909
2	1.970	1.942	1.913	1.886	1.859	1.833	1.808	1.3783	1.759	1.736
3	2.941	2.884	2.829	2.775	2.723	2.673	2.624	2.577	2.531	2.487
4	3.902	3.808	3.717	3.630	3.546	3.465	3.387	3.312	3.240	3.170
5	4.853	4.713	4.580	4.452	4.329	4.212	4.100	3.993	3.890	3.791
6	5.795	5.601	5.417	5.242	5.076	4.917	4.767	5.623	4.486	4.355
7	6.728	6.472	6.230	6.002	5.786	5.582	5.389	5.206	5.033	4.868
8	7.652	7.326	7.020	6.733	6.463	6.210	5.971	5.747	5.535	5.335
9	8.566	8.162	7.786	7.435	7.108	6.802	6.515	6.247	5.995	5.759
10	9.471	8.983	8.530	8.111	7.722	7.360	7.024	6.710	6.418	6.145
11	10.368	9.787	9.253	8.760	8.306	7.887	7.499	7.139	6.805	6.495
12	11.255	10.575	9.954	9.385	8.863	8.384	7.943	7.536	7.161	6.814
13	12.134	11.348	10.635	9.986	9.394	8.853	8.358	7.904	7.487	7.103
14	13.004	12.106	11.296	10.563	9.899	9.295	8.746	8.244	7.786	7.367
15	13.865	12.849	11.938	11.118	10.380	9.712	9.108	8.560	8.061	7.606
16	14.718	13.578	12.561	11.652	10.838	10.106	9.447	8.851	8.313	7.824
17	15.562	14.292	13.166	12.166	11.274	10.477	9.763	9.122	8.544	8.022
18	16.398	14.992	13.754	12.659	11.690	10.828	10.059	9.372	8.756	8.201
19	17.226	15.679	14.324	13.134	12.085	11.158	10.336	9.604	8.950	8.365
20	18.046	16.352	14.878	13.590	12.462	11.470	10.594	9.818	9.129	8.514
21	18.857	17.011	15.415	14.029	12.821	11.764	10.836	10.017	9.292	8.649
22	19.661	17.658	15.937	14.451	13.163	12.042	11.061	10.201	9.442	8.772
23	20.456	18.292	16.444	14.857	13.489	12.303	11.272	10.371	9.580	8.883
24	21.244	18.914	16.936	15.247	13.799	12.550	11.469	10.529	9.707	8.985
25	22.023	19.524	17.413	15.622	14.094	12.783	11.654	10.675	9.823	9.077
30	25.808	22.397	19.601	17.292	15.373	13.765	12.409	11.258	10.274	9.427
40	32.835	27.356	23.115	19.793	17.159	15.046	13.332	11.925	10.757	9.779
50	39.197	31.424	25.730	21.482	18.256	15.762	13.801	12.234	10.962	9.915

n	11%	12%	13%	14%	15%	16%	17%	18%	19%	20%
1	.901	.893	.885	.877	.870	.862	.855	.847	.840	.833
2	1.713	1.690	1.668	1.647	1.626	1.605	1.585	1.566	1.547	1.528
3	2.444	2.402	2.361	2.322	2.283	2.246	2.210	2.174	2.140	2.106
4	3.102	3.037	2.974	2.914	2.855	2.798	2.743	2.690	2.639	2.589
5	3.696	3.605	3.517	3.433	3.352	3.274	3.199	3.127	3.058	2.991
6	4.231	4.111	3.998	3.889	3.784	3.685	3.589	3.498	3.410	3.326
7	4.712	4.564	4.423	4.288	4.160	4.039	3.922	3.812	3.706	3.605
8	5.146	4.968	4.799	4.639	4.487	4.344	4.207	4.078	3.954	3.837
9	5.537	5.328	5.132	4.946	4.772	4.607	4.451	4.303	4.163	4.031
10	5.889	5.650	5.246	5.216	5.019	4.833	4.659	4.494	4.339	4.192
11	6.207	5.938	5.687	5.453	5.234	5.029	4.836	4.656	4.487	4.327
12	6.492	6.194	5.918	5.660	5.421	5.197	4.988	4.793	4.611	4.439
13	6.750	6.424	6.122	5.842	5.583	5.342	5.118	4.910	4.715	4.533
14	6.982	6.628	6.303	6.002	5.724	5.468	5.229	5.008	4.802	4.611
15	7.191	6.811	6.462	6.142	5.847	5.575	5.324	5.092	4.876	4.675

n	11%	12%	13%	14%	15%	16%	17%	18%	19%	20%
16	7.379	6.974	6.604	6.265	5.954	5.669	5.405	5.162	4.938	4.730
17	7.549	7.120	6.729	6.373	6.047	5.749	5.475	5.222	4.990	4.775
18	7.702	7.250	6.840	6.467	6.128	5.818	5.534	5.273	5.033	4.812
19	7.839	7.366	6.938	6.550	6.198	5.877	5.585	5.316	5.070	4.843
20	7.963	7.469	7.025	6.623	6.259	5.929	5.628	5.353	5.101	4.870
21	8.075	7.562	7.102	6.687	6.312	5.973	5.665	5.384	5.127	4.891
22	8.176	7.645	7.170	6.743	6.359	6.011	5.696	5.410	5.149	4.909
23	8.266	7.718	7.230	6.792	6.399	6.044	5.723	5.432	5.167	4.925
24	8.348	7.784	7.283	6.835	6.434	6.073	5.747	5.451	5.182	4.937
25	8.422	7.843	7.330	6.873	6.464	6.097	5.766	5.467	5.195	4.948
30	8.694	8.055	7.496	7.003	6.566	6.177	5.829	5.517	5.235	4.979
40	8.951	8.244	7.634	7.105	6.642	6.233	5.871	5.548	5.258	4.997
50	9.042	8.305	7.675	7.133	6.661	6.246	5.880	5.554	5.262	4.999

n	21%	22%	23%	24%	25%	26%	27%	28%	29%	30%
1	.826	.820	.813	.806	.800	.794	.787	.781	.775	.769
2	1.509	1.492	1.474	1.457	1.440	1.424	1.407	1.392	1.376	1.361
3	2.074	2.042	2.011	1.981	1.952	1.923	1.896	1.868	1.842	1.816
4	2.540	2.494	2.448	2.404	2.362	2.320	2.280	2.241	2.203	2.166
5	2.926	2.864	2.803	2.745	2.689	2.635	2.583	2.532	2.483	2.436
6	3.245	3.167	3.092	3.020	2.951	2.885	2.821	2.759	2.700	2.643
7	3.508	3.416	3.327	3.242	3.161	3.083	3.009	2.937	2.868	2.802
8	3.726	3.619	3.518	3.421	3.329	3.241	3.156	3.076	2.999	2.925
9	3.905	3.786	3.673	3.566	3.463	3.366	3.273	3.184	3.100	3.019
10	4.054	3.923	3.799	3.682	3.570	3.465	3.364	3.269	3.178	3.092
11	4.177	4.035	3.902	3.776	3.656	3.544	3.437	3.335	3.329	3.147
12	4.278	4.127	3.985	3.851	3.725	3.606	3.493	3.387	3.286	3.190
13	4.362	4.203	4.053	3.912	3.780	3.656	3.538	3.427	3.322	3.223
14	4.432	4.265	4.108	3.962	3.824	3.695	3.573	3.459	3.351	3.249
15	4.489	4.315	4.153	4.001	3.859	3.726	3.601	3.483	3.373	3.268
16	4.536	4.357	4.189	4.003	3.887	3.751	3.623	3.503	3.390	3.283
17	4.576	4.391	4.219	4.059	3.910	3.771	3.640	3.518	3.403	3.295
18	4.608	4.419	4.243	4.080	3.928	3.786	3.654	3.529	3.413	3.304
19	4.635	4.442	4.263	4.097	3.942	3.799	3.664	3.539	3.421	3.311
20	4.657	4.460	4.279	4.110	3.954	3.808	3.673	3.546	3.427	3.316
21	4.675	4.476	4.292	4.121	3.963	3.816	3.679	3.551	3.432	3.320
22	4.690	4.488	4.302	4.130	3.970	3.822	3.684	3.556	3.436	3.323
23	4.703	4.499	4.311	4.137	3.976	3.827	3.689	3.559	3.438	3.325
24	4.713	4.507	4.318	4.143	3.981	3.831	3.692	3.562	3.441	3.327
25	4.721	4.514	4.323	4.147	3.985	3.834	3.694	3.564	3.442	3.329
30	4.746	4.534	4.339	4.160	3.995	3.842	3.701	3.569	3.447	3.332
40	4.760	4.544	4.347	4.166	3.999	3.846	3.703	3.571	3.448	3.333
50	4.762	4.545	4.348	4.167	4.000	3.846	3.704	3.571	3.448	3.333

n	31%	32%	33%	34%	35%	36%	37%	38%	39%	40%
1	.763	.758	.752	.746	.741	.735	.730	.725	.719	.714
2	1.346	1.331	1.317	1.303	1.289	1.276	1.263	1.250	1.237	1.224
3	1.791	1.766	1.742	1.719	1.696	1.673	1.652	1.630	1.609	1.589
4	2.130	2.096	2.062	2.029	1.997	1.966	1.935	1.906	1.877	1.849
5	2.390	2.345	2.302	2.260	2.220	2.181	2.143	2.106	2.070	2.035
6	2.588	2.534	2.483	2.433	2.385	2.339	2.294	2.251	2.209	2.168
7	2.739	2.677	2.619	2.562	2.508	2.455	2.404	2.355	2.308	2.263
8	2.854	2.786	2.721	2.658	2.598	2.540	2.485	2.432	2.380	2.331

n	31%	32%	33%	34%	35%	36%	37%	38%	39%	40%
9	2.942	2.868	2.798	2.730	2.665	2.603	2.544	2.487	2.432	2.379
10	3.009	2.930	2.855	2.784	2.715	2.649	2.587	2.527	2.469	2.414
11	3.060	2.978	2.899	2.824	2.752	2.683	2.618	2.555	2.496	2.438
12	3.100	3.013	2.931	2.853	2.779	2.708	2.641	2.576	2.515	2.456
13	3.129	3.040	2.956	2.876	2.799	2.727	2.658	2.592	2.529	2.469
14	3.152	3.061	2.974	2.892	2.814	2.740	2.670	2.603	2.539	2.477
15	3.170	3.076	2.988	2.905	2.825	2.750	2.679	2.611	2.546	2.484
16	3.183	3.088	2.999	2.914	2.834	2.757	2.685	2.616	2.551	2.489
17	3.193	3.097	3.007	2.921	2.840	2.763	2.690	2.621	2.555	2.492
18	3.201	3.104	3.012	2.926	2.844	2.767	2.693	2.624	2.557	2.494
19	3.207	3.109	3.017	2.930	2.848	2.770	2.696	2.626	2.559	2.496
20	3.211	3.113	3.020	2.933	2.850	2.772	2.698	2.627	2.561	2.497
21	3.215	3.116	3.023	2.935	2.852	2.773	2.699	2.629	2.562	2.498
22	3.217	3.118	3.025	2.936	2.853	2.775	2.700	2.629	2.562	2.498
23	3.219	3.120	3.026	2.938	2.854	2.775	2.701	2.630	2.563	2.499
24	3.221	3.121	3.027	2.939	2.855	2.776	2.701	2.630	2.563	2.499
25	3.222	3.122	3.028	2.939	2.856	2.776	2.702	2.631	2.563	2.499
30	3.225	2.124	3.030	2.941	2.857	2.777	2.702	2.631	2.564	2.500
40	3.226	2.125	3.030	2.941	2.857	2.778	2.703	2.632	2.564	2.500
50	3.226	2.125	3.030	2.941	2.857	2.778	2.703	2.632	2.564	2.500

APPENDIX F
Check Figures for Selected End-of-Chapter Study Problems

CHAPTER 1

1–1. Taxable income = $526,800
Tax liability = $179,112
1–3. Taxable income = $365,000
Tax liability = $124,100
1–5. Taxable income = ($38,000)
Tax liability = $0
1–7. Taxable income = $153,600
Tax liability = $43,154
1–9. Taxable income = $370,000
Tax liability = $125,800
1–11. Taxable income = $1,813,000
Tax liability = $616,420

CHAPTER 2

2–1. Inferred real rate on Treasury bills: 1.56%
Inferred real rate on Treasury bonds: 4.55%
2–2. 11.28%
2–4. 12.35%
2–5. **a.** The logic here is based on the expectations theory of the term structure of interest rates.

CHAPTER 3

3–1. $120,650
3–3. No numerical solution
3–5. Free cash flow ($8)
3–7. Free cash flow $53,800

CHAPTER 4

4–1. $500,000
4–3. **a.** Total assets turnover = 2
b. Sales = $17.5m
Percentage increase = 75%
c. For last year, OIROI = 20%
Projected OIROI = 35%
4–5.

RATIO	2000
Current ratio	4.0x
Acid-test (quick) ratio	1.92x
Average collection period	107 days
Inventory turnover	1.36x
Operating income return on investment	13.8%
Operating profit margin	24.8%
Total asset turnover	.56x
Inventory turnover	1.36x
Fixed asset turnover	1.04x

Debt ratio	34.6%
Times interest eraned	5.63x
Return on common equity	10.5%

4–7. **a.** Current ratio = 1.84
Acid-test ratio = .72
Debt ratio = .55
Times interest earned = 8
Inventory turnover = 5.48
Fixed asset turnover = 2.22
Return on equity = 23.4%

CHAPTER 5

5–1. Total assets = $11.75 million
5–3. Total assets = $1.8 million
Fixed assets = $1 million
5–5.

Cash	$100,000
Accounts receivable	$100,000
Current liabilities	$600,000
Net fixed assets	$800,000
Total assets	$2,000,000

5–9. **a.** Notes payable $1.11 million
b. Current ratio (before) = 2 times
Current ratio (after) = 1.12 times
5–11. Cummulative borrowing (March) = $52,100
Ending cash balance (July) = $223,285
5–13.

	20×0	19×7
a. Sales growth rate	7.1%	20.0%
b. Sustainable rate of growth	8.6%	6.7%

CHAPTER 6

6–1. **a.** $12,970
c. $3,019.40
6–2. **a.** $n = 15$ years
6–3. **b.** 5%
c. 9%
6–4. **b.** $PV = $235.20
6–5. **a.** $6,289
c. $302.89
6–6. **c.** $1,562.96
6–7. **a.** $FV_1 = $10,600
$FV_5 = $13,380
$FV_{15} = $23,970
6–9. **a.** $6,690
b. Semiannual: $6,720
Bimonthly: $6,740

6–11. Year 1: 18,000 books
Year 2: 21,600 books
Year 3: 25,920 books
6–13. $6,108.11
6–15. 8%
6–17. $658,197.85
6–21. b. $8,333.33
6–24. $6,509
6–26. 22%
6–27. $6,934.81
6–30. a. $1,989.73
6–33. $15,912

CHAPTER 7

7–1. $752.52
7–3. 4.79% semiannually
9.8% compounded annually
7–5. 5.28%
7–7. a. $863.78
   b. Market value $707.63 when required rate of return is 15%
   Market value $1,171.19 when required rate of return is 8%
7–9. $513

CHAPTER 8

8–1. $116.67
8–3. a. 8.5%
   b. $42.50
8–5. a. 18.9%
   b. $28.57
8–7. 7.2%
8–9. $39.96
8–11. a. 10.91%
   b. $36
8–13. $50

CHAPTER 9

9–1. $\bar{k} = 9.1\%$; $\sigma^2 = 9.38\%$; $\sigma = 3.06\%$
9–3. A: $\bar{k} = 16.7\%$; $\sigma^2 = 102.5\%$; $\sigma = 10.12\%$
B: $\bar{k} = 9.2\%$; $\sigma^2 = 12.76\%$; $\sigma = 3.57\%$
9–5. The beta is approximately 0.5.
9–7. 10.56%
9–9. a. Asman: For time = 2, 20%; Salinas: for time = 3, 14.29%
9–11. a. 15.8%
   b. 0.95

CHAPTER 10

10–1. a. $IRR = 7\%$
   b. $IRR = 17\%$
10–3. a. IRR = approximately 19%
10–5. a. payback period = 4 years

10–7. a. Project A:
   payback period = 2.5 years
10–11. a. $NPV_A = \$136.30$
   $NPV_B = \$455$
   b. $PI_A = 1.2726$
   $PI_B = 1.09$
   c. $IRR_A = 40\%$
   $IRR_B = 20\%$
10–13. a. Payback A = 1.589 years
   Payback B = 3.019 years
   b. $NPV_A = \$8,743$
   $NPV_B = \$11,615$
   c. $IRR_A = 40\%$
   $IRR_B = 30\%$

CHAPTER 11

11–1. a. $6,800
   b. $3,400
   c. No taxes
   d. $1,020
11–3. a. 2.75 years
   b. $10,628.16
11–5. a. $560,000
   b. Cash flow after tax: $116,170
11–7. $NPV_A = \$8,025$
$NPV_B = \$10,112$

CHAPTER 12

12–1. a. $k_d (1 - t) = 6.53\%$
   b. $k_{nc} = 14.37\%$
   c. $k_c = 15.14\%$
   d. $k_p = 8.77\%$
   e. $k_d (1 - t) = 7.92\%$
12–3. $k_{nc} = 12.06\%$
12–5. $k_p = 7.69\%$
12–7. $k_p = 14.29\%$
12–9. a. $k_c = 17.59\%$
   b. $k_{nc} = 18.25\%$
12–11. $P_0 = \$1,063.80$
   $NP_0 = \$952.10$
   Number of bonds = 525
   $k_d (1 - t) = 7.14\%$
12–13. a.

	Incentive Compensation		
	80%	100%	120%
CEO	$540,000	$675,000	$810,000

   b.

	60%	150%
CEO	$405,000	$1,012,500

CHAPTER 13

13–1. a. 1.67 times
   b. 1.11 times
   c. 1.85 times

13–3. **a.** 1.67 times
    b. 1.11 times
    c. 1.85 times
    d. $18,326,693.23
    e. (25%) (1.85) = 46.25%

13–5. **a.** F = $780,000
    b. S_B = $1,560,000

13–7. **a.** P = $6.875 (selling price per unit)

13–8. **a.** 1,200 units
    b. $600,000
    c. 1.316 times
    d. 26.32%

13–11. **a.** EBIT = $2,000,000
    b. EPS will be $1.00 for each plan
    d. Plan B

CHAPTER 14

14–1. 95,238 shares; $11,428,560

14–3. Value before and after dividend: $275

14–5. **a.**

Year	Dividend
1	$0.70
3	$0.93

    b. Target dividend: $0.90

14–7. 163,743 shares; $15,555,556

CHAPTER 15

15–1. Rate = 13.79%

15–3. **a.** Rate = 36.73%
    b. Rate = 74.23%

15–7. **a.** Rate = 16.27%

15–11. **a.** APR = 10%
    b. APR = 11.76%
    c. APR = 12.5%

15–13. **a.**

	Jan-96	Jan-00
CCC	44.25 days	2.25 days

CHAPTER 16

16–1. Yes; the company will save $250,000 annually by switching to the new concentration-banking system.

16–4. **a.** Need to speed up collections by more than 0.5214 day.
    b. Cash collections would have to be accelerated by more than 0.8110 day.

16–6. **a.** $4 million
    b. $240,000
    c. $48,600
    d. Yes; net annual gain = $191,400

16–8. **a.** $5,333

16–10. **a.** $912.44
    b. The loss will be $87.56.
    c. The capital loss here would be only $17.59.
    d. Interest rate risk. This leads to the maturity premium discussed in Chapter 2.

16–12. **a.** 36.36%
    b. 36.73%
    c. 55.67%

16–14. **a.** Average inventory = $90,000
    b. $53,333

16–16. **a.** EOQ = 7,071 units, or rounded to 7,100
    b. 35.2 orders per year

CHAPTER 17

17–1. **a.** $8,437
    b. $9,368
    c. $25,695

17–3. Canada: 1.1853; 1.1881; 1.1912
    Japan: 213.4927; 211.9992; 209.1613
    Switzerland: 1.9459; 1.9346; 1.8815

17–5. Net gain = $149.02

GLOSSARY

Accelerated Depreciation Techniques. Techniques that allow the owner of the asset to take greater amounts of depreciation during the early years of its life, thereby deferring some of the taxes until later years.

Accounts-Receivable Turnover Ratio. A ratio, credit sales divided by accounts receivable, that expresses how often accounts receivable are "rolled over" during a year.

Accrual Method. A method of accounting whereby income is recorded when earned, whether or not the money has been received at that time, and expenses are recorded when incurred, whether or not any money has actually been paid out.

Acid-Test Ratio. (Current assets − inventories) ÷ current liabilities. This ratio is a more stringent measure of liquidity than the current ratio in that it subtracts inventories (the least liquid current asset) from current assets.

Acquisition. A combination of two or more businesses into a single operational entity.

Agency Costs. The costs, such as a reduced stock price, associated with potential conflict between managers and investors when these two groups are not the same.

Agency Problem. Problems and conflicts resulting from the separation of the management and ownership of the firm.

Amortized Loans. Loans that are paid off in equal periodic payments.

Analytical Income Statement. A financial statement used by internal analysts that differs in composition from audited or published financial statements.

Annuity. A series of equal dollar payments for a specified number of years.

Annuity Due. An annuity in which the payments occur at the beginning of each period.

Anticipatory Buying. Buying in anticipation of a price increase to secure goods at a lower cost.

Arbitrage-Pricing Model. A theory that relates stock returns and risk. The theory maintains that security returns vary from their expected amounts when there are unanticipated changes in basic economic forces. Such forces would include unexpected changes in industrial production, inflation rates, term structure of interest rates, and the difference between interest rates of high- and low-risk bonds.

Arbitrageur. A person involved in the process of buying and selling in more than one market to make riskless profits.

Arrearage. An overdue payment, generally referring to omitted preferred stock dividends.

Asked Rate. The rate a bank or foreign exchange trader "asks" the customer to pay in home currency for foreign currency when the bank is selling and the customer is buying.

Asset Allocation. Identifying and selecting the asset classes appropriate for a specific investment portfolio and determining the proportions of those assets within the portfolio.

Automated Depository Transfer Check (DTC) System. A cash management tool that moves funds from local bank accounts to concentration bank accounts electronically. This eliminates the mail float from the local bank to the concentration bank.

Average Collection Period. Accounts receivable divided by (annual credit sales divided by 365). A ratio that expresses how rapidly the firm is collecting its credit accounts.

Balance Sheet. A basic accounting statement that represents the financial position of a firm on a given date.

Balance-Sheet Leverage Ratios. Financial ratios used to measure the extent of a firm's use of borrowed funds, calculated using information found in the firm's balance sheet.

Bankers' Acceptances. A draft (order to pay) drawn on a specific bank by a seller of goods in order to obtain payment for goods that have been shipped (sold) to a customer. The customer maintains an account with that specific bank.

Bank Wire. A private wire service used and supported by approximately 250 banks in the United States for transferring funds, exchanging credit information, or effecting securities transactions.

Benefit-Cost Ratio. See **Profitability Index.**

Beta. The relationship between an investment's returns and the market returns. This is a measure of the investment's nondiversifiable risk.

Bid-Ask Spread. The difference between the bid quote and ask quote.

Bird-in-the-Hand Dividend Theory. The view that dividends are more certain than capital gains.

Bond. A long-term (10-year or more) promissory note issued by the borrower, promising to pay the owner of the security a predetermined and fixed amount of interest each year.

Bond Par Value. The face value appearing on the bond, which is to be returned to the bondholder at maturity.

Book Value. (1) The value of an asset as shown on the firm's balance sheet. It represents the historical cost of the asset rather than its current market value or replacement cost. (2) The depreciated value of a company's assets (original cost less accumulated depreciation) less the outstanding liabilities.

Book-Value Weights. The percentage of financing provided by different capital sources as measured by their book values from the company's balance sheet.

Break-even Analysis. An analytical technique used to determine the quantity of output or sales that results in a zero level of earnings before interest and taxes (EBIT). Relationships among the firm's cost structure, volume of output, and EBIT are studied.

Business Risk. The relative dispersion or variability in the firm's expected earnings before interest and taxes (EBIT). The nature of the firm's operations causes its business risk. This type of risk is affected by the firm's cost structure, product demand characteristics, and intra-industry competitive position. In capital structure theory, business risk is distinguished from financial risk. Compare **Financial Risk.**

Buying Rate. The bid rate in a currency transaction.

Call Option. The right to purchase a given number of shares of stock or some other asset at a specified price over a given time period.

Call Premium. The difference between the call price and the security's par value.

Call Provision. A provision that entitles the corporation to repurchase its preferred stock from their investors at stated prices over specified periods.

Capital Asset. All property used in conducting a business other than assets held primarily for sale in the ordinary course of business or depreciable and real property used in conducting a business.

Capital Asset Pricing Model (CAPM). An equation stating that the expected rate of return on a project is a function of (1) the risk-free rate, (2) the investment's systematic risk, and (3) the expected risk premium for the market portfolio of all risky securities.

Capital Budgeting. The decision-making process with respect to investment in fixed assets. Specifically, it involves measuring the incremental cash flows associated with investment proposals and evaluating those proposed investments.

Capital Gain or Loss. As defined by the revenue code, a gain or loss resulting from the sale or exchange of a capital asset.

Capital Market. All institutions and procedures that facilitate transactions in long-term financial instruments.

Capital Rationing. The placing of a limit by the firm on the dollar size of the capital budget.

Capital Structure. The mix of long-term sources of funds used by the firm. This is also called the firm's capitalization. The relative total (percentage) of each type of fund is emphasized.

Cash. Currency and coins plus demand deposit accounts.

Cash Break-even Analysis. Another version of break-even analysis that includes only the cash costs of production within the cost components. This means noncash expenses, like depreciation, are omitted in the analysis.

Cash Budget. A detailed plan of future cash flows. This budget is composed of four elements: cash receipts, cash disbursements, net change in cash for the period, and new financing needed.

Cash Flow Process. The process of cash generation and disposition in a typical business setting.

Cash Flow Statement. An accounting statement that computes the firm's cash inflows and outflows for a given time period.

Cash Flows from Investment Activities. Cash flows that include the purchase of fixed assets and other assets.

Cash Flows from Financing Activities. Cash flows that include proceeds from long-term debt or issuing common stock, and payments made for stock dividends.

Cash Flows from Operations. Cash flows that consist of (1) collections from customers; (2) payments to suppliers for the purchase of materials; (3) other operating cash flows such as marketing and administrative expenses and interest payments; (4) and cash tax payments.

Certainty Equivalents. The amount of cash a person would require with certainty to make him or her indifferent between this certain sum and a particular risky or uncertain sum.

Characteristic Line. The line of "best fit" through a series of returns for a firm's stock relative to the market returns. The slope of the line, frequently called beta, represents the average movement of the firm's stock returns in response to a movement in the market's returns.

Chattel Mortgage Agreement. A loan agreement in which the lender can increase his or her security interest by having specific items of inventory identified in the loan agreement. The borrower retains title to the inventory but cannot sell the items without the lender's consent.

Clientele Effect. The belief that individuals and institutions that need current income will invest in companies that have high dividend payouts. Other investors prefer to avoid taxes by holding securities that offer only small dividend income but large capital gains. Thus, we have a "clientele" of investors.

Commercial Paper. Short-term unsecured promissory notes sold by large businesses in order to raise cash. Unlike most other money-market instruments, commercial paper has no developed secondary market.

Common Stock. Shares that represent the ownership in a corporation.

Company-Unique Risk. See **Unsystematic Risk.**

Compensating Balance. A balance of a given amount that the firm maintains in its demand deposit account. It may be required by either a formal or informal agreement with the firm's commercial bank. Such balances are usually required by the bank (1) on the unused portion of a loan commitment, (2) on the unpaid portion of an outstanding loan, or (3) in exchange for certain services provided by the bank, such as check-clearing or credit information. These balances raise the effective rate of interest paid on borrowed funds.

Compound Annuity. Depositing an equal sum of money at the end of each year for a certain number of years and allowing it to grow.

Compound Interest. The situation in which interest paid on the investment during the first period is added to the principal and, during the second period, interest is earned on the original principal plus the interest earned during the first period.

Compounding. The process of determining the future value of a payment or series of payments when applying the concept of compound interest.

Concentration Bank. A bank where a firm maintains a major disbursing account.

Concentration Banking. The selection of a few major banks where the firm maintains significant disbursing accounts.

Constant Dividend Payout Ratio. A dividend payment policy in which the percentage of earnings paid out in dividends is held constant. The dollar amount fluctuates from year to year as profits vary.

Contractual Interest Rate. The interest rate to be paid on a bond expressed as a percent of par value.

Contribution Margin. The difference between a product's selling price and its unit variable costs. It is usually measured on a per unit basis.

Contribution-to-Firm Risk. The amount of risk that a project contributes to the firm as a whole. This measure considers the fact that some of the project's risk will be diversified away as the project is combined with the firm's other projects and assets, but ignores the effects of diversification of the firm's shareholders.

Convertible Debt. A hybrid security that combines debt or preferred stock with an option on the firm's common stock.

Convertible Preferred Stock. Stock that allows the stockholder to convert the preferred stock into a predetermined number of shares of common stock, if he or she so chooses.

Convertible Security. Preferred stock or debentures that can be exchanged for a specified number of shares of common stock at the will of the owner.

Corporate Bylaws. Regulations that govern the internal affairs of the corporation, designating such items as the time and place of the shareholders' meetings, voting rights, the election process for selecting members of the board of directors, the procedures for issuing and transferring stock certificates, and the policies relating to the corporate records.

Corporation. An entity that *legally* functions separate and apart from its owners.

Cost of Capital. See **Weighted Cost of Capital.**

Cost of Common Stock. The rate of return a firm must earn in order for the common stockholders to receive their required rate of return. The rate is based on the opportunity cost of funds for the common stockholders in the capital markets.

Cost of Debt. The rate that has to be received from an investment in order to achieve the required rate of return for the creditors. The cost is based on the debtholders' opportunity cost of debt in the capital markets.

Cost of Preferred Stock. The rate of return that must be earned on the preferred stockholders' investment to satisfy their required rate of return. The cost is based on the preferred stockholders' opportunity cost of preferred stock in the capital markets.

Cost-Volume-Profit Analysis. Another way of referring to ordinary breakeven analysis.

Coupon Interest Rate. The interest to be paid annually on a bond as a percent of par value, which is specified in the contractual agreement.

Coverage Ratios. A group of ratios that measure a firm's ability to meet its recurring fixed-charge obligations, such as interest on long-term debt, lease payments, and/or preferred stock dividends.

Covered Interest Arbitrage. Arbitrage designed to eliminate differentials across currency and interest rate markets.

Credit Scoring. The numerical evaluation of credit applicants where the score is evaluated relative to a predetermined standard.

Cross Rate. The computation of an exchange rate for a currency from the exchange rates of two other currencies.

Cumulative Feature. A requirement that all past unpaid preferred stock dividends be paid before any common stock dividends are declared.

Cumulative Voting. Voting in which each share of stock allows the shareholder a number of votes equal to the number of directors being elected. The shareholder can then cast all of his or her votes for a single candidate or split them among the various candidates.

Current Assets. Assets consisting primarily of cash, marketable securities, accounts receivable, inventories, and prepaid expenses.

Current Ratio. Current assets divided by current liabilities. A ratio that indicates a firm's degree of liquidity by comparing its current assets to its current liabilities.

Current Yield. The ratio of the annual interest payment to the bond's market price.

Date of Record. Date at which the stock transfer books are to be closed for determining the investor to receive the next dividend payment. See **Ex-Dividend Date.**

Debenture. Any unsecured long-term debt.

Debt. Liabilities consisting of such sources as credit extended by suppliers or a loan from a bank.

Debt Capacity. The maximum proportion of debt that the firm can include in its capital structure and still maintain its lowest composite cost of capital.

Debt Ratio. Total liabilities divided by total assets. A ratio that measures the extent to which a firm has been financed with debt.

Declaration Date. The date upon which a dividend is formally declared by the board of directors.

Default Risk. The uncertainty of expected returns from a security attributable to possible changes in the financial capacity of the security issuer to make future payments to the security owner. Treasury securities are considered default-free. Default risk is also referred to as "financial risk" in the context of marketable-securities management.

Degree of Combined Leverage. The percentage change in earnings per share caused by a percentage change in sales. It is the product of the degree of operating leverage and the degree of financial leverage.

Delivery-Time Stock. The inventory needed between the order date and the receipt of the inventory ordered.

Depository Transfer Checks (DTCs). A means for moving funds from local bank accounts to concentration bank accounts. The depository transfer check itself is an unsigned, nonnegotiable instrument. It is payable only to the bank deposit for credit to the firm's specific account.

Depreciation. The means by which an asset's value is expensed over its useful life for federal income tax purposes.

Direct Costs. See **Variable Costs.**

Direct Method. A format used to measure cash flow from operations, by which the different cash outflows occurring in regular operations of a business are subtracted from the cash flow collected from customers.

Direct Placement. See **Private Placement.**

Direct Quote. The exchange rate that indicates the number of units of the home currency required to buy one unit of foreign currency.

Direct Sale. The sale of securities by the corporation to the investing public without the services of an investment-banking firm.

Direct Securities. The pure financial claims issued by economic units to savers. These can later be transformed into indirect securities.

Disbursing Float. Funds available in the company's bank account until its payment check has cleared through the banking system.

Discount Bond. A bond that sells at a discount below par value.

Discounting. The inverse of compounding. This process is used to determine the present value of a cash flow.

Discount Rate. The interest rate used in the discounting process.

Discretionary Financing. Sources of financing that require an explicit decision on the part of the firm's management every time funds are raised. An example is a bank note which requires that negotiations be undertaken and an agreement signed setting forth the terms and conditions of the financing.

Diversifiable Risk. See **Unsystematic Risk.**

Dividend Payout Ratio. The amount of dividends relative to the company's net income or earnings per share.

Dividend Yield. The dividend per share divided by the price of the security.

Dunning Letters. Past-due letters sent out to delinquent accounts.

DuPont Analysis. A method used to evaluate a firm's profitability and return on equity.

Earnings Before Interest and Taxes (EBIT). Profits from sales minus total operating expenses. Also called **Operating Income.**

Earnings Before Taxes (EBT). Operating income minus interest expense.

EBIT-EPS Indifference Point. The level of earnings before interest and taxes (EBIT) that will equate earnings per share (EPS) between two different financing plans.

Economic Failure. Situation in which a company's costs exceed its revenues. Stated differently, the internal rates of return on investments are less than the firm's cost of capital.

Efficient Market. A market in which the values of securities at any instant in time fully reflect all available information, which results in the market value and the intrinsic value being the same.

EPS. Typical financial notation for earnings per (common) share.

Equity. Stockholders' investment in the firm and the cumulative profits retained in the business up to the date of the balance sheet.

Equivalent Annual Annuity (EAA). An annuity cash flow that yields the same present value as the project's NPV. It is calculated by dividing the projects' NPV by the appropriate $PVIFA_{i,n}$.

Eurobond. A bond issued in a country different from the one in whose currency the bond is denominated; for example, a bond issued in Europe or Asia by an American company that pays interest and principal to the lender in U.S. dollars.

Eurodollar Market. This is a banking market in U.S. dollars outside the United States. Large sums of U.S. dollars can be borrowed or invested in this unregulated financial market. Similar external markets exist in Europe and Asia and for other major currencies.

Exchange Rate. The price of a foreign currency stated in terms of the domestic or home currency.

Exchange Rate Risk. The risk that tomorrow's exchange rate will differ from today's rate.

Ex-Dividend Date. The date upon which stock brokerage companies have uniformly decided to terminate the right of ownership to the dividend, which is two days prior to the date of record.

Expectations Theory. The concept that, no matter what the decision area, how the market price responds to management's actions is not determined entirely by the action itself; it is also affected by investors' expectations about the ultimate decision to be made by management.

Expected Rate of Return. (1) The discount rate that equates the present value of the future cash flows (interest and maturity value) with the current market price of a bond. It is the rate of return an investor will earn if the bond is held to maturity. (2) The rate of return the investor expects to receive on an investment by paying the existing market price of the security. (3) The arithmetic mean or average of all possible outcomes where those outcomes are weighted by the probability that each will occur.

Ex-Rights Date. The date on or after which the stock sells without rights.

External Common Equity. A new issue of common stock.

Factor. A firm that, in acquiring the receivables of other firms, bears the risk of collection and, for a fee, services the accounts.

Factoring Accounts Receivable. The outright sale of a firm's accounts receivable to another party (the factor) without recourse. The factor, in turn, bears the risk of collection.

Fair Value. The present value of an asset's expected future cash flows.

Federal Agency Securities. Debt obligations of corporations and agencies created to carry out the lending programs of the U.S. government.

Federal Reserve System. The U.S. central banking system.

Field Warehouse–Financing Agreement. A security agreement in which inventories pledged as collateral are physically separated from the firm's other inventories and placed under the control of a third-party field-warehousing firm.

Financial Analysis. The assessment of a firm's financial condition or well-being. Its objectives are to determine the firm's financial strengths and to identify its weaknesses. The primary tool of financial analysis is the financial ratio.

Financial Assets. Claims for future payment by one economic unit upon another.

Financial Intermediaries. Major financial institutions, such as commercial banks, savings and loan associations, credit unions, life insurance companies, and mutual funds, that assist the transfer of savings from economic units with excess savings to those with a shortage of savings.

Financial Leverage. The use of securities bearing a fixed (limited) rate of return to finance a portion of a firm's assets. Financial leverage can arise from the use of either debt or preferred stock financing. The use of financial leverage exposes the firm to financial risk.

Financial Markets. Institutions and procedures that facilitate transactions in all types of financial claims (securities).

Financial Policy. The firm's policies regarding the sources of financing it plans to use and the particular mix (proportions) in which they will be used.

Financial Ratios. Accounting data restated in relative terms to identify some of the financial strengths and weaknesses of a company.

Financial Risk. The added variability in earnings available to a firm's common shareholders, and the added chance of insolvency caused by the use of securities bearing a limited rate of return in the firm's financial structure. The use of financial leverage gives rise to financial risk.

Financial Structure. The mix of all funds sources that appear on the right-hand side of the balance sheet.

Financial Structure Design. The activity of seeking the proper mixture of a firm's short-term, long-term, and permanent financing components to minimize the cost of raising a given amount of funds.

Financing Costs. Cost incurred by a company that often include interest expenses and preferred dividends.

Finished-Goods Inventory. Goods on which the production has been completed but that are not yet sold.

Fixed-Asset Turnover. Sales divided by fixed assets. A ratio indicating how effectively a firm is using its fixed assets to generate sales.

Fixed Costs. Costs that do not vary in total dollar amount as sales volume or quantity of output changes. Also called Indirect Costs.

Fixed or Long-Term Assets. Assets comprising equipment, buildings, and land.

Float. The length of time from when a check is written until the actual recipient can draw upon or use the "good funds."

Floating Lien Agreement. An agreement, generally associated with a loan, whereby the borrower gives the lender a lien against all its inventory.

Floating Rate International Currency System. An international currency system in which exchange rates between different national currencies are allowed to fluctuate with supply and demand conditions. This contrasts with a fixed rate system in which exchange rates are pegged for extended periods of time and adjusted infrequently.

Flotation Costs. The transaction cost incurred when a firm raises funds by issuing a particular type of security.

Foreign Direct Investment. Physical assets, such as plant and equipment, acquired outside a corporation's home country but operated and controlled by that corporation.

Formal Control. Control vested in the stockholders having the majority of the voting common shares.

Forward Exchange Contract. A contract that requires delivery on a specified future date of one currency in return for a specified amount of another currency.

Forward-Spot Differential. The premium or discount between forward and spot currency exchange rates.

Future-Value Interest Factor (*FVIF$_{i,n}$*). The value $(1 + i)^n$ used as a multiplier to calculate an amount's future value.

Future-Value Interest Factor for an Annuity (*FVIFA$_{i,n}$*). The value $\left[\sum_{t=0}^{n-1} (1 + i)^t\right]$ used as a multiplier to calculate the future value of an annuity.

Futures Contract. A contract to buy or sell a stated commodity (such as soybeans or corn) or financial claim (such as U.S. Treasury bonds) at a specified price at a specified future time.

General Partnership. A partnership in which all partners are fully liable for the indebtedness incurred by the partnership.

Gross Income. A firm's dollar sales from its product or services less the cost of producing or acquiring the product or service.

Gross Profit Margin. Gross profit divided by net sales. A ratio denoting the gross profit of the firm as a percentage of net sales.

Hedge. A means to neutralize exchange rate risk on an exposed asset position, whereby a liability of the same amount and maturity is created in a foreign currency.

Hedging Principle. A working-capital management policy which states that the cash flow–generating characteristics of a firm's investments should be matched with the cash flow requirements of the firm's sources of financing. Very simply, short-lived assets should be financed with short-term sources of financing while long-lived assets should be financed with long-term sources of financing.

High-Yield Bond. See **Junk Bond.**

Holding-Period Return. The return an investor would receive from holding a security for a designated period of time. For example, a monthly holding-period return would be the return for holding a security for a month.

Hostile Takeover. A merger or acquisition in which management resists the group initiating the transaction.

Hurdle Rate. The required rate of return used in capital budgeting.

Income Statement. A basic accounting statement that measures the results of a firm's operations over a specified period, commonly one year. Also known as the profit and loss statement. The bottom line of the income statement shows the firm's profit or loss for the period.

Increasing-Stream Hypothesis of Dividend Policy. The hypothesis that dividend stability is essentially a smoothing of the dividend stream to minimize the effect of other types of company reversals. Thus, corporate managers make every effort to avoid a dividend cut, attempting instead to develop a gradually increasing dividend series over the long-term future.

Incremental Cash Flows. The cash flows that result from the acceptance of a capital-budgeting project.

Indenture. The legal agreement between a firm issuing bonds and the bond trustee who represents the bondholders, providing the specific terms of the loan agreement.

Indirect Costs. See **Fixed Costs.**

Indirect Method. An approach used to measure cash flows from operations, by which all operating expenses that did not result in a cash outflow for the period are added to net income.

Indirect Quote. The exchange rate that expresses the number of units of foreign currency that can be bought for one unit of home currency.

Indirect Securities. The unique financial claims issued by financial intermediaries. Mutual fund shares are an example.

Information Asymmetry. The difference in accessibility to information between managers and investors, which may result in a lower stock price than would be true in conditions of certainty.

Initial Outlay. The immediate cash outflow necessary to purchase an asset and put it in operating order.

Insolvency. The inability to meet interest payments or to repay debt at maturity.

Interest-Rate Parity Theory. The forward premium or discount should be equal and opposite in size to the differences in the national interest rates for the same maturity.

Interest Rate Risk. (1) The variability in a bond's value (risk) caused by changing interest. (2) The uncertainty that envelops the expected returns from a security caused by changes in interest rates. Price changes induced by interest rate changes are greater for long-term than for short-term financial instruments.

Internal Common Equity. Profits retained within the business for investment purposes.

Internal Growth. A firm's growth rate in earnings resulting from reinvesting company profits rather than distributing the earnings in the form of dividends. The growth rate is a function of the amount retained and the return earned on the retained funds.

Internal Rate of Return (IRR). A capital-budgeting technique that reflects the rate of return a project earns. Mathematically, it is the discount rate that equates the present value of the inflows with the present value of the outflows.

Intrinsic or Economic Value. The present value of an asset's expected future cash flows. This value is the amount the investor considers to be fair value, given the amount, timing, and riskiness of future cash flows.

Inventory Loans. Loans secured by inventories. Examples include floating or blanket lien agreements, chattel mortgage agreements, field-warehouse receipt loans, and terminal-warehouse receipt loans.

Inventory Management. The control of assets used in the production process or produced to be sold in the normal course of the firm's operations.

Inventory Turnover Ratio. Cost of goods sold divided by inventory. A ratio that measures the number of times a firm's inventories are sold and replaced during the year. This ratio reflects the relative liquidity of inventories.

Investment Banker. A financial specialist who underwrites and distributes new securities and advises corporate clients about raising new funds.

Investor's Required Rate of Return. The minimum rate of return necessary to attract an investor to purchase or hold a security. It is also the discount rate that equates the present value of the cash flows with the value of the security.

Junk Bond. Any bond rated BB or below.

Just-in-Time Inventory Control System. A production and management system in which inventory is cut down to a minimum through adjustments to the time and physical distance between the various production operations. Under this system the firm keeps a minimum level of inventory on hand, relying upon suppliers to furnish parts "just in time" for them to be assembled.

Law of One Price. The proposition that in competitive markets the same goods should sell for the same price where prices are stated in terms of a single currency.

Lead and Lag Strategies. Techniques used to reduce exchange rate risk where the firm maximizes its asset position in the stronger currency and its liability position in the weaker currency.

Least-Square Regression. A procedure for "fitting" a line through a scatter of observed data points in a way that minimizes the sum of the squared deviations of the points from the fitted line.

Leveraged Buyout (LBO). A corporate restructuring where the existing shareholders sell their shares to a small group of investors. The purchasers of the stock use the firm's unused debt capacity to borrow the funds to pay for the stock.

Limited Liability. A protective provision whereby the investor is not liable for more than the amount invested in the firm.

Limited Partnership. A partnership in which one or more of the partners has limited liability, restricted to the amount of capital he or she invests in the partnership.

Line of Credit. Generally an informal agreement or understanding between a borrower and a bank as to the maximum amount of credit the bank will provide the borrower at any one time. Under this type of agreement there is no "legal" commitment on the part of the bank to provide the stated credit. Compare **Revolving Credit Agreement.**

Liquidation Value.   The dollar sum that could be realized if an asset were sold independently of the going concern.

Liquidity.   A firm's ability to pay its bills on time. Liquidity is related to the ease and quickness with which a firm can convert its noncash assets into cash, as well as the size of the firm's investment in noncash assets vis-à-vis its short-term liabilities.

Liquidity Preference Theory.   The shape of the term structure of interest rates is determined by an investor's additional required interest rate in compensation of additional risks.

Liquidity Ratios.   Financial ratios used to assess the ability of a firm to pay its bills on time. Examples of liquidity ratios include the current ratio and the acid-test ratio.

Loan Amortization Schedule.   A breakdown of the interest and principle payments on an amortized loan.

Long-Term Residual Dividend Policy.   A dividend plan by which the residual capital is distributed smoothly to the investors over the planning period.

Mail Float.   Funds tied up during the time that elapses from the moment a customer mails his or her remittance check until the firm begins to process it.

Majority Voting.   Voting in which each share of stock allows the shareholder one vote, and each position on the board of directors is voted on separately. As a result, a majority of shares has the power to elect the entire board of directors.

Marginal Cost of Capital.   The cost of capital that represents the weighted cost of each additional dollar of financing from all sources, debt, preferred stock, and common stock.

Marginal Tax Rate.   The tax rate that would be applied to the next dollar of income.

Market Equilibrium.   The situation in which expected returns equal required returns.

Market Risk.   See **Systematic Risk.**

Market Segmentation Theory.   The shape of the term structure of interest rates implies that the rate of interest for a particular maturity is determined solely by demand and supply for a given maturity. This rate is independent of the demand and supply for securities having different maturities.

Market Value.   The value observed in the marketplace, where buyers and sellers negotiate a mutually acceptable price for the asset.

Market-Value Weights.   The percentage of financing provided by different capital sources, measured by the current market prices of the firm's bonds and preferred and common stock.

Marketable Securities.   Security investments (financial assets) the firm can quickly convert to cash balances. Also known as near cash or near-cash assets.

Maturity.   The length of time until the bond issuer returns the par value to the bondholder and terminates the bond.

Maturity Date.   The date upon which a borrower is to repay a loan.

Merger.   A combination of two or more businesses into a single operational entity.

Money Market.   All institutions and procedures that facilitate transactions in short-term instruments issued by borrowers with very high credit ratings.

Money-Market Mutual Funds.   Investment companies that purchase a diversified array of short-term, high-grade (money-market) debt instruments.

Monitoring Costs.   A form of agency costs. Typically these costs arise when bond investors take steps to ensure that protective covenants in the bond indenture are adhered to by management.

Mortgage Bond.   A bond secured by a lien on real property.

Multinational Corporation (MNC).   A corporation with holdings and/or operations in more than one country.

Mutually Exclusive Projects.   A set of projects that perform essentially the same task, so that acceptance of one will necessarily mean rejection of the others.

Negotiable Certificates of Deposit.   Marketable receipts for funds deposited in a bank for a fixed period. The deposited funds earn a fixed rate of interest. More commonly, these are called CDs.

Net Income.   A figure representing a firm's profit or loss for the period. It also represents the earnings available to the firm's common *and* preferred stockholders.

Net Income Available to Common Equity (also **Net Common Stock Earnings**).   Net income after interest, taxes, and preferred dividends.

Net Income Available to Common Stockholders (Net Income).   A figure representing a firm's profit or loss for a period. It also represents the earnings available to the firm's common and preferred stockholders.

Net Operating Loss Carryback and Carryforward.   A tax provision that permits the taxpayer first to apply the loss against the profits in the three prior years (carryback). If the loss has not been completely absorbed by the profits in these three years, it may be applied to taxable profits in each of the 15 following years (carryforward).

Net Present Value (NPV). A capital-budgeting concept defined as the present value of the project's annual net cash flows after tax less the project's initial outlay.

Net Profit Margin. Net income divided by sales. A ratio that measures the net income of the firm as a percent of sales.

Net Working Capital. The difference between the firm's current assets and its current liabilities.

Nondiversifiable Risk. See **Systematic Risk.**

Nominal Interest Rate. The interest rate paid on debt securities without an adjustment for any loss in purchasing power.

Normal Probability Distribution. A special class of bell-shaped distributions with symmetrically decreasing density, where the curve approaches but never reaches the X axis.

Offer Rate. Same as asked rate.

Operating Income. See **Earnings Before Interest and Taxes (EBIT).**

Operating Income Return on Investment. The ratio of net operating income divided by total assets.

Operating Leverage. The incurring of fixed operating costs in a firm's income stream.

Operating Profit Margin. Net operating income divided by sales. A firm's earnings before interest and taxes. This ratio serves as an overall measure of operating effectiveness.

Opportunity Cost of Funds. The next-best rate of return available to the investor for a given level of risk.

Optimal Capital Structure. The capital structure that minimizes the firm's composite cost of capital (maximizes the common stock price) for raising a given amount of funds.

Optimal Range of Financial Leverage. The range of various capital structure combinations that yield the lowest overall cost of capital for the firm.

Option Contract. The right to buy or sell a fixed number of shares at a specified price over a limited time period.

Order Point Problem. Determining how low inventory should be depleted before it is reordered.

Order Quantity Problem. Determining the optimal order size for an inventory item given its usage, carrying costs, and ordering costs.

Organized Security Exchanges. Formal organizations involved in the trading of securities. Such exchanges are tangible entities that conduct auction markets in listed securities.

Other Assets. Assets not otherwise included in current assets or fixed assets.

Over-the-Counter Markets. All security markets except the organized exchanges. The money market is an over-the-counter market. Most corporate bonds also are traded in this market.

Partnership. An association of two or more individuals joining together as co-owners to operate a business for profit.

Par Value. On the face of a bond, the stated amount that the firm is to repay upon the maturity date.

Payable-Through Draft (PTD). A legal instrument that has the physical appearance of an ordinary check but is not drawn on a bank. A payable-through draft is drawn on and paid by the issuing firm. The bank serves as a collection point and passes the draft on to the firm.

Payback Period. A capital-budgeting criterion defined as the number of years required to recover the initial cash investment.

Payment Date. The date on which the company mails a dividend check to each investor of record.

Percent of Sales Method. A method of financial forecasting that involves estimating the level of an expense, asset, or liability for a future period as a percent of the sales forecast.

Perfect Capital Market. An assumption that allows one to study the effect of dividend decisions in isolation. It assumes that (1) investors can buy and sell stocks without incurring any transaction costs, such as brokerage commissions; (2) companies can issue stocks without any cost of doing so; (3) there are no corporate or personal taxes; (4) complete information about the firm is readily available; (5) there are no conflicts of interest between management and stockholders; and (6) financial distress and bankruptcy costs are nonexistent.

Permanent Investment. An investment that the firm expects to hold longer than one year. The firm makes permanent investments in fixed and current assets. Compare **Temporary Investments.**

Perpetuity. An annuity with an infinite life.

Pledging Accounts Receivable. A loan the firm obtains from a commercial bank or a finance company using its accounts receivable as collateral.

Plowback Ratio. The fraction of earnings that are reinvested, or plowed back, into the firm.

Portfolio Beta. The relationship between a portfolio's returns and the market returns. It is a measure of the portfolio's nondiversifiable risk.

Portfolio Diversification Effect. The fact that variations of the returns from a portfolio or combination of assets may be less than the sum of the variation of the individual assets making up the portfolio.

Preauthorized Check (PAC). A check that resembles an ordinary check but does not contain or require the signature of the person on whose account it is being drawn. A PAC is created only with the individual's legal authorization. The PAC system is advantageous when the firm regularly receives a large volume of payments of a fixed amount from the same customer over a long period.

Preemptive Right. The right entitling the common shareholder to maintain his or her proportionate share of ownership in the firm.

Preferred Stock. A hybrid security with characteristics of both common stock and bonds. It is similar to common stock in that it has no fixed maturity date, the nonpayment of dividends does not bring on bankruptcy, and dividends are not deductible for tax purposes. It is similar to bonds in that dividends are limited in amount.

Premium Bond. A bond that is selling above its par value.

Present Value. The value in today's dollars of a future payment discounted back to present at the required rate of return.

Present-Value Interest Factor ($PVIF_{i,n}$). The value $[1/(1 + i)^n]$ used as a multiplier to calculate an amount's present value.

Present-Value Interest Factor for an Annuity ($PVIFA_{i,n}$). The value $\left[\sum_{t=1}^{n} \frac{1}{(1 + i)^t}\right]$ used as a multiplier to calculate the present value of an annuity.

Price-Earnings (P/E) Ratio. The price the market places on $1 of a firm's earnings. For example, if a firm has an earnings per share of $2, and a stock price of $30, its price-earnings ratio is 15 ($30 ÷ $2).

Primary Markets. Transactions in securities offered for the first time to potential investors.

Principle of Self-Liquidating Debt. See **Hedging Principle.**

Private Placement. A security offering limited to a small number of potential investors.

Privileged Subscription. The process of marketing a new security issue to a select group of investors.

Processing Float. Funds tied up during the time required for the firm to process remittance checks before they can be deposited in the bank.

Profit Budget. A budget of forecasted profits based on information gleaned from the cost and sales budgets.

Profit Margins. Financial ratios (sometimes simply referred to as margins) that reflect the level of firm profits relative to sales. Examples include the gross profit margin (gross profit divided by sales), operating profit margin (operating earnings divided by sales), and the net profit margin (net profit divided by sales).

Profitability Index (PI). A capital-budgeting criterion defined as the ratio of the present value of the future net cash flows to the initial outlay. Also called **Benefit-Cost Ratio.**

Pro Forma Income Statement. A statement of planned profit or loss for a future period.

Prospectus. A condensed version of the full registration statement filed with the Securities and Exchange Commission that describes a new security issue.

Protective Provisions. Provisions for preferred stock included in terms of the issue to protect the investor's interest. For instance, provisions generally allow for voting in the event of nonpayment of dividends, or they restrict the payment of common stock dividends if sinking-fund payments are not met or if the firm is in financial difficulty.

Proxy. A means of voting in which a designated party is provided with the temporary power of attorney to vote for the signee at the corporation's annual meeting.

Proxy Fight. A battle between rival groups for proxy votes in order to control the decisions made in a stockholders' meeting.

Public Offering. A security offering where all investors have the opportunity to acquire a portion of the financial claims being sold.

Purchasing Power Parity Theory. In the long run, exchange rates adjust so that the purchasing power of each currency tends to be the same.

Pure Play Method. A method of estimating a project's beta that involves looking for a publicly traded firm on the outside that looks like the project and using that outside firm's required rate of return to judge the project.

Put Option. The right to sell a given number of shares of common stock or some other asset at a specified price over a given time period.

Quick Ratio. See **Acid-Test Ratio.**

Raw-Materials Inventory. The basic materials purchased from other firms to be used in the firm's production operations.

Real Assets. Tangible assets like houses, equipment, and inventories; real assets are distinguished from financial assets.

Real Interest Rate. The nominal rate of interest less any loss in purchasing power of the dollar during the time of the investment.

Remote Disbursing. A cash management service specifically designed to extend disbursing float.

Repurchase Agreements. Legal contracts that involve the sale of short-term securities by a borrower to a lender of funds. The borrower commits to repurchase the securities at a later date at the contract price plus a stated interest charge.

Required Rate of Return. See **Investor's Required Rate of Return.**

Residual Dividend Theory. A theory that a company's dividend payment should equal the cash left after financial all the investments that have positive net present values.

Restrictive Covenants. Provisions in the loan agreement that place restrictions on the borrower and make the loan immediately payable and due when violated. These restrictive covenants are designed to maintain the borrower's financial condition on a par with that which existed at the time the loan was made.

Retained Earnings. Cumulative profits retained in a business up to the date of the balance sheet.

Return on Common Equity. Net income available to the common stockholders divided by common equity. A ratio relating earned income to the common stockholder's investment.

Return on Total Assets. Net income divided by total assets. This ratio determines the yield on the firm's assets by relating net income to total assets.

Return-Risk Line. A specification of the appropriate required rates of return for investments having different amounts of risk.

Revolving Credit Agreement. An understanding between the borrower and the bank as to the amount of credit the bank will be legally obligated to provide the borrower. Compare **Line of Credit.**

Right. A certificate issued to common stockholders giving them an option to purchase a stated number of new shares at a specified price during a 2- to 10-week period.

Risk. Potential variability in future cash flows. The likely variability associated with revenue or income streams. This concept has been measured operationally as the standard deviation or beta.

Risk-Adjusted Discount Rate. A method for incorporating a project's level of risk into the capital-budgeting process, in which the discount rate is adjusted upward to compensate for higher-than-normal risk or downward to compensate for lower-than-normal risk.

Risk-Free Rate of Return. The rate of return on risk-free investments. The interest rates on short-term U.S. government securities are commonly used to measure this rate.

Risk Premium. The additional return expected for assuming risk.

Safety Stock. Inventory held to accommodate any unusually large and unexpected usage during delivery time.

Sales Forecast. Projection of future sales.

Salvage Value. The value of an asset or investment project at the end of its usable life.

Scenario Analysis. Simulation analysis that focuses on an examination of the range of possible outcomes.

Secondary Market. Transactions in currently outstanding securities. This is distinguished from the new issues or primary market.

Secured Loans. Sources of credit that require security in the form of pledged assets. In the event the borrower defaults in payment of principal or interest, the lender can seize the pledged assets and sell them to settle the debt.

Securities and Exchange Commission (SEC). The federal agency created by the Securities Exchange Act of 1934 to enforce federal securities laws.

Securities Exchange Act of 1933. A regulation that requires registration of certain new issues of public securities with the Securities and Exchange Commission (SEC). The registration statement should disclose all facts relevant to the new issue that will permit an investor to make an informed decision.

Securities Exchange Act of 1934. This act enables the SEC to enforce federal securities laws. The major aspects of the 1934 act include (1) major securities exchanges are required to register with the SEC; (2) insider-trading is regulated; (3) stock price manipulation by investors is prohibited; (4) the SEC has control over proxy procedures; and (5) the Board of Governors of the Federal Reserve System is given the responsibility of setting margin requirements.

Security Market Line. The return line that reflects the attitudes of investors regarding the minimum acceptable return for a given level of systematic risk.

Selling Group. A collection of securities dealers that participates in the distribution of new issues to final investors. A selling-group agreement links these dealers to the underwriting syndicate.

Selling Rate. Same as the asked rate.

Sell-off. The sale of a subsidiary, division, or product line by one firm to another.

Semifixed Costs. See **Semivariable Costs.**

Semivariable Costs. Costs that exhibit the joint characteristics of both fixed and variable costs over different ranges of output. Also called **Semifixed Costs.**

Sensitivity Analysis. The process of determining how the distribution of possible net present values or internal rates of return for a particular project is affected by a change in one particular input variable.

Shelf Offering. See **Shelf Registration.**

Shelf Registration. A procedure for issuing new securities where the firm obtains a master registration statement approved by the SEC.

Simple Arbitrage. Trading to eliminate exchange rate differentials across the markets for a single currency, e.g. for the New York and London markets.

Simulation. The process of imitating the performance of an investment project through repeated evaluations, usually using a computer. In the general case, experimentation upon a mathematical model that has been designed to capture the critical realities of the decision-making situation.

Sinking-Fund Provision. A protective provision that requires the firm periodically to set aside an amount of money for the retirement of its preferred stock. This money is then used to purchase the preferred stock in the open market or through the use of the call provision, whichever method is cheaper.

Small, Regular Dividend Plus a Year-End Extra. A corporate policy of paying a small regular dollar dividend plus a year-end extra dividend in prosperous years to avoid the connotation of a permanent dividend.

Sole Proprietorship. A business owned by a single individual.

Spin-off. The separation of a subsidiary from its parent, with no change in the equity ownership. The management of the parent company gives up operating control over the subsidiary, but the shareholders maintain their same percentage ownership in both firms. New shares representing ownership in the averted company are issued to the original shareholders on a pro rata basis.

Spontaneous Financing. The trade credit and other accounts payable that arise "spontaneously" in the firm's day-to-day operations.

Spot Transaction. A transaction made immediately in the marketplace at the market price.

Stable Dollar Dividend per Share. A dividend policy that maintains a relatively stable dollar dividend per share over time.

Standard Deviation. A statistical measure of the spread of a probability distribution calculated by squaring the difference between each outcome and its expected value, weighting each value by its probability, summing over all possible outcomes, and taking the square root of this sum.

Stock Buyback. See **Stock Repurchase.**

Stock Dividend. A distribution of shares of up to 25 percent of the number of shares currently outstanding, issued on a pro rata basis to the current stockholders.

Stock Market Value. (See **Market Value.**)

Stock Repurchase. The repurchase of common stock by the issuing firm for any of a variety of reasons, resulting in a reduction of shares outstanding. Also called **Stock Buyback.**

Stock Split. A stock dividend exceeding 25 percent of the number of shares currently outstanding.

Straight-Line Depreciation. A method for computing depreciation expenses in which the cost of the asset is divided by the asset's useful life.

Stretching on Trade Credit. Failing to pay within the prescribed credit period. For example, under credit terms of 2/10, net 30, a firm would be stretching its trade credit if it failed to pay by the thirtieth day and paid on the sixtieth day.

Subchapter S Corporation. A corporation that, because of specific qualifications, is taxed as though it were a partnership.

Subordinated Debenture. A debenture that is subordinated to other debentures in being paid in case of insolvency.

Subscription Price. The price for which the security may be purchased in a rights offering.

Sustainable Rate of Growth. The rate at which a firm's sales can grow if it wants to maintain its present financial ratios and does not want to resort to the sale of new equity shares.

Syndicate. A group of investment bankers who contractually assist in the buying and selling of a new security issue.

Systematic Risk. (1) The portion of variations in investment returns that cannot be eliminated through investor diversification. This variation results from factors that affect all stocks. Also called **Market Risk** or **Nondiversifiable Risk.** (2) The risk of a project from the viewpoint of a well-diversified shareholder. This measure takes into account that some of the project's risk will be diversified away as the project is combined with the firm's other projects, and, in addition, some of the remaining risk will be diversified away by shareholders as they combine this stock with other stocks in their portfolios.

Target Capital Structure Mix. The mix of financing sources that a firm plans to maintain through time.

Target Debt Ratio. A desired proportion of long-term debt in a firm's capital structure. Alternatively, it may be the desired proportion of total debt in the firm's financial structure.

Taxable Income. Gross income from all sources, except for allowable exclusions, less any tax-deductible expenses.

Tax Expenses. Tax liability determined by earnings before taxes.

Tax Liability. The amount owed the federal, state, or local taxing authorities.

Tax Shield. The element from the federal tax code that permits interest costs to be deductible when computing a firm's tax bill. The dollar difference (the shield) flows to the firm's security holders.

Temporary Financing. Financing (other than spontaneous sources) that will be repaid within a period of one year or less. Included among these sources of short-term debt are secured and unsecured bank loans, commercial paper, loans secured by accounts receivable, and loans secured by inventories.

Temporary Investments. A firm's investments in current assets that will be liquidated and not replaced within a period of one year or less. Examples include seasonal expansions in inventories and accounts receivable. Compare **Permanent Investments.**

Tender Offer. A formal offer by the company to buy a specified number of shares at a predetermined and stated price. The tender price is set above the current market price in order to attract sellers.

Terminal Warehouse Agreement. A security agreement in which the inventories pledged as collateral are transported to a public warehouse that is physically removed from the borrower's premises. This is the safest (though costly) form of financing secured by inventory.

Term Loans. Loans that have maturities of 1 to 10 years and are repaid in periodic installments over the life of the loan. Term loans are usually secured by a chattel mortgage on equipment or a mortgage on real property.

Terms of Sale. The credit terms identifying the possible discount for early payment.

Term Structure of Interest Rates. The relationship between interest rates and the term to maturity, where the risk of default is held constant.

Times Interest Earned Ratio. Earnings before interest and taxes (EBIT) divided by interest expense. A ratio that measures a firm's ability to meet its interest payments from its annual operating earnings.

Total Asset Turnover. Sales divided by total tangible assets. An overall measure of the relation between a firm's tangible assets and the sales they generate.

Total Project Risk. A project's risk ignoring the fact that much of the risk will be diversified away as the project is combined with the firm's other projects and assets.

Total Revenue. Total sales dollars.

Trade Credit. Credit made available by a firm's suppliers in conjunction with the acquisition of materials. Trade credit appears on the balance sheet as accounts payable.

Transaction Loan. A loan where the proceeds are designated for a specific purpose—for example, a bank loan used to finance the acquisition of a piece of equipment.

Transfer Price. The price a subsidiary or a parent company charges other companies that are part of the same MNC for its goods or services.

Transit Float. Funds tied up during the time necessary for a deposited check to clear through the commercial banking system and become usable funds to the company.

Treasury Bills. Direct debt obligations of the U.S. government sold on a regular basis by the U.S. Treasury.

Trend Analysis. An analysis of a firm's financial ratios over time.

Triangular Arbitrage. Arbitrage across the markets for all currencies.

Unbiased Expectations Theory. The shape of the term structure of interest rates is determined by an investor's expectations about future interest rates.

Underwriting. The purchase and subsequent resale of a new security issue. The risk of selling the new issue at a satisfactory (profitable) price is assumed (underwritten) by the investment banker.

Underwriting Syndicate. A temporary association of investment bankers formed to purchase a new security issue and quickly resell it at a profit. Formation of the syndicate spreads the risk of loss among several investment bankers, thereby minimizing the risk exposure of any single underwriter.

Undiversifiable Risk. The portion of the variation in investment returns that cannot be eliminated through investor diversification.

Unique Risk. See **Unsystematic Risk.**

Unsecured Loans. All sources of credit that have as their security only the lender's faith in the borrower's ability to repay the funds when due.

Unsystematic Risk. The portion of the variation in investment returns that can be eliminated through investor diversification. This diversifiable risk is the result of factors that are unique to the particular firm. Also called **Company-Unique Risk** or **Diversifiable Risk.**

Value of a Bond. The present value of the interest payments, I_1 in period t, plus the present value of the redemption or par value of the indebtedness, M, at the maturity date.

Value of a Security. The present value of all future cash inflows expected to be received by the investor owning the security.

Variable Costs. Costs that are fixed per unit of output but vary in total as output changes. Also called **Direct Costs.**

Volume of Output. A firm's level of operations expressed either in sales dollars or as units of output.

Weighted Cost of Capital. A composite of the individual costs of financing incurred by each capital source. A firm's weighted cost of capital is a function of (1) the individual costs of capital, (2) the capital structure mix, and (3) the level of financing necessary to make the investment.

Weighted Marginal Cost of Capital. The composite cost for each additional dollar of financing. The marginal cost of capital represents the appropriate criterion for making investment decisions.

Wire Transfers. A method of moving funds electronically between bank accounts in order to eliminate transit float. The wired funds are immediately usable at the receiving bank.

Working Capital. A concept traditionally defined as a firm's investment in current assets. Compare **Net Working Capital.**

Work-in-Process Inventory. Partially finished goods requiring additional work before they become finished goods.

Yield to Maturity. (1) See Term **Structure of Interest Rates.** (2) The rate of return a bondholder will receive if the bond is held to maturity. (Equivalent to the expected rate of return.)

Zero and Very Low Coupon Bond. A bond issued at a substantial discount from its $1,000 face value and that pays little or no interest.

Zero Balance Accounts (ZBA). A cash management tool that permits centralized control over cash outflow while maintaining divisional disbursing authority. Objectives are (1) to achieve better control over cash payments; (2) to reduce excess cash balances held in regional banks for disbursing purposes; and (3) to increase disbursing float.

INDEX

C

Callable preferred, 233
Call provision, 233
Capital
  assets. *See* Capital asset pricing model
    (CAPM)
  budgeting. *See* Capital budgeting
  costs. *See* Capital costs
  curve, saucer-shaped cost of, 426–27
  formation, rate of, 38
  funds, nonfinancial sources, 35
  gains, 11
    raising, 5–6
  investments
    capital costs and, 378–80
    evaluating new, 378–80
  losses, 11
  markets, 17, 33
    mix of corporate securities in, 34–37
  par value and paid in, 83
  rationing, 305–7
    IRR problems and, 307–12
    project selection and, 306
    rationale for, 305–6
  structures. *See* Capital structures
  weighted average cost of, 364
Capital asset pricing model (CAPM), 274
  implementing, 369–71
Capital budgeting, 290–91, 338–41, 351
  cash flows and, 327–28
    vs. accounting profits, 328–29
  comprehensive, 339
  criteria for, 294, 316–17
    decision, 291–304
  ethics in, 312
  guidelines for, 328–31
  incidental or synergistic effects, 329–30
  incorporating risk into, 345–49
  incremental thinking, 329
  multinational firm, 314–15
  practices of, 313–14
    and techniques, 289–91
  risk and, 343–44
Capital costs, 56, 361–63. *See also* Costs,
    Debt, Preferred stock, etc.
  asset and financial structure, 401
  calculating, 373n
    divisional, 376–78
  definitions and concepts, 363–64
  determining individual, 364–71
  financial leverage and, 427
  financial policy, 364
  formulas of, 379
  investments and, 378–80
  investor opportunity, 363–64
  overall, 56

required rates of return, 363–64
  structure and, 438
  weighted average, 372–76
    calculation, 374–76
Capital structures, 372, 414, 420–21
  analytical setting, 422–24
  costs and, 438
  design, firm value and, 423
  enterprise valuation and, 431n
  of growth firm, 373
  importance of, 422
  management of
    basic tools, 432–34
    business risk, 440–41
    debt capacity, 440
    target debt ratios, 439–40
  possible, 433
  theory, 422–31
    managerial implications, 431
    moderate position, 425
  weights, 372–73
CAPM. *See* Capital asset pricing model
Cash, 512
  -basis accounting, 87
  budget, 151–52
  collection
    disbursal technique features, 528–29
    system, 518
    compared to lockbox system, 520
  conversion cycles (CCC), 492
  vs. earnings, 90
  flows. *See* Cash flows
  generation, disposition process, 513
  holding, 513–15
    precautionary motive, 514–15
    speculative motive, 515
    transactions motive, 514
  inflow, 516–17
  management
    cost evaluation of services, 527–28
    objectives and decisions, 515–16
    outflow, 524–27
  vs. profits, 14–15
  stock of, 542
  tax payment, 88
Cash flows
  vs. accounting profits, 328–29
  after-tax, 18
    basis, 338
  calculating free, 87–88
  capital budgeting and, 327–28
  differential, 334–37, 340
  diverting, 329
  financial statements and, 75–76
  incremental, 15, 331
    after-tax, 329
  measuring, 86–92

  in multinational firm, 352–53
  multiple, uneven, 178–79
  over project life, 334–37
  potential future variability, 257
  process, 513–14
  sunk costs and, 330–31
  terminal, 337–38
CCC. *See* Cash, conversion cycles
CDs. *See* Negotiable certificates of deposit
CEO. *See* Chief Executive Officer
CFO. *See* Chief Financial Officer
Characteristic line, 266
Chattel mortgage agreement, 504
Checks, dishonored, 520
Chicago Stock Exchange, 44
Chief Executive Officer (CEO), 6
Chief Financial Officer (CFO), 6
Cincinnati Stock Exchange, 44
Clerical functions, elimination of, 520
Clientele effect, 459
Collection, disbursement procedures and,
    516–27
Commercial bank prime lending rate, 32
Commercial paper, 534–35
  cost estimation of, 501
  short-term credit and, 500–1
Common equity, cost of, 367
Common stock, 235–44
  characteristics, 235–38
    claim on assets, 236
    claim on income, 236
    cumulative voting, 237–38
    majority voting, 237
    proxy, 237
    proxy fights, 237
    voting rights, 237–38
  features of, 235–38
  valuing, 238–44
    growth factor in, 238–40
    multiple holding period, 241–44
    single holding period, 240–42
Common stockholders, 83
  expected rate of return, 245–47
Company-unique risk, 262
Compensating balance, 498
Competitive markets, 15–16
Compound annuities, 179
Compound interest
  calculations, 170
  future value and, 168–75
  with nonannual periods, 187–89
Concentration banking, 522
Conflicts of interest, 428
Constant dividend payment ratio, 465
Contribution-to-firm risk, 343
Controller, 6
Convertible preferred stock, 232–33

Return on equity (ROE), 119, 123, 147, 156
  common, 118
  measuring, 120–26
Returns
  average annual and standard deviations of, 57
  distribution of, 257n
  monthly holding-period, 265
  probability distribution of, 258
Revaluation, 559
Revenue
  output and, 406
  total, 406
Revenue Reconciliation Act (1993), 8, 335
Revolving credit agreement, 498
Risk
  capital budgeting and, 343–44
    measure, 344
  defined and measured, 256–257
  diversification and, 19, 261–64, 270–72
  international dimension of, 352–53
  investment and, 341–45
  meaning of, 257–59
  premiums, 61–63, 273
  simulation of, 349–52
Risk-adjusted discount rates, 345–48
Risk-free rate of return, 272
Risk-return
  diversification effect, 271
  meaning and measurement of, 253–54, 259
  relationship, 346
  trade-off, 13, 19, 192–94, 515
ROA. *See* Return on assets
ROE. *See* Return on equity

Security market line, 275
Selling rate, 564
Sensitivity analysis, 350–52
Shareholders
  value-based management (SVBM), 362, 382–86
  value created for, 127
  wealth, maximization of, 3
Share repurchase, as dividend decision, 472–73
Shelf offering and registration, 55–56
Simple arbitrage, 564
Simulation, 349–52
Sinking-fund provision, 233
Sinquefield, Rex A., 56n
Small-issues exemption, 54
Smithian value system, 376
Social responsibility, 24
Sole proprietorship, 4
Solon, 256
Spontaneous financing, 141, 490–91
Spot transactions, 561
Stable dollar dividend per share, 466
Standard and Poor's, 204, 208
  corporate bond ratings, 209
Standard deviation, 258–59
  of returns, 57–58
Stern Stewart performance 1000, 384
Stock
  buyback, 471
  dividends
    defined, 469
    rationale for, 470–71
    vs. split, 469–70
    stock splits and, 468–71
  preferred, 230–35
  repurchases, 471-75
    financing, 474
    investment decision, 474
    investor choice, 473–74
    procedure, 474
  split, 469
    rationale for, 470–71
  valuation and characteristics of, 229–30
Stockholders
  plus dividends paid to, 91
  return on investment, 118–20
Subordinated debentures, 202–3
Sustainable rate of growth, 155
  calculating, 147–48
SVBM. *See* Shareholders, value–based management
Syndicate, 48
Systematic risk, 262, 343
  measurement of, 347–48

T

Target capital structure proportions, 373
Taxable income, 8
Tax computations, 12
Tax effects, sale of old machine, 333–34
Taxes
  business decisions and, 18–19, 457
  computing owed, 8–10
  corporate rates, 9
  environment of, 7–12
  expenses, 77
  shield, 425
Taxpayers, types of, 7–8
Tax Reform Act (1986), 335
Temporary assets, 490
Temporary financing, 490–91
Temporary investments, 490
Tender offer, 474
Terminal warehouse agreement, 504
Term structure
  of interest rates, 65
  shape of, 67–69
Third World governments, 579
Times interest earned, 117
Time value of money, 14, 167–68
  in multinational firms, 192–94
  solving problems with financial calculator, 173–75
Tobias, Andrew, 167–68
Total asset turnover, 115
Total revenue, 406
Trade credit, 490, 496–97
  advantages, 497–98
  stretching, 497
Transaction
  exposure, 573
  loans, 499–500
Transit float, 517
Translation exposure, 572–73
Treasurer, 6
Treasury bills, 43, 58
Treasury stock, 83
Triangular arbitrage, 564

U

Ukraine, 580
Unbiased expectations theory, 67–68
Uneven stream, present value of, 189–91
U.S. Overseas Private Investment Corporation, 580
U.S. Treasury bills, 532–33
Unsystematic risk, 262